Show Me the Money

Writing Business and Economics Stories for Mass Communication

LEA'S COMMUNICATION SERIES

Jennings Bryant/Dolf Zillmann, General Editors

For a complete list of titles in LEA's Communication Series, please contact Lawrence Erlbaum Associates, Publishers, at www.erlbaum.com.

Show Me the Money

Writing Business and Economics Stories for Mass Communication

Chris Roush

University of North Carolina at Chapel Hill

LAWRENCE ERLBAUM ASSOCIATES, PUBLISHERS
2004   Mahwah, New Jersey   London

Senior Acquisitions Editor:	Linda Bathgate
Assistant Editor:	Karin Wittig Bates
Cover Design:	Kathryn Houghtaling Lacey
Textbook Production Manager:	Paul Smolenski
Full-Service Compositor:	TechBooks
Text and Cover Printer:	Hamilton Printing Company

This book was typeset in 10/12 pt. Times, LucidaSans, LucidaSansBold.
The heads were typeset in Times, LucidaSans, LucidaSansBold.

Lawrence Erlbaum Associates, Inc., Publishers
10 Industrial Avenue
Mahwah, New Jersey 07430
www.erlbaum.com

Library of Congress Cataloging-in-Publication Data

Roush, Chris.
  Show me the money : writing business and economics stories for mass communication / Chris Roush.
    p.   cm.
  Includes bibliographical references and index.
  ISBN 0-8058-4954-8 (case : alk. paper)—ISBN 0-8058-4955-6 (pbk. : alk. paper)
  1. Journalism, Commercial.   I.Title.

  PN4784.C7R68   2004
  070.4'4965—dc22   2004001743

Books published by Lawrence Erlbaum Associates are printed on
acid-free paper, and their bindings are chosen for strength and
durability.

Printed in the United States of America
10 9 8 7 6 5 4 3 2 1

To my wife Mindy
and my sons Andrew and Tyler.

Contents

Foreword

The request was urgent. The CEO of a local company was retiring and rumors were that he was walking out the door with a hefty bonus.

The call was from a young reporter at a medium-sized newspaper in the South. His editor, reading wire stories about the latest scandal on Wall Street, assigned him to investigate the local CEO's golden parachute. The reporter was on a tight deadline. He needed help in finding the answers, and could the professor help?

The questions poured out: What documents do I need to find? Are they available online? What's the average retirement for executives in that same industry? What's the proper method to evaluate the stock options the CEO was given? How do I write the story fairly?

The reporter was overwhelmed. Like many of his colleagues, he had a journalism degree but no specific business education besides Econ 101 in college. But as a result of recent events on Wall Street, readers and viewers of business news are demanding to know more about the inside deals of American and foreign companies. For today's Americans a lot more is at stake—their retirement savings, their children's education—not to mention the future of their weekly paychecks.

Companies like Enron have unraveled, ripping away the life savings of thousands of workers and investors. Events in remote villages have sent prices at the corner gas station spiraling. It's no wonder that with world terror at an all-time high, most Americans' chief concern is still the economy.

Americans want and expect business journalists to be watchdogs of "Big Business." Just like their colleagues on the metro or political desks, business reporters must be vigilant in protecting and representing the interests of the masses. Today's public face of business goes beyond the interests of shareholders, workers, and consumers. Business and government increasingly intersect, with public tax monies used to lure workers to jobs, or build new roads or sports stadiums in the guise of economic development.

That means that journalists—even those working at smaller publications—must have knowledge of the inner workings of publicly and privately held companies. Journalists must be able to apply government statistics to local circumstances and help citizens evaluate the costs and consequences of tax breaks that fund economic development. In short, they must effectively translate the workings of Wall Street and Washington for a "Main Street" audience.

Knowledge is the key, but taking classes in accounting or statistics is not enough. Journalists need specialized business education to learn technique as well as theory. It is one thing to know, it is another to be able to tell. That is why tailored education for business and financial journalists is vital. In the following pages, you will learn to demystify corporate structure and untangle government regulations, understand the elements of profit and loss, and grasp the global view.

There is no more important work in today's media than that of the financial journalist. Financial information, available to all, promotes world prosperity; and prosperous nations, in general, promote peace. It is no wonder that strong business journalism is being encouraged in emerging democracies and emerging economies.

Your guide in these pages is an experienced financial journalist who has worked for major newspapers and financial news services. He knows firsthand what it takes to tell the truth about today's financial events. He knows the importance of accuracy, ethics, and bringing the story home.

For the student journalist, consider this text an introduction to the world of business journalism; for working reporters, consider this text a welcome friend that can lead you to new journalistic excellence. The result should be the same—shedding light on an area of vital importance to the American public.

—Martha Steffens
SABEW Chair in Business and Economic Reporting
University of Missouri

Preface

My first week as a business reporter seems like yesterday. At the Manatee County bureau of the *Sarasota Herald-Tribune* in May 1989, I spent the first week being trained by my predecessor, who was transferring to the newspaper's main office. After a week, she left. I panicked.

I had never been a business reporter before. My previous job was covering cops and courts in the Pasco County bureau of the *St. Petersburg Times*—a job, I might add, I hated. I wanted to do anything other than look at dead bodies. So I called a friend in Sarasota who told me about the business opening. After the first week, I got over the panic, made some mistakes, and learned what to do on the job.

It was the break I needed, and the right career move. Becoming a business reporter put me in the fastest-growing part of editorial content in newspapers, magazines, and, later, the Internet. Reporters who knew something about business were recruited by other publications, and my career took off, like the careers of many others.

After a year in Sarasota, the business editor at the *Tampa Tribune* called me. I had no idea who he was, or what stories of mine he had seen. But he wanted to hire me, and offered me more money and the opportunity to work at a larger newspaper. The trend continued. *BusinessWeek* needed someone in its Connecticut bureau who knew how to write about insurance. Bloomberg News wanted someone in its Atlanta office that had covered the beverage industry. A publishing company in Virginia hired a recruiter to find someone who could start an insurance magazine.

Business news, whatever the form, has been the growth industry of mass communication for the last 15 years. Yet, during the entire progression of my career, I kept thinking back to that first job and my lack of experience. I learned on the job, just like many others in the field, about the differences between revenue and profits, and net income and operating income. I discovered public company filings the way other reporters did—someone with more experience told me about them and what they contained.

And as my career has transitioned into teaching, I have thought even more about how most business reporters get into the business. Why should they start off with little or no knowledge of corporate America?

The answer is they shouldn't. The public deserves to have information about the business world from all forms of mass communication written and edited by journalists who are knowledgeable and who can explain the significance of stories to consumers in a way anybody can understand.

Yet higher education and mass communication have failed miserably in effectively training journalists for careers in business reporting. In a 2002 survey by Selzer & Co. for the American Press Institute and the Reynolds Foundation, not one journalism school administrator rated his or her program as doing an excellent job of training students for careers in business journalism. Only 28% said their program does a good job. And news executives say hiring business reporters is the hardest beat for which to find qualified workers; just 38% of them say that business is a high priority in their newsrooms, showing the lack of emphasis placed on this important field.

Universities and colleges across the country need to team with mass communication outlets to provide more training and teaching in business journalism. In some areas, this is happening. Business journalism programs exist at major schools such as the University of Missouri, Northwestern, Columbia, and Boston Universities, as well as others, including the University of Illinois, Baruch College in New York, and Washington & Lee University.

In addition, newspapers, magazines, TV stations, and Web sites are sending their reporters and editors to more and more conferences for training and tips. The Society of American Business Editors and Writers, along with the American Press Institute and the Reynolds Foundation, are also making concerted efforts to improve business journalism education and knowledge.

This book strives to be a guide for both the beginning business reporter and one who has worked the beat for years. It provides guidance on important topics and issues that everyone who writes a business-related story encounters. It starts off with a basic history lesson on the importance of business journalism to everyone, and then seeks to teach readers what every business reporter should know—from reading an income statement and balance sheet for a company to what to look for in Securities and Exchange Commission (SEC) filings.

Although there have been other books to help business reporters along the way, there has never been a guide to show them specifically how to write stories about companies and the economy.

These are skills I wish I had back in 1989. Now, business journalists will not have to start their jobs without this knowledge.

Though this book is written primarily from the viewpoint of the newspaper business editor, I have also included examples of excellent business journalism from television, the Internet, and magazines. All of the reporting techniques and methods discussed herein are relevant to any media.

Acknowledgments

A lot of people offered great advice to make this book the best reference guide possible for new and experienced business reporters.

I thank Jan Yopp, who heads the news–editorial program at the University of North Carolina at Chapel Hill, for looking at the proposal for this book, offering suggestions, and providing some guidance on the textbook-writing process; Cindy Elmore, a former business journalist who was a graduate student in Chapel Hill and who is now a journalism professor at East Carolina University, for reviewing early chapters and the proposal and making suggestions; Carol Pardun, another UNC faculty member, for giving me the name and phone number of Linda Bathgate, an editor at Lawrence Erlbaum Associates, a well-known mass-communication textbook publisher. Linda enthusiastically took on the project and made me feel welcome.

I also thank two colleagues, Pamela Luecke at Washington & Lee University and Marty Steffens at the University of Missouri, who teach business journalism classes, for reviewing the proposal and some chapters. Both suggested additional chapters, as well as other topics that needed to be covered, to make the book more complete. Their teaching expertise and knowledge were invaluable. In addition, Rusty Todd at the University of Texas at Austin reviewed the entire manuscript and made suggestions. Professors at the Kenan-Flagler Business School at the University of North Carolina also reviewed some of the chapters and made similar comments and suggestions.

Parts of the text were shown to professional journalists, including Adam Levy of Bloomberg News, online journalists Michael Crittenden and Dail Willis, among others, to get a sense of what they would want in such a book. In addition, Keith Allen, an accounting research manager at Coca-Cola Company, reviewed chapter 4, which contains recent examples of the company's financial statement, balance sheet, and cash flow statement. I appreciate all of their comments and suggestions.

I thank Dean Richard Cole, who runs the School of Journalism and Mass Communication at Chapel Hill, for his enthusiastic support of my interest in business journalism education and for giving his approval to the creation of the Carolina Business News Initiative, a program designed to teach students and professionals.

I thank the Society of American Business Editors and Writers and the National Newspaper Association for allowing me to judge some of their business writing contests during the past year. Judging these events allowed me to review top-notch business reporting and writing and gave me access to many of the story examples used in this text.

Finally, I thank the students to whom I have taught business reporting at Washington & Lee University, the University of Richmond, and now at UNC Chapel Hill. Most of the information in this book has been tried out on them in the classroom— with some degree of success, I will modestly add. Their feedback helped refine much of what you are about to read. One student in particular, John Kuka, spent a summer reading a preliminary version of this book and made helpful suggestions.

I am sure that I am forgetting someone. Please accept my apologies and know that it was not intentional—just a sign of an absent-minded professor.

—Chris Roush
University of North Carolina at Chapel Hill

Show Me the Money

Writing Business and Economics Stories for Mass Communication

1

Why Business Reporting Is Important

KNOWLEDGE OF CORPORATE AMERICA GOES A LONG WAY

A former editor of a Kentucky newspaper likes to tell the story about how one of her business reporters went to interview the CEO of Humana Incorporated, a locally based managed care company.

The CEO began talking about the SEC. After several minutes, the reporter, who was new to the beat, interrupted the CEO and asked, "Excuse me, but what does the Southeastern Conference have to do with your business?"

At that point, the annoyed CEO abruptly ended the interview. He was not talking about the conference of universities from Kentucky to Florida that compete in sports ranging from football to swimming. He was talking about the Securities and Exchange Commission, the federal agency that regulates thousands and thousands of companies across the country.

Business reporting is just like reporting any other beat. You have to know what you are writing about, what documents to look for, and the correct sources. Even though the quality of business journalism has improved in the last 15 years, there are still concerns that reporters in the field are not fully knowledgeable about their topics. Some business reporters and editors also do not know the appropriate place to look for the information they need to get the story, or to make the story they already have even better. Still others do not understand the basic principles of economics that help a company's profits rise and fall, and even more do not understand the importance of the stock market and trade relations to a business's future prospects.

Sources and documents can help explain all of these topics and more. But it is also important for reporters to take this knowledge of business and do something with it. That is why furthering the knowledge of business reporters and editors will help them do a better job in the future.

Will this have an effect on future business reporting? One can only hope that the quality will improve. On February 5, 2001, *Fortune* magazine named Enron Corporation the "Most Innovative Company in America." The company also placed 18th overall in the magazine's list of "Most Admired Companies" in the country.

To be sure, Enron was innovative and perhaps even admired by competitors and other corporate executives. However, a skeptical reporter for that magazine, Bethany McLean, believed what some sources were telling her: Something was amiss at the Houston-based company, and that it was not to be admired or considered innovative, except in finding creative ways to skirt the law. She dug into the company's financial filings, and discovered that it was hard to determine exactly where the company was making money.

"It's a really important lesson for reporters to keep in mind, as well as other supposedly sophisticated people, that sometimes the most obvious question really is the question," said McLean in an interview. "In Enron's case: How do you make money? It's such an obvious question that you almost feel stupid asking it" (Smith, 2002).

Despite protests from company management to her editors and being turned away by the company when she asked for information, McLean continued researching her story, which ran in March 2001. By the end of the year, the company's financial performance unraveled, and Enron had filed for bankruptcy court protection. People who read McLean's article and became scared by what she reported likely sold their stock in the company at around $80 per share, saving themselves millions. Today, Enron's shares are worthless.

Business reporting, particularly for stories as complicated as Enron, is not easy. At least in this case, arcane accounting techniques and subsidiaries that were not on its balance sheet hid Enron's problems to all but the very skeptical and expert business journalists. There were clues, however. A business reporter who had watched the dramatic rise in Enron's stock price the previous year would have noticed that increase was in direct opposition to how the rest of the market was performing. In the first nine months of 2000, Enron's stock more than doubled, but its revenues and profits did not match that strong growth rate. It is a basic economic principle that in the long run, most companies see their stock price rise at the same rate as their revenue and profits. These were clues that maybe something was not right.

A red flag would likely have been raised to a critical-minded business reporter making this simple analysis, likely causing him or her to more closely investigate the company. Yet few who covered Enron at the time made such a connection. Though uncovering Enron's troubles became far more complicated than just comparing stock prices, the discontinuity between Enron's success and the rest of the market should have been the first indicator of deeper problems. A case could be made that some reporters did not understand how a company's financial performance is related to its stock price and how that should have led them to question Enron's tactics.

"Business journalism in what has been its glory days has been the dog that didn't bark—the watchdog that didn't bark," said Jim Michaels, editor of *Forbes* magazine for 38 years. (Barnhart, 2001)

Many Enron executives were selling their company stock, a story tracked by numerous wire service reporters. What should this tell a reporter who understands the significance? That these executives, who had an intimate knowledge of Enron's future prospects, did not think the stock price was going to get higher than where it was anytime soon. It is not that hard for reporters, at least those willing to take the time to learn, to recognize what these and other actions mean and to connect the dots into a story that tells the reader what he or she needs to know about a business.

The stock market has dropped more than 25% from its all-time high, and dozens of companies have failed in spectacular crashes. Many blame business journalists for the Wall Street bubble. Why couldn't the media have done a better job in uncovering Enron, WorldCom, and Adelphia, to name a few? The answer is they could, although journalists are not to blame for the misdeeds that caused these and other companies to fail. But business reporters can learn lessons from what went wrong in the past. One of the best ways for business journalists to produce better work is to give them training that will enable them to understand the significance of events and of what they are writing.

Although reporting and writing in business sections is much better than it was three decades ago, some of it still lacks the contextualization that would help local readers better understand what business means to them. In addition, savvy readers who want good business news are eschewing their local newspapers for Internet sites that provide the in-depth coverage they want. For newspapers, magazines, and television stations struggling to keep circulation and viewership up, the message is clear: To retain consumers of business news, more breadth and depth of coverage is needed.

The chief problem appears to be a reporting and editing staff that does not fully understand business issues and complicated economic topics. Few business reporters and editors have business-related degrees, and they have not been trained in how to cover corporations and the economy. Because of the rapid demand for business news coverage in the past two decades, reporters and editors were thrown into the topic. "Many reporters made the switch with only a rudimentary understanding of how to read a balance sheet," noted *San Francisco Chronicle* media columnist Dan Fost in early 2002 (p. 61).

The result has been shallow reporting that sometimes misses the point entirely. Business journalism "pumped up stocks before the market collapsed, failed to sound a bear alarm until the mauling was well underway, and were ignorant to the scope of corporate corruption," said personal finance editor Chris Pummer (2002) on CBS.MarketWatch.com.

The solution, according to an article in the Spring/Summer 2002 *Newspaper Research Journal,* is better training and education. In a study of West Coast newspaper business editors and reporters, nearly all agreed that "business reporters and editors need classes or training in business and economics to provide them with the tools necessary for their work." The study also said that those surveyed "were also emphatic that a basic understanding of business economics isn't necessary just for business journalists, but for all journalists" (Ludwig, p. 139).

Improving the understanding of business and economics among reporters and editors can strengthen the quality of understanding of how corporate decisions and economic factors impact everyday life for readers around the world. With a better understanding of how business affects all consumers, newspapers, television stations, magazines, Web sites, and other media can provide more effective coverage, allowing readers to make more informed decisions with their money and their lives.

Imagine you walk into your local McDonald's today and buy a hamburger. That simple purchase ultimately has an effect on the company's profits. In turn, that decision also affects the performance of dozens of competitors, including Burger King and Wendy's. In addition, all of these companies have spent money on advertising and developing products in an attempt to woo you into their restaurants. But imagine money was tight, and you decided against eating at a fast-food restaurant, your economic decision still impacts these companies. If you instead decide to go purchase hamburger meat and buns at your local grocery store, you are also affecting the financial results of the company that processed the meat, as well as the grocery store. Your decision to drive to the grocery store, or the restaurant, also affects other companies. What gas station did you buy fuel at to allow you to make that trip? What influenced the decision to purchase the car you are driving?

We are just talking about one decision about eating lunch. Imagine all of the other decisions that you and other consumers make each day, and think how those decisions affect the local economy, the national economy, and the performance of the companies whose goods, products, and services you are or are not purchasing. Now, how are you going to explain the effect of all of those decisions to readers of your local newspaper, or viewers of the evening news, or listeners of your radio station?

HOW BUSINESS—AND THE COVERAGE OF IT—HAS CHANGED OUR LIVES

Business journalism has had a profound effect on this country and the millions of people who interact with companies on an everyday basis by purchasing their goods, products, and services.

The early settlers in America depended on newspapers to provide them details of crop and livestock prices, information about what ships had entered the port, and what goods they contained. By the 19th century, newspapers devoted solely to business news were established. *The Journal of Commerce* began in 1827. *The Wall Street Journal* came along in 1889. But some of the most important stories in business journalism during this time ran in mainstream papers.

In the late 1850s, Horace Greeley of the New York *Tribune* pushed for a railroad that would connect the west with the east. His stories were the first major push to combine the regional economies of a growing country. Greeley also wrote about the need for low-cost homestead lands, another important development in the U.S. economy. A decade later, the New York *Sun* exposed how the construction company that helped build the first intercontinental railroad had been formed by the railroad companies themselves, essentially making contracts with themselves and bribing members of Congress to keep quiet by selling them shares in the company at a discounted price. The story led to the first major Congressional investigation into a corporation, foreshadowing later hearings on the downfall of Enron, WorldCom, and others.

Newspapers also influenced how government regulated business. At around the same time Greeley was pushing for a railroad, another newspaper in New York, *Frank Leslie's Illustrated Newspaper,* exposed how bad milk was killing children. The article pushed regulators into passing laws banning swill milk. The milk exposé was not the first in journalism that took aim at a business or corporation. Throughout the late 1890s and the early part of the 20th century, many newspapers directed reporters to investigate how companies were affecting the lives of people. In 1899, the *Chicago Daily Tribune* began publishing stories about how firecrackers and other explosives sold to celebrate the Fourth of July were killing people every year. Its stories led to restrictions on how fireworks were manufactured and sold.

The most famous examples of business journalism that led to business operation reforms occurred with Upton Sinclair, who, in his novel, *The Jungle,* documented the unsanitary conditions of the meat-packing industry; and Ida Tarbell, who wrote in *McClure's* magazine about how Standard Oil had forced competitors out of business. Their brand of muckraking journalism successfully advocated for reforms in how government regulated business. After reading Sinclair's novel, Theodore Roosevelt ordered an investigation which culminated in the passing of the Pure Food and Drugs Act and the Meat Inspection Act in 1906. And in 1911, the U.S. Supreme Court ordered Standard Oil to be split up. After the turn of the century other articles in *McClure's* attacked the railroad industry, which led to laws limiting shipping charges on goods and products transported by rail. In *Cosmopolitan,* a 1906 article about child labor helped discontinue the abuse of young workers in factories across the country.

Journalists also turned their attention to investments. In 1920, the *Boston Post* uncovered the financial wrongdoings of Charles Ponzi, a local financial expert, who promised huge returns to investors. Ponzi was arrested and convicted based on the articles, and spent time in prison. His name, of course, lives on in the business world, as the term Ponzi scheme is now used to explain any illegal pyramid scheme in which investors are paid with money from other investors.

More recently, publications have led the way for improved living conditions by educating consumers thereby leading them to purchase safer products. For example, *Reader's Digest,* not known today for breaking stories or leading causes, was the first broad publication to expose the potential dangers of smoking and link it to cancer. The December 1952 article is credited with starting the antismoking debate and forcing the cigarette industry to admit its products were harmful.

With an article in *The Nation* in April 1959, well-known consumer advocate Ralph Nader began his investigation into automobile safety that eventually led to new federal regulations requiring seat belts, recalls, crash tests, and air bags in most vehicles. His argument gained clout after it was disclosed that General Motors Corporation had hired private investigators to track Nader.

In the 1960s, the *Des Moines Register* printed articles that led to Congress closing loopholes in inspections that allowed for unsanitary plants and for diseased animals to be turned into meat sold in grocery stores. A 1977 article in *Mother Jones* exposed readers to the dangers of driving a Pinto, which, because of its poorly designed fuel tank, easily exploded when hit from behind. The article led to a recall of the Ford Motor Company's car and the end of its production. More than two decades later, a television reporter at KHOU in Houston found an unsettling pattern of crashes involving Ford SUVs and Firestone tires. The resulting coverage led to a recall of millions of tires.

What most of these articles have in common is that they were researched and written by reporters who understood the importance of business in society and exposed the problems, warts and all. Some of these reporters were not specifically trained in understanding how businesses operate, but learned the vital information about how companies work and how they make money, thus they turned dogged reporting into stories that changed our economy and our lives. That is the standard that today's business reporters need to strive to match. Many other reporters and editors have changed business journalism over the last 100 years, evolving the art of reporting and writing about companies and the economy into arguably the most important journalism of the last 20 years.

BusinessWeek magazine was founded in 1929, just weeks before the stock market crash that led to the Great Depression. *Fortune* magazine, created by *Time* founder Henry Luce, followed a year later. Both publications, along with *Forbes,* spent the next seven decades defining business journalism in a magazine format, printing long articles about industries and Wall Street and labor—all important topics that gave readers a broad understanding of the effects of business on the country.

New and interesting reporting styles also developed. In 1935, Sylvia F. Porter began writing a column in the *New York Post* on financial news. Her writing defined personal finance reporting, explaining to readers in simple terms how they should take care of their hard-earned money, and it landed her on the cover of *Time* in 1960. At the height of her career, Porter's column ran in more than 450 newspapers around the world, and her style spawned other well-known personal finance writers such as Jane Bryant Quinn and Kathy Kristof, who today continue the tradition of bringing sound, basic personal finance advice to millions. Without these reporters, many people would have never understood how a 401(k) plan works and the difference between growth stocks and value stocks.

Barney Kilgore took control of the *Wall Street Journal* at the age of 32 and turned a newspaper that basically catered to a small subscriber base in New York City into an international newspaper that day in and day out publishes the best business journalism in the world. Kilgore, considered the father of modern business journalism, took a financial newspaper and turned it into a publication that explained the relationship between labor, capital, and enterprise. "He also believed that those who had to deal with these problems would value a newspaper that informed them in depth and without sensation about the world they live in all its variety," said Peter Kann, CEO of Dow Jones & Company, the newspaper's owner (Kann, 2000, p. 1). In 1941, when Kilgore began running the paper, it had 41,000 subscribers. By the time he died in 1967, it had a circulation of more than 1.1 million. And since 1977, it has sold more copies each business day than any other paper in the United States. Kilgore understood that the best business reporting was written for the broadest audience possible. A banker needed to understand the same information about the economy as did a consumer wanting to borrow money from the bank. A seasoned Wall Street investor needed to know why the stock market was falling in the same simple terms that a grandmother in Thomasville, Georgia, could comprehend. Franklin Delano Roosevelt so trusted Kilgore's descriptive ability that he told other reporters attempting to understand the economics of the new Social Security system to "go ask Kilgore."

In 1970, Louis Rukeyser began hosting "Wall Street Week" on public television, becoming the first show broadcast to millions of viewers that discussed nothing but the stock market and the economy. The program became the standard television show for understanding how Wall Street affected Main Street and was the precursor of other television shows and even networks such as CNBC that now report exclusively about business and the economy. Viewers around the world now think nothing of turning on CNBC in their offices and leaving it on all day. Two decades ago, the mere thought of someone who wanted to constantly watch a television network devoted solely to business news would have earned that person a well-earned vacation. Now, it is considered almost standard for large segments of our society.

Even today, the shape of business journalism continues to evolve. Bloomberg News, an international wire service, is slightly more than a decade old, but its aggressive coverage of Wall Street and corporations has forced others to pay more attention to daily coverage. Dow Jones and Reuters are also major players, competing against Bloomberg for breaking business news stories. In many ways, business news has become immediate, supplied to us almost instantaneously. For example, the *Journal's* coverage of mergers and acquisitions, breaking many big deals before they were officially announced, has significantly changed the style and structure of how others write about business deals.

Increasingly, reporting and writing with strong business overtones wins Pulitzer Prizes. In 1999, a reporter for *The Oregonian* in Portland won a Pulitzer Prize for explaining the effect of the Asian economic downturn on the Pacific Northwest by tracing shipments of frozen French fries from the United States to Asia. The increasing number of stories winning awards in mainstream journalism prize competitions validates the importance of business journalism in newspapers around the country.

More than ever, business journalism is comforting the afflicted, and afflicting the comfortable. Budding students interested in the field need to understand the ins and outs of business journalism, where it has come from and where it is headed. There have been numerous successes and advances as a result of business journalism; and, for that, we should all be thankful. As business has become a major focus of everyday life, the role of the business journalist has become increasingly more important to both media and society.

BUSINESS REPORTING HAS MISSED SOME BIG STORIES

Yet for all of the advancements and impact brought upon society by reporting and writing that has focused on business and the economy, business journalism must also rightly take the blame for some of the problems in the world, past and present.

At the same time that the muckrakers were exposing unsanitary conditions in meat-packing plants and monopolistic business practices, companies were turning to experts to help them deal with the media. These forebears of public relations professionals brought a new twist to business journalism. CEOs attacked in newspaper stories wanted a way to respond. In the 1920s and 1930s, many major corporations such as General Electric and General Motors hired public relations experts to answer questions from the media and to try to persuade reporters that these for-profit businesses were not as evil as many believed. After World War II, public relations jobs proliferated as the economy grew. The task of the public relations professionals was to tell the media the good things that their companies were doing.

In a way, the rise in public relations led to an overall down period for business journalism. In the 1950s and 1960s, the business desk became a place where newspapers put reporters who could not hack it covering city hall or state government. Older reporters were put out to pasture with an assignment to cover business. With a few notable exceptions, business reporting took a back seat to writing about the Vietnam War or the race riots.

A journalism textbook of the era, *Modern Journalism,* devoted only one chapter to what it called "Economic News." The chapter included sections on how to write stories about labor and agriculture—two valuable parts of the country's economy, certainly, but which have since diminished in importance to more pressing industries and topics in today's media. And, the chapter did nothing to help the budding reporter understand how to read a company's balance sheet or where to look for information in SEC filings.

The 1980s and 1990s were better. The quality of business journalism improved as reporters and editors gained experience, but major stories were still missed. And business reporting took some hits. Foster Winans wrote the popular "Heard on the Street" column for *The Wall Street Journal* in the early 1980s. The stories disclosed whether professional investors were bullish or bearish on certain stocks. Winans started leaking what was in his stories before publication and was eventually caught and served time in prison. A decade later, well-known business columnist Dan Dorfman was fired from *Money* magazine for failing to disclose his sources to his editor after reports in other publications noted his close relationship with investors.

Along the way, few reporters were warning readers about impending problems. There were no glaring headlines in early October 1987 urging investors to take their money out of the stock market before it fell. A decade later, business sections and magazines lauded the management of Enron in prose that now seems ludicrous. In the *Dallas Morning News,* Enron was dubbed in a headline as a "global e-commerce leader" (North, 2002). A reporter for the *Houston Business Journal* wrote, "Enron has shown a widely recognized knack for innovation that consistently generates additional sources of revenue, potential profits and more capital" (North, 2002).

The boosterism was not confined to local publications touting hometown companies. Even the magazines and publications that were the so-called experts in writing about these new industries and businesses missed out on notifying readers of the problems. "Too often the new magazines and Web sites acted as incurious cheerleaders, championing executives and innovative companies without questioning their books," said James Ledbetter, business editor of *Time Europe* and a former employee of *The Industry Standard,* one of the publications that chronicled the meteoric rise of many Internet companies without realizing that many of them were doomed to failure. "Do a search, for example, of the word 'Enron' in the databases of those publications prior to 2000 and you'll find little but praise for its market innovations" (2003, p. A17).

Even well-respected and revered mass communication outlets failed in their watchdog role. *The New York Times* called Enron's president an "idea machine"

(Salpukas, p. C1). "Not only did the press miss the Enron scandal, it actively helped create the Enron scandal," said Jeffrey Madick, editor of *Challenge,* an economics magazine. "It not only missed the complications of Enron's fancy partnerships, which are indeed complicated, but it extolled Enron's virtues beyond almost any company. *Fortune* named Enron the most innovative company five or six years in a row, presumably without once checking the books" (2003, p. 3).

And even when mass communication outlets investigated serious business issues, such as the series run by *The New York Times* in March 1996 that examined why people around the country were losing their jobs despite strong economic growth, gaps remained. The series made faulty assertions such as the economy was not producing workers who stayed in the same jobs for long periods of time, that it was harder for a laid-off worker to find a new job, and that many of the jobs being created were low paying service jobs, not higher paying manufacturing jobs.

"The problem with business coverage in the 1990s was not that journalists weren't smart enough to root out the corruption," wrote Charles Layton in *American Journalism Review* in March 2003. "Reading the coverage of the past half-decade, one is struck by how much certain reporters *did* uncover. But even within their own news organizations, their insights were lost in a cacophony of naïve reportage that reassured us the system was sound, analysts and auditors and CEOs were basically trustworthy, and the market boom might go on forever" (p. 22).

With a dose of reality now entering business reporting, is it any wonder that confidence in the quality of work by business journalists remains low, particularly among those who regularly read the business section, namely, corporate executives? Even in newsrooms and among journalists, business reporting is still considered a backwater in knowledge and expertise. In a 1992 poll by Louis Harris, 46% of executives rated the overall quality of business journalism as negative, whereas just 21% of journalists gave business reporting a negative rating. Furthermore, 17% of executives felt that the quality of business journalism had actually declined since 1967 (Louis Harris Poll, 1992). In the same survey, more than three-fourths of executives—and nearly the same amount of journalism academics—agreed that too much emphasis was being placed on "personality" reporting, or writing stories about the CEO. Only 34% of journalists agreed, resulting in stories that made heroes of CEOs that later fell from grace as their companies faltered. But the most telling numbers are these: 92% of executives and 72% of journalists and journalism academics were concerned about a reporter's knowledge of the businesses they were covering.

Two years later, the Freedom Forum First Amendment Center published a study called "The Headline vs. The Bottom Line: Mutual Distrust Between Business and the News Media." The study found that more than two-thirds of journalists believed that they did not make mistakes on the technical details of business stories. However, more than three-fourths of executives felt the opposite way. (Haggerty and Rasmussen, 1994, p. 12) In addition, the same survey found that nearly half of all journalists believed they were not adequately trained for reporting about business, whereas 7 out of 10 executives were convinced that reporters did not have the business background they needed (Haggerty and Rasmussen, 1994, p. 10).

Ten years later, many of the same attitudes and beliefs exist about the value of business journalism. A 2002 survey conducted by Seltzer & Company for the Reynolds Foundation and the American Press Institute concluded that the nation's business leaders are unimpressed with the quality of business reporting in most daily newspapers and describe business journalists as lacking a basic understanding of how businesses operate. "They don't ask questions that probe below the surface and so their reports do not convey the detailed information business leaders need," said the report (Seltzer, 2002, p. 2).

The survey also found that when newsroom executives rated five beats, business desk reporters earned the lowest ratings, and that business was a low priority for resources in the newsroom—even though a number of solid—even brilliant— stories in business journalism have helped readers understand complex issues and warned them of future problems. In fact, Pulitzer Prizes were awarded to business reporters in both 2001 and 2002.

Why then is business journalism held in such low esteem, given that the quality of stories and the content in business coverage has improved overall and is more objective than it was 50 years ago?

Part of the problem is perception. Business stories are considered by many to be staid and unwieldy, with too many numbers and complicated topics to be of any interest to the average reader. Business is too often covered for the elite in business.

But business writing can—and should—be interesting to the masses, and it should be some of the best journalism today in newspapers, magazines, and on television. Virtually every person in this country spends time each day thinking about how much money they make, or whether they have job security, or whether they should be looking for a new job. They want to know if now is the time to refinance a home mortgage, or whether the CEO of the company where they work is considering selling the business. They want to know what companies are in financial trouble so they do not invest in their stocks. And they want to know what businesses might be good places to work.

Simply put, they want better business coverage.

THE KEYS ARE UNDERSTANDING AND ANALYZING

The most important aspect for business journalists around the world is to understand and comprehend what they are writing about. A business editor at a large metropolitan newspaper recoils at remembering his first story as a professional writer 15 years earlier, when he confused revenue with net income. That mistake, if it had not been caught by a careful editor, would have called into question the facts throughout that story and the entire business section.

But as we've seen, mass communication outlets have never placed much emphasis on training and teaching their business reporters and editors the ins and outs of the business world. It is not just reporters on the business desk, unfortunately, who need this understanding of business topics and concepts. Reporters throughout every section of every newspaper and every magazine and every Internet news site and every television news station will eventually come across a story that involves money or business in some fashion. Without the knowledge to cover the story adequately, they will be doing a disservice to their readers or listeners.

And it's not just the journalists. Public relations professionals also often do not understand many of the concepts and ideas that they are writing about in press releases for companies. They too have not gone to school to learn how to read a balance sheet or analyze an executive's compensation package.

There is so much for a business journalist to learn to be an effective reporter. They need to know how to report and write about the economy and about government regulation and taxes affecting businesses. They need to understand how businesses operate, and why some businesses make money whereas others lose money. They need to know the role of executives and other managers inside a company, and that some businesses do not exist to make money, but to serve the community.

Without all of this knowledge and more, mistakes get into the story that hurts all business journalists. Some business journalism experts resort to letting their readers know when others in the field are making mistakes. The following column by *St. Paul Pioneer Press* writer Edward Lotterman shows how a reporter can make assertions about business and the economy that may be refuted by others.

Some members of the financial press continue to flub international economic issues. Consider an Associated Press article published in this newspaper Tuesday.

Under the headline of "Dollar still lags against euro, yen," it states: "The dollar continued to languish Monday at its lowest levels against the euro and yen since around the end of last year. The dollar and U.S. equities sustained a blow from the Conference Board's composite Index of Leading Indicators."

Later, it notes, "Much of the foreign exchange market's focus was on the dollar's fragility against the Japanese currency."

This same wire service reported three days earlier that "the U.S. trade deficit improved slightly in March as growth in exports . . . outpaced the growth in imports."

Associated Press editors and writers apparently don't see any irony in reporting a trade deficit as bad news, then three days later describing an infinitesimally weaker dollar in negative terms, such as lags and languish.

This could be compared to a weather forecaster who cheerily reports we had another beautiful day with no rain to interrupt anyone's activities. Then, after a commercial, he notes that "the devastating drought" continues.

Our imports exceed our exports precisely because the dollar is strong, just as a drought occurs when there are many sunny, rainless days. It is as idiotic to cheer a narrowing trade gap and decry a weaker dollar, as it is to cheer a bright, clear day and moan about the lack of rain.

The U.S. dollar is overvalued by any number of measures. This helps consumers, but hurts producers, especially those firms that export goods or compete with imports.

A "strong" dollar clearly equals "expensive" American products abroad.

The irony of Tuesday's article is that it ended with the following observation: "Japanese pension funds have been getting pressure to buy foreign assets to generate capital outflow that is necessary to keep the yen from appreciating."

If a "strong" currency were good for the economy, why would the Japanese government initiate actions to keep the yen weak? Does the Japanese economy function in a fundamentally different way from that of the United States? No, it doesn't.

Japanese business and government know that an expensive yen is bad for Japanese output and production, just as an expensive dollar is bad for U.S. producers and employment.

History tells us that when nations incur long-running deficits in their current account sections of balance-of-payments tabulations—which include imports and exports—currencies inevitably decline in value.

When the dollar gets cheaper, American consumers will buy fewer newly expensive imports, and U.S. producers will sell more newly inexpensive exports.

This can occur gradually, giving consumers and businesses time to adjust strategies, or it can occur abruptly in a few months or quarters. Again, history tells us that gradual adjustments usually are less disruptive than harsh ones.

Thoughtful U.S. citizens should welcome gradual weakening of the dollar over a sustained period. There's no reason other than misguided xenophobia for Americans to cling to a strong dollar.

But the media continue to report any decline in the value of the dollar as bad news and any increase as good news.

The media play a vital role in a democracy. Articles that enlighten the public foster better economic policies and a better level of living.[1]

After reading that critique, you become nervous about writing that first story about the economy, don't you? Not to worry. It is not as hard as it seems.

The simplicity of Lotterman's explanations of a strong currency and trade help any reader understand what he is writing about. (A contrary argument to Lotterman's can also be made, that is, if the dollar weakens too much, foreigners who own U.S. financial stocks may sell them, causing a rapid rise in interest rates.) Yet too many journalists, including business journalists, seek to impress their readers by using multisyllable words in explaining arcane topics the meaning of which many of them quietly admit they are not 100% sure about.

In addition, many reporters simply regurgitate what they have been told or have read regarding a business topic without questioning the validity of the meaning or fully understanding what they are writing about. And that can lead to problems, for both the reporter and the reader or listener. As we have seen in numerous surveys, business executives and other readers can easily tell by reading a story when a reporter does not fully understand what he or she is writing. That should not be the case. True, newsrooms are places where deadline pressure prohibits reporters from spending a day or two researching a topic until they feel comfortable writing

---

[1]From "Media Need to Know Value of Dollar vs. Trade Defecit," by E. Lotterman, May 26, 2002, *St. Paul Pioneer Press*, p. 1C. Copyright 2002 by *St. Paul Pioneer Press*. Reprinted with permission.

about it. But that is where an editor with the knowledge should take the time and care to guide the reporter along, imparting his or her wisdom.

So knowledge and understanding of business topics is vital not just for reporters, but for their editors as well. Reporters who cover county or city government have a basic understanding of how governments operate from their high school and college political science classes. And many sports reporters have spent countless hours as youths watching and playing the games that they now write stories about.

Yet few business reporters and editors ever took a class or majored in business to obtain the knowledge that they needed to do their job. "Nobody would send someone to cover the Red Sox who doesn't know what a shortstop is," said *New York Times* business columnist Floyd Norris at the 2003 Society of American Business Editors and Writers annual conference. Yet "many people send reporters to cover business who are not real sure what earnings per share means" (Nelson, 2003, p. 6).

BUSINESS REPORTING CONCEPTS IMPORTANT IN ALL JOURNALISM

But for the government reporter and the sports reporter, as well as reporters covering education, the police beat, or the courts, it can be important for them to know and understand how businesses operate. Every single story in the newspaper or on the nightly news or on an Internet Web site can be traced back to one single important common denominator: money.

Money is important in every part of society. Throughout society, most of that money is generated from business and the economy. Governments receive tax money to operate. Where does the tax money come from? From consumers and businesses who either live in or are located in the government's jurisdiction. Sports teams need money to pay athletes and to build stadiums and arenas. Where does that money come from? From the people and corporations who pay to sit and watch the games. Business and the economy are related to everything. Private companies are now running schools. Universities now rely more on their endowments and how that money is invested on Wall Street to pay for faculty salaries and to keep tuition costs low. Murders, thefts, and robberies often revolve around one person's need to obtain more money or material items purchased for large sums of money.

Here's an excellent example of a story on the front page of *The News & Observer* in Raleigh, NC that shows how a decline in interest rates—one of those business topics that a few reporters may not fully understand even though they have written stories mentioning it—has had far-reaching effects, likely across the country:

> Cities across the state, including in the Triangle, saw huge declines in investment earnings this past year, a financial setback that complicates matters for officials who are putting budgets together and trying to hold the line on property taxes. To many

local governments, the losses amounted to as much or more than what Gov. Mike Easley withheld last year in settling state budget woes.

"It's a big hit," Raleigh Finance Director Perry James said. "You can't do as much with the money, naturally, if you've got less of it."

But the municipalities can't fault the governor for the poor investment showing. Blame the Fed.

Trying to boost the economy, the Federal Reserve cut short-term interest rates 11 times in 2001, and then once more last November.

With each cut, the Fed lopped off potential returns for local governments, which by state law must put most of their cash in conservative investments tied to the federal fund rate— things such as certificates of deposit and treasury bills.

As a result, after several years of rosy returns, those investments tanked in the fiscal year that ended June 30, 2002.

Just about any portfolio tied to the stock markets did, too, including the state pension fund, which lost $3.3 billion a year ago, or 5.8 percent of its assets.

While no one can predict the future of markets, the returns for local governments are expected to remain weak this year as the Fed keeps the fund rate at its lowest level in decades.

There is a bright side: Local governments are getting lower interest rates on money they borrow to erect buildings and other infrastructure projects, though much of that activity has slowed with the uncertain economy and budget picture.

For local budget writers and finance officers, the low earnings make already tight budgets even more difficult.

Raleigh pocketed about $12 million on its investments in the 2001–02 fiscal year, state records show. That's a steep, 46 percent decline from the $22.1 million it made the previous fiscal year and $20.6 million the year before that.

Durham pulled in $7 million on its investments in 2002. But that's $6.7 million, or 49 percent, less than the year before.

"This had been, in some years, a really big source of income for us," said Julie Brenman, Durham's budget director. "It was nice to generate money through investments and not by going to the citizens. Without it, you have to make service cuts or go find other ways to get revenue."

For both Raleigh and Durham, those investment losses exceeded what Easley withheld in reimbursements and other payments to local governments, an action that prompted an outcry from local officials and threats of lawsuits.

In Chapel Hill, where less money is invested overall, the town saw a $700,000 decrease in 2002. That's 57 percent below the $1.2 million it made on investments in 2001.

Cary did the best of all the large local Triangle governments, bringing in about $3.1 million less in fiscal 2002 than the year before, a 23.8 percent decline.

None of the Triangle cities fared as badly as Winston-Salem, one of the few governments in North Carolina with permission from the General Assembly to invest money in more volatile stocks.

Winston-Salem posted an actual loss— not just a lower gain— on its investments in fiscal 2002 and 2001, losing a combined $51.4 million. In the previous three years, however, Winston-Salem rode the booming stock market, outperforming all other cities in the state and bringing in $137 million in combined investment profits.

Last summer, Durham's representatives in the General Assembly won authority to let Durham City and Durham County invest taxpayer money the same way Winston-Salem does: By putting up to half its cash not needed for at least five years into stocks.

So far, Bull City officials said, they haven't followed through because of what has happened in Winston-Salem.

Durham, like other cities, has three priorities for its available cash: The top two are safety and "liquidity," which means not locking it up in long-term investments. Next is the yield, or earnings.

Vance Holloman, deputy director of the state's Local Government Finance Commission, which monitors investments, said the losses have been significant.

"It's another revenue there's less of," he said. "And it adds to the fact that sales taxes are down and haven't grown."

For now, though, most local governments say they will ride out the losses and wait for better times. There's no concerted lobbying effort to allow municipalities to put more money in stocks, according to the N.C. League of Municipalities.

More flexibility brings greater risk—as Winston-Salem has seen.

"Mostly, people are focused on getting this economy improved," said Margot Christensen, a league spokeswoman. "That way, the investments they are in already will do better and perform better."[2]

This story explains simply the effects of lower interest rates and a falling stock market to anyone who lives in these towns. The bottom line: There is less money in the bank accounts of these city governments to spend on the services that it provides the people living in their areas. And explained that way, it is a concept even the self-admitted business illiterate can understand.

Here is a story in which the reporters have gone through the tedious and often boring task of reading public documents filed with the SEC to explain the relationship between an aircraft manufacturer, an airline that owned a plane that crashed, and a company that was supposed to service and maintain the airplane. The story ran on the front page of the "City and State" section of *The News & Observer*—not in the business section. And it was co-written by a metro reporter, not someone with extensive knowledge of business documents. Despite the reporters' limited understanding of what these documents mean, the story clearly explains the conflict of interest in the business relationship.

The company that built the 19-seat turboprop commuter plane that crashed in a fireball last Wednesday has a financial stake in both the airline that flew the plane and the firm that did maintenance on it earlier in the week.

With the airline's parent losing millions in recent years and actively trying to cut costs, the companies' financial ties have raised questions whether safety may have been compromised, according to some industry experts.

"If the vendor whose feet you're supposed to hold to the fire for quality control was also one of your owners, how robust can you be about [demanding] everything being done to the highest standard?" said Jim Burnett, a former chairman of the National

---

[2]From "Fed's low rates zap city budgets: Investment + Income goes into free fall," by Andrew Curliss, February 10, 2003, *The News & Observer*, p. 1A. Copyright 2003 by the Raleigh News & Observer. Reprinted with permission.

Transportation Safety Board, the federal agency that investigates crash causes. "There could be a safety issue there."

But others say such relationships are common in the airline industry and pose no conflict. And a spokesman for the manufacturer, Raytheon Aircraft, said it had no active role in the operations of either the repair company, Raytheon Aerospace, or the owner-airline, Air Midwest.

"We don't have any involvement in the day-to-day operations of either company," said Tim Travis, a spokesman for the manufacturer, Raytheon Aircraft Co. of Wichita, Kan.

The financial links are being scrutinized because the plane crashed only a few days after repairs were made to the tail elevator control assembly by Raytheon Aerospace, a company based in Madison, Miss. Those repairs, along with a heavy load of baggage, have emerged as possible causes of the crash.

The company that did the repair is 26 percent owned by the plane's manufacturer and, formerly, was a wholly owned subsidiary. Raytheon Aircraft sold off a majority stake in the repair subsidiary to privately held Veritas Capital of New York for $270 million in June 2001.

The financial ties between the companies spread a few months later when the manufacturer got partial ownership of Air Midwest's parent company, Phoenix-based Mesa Air Group.

According to documents filed by Mesa Air Group with the U.S. Securities and Exchange Commission, the manufacturer last February agreed to pay Mesa up to $5.5 million annually so Mesa could keep up with payments on planes it had acquired from Raytheon Aircraft. In turn, Mesa gave the manufacturer warrants to buy 233,068 shares of Mesa stock at $10 a share.

To date, Raytheon Aircraft has bought nearly $1.3 million in Mesa stock and still holds warrants to buy another 103,133 shares. Last Wednesday, the manufacturer took a partial interest in another airline, too.

Cheyenne, Wyo.-based Great Lakes Aviation, which flies dozens of the Beech 1900s, was late on the payments for many of the aircraft and gave the manufacturer a 36 percent stake in the airline to reduce debt.

Air Midwest did not return repeated calls. But the airline, which, like the manufacturer, is based in Wichita, has been shedding planes from its fleet of 1990 Beech commuters. Many passengers prefer jets, and during the past fiscal year, Air Midwest returned 12 of the Beech 1900s. The airline currently has a fleet of 43 of the planes.

Air Midwest's parent company also has been trying to reduce its maintenance bills. During its last fiscal year, which ended Sept. 30, Mesa Air Group reached a cost reduction agreement with the repair company that resulted in $3.4 million in savings along with reduced turboprop flights, according to SEC documents.

Like most other airlines, Mesa has been hit hard by the sluggish economy and sharp dropoff in passengers following the September 2001 terrorist attacks. After earning almost $59 million in 2000, the company lost $48 million in 2001 and lost $9.3 million during the latest fiscal year. In December the company asked its 3,300 employees to voluntarily take a 5 percent, one-year pay cut in return for bonuses.

Burnett, the former NTSB member, said the web of shared ownership poses risks.

"Right now we don't know if there was a problem, but the potential is there," said Burnett, now a lawyer in Arkansas. "It makes it very difficult for Air Midwest to say, 'We're not satisfied with the service; we're going somewhere else.'"

"It would be better from a safety standpoint to have an arms-length relationship," Burnett said.

Other industry experts disagreed.

"There's no conflict because it's in the manufacturer's best interest to keep the planes flying and safe because it's their product," said Michael Boyd, president of the Boyd Group, an Evergreen, Colo.-based aviation consulting firm. "Ultimately it's their reputation on the line and their liability, too." If a plane goes down, everybody looks at them.

"Who is better to be involved than those who built it?" Boyd said.

Boyd and longtime aviation consultant Mort Beyer of Arlington, Va., pointed to General Electric, which for years has financed airlines' purchases of jet engines, which the company builds. GE also overhauls the same engines, they said.

Beyer compared it to auto dealerships that offer financing deals for car buyers.

"It is not a unique arrangement," Beyer said of the Mesa-Raytheon deals. "I think it's an area of opportunity. It enables airlines to get airplanes and to fly them and maintain them efficiently. It also helps passengers, because they have air service, which they might otherwise not have."

Boyd said, "I'd rather have Raytheon do the work than someone else because they know the product. If it isn't being done right, Air Midwest is the one that gets burned; the repair company gets burned; and the manufacturer gets burned."[3]

A reader looking at the *News & Observer* story gets a great explanation of how these three companies are tied together, and why some aviation experts object to such relationships. For the families who lost relatives on the flight, the story points to what might have gone wrong. Again, this is not a business story, per se. But it takes an understanding of business to fully explain the topic in such a way that the reader can grasp its importance and reach his or her own conclusions about what might have happened to cause the plane to crash.

DOING BETTER FOR AUDIENCES

Thus we see that business journalism has made great strides and has made the world a better place to live in, but still falls short of being as good as it can be. But, small changes are occurring in business journalism. More editors and reporters have realized that they need more and better training to do their jobs. Membership in the Society of American Business Editors and Writers, an industry group that recently celebrated its 40th anniversary, is at an all-time high, and hundreds attend its seminars and conferences to learn how to do a better job.

Others interested in the quality of business journalism are taking steps to improve quality. The Reynolds Foundation recently gave a $3 million grant to the American Press Institute to develop seminars and a Web site to teach business journalists all around the country. And on college campuses across the country, more journalism schools are teaching business and economics reporting classes

---

[3]From "Crash Raises Vendor Issue," by D. Price and L. Perez, January 12, 2003, *The News & Observer,* p. 1B. Copyright 2003 by The Raleigh News & Observer. Reprinted with permission.

than ever before, giving students some basic training and understanding. Most important, however, there appears to be a newfound diligence on the part of newspapers, magazines, Web sites, and television stations to be more critical in their business coverage.

Peter Carlson (2002) who critiques magazines for *The Washington Post*, lauded this change of heart recently after reading two important articles: one in *Fortune* that exposed white-collar crime and another in *Business 2.0* that skewered American business. "Business magazines have turned into pit bulls, printing stories excoriating these once-deified entrepreneurs as crooked, mendacious, rapacious robber barons," wrote Carlson (p. C4). "To tell you the truth, I much prefer these new stories," he added. "They're a lot more fun—and probably a lot more accurate, too" (p. C4).

Harder, tougher, more thorough business reporting done by reporters who have been properly trained and who better understand what they are writing about will dramatically raise the quality of stories and topics discussed in mass communication today.

Many consider the 1990s a golden age for business journalism, a time in which coverage expanded dramatically and more stories were written. Others would argue that business journalism has yet to reach its peak. Quality reporting and editing is needed now more than ever, as more and more consumers cope with job losses and harder-to-find investment ideas. Business journalism has helped them in the past, but not as much as it could. "It is time for business journalists to be more ambitious," said Martin Baron, editor of *The Boston Globe*, "to set their sights higher, to routinely produce the finest journalism in America" (Baron, 2001).

The readers need and want better business journalism.

REFERENCES

Barhart, B. (2002, January). Downturn brings out the critics. *The Business Journalist.* p. 8.

Baron, M. (2001, October 15). Business Journalism: Is the boom over? Speech to the Society of American Business Editors and Writers. Retrieved September 1, 2002 from http://www.sabew.org.

Caldwell, C. (1996, Fall). Trading places. *Forbes Media Critic,* vol. 3, No. 4. pp. 80–86.

Carlson, P. (2002, March 26). Post-Enron, a reversal of fortune. *The Washington Post.* p. C4.

Curliss, J. A. (2003, February 10). Fed's low rates zap city budgets: Investment income goes into free fall. *The* (Raleigh) *News & Observer.* p. 1A.

Fost, D. (2002, March 3). Stung by Enron, business journalists increase their vigilance. *San Francisco Chronicle.* p. G1.

Haggerty, M., & Rasmussen, W. (1994). Mutual distrust between business and the news media. Nashville, TN: Freedom Forum First Amendment Center. pp. 1–92.

Kann, P. (2000, March 14). Peter Kann talks about Barney Kilgore, *Princeton Packet.* p. 1.

Layton, C. (2003, March). Ignoring the alarm. *American Journalism Review.* pp. 21–28.

Ledbetter, J. (2003, January 2). The boys in the bubble. *New York Times.* p. A17.

Lewis Harris Poll (1992). The quality of business journalism in America. [Brochure]. Boston: John Hancock Financial Services.

Lotterman, E. (2002, May 26). Media need to know value of dollar vs. trade deficit. *St. Paul Pioneer Press.* p. 1C.

Ludwig, M. (Spring/Summer 2002). Business journalists need specialized finance training. *Newspaper Research Journal* Vol. 23, No. 213, pp. 129–141.

Madick, J. (2003, Winter). Financial reporting: Lessons of the Enron collapse. *The Harvard International Journal of Press/Politics.* pp. 3–7.

Nelson, D. (2003, July). It's a question of ethics. *The Businness Journalist.* p. 6.

North, G. (2002, February 6). Enron, spawn of Business Journalism. LewRockwell.com. Retrieved Dec. 11, 2002. From http://www.lewrockwell.com/north.

Price, D., & Perez, L. (2003, January 12). Crash raises vendor issue. *The* (Raleigh) *News & Observer.* p. 1B.

Pummer, C. (2002, August 29). How business media is failing its audience. CBS.Market Watch.com. Retrieved September 1, 2002 from http://www.cbs.MarketWatch.com/news.

Salpukas, A. (1999, June 27). Firing up an Idea Machine. *New York Times.* p. C1.

Seltzer & Co. (2000). Business Journalism Surveys. Reston, VA: American Press Institute.

Smith, T. (2002, February 19). Asleep at the switch. News Hour with Jim Lehrev. Retrieved Nov. 25, 2003. From http://www.pbs.org/newshour.

Other Books About Business Journalism and Business Journalism History

Dealy, F. X. (1993). *The power and the money: Inside the Wall Street Journal.* New York Birch Lane Press.

Emery, E., & Emery, M. (1984). *The press and America.* Englewood Cliffs, NJ: Prentice-Hall.

Quirt, J. (1993). *The press and the world of money.*Byrou, CA: Anton/California-Courier.

Rosenberg, J. M. (1982). *Inside the Wall Street Journal: The history and the power of Dow Jones and Company and America's most influential newspaper.* New York: MacMillan.

Scharff, E. (1982). *Worldly power: The making of the Wall Street Journal.* New York Beaufort Books.

SUGGESTED EXERCISES

1. Write a 500-word essay explaining how business has affected your life, from the products and services you purchase to where your parents work. How would your life be different without one or two of those businesses being in operation?

2. Review a newspaper's business section for a week. Bring in the sections and discuss with the class what stories you thought were informative and what stories you did not understand. What helped you understand the stories? What was hard to decipher?

3. With the rest of the class, discuss the relationship between a CEO and a business reporter. Should a CEO attempt to help educate a reporter that he or she sees is struggling with a topic?
4. In a group discussion, talk about the qualifications for being a business reporter or editor. What skills should they have? What should they know about how business and the economy operate? Where should they obtain that knowledge?

2

Building a Foundation

DEFINING PUBLIC AND PRIVATE COMPANIES

Read the business section of almost any major metropolitan newspaper, and you will find that most of the stories are written about large companies with stock traded on an exchange in New York.

For example, the front page of the business section of the *News & Observer* in Raleigh, NC, on December 12, 2002 featured articles about Quintiles Transnational, a Durham-based drug company that is a public company, as well as Bank of America, the Charlotte-based bank that is also public. Inside the section were articles about defense contractor Northrop Grumman and phone company Sprint, also public companies. All of these stories mentioned how big these companies are in terms of revenue or profits.

But read the business section of a paper in a smaller town or city, and the stories are likely about small, private companies that are not required to disclose information about their operations. For example, the December 12, 2002 front page of the business section of the *Huntsville Times* in Alabama contained a story about Alterations & More, a one-woman alteration and sewing business. As a private company, this alteration business was not required to disclose its revenue and profits. As such, those details are omitted from the story. The reporter likely never asked for them. The dichotomy is evident. A public company sells stock to the public and its stock is traded on an exchange. Because of this, the public company is required to file information with the Securities and Exchange Commission (SEC), making it easy for business reporters to obtain facts for their stories.

Private companies, for the most part, are not required to file such information. (We will learn later where to find financial information about some private companies.) As such, there are few financial numbers to use to flesh out a story about a private company, unless the company willingly discloses its performance. Still, learning how to read and dissect financial information available on public companies with a stock that is traded daily can be valuable for every reporter. Public companies operate similar to private companies. They are both in business to make money. And they are both typically run by a CEO.

There are advantages and disadvantages to both structures. An advantage is that public companies are able to more easily raise cash to expand. However, they are also required to disclose their financial performance every three months. That can be a disadvantage, particularly after a bad quarter. In contrast, private companies often have a harder time raising the money to expand. That can be a disadvantage for them, particularly if they need to expand quickly to take advantage of a business opportunity. But if they have a bad quarter, few people know. That can be an advantage, particularly in businesses where perception is important.

Bill Smartt, an executive vice president and chief financial officer (CFO) at DHL Airways, a California-based airfreight carrier, said that private ownership allows the company to maintain a low profile. If it had to file information with the SEC as a public company, competitors like Federal Express could analyze those facts for a competitive advantage. In the end though, public companies and private companies are similar in how they measure success, that is, by increased sales or revenues and improved profits. These are, unfortunately, concepts that many inexperienced business reporters confuse.

This chapter explores some basic concepts that every business reporter and editor should know, beginning with how the business journalist does his or her job. Business reporting and editing is just like any other beat at a newspaper, or at a television or radio station, or even at an Internet site. It requires knowledge of who the best sources are and where to find documents that will answer questions and provide the details to make good, and often great, stories.

Business reporting also requires knowing something about how business operates, much like the school reporter needs to know how the school board works and when it meets. Businesses have a reputation of being tight-lipped and unwilling to provide information. But knowing when they are required to provide information can give reporters an edge. Knowing something about business will also make sources such as company executives more willing to talk when they see the reporter as a knowledgeable person.

Sometimes, the world of public and private companies can overlap, and not just for the business reporter. The CEO of a public company may also own private businesses that could be affected by the performance of the public corporation. When regulators went after former HealthSouth CEO Richard Scrushy for allegedly inflating earnings at the medical rehabilitation company, they sought to freeze the assets at his other private businesses.

In another example, The owner of the Carolina Hurricanes hockey team was asked questions, during a conference call, about whether his public company (Compuware) was for sale and, if so, how that might affect his ownership of the privately held hockey business:

Days after shutting down part of his youth hockey operation, Carolina Hurricanes owner Peter Karmanos said he had been approached about selling part of his software company, Compuware.

Karmanos confirmed he had spoken with other companies about a sale but had no interest in breaking up Compuware.

"The company is not up for sale, and divisions of the company are not up for sale," Karmanos said in a conference call with analysts Wednesday to discuss Compuware's fourth-quarter earnings. "Some people have inquired. That's about it. All kinds of people inquire.... There's no active discussion going on at this point in time."

The Dow Jones news service reported that BMC Software and Texas Pacific Group were potential buyers for part of Compuware.

Over the past $3^{1}/_{2}$ years, Karmanos has seen his net worth take a beating as Compuware's stock has plummeted. According to SEC filings, Karmanos owns 15.7 million shares of Compuware, worth about $75 million. Compuware is valued at about $1.8 billion.

Karmanos founded Compuware with two friends in 1973. Long a supporter of youth hockey in his hometown of Detroit, he purchased the Hartford Whalers NHL franchise in 1994 and moved the team to North Carolina to become the Hurricanes in 1997.

Karmanos this week decided to fold the Compuware Ambassadors rather than move them to a new, more expensive league. Eric Lindros and Pat LaFontaine played for the Ambassadors as teenagers.

The Ambassadors, based in Plymouth, Michigan, played in the North American Hockey League, a struggling junior league for college-bound players. Many of its teams are either folding or joining rival junior leagues.

Karmanos will continue to fund Compuware's large Michigan youth hockey program.

In addition to the Hurricanes, Karmanos still owns the Plymouth Whalers of the Ontario Hockey League, which is a semi-pro junior league for NHL hopefuls, and the Florida Everblades of the minor-league East Coast Hockey League. He also owns the arenas in which those two teams play.

The Ambassadors are not part of Gale Force Holdings, the Canes' holding company.

"It's not related to Gale Force in any way," general manager Jim Rutherford said.

Compuware stock closed at $4.81 on Thursday. That's down from $7.37 last May and $37.25 in December 1999. The company said this week it plans to buy back $125 million of its stock to boost the price.

Compuware has had 11 straight quarters of declining sales but reported net fourth-quarter income of $21.4 million, compared to a loss of $335.9 million a year ago.

"It's been a tough year, but we believe we have turned the corner," Karmanos said.

Karmanos has said he maintains more than $400 million in "liquid" assets not tied to Compuware.[1]

Public companies and private companies also interact with each other on a daily basis, even though they may not have the same owner. Public companies sell their products and services to private companies, and vice versa. In many ways, the success of public companies and private companies are intertwined. If there is a business relationship, a company will want its business partner to succeed. If the business that it is working with does not succeed, then it may not be able to pay its bills, which could hurt the company. And both types of companies are vitally important to the U.S. economy. There are many more private companies than there are public companies. Think of all of the small businesses in a community, no matter if they are one-person shops or factories with 1,000 workers. Virtually all of them are likely to be private companies.

But think about the companies providing products you may buy the most. Nike shoes, clothes from The Gap, drinks from Coca-Cola, computers from Dell, software from Microsoft, cars from General Motors, a homes from D.R. Horton, gasoline from Chevron. All of these companies are public companies with stock that is traded every day by investors.

WHY MANY MEDIA OUTLETS WRITE PRIMARILY ABOUT PUBLIC COMPANIES

In fact, as mentioned at the beginning of this chapter, most medium- and large-sized newspapers focus most of their coverage of business news on public companies. The focus of Internet news sites such as CBS.MarketWatch.com and the Bloomberg News site and television stations is also on public companies. Newspapers in major metropolitan areas such as New York and Washington spend the bulk of their coverage on public businesses. The reason behind this is simple: For the reporters and editors, there is more information available with which to write stories about public companies than there is about private companies. Because of the nature of public companies, they are required by law to disclose information. Many times, it is information that executives may not want to disclose, but that they have to. Most private companies are under no such restrictions.

---

[1] From "Hurricanes' owner says his company isn't for sale," by L. De Cock, May 9, 2003, *The News & Observer,* p. C1. Copyright 2003 by The Raleigh News & Observer. Reprinted with permission.

As mentioned earlier, public companies are regulated by the SEC, a federal agency created in the 1930s to provide protection for investors against unscrupulous companies duping people into buying worthless stock. One of the ways the SEC has gone about its job of protecting investors and maintaining the integrity of the stock markets is to require companies with stock that is publicly traded to provide information that anyone can read. The SEC does this by requiring companies to file documents disclosing certain information. For example, financial performance must be filed every quarter by a certain deadline. Public companies are also required to file a documents with the SEC to disclose important events in their existences, such as changes in auditors, mergers, or acquisitions. In addition, the SEC regulates other parties involved in the investment industry, including companies who buy and sell stocks and mutual funds, like, for example, large money management companies who pool stock purchases into funds to limit the risk for investors. These companies are also required to disclose information to the public.

Although these filings are intended for investors to decide whether they want to put their money in the company's stock, the documents are available for anyone to read on the SEC's Web site at www.sec.gov and at other sites. Increasingly, companies have started providing access to their SEC filings on their own Web sites as well. These documents, as detailed in later chapters, can be invaluable sources of information for reporters writing stories about companies and other business topics. In fact, they have become required reading for any serious business reporter as they are often filled with interesting revelations, such as lawsuits and severance packages for departing executives, both of which are events that companies are required to detail.

If the SEC believes, on the basis of the filings, that a company or someone has violated its rules, it will investigate the business or person. Often, the SEC will levy fines, or set restrictions on the future involvement of that business or person in public companies or trading stocks. The staff of the SEC (made up of five commissioners who are appointed by the president) writes rules when it is determined that new regulations are needed. Once a rule is proposed, the SEC invites companies and others to comment on the proposal. These comments are available for review by any reporter, and can often make for an interesting story, particularly if companies are opposed to the new regulations.

One of the most important rules—at least for reporters writing stories about public companies—passed by the SEC in recent years is Regulation Fair Disclosure (FD), which went into effect in 2000. Regulation FD requires public companies to provide information to every investor at the same time. This has resulted in companies providing telephone and Internet access to discussions their managements have with investors and analysts, and to more filings with the SEC disclosing pertinent company information. Many reporters have taken advantage of Regulation FD to increase their access to information from public companies. Reporters can listen to these earnings conference calls or presentations at investor conferences along with everyone else.

Another important SEC regulation also provides business reporters access to the inner workings of a company. Each public corporation is required to hold an annual meeting of its shareholders once a year. The invitation to the meeting is in the form of an SEC filing that is sent to every shareholder of the company, even if they just own one share of stock. In fact, many business journalists or business news departments in the past would purchase one share of stock for each company they covered to make sure they received this invitation.

The annual meeting, as it is commonly known, is often held near or at the company's headquarters, but sometimes it may be held at another company location. Large corporations such as Anheuser-Busch and General Electric rotate the location of their annual meeting among their various locations. Anheuser-Busch, for example, prefers to hold its meetings at its theme parks and breweries. Although journalists are not specifically invited to annual meetings by law, virtually every public company allows reporters to attend the meetings.

At these meetings, the companies discuss some of their business. For example, an auditor may be elected to review the company's books. Or new board members are elected. Each shareholder can vote on the proposals presented at the annual meeting, even if they don not attend the meeting. Other shareholders can also make proposals to be voted on at the annual meeting, so it is important to do some homework before the event. These proposals are detailed in the invitation to the meeting, which is known as the proxy statement. In the proxy statement, the shareholders explain their proposal and why they think it is good for the company. The company likely responds and states whether it supports or is opposed to the shareholder proposal.

Such conflict is common between public companies and shareholders, but these proposals can often make good stories, or serve as examples and anecdotes for a larger trend story. Here is an example of a shareholder proposal in Coca-Cola's 2003 invitation to its shareholders:

The Amalgamated Bank LongView Collective Investment Fund, 11-15 Union Square, New York, New York 10003, owner of 819,209 shares of The Coca-Cola Company Common Stock, submitted the following proposal:

RESOLVED: The shareholders request that the Board of Directors of The Coca-Cola Company ("Coca-Cola" or the "Company") adopt an enforceable policy to be followed by the Company, its subsidiaries, bottlers and distributors with respect to operations in Colombia, said policy to be based on the International Labor Organization's Declaration on Fundamental Principles and Rights at Work and to include the following:

—All workers have the right to form and join trade unions and to bargain collectively (Conventions 87 and 98);

—There shall be no discrimination or intimidation in employment. Coca-Cola shall provide equality of opportunity and treatment regardless of race, color, sex, religion, political opinion, age, nationality, social origin or other distinguishing characteristics (Conventions 100 and 111);

—Employment shall be freely chosen. There shall be no use of forced, including bonded or voluntary prison, labor or of child labor (Conventions 29 and 105,

138 and 182); and prepare a report at reasonable cost to shareholders concerning implementation of this policy.

SUPPORTING STATEMENT: As a global corporation, Coca-Cola faces many regulatory regimes and public pressures exposing it to various risks. Managing operations effectively and increasing shareholder value depend on public and governmental goodwill. A company's record of good corporate citizenship is a valuable asset.

This proposal addresses Coca-Cola's risk with respect to human rights violations in Colombia. Coca-Cola's operations there have become controversial in recent years. In December 1996 several gunmen went to a bottling plant in Carepa, Colombia, asked to see union leader Isidro Gil and shot him to death. Mr. Gil was one of more than 1500 Colombia trade unionists who have been killed in the past decade. Human rights groups contend that many of these killings are carried out by a paramilitary group.

Coca-Cola is a defendant in a lawsuit filed by Mr. Gil's family. The suit alleges that managers at the Carepa bottling plant hired paramilitary gunmen to kill two union organizers in 1994. The gunmen then allegedly threatened workers, and the executive board of the union was forced to resign. A new board that included Mr. Gil was then elected. The suit also alleges that the plant manager told workers that he had given paramilitary gunmen an order to destroy the union and that two days after Mr. Gil's death, plant managers passed out union resignation forms, and dozens of workers resigned shortly after that.

Workers at other bottling plants are also plaintiffs in the suit and allege that they were threatened, falsely imprisoned and tortured by paramilitary gunmen. Coca-Cola and the other defendants have denied these allegations and have moved to dismiss the case on legal grounds. Their motion is pending.

In our view, the situation in Colombia warrants the pursuit of a more active policy to protect human rights in connection with the Company's operations and those of its subsidiaries and distributors in Colombia.

WE URGE YOU TO VOTE **FOR** THIS RESOLUTION.

Statement Against Share-Owner Proposal Regarding Company Policy in Colombia

We believe that through the Company's existing policies and activities we already comply with both the spirit and intent of the proposal.

As the proponents of this proposal are aware, our current policies substantially address the subjects raised in the proposal. For example, our policies affirm the lawful right to third-party representation, prohibit the use of forced labor and child labor, and provide for equality of opportunity. We have similar written expectations of our suppliers, vendors and contractors. Many of our bottlers have developed parallel statements of principle. These commitments are essentially identical to those sought in the proposal.

Moreover, we believe that, as a truly global corporation, the best course is to operate by a uniform set of standards and principles applicable to all our worldwide operations—such as what we have in place—rather than with a set of principles which, like those proposed, apply only to a single country or region.

For these reasons, we do not believe that this proposal is in the best interests of our business or our share owners.

It is important to note that this proposal repeats allegations contained in a lawsuit against the Company and its bottling partners. An investigation has revealed no evidence to support the allegations. Neither The Coca-Cola Company nor its bottler partners have committed or directed abuses against Colombia's trade unionists, or condoned any such abuses.

The Board of Directors recommends a vote AGAINST the proposal regarding Company policy in Colombia.[2]

After reading this proposal in Coca-Cola's filing, a reporter might feel there is a story to be written examining the conditions of union workers in Coca-Cola bottling plants around the world or just in South America. Or a reporter could use the proposal to examine the company's relationship with unions.

Annual meetings are also good for reporters to attend because the CEO and other executives will often make a presentation about the company's past performance and future direction, and take questions from those in attendance. If the company is small, there might not be many shareholders in the audience, and the reporter might be able to ask a lot of questions, getting answers from executives that might not otherwise have been as candid if the reporter had tried calling on the telephone or going through the company's public relations staff. Other companies will set aside time after the annual meeting for its executives to meet with the media attending the annual meeting. This too can be valuable for a reporter to attend. The more time a reporter can show his or her face to an executive and demonstrate that s/he is interested in learning about a company and its operations, then the more likely the CEO or president will answer questions the next time that reporter calls by phone.

Listening to the questions being asked by the shareholders at the meeting can also elicit story ideas. The question-and-answer period at some large company annual meetings can last for hours. Some shareholders may be angry about a company's poor performance and may ask the CEO and president pointed questions about how they are going to turn it around. Others may want the company to take on an environmental cause. There are even shareholders who attend dozens of annual meetings a year, simply to harangue executives and ask for better performance. The most famous of these is Evelyn Y. Davis, a Washington, DC resident who writes a newsletter for shareholders and who once told a CEO that he was better looking than his predecessor.

In addition, an annual meeting can often be a barometer of a company's current standing. If there are many negative questions asked at an annual meeting, then that likely means the business has performed better in the past, and shareholders would like the corporation to return to that level. If there are few negative questions, then the company has likely been performing well financially and with the interest of its shareholders in the fore. Watch the mood of the attendees and the executives to get a feel for where a company is headed and where it has been.

Public companies are a vital part of news for any mass communication outlet, particularly regional or local publications, because many area residents are likely shareholders of the company. Because many companies offer their employees

---

[2]From Form DEF14A, by the Coca-Cola Company, March 5, 2003, SEC Publication No. 0000950144-93-002640. Washington DC: Securities and Exchange Commission.

stock ownership plans, the workers are also likely shareholders and would want to know information about the company from an independent source. In Atlanta, for example, thousands of residents own stock in Coca-Cola, and Home Depot has made millionaires out of hundreds of its store employees. The same situation exists across the country in the Seattle area, where Microsoft's stock has made many people, besides Bill Gates, rich—even by today's standards. Find out what stocks are owned by residents in your circulation or distribution area. Those are likely to be the companies that they will want to read stories about.

PRIVATE COMPANIES STILL IMPORTANT TO EVERY ECONOMY

Private companies, on the other hand, are not required to discuss disagreements with its shareholders in public, and they do not hold annual meetings and allow reporters to attend. Still, private companies are vital to the readers or viewers of any mass communication outlet that reports on business news. The largest private companies in the country include businesses such as grocer Publix Super Markets, accounting firms PricewaterhouseCoopers and Ernst & Young, Enterprise Rent-A-Car, jeans maker Levi Strauss & Co., and Hallmark Cards—all businesses that have touched our lives in one way or another. These are multibillion dollar corporations equal in size or larger than many of their public competitors.

In fact, there are more than 250 private companies in the United States with more than $1 billion in annual revenue. According to *Forbes* magazine, these companies have more than 3 million employees combined and contribute more than $700 billion in products and services to the country's economy.

Think again about the businesses that are part of your everyday life, such as the corner gas station, the local bank branch, or the restaurant downtown where you might eat dinner tonight with your spouse or significant other. Chances are these businesses are privately held enterprises owned by maybe just one person or a handful of investors, with no intention to ever sell shares of stock to the public. For every public company, there are likely to be dozens of private competitors. These are companies, especially in small- and medium-sized towns and cities, that could be the largest employers in the area. Many local hospitals are privately owned, as are factories and manufacturers. Yet despite their status as private companies, they still can make for compelling stories that readers and viewers will want to know about.

However, there is more work involved in finding information about private companies. In fact, many business journalism experts believe that the easier job is to write stories about public companies because much of the information needed to explain a company and its strategy, as mentioned earlier, is available in SEC documents. Thus, a reporter can earn his or her stripes as a top-notch business journalist by writing a story about a private company because the information about which will be much harder to find and company executives may not want the exposure.

There is still a lot of information to be found in public documents about private companies. It just may not necessarily be with the SEC, although there are many private businesses that do have to file documents with the federal regulatory agency. For example, private companies that have issued bonds to investors will file documents with the SEC although they are still considered a private business. But there are plenty of other places to get information on a private enterprise. All businesses have to incorporate themselves with the state in which they are operating. This is typically done with the Secretary of State's office or a regulatory entity such as the State Corporation Commission, as it is called in Virginia. These documents will often tell a reporter who owns the business, who the executives are, and where it is located.

Other state regulatory agencies also have plenty of information about private companies. Most businesses, from a barbershop to a bank, are regulated in some form or another by a state agency. Many of these state agencies will have information about the performance of the business in their files. Federal agencies such as the Occupational Safety and Health Administration within the U.S. Department of Labor and the Federal Trade Commission also have jurisdiction over thousands of private companies. They are worthy places to look for information if you are writing about a business with stock that is not publicly traded.

Although most small private businesses are possibly owned by only one or two people, other private companies have solicited investors, just not in the same way that public companies sell stock to investors. Many private businesses, seeking capital to expand, will go to investment firms that specifically invest in small operations. These firms provide what is typically known as venture capital funding.

Venture capital firms give private companies money—sometimes millions of dollars—to expand their operation. In return, the owners of the private company give the venture capital operation an ownership stake in their business. The venture capital executives may want to have a say in how the company is operated after they invest money. But they are hoping that the business will take their money and put it to good use, expanding their operations in a prudent manner and creating additional profits, making the private business more valuable. Often, a venture capital firm will sit on its investment in a private company for five to seven years, and then sell it to another investor, or sell its stake in the company to public investors in an initial public offering, making the private company a public operation.

In the 1990s, dozens and dozens of venture capital firms poured billions of dollars into private businesses in the hopes that the money would provide huge investment returns. Much of that money went into Internet, technology, and telecommunications companies. However, because many of these companies went out of business, leaving venture capital investors with nothing in return, such investments are now done with closer scrutiny.

Here is a story from the *Kansas City Star* that explains the process many private companies in the Midwest went through to try to entice venture capital firms into investing money into their companies:

Money doesn't grow on trees the way it used to.

Venture capitalists have long since stopped scribbling out checks to companies they've just met. And in many instances they've stopped writing checks altogether.

According to a quarterly survey of venture capital investment by Pricewaterhouse-Coopers, only $3.8 billion in venture capital was invested in the first quarter. That's a five-year low, and a far cry from the $28.6 billion invested in the first quarter of 2000.

But those facts didn't seem to dampen the enthusiasm of the 20 companies on stage Thursday morning at InvestMidwest, a venture capital forum in Kansas City designed to link high-growth companies with investors.

The fourth annual event, which alternates between Kansas City and St. Louis, drew representatives from more than 30 venture capital firms. Companies from throughout the Midwest got 10 minutes each to introduce themselves and explain why they were looking for venture financing.

"If we would have had this venture conference last year in Kansas City, it would have been voices in the wilderness," said Abel Mojica, a partner with Kansas City Equity Partners. "No one would have been here to listen."

But Thursday morning, sitting around tables in a hotel ballroom at the Hyatt Regency Crown Center hotel, investors were listening—even if their pens weren't poised over blank checks.

"For three years they've hunkered down and covered their heads up and said, 'We're just going to cover ourselves," said David Lazenby of ScenarioNow Inc., a St. Louis technology company.

After making his presentation to investors, Lazenby said he was confident the situation was finally beginning to turn. Money has been piling up, he said, and investors are starting to uncover their heads.

Thomas Marshall, a partner with Hickory Venture Capital in Huntsville, Ala., said his firm was still very cautious and, like many venture firms, was likely to continue to be much more wary of risky early-stage investments.

His firm wants potential investments to already have at least $1 million in revenue. Not exactly early stage.

Doug Elliott, a partner with Duff & Phelps Capital Partners in Chicago, said venture firms had learned from the past two years. They're looking for better deals–a bigger ownership stake for their investments—which is easier to come by in lean times.

Of course, investors are also looking for the next big success story.

"Everyone's looking for the next Microsoft or Amgen," Elliott said.

Companies seemed to understand what the investors wanted. They pointed to rising revenue lines, new customers and estimates for continued growth as they made their pitches for funding in sums of $2 million to $12 million.

"We intentionally made the decision 2½ years ago to focus on getting customers rather than growing," Lazenby said.

Now the company can pull out figures for solid sales and customers when it talks to investors.

Tim Donnelly, president and CEO of SoftVu, a Leawood company that specializes in e-mail marketing, started in his basement on a shoestring. He points to that as an advantage.

"Our competitors who received 20, 30, 40 million dollars in capital went through it a little too quickly," Donnelly said. "We went from seed company in my basement, and we've been able to learn from some tough situations' before large investments were at stake."

The area firms making presentations Thursday were SoftVu, Deciphera Pharmaceuticals Inc. of Lawrence, Felton International Inc. of Lenexa, Chemidex of Lenexa, K2B Inc. of Kansas City, Nexgenesis of Lenexa, and Proteon Therapeutics of Kansas City.[3]

Venture capital meetings are great places to meet owners of small, local, private businesses and get a feel for the companies. At these meetings, private companies are essentially trying to sell themselves and their business to investors, much the same way a public company does when it sells stock to the public. In that regard, private companies can be just like public businesses. And if a private company gets an investment from a venture capital firm, it can be a story for the business reporter. What will they do with the money? How much of an ownership stake in the company are the venture capital investors receiving in return?

Ownership in private companies can come in all shapes and sizes. Private companies also often offer shares to their employees, just like many public companies. Ownership in a private company such as an insurance agency or a barbershop can be controlled by one person. These owners can be valuable resources for stories— besides those about their companies. As business owners, they are often cognizant of the economy and make decisions on a daily basis such as whether they should spend money to expand or hold back until times get better. If a business reporter is writing a story about economic conditions in his or her community, then private business owners can be the best interviews.

In addition, private business owners often band together in groups such as the local Chamber of Commerce. The business reporter should attend their functions and get to know them; one can never know when those contacts will come in handy. As mentioned earlier, private businesses far outnumber public companies in every community. The reporter should find out who these private businesses are and how they are doing, and he or she will likely get a better picture of the area than he or she would by talking to executives at a public company, which may only have a local subsidiary run by a manager who reports to higher ups in another state or country.

WRITING BUSINESS-RELATED STORIES

Writing business stories appears daunting at first. They are filled with numbers, and use terms such as adjustable rate mortgage or off-balance sheet financing that the average reader may not understand. And then there is the whole idea of

---

[3]From "Companies make pitch for venture capital funds," by S. King, May 23, 2003, *Kansas City Star,* p. C3. Copyright 2003 by the Kansas City Star Company. Reprinted with permission.

10 tips for newcomers to business coverage, by Shelly Haskins, business editor, *Huntsville Times.*

1. *Write for the reader, not for the company:* Companies will try to spin information to their benefit. Consider the source, and seek our objective opinions. For example, if a company announces a layoff, make sure you consider whom that affects, whether it be the laid-off employees, customers who might see a decline in service, or investors, who might see their stock go up or down, depending on the severity of the company's financial picture.

2. *Business coverage is not just company coverage:* It's the economy, it's saving and spending, it's investing. Do personal finance stories on ways to save or invest money. Keep your eye on the local economy. Is unemployment up? How are workers getting by without jobs, or what are people doing with their money in boom times?

3. *Know the difference between news and advertising:* When you profile a business or a product, make sure there is news value there. Our advertising side gets paid to bring in ads. When you write about a business, make sure there is something there for your readers. How did it survive rough times? What strategies do the owners use to keep their employees and customers happy? And be careful about profiling brand new businesses. Their business plan hasn't stood the test of time.

4. *Keep your eye out for trends:* For example, Alabama has landed several auto industry companies in recent years—Mercedes, Honda, Toyota and Navistar. The auto industry provides high-paying jobs, but auto and truck sales go up and down with the economy. Is your local economy diversified enough to survive an economic downturn? Why, or why not?

5. *Try to take the reader behind the scenes:* When Toyota chose Huntsville to build the engine for its popular Tundra truck, the deal—like all other big economic development projects—was done behind closed doors. When it's over, use your reporting skills to reconstruct how the deal came down. You'll get some revealing and even fun anecdotes, such as how many dozen hushpuppies from Greenbrier Barbecue does it take to land a Target Corporation distribution center, and insight into how the recruiting process works.

6. *Don't forget small business:* Make a special effort to profile small businesses. They provide 85 percent of the jobs, but don't get as much attention as the large employers. Encourage business owners to send you information on recent employee training or industry honors—it will give you a peek into their success, as well as provide fodder for briefs.

7. *Know your community:* It's all a matter of scale. Deciding what is and isn't an important business story depends on how your readers are. In Huntsville or Birmingham, the corner grocery store might close or change hands without us giving it muck ink. In Scottsboro, the fact that the local FoodWorld is now a Bi-Lo is front-page news.

8. *Get to know the business people in your community, and find out their concerns and agendas.* Just because you go to the chamber functions and press the flesh doesn't mean that you're a chamber lackey. You'll get better results from sources if they know you. Imagine how you'd feel if someone you'd never met called you up cold and

wrote down everything you said for publication. Many business people don't trust the media, and, for the most part, they don't have to talk to you. Establish relationships and build trust.

9. *Read business publications for background and story ideas:* More often than not, I'll come away from *BusinessWeek* or the *Wall Street Journal* with a story idea that can be localized to Huntsville. At the least, it gives you an idea of the economic landscape, or just conversation fodder for those chamber functions.

10. *Read your own small print.* The stuff your own newspaper runs in agate can be gold. Building permits, particularly, can give you an idea of where the biggest homes are going, what kind of projects are underway, etc. Bankruptcy listings might tip you off to a declining business segment. Legal advertising can also signal changes in ownership, or who has tax liens. Business licenses can lead you to interesting new business trends to write about. One *Huntsville Times* writer found a business called "Clip at your Curb," in the business license renewals. That turned us onto a growing trend of "come to you" businesses that will do everything from washing your car to washing your dog. Another writer at another newspaper got a tip that their city was being considered as a potential site for a new telemarketing center, with 450 new jobs. Seems the company placed a blind ad for hundreds of workers with phone skills—it was a test to see how many job seekers would respond. The newspaper did a story; the city later landed the new company.[4]

whom a business reporter must interview to get the information to write a story. CEOs and presidents of large corporations are busy people, and sometimes appear curt in responding to questions because they have other topics on their mind—like running their company. Other sources in the business world are also difficult to reach and even harder to interview. Many of them do not have to talk to a reporter; it is not part of their job description. However, a reporter should not get discouraged. These people started out with a limited knowledge of the business world as well. With a little experience and some training, the reporter will be able to talk like an expert with these sources, opening them up, and will begin writing stories that read as if the writer knows more about the copper tubing industry than the company executive.

Business stories can come from a number of different places. Some of the best business stories are developed in a reporter or editor's mind by watching trends and understanding economic numbers or by tracking a company for months or years at a time. Great business stories are not always readily apparent. They can take time to report and write as well. The bulk of business stories written today come from basic sources, such as company news releases or releases from regulatory agencies. Stories can also come from regulatory filings made by companies or from lawsuits or other documents filed in a courthouse. Stories can come from source tips such

---

[4]From "10 tips for newcomers to business coverage," by S. Haskins, *The Huntsville Times*. Reprinted with permission.

as union officials or from people who overheard a conversation. Business stories can also come from attending meetings such as zoning or planning commissions.

Part of the skill in being a good business reporter is knowing where to find these stories, and what sources are important to a specific beat. For some business writers, the bulk of their daily stories may come from company or regulatory agency announcements. For others, stories may be developed from documents such as lawsuits or zoning requests. Reporters should be knowledgeable enough about their beats to write stories that show the reader or listener that the writer knows what he or she is discussing. Part of the job is understanding what a company or a regulatory agency is saying in a release. Sometimes, the hardest part is translating the release into a story that the average reader can understand.

The problem with news releases is that they are sometimes written or approved by lawyers and the language may not be clear. Or the release can be written in such a way as to downplay or hide what may be the actual news. A company could issue a release announcing its quarterly dividend of 20 cents per share. But what the release does not state is actually the news—that the dividend has been reduced from the 40 cents per share the company has been paying its shareholders in previous quarters. Or a company could announce a new advertising campaign for its major product, without disclosing that its commercials from last year were a total flop and the company slogan has been changed. It is important, therefore, for any writer to research any topic they are writing about. Even the most mundane and basic announcements could have a hidden news peg just waiting to be found.

Using numbers effectively and correctly in business-related stories is also a key to success in making your writing understandable to readers and viewers. Make sure that numbers are used sparingly in most cases. Numbers can bog down a story, and make the reader disinterested. If the story requires a lot of numbers, such as a story about a company's earnings, make sure the numbers are spread out. Do not put revenue and earnings numbers in the same paragraph. Make sure they are used in separate parts of the story, with explanations as to why the numbers rose and fell. Behind every number is a story.

Numbers can be tricky in other ways. Make sure you are comparing applicable numbers. For example, it is not valid to compare earnings growth from the second quarter with that from the third quarter, but it is valid to compare earnings from the third quarter of one year with the third quarter from the previous year. Earnings for quarters can fluctuate on the basis of what a company is selling, or moves made by the company itself to boost sales. For example, Coca-Cola's revenues and earnings are stronger in the second and third quarters of a year because that is when the weather is hottest and consumers want drinks to quench their thirst. So it would not be a meaningful to compare the company's earnings in the warm second quarter with earnings in the chilly first quarter. But it would be meaningful to look at earnings at the second quarter of this year compared with earnings from the second quarter of last year.

Follow the money. How is the money being spent? Where is the money coming from? Who decides how the money gets spent? What is the money being spent on? The business reporter who answers these questions in virtually any business story will write a story that will be compelling and will help explain an issue to readers. Thus, knowledge of key business terms is also critical. A reporter who does not know the difference between revenue and earnings should look them up, or ask

---

The craft of business writing, by Bill Choyke, business editor of the *Norfolk Virginian-Pilot.*

1. *What's the best story?* What's the most interesting development, story line or trend, and then focus, but keep an open mind.
2. *Read, read, read:* Best practices works in journalism too. Read the *Wall Street Journal, New York Times* and other metros and read not only for content but storytelling and structure. Read more, of course, but make an effort to read, digest and even study several stories per week.
3. *Think presentation from the beginning:* Yes, *USA Today* has changed the world, like it or not. From the outset, think how the words, graphics, photo and even design can work together. Brainstorm with your design/graphic folks. They can make the writing easier.
4. *Don't be afraid of numbers.* Numbers often don't lead to the truth, only to other numbers. Still, follow the numbers, including the money, and give the story a business feel. Numbers don't bite.
5. *Be creative within the parameters of your reporting:* Report, report, report, and then think creatively how you can creatively present your material within the parameters of your reporting.
6. *Understand before you write:* I plead guilty; unfortunately we all have done it. Make sure you know what the source/expert is saying before you write it. If in doubt, ask. If still in doubt, don't use it. Don't ask the reader to understand something that you have no idea what it means.
7. *You are your best editor:* Read aloud. If it distracts others, do it softly. Edit yourself and if you have time before you turn it in, read a hard copy one more time, and/or read a hard copy after the edit.
8. *Think globally, write and edit locally.* Think context and more. A good newspaper is first with local news, occasionally localizes the national news and reaches for excellence with it nationalizes (or regionalizes) the local news.
9. *Don't empty your notebook.* Report extensively, but write to fit—fit the news. Resist the urge to unload everything. Be selective with focus and purpose.
10. *Open yourself to feedback:* Don't resist constructive criticism and open yourself to ideas and suggestions or co-workers, friends and family, and even editors.[5]

---

[5]From "The craft of business writing," by B. Chouke, the *Norfolk Virginian-Pilot.* Reprinted with permission.

another reporter or an editor to explain the terms. Misusing business terms in a story that is published or appears on the air can cost the media outlet, the reporter, and the entire journalism community some credibility.

Above all, a journalist taking on the task of reporting and writing a business story should write with as much clarity as possible. Explain in simple words what is going on, avoiding the jargon terms permeating the corporate world today. Do not write about a "reduction in force." Call it a "layoff" or a "firing." When a company "agrees to divest certain assets," it's "selling" a business. Let your reader know what's happening in terms that they can read and understand.

Terms commonly used by corporations in releases that may need to be explained to average readers include market capitalization, takeover, joint venture, charges, forecasts, stock split, debt, liabilities, strategic alternatives, margins, shortfall, and reserves. Many of these are defined at the end of this chapter.

Corporate America can seem daunting. It may not be as easy to understand as writing about crime or government. What can be easy to understand, however, is that virtually every business story comes down to money. Businesses are trying to make more money. The more money they make, the happier their shareholders— public or private—will be. Increased profits send up the stock price of public companies, whereas increased profits make a private company more valuable, also increasing the value of a private shareholder's stake. The business world is fascinating. There are con artists and people trying to make the world a better place to live. The job is try write about both in a way that will attract the widest audience possible.

LABOR AND CONSUMER ISSUES

When writing business stories, the reporter should think about the impact the topic of the story is going to have on readers or viewers. Is the story about a large, local company that has lost money? That could mean that the business might have to lay off some of its workers, or that it might even be headed toward bankruptcy court. That is information that its workers, as well as its customers, will want to know. Is a local company adding new jobs to its plant? That could mean more jobs being added to the community, improving the area's unemployment rate and boosting the economy by adding more workers to the area who have money to spend on groceries, housing, and other goods and services. That is also information that people will want to read about.

All too often business journalism forgets about the worker and the consumer. Yet, arguably, these two constituents are the most vital to writing about business and the economy. Without workers, companies would not have the ability to produce and sell their products and services; and without consumers going into stores every day, these companies would not have anyone to sell their goods and services to.

The best business writers do not lose sight of this important fact. They write stories for the employees and for the consumers of a company, making sure the ramifications of those readers are explained in a story.

Merger and acquisition stories are not just about Company A purchasing Company B. In virtually every case, it is also a story about employees losing jobs as the two companies merge operations and no longer need two secretaries for the CEO, or two CFOs for that matter. Product recall stories are not just about the millions of dollars an automaker will have to spend to fix a defective seatbelt on its latest model. It is also a story about the consumers who purchased that car who were injured or killed when the seatbelt did not properly protect them in an accident. Stories about stores closing are not just about going-out-of-business sales. They are about competition, and the workers who are losing their jobs, or external forces that have caused a business's decline. The beginning of this story from the *Door County Advocate* in Sturgeon Bay, Wisconsin, is a classic example:

> The ailments of the aging Michigan Street bridge probably are the biggest reason Sturgeon Bay is losing a grocery store.
> Nick Swinarski said he hates to beat a dead horse but in this case, he can't help it. After 10 years of owning Nick's SuperValu in downtown Sturgeon Bay, Swinarski is bowing to the pressures of the long and frequent bridge closings.
> The bridge problems are the primary reason he and his wife, Cindy, are closing their Third Avenue grocery store.
> While it may be difficult for most residents to assign a dollar value to the inconvenience caused by the Michigan Avenue bridge closings, it's not difficult for business owners like Swinarski. Each time the bridge closed, Nick's SuperValu recorded a 35 percent drop in sales.
> Over the past three years, Swinarski was forced to slash his peak workforce of 40 to the 18 employees who current work for him. The job cuts were directly attributable to eroding sales and decreased profits, a downward trend like a kind of snowball effect that all started when traffic flow across the bay was interrupted due to bridge repairs.[6]

The story goes on to explain how many times the bridge has been closed by repairs, how many grocery stores will remain in the town—a vital piece of information for downtown grocery shoppers in Sturgeon Bay—and the fact that Swinarski tried to sell his store, but could not find any takers.

The best business writers think of what they would want to know if they were a consumer or an employee when writing such stories. The reporters who covered the Firestone tire recall pointed out how people could go out to their driveways and read the writing on their tires to determine if they had come from one of the factories that had been producing faulty tires. They explained it because they

---

[6]From "Nick's bows to bridge pressures," by D. Fitzgerald, August 16, 2002, *Door County Advocate*. Copyright by the Door County (Wisconsin) Advocate. Reprinted with permission.

thought of their audience. Good business journalism has a particular audience in mind. Many reporters try to think of a relative, like their mother or father, or even a grandmother, and write their stories on the basis of information they know that person would understand.

Business journalism is full of stories that help consumers and workers. Publications call these stories "news you can use" or personal finance reporting. They are stories offering advice on how to write resumes, or how to go into a job interview prepared for the tough questions. These stories show readers what to wear to work, or proper e-mail etiquette. But, it is also much more. Personal finance journalism can run the gamut from everything to picking the correct stocks in a down market to how to read your life insurance policy and understand what it means. Stories that provide a service to readers are valuable commodities in business journalism, and many publications and Web sites are devoted solely to this type of reporting.

Writing business stories is also thinking of consumers for stories that may not even be in the business section, but have a business angle. If a town can maintain its high credit ratings, then it can borrow money at a lower rate than other cities and keep its taxes for its residents down, as this local news story from *The Herald-Sun* in Durham, NC explained:

> The city of Durham's financial health is good enough for three national agencies to give it their entire AAA credit rating, a status that allows the city to borrow money at lower interest rates.
>
> In fact, with the help of the ratings and unusually low interest rates, the city recently refinanced roughly $45 million in outstanding debt at 2.505 percent. Before, the city had been paying about 5 percent to 6 percent on the money.
>
> But one firm warned that the city should stop dipping into its savings account to cover operating costs, as it did last year.[7]

The business reporter should think about employees and consumers with any business story he or she writes, and should include the impact on these people in the story. The previously arcane story about Coca-Cola's earnings falling as a result of rising prices will have more meaning to consumers if the reporter explains that fewer grocery shoppers bought the company's 12 packs after it raised its prices in the last quarter.

BUSINESS JOURNALISM ETHICS

At one time or another, anyone involved in the reporting, writing and editing of news will be faced with an ethical dilemma. It is no different in reporting on

---

[7]From "Durham gets AAA credit rating from 3 agencies," by B. Evans, May 22, 2003, *Durham Herald-Sun,* p. B3. Copyright 2003 by the Durham Herald Company Inc. Reprinted with permission.

business and economic topics. In fact, it can be argued that because everyone who is involved with business reporting is an investor or a consumer of products, then everything they do in their lives results in an ethical question. Is a reporter covering the beverage industry showing favoritism by drinking Pepsi instead of Coke? Can a reporter who only does grocery shopping at Kroger because it is her favorite store write objectively about the Cincinnati-based company? These questions may seem silly, but they have been raised in one form or another at business journalism seminars and conferences.

One of the major potential areas of conflict for business journalists is Wall Street. Many business reporters and editors own stock in companies or shares in mutual funds. Should that prevent them from writing or editing stories about investing or stories about companies or industries in which they own stock? There is no clear-cut answer to this question, unfortunately. Media outlets handle it differently, and some handle it on a case-by-case basis. Bloomberg News, for example, allows reporters to write about events of companies in which they have a financial interest as long as they disclose that interest to their supervisor and state that this interest will not prevent them from covering the topic in an unbiased manner.

But the ethical guidelines at *Business Week* are strict. Its guidelines state that staff members may not "report, write, or edit a story about a company in which they or members of their immediate family own securities" (Business Week Editorial Handbook, 1992, p. 2). The magazine says that its prohibition extends to securities in companies in industries that a reporter covers or is reasonably likely to cover, but does not include mutual funds, Treasury bills, or municipal bonds. So, theoretically, the magazine's mutual funds reporter in Boston who follows Fidelity can invest in some of that company's mutual funds.

CNNmoney.com's Web site for business news goes one step further. With each of its stock-related stories, it uses a disclaimer that reads, in part, "Stock recommendations and comments presented on CNNmoney.com are solely those of the analysts and experts quoted. They do not represent the opinions of CNNmoney on whether to buy, sell, or hold shares of a particular stock" (CNNmoney.com, 2003).

The trust of a business reporter and editor is vital. If that trust is violated, then the readers and viewers may not believe the next story. But, more important, reporters and editors who violate these rules have been fired. In 1990, the *St. Petersburg Times* fired its banking reporter after he shorted—or bet that the stock would fall—shares of a bank that he mentioned in a story. Many journalism ethics codes, including the one for Dow Jones, the parent of the *Wall Street Journal,* prohibits any of its reporters from shorting stocks. Some publications go as far as to require their reporters and editors to disclose their financial holdings to bosses. These financial holdings can include stocks, bonds, and other securities. Some even require that these investments be disclosed for their spouses and immediate families.

Do such situations always result in an ethical conflict? Not necessarily. For example, when I was a reporter at the *Atlanta Journal-Constitution,* I inherited

Southern Co. stock when my grandfather died, and then I was asked to cover a speech by the company's CEO on downtown redevelopment. I went to my boss and explained the stock ownership, but told the editor that I did not think a speech on downtown development had anything to do with Southern, the largest utility in Georgia. The editor allowed me to cover the speech.

Another ethical issue that many business-related journalists encounter is when they have obtained information during the writing of a story that they believe will move a company's stock up or down once it is published. Virtually all ethics codes prohibit reporters from acting on the information that they obtain in the course of their job. However, the temptation can be great. Suppose a reporter for the *Seattle Times* was told by someone within Microsoft Corporation that the software maker would greatly miss analyst earnings projections for the quarter. Such information would likely send the company's stock crashing downward. A reporter could short a large amount of the company's shares, and likely make a profit if that were the case. But the reporter, and the newspaper, would also lose the trust of readers if the trade was disclosed. Becky Bisbee, the business editor at the *Times,* would likely fire this reporter. The Dow Jones ethics codes prevents its reporters and editors from trading in the stock of any company mentioned in one of its stories until the third trading day after the article has appeared.

Does stock trading still occur among business staff personnel? Yes, it likely does. But the stock trading and ownership likely should be confined to companies and industries outside of the reporter's beat. In some cases, however, some media outlets have made exceptions. For example, professional investors and money managers have been allowed to write columns for online publications and other outlets. Media managers argue that these people provide an insight into stock ownership and trading that journalists can not offer. In many cases, the stock ownership of the Wall Street pro is disclosed at the end of the column or article. In many cases, the writer will even disclose that he owns a stock when it is mentioned in the writing.

Other ethical situations often arise when a journalist is reporting or writing business stories. For example, imagine you are a reporter interviewing the president of a local grocery store chain, and at the end of the interview he gives you some loaves of bread, baked fresh from one of the locations, to take home. Do you take them? If you do not take them, do you think the executive would be upset, or not understand why you are turning him down? Most business publications frown on their reporters and editors accepting anything of value, but that value often has a limit. Some newspapers do not allow its reporters and editors to accept anything that is worth more than $25. In many cases, this is done to allow a public relations person or another source to buy a reporter lunch. But most media outlets would like their reporters to repay the favor the next time the staffer has lunch with the source.

Nothing should be accepted in return for coverage. A personal finance writer should not accept an offer to refinance her mortgage at a lower rate by a banker she is interviewing for a story. The situation can arise with even the most innocuous of stories. An executive at the advertising agency that handles the famous AFLAC duck commercials once offered to let a reporter pick the next AFLAC trivia question for a televised sporting event. Was the request just an honest, friendly gesture? Perhaps, but the reporter turned down the offer, not wanting anyone to think his coverage of the ad campaign had been tainted. In addition, companies will often send their products and promotional material to business desks along with news releases. In many cases, the material can be worth well more than $25. PepsiCo, when it announced several years ago its huge Pepsi Stuff promotion in which consumers could win everything from leather jackets to T-shirts, sent a huge box of the material to dozens of newsrooms. Many reporters promptly shipped the goods back, while others donated the clothing to charity.

A journalist's interviewing and reporting tactics can often raise problems as well. In possibly the most famous case of an ethical transgression in business journalism, a reporter for the *Cincinnati Enquirer* was fired after spending a year reporting and writing a huge series of stories on Chiquita Brands International, Inc. The reporter had illegally broken into the company's voicemail system.

Business publications should not allow their reporters and editors to break the law when trying to find news. Many of them do not allow their staff members to disclose their identities or lie when obtaining news. "This does not mean we cannot use extraordinary efforts to obtain information, but we must always do so above board and as clearly identified members of the staff of this magazine," states *BusinessWeek's* code (1992, p. 3). "Anything else could compromise the use of the material so obtained and could give rise to a legal claim for misrepresentation, invasion of privacy, or trespass."

Other standard rules of journalism conduct apply to business reporting. Sources should not be made up. Quotes should not be faked. (The recent example of former *New York Times* reporter Jayson Blair, who fabricated dozens of interviews, should make this clear to everyone.) Reporters and writers should not use their position as members of the media for personal gain. Paid trips should not be accepted. Above all, it is the business reporter's job to maintain integrity. If there is anything that might give even the appearance of impropriety, then it is something that the reporter should not do. As Bloomberg News' ethics code states, "You must abide by the highest standards of journalistic ethics and perform your duties with objectivity and without intent to achieve financial gain for yourself, directly or indirectly" (Bloomberg Way, 1995, p. 176). Are there gray areas? Of course. Any reporter should discuss what he plans to do with his editor or a superior before any action is taken.

APPENDIX

Society of American Business Editors and Writers Code of Ethics

Statement of purpose: It is not enough that we be incorruptible and act with honest motives. We must conduct all aspects of our lives in a manner that averts even the appearance of conflict of interest or misuse of the power of the press.

A business, financial and economics writer should:

1. Recognize the trust, confidence and responsibility placed in him or her by the publication's readers and do nothing to abuse this obligation. To this end, a clear-cut delineation between advertising and editorial matters should be maintained at all times.

2. Avoid any practice which might compromise or appear to compromise his objectivity or fairness. He or she should not let any personal investments influence what he or she writes. On some occasions, it may be desirable for him or her to disclose his or her investment positions to a superior.

3. Avoid active trading and other short-term profit-seeking opportunities. Active participation in the markets which such activities require is not compatible with the role of the business and financial journalist as disinterested trustee of the public interest.

4. Not take advantage in his or her personal investing of any inside information and be sure any relevant information he or she may have is widely disseminated before he buys or sells.

5. Make every effort to insure the confidentiality of information held for publication to keep such information from finding its way to those who might use it for gain before it becomes available to the public.

6. Accept no gift, special treatment or any other thing of more than token value given in the course of his professional activities. In addition, he or she will accept no out-of-town travel paid for by anyone other than his or her employer for the ostensible purpose of covering or backgrounding news. Free-lance writing opportunities and honoraria for speeches should be examined carefully to assure that they are not in fact disguised gratuities. Food and refreshments of ordinary value may be accepted where necessary during the normal course of business.

7. Encourage the observance of these minimum standards by all business writers.

Addendum to Code of Ethics

Guidelines to Insure Editorial Integrity of Business News Coverage:

1. A clear-cut delineation between advertising and editorial matters should be maintained at all times.
2. Material produced by an editorial staff or news service should be used only in sections controlled by editorial departments.
3. Sections controlled by advertising departments should be distinctly different from news sections in typeface, layout and design.
4. Promising a story in exchange for advertising is unethical.

5. Publishers, broadcasters and top newsroom editors should establish policies
   and guidelines to protect the integrity of business news coverage.

Cautions On Use Of Non-Journalists With
Conflicts Of Interest In The Subject Matter:
Using articles or columns written by non-journalists is potentially deceptive and
poses inherent conflicts of interest that editors should guard against. This does not
apply to clearly labeled op-ed or viewpoint sections or "Letters to the Editor."[8]

GLOSSARY

annual meeting: A meeting held at least once a year by public companies where
   shareholders are invited to attend and vote on matters. Company executives
   typically give presentations about the performance of the business at the
   meeting, and answer questions from shareholders in the audience.

charge: A one-time expense by a company that negatively affects earnings.

forecast: A company or analyst's estimate of the company's future earnings.

joint venture: Agreement by two or more parties to work on a project together.

market capitalization: Value of a corporation as determined by the market
   price of its issued and outstanding common stock. It is calculated by multiplying the number of outstanding shares buy the current market price of a share.

private company: A business whose ownership is confined to a handful of
   people, or whose ownership cannot be traded on a stock exchange.

proxy statement: A document sent to shareholders of public companies to
   invite owners of the company's stock to its annual meeting. The proxy
   statement will include information about proposals to be voted on at the
   annual meeting.

public company: A business whose ownership includes stockholders that
   have purchased shares on Wall Street.

reserve: Money set aside by a company from earnings to pay for other
   expenses, such as a pending lawsuit or other contingencies.

restructuring: General term for major corporate changes aimed at greater
   efficiency and adaptation to changing markets. This can also be called a
   downsizing, a recapitalization and a major management realignment.

Securities and Exchange Commission: A federal regulatory agency that
   oversees all publicly traded companies. As part of its mission to protect
   investors and the investment community, the SEC required public companies
   to file documents disclosing financial information and other material so that
   it can be read by anyone.

shortfall: Amount by which a financial objective has not been met.

---

[8]From Society of American Business Editors and Writers Code of Ethics. Copyright by
the Society of American Business Editors and Writers Inc. Reprinted with permission.

stock split: Increase in a corporation's number of outstanding shares of stock without any change in the shareholders' equity or the aggregate market value at the time of the split. In a split, the share price declines.

strategic alternatives: Anything up to and including the sale of a company.

takeover: Change in controlling interest of a corporation. A takeover may be a friendly acquisition or an unfriendly bid that the target company may fight.

venture capital: Funds made available to start-up companies and small businesses, typically in return for an ownership stake and a say in how the operation is managed. A venture capital firm invests money in such companies, expecting that the company receiving the funds will grow and become successful.

REFERENCES

Blum, A. (1998, August–September). The long, hot summer: Chiquita, other retractions, firings shake newsroom ethics to the core. *The Business Journalist.* pp. 1, 12–14.

Business Week Editorial Handbook (1992). Statement of values and code of ethics. pp. 2–4.

DeCock, L. (2003, May 9). Hurricanes' owner says his company isn't for sale. *The News & Observer.* p. C1.

Disclaimer (2003) CNNmoney.com. Retrieved November 27, 2003 at http://money.cnn.com/services/disclaimer.html.

Evans, B. (2003, May 22). Durham gets AAA credit rating from 3 agencies. *The Herald-Sun.* p. B3.

Fitzgerald, D. (2002, August 16). Nick's bows to bridge pressures. *Door County Advocate.* p. 1.

Coca-Cola Company. (2003, March 5). Form DEF14A. (SEC Publication No. 0000 950144-03-002640, pp. 57–71. Washington, DC: Securities and Exchange Commission.

King, S. (2003, May 23). Companies make pitch for venture capital funds. *Kansas City Star.* p. C3

Society of American Business Editors and Writers. (2001) Code of Ethics, sabew.org. Reprinted June 19, 2003 from http://www.sabew.org.

Tannenbaum, A. (1990, November). Ruminations: A self-inflicted scandal. *TJFR: Business News Reporter.* pp. 1, 4–5, 10–11.

The Bloomberg Way. (1995). New York: Bloomberg Business News. pp. 174–176.

Other Books About Business Reporting

Clinton, P. (1997). *Guide to writing for the business press.* Lincolnwood, IL: American Business Press.

Fink, C. (2000). *Bottom line writing: Reporting the sense of dollars.* Ames, IA: Iowa State University Press.

Kurtz, H. (2000). *The fortune tellers: Inside Wall Street's game of money, media and manipulation.* New York: Simon & Schuster.

Leckey, A., & Sloan, A. (Eds.) (2003). *The best business stories of the year: 2003 Edition.* New York: Vintage Books.

Martin, P. R. (2002). *The Wall Street Journal guide to business style and usage.* New York: Wall Street Journal Books.

Surowiecki, J. (Ed.) (2002). *Best business crime writing of the year.* New York: Anchor Books.

Thompson, T. (Ed.) (2001). *Writing about business: The New Columbia Knight-Bagehot guide to economics & business journalism.* New York: Columbia University Press.

SUGGESTED EXERCISES

1. Find 10 companies in your state that are public companies and 10 companies in your state that are private companies. What information is available for each company? How does the information between the two groups compare?

2. Read the Society of American Business Editors and Writers ethics code. Discuss what it says about stock ownership. Do you think that you can write objectively about a company in which you own stock? What about a company in which you've shorted stock?

3. You're writing a story about rising gasoline prices in your community. How would you go about finding consumers to interview for this story? What types of questions would you ask them?

4. Discuss what you would do if you were a reporter for a newspaper covering Walt Disney Co. and someone from its corporate communications department offered you and your family free passes to one of its theme parks for the weekend. Would you take them? If you did take them, why would you?

5. Write down 10 important pieces of information or facts that you think every business reporter and editor should know. Do you think that every person working on the business desk at your local newspaper knows this information? Why, or why not?

3

The Economy and Business

COMPANIES DRIVE LOCAL AND NATIONAL ECONOMIES

The economy of any town, city, county, state, or country can seem to be a nebulous concept for a reporter to grasp. What exactly makes an economy? An economy can be defined as the activities surrounding the production and distribution of goods and services for consumption in a region. Those activities include paying workers to manufacture products that are then sold. The money paid to those employees goes to work in the region as they purchase other goods and services to live. Economies can grow, and they can contract. If a country or region's economy is growing, that means that jobs are being created. For a business reporter interested in the economy, a story could be written about what kind of jobs are available, for what pay, and in what industries. The converse is also true. When the economy starts to slow down, or decline, that means that there is not as much demand for a company's goods and services as there was in the past. When companies are faced with such an economic slowdown, they are often forced to lay off or fire workers.

Companies—public and private, large and small—will increase or decrease their capital expenditures on the basis of where they believe the national or regional economy is headed. If the CEO and other executives at a company decide that the economy is going to keep growing and that consumers are going to spend more money in the future, then they will likely increase capital expenditures. Capital expenditures can be defined as the money spent by a company to expand or build its business.

Companies will also decrease their spending when they think that there will not be as much of a demand for their products. Raleigh, NC-based Martin Marietta Materials Incorporated makes products that help build roads and bridges, among other things. CEO Steve Zelnak decreased the capital expenditures for the company in 2003 after deciding that the economy, particularly the spending on new construction for neighborhood roads, was not going to grow as fast as it had in previous years. Thus, any business reporter looking for clues about the economy in his or her region will want to talk to business executives. Company managements watch the economy and economic indicators closely. They do not want to be caught with too much of their product sitting in warehouses when there is no demand, and they do not want to be caught with too little of their goods being manufactured when demand is great because they are likely to lose sales.

Others are interested in what companies are doing. If a company's executive team decides that the economy is about to grow stronger than it has in the past, then it will increase its production raising the possibility that it will sell more of its goods. If it sells more of its goods, then it might have higher revenue and profits. That is something that will attract the interest of investors on Wall Street, who might want to buy the company's stock.

On the national level, a key economic indicator is a report from the Department of Commerce's Bureau of the Census, which measures shipments by manufacturers, new orders, inventories, and unfilled orders. If new orders to manufacturers are rising, that means that likely there will soon be more goods shipped. That can be seen as a positive indicator for the economy. Or if the inventory level for manufacturers is going up, that means that they are not selling as many of their goods as they once were and their warehouses are filling up. That is a negative indicator for the economy.

The Federal Reserve Board also looks at industrial production by industry—manufacturing, mining, and utilities. And it also breaks its production report down by market group, such as consumer goods, business equipment and materials, for example. The information is typically released around the 15th of every month, and is also closely watched by those interested in whether the economy is growing or contracting.

Here is how a story on the Fed's report on industrial production is typically covered by the Associated Press (AP):

> Industrial production roared back to life in January, rising by 0.7 percent while businesses boosted their stockpiles of unsold goods the month before—a pair of promising signs for an ailing economy.

The latest snapshot of activity at the nation's factories, mines and utilities—the sector of the economy hardest hit by the 2001 recession—showed an impressive rebound.

The 0.7 percent over-the-month jump in industrial activity marked a turnaround from the steep 0.4 percent drop registered in December, the Federal Reserve reported Friday.

January's increase marked the best performance since July when industrial activity also rose by 0.7 percent. The strong showing surprised economists, who were predicting a 0.3 percent advance.

The industrial sector has been the weakest link for the economy's ability to get back to full throttle, but Friday's report offered hope that the battered sector may seeing more better days ahead.

The increase in business inventories was the largest in three months as retailers apparently were betting that cautious consumers would have a stronger appetite to spend during the holidays.

December's increase was two times bigger than the 0.3 percent boost in supplies of unsold goods on shelves and back lots, which was recorded in November, the Commerce Department said in a second report Friday.

At the same time, business sales edged up by 0.2 percent in December, up from a 0.1 percent rise.

On Wall Street, the pair of economic reports gave stocks a lift. The Dow Jones industrial average was up 13 points and the Nasdaq was up 4 points in the first half-hour of trading.

At factories, which account for most industrial output tracked by the Fed, production rose by a solid 0.5 percent in January, largely reflecting a boost in automobile production. That marked a big improvement over the 0.4 percent drop in factory output registered in December.

Production at gas and electric utilities jumped by 4 percent last month, compared with a 1.4 percent drop in December, as demand was stoked by colder weather.

At mines, however, production fell by 1.2 percent, more than reversing a 1 percent gain posted in December.

The economy has been coping with uneven growth as a quarter of strength has been followed by a three-month period of weakness. And businesses have been struggling, especially, to try and gauge demand for their goods during these muddled economic times.

The biggest factor holding back the economy's recovery: Businesses have been reluctant to make big commitments in hiring and in capital spending, due in part to uneasiness about the possibility of war and also generally to an uncertain business environment.

Federal Reserve Chairman Alan Greenspan told Congress this week he was hopeful that once such 'geopolitical' uncertainties lift, businesses would be much more willing to step up capital investment and hiring, forces that would boost economic growth.

Against that backdrop, Greenspan said President Bush's proposed 10-year, $1.3 trillion tax-cut package isn't needed to stimulate the economy, dealing a blow to the president's efforts to sell the plan to Congress.

The 0.6 percent increase in inventories was stronger than the 0.2 percent rise economists were predicting and represented the biggest boost since September.

Even though December's increase marked the eighth straight month that businesses have added to their stockpiles, economists say that the levels are still lean, reflecting companies' wariness about the economic climate.

In the inventories report, retailers boosted supplies by 0.6 percent in December and sales rose by a solid 2 percent.

Factories saw their stockpiles rise by 0.5 percent in December as sales slid by 0.6 percent. At wholesalers, supplies rose by 0.8 percent as sales fell by the same amount.

The Fed last month decided to leave a key interest rate at a 41-year low of 1.25 percent, with the hope that will encourage consumers and businesses to spend and invest more and help along the recovery.

In addition to Friday's industrial production report, there have been some other hopeful signs for the economy recently.

Retail sales for merchants other than car dealers were solid in January, suggesting that consumers—the main force keeping the economy going—still have an appetite to spend even amid all the global and economic turmoil.

And, the nation's unemployment rate dipped to 5.7 percent in January as the economy added 143,000 jobs, the largest amount since November 2000.[1]

The writer showed how the stock market reacted to the Fed's industrial production report favorably. But if the industrial production numbers had been below what economists were expecting, then stock prices might have fallen, as investors could have become worried that companies were not making as much of their goods to stimulate higher earnings.

Plenty of other reports from a variety of groups also examine what companies are doing as far as production, how much inventory they are keeping, what their orders are, and how much product they are shipping. For example, the Institute for Supply Management, formerly the National Association of Purchasing Management, produces a monthly report that is a national survey of manufacturing activity. The highlight of this report is a measurement called the Purchasing Managers' Index, or the PMI, which takes into account new orders, production, employment, deliveries, and inventories. Big moves in the PMI can signal a change in the economy. The Reserve Bank in Philadelphia also issues a monthly report that looks at manufacturing activity in the region. The survey is more of an outlook of business activity in the region and is based on a survey sent to about 250 manufacturers in the area. All of these reports on production by companies are closely watched. Although they often move in tandem, one moving in the opposite direction of the others may be the first sign that the economy is changing. That is why everyone wants to examine these reports.

In discussions of other important economic barometers, we must understand that it is the millions of businesses in the country that are the driving force of the economy. Businesses in any county or region may actually be increasing production or shipments while the rest of the state or country may be decreasing production and shipments. It always helps to keep close tabs on what local businesses are doing. When a report on industrial production comes out, the business

---

[1]From "Industrial production surges in January," by J. Aversa, Feb. 14, 2003, Associated Press. Copyright 2003 by The Associated Press. Reprinted with permission.

reporter should be sure to check with a few of them. For example, some local economies try to entice businesses to move to their regions by offering tax incentives or zones where goods can be shipped tax free. Others have economic development areas around downtown areas or other regions to stimulate growth. These too may have an impact on the local economy that does not show up in these reports.

Economics is not an exact science, and neither is writing about the economy. The economy can send mixed signals. It is important for any writer trying to make sense of economic indicators or factors to understand what they are writing about. Otherwise their stories will also send mixed signals. Although the economic picture may be cloudy, writing about it should be clear.

WRITING ECONOMICS STORIES THAT MAKE SENSE

The best economics reporting, says Noam Neusner, who covered the economy for Bloomberg News and *U.S. News & World Report,* is all about spotting important trends. So while it is important for any reporter to understand the content and nature of reports from the federal government that gauge different parts of the economy, the bigger focus needs to be on a few big ideas, says Neusner. For example, inflation, or the price levels of goods and services, is an important economic barometer. If inflation is rising, the cost of goods and services for consumers is going up. But the business writer should not simply report that inflation is rising. In most cases, the story will be much more informative if the reporter finds consumers who are being affected by inflation at the grocery store or someplace else they shop. Consumers should be used in the story to let a reader see firsthand how a nebulous economic term such as inflation is changing the lives of everyone.

Here is a story from CBSMarketWatch.com that discusses the Consumer Price Index (CPI), a barometer of inflation measured by the Labor Department that does not include consumers:

> A reversal in oil and gasoline prices pushed down consumer prices in April. Without volatile energy and food components, retail prices were flat for a second month in a row for the first time since 1982, government figures showed Friday.
>
> The consumer price index fell 0.3 percent, the Labor Department said, even bigger than the 0.1 percent drop economists expected. The CBS MarketWatch.com survey called for a 0.1 percent gain in the core rate.
>
> The flat and falling price data spooked investors worried about returns in a declining price environment.
>
> The CPI drop was enough to push a benchmark 10-year Treasury yield to a fresh 1950s low.
>
> A separate report Friday showed consumer sentiment, as measured by University of Michigan researchers, rebounded to its highest mark in a year, but the number had little impact on financial markets. The latest housing start results were also released, falling amid job cuts and poor weather.

The CPI results follow a record 1.9 percent drop reported for wholesale prices Thursday. The core producer price index fell 0.9 percent or the most for one month in nine years.

Despite initial worries about deflation sparked by the Fed's post-meeting policy statement last week, some economists have since been arguing they see only slim or no risks for actual deflation-sustained price drops—even though most expect inflation to remain contained.

"Deflation is indeed a meaningful threat, largely because inflation is already so low and the economy continues to struggle," said Economy.com's Mark Zandi. "Still, while deflationary scenarios are not difficult to construct, they remain highly unlikely."

Low levels of inflation are likely to persist, allowing the Fed to keep interest rates low.

On a year-over-year comparison, core CPI is up just 1.5 percent, the lowest since 1966, Labor officials confirmed.

Many companies continue to have little to no pricing power, which could have import repercussions for investment and hiring. Cheaper energy bills should help the profit outlook and most economists are sticking with predictions for at least subtle improvement in U.S. growth by the end of the year.

"The recent strong rallies in the stock and corporate bond markets and improving business and consumer confidence suggest that the economy should soon find its footing. The job losses are expected to abate and give way to job gains later this year," said Zandi.

Carl Tannenbaum, chief economist with ABN AMRO North America, said he thinks the impact from energy swings in the lead-up to war in Iraq and then relatively quick conclusion to combat is unduly causing deflation jitters.

Still, he conceded, clients who previously cared little about what deflation means or weren't worried about it are now asking for some explanation, "and that's not good" for investor sentiment.

Energy prices fell 4.6 percent, the biggest drop since November 2001 and completely reclaiming a like-size jump in March. Fuel oil tumbled 14.9 percent, the biggest drop since early in 1990. Gasoline prices fell 8.3 percent.

Food prices slipped 0.1 percent last month amid cheaper fruits and vegetables.

Transportation costs slumped 1.7 percent, in part on a 0.4 percent drop in car prices. Airfares were 0.9 percent more expensive however.

Clothing prices were 0.6 percent lower and housing prices eased 0.1 percent. Cigarette prices rose 0.1 percent. Medical care was 0.2 percent more expensive, although prescription drug prices eased 0.1 percent.[2]

Why does this story not include consumers? Probably because of the typical audience for CBSMarketWatch.com is more investor focused. This Web site is primarily read by Wall Street investors, analysts, and money managers looking to get economic and business news fast. They know how inflation affects consumers and do not need it explained to them. That may also be the case for business magazines that cater to highly educated readers, but may not be the case for the readers of

---

[2]From "CPI drops on energy drop; core flat," by R. Konin, May 16, 2003, CBS.MarketWatch.com. Copyright 2003 by CBS.MarketWatch.com. Reprinted with permission.

most newspapers who may have never actually thought about what inflation does to their own wallets. Explain to these readers that the CPI shows that they are paying more for goods and services, and that is a concept they will understand.

An economic topic most readers think they understand is the unemployment rate, but this can also be misinterpreted. The unemployment rate is the percentage of the labor force that does not have a job but is looking for work. It does not count the number of workers without a job who are not looking to become employed. So the unemployment rate may not always be an accurate barometer of how many people are without a job in any town or community.

Unemployment figures are collected for the country and for each state. If in one state the unemployment rate is lower than that of the rest of the country, a good story may be found in why that is happening. Perhaps that state has more service-related jobs, and the bulk of job losses elsewhere in the county have occurred in manufacturing jobs. Consumers are especially important when writing about employment or unemployment. Workers without a job can typically be found at the local unemployment office trying to find work. What are they doing to find a new job? Have they considered a job in a different field from their previous work experience? Will they need to be trained with new skills to make themselves more marketable to potential employers?

Sometimes workers stop looking for jobs and are not counted as part of the unemployment rate. But when they reenter the job hunt, they are counted once again. This may actually cause the unemployment rate to rise. Typically, out-of-work consumers start looking for jobs again when they believe the economy is getting better and work may have become available. Ironically, then, the first signal of a stronger economy may be a higher unemployment rate.

The business reporter should not simply focus on the low-end paying jobs. In many communities, the hardest hit in the unemployment line have been those who were once making six-figure salaries and higher. They are often the workers who also have the toughest time finding a new job, and they may need to take a step down in pay to become employed again.

Thus, as Neusner suggested, it behooves the business reporter to look at the big picture. As mentioned earlier, business reporters should not simply write about the unemployment rate rising or falling without looking at what it means. One should take the national and state figures and apply them to the local community as well. Maybe what has been happening in the rest of the country is now what is occurring locally. It is easy to write about workers getting laid off or hired at one company. It is harder to write about the broader employment trend.

Productivity is another important economic factor that few readers may understand except for the economics wonks. Productivity measures how the workforce is producing goods, and can be thought of as a simple mathematical equation:

$$\frac{\text{Output (Goods and services)}}{\text{Input (Number of worker hours)}}$$

The higher the productivity level, the more efficient companies become in producing goods while holding down costs. Businesses may try to get away with making their workers perform at higher levels or for longer hours without raising their pay to increase productivity, as the beginning of this Bloomberg News story suggests:

> U.S. worker productivity rose in the first quarter at twice the pace of the previous three months as the economy expanded and companies held down payrolls.
>
> The measure of how much an employee produces for every hour of work grew at a 1.6 percent annual pace in the first three months of the year, the Labor Department said, after 0.7 percent in the fourth quarter. The productivity gain accounts for all of the 1.6 percent increase in first-quarter gross domestic product. The cost of labor for each unit of production rose at a 1.9 percent rate after a 3.2 percent gain.
>
> U.S. corporate profits in the first quarter jumped the most in 2½ years, bolstered by job cuts, based on reports through last week by companies in the Standard & Poor's 500 Index. Technological gains in the last decade enabled companies to produce as many goods or services with fewer workers and helped them weather an uneven recovery. In the first quarter, the economy shed 262,000 jobs.
>
> "We're going to need to get economic growth rising at a pace sufficiently in excess of the rate of growth in productivity in order to get the job market viable again," Federal Reserve Chairman Alan Greenspan said yesterday in testimony before the House Financial Services Committee.[3]

If workers or readers can understand productivity and why it is important to the economy, then they can understand how an employer trying to increase productivity will affect them. That boss may ask the worker to work longer hours, or to take on additional tasks on the job. That is something that everyone can relate to and comprehend.

A consumer's level of credit is also an economic factor that most readers can understand as long as it is explained to them properly. The Federal Reserve Board, which is discussed later in the chapter, tracks consumer credit in monthly reports. If consumer credit card use is being used increasingly to make purchases, then consumers may have difficultly paying off those bills down the road, in turn hurting the economy.

The Charlotte Sun in Southwest Florida is not a newspaper that many readers would consider looking at to get an idea of broad economic factors affecting consumers. But in April, 2002 it covered the rising problem of credit card debt on its front page in a package that explained the issue to any reader with a Visa or MasterCard in his or her wallet. The story began:

> When you're overwhelmed with debt, every thought focuses on unpaid bills.
>
> Instead of sleeping, nights you spend pacing the floor. Arguments at home take place more frequently. And the most dreaded sound is the phone ringing.

---

[3]From "U.S. first-quarter productivity rises at 1.6% rate," by W. Edwards, May 1, 2003, Bloomberg News. Copyright 2003 by Bloomberg News. Reprinted with permission.

"They hate the telephone," said Lennie Eisenberg, office manager of Consumer Budget Counseling Inc. in Southwest Florida, of his debt management clients. "People come in very stressed. Creditors are calling day and night and are very nasty. They're calling people at work. It gets to the point people don't even want to answer the phone—they feel haunted."

Debt is a problem for one out of every 10 adults in the United States, according to Myvesta.org, a financial crisis treatment center in Gaithersburg, Md. And financial problems tend to trigger depression—more than death, family illness, work worries or marital problems—according to 88 percent of people surveyed for the National Depression Campaign.[4]

Does the above read like a business story? No, it does not. Yet it is tackling a serious economic issue that faces millions of consumers across the country. That is the type of writing about an economic topic that helps bring the reporting home to readers. Readers will also understand how their household debt affects personal spending habits. The more debt they have, the more of their income must go to paying off that debt, plus interest. The Federal Reserve releases a quarterly report on the household debt service burden, which at the end of 2002 was at its highest level in the past two decades. If the reporter finds some readers with too much debt, then he or she will have a story that ties nicely into these statistics and one that backs up a national trend.

Business and economics reporters need to expand their ideas of what makes a good story about the economy. Too often, these stories simply report the numbers from a government report. That is too boring. Reporters need to take the extra step and explain what the numbers mean, and put a face to the numbers by offering the reader personal examples and anecdotes based on interviews.

Greg McCune, Midwest bureau chief for Reuters, suggests that reporters can get clues that will help their economics reporting by watching what friends and neighbors are purchasing, or by examining the stores opening and closing at the nearest mall. He believes the economy should be covered from the bottom up, not the top down, according to Peters and Zuber (2002) in *The Business Journalist.*

Paul Solman, the business and economics correspondent for *The NewsHour with Jim Lehrer,* explained his style of economic reporting to online journalism web site Poynter.org:

When I try to figure out is what I can teach people that may be useful to them in understanding the material world and thus feel more like citizens who can make educated economic decisions, as we're all supposed to be able to in a democracy. I use interesting stories as my pretext to try to teach people how the material world works. And since there are innumerable facts to the world, there's no end of stories to do.

---

[4]From "Anguish, bills go hand in hand," by R. LePere, April 7, 2002, *The Charlotte* (Florida) *Sun,* p. 1–A. Copyright 2002 by *The Charlotte Sun.* Reprinted with permission.

"When I do my storytelling, I think of myself as demystifying economics," added Solman. When people tell me I've made things so simple that even THEY can understand it, that's when I feel I've succeeded.

Simplicity and explanation are most important elements of writing about the economy. Without those things, the reader will be lost.

THE FEDERAL RESERVE AND ITS INFLUENCE

When Alan Greenspan talks, people listen—especially reporters. The chairman of the Federal Reserve Board is likely the most powerful man in the country next to the president. And he is one of the few people who will take on the president. When President Bush announced his tax cut in early 2003 as a way to get the economy growing, Greenspan retorted that the cut was not needed. But, besides knowing the name of this man with the oversized glasses and balding head, few readers of newspapers, Web sites, or watchers of the evening news fully understand Greenspan's job or the important role played by the Federal Reserve, or the Fed as it is commonly known, in managing the country's economy.

The Federal Reserve system serves as the country's central bank and was created in 1913. There are seven on the board of governors, each of whom is appointed by the president and confirmed by Congress, and each one of those members serves a 14-year term. The primary responsibility of the board is to set the country's monetary policy, which may seem like a vague term. Put simply, the Fed's monetary policies aim to stimulate economic growth without causing too much inflation. The Fed tries to make the economy grow when the board members believe it is slowing and slow down the growth when they believe it is growing too fast, which could cause prices of goods and services to rise faster than wages. The Fed accomplishes its goals by controlling the economy's money flow and available credit.

The seven board members make up a majority of the Federal Open Market Committee. There are five other members of the committee who are presidents of regional Federal Reserve Banks including the Federal Reserve Bank of New York. There are Federal Reserve Bank locations in major cities across the country, including Philadelphia, Chicago, Richmond, Atlanta, Kansas City, and San Francisco.

This committee meets eight times each year to discuss the state of the country's economy and whether the group should take action on the basis of their assessment of various economic indicators. If the committee believes that economic growth is slowing, they might lower the federal funds rate to stimulate spending. Conversely, if, in the opinion of the committee, the economy is growing too fast they might raise the federal funds rate to slow spending. The federal funds rate refers to the interest rate at which depository institutions lend balances at the Federal Reserve to other depository institutions overnight. It affects other economic factors, including the interest rate that banks and other lenders charge when a consumer purchases a home or a car. If banks and lenders start charging a higher interest rate, for example, consumers might hold off on purchasing an item using a loan. This could cause economic growth to slow.

Fed officials have no better idea than most economists or anyone else as to what is going to happen with the economy. What they do is forecast where the economy is headed with their monetary policy. Because they are making a forecast, they are constantly looking at the trends in major economic barometers—many of which are discussed later in this chapter. Those include the unemployment rate, the CPI, auto and home sales, and consumer confidence. Unemployment and inflation are two of the Fed's biggest concerns.

After each committee meeting, the Fed issues a press release stating the action taken by the committee, even if no action was taken. This is always a story, particularly for major newspapers and other large media outlets. The release would read something like this:

> The Federal Open Market Committee decided to keep its target for the federal funds rate unchanged at $1\frac{1}{4}$ percent.
>
> Recent readings on production and employment, though mostly reflecting decisions made before the conclusion of hostilities, have proven disappointing. However, the ebbing of geopolitical tensions has rolled back oil prices, bolstered consumer confidence, and strengthened debt and equity markets. These developments, along with the accommodative stance of monetary policy and ongoing growth in productivity, should foster an improving economic climate over time.
>
> Although the timing and extent of that improvement remain uncertain, the Committee perceives that over the next few quarters the upside and downside risks to the attainment of sustainable growth are roughly equal. In contrast, over the same period, the probability of an unwelcome substantial fall in inflation, though minor, exceeds that of a pickup in inflation from its already low level. The Committee believes that, taken together, the balance of risks to achieving its goals is weighted toward weakness over the foreseeable future.
>
> Voting for the FOMC monetary policy action were Alan Greenspan, Chairman; William J. McDonough, Vice Chairman; Ben S. Bernanke; Susan S. Bies; J. Alfred Broaddus, Jr.; Roger W. Ferguson, Jr.; Edward M. Gramlich; Jack Guynn; Donald L. Kohn; Michael H. Moskow; Mark W. Olson; and Robert T. Parry.[5]

This four paragraph release was covered by the Associated Press this way:

> The Federal Reserve left interest rates unchanged Tuesday but signaled that cuts could be coming, given worries about the economy's uncertain recovery and the possibility of a destabilizing fall in prices.
>
> Many analysts said an unusually detailed statement by Federal Reserve Chairman Alan Greenspan and his colleagues convinced them the central bank would cut rates

---

[5]From Federal Open Markets Committee news release, May 6, 2003, Federal Reserve Board.

at its next meeting June 24 and 25 if the economy has not started to post stronger growth.

"By June, I think there will be hints of an economic rebound, but it will be a highly uncertain thing, and the Fed does not want to take any chances here," said economist David Jones, author of four books on the Greenspan Fed.

The Fed has not reduced its target for the federal funds rate, the interest that banks charge each other; since Nov. 6 when it slashed it by a half-point to a 41-year low of 1.25 percent, the 12th reduction in an aggressive easing campaign that began in January 2001.

Those low rates have driven mortgage rates to their lowest levels since the early 1960s, triggering record sales of new and existing homes and a surge in mortgage refinancing.

However, except for housing, the economy has been moving sideways for six months as consumer confidence plunged during the runup to the Iraq war and businesses, with excess capacity, remained reluctant to invest in new plants and equipment. The nation's unemployment rate returned to an eight-year high of 6 percent in April with more than a half-million jobs lost over three months.

In its statement explaining the decision to leave rates unchanged, the Fed mentioned recent disappointing statistics on employment and factory production, although it said that data "was mostly reflecting decisions made before the conclusion of hostilities."

With the end of the Iraq war, oil prices have fallen and consumer confidence and financial markets have rebounded, the Fed said, observing that this should "foster an improving economic climate over time."

However, the central bank's statement noted a new, although it said remote, concern that the United States, which has been struggling for three years to overcome the bursting of the U.S. stock market bubble, could go the way of Japan and encounter a bout of falling prices.

Japan, which saw real-estate prices fall in the late 1980s, has been mired in more than a decade of weak growth compounded now by a prolonged bout of deflation— falling prices.

Economists view deflation as a far more serious threat than inflation because interest rate changes have only a limited effect once a deflationary spiral begins. The last bout of deflation in the United States was during the Great Depression of the 1930s.

"The probability of an unwelcome substantial fall in inflation, though minor, exceeds that of a pickup in inflation from its already low level," the Fed said in Tuesday's statement.

For that reason, the central bank said it believed the "balance of risks" going forward was 'weighted toward weakness over the foreseeable future.'

At its last meeting March 18, the Fed had refrained from offering a risk assessment, on grounds there were too many uncertainties in the period before the Iraq war.

Most economists had expected the Fed to leave its target for the federal funds rate unchanged. But the concerned tone of the Fed's statement appeared to shed light on an emerging disagreement between Greenspan and some of his colleagues.

The combination of the announcement and a unanimous vote in favor of holding rates unchanged "has 'compromise' written all over it," said Ian Shepherdson, the chief domestic economist at High Frequency Economics in Valhalla, N.Y.[6]

---

[6]From "Fed warns of risks ahead: Interest rates are left alone, but are likely to be lowered soon if things don't improve," by M. Crutsinger, May 6, 2003, Associated Press. Copyright 2003 by The Associated Press. Reprinted with permission.

The story quotes from the release, but also provides analyses from economists who have viewed the statement giving insight into what the Fed's board may be thinking.

Later, the Federal Reserve release minutes from the meetings. While the newsworthiness of what was discussed in these meetings if often muted as a result, the sometimes can show disagreements among the members.

The Fed also presents a report on the economy to Congress twice a year, and the chairman is called to testify before Congress. And as chairman, Alan Greenspan carries tremendous clout in influencing the economy.

Greenspan has been chairman of the Fed since 1987, and during that time he's overseen one of the longest periods of economic prosperity this country has ever seen. Because of that, his influence among the other board members is tremendous. They often vote based on what Greenspan says and believes.

Because of that influence, when Greenspan talks, his words are carefully chronicled by reporters and analyzed as to what they mean. His speeches before Congress and other events are considered major news, especially when he provides warnings about the economy, such as he did in December 1996 at a speech before The American Enterprise Institute for Public Policy Research, where he used the famous term "irrational exuberance" to describe the mood of investors in the fast-rising stock market.

The Fed makes copies of Greenspan's speeches, and speeches of other board members and bank presidents, readily available to the media. Reporters who have spent years covering the Fed and monetary policy will look for clues as to what board members are thinking about the economy in these speeches.

Be forwarned, however. These speeches can be tedious to read unless you're a fan of academic writing. Many of these public comments are filled with long and complicated explanations of where the economy is going. The job for any reporter covering the Fed is to boil the speech down to its simplest form.

Here's how a reporter for CBSMarketWatch.com began a story about a Greenspan speech to Congress:

> The outlook for the U.S. economy is still uncertain, but the most likely course is stronger growth and low inflation, Federal Reserve Chairman Alan Greenspan said Wednesday in congressional testimony.
>
> While noting that the end of the Iraq war had pushed down oil prices and boosted confidence, "we do not yet have sufficient information...to make a firm judgment about the current underlying strength of the real economy," he said.
>
> Much of Greenspan's testimony to the Joint Economic Committee repeated his remarks of three weeks ago before the House Financial Services Committee.
>
> "Looking ahead, the consensus expectation for a pickup in economic activity is not unreasonable, though the timing and extent of that improvement continue to be uncertain," he said. Conditions in financial markets, including the Fed's monetary policy, are ripe for growth, he noted.
>
> Recent employment and production data have been "disappointing," he said, but these reflect business decisions that were likely made before the end of the war.

"Many more weeks of data will be needed to confidently discern the underlying trends in these areas," he said.

"Firms still appear hesitant to spend and hire, and we need to remain mindful of the possibility that lingering business caution could be an impediment to improved economic performance," he said.

Financial markets reacted quickly to Greenspan's apparent patience.

At the Chicago Board of Trade, federal funds futures priced in a 78 percent chance of a 25 basis-point rate cut at the June 25 meeting, instead of the 70 percent chance of a 50 basis-point cut that had been priced in before Greenspan spoke.[7]

Investors also react to what Greenspan says. If Greenspan warns that the economy is growing faster than it should, investors are likely to sell stocks because that means the Fed might raise interest rates to slow growth, causing profits for companies to ease. Or, if Greenspan believes that the economy needs a boost, some might believe that interest rates will be lowered, leading investors to want to buy stocks because of the potential for higher profits. It has been common in the past for the Dow Jones Industrial Average and other stock indexes to jump or fall based on Greenspan's comments or a decision by the Federal Open Market Committee.

Myron Kandel, the CNN Financial Editor and one of the long-time business journalist experts on the economy, noted that Greenspan can be evasive in what he actually means when talking about the economy, and points out how the media can come away from his public pronouncements with different takes (Kandel, 2003). After Greenspan spoke in May 2003 before the Joint Economic Committee of Congress, Kandel wrote that even the media that covers Greenspan and the Fed the most could not come to a consensus as to what he said. The *New York Times* headline read, "Greenspan, Broadly Positive, Spells Out Deflation Worries," whereas The *Financial Times* echoed the deflation theme with this headline: "Greenspan says Fed is ready to tackle deflation." But the *Wall Street Journal* played down deflation, with the headline: "Greenspan Says Deflation Risk Is Low." Both the *Washington Post* and *USA Today* took different tacks. The *Post* headline read: "Greenspan Hints at Another Rate Cut," with the subhead: "Fed Chief Likens Step to 'Taking Out Insurance' Against Dangers of Deflation." *USA Today* had a similar headline: "Greenspan hints at more rate cuts," with the subhead: "Deflation's 'minor' threat may call for action by Fed." "So there they are," wrote Kandel. "Five leading papers with their somewhat differing takes on the same event, as each focuses on what it thinks is the most important. My view is watch out for more signs of deflation, forget about inflation any time soon, and expect at least another interest rate cut in the weeks ahead" (Kandel, 2003).

Greenspan will not be chairman of the Fed forever. And it may take some time for his successor to gain as much stature. But the chairman of the Fed carries

---

[7]From "Outlook still cloudy, Greenspan says," by R. Nutting, May 21, 2003, CBS.MarketWatch.com. Copyright 2003 by CBS.MarketWatch.com. Reprinted with permission.

tremendous influence in how the country's economy operates. And that is why it is important to hang on his every word.

UNEMPLOYMENT RATES

As mentioned earlier, one of the economic concepts that most readers can understand is whether or not they have a job. If they do not have a job, they are unemployed and likely looking for work. If they do have a job, they could be looking for a new job, or higher wages. The number of jobs in a region or the country increases as the economy improves. When people start buying more products and services, the companies that make them may decide they need to hire more workers to meet that demand. Or, if fewer people are purchasing goods and services, businesses may lay off or fire workers they no longer need to make those goods.

The unemployment rate is a measure of this part of the economy. The unemployment rate rises when more people have lost jobs and are looking for new jobs, and it falls when more people find jobs who previously did not have jobs. Workers out of a job have a broader effect on the economy. Because they no longer have an income, they are likely to spend less on goods that may not necessarily be required for them to survive. Unemployed workers who then get jobs may help stimulate the economy by purchasing goods they may have held off buying until they found employment.

Unemployment is one of the major macroeconomic issues that the Federal Reserve follows. They want to know if unemployment is rising or following and stimulate the economy to produce jobs if needed. The unemployment rate measures the number of workers out of a job who are actively seeking employment. It does not measure workers who have lost a job but are not trying to find a new one. This can be an important distinction when writing about the economy. Often, laid-off or fired workers will try to find a new job immediately after they have lost their previous one. But after several months, many become discouraged and stop looking. When that happens, they are no longer counted in the unemployment rate. However, if they later feel like the economy has improved and there are more jobs available, they may start looking for another job. When that happens, they are counted as part of the unemployment rate again.

The unemployment rate is measured as a percentage. The national unemployment report is typically released on the first Friday of the month by the Bureau of Labor Statistics. (State data is also typically available, as is data for metropolitan statistical areas.) But in addition to the unemployment rate, this report also details the number of new jobs created each month. Job growth can indicate economic growth, and is a number that is almost as important as the unemployment rate. Job gains can also signal the potential for inflation if there are a number of new workers willing to pay higher for goods and services now that they are getting a regular paycheck.

Here is how the monthly unemployment rate should be covered:

North Carolina's unemployment rate edged up to 6 percent in March as employers continued to slash jobs and postpone hiring.

A month earlier, the state had a seasonally adjusted rate of 5.8 percent, suggesting that the economy is still far from a full recovery, the state said Tuesday in its monthly unemployment report.

About 76,724 workers reported losing their jobs in March, 4,700 more than in February, while an additional 36,191 reported being out of a job six months or longer.

The biggest losses were in manufacturing, as employers moved jobs overseas and took advantage of productivity gains. The construction industry also suffered a decline in jobs, largely because of bad weather and a sharp slowdown in demand for commercial real estate.

"The economy is just not growing fast enough to create jobs," said Harry M. Davis, an economist for the N.C. Bankers Association.

Davis, who teaches economics at Appalachian State University, said the state's economic output is increasing at an annual rate of 2 percent, well below the 3 percent rate needed for unemployment to fall.

But with the major fighting in Iraq over, the job market is expected to gradually improve during the next few months, Davis said. He pointed to recent increases in consumer confidence, corporate profits and business investment as evidence that employers are likely to start hiring again.

Michael L. Walden, an economist at N.C. State University, predicts the unemployment rate will remain above 5 percent this year. "We went into this recession with 3.1 percent unemployment, and we're not likely to get down to that anytime soon," Walden said.

Nationally, unemployment was 5.8 percent in March and 6 percent in April.

A year ago, North Carolina's unemployment rate was 0.9 percent age points higher, at 6.9 percent, but state officials said the decline since then is misleading and largely the result of changes in the way the rate is calculated.

Nevertheless, year-to-year comparisons of the employed and unemployed in North Carolina indicate that the job market is better than this time last year, the state said. The number of workers out of a job fell by 37,669 from March 2002 to 249,488, while the number of workers with jobs increased by 9,811 to 3.9 million.

On the downside, the state's labor force—made up of people who are working or looking for work—decreased by 27,858 from a year ago to 4.15 million. Economists said a decline of that magnitude is evidence that workers are moving out of the state or giving up on their job searches until the economy improves.

"Normally, when the economy begins to recover, the labor force grows. We're just not seeing that right now, and that's signaling that people are discouraged," said Lisa Anderson, who follows North Carolina for Economy.com.

Two years of rising joblessness has emptied the state's unemployment insurance trust fund. Supported by quarterly taxes on employers, the fund provides jobless benefits to workers who lose their jobs through no fault of their own.

Before collecting first-quarter taxes this week, the state borrowed $53 million from the federal government to continue paying benefits. The state paid the federal government back with the recent tax collections and now has $20.6 million in the trust fund, said Michele Walker, a spokeswoman for the Employment Security Commission. The state still expects to collect about $200 million from employers this month.[8]

The story focuses on the fact that jobs were created in some industries, but lost in others, and points out that many workers who have lost jobs may have left the state to find employment or simply stopped looking.

How could this story have been improved? If the writer had been able to find a worker who had lost his or her job within the past month and used an anecdote of that situation, the story would have brought home to the reader what it is like to be looking for work. But it has plenty of expert quotes analyzing the local job market. There are plenty of other ways that a business reporter can track employment in his or her region without simply reporting the numbers of an unemployment rate. Many of these help give a more short-term overview of what may be happening with jobs.

When companies hire workers, particularly a large number of workers, they are likely to announce this move with a news release heralding the event. "XYZ Products to expand local plant and add 200 workers," will likely be the headline on such a release. These stories can be informative to readers, particularly those who think they might be able to fill one of these jobs. Such stories provide a service to the readers if they give information on how to apply for the jobs, or what type of jobs the company is looking to fill—manual labor, factory, administrative assistants, software development, etc.

The Blackshear Times in south Georgia began a front-page story on a business adding jobs to its community this way:

> A Jacksonville, Florida company that customizes vans and trucks for major Detroit automakers will build a $2.4 million plant in Waycross' industrial park.
>   Sherrod Vans, a 23-year-old firm, will break ground Thursday at 9 a.m. on a 69,000 square-foot building located on 25 acres just across Industrial Boulevard from Clayton Homes. The company hopes to be in operation in approximatelybreak 10 months, employing at least 100 workers from this area with plans to expand to 150 soon after. Annual payroll for the company is expected to top $6 million.[9]

An enterprising reporter can sometimes find out about a company's intent to hire local workers by scanning his newspaper's classified ads. Often, a business will advertise for the jobs in an area to see what kind of demand they will get from the local work force before announcing the move. Also note that the Conference

---

[8]From "State's jobless rate rises to 6%; up after 2 months of declines," by A. Martinez, May 7, 2003, *The News & Observer,* p. D1. Copyright 2003 by *The News & Observer.* Reprinted with permission.
    [9]From "Customizing van facility means 100 + jobs for area," by R. Williams, Sept. 25, 2002, *The Blackshear* (Georgia) *Times,* p. 1. Copyright 2002 by *The Blackshear Times.* Reprinted with permission.

Board releases a monthly Help-Wanted Index that tracks the demand for workers by surveying advertising in major newspapers across the country. In addition, individual company layoffs can also be important stories. Sometimes, they signal for the first time that a business may be in financial trouble. Layoffs can also be an indication that an industry is slumping, or that a new competitor is taking away business. Many companies are not likely to want to discuss layoffs and rarely announce decisions like this with a release, but disgruntled workers may call reporters and let them know. If an executive at the business writes a memo to employees explaining the decision, that memo can often show up anonymously on the newsroom fax machine, especially if reporters have cultivated relationships with workers.

There is another, more reliable method to find out about layoffs in a timely manner, however. A federal law known as the Worker Adjustment and Retraining Notification Act, or more commonly referred to as the WARN Act, requires businesses to notify their workers within 60 days of a plant closing or a layoff. These notifications are filed with state Labor Departments and local government officials, and can be reviewed by the public. The WARN Act notices are also given to labor officials if the affected workers are represented by a union. If a reporter has never looked at a WARN Act filing, he or she should find out who in the area oversees these documents. They can be filled with stories of which the local media outlet was unaware. In general, businesses must file WARN Act notices if they have 100 or more workers, as long as the workers have been on the job for at least six months and work more than 20 hours per week. Plant closings are covered if the shut down will result in the loss of work for at least 50 workers for more than 30 days. Layoffs are covered under the law if the company has more than 500 workers, or more than 50 employees if the layoff will result in at least one third of them losing their job.

Finding workers who have made shifts in their jobs, or have gone back to work to meet other needs can also be interesting employment stories that give a glimpse into the local economy. Is there a nursing shortage at the local hospital? If so, what are administrators doing to attract more nurses to the area? Drug store chains such as CVS often provide incentives for pharmacists to move to small towns for a certain time period. Another interesting employment trend may be that elderly workers who have already retired are rejoining the workforce. This may be for various reasons, but could include the fact that they did not save enough for retirement, or simply became bored with staying at home.

AUTO AND HOME SALES

When people spend money to live, buying goods and services, their expenditures are tracked and watched closely by economists and others wanting to get a feel for consumer spending trends. Two of the biggest items tracked are sales of automobiles and sales of houses. Increases and decreases in both of these big-ticket items can give a good picture of where the economy is headed. Whereas employment information may tell readers whether a consumer has the ability to spend money, information about sales for specific items gives an even better picture because it shows how willing a consumer is to spend that money.

Individual automakers and the Bureau of Economic Analysis release sales statistics for cars and trucks typically right after the end of the month. Auto sales can be cyclical, depending on the economy, and are tied to interest rates as well. If interest rates are low, then there is an incentive for consumers to purchase cars. After the 9/11 terrorist attacks, many automakers enticed consumers to continue purchasing cars by offering 0% interest rates. Car sales are about 5% of the country's Gross Domestic Product, but since vehicle sales are what are considered "discretionary" purchases, they are often examined as a barometer for consumer behavior. Increasing car sales likely mean that consumers are happy with their jobs and the economy and feel comfortable spending money on a new vehicle. If car sales slump, the decline could be an indication that consumers are worried about the economy.

Here is how *The Detroit News,* a paper that spends a lot of reporter resources and time covering the auto industry, typically covers car sales:

U.S. auto sales rose 2.8 percent in April—the first gain of the year—as generous incentives, popular new products and an improving national economy drew shoppers to showrooms.

"Consumer confidence remains very strong," said Art Spinella, a consultant with CNW Marketing in Bandon, Ore. "I'm not sure there's any other reason (for the strong showing) than continued incentives."

Automakers sold an estimated 1.45 million new vehicles in April, up from 1.35 million in April 2001.

New cars, pickups, minivans and SUVs sold at an annualized rate of 17.4 million units in April, compared with 16.65 million a year earlier, according to Autodata Corp.

With incomes rising, unemployment falling and other signs of a healthy economy, automakers now forecast U.S. auto sales could rise to 17 million units or more this year, up from previous estimates as low as 15 million units.

So far this year, demand for new cars and light trucks is off just 1.7 percent from strong 2001 levels.

April's showing prompted General Motors Corp. to bump up planned output during the second quarter to 1.53 million vehicles from an earlier forecast of 1.5 million. Chrysler plans to run overtime at 14 of 17 North American factories.

With sales shaping up much stronger than expected, automakers are starting to pull back on the expensive discounts and financing deals that helped sustain demand after the Sept. 11 terrorist attacks. This could improve their profit pictures.

GM led the way in April with a 12.4 percent sales gain for its domestic brands. DaimlerChrysler AG's Chrysler Group logged a 2.8 percent improvement. Only troubled Ford Motor Co. finished the month with a decline of 8 percent.

Asian automakers continued to gain sales in the U.S. market, with Toyota Motor Corp. sales rising 0.3 percent, demand at Honda Motor Co. up 1.1 percent and Nissan Motor Co. up 14.8 percent. Mitsubishi Motors Corp. sales rose 8.4 percent and Hyundai Motor Co. sales were up more than 13 percent.

Among German automakers, Mercedes-Benz posted a 7.2 percent gain and BMW AG sales rose 15.1 percent while Volkswagen AG posted a 0.4 percent decline.

GM eliminated Tuesday free loans and reduced some rebates on selected new cars and trucks. Buyers can get financing of 1.9 percent to 3.9 percent or $1,000, $2,000 or $3,000 cash back. That's down from a minimum of $2,000.

The automaker hopes the program compels consumers to continue buying while saving GM money, said GM sales analyst Paul Ballew.

For now, neither Chrysler nor Ford is following GM's latest move to curtail rebate offers.

Lower incentive spending, combined with stable or growing sales, would help both automakers as they execute massive turnarounds. Ford is expected to announce a new round of incentives today.

Chrysler will continue to offer up to $2,500 cash back or low-rate financing on most Chrysler, Dodge and Jeep vehicles, along with a seven-year, 100,000-mile powertrain warranty.

"What we see right now, it wouldn't make us jump," Gary Dilts, Chrysler's senior vice-president of sales, said of GM's new discounts. "One size does not fit all."

Analysts said automakers are hoping to adjust incentives enough so that sales remain robust while factories keep humming without carving too deeply into profits. "They don't want another 17 million year if it costs them billions in rebates," said Walter McManus, executive director of forecasting for J.D. Power and Associates in Troy.

GM's April sales gain reflected strong demand for trucks and a slight improvement in car sales. Retail sales climbed 15 percent for the month.

The No. 1 automaker was helped by strong demand for SUVs and pickups. GM truck sales soared 24 percent, led by the GMC Envoy and Chevrolet TrailBlazer SUVs and Chevrolet S-10 pickup.[10]

The story explains why car sales have increased, and gives perspective as to when the last time sales increased for the industry. Although the story is numbers intensive, it also gives a broad overview of the industry and how it is affecting the economy. Missing, perhaps, are comments from consumers who either recently made a car purchase or are considering a car purchase.

Car sales data can sometimes fluctuate wildly, depending on manufacturer's incentives and dealer rebates. Sales may be strong one month, but not the next month. New model introductions also influence sales. For smaller media outlets, however, new car sales can be a vital story in explaining the local economy, particularly if there are just one or two new car dealers in the area. Getting information

---

[10]From "Incentives spark April auto sales; consumer confidence drives 2.8% gain," by S. Carney, May 2, 2002, *The Detroit News*, p. 1A. Copyright 2002 by *Detroit News*. Reprinted with permission.

about new sales from those dealers can sometimes be hard to obtain, but they are likely the best gauge of a local economy's potential for growth—or decline.

Buying a home is the one purchase a consumer will make that will be worth more than a vehicle. Buying a home can be a stressful event, and many consumers go to great lengths to ensure that they are getting the right house for their needs. Nationally, new home sales are tracked by the Bureau of the Census, which typically reports on a monthly basis. New home sales make up about 15% of total sales. Existing home sales are measured by the National Association of Realtors, which also issues a report on a monthly basis.

Existing home sales make up about 85% of total sales. Still, new home sales are important for the overall economy because they reflect new ownership, whereas existing home sales are typically current homeowners buying a new home and selling the old. Existing home sales numbers are based on contract closings, whereas new home sales data is based on the signing of a sales contract. In many communities, home sales data can be found by contacting a local realtors association. These local numbers are frequently more valuable to your readers than the national data, as this *Buffalo News* story suggests:

Area home sales got off to a strong start this year, rising 4.5 percent from a year ago.

A total of 673 homes were sold in Erie and Niagara counties, according to the Buffalo Niagara Association of Realtors.

Low mortgage rates continued to make homebuying attractive. Peter F. Hunt, president and chief executive officer of Hunt Real Estate ERA, said home sales remained robust in spite of some unpleasant weather last month.

"We had lots of snow, but I still believe that real estate is an investment of choice today," Hunt said.

The median sale price for a single-family home in the area dropped 5 percent from a year ago, to $79,500, the Realtors association said.

The median price means half the number of homes sold for more than that amount, and half sold for less. It's less affected by exceptionally high or low-priced homes than the average price.

The average price of homes sold in the area fell slightly from a year ago, to just below $97,000.

Prospective homebuyers once again had fewer properties to choose from than they did a year ago, continuing a lengthy trend. The number of homes for sale dropped 12 percent, to less than 4,000.

Hunt said that homes that are coming onto the market are turning over rapidly, forcing prospective buyers to be ready to act quickly when they see something they like. On one day last month, he said, six offers were made for one property listed with Hunt Real Estate. Another property had five offers in one day.

"Those nine families that didn't win are back in the market," Hunt said.

Lower-priced homes helped drive the overall increase in the number of homes sold. Homes that sold for between $50,000 and $60,000 recorded the largest percentage gain—44 percent—of any segment from a year ago.

Still, there was also slightly higher demand for homes at the higher end. Fifteen homes sold for at least $300,000, up from 11 a year ago.

The median price for homes with four or more bedrooms increased 5.5 percent, to $115,000.

If a National Association of Realtors forecast proves correct, homebuying conditions this year should remain favorable across the country.

The organization projects that the 30-year fixed interest mortgage rate will average 6.2 percent during the first half of the year, before rising to 6.6 percent in the fourth quarter.[11]

Just like car sales, home sales are influenced by interest rates. When interest rates rise, home sales often decrease because potential buyers want to purchase at the lowest interest rate possible. When rates fall, buyers enter the market, as many may have been waiting to lock in a lower rate before signing a contract.

In addition, there are groups tracking other economic barometers that relate to home sales. For example, the Mortgage Bankers' Association publishes a weekly report that tracks the number of mortgage applications across the county and looks at the number of consumers refinancing a loan at a lower interest rate. This can be important to watch, because when consumers are refinancing a loan, they are often freeing up more cash to use to spend on other goods and services. The National Association of Home Builders also issues a monthly report based on three factors—current sales, expected sales during the next three months, and potential buyer traffic at new home sites. Although this report is not as closely watched as other housing market data, it is more timely. The Census Bureau also issues a monthly report on housing construction starts and permits. The report tracks single-family home and apartment construction as well as permits authorized by local building authorities. The construction starts tend to get more attention than the permits, although it can be argued that the permit data is more reliable.

Another key indicator of consumer spending is retail sales. When consumers spend more at retailers, it is an indication that the economy is growing, whereas declining retail sales indicate that the economy is in trouble. Retail sales are measured by the Census Bureau as well, and those reports are also released on a monthly basis. Retail sales figures are broken down into sectors, which include furniture, electronics and appliances, food and beverage, clothing, gasoline, sporting goods, and general merchandise. Because retail sales are almost 30% of the Gross Domestic Product (GDP), the information can provide valuable insight into consumer spending trends and give readers and others an indication of where the economy is headed. Large retailers and some Wall Street investment banks also issue sales reports. Big retailers such as Wal-Mart and Target issue monthly sales reports based on the performance at their stores. Business reporters should watch these reports closely. They may provide the first signal that the economy is turning.

---

[11]From "Area home sales rise, but median prices decline," by M. Glynn, February 21, 2003, *The Buffalo News*, p. B-5. Copyright 2003 by *The Buffalo News*. Reprinted with permission.

They can also be used to show what consumers in small- and medium-sized towns are doing with their money.

INTERNATIONAL TRADE

When retailers, automakers, homebuilders, and other U.S. companies are not selling goods and services to consumers in this country, they are trying to sell their products in other countries. Likewise, foreign companies are interested in selling their products to American consumers.

When the U.S. economy exports more goods than it imports, there is a trade surplus. When it imports more goods than it exports, there is a trade deficit. An understanding of how our economy is interacting with economies of other countries can be an important factor in business growth.

In 2001, the U.S. economy imported approximately $330 billion more in goods and services into the country than it exported. Most of the deficit results from goods such as automobiles, industrial supplies and materials, and consumer goods. The country is actually exporting more in services than it is importing.

Simply comparing the import and export figures, however, paints an incomplete picture of international trade. Foreign markets are much more open to U.S. goods and services than they were a decade ago, and the United States is also importing more goods than previously. Imports and exports were less than 10% of the GDP in 1960. But now they account for nearly a quarter of the GDP.

International trade is measured by the Census Bureau at the Commerce Department. Each month, the agency releases a report on imports and exports, breaking down the results by industry. A typical story covering trade would begin like this one from the *Milwaukee Journal-Sentinel:*

> The United States, which has not posted a trade surplus since 1975, saw its chronic trade deficit widen in March to the second-highest monthly shortfall on record, the Commerce Department reported Tuesday.
> The $43.5 billion trade gap in March was second only to December's record trade deficit of $44.9 billion, reflecting what economists call one of the weightiest imbalances in the world's biggest economy.
> "We consume more than we produce," said Peter Kretzmer, senior economist in New York for the Bank of America.
> America's insatiable thirst for imported oil and its demand for foreign cars both hit records in the month.
> The U.S., which has 5 percent of the world's population and consumes 30 percent of the world's petroleum, imported a record $9.1 billion in crude oil, up from $7.5 billion in February, the agency said.
> The nation increased its oil stocks on fears that the war in Iraq could disrupt supplies, economists said. According to the Commerce Department, the U.S. soaked up 300.7 million barrels of oil in March, up from 247.1 million barrels in February.

Americans purchased an unprecedented 3.53 million imported vehicles in March, the agency reported. In dollar terms, sales of imported cars and car parts rose 2.1 percent to $17.2 billion.[12]

Why is international trade important? It lets businesses—and the workers who rely on jobs at those businesses—know how successful they have been in selling their goods to countries overseas. For many businesses, the more products they sell overseas, the more successful they are. Many U.S. companies make a large portion of their sales outside of this country. Coca-Cola is considered one of the many all-American companies, and yet this business sells approximately two-thirds of all of its drinks in international markets. Another U.S. company, Boeing, sells more than half of its airplanes to foreign markets.

But there is more to understanding international trade than sales. Many companies depend on strong international currencies for profits. When the currency in countries where businesses sell goods falls in comparison with the dollar, they receive less revenue and, thus, less profits when they convert that currency into U.S. cash. So many companies with large international operations or that sell their products to international markets actually want a weak dollar—a fact that can be surprising to some readers.

Because of wild fluctuations in the value of their currencies, many foreign economies are considered unstable, whereas the U.S. economy is viewed as relatively stable. Unstable economies often have huge ups and downs in inflation, and hence the value of their currencies, which can make doing business in a foreign economy a risky proposition. Business reporters should find out whether any companies they are writing about have business in foreign countries. Then they should research those countries to see whether their economies have had any upswings or downswings recently. That may be the cause of an increase or decrease in a company's profits.

The Bureau of Labor Statistics compiles import and export price indexes that measure prices of goods and services imported to or exported from the country. These monthly reports reflect changes in the prices paid by importers or the prices at which exporters sell their goods. Import price changes are often affected by commodity products such as oil, and agriculture products such as wheat.

Knowing what is happening in foreign economies can be important to writing about the U.S. economy and to writing about specific American companies. It is also vital to have an understanding of foreign corporations that may have local, regional operations. These foreign businesses may be affected by economic events back home, whereas the U.S. subsidiary is operating smoothly. Although

---

[12]From "Trade deficit 2nd highest ever as U.S. continues to consume; Crude oil imports climb to $9.1 billion over Iraq war fears," by J. Schmid, May 14, 2003, *Milwaukee Journal Sentinel*, p. 1D. Copyright 2003 by Journal Communications. Reprinted with permission.

the information about foreign companies is limited, documents and other filings on foreign companies can be obtained from U.S. regulatory agencies that help explain trade with other countries.

CONSUMER CONFIDENCE

Gauging the economy and where it is headed is almost like being a psychologist for the country or a region. Many times, it is necessary to get inside the head of consumers to determine what they are thinking.

Consumer confidence reports are widely watched by economists, Wall Street investors, and corporations because they are considered a leading indicator of where the economy is headed. If consumer confidence is on the rise, people are more likely to spend money in the future on goods and services; if consumer confidence falls, those purchases may be delayed. Many factors influence consumer confidence. The two most widely known consumer confidence reports come from The Conference Board and the University of Michigan. The Conference Board, which polls 5,000 households every month, asks questions such as: *How would you rate the present general business conditions in your area? Good, normal, or bad?* and *how would you guess your total family income to be six months from now? Higher, same, or lower?* The Michigan report asks questions such as: *Would you say that you and your family living with you are better off or worse off financially than you were a year ago?* and *Now looking ahead, do you think that a year from now you and your family living with you will be better off financially, worse off, or just about the same as now?* The Conference Board questions emphasize labor conditions, whereas the Michigan survey focuses on financial conditions. But each comes out with a number reflecting the change in consumer sentiment from the previous month based on an overall index. Consumer sentiment can be affected by other events as well, such as the 9/11 terrorist attacks. After that, consumer confidence fell.

A Reuters reporter tied in consumer confidence to other economic factors such as lower interest rates and incentives from car manufacturers when he filed a report that noted that consumer confidence increased in the second half of July, 2002. Despite their ability to refinance home mortgages at lower rates and buy new cars with little or no interest, consumers were still concerned about the economy though. The report also noted that in July, 2002 consumer confidence had hit its lowest level since the previous November, but that the level of consumer confidence was higher than forecasted by economists.

Consumer confidence reports can be timely, issued within days of when consumers have been asked questions, so their findings are closely watched. For a reporter interested in writing about the economy, the results of these studies on consumer confidence can be followed up by interviewing local consumers and getting their feelings about the economy and spending. Also note that another good picture of the economy comes from the Conference Board's Expectations Index, which projects consumer feelings about six months in the future. If that index falls below a rating of 80 for two months, then economists believe a recession is coming. Although the Conference Board and the Michigan reports are the two most widely

---

"Top Economic Issues Reporters Should Consider," by James F. Smith, senior fellow and director of the Center for Business Forecasting at the Kenan Institute of Private Enterprise in the Kenan-Flagler Business School at the University of North Carolina at Chapel Hill and chief economist, Society of Industrial and Office Realtors.

1. Consumers account for nearly 70% of GDP with their purchases. What are consumers doing now in your area?
2. Stock price volatility gains headlines, but less than one half of all households own a stock or a mutual fund directly. Only 10% of households own 90% of stocks. Interview consumers to see if stock prices have any impact on their spending plans.
3. More than two-thirds of consumers own a home. Capital gains from rising house prices have supported consumer spending, especially cars and trucks. Interview homeowners to see how they respond to market incentives. Have they refinanced? What did they do with the money?
4. Unemployment and layoffs grab headlines. New job creation rarely does. Working for the same employer for a decade or more almost never rates a story. Interview a sample of people to find people in the two latter categories and tell their stories.
5. People who lose their jobs are rarely unemployed for very long. Interview a sample of people who've lost their jobs to see how long it took to find a new one.
6. Community colleges are the unsung heroes of the U.S. educational system. Globally, only the United States and Canada have this type of institution. If your area has one, interview some students to find out their career goals and aspirations.
7. The people in the bottom 10% of the income distribution on average spend 3–4 times their income each year. This suggests that temporary periods of very low income are planned for by many people. Interview people in this income segment to see if this is true in your area.
8. Turnover in the top 10% of the income distribution is very high. Interview people in this income segment to see how long they've been in that group. Find some inspiring examples to uplift readers.
9. During the past 20 years, more than 40 million net new jobs have been created in the United States. Interview a sample of people in your area and find people in these new jobs. Tell their stories.
10. About half the people in the labor force work for companies with fewer than 10 employees. These companies rarely make the news, yet they are the most dynamic companies in the country. Find some of these companies in your area and tell their stories.

cited in stories, other reports also gauge consumer sentiment, including one by ABC News and *Money* magazine.

Reporting about the economy can be one of the most fascinating parts of business journalism. It puts reporters in touch with what average, everyday people are doing with their money and what they might be thinking. And it does not take a broad understanding of economic theory, just an understanding of how and why people spend money and for what.

GLOSSARY

Consumer Confidence Index: A measurement by the Conference Board on whether consumers are feeling optimistic or pessimistic about the economy.

Consumer Price Index: A measure of the price change of consumer goods such as gasoline, food, and automobiles.

deflation: The opposite of inflation. This is the rate at which the price of goods and services in the economy is falling.

depression: A severe and prolonged recession in the economy marked by lower productivity, higher unemployment, and falling prices.

durable good orders: Measures spending on products consumers purchase that they don't necessarily need, such as dishwashers, sports equipment, jewelry, and lawn and garden equipment.

economics: The science dealing with the production, distribution and consumption of goods and services and with the issues of labor, finance, and taxation.

existing home sales: The resale of an existing home by the current owner to a new owner. Not to be confused with new home sales.

Federal Reserve Board: The governing body of the Federal Reserve System. They are appointed to the Board of Governors by the president, but must be approved by the Senate.

Gross Domestic Product: The monetary value of all goods, services and products made by an economy during a certain time period. It includes purchased, investments and exports minus imports.

housing starts: The number of residential buildings that have begun construction in any month.

inflation: The rate at which the average price of all goods and services in the economy from one year to the next is rising, and therefore, purchasing power is falling.

interest rate: The rate paid on money borrowed, or received on money lent if you are the lender. It is typically expressed as a percent. $1,000 borrowed at a 6% interest rate means the person pays $60 a year in interest.

lagging indicators: An economic measurement that begins to change after the economy has already moved in that direction.

leading indicators: An economic measurement that begins to change before the economy moves in that direction.

new car sales: Reported by the major automobile dealers, typically five days after the end of the month. The sales can give an indication about the economy because they indicate consumer demand.

new home sales: The sale of a newly built home to a buyer from the builder. An increase in new home sales can be a sign of a growing economy.

Producer Price Index: A measure of price change from the perspective of the seller, it measures selling prices for goods and services.

productivity: Output divided by input, with output being the goods and services produced and input being the number of worker hours.

recession: A decline in the Gross Domestic Product for at least two consecutive quarters.

trade deficit: When the buying and selling of goods and services between two economies results in fewer exports than imports.

unemployment rate: A measure of how many people are out of the labor force but are looking for work.

REFERENCES

Aversa, J. (2003, February 14). Industrial production surges in January. Associated Press.

Burroughs, E. (2002, July 26). Consumer sentiment improves in late July. Reuters.

Carney, S. (2002, May 2). Incentives spark April auto sales; Consumer confidence drives 2.8% gain. *Detroit News.* p. 1A.

Crutsinger, M. (2003, May 6). Fed warns of risks ahead: Interest rates are left alone, but are likely to be lowered soon if things don't improve. Associated Press.

Edwards, W. (2003, May 1). U.S. first-quarter productivity rises at 1.6% rate. Bloomberg News.

Federal Open Markets Committee. (2003, May 6). News release. Washington, DC: Federal Reserve Board.

Glynn, M. (2003, February 21). Area home sales rise, but median prices decline. *Buffalo News.* p. B-5.

Kandel, M. (2003, May 22). Reading Greenspan's speak: The Fed chief warned of deflation, but how seriously depends on the headline. Retrieved May 30, 2003 from http://www.money.cnn.com.

Konin, R. (2003, May 16). CPI drops on energy drop; core flat. CBS.MarketWatch.com.

LePere, R. (2002, April 7). Anguish, bills go hand in hand. *The Charlotte* (Florida) *Sun.* pp. 1A–2A.

Martinez, A. (2003, May 7). State's jobless rate rises to 6%; Up after 2 months of declines. *The* (Raleigh) *News & Observer.* p. D1.

McCartney, M. S. (2000, April 18). Teaching' economics to the masses. Poynter.org. Retrieved Dec. 10, 2002 from http:// www.poynter.org.

Nutting, R. (2003, May 21). Outlook still cloudy, Greenspan says. CBS.MarketWatch.com.

Peters, J., & Zuber, A. (2001, December). Energizing Economics. *The Business Journalist.* pp. 1, 12.

Schmid, J. (2003, May 14). Trade deficit 2nd highest ever as U.S. continues to consume; crude oil imports climb to $9.1 billion over Iraq war fears. *Milwaukee Journal Sentinel,* p. 1D.

Williams, R. (2002, September 25). Customizing van facility means 100+ jobs for area. *The Blackshear Times.* p. 1.

Other Books on the Economy

Cleaver, T. (2002). *Understanding the world economy* (2nd ed.). New York: Routledge.

Rothbard, M. N. (1994). *The case against the Fed.* Auburn, AL: Ludwig von Mises Institute.

Stein, H. (1996). *The fiscal revolution in America: Policy in pursuit of reality.* Washington, DC: AEI Press.

Tuccille, J. (2002). *Alan shrugged: Alan Greenspan, the world's most powerful banker.* New York: Wiley.

Woodward, B. (2002). *Maestro: Greenspan's Fed and the American boom.* New York: Simon & Schuster.

SUGGESTED EXERCISES

1. Pick one stock or a set number of stocks at the beginning of the semester. Track the prices of the stocks you picked throughout the semester. At the end of the semester, compare the performance of your stocks with others in the class. What economic factors do you think influenced the rise or fall of your stocks?

2. Pick a day of the week and look at a dozen stocks in your community or in your state. Did they rise or fall for the day? How did they do compared to the rest of the stock market? Was there something that happened during the day that caused stocks of companies in one industry to rise or fall while the rest of the stock market moved in the opposite direction?

3. Go around the class asking your fellow students what type of jobs they've had during summer vacations or other times in their lives. How did they get these jobs? What was it like to be in the workforce? Were any of them ever afraid of losing their job? How hard was it to find a job?

4. Conduct a consumer confidence survey of 30 students on campus using some of the questions used by the Conference Board and the University of Michigan and report your findings in class. Do your results differ from other students who asked the same questions? Why do you think there's a difference in opinion?

4

The Basics of Company Financial Reporting

INCOME STATEMENTS AND BALANCE SHEETS

A company is in operation to make money. If it is not making money, then it needs to change its business in a way that could enable it to be profitable. But how does one determine whether a company is making money? Public companies and private companies provide charts of financial numbers to the SEC and state regulatory agencies that are important to read and analyze. One is called the income statement, and the other is called the balance sheet. Both are equally valuable in the information they contain and the story they convey about a company's performance. Yet, too often, business writers focus on the income statement and ignore the balance sheet, as well as another, the cash-flow statement.

An income statement is a chart that records a company's financial performance. To the experienced reader, the income statement tells dozens of stories and gives plenty of clues about a company's financial performance. It details a company's sales, its expenses, and its profits. A company typically provides its income statement for a 3-month period, known as a fiscal quarter, and compares the performance in that time with the same three months of the previous year. Analysts should not compare one quarter with the previous quarter. The comparison may not be valid, particularly if a company's business is seasonal. For example, Coca-Cola sells more soft drinks in the second and third quarters of the year than it does in the first and fourth quarters. Why? It is hotter in the second and third quarters, so people purchase more soft drinks.

An income statement is an important barometer of a company's success and health. A business reporter should review the performance in the income statement, and compare the growth rates of revenues, expenses, and profits with each other. If revenues are growing faster than profits, one interpretation of those two numbers could be that a company is cutting the cost of its products. If profits are increasing faster than revenue, then a company could be cutting expenses. If expenses are rising faster than revenues or profits, then a business might have begun an advertising campaign that has yet to boost sales. There are three possible story ideas right in the income statement.

Table 4.1 shows what a typical financial statement for a fiscal quarter might look like.

The income statement of a company such as Coca-Cola is basic enough for anyone to understand if they know what they are looking at. The top line in this

TABLE 4.1
CONDENSED CONSOLIDATED STATEMENTS OF INCOME
The Coca-Cola Company and Subsidiaries
(Unaudited)

Three Months Ended June 30	2002	2001
(In millions except per share data)		
Net operating revenues	$ 5,368	$ 4,653
Cost of goods sold	1,927	1,579
Gross profit	3,441	3,074
Selling, general and administrative expenses	1,789	1,561
Operating income	1,652	1,513
Interest income	52	78
Interest expense	58	77
Equity income (loss)—net	176	101
Other income (loss)—net	(55)	(18)
Income before income taxes and cumulative effect of accounting change	1,767	1,597
Income taxes	477	479
Net income	$ 1,290	$ 1,118
Basic net income per share	$ .52	$ .45
Dividends per share	$ .20	$ .18
Average shares outstanding	2,481	2,488

Note. From Coca-Cola Company, Form 10-Q, filed with the securities and Exchange Commission on August 13, 2002.

statement is called "Net operating revenues." What this means for a company such as Coca-Cola is that during the months of April, May, and June of 2002 it sold $5.4 billion worth of Coke Classic, Diet Coke, Fanta, Mr. Pibb, and other drinks. That is an increase of 15.4% over the $4.7 billion worth of soft drinks it sold during the same three months of 2001.

The next line is called "Cost of goods sold." This line includes how much money it cost Coca-Cola to make the concentrates and syrups used to make the soft drinks. For this quarter, it cost the company $1.9 billion, up 22.0% from the nearly $1.6 billion it cost in the same quarter of 2001. Note that the cost to make the soft drinks for the company rose faster than sales. Why did this happen? Maybe Coca-Cola was charged more by its suppliers for the cost of the ingredients, such as artificial sweeteners, used to make its drinks. Understanding that a change in growth rates always has an underlying reason enables the business writer to ask the right questions of executives and Wall Street experts. (Hint: The reason is also outlined later in the filing under "Management's Discussion and Analysis.")

Next is "Gross profit." This figure is essentially sales minus the cost to produce the product. It excludes company expenses for running the business, which appear in the next line, called "Selling, general and administrative expenses." This line is also commonly called SG&A. These expenses include everything from advertising to executive and employee salaries to the cost of heating corporate headquarters and the company's telephone bill. At Coca-Cola during this quarter, the SG&A costs were nearly $1.8 billion, up 14.6% from the same quarter the previous year. For a quick comparison of the numbers on an income statement, the back of the 10-Q contains a section called "Results of Operations." Here, a company will review its performance for the time period, typically explaining the increase or decrease in each number listed in the income statement.

To review, we have a company for which revenue, or sales, increased by 15.4%, its cost of making its product rose 22.0%, and its SG&A expenses jumped 14.6%. By comparing the growth rates of these three figures, the business reporter should begin to understand what happened at the company that quarter. In the case of Coca-Cola, revenue rose faster than its SG&A expenses. That is an indication that the company is tightening the belt around the expenses it can control, such as travel and pay. But it is also evident that the cost to produce all those soft drinks rose faster than the company could increase sales, which could mean that the company received price hikes from its suppliers. Somewhere, spending increased.

By taking the revenue, or sales figure, and subtracting the cost of the goods and the SG&A expenses, a company arrives at its operating income, or the amount of money it made or lost before paying taxes and before other accounting effects. The operating income figure gives a business reporter an indication of how the company's core business is performing. In this case, Coca-Cola's operating income rose 9.2% when compared to the same quarter of last year. This growth is less than its sales, or revenue growth, because of the increase in the cost of goods sold.

The next few lines in the income statement reflect the money made or lost by the company from its investments and from money it holds in bank accounts. This information typically does not heavily influence most companies' earnings. However, in some industries, it can have an impact. For example, insurance companies typically take premiums from consumers and invest that money in stocks and bonds. They then record income or losses from those investments here. Note that the losses reflected here are in parentheses instead of a minus sign before a number. Don't report that a number from a company's earnings was positive when it has parentheses around it. A number inside parentheses means that it's a negative number.

After adding and subtracting interest income and expenses, as well as income and losses from investments, the company arrives at an earnings figure before paying taxes. It then subtracts the amount of taxes paid in the quarter to arrive at a net income amount. This is the number that is arguably most important for the business reporter to assess, because it reflects how much money a company made, or lost, during the quarter. Coca-Cola reported net income of just under $1.3 billion, a gain of 15.4% above the net income figure it reported in the same quarter the previous year.

Public companies such as Coca-Cola break down its net income figure to show how much money was made for each share of its outstanding stock. This is called "Basic net income per share" in Table 4.1, but is typically known simply as earnings per share, or EPS. This number is calculated by dividing the net income by the total number of shares outstanding. The math done here for Coca-Cola is dividing the $1.3 billion in net income by the 2.48 billion shares outstanding to arrive at the 52 cents per share figure.

Earnings per share is a barometer for Wall Street to measure a company's earnings. Many Wall Street analysts estimate a company's EPS on the basis of projections and computer models before a company actually reports the figure. If the company's actual EPS beats what the Wall Street analysts estimated, then the company's stock could rise. If its EPS is lower than the estimate, then the stock price could fall.

The following fictional excerpt explains how the above numbers could have been used to help explain Coca-Cola's earnings to readers:

The Coca-Cola Co. reported second-quarter earnings that rose 15 percent as new products and strong sales in North America and Asia overcame slumping economies in other markets.

The Atlanta-based company reported net income of $1.29 billion, or 52 cents a share, compared with $1.12 billion, or 45 cents a share, in the quarter in 2001. The results were in line with Wall Street analyst expectations. Revenue increased 15 percent, to $5.37 billion from $4.65 billion.

The world's largest beverage company also said that it was comfortable with analysts' estimates for 2002 earnings and that it would stand by its projections for volume growth in its beverages.

According to analysts surveyed by Thomson First Call, the company will earn $1.75 to $1.80 a share for all of 2002.

The company's stock fell 37 cents, at $50 a share as investors questioned whether too much of Coke's volume growth came from its lower-margin juice brands, analysts said.

Note the emphasis in the lead is on the growth in earnings, or net income. The actual net income numbers are not included until the second paragraph, in which the reporter also assesses where the EPS was in relation to estimates. For a more in-depth treatment of writing earnings stories and earnings estimates. See the "Writing the Earnings Story" section of this chapter.

Balance sheets are also important barometers of a company's financial status, but rarely do you see reporters writing stories about the company's balance sheet. They should, because the balance sheet shows the company's assets and its debts. Though a company reports net income, it could have more liabilities than assets— possibly a truer reflection of that company's health. You can find out important information about a company by assessing the balance sheet.

The balance sheet is just what its name implies. The assets of a company on its balance sheet should be equal to the sum of its liabilities and the shareholders' equity in the company. Assets are typically divided into three areas: current; property, plant and equipment; and intangible assets. These will be explained in more detail after we look at a sample balance sheet.

Since we've discussed Coca-Cola earlier, let's look at its balance sheet at the end of the same quarter.

Table 4.2 reflects the listing of the company's total assets as of June 30. The worth of these assets can change every day, particularly for items such as cash and cash equivalents, so it is important to view these numbers as a snapshot of a company's assets on just that day.

The top section lists how much cash Coca-Cola has in its bank accounts as of June 30. It also details the value of the inventory of soft drink ingredients and other materials the company had at the end of the quarter. This is called "Inventories." Another large item in this section is "Prepaid expenses and other assets." This line could include items such as money Coca-Cola has paid for advertising on television, but has not yet used.

The next section of the list of assets is called "Investments and other assets." These columns list investments Coca-Cola has made in other companies around the world, either by purchasing stock or by adding money into the company. The investments listed by Coca-Cola are in companies that bottle and ship its soft drinks to retailers. Coca-Cola Enterprises, for example, is the largest soft-drink bottler in the United States. Coca-Cola Amatil is a large bottler in Australia.

Why does Coca-Cola invest in these companies? Maybe it is because company executives know that the success of these businesses is intertwined with the company's own success. Such investments can be very important for a company— which is why this section of the balance sheet is vital for a business reporter to evaluate. If a company is making investments in other companies that have nothing to do with its business, then maybe these assets need closer examination. (Why would a beverage company invest in a software developer, for example? There should be some valid business reason for the investment.) A business reporter also wants to see whether these investments are increasing in value for the

TABLE 4.2
CONDENSED CONSOLIDATED BALANCE SHEETS
The Coca-Cola Company and Subsidiaries
(Unaudited)

ASSETS

Three Months Ended	*June 30, 2002*	*December 31, 2001*
(In millions except share data)		
Current		
Cash and cash equivalents	$ 2,671	$ 1,866
Marketable securities	165	68
Trade accounts receivable, less allowances		
of $58 at June 30 and $59 at December 31	2,334	1,882
Inventories	1,385	1,055
Prepaid expenses and other assets	1,995	2,300
Total current assets	8,550	7,171
Investments and other assets		
Equity method investments		
Coca-Cola Enterprises Inc.	841	788
Coca-Cola Amatil Ltd.	502	432
Coca-Cola Hellenic Bottling Company S.A.	789	791
Other, principally bottling companies	2,397	3,117
Cost method investments, principally		
bottling companies	275	294
Other assets	3,038	2,792
Total investments and other assets	7,842	8,214
Property, plant and equipment		
Land	349	217
Buildings and improvements	2,194	1,812
Machinery and equipment	5,469	4,881
Containers	336	195
Subtotal property, plant and equipment assets	8,348	7,105
Less allowances for depreciation	2,882	2,652
Total property, plant and equipment assets	5,466	4,453
Trademarks and other intangible Assets	3,429	2,579
Total assets	$25,287	$22,417

Note. From Coca-Cola Company, Form 10-Q, filed with the Securities and Exchange Commission, on August 13, 2002.

company. If they are not increasing, then maybe the company's strategy of investing in other companies needs to be assessed. That review could turn into a story.

Following its investments, Coca-Cola lists the value of its property, plant, and equipment. This is the land its headquarters is on, its other buildings, its computers, company cars, trucks, and other items such as vending machines. The value of these items decreases regularly as a result of an accounting measure called depreciation. Depreciation can be thought of this way: When a consumer buys a car, the worth of that car immediately declines as it is driven off the lot. That is the depreciation of the value of the car. If it is a Mercedes, then the value may not decrease as fast as a Chevrolet. The same depreciation in value happens with other items, such as computers and vending machines.

Last, the company lists the value of its trademarks and other intangible assets. Here, Coca-Cola assessed the value of the franchise rights it grants to bottlers. A breakdown of these assets can also be found in the filing.

All of these assets, minus depreciation, totaled $25.3 billion as of June 30. That is an increase in nearly $3 billion in assets for the company in the first six months of 2002. And although this number may seem impressive, it is always smart to find out why assets are rising or falling. Typically, a company will explain this in the financial filing somewhere. In the case of Coca-Cola, the increase in assets is partly attributed to its acquisition of a bottler during the time period. (Information about the deal is found elsewhere in the filing.) The acquisition also affected its liabilities.

Now, let's look at the other side of the balance sheet, the liabilities and shareowners' equity (Table 4.3). This side of the balance sheet should equal the company's assets.

The "Accounts payable and accrued expenses" section of the liabilities side of the balance sheet lists the money that the company owes various suppliers and vendors for the ingredients to make its soft drinks and other items. "Loans and notes payable" details the money that the company owes banks and other lenders. These are both included in current liabilities, which are generally obligations that a company must pay within a year. Under this section, Coca-Cola lists how much long-term debt it owes. Long-term debt is typically payable for more than a year. Note that the long-term debt for the company more than doubled during the 6-month timeframe. Whenever you see a number increase by a significant amount, you should look further into the reasons. In the case of Coca-Cola, part of the reason for the increase in long-term debt was attributable to its acquisition of the bottler, causing it to put the bottler's debt onto its balance sheet. The increase in "Other liabilities" is also due to the acquisition. (For more on mergers and acquisitions, see chap. 6.)

Finally, the company lists the value of the shareowners' equity, which is also commonly referred to as the book value of the company. This is essentially how much money shareholders would receive if the company sold everything in its possession, went out of business, and paid its investors the money.

TABLE 4.3
CONDENSED CONSOLIDATED BALANCE SHEETS
The Coca-Cola Company and Subsidiaries
(Unaudited)

LIABILITIES AND SHARE-OWNERS' EQUITY

	June 30, 2002	December 31, 2001
(In millions except share data)		
Current		
Accounts payable and accrued expenses	$ 4,485	$ 3,679
Loans and notes payable	2,967	3,743
Current maturities of long-term debt	203	156
Accrued income taxes	1,208	851
Total current liabilities	8,863	8,429
Long-term debt	2,774	1,219
Other liabilities	1,759	961
Deferred income taxes	540	442
Share-owners' equity		
Common stock, $.25 par value		
Authorized: 5,600,000,000 shares		
Issued: 3,494,331,099 shares at June 30;		
3,491,465,016 shares at December 31	874	873
Capital surplus	3,641	3,520
Reinvested earnings	23,614	23,443
Accumulated other comprehensive income and		
unearned compensation on restricted stock	(2,792)	(2,788)
Subtotal Share-owners' equity	25,337	25,048
Less treasury stock, at cost		
(1,011,322,527 shares at June 30;		
1,005,237,693 shares at December 31)	13,986	13,682
Total Share-owners' equity	11,351	11,366
Total liabilities and Share-owners' equity	$25,287	$22,417

Note. From Coca-Cola Company, Form 10-Q, filed with the Securities and Exchange Commission, on August 13, 2002.

Again, most companies discuss the increase or decrease in each of these numbers later in their financial disclosures. But it is important to compare the "Total current assets" side of the balance sheet with the "Total current liabilities" side primarily because companies typically pay the liabilities with the assets. If liabilities are exceeding assets, then a company may have to borrow money to pay some of those liabilities. That might be the case here with Coca-Cola. Obviously, it is important to look at these balance sheet numbers for any large increases or decreases that might be a signal of something else going on at the company that could result in a story.

Because of the failure of Enron Corporation, many casual readers of the business page may have heard of an "Off-Balance sheet transaction." These are deals that a company enters into that are not included on a balance sheet. They may be the creation of a joint venture with another company, or they may be a loan to another company to help it get started. For example, oil companies create off-balance sheet subsidiaries to explore for new oil wells. Generally accepted accounting rules allow for these to be excluded from a company's balance sheet, but most of them must be detailed in the footnotes. These footnotes can be difficult to read and even harder to understand because they are written by accountants and reviewed by attorneys. If footnotes for an off-balance sheet transaction are encountered, it would be wise to take the information to an accountant, lawyer, or another expert who understands what the disclosure is stating. In the case of Enron, the company was using the off-balance sheet transactions to pump up its earnings and mask enormous losses in many businesses.

FINANCIAL STATEMENTS ARE ALIKE FOR PUBLIC AND PRIVATE COMPANIES

The first part of this chapter assesses the financial performance of a public company. Shares of Coca-Cola are traded on the New York Stock Exchange (NYSE). Because anyone can purchase its stock if he or she has the money, it is considered a public company. Yet, Coca-Cola's financial statements are constructed not much differently than financial statements for a private company. That is why understanding how a company derives the numbers in its income statement and balance sheet can be important for any type of business reporting—whether the company is public or private.

Many beginning business reporters operate under the assumption that a private company is just that—private. They think that because its stock is not owned by investors across the country, it is therefore not required to divulge its financial performance. Nothing could be further from the truth. Many business reporters are surprised to learn that there are numerous private companies that also file financial performance statements with the SEC. Thousands of private companies, such as banks and insurance companies, are required to file documents with state regulators disclosing their financial performance.

In fact, private companies may be more public in disclosing information than one might think. For example, when Publix Super Markets Incorporated, one of the country's largest grocery store chains, began expanding its operations out of Florida northward into Georgia, Alabama, and South Carolina in the 1990s, smart newspaper reporters in those states delved into the company's financial performance disclosed to the SEC, even though the Lakeland, Florida-based company is considered private. Why was Publix providing this information? Because companies with more than $10 million in assets with securities that are held by more than 500 owners must file annual and other periodic reports. Publix fits this description. Its stock is held by hundreds of store employees and the Jenkins family. Still, when it files this information, it is news. The company's competitors want to know how it is performing, and so do the thousands of employees in its stores. Yet few reporters bother to look for this information. Here is a story from Bloomberg News that provided the results:

> Publix Super Markets Inc., a closely held supermarket company, said its profit last year was unchanged at $530.4 million.
> Per-share earnings rose to $2.62 from $2.52 a year earlier, as the company had fewer shares outstanding. Sales rose 4.8 percent to $15.3 billion from $14.6 billion in 2000, which had an extra week in the period, Publix said in a statement.
> Same-store sales rose 3.2 percent. Sales in stores open at least a year are a key indicator of a retailer's business because they exclude new and closed locations.
> Shares of Lakeland, Florida-based Publix, with 691 stores in Florida, Georgia, South Carolina and Alabama, are owned by family members and Publix employees and directors. The shares are valued at $41.[1]

The information in this story about a private company is the same as for a public company. The lead emphasizes the company's profit, similar to the lead in the story on Coca-Cola's earnings. Sales, or revenue, is just as important a barometer for a private company as for public one. All companies, whether they are public or private, strive to make money and keep increasing the amount of money they make. A company, public or private, is considered healthy if it continues to increase its sales and profits.

Similar financial information can be obtained from other regulatory agencies for private companies in other industries. For example, the insurance industry is regulated by state commissioners. Insurance companies that do business in a state are required to file financial information with the commissioner. (For more information about what is available from regulatory agencies, see chap. 14.)

Although public and private companies report similar financial information, how a reporter interprets those numbers should be different. Public companies are in the business of increasing the stock price of their shareholders. To do that, many of them engage in practices such as cutting SG&A expenses to increase their profits. A private company, however, may not be as interested in improving profits. Management at a private company, particularly one that is run by its owners and has no interest in becoming public, may actually lower earnings for a year or

---

[1] From "Publix Super Markets annual profit unchanged at $530.4 million," by S. Elam, March 1, 2002, Bloomberg News. Copyright 2002 by Bloomberg News. All rights reserved. Reprinted with permission.

two and use that money to build a new plant or add a new corporate headquarters building. Many private companies, particularly private businesses that have few shareholders, do not worry about earnings per share (EPS). And for very small private companies, there may be only one owner.

HOW AND WHY COMPANIES DISCLOSE FINANCIAL INFORMATION

Imagine for a minute that no company, public or private, ever divulged how much money it was making, how much money it was losing, how its sales rose or fell from quarter to quarter or from year to year. How would potential investors assess whether to purchase stock in such companies? Would they just have to believe what the company told them? What about consumers deciding whether to buy a product from Company A or Company B? Obviously, there are some companies whose word is not to be trusted. Companies know that by releasing financial information about their performance, they build confidence among their customers that they are not going to go out of business, and they may convince investors to buy their stock if their executives can demonstrate an ability to increase revenue and profits.

Our business world is set up in a way that requires companies to release detailed information about their financial performance to a multitude of audiences. Companies with stock that is traded on an exchange regularly file documents with the SEC that disclose their profits, losses, sales, and many other financial measures. Private companies also disclose financial information, although it may be tougher to obtain. Many of them provide results to the SEC, a fact that is surprising to many reporters. Other private companies disclose their financial performance to lenders, rating agencies, and state regulators. In short, all companies keep close tabs on where they are spending their money, and where they are making their money. The business reporter can find this kind of information for thousands of companies by carefully reading the financial statements filed with the SEC and state regulatory agencies.

Being able to read and assess a company's financial statement is the cornerstone of a business reporter's job. The writer needs to be able to analyze how a company is performing and how that performance compares with the performance of its competitors. It can be argued that assessing a company's financial numbers is the root of everything else important in a business reporter's job. Without a proper understanding of profits, sales, revenue, and other measures, a business reporter can not (a) interview a CEO about his or her company's performance, (b) begin to properly understand why a company might want to acquire a competitor, or (c) comprehend a board member's opinion that management needs to be changed.

As mentioned above, the SEC regulates all companies that regularly trade stocks or bonds. Because the SEC is there to protect the investor, it requires a lot of information to be filed for public dissemination. This can be a treasure trove for business reporters—if they know what they are looking for and where to find it.

Why does the SEC require these filings? The answer is simple: If the SEC requires companies to file information about their operations on a regular basis, then investors and potential investors will be able to read that information and assess for themselves whether the company's performance is improving or waning. The bad information disclosed, most likely in an SEC filing and not in a news release, will likely send a company's stock price down. The good information, likely disclosed in a release with horns blaring and whistles blowing, will send the stock price up.

Professional investors on Wall Street review these filings every day for this type of information. That is also why the good business reporter reads the SEC filings. If he or she can find this information before anyone else and write a story about it, then he or she has a scoop. It is not always that easy, however. Many business reporters can read an SEC filing just like anyone else. But they need to be able to understand what they are reading, and they need to be able to analyze the importance of what is in the filings. Last, and most important, business reporters need to be able to then take that newsworthy information and write about it in a story that makes sense to a reader who may not have the time to go looking through the SEC filings.

HOW TO EVALUATE A COMPANY'S FINANCIAL HEALTH

This chapter, and the previous chapters, outline the basics of how and where to look to assess whether a company is making or losing money. Essentially, a company that reports increasing profits and rising revenues is generally considered to be a healthy company, whether it is public or private. This section discusses some of the financial information a company discloses that can be manipulated to determine barometers of health or sickness.

The cash-flow statement is another table of financial information that every company discloses in its SEC filings along with its income statement and its balance sheet (Table 4.4). This statement helps a business reporter analyze where a company is getting its money and how that money is being used.

As the first section of this chapter shows, assessing the income statement and balance sheet has required only simple addition, subtraction, and division. There is no need to know complicated formulas or understand algorithms to asses how a company is performing. The same holds true for a cash-flow statement. It is a simple table that shows how much money a company is getting from its operations, investments, and financing. The basic test of health is whether a company is generating positive cash flow, that is, is more money coming into the company than flowing out? If the company is generating more money than it is spending, then this is the sign of a healthy company.

Here is what the table would look like, again for Coca-Cola:

TABLE 4.4
CONDENSED CONSOLIDATED STATEMENTS OF CASH FLOWS
The Coca-Cola Company and Subsidiaries
(Unaudited)

Six Months Ended June 30	*2002*	*2001*
(In millions)		
Operating activities		
Net income	$ 1,165	$ 1,981
Depreciation and amortization	398	385
Deferred income taxes	(145)	(84)
Equity income or loss, net of dividends	(173)	4
Foreign currency adjustments	16	7
Cumulative effect of accounting changes	926	10
Other items	225	25
Net change in operating assets and liabilities	(256)	(233)
Net cash provided by operating activities	2,156	2,095
Investing activities		
Acquisitions and investments, principally trademarks and bottling companies	(267)	(241)
Purchases of investments and other assets	(62)	(340)
Proceeds from disposals of investments and other assets	46	140
Purchases of property, plant and equipment	(374)	(313)
Proceeds from disposals of property, plant and equipment	35	55
Other investing activities	36	104
Net cash used in investing activities	(586)	(595)
Net cash provided by operations after reinvestment	1,570	1,500
Financing activities		
Issuances of debt	1,189	2,307
Payments of debt	(1,272)	(2,523)
Issuances of stock	85	125
Purchases of stock for treasury	(301)	(132)
Dividends	(497)	(448)
Net cash used in financing activities	(796)	(671)
Effect of exchange rate changes on cash and cash equivalents	31	(49)
Cash and cash equivalents		
Net increase during the period	805	780
Balance at beginning of period	1,866	1,819
Balance at end of period	$ 2,671	$ 2,599

Note. From the Coca-Cola Company, Form 10-Q, Filed with the Securities and Exchange Commission on August 13, 2002.

The cash flow from operations is an indication of the money the company is receiving from selling its product or services. If the cash flow from operations is increasing, that is a sign of a healthy company. If it is decreasing, the company may be having some problems selling its goods or services. That could be a sign to a business reporter to check further into the company.

The cash flow from investing activities explains how the company is investing its excess money and how it is trying to use that money to expand its operations. In the case of Coca-Cola, there is spending to purchase bottling companies and property, plant, and equipment (represented by values in parentheses). Business reporters should be wary of the money a company spends on investing activities. If this money has increased dramatically, why has the company determined that it needs to spend even more to expand its operations? What is the new business opportunity that was not available at the same time last year?

The last section of the cash-flow statement shows cash spent on financing. This shows how companies get extra money to grow their business, and whether they are paying off their debts. It is vital to see a company paying its debts. If a company does not pay its debt, interest keeps adding to the total, making the debt higher and higher. The higher the debt gets, the more difficult it becomes to pay off. Companies that keep borrowing money by issuing debt will eventually have to pay off that debt. Some companies wind up in bankruptcy court if they can not pay off that debt.

Healthy companies have an overall positive cash flow. If the overall cash flow number is negative, the company is spending more money to operate the business than is coming in through the sale of products and services. In healthy companies, cash flow continues to increase from time period to time period. In the case of Coca-Cola, its cash in the first six months of 2002 was $805 million, up from the $780 million in the first six months of 2001.

A public company's financial performance is also measured by Wall Street investors and business reporters in other ways. One of these measures is analysis of a company's profit margin. Profit margins can be high for some industries and low for others. The profit margin for grocery retailers is low, sometimes as low as 2%. However, whether, high or low, a profit margin divides the net income by the revenue. If we look back at Coca-Cola's profit margin, the net income of nearly $1.3 billion can be divided by its revenue of nearly $5.4 billion showing a profit margin of a little more than 24.0%. With this information, investors and reporters can see how Coca-Cola's profit margin compared with that of its rival PepsiCo, for example. One must simply find the same numbers for PepsiCo and do the math. In this example, investors and reporters will find that Coca-Cola has a higher profit margin (24.0%) than its competitor (15.2%). A similar measure of a company's health is its operating margin, which is another case of simple division, where operating costs are divided by sales. Again, this number for a specific company should be compared with competitors and the overall industry.

Another measure of a company that is useful in comparing it with other companies in the same industry is return on equity (ROE). This measure divides net income by shareholders' equity. ROE assesses how well a company uses the money shareholders put into it. Many well-run companies have ROEs above 20%. In simple terms, this means that 20 cents in company profits have been created for every $1 invested in the company.

A similar measure of a company's performance is called return on assets (ROA), or return on investment. This is another division problem where a company's net income plus its interest expense is divided by its total assets. All three of these numbers can be found on the income statement and the balance sheet. A company looks at its ROA to determine whether to take on new projects. If its ROA is 5%, for example, the company may not decide to borrow money to build a new plant if it is going to have to pay its lender 7% interest.

One of the most basic measures investors use to examine a company is a price-to-earnings (P/E) ratio. This is a simple equation where the stock price of a company is divided by the EPS. For example, if a company has a stock that is trading at $60, and it has earned $2.50 per share in earnings, then it has a P/E ratio of 24. This number is then compared with competitors' P/E ratios and the overall stock market.

If the above company with the P/E ratio of 24 has a competitor with a P/E ratio of 30, there may be something about the competitor that causes its stock price to be higher. Maybe it has a management team that is considered more valuable. Or maybe the company with the lower P/E has had some financial problems in the past, and investors are not willing to give it the benefit of a higher ratio just yet. Such a comparison can be useful to a business reporter evaluating a company's strategy and where it stands in relation to its peers. Companies with higher P/E ratios are generally considered to be businesses with greater growth potential than those with lower P/Es. In addition, some industries generally have higher P/E ratios than other sectors of the economy—always evaluate this number within an industry.

Another important barometer of a company used by both Wall Street and business journalists is the price-to-book (P/B) ratio. This equation divides the price of the company's stock by the company's book value. A company's book value per share is often provided in SEC filings, and is arrived at by dividing its assets by the number of shares outstanding. If a company has a stock price of $60 per share, but its book value is $50 per share, then it is said that the stock is trading above book value. Put another way, the stock price is 1.2 times the book value.

Again, the P/B ratio is a measure that can be valuable to business reporters assessing a company's performance in the stock market relative to competitors. Companies with stock that trades below book value may be considered cheap by investors. But there may also be a reason why the stock is trading below book value. Maybe the company has been reporting losses, or revenue has been falling. Investors, scared that the company could be in trouble, may be selling the stock, depressing its value. Overall, the stock market trades slightly above book value. The stock of some companies may trade at three or four times its book value. Microsoft is a good example of a company that is valued by investors for always reporting solid earnings, and is therefore rewarded by being traded at higher values.

WRITING THE EARNINGS STORY

This chapter first discussed the information contained in a Form 10-Q and Form 10-K before discussing the information companies release in quarterly earnings news releases. That is because the information and analysis is more detailed in the filings than it is in releases. The filings expose a complete, often unfettered, picture of a company's financial health, whereas the releases provide the company's interpretation of its performance. The two may not always correlate.

Unfortunately for business writers, a company rarely, if ever, files its quarterly 10-Q or annual 10-K with the SEC before it discloses its earnings in a press release. As a result, most stories about a company's earnings are written on the basis of information that is disclosed in the release, not in the filing. By the time a company gets around to filing a 10-Q or 10-K with the SEC, most reporters forget to look at it and, consequently, may be missing a story. That's why those filings have been emphasized first in this chapter because they often contain important nuggets of information.

Many companies like to put out earnings releases before the stock market opens at 9:30 a.m. or after the stock market closes for trading at 4 p.m. For many reporters, particularly those that work at a wire service such as the Associated Press, Reuters, Dow Jones, or Bloomberg News, this means that the morning and afternoon can be busy times during earnings season.

It is important to note again that a company can use its earnings releases to put a spin on its performance. Sometimes a company will emphasize strong growth in revenue or sales to mask the fact that it spent a lot of money that quarter on advertising or something else, making earnings lower than expected. Other times, companies will trumpet strong earnings growth despite weak sales. That is why the business reporter needs to look at the complete picture in an earnings release. Although Wall Street analysts and investors primarily focus on whether the company "made" its earnings projections, a better story may be told by looking at the overall performance of the company.

Let's look at how a typical earnings release begins from a company:

> The Home Depot, the world's largest home improvement retailer, today reported record net earnings of $940 million, or $0.40 per diluted share, for the third quarter of fiscal 2002, an increase of 21 percent compared with net earnings of $778 million, or $0.33 per diluted share, in fiscal 2001. Sales for the quarter increased 9 percent to $14.5 billion and comparable store sales decreased 2 percent.
>
> "The Home Depot delivered strong earnings in the third quarter as we continue to reinvest in our facilities and associates. The operational initiatives we launched a year ago are delivering results, thanks to our dedicated associates, loyal customers

and vendor partners," said Bob Nardelli, Chairman, President & CEO of The Home Depot. "The current retail environment, coupled with merchandising changes and resets within our stores, affected customer traffic. Throughout the quarter, however, we saw customers respond to great values in areas like appliances, flooring, and power tools, supporting growth in our average ticket."

"Looking forward, our customers can be assured of everyday low prices, broader assortments and excellent service at the heart of our activities through the fourth quarter and into the next fiscal year," Nardelli said. "While we remain cautious on the outlook for the economy into next year, the strength of our balance sheet and our operating performance allows us to stay on strategy."

"This year we will open 200 new stores and add 40,000 associates. Our financial condition remains unsurpassed in retail, with $4.0 billion in cash and more than $20 billion in equity at the end of the quarter," Nardelli said.

During the quarter, The Home Depot added 34 stores, including two stores in Mexico. At the end of the quarter, the company operated a total of 1,471 stores.

The Home Depot reconfirmed that it expects to earn $0.31 diluted earnings per share for the fourth quarter of fiscal 2002, an increase of 15 percent over the fourth quarter of 2001 on a 13-week basis. The company also indicated that it is comfortable with $1.57 diluted earnings per share for the fiscal year, a 25 percent increase over fiscal 2001 on a 52-week basis.[2]

This earnings release begins with the numbers that everyone will care about: The net income and net income per share figures. At Home Depot during the above quarter, the profit increased by 21% from the same quarter in the previous year. Note that the comparison is not made with the prior quarter in the same year, but with the same quarter a year ago, to provide a more accurate picture of how the company is performing. The business reporter should be leery of any company that tries to compare earnings from two consecutive quarters. That is not how Wall Street assesses earnings, and that is not how reporters should either. It is also smart to check the company's math. For example, a reporter should look at the 21% growth in earnings figure that is given by Home Depot. Does that number apply to the growth in net income, or the growth in net income per share? If one does the math, the actual figure is 20.8% growth in net income, and 21.2% in net income per share, so the 21% growth reported, by the company could reflect either the growth in net income or net income per share.

For other companies, however, the percentage increase in earnings may not be uniform. The lead paragraph of an Intel Corporation earnings release (2002) began with the statement that third-quarter revenue was up 3% from the previous quarter and even from the same quarter a year ago before mentioning in the second paragraph that net income rose. The net income figure was up 547% from the same quarter of the previous year, but net income per share was up 400%. Why does this happen? Intel had more shares outstanding in the recent quarter. Because a company issues more stock, or often repurchases stock to make its net income

---

[2]From "Third quarter 2002 earnings release," by Home Depot Incorporated, November 19, 2002. Copyright 2002 by Home Depot. Reprinted with permission.

per share figure grow at a faster rate than its net income, a better barometer of a company's earnings growth is the percentage gain in net income, not the percentage gain in net income per share. A business reporter should not fall into this trap, but focus on the growth or decline in the dollar amount noted in net income.

Intel mentioned its revenue first before it mentioned its earnings, whereas Home Depot mentioned its earnings before it mentioned its revenue, or sales. In some industries, revenue and sales can be more important than profits as barometers of how a company is performing. This is often the case in the computer industry, for example. However, the success of most companies is still measured by their profits.

Other industry barometers are also important in earnings releases. For retailers such as Home Depot and Wal-Mart, many experts like to measure their success by comparable, or same-store, sales, a figure mentioned in the first paragraph of the Home Depot release. This figure tells how sales have done at stores that have been open for at least a year. In the case of Home Depot, these sales fell by 2%, but the company was still able to increase its overall sales by 9%. The company achieved this by opening new stores during the quarter, thereby boosting total sales.

Other industries have similar measures of performance that a business reporter will want to look for in the earnings statement. Beverage companies such as Coca-Cola and Pepsi report increases or declines in the number of cases of soft drinks sold during a quarter. Anheuser-Busch and Coors report gains or losses in the number of barrels of beer sold during a quarter. In the table that accompanied Home Depot's earnings release, the company also disclosed information such as the average purchase at one of its stores.

Business writers typically receive the earnings release from a company by facsimile or, increasingly, by e-mail. Here is how a reporter in Bloomberg's Atlanta bureau took the information from the Home Depot release and explained what was important. This story was sent out on Bloomberg's wire at 9:50 a.m., less than two hours after the earnings were released. The conference call mentioned in the story began at 9 a.m.:

> Home Depot Inc., the world's largest home-improvement retailer, said third-quarter earnings rose 21 percent as the company controlled expenses. Sales at stores open at least a year declined.
>
> Net income increased to $940 million, or 40 cents a share, from $778 million, or 33 cents, a year earlier. Sales in the three months ended Nov. 3 rose 8.9 percent to $14.5 billion, Home Depot said in a statement. The company's shares dropped as much as 12 percent.
>
> Home Depot's sales at stores open at least a year fell 2 percent, the second-biggest decline in Robert Nardelli's two years as chief executive. The company had forecast a gain of as much as 4 percent. Home Depot is grappling with slower growth after saturating the U.S. market. Smaller rival Lowe's Cos. is also entering Home Depot's turf in bigger cities such as Boston.
>
> "I'm disappointed with my sales performance," Nardelli told investors on a conference call. "The operational programs set in place a year ago are (helping) to expand gross margins. They are not all perfect, but it's better than doing nothing."

Nardelli said the company won't meet its revenue-growth forecast of 15 percent to 20 percent this year. Same-store sales are expected to fall 3 percent to 5 percent in the fourth quarter, Chief Financial Officer Carol Tome said on the call.

Home Depot has enlarged the appliance and home-decor departments in its stores to attract customers. The moves hurt sales, spokesman Bob Burton said. The changes reduced same-store sales by 2 percent to 3 percent in the second quarter, according to a regulatory filing.

"They've been running so far behind Lowe's. It's a company that's trying to get its footing," said Arnhold & S. Bleichroeder Inc. analyst Barbara Allen, who rates Home Depot a "neutral" and doesn't own the shares. "I don't have a good sense whether Nardelli understands what Home Depot really needs."

Falling lumber prices trimmed same-store sales by 1 percent, while new Home Depot stores pulling business from older ones hurt sales by 4 percent, Tome said.

Shares of Atlanta-based Home Depot fell $2.72 to $25.88 at 9:45 a.m. in New York Stock Exchange composite trading, after dropping to $25.05. The stock had tumbled 44 percent this year, making it the biggest decliner in the 30-member Dow Jones Industrial Average.

Home Depot, in a statement, reiterated a fourth-quarter profit forecast of 31 cents a share, one cent less than the average analyst estimate from Thomson First Call. Third-quarter earnings met the analysts' average forecast.

Same-store sales fell 3 percent in the first quarter of 2001, the biggest decline under Nardelli.[3]

The reporter who wrote this story, Maxine Clayton, had covered Home Depot for a couple of years and began working at Bloomberg just after graduating from college. Yet her story shows that she understands what is important to Home Depot's results and conveys her knowledge of the retail industry. Her lead paragraph explains why profits rose faster than sales—the company cut its expenses for running its stores. The story explains why sales fell at Home Depot stores open for more than one year, and Clayton adds comments from the conference call that she knows her readers will want to know about, such as sales estimates for the next quarter. In addition, the story includes reaction to what other people think about the results, with a comment from an analyst and a description of how the stock price fell after the earnings were released. Also note that in the next-to-last paragraph of the story, this reporter tells readers that the earnings reported by Home Depot were in line with analyst estimates. This is an important barometer when writing about a company's earnings performance. If the earnings had come in below or above Wall Street estimates, then that likely would have been mentioned earlier in Clayton's story. Last, she reports the earnings Home Depot expects to report in the next quarter—31 cents per share—and points out that this guidance from the company is a penny lower than what analysts were expecting at the time of the release. Maybe that is why the stock price fell.

---

[3]From "Home Depot 3rd-qtr earnings rise 21% on cost controls," by M. Clayton, November 19, 2002, Bloomberg News. Copyright 2002 by Bloomberg News. All rights reserved. Reprinted with permission.

Earnings guidance like this is important for business writers to track, because the stock prices of companies can rise and fall dramatically on the basis of the release of this information. Anytime a company issues a statement forecasting what it expects to report in earnings for a quarter or a year, a business reporter should compare those numbers against both Wall Street expectations and earlier guidance given by the company. The reasoning for this is simple, but important. If a company issues earnings guidance that is higher than it previously stated or higher than Wall Street thought, its stock price is likely to rise that day. Many investors decide how much they are willing to pay for a stock on the basis of how much a company is expected to report in earnings that year. If the company expects to report higher earnings, investors will be willing to pay a higher price for the stock. The reverse is also true. If a company discloses that it expects to report earnings lower than it previously stated or that Wall Street estimated, the stock price is likely to fall. A business reporter's story on the release of new guidance should emphasize why the earnings estimate has changed, for the good or the bad. In most cases, the reason is that the company's business is performing better than expected, or worse than expected.

The following is how a company will typically release such information:

UnitedHealth Group anticipates a continuation of its strong growth and operating per-formance in 2003, expecting that its operating margins will increase in the aggregate, with every business segment showing stable or expanded margins next year.

At its annual Investor Conference last week, management provided the following key data points for 2003:

- Revenues of approximately $29 billion, supported by 13 percent organic rev-enue growth across the aggregate of the company's businesses.
- Operating earnings at or above $2.57 billion.
- Margins expanding from an estimated 8.7 percent in 2002 to 8.9 percent or more in 2003.
- Earnings per share increasing to at least $5.05 per share, representing the high side of the Company's guidance range, 20 percent above $4.20 in earnings per share currently expected in 2002.
- Cash flows from operations exceeding $2.6 billion in 2003, up from $2.3 billion in 2002.
- Return on equity at or above 34 percent.[4]

The fourth bullet point in this release is the earnings guidance, and it indicates that UnitedHealth, a managed care company, believes that its earnings for 2003 will be higher than it expected earlier. This news release was issued shortly after 6 a.m. Though it's doubtful that many reporters were in their newsrooms at that time, many companies like to issue releases early in the morning, because executives know that editors will assign the story to reporters before the day gets busy.

---

[4]United Health Group Inc. news release, November 26, 2002. Copyright 2002 by United Health Group Inc. Reprinted with permission.

A Reuters reporter took the UnitedHealth information and explained why the company released the information—to counteract a drop in its stock price the previous day which was based on concerns by an analyst and how the stock market reacted. The reporter noted that the earnings outlook came a day after a Wall Street analyst downgraded UnitedHealth, which caused its stock to fall by nearly 10%. After the company released its earnings projection, the stock rose about 3.5%. The story also noted that the company's earnings projections for 2003 were slightly higher than analyst estimates, and that its revenue projections were in line with previous expectations. This comparison should be in every earnings-related story.

Company releases explaining earnings for the previous quarter or projections for the next quarter contain some of the most important news of a business. These releases can be a barometer of the company's performance, letting the rest of the world know whether the business is healthy or sick. That is why it is important for a business writer to know how to read these releases and turn the information into a story that will explain what is going on.

OTHER NEWS IN A CORPORATE FINANCIAL REPORT

Besides the earnings reporters can find information in the SEC filings—Forms 10-Q and 10-K— that detail a company's financial performance, there is a lot of other good, useful information in these filings that at first glance may not seem to be telling anyone a story.

The best known SEC filing is a Form 10-Q. This is the quarterly financial statement for each company that falls under SEC's regulations. This form must be filed with the SEC within 45 days following the end of the quarter. Because the fiscal year of most companies is the same as the calendar year, May 15, August 15, and November 15 are busy reading days for most business reporters. Quarters typically end on March 31, June 30, September 30 and December 31. Companies that do not file within this time frame typically ask for extensions, and usually are having some sort of financial problem.

Form 10-Q filings have a section which discusses the financial performance for the previous quarter, explaining the ups and downs of revenues and profits. In addition, these filings tell the business reporter whether the company is buying its own stock. This is an interesting disclosure, and one that could turn into a potential story, because it tells investors whether the company's executives believe the stock is cheap or expensive. If a company has been repurchasing a large amount of its stock in the recent quarter, the CFO or CEO probably think it is a good investment. If they have not purchased a significant amount of its stock, then maybe they think the stock price is high. That is information a business reporter would want to tell his or her readers, because those readers often buy and sell stocks on the basis of this information.

The following excerpt shows how this information is disclosed in a 10-Q:

The Company may repurchase as much as $120 million of its outstanding Class A common stock through December 31, 2002. During the second quarter of 2001, 25,500 shares were repurchased at a total cost of $734,295 or an average price of $28.80. The Company repurchased 149,957 shares at a total cost of $4,300,216 during the second quarter of 2000. (Form 10-Q, Erie Indemnity, 2001, p. 20)

What does this tell the business reporter? This statement implies that whoever is in charge of this company's stock buyback plan may have thought the stock was a lot cheaper in the second three months of 2000, during which time $4.3 million was spent to buy stock, than in the second quarter of 2001, during which time only $734,000 was spent to buy stock. Again, companies tend to buy their own stock when it is cheap and they believe it is going to go up.

More important, stock repurchasing might be an indication to the business writer of the company's future prospects. If a company is buying back its shares, it probably thinks that its future performance is going to be good, which will drive up the price. If the company is not buying its own stock, maybe the executives do not see a catalyst in its business that will drive up the price.

The 10-K is a company's annual filing with the SEC, and it must be filed within 75 days of the end of the fiscal year, which typically makes the end of March a busy time for business writers who read these filings. Note that the deadlines for filing a 10-Q and a 10-K will be lowered to 35 days after the end of a quarter and 60 days for the year by Dec. 15, 2005. The 10-K provides a history and an overview of the company's business that is informative reading for a reporter just beginning to cover the company. It also details the number of employees a company has and the property it owns.

If a reporter knows how to compare the growth rate of two numbers provided in a filing, that information might make a story. As Bill Barnhart, financial markets columnist for the *Chicago Tribune,* wrote: It is important to determine whether there is a variance in the numbers. "Identify these variances before you read management's discussion of results," said Barnhart. "Often an interesting trend or anomaly will appear in the financial statements that the company fails to address in the report text. You may have a story. This is particularly true during sluggish economic times, when a company may grow profits by tweaking seemingly incidental line items" (Barnhart, 2001, p. 1).

For example, Barnhart reviewed a filing from McDonald's Corporation that showed the company issued $2.4 billion in long-term debt, boosting the company's debt-to-equity ratio to its highest level since 1991. Barnhart noted that the company used nearly all of that money to repurchase its shares, causing its net income per share to increase, even as cash flow from its business declined during a tough year. In other words, McDonald's did not have a great year. But it looked like it did to the unsophisticated business reporter who could not connect the stock repurchases to the increase in net income per share.

Another important disclosure that is often found in these filings is an estimate of a company's future spending to improve its infrastructure or other operations. This may involve building a new factory or adding new computers. Not every company reports this in a 10-Q or 10-K filing, but when it does, it can estimate the financial impact to future earnings—something that investors will look for. If a business writer can write a story about this information before anyone else finds it, then his or her story may move the company's stock price.

Disclosures like this can read something like the following:

> In 2001, the Company began the development of several eCommerce initiatives in support of the Erie Insurance Group's business model of distributing insurance products exclusively through independent agents. The eCommerce program includes initiatives to replace property/casualty policy administration systems as well as customer interaction systems. The eCommerce program also includes significant information technology infrastructure expenditures. The program is intended to improve service and efficiency, as well as result in increased sales. Total five-year expenditures for the program are estimated at $150 to $175 million. The cost of these initiatives will be shared among several companies of the Erie Insurance Group, including the Company. Based on preliminary estimates, which will be further refined in the second half of 2001, the after-tax effect on net income of the Company is estimated to reduce earnings per share between $0.08 and $0.12 for 2001 and between $0.05 and $0.07 per share for each of the next four years of the program. (Form 10-Q, Erie Indemnity Group, 2001, p. 21)

A business writer who discovers information like this in a 10-Q or 10-K should immediately try to find out if Wall Street has factored in this expenditure and lower earnings guidance into the stock price. It is also important to assess what the company's competitors are doing. If they are not building new plants or adding new product lines when the company you are writing about is, there could be a good reason to add that information to your story.

Litigation is also frequently discussed in 10-Q and 10-K filings. Business lawsuits are discussed in depth in chapter 11, but suffice it to say for now that these filings can give the business writer clues as to where to look for this information. Business lawsuits can be quite nasty and can affect stock prices. Companies will often set aside money to pay for potential settlements or adverse rulings resulting from lawsuits. This information can be even more important to readers if the litigation involves two companies.

In Coca-Cola's 10-K filed in March 2002, the company disclosed that it and some of its executives were sued in U.S. District Court for the Northern District of Georgia on October 27, 2000. The lawsuit alleges that the executives misrepresented the company's financial performance. A second similar lawsuit was filed on November 9, 2000. The filing notes that a judge consolidated these two lawsuits in 2001 and that the company filed a motion to dismiss in September 2001. The company noted in the filing that it expected a decision on its motion in 2002. Reporters who read this in the filing may not see any news in this background. But if they were curious, they could go to the courthouse and read the motions and other documents in the file to see if there is a bigger story. The reporter could also research the background of the case to be prepared to write a story when the judge issues a ruling on the motion.

A review of the litigation sections for competitors of the company a reporter is writing about may also have value. For example, if a reporter for the *Richmond Times-Dispatch,* whose beat includes writing stories about Markel Corporation—a local company that provides insurance for everything from horse farms to day care centers—would want to read the litigation sections of 10-Q filings of other insurance companies.

In a recent Markel 10-Q filing, the company disclosed the following litigation:

> On January 31, 2001, the Company received notice of a lawsuit filed in the United States District Court for the Southern District of New York against Terra Nova Insurance Company Limited by Palladium Insurance Limited and Bank of America, N.A. seeking approximately $27 million plus exemplary damages in connection with alleged reinsurance agreements. The Company believes it has numerous defenses to these claims, including the defense that the alleged reinsurance agreements were not valid. The Company intends to vigorously defend this matter; however, it cannot predict the outcome at this time.
>
> On May 29, 2001, Reliance Insurance Company was placed in rehabilitation by the Pennsylvania Insurance Department. At June 30, 2001 and December 31, 2000, Reliance Insurance Company and its affiliates owed the Company approximately $33.4 million in reinsurance recoverables for paid and unpaid losses. These balances were considered in the normal course of assessing the collectability of reinsurance recoverables. (Form 10-Q, Market Corporation, 2001, p. 13)

However, the filing did not disclose other litigation that involved Markel. If the reporter covering the company had spent some time reading the litigation sections of 10-Q filings by other insurers, they would have discovered this entry from PXRE Group:

> PXRE entered into weather option agreements in May 1999 with two counter-parties. In April 2000, these counter-parties submitted invoices to PXRE Delaware in the aggregate sum of $8,252,500 seeking payment under the weather option agreements, which invoices have been paid. PXRE Delaware insured its obligations under these weather option agreements through two Commercial Inland Marine Weather Insurance Policies issued by Terra Nova Insurance Company Limited ('Terra Nova'). PXRE Delaware submitted claims under these policies to Terra Nova in April 2000. Terra Nova has denied coverage, contending that its Managing General Agent had no authority to issue these policies. PXRE Delaware disagrees with Terra Nova's denial and has filed suit against Terra Nova in the United States District Court for the District of New Jersey. Both parties have submitted motions for summary judgment to the court and the trial of this matter has been postponed pending the court's ruling

on the pending summary judgment motions. The aggregate sum of $8,252,500 is included in Other Assets; management has concluded that it is realizable and no valuation allowance is necessary. (Form 10-Q, PXRE Group Limited, 2001, p. 15)

The reporter who writes stories about Markel has just found himself a story. Because the reporter has been covering the company for several years, he knows that Markel recently acquired another insurance company called Terra Nova, which is having a dispute with PXRE that appears to have the potential to cost the company some money. If Markel is forced to pay that money to PXRE, its profits could be less than investors expected.

Quite often, a company will disclose the sale price, or purchase price, of a recent deal in a 10-Q or 10-K. Or it may use the 10-Q as a way to update investors on the progress of a recent acquisition. Business reporters are always interested in these nuggets of information, because the price likely has not been disclosed elsewhere, or it likely contains numbers that have not been seen before. Here are some examples from property and casualty insurer St. Paul and MetLife:

St. Paul's update on an acquisition read the following way:

In connection with the MMI purchase, we established a reserve of $28 million, including $4 million in employee-related costs and $24 million in occupancy-related costs. The employee-related costs represent severance and related benefits such as outplacement counseling to be paid to, or incurred on behalf of, terminated employees. We estimated that approximately 130 employee positions would be eliminated, at all levels throughout MMI. Through June 30, 2001, 118 employees had been terminated, with payments totaling $4 million. Our remaining obligations for employee-related costs at MMI are expected to be less than $1 million. (Form 10-Q, St. Paul Companies, 2001, p. 23)

In this case, the reserve charge had been previously reported, but not how much had been paid. Also, if this statement is read carefully, St. Paul appears to be saying that it is spending more to fire MMI employees than originally estimated.

The following is another entry from a 10-Q filed by MetLife, the large life insurer and money manager based in New York:

On July 2, 2001, the Company completed its sale of Conning Corporation ("Conning"), an affiliate acquired in the acquisition of GenAmerica Financial Corporation. Conning specializes in asset management for insurance company investment portfolios and investment research. The Company received $108 million in the transaction and will report a gain of approximately $17 million, net of income taxes of $11 million, in the third quarter. The sale price is subject to adjustment under certain provisions of the sale contract. (Form 10-Q, MetLife Incorporated, 2001, p. 20)

In this filing, MetLife discloses for the first time how much money it will receive for the sale of a subsidiary and how the sale is going to affect its earnings in the upcoming quarter. These numbers, particularly because they have not been disclosed before, should be the basis of a story for a reporter.

Companies also disclose important information about other business transactions in its filings. For example, in the back of the 10-Q for Coca-Cola that was used in the beginning of the chapter to review income statements and balance sheets is a section called "Recent Developments." At the bottom of this section is a paragraph detailing two business contracts designed to promote the company's drinks:

> In July 2002, our Company announced long-term agreements with the National Collegiate Athletic Association (NCAA) and CBS, and with the Houston Astros Baseball Club with a combined value of approximately $650 million to $800 million. Our Company, CBS and the NCAA will participate in an integrated marketing and media program that includes, for our Company, beverage marketing and media rights to 87 NCAA championships in 22 sports. Additionally, The Minute Maid Company, an operating unit of our Company, and the Houston Astros Baseball Club will participate in a long-term marketing and community partnership, including naming rights for Astros Field, which will be renamed "Minute Maid Park." (Form 10-Q, Coca-Cola Company, 2002, p. 27)

Now, these deals may not be news, particularly because the company issued releases about both of them, but what is news is the value of the agreements. Even for a company such as Coca-Cola, more than $650 million is a lot. That is the story contained in the above disclosure.

However, as can be gleaned from the following, these disclosures may not always be good news.

> In late July, the [Commerce Insurance] Company received notice from the Massachusetts Teachers Association (MTA) that the MTA is terminating its agency relationship with the Company and has withdrawn their endorsement, effective January 1, 2002, of the personal automobile group-marketing plan made available to members of the MTA by The Commerce Insurance Company. Commerce expects that approximately $16.7 million of premiums written will not be renewed as a result of this. (Form 10-Q, Commerce Group, 2001, p. 14)

Commerce Group lost nearly $17 million when MTA terminated its contract with the insurer. For a mid-size business like Commerce, the loss of that money will hurt.

This information is not always contained in the same place for every 10-Q or 10-K. The lawsuit information is commonly under a header called "Contingency," whereas the information about rate increases and business decisions can sometimes be found under "Management's Discussion." In other 10-Qs this information is located in a footnote. Sometimes it pays to read the entire filing.

With a good understanding of how to read and analyze a company's financial statements, as well as the related information that many businesses disclose, a business reporter has begun taking the steps to a better understanding of how he can use these numbers to tell better stories about a company.

READING ANNUAL REPORTS AND
PROXY STATEMENTS

Culling corporate annual reports and proxy statements for financial information is usually a job for professionals.

After all, securities analysts and accountants get paid big bucks to give investors their opinions on the company's real value. But the fallout from the Enron debacle has created a wake-up call for many investors. Maybe the pros can't be trusted.

How can the typical armchair investor sift through the annual influx of corporate financial material and make sense of it all? Does it take heavy-duty computers crunching numbers to get an idea about what is going on within a company?

Armed with only an annual report and a proxy statement, investors can use a dose of logic and add a dab of common sense to get a pretty good idea of the financial prospects of a company. A cheap calculator might help, but it is not required.

As the name implies, a company's annual report summarizes activities during the past year. While certain information is required by the U.S. Securities & Exchange Commission, a portion of the annual report gives company executives a chance to put their own spin on financial results and operational activities.

The glossy, colorful pages in the front of the annual report usually read like a sales brochure, exulting management's achievements. Investors should at least scan the material, since it often includes a company mission statement as well as the chief executive officer's letter.

Yet the armchair investor should take special note of the section labeled "Management's Discussion & Analysis," tucked near the back of the annual report. This section, required by the SEC, summarizes financial results and provides greater details without the platitudes found elsewhere in the report.

The annual report also contains three important financial tables—the income statement, often called a profit and loss statement; the balance sheet listing assets and liabilities; and the cash flow statement.

On the income statement, most investors need only look at the top line revenues and the bottom line net profit and earnings per share. Results for three or more years are typically shown.

In a perfect world, sales and profits will show consistent growth, with profits increasing slightly faster than sales. If not, "Management's Discussion & Analysis" section should explain why.

The balance sheet provides a snapshot of three key financial categories:

- assets, such as plants, inventories and cash;
- liabilities, including vendor invoices, bank debt and taxes due; and
- shareholders' equity or the "book value" of a company.

Most investors need only look at a couple of summary lines. Current assets should be greater than current liabilities. If not, the company may not be able to pay its bills and could be a candidate for bankruptcy.

If a company has substantial cash on its balance sheet, investors should investigate.

While cash earns interest, a well-run company can generate a significantly greater return by using cash to purchase additional operating assets. A cash hoard often indicates that the company might be contemplating an acquisition, a stock buy-back or some other cash-related financial transaction.

Investors also should compare long-term debt to shareholders' equity. In today's investment world, equity should normally be equal to or greater than long-term debt.

The third critical financial table is the cash flow statement, which is the most complex financial document in the annual report.

But don't fret. There are only four lines that the typical armchair investor needs to understand—net income; depreciation and amortization; capital expenditure; and cash dividends.

These four key cash flow lines relate directly to the company's ability to financially reinvigorate itself for the long term.

If the sum of the year's net profits plus depreciation and amortization is greater than the sum of capital expenditures plus cash dividends, the company's cash flow is probably reasonably sound. Most of the other information on the cash flow statement relates to short term cash flow, which is of interest primarily to commercial bankers and the company's suppliers.

Following the financial tables, company annual reports always include a section of "Notes." While the notes section appears to be a lot of fine print, there are nuggets for investors.

Investors should scan the headings, stopping to linger at "Subsequent Events," the "Related Party Transactions," and the "Commitments and Contingencies."

The other key document investors should comb is the proxy statement. It contains information investors need to read before casting their ballot. The proxy statement summarizes activities of the board of directors and reports from the various board committees, including those that oversee audit, nominations and compensation. And it details the salaries and bonuses, including any stock options, for the company's highest paid employees.

The proxy also lists the date, time, and place of the annual shareholders' meeting.

It is important to review the qualifications of company directors. There should be a significant number of nonemployee directors, whose primary function is to represent outside shareholders. Directors should be chosen for their strong financial and operational qualifications.

A proxy seeks shareholder approval to elect directors, ratify the selection of the outside auditors, and, perhaps, approve a stock option plan.

Shareholders may vote by mail, e-mail, fax, or telephone, or they may vote in person at the annual meeting. Any shareholder can place items on the ballot. Social activists often put special interest matters to a vote on corporate proxies. Another key section of the proxy statement is the "Certain Relationships and Related Trans-actions."

Disclosed in this section will be annual fees paid to the outside counsel if someone from the company's law firm is on the board. Same is true for familial relationships between directors, officers and major vendors. If this section is more than a half-page long, investors should be wary.

Devouring an annual report and a proxy statement is something like a gourmet meal experience: investors should feel satisfied when finished.

If there is any hint of indigestion, investors can call the company's investor relations department for further information. If the heartburn lingers, invest elsewhere.

—Kenneth M. Gassman Jr.
Former stock analyst
Richmond Times-Dispatch

GLOSSARY

asset: Anything that an individual or a corporation owns that has value. Asset is also a balance sheet item showing what a firm owns. Assets are bought to increase the value of a business or benefit the firm's operations.

balance sheet: A company's financial statement. It reports the company's assets, liabilities and net worth at a specific time, typically the end of a quarter.

cash flow: The amount of cash a company generates and uses during a period, calculated by adding non-cash charges (such as depreciation) to the net income after taxes. Cash flow can be used as an indication of a company's financial strength.

debt-to-equity ratio: A company's total long-term debt expressed as a percentage of shareholders' equity.

earnings guidance: A report by a company that its earnings may vary considerably, either positively or negatively, from Wall Street expectations, or that its earnings will still be in line with expectations.

earnings per share: The portion of a company's profit allocated to each outstanding share of common stock.

Form 10-K: This is the annual report that companies file with the SEC. It provides a comprehensive overview of its business. The report must be filed within 90 days after the end of the company's fiscal year.

Form 10-Q: A report filed quarterly by public companies. It includes unaudited financial statements and provides a view of its financial position during the year. The report must be filed for each of the first three fiscal quarters of the fiscal year and is due within 45 days of the close of the quarter.

income statement: An accounting of sales, expenses, and net profit for a given period.

liability: A legal debt or obligation estimated via accrual accounting. Recorded on the balance sheet, current liabilities are debts payable within one year. Long-term liabilities are debts payable over a longer period.

net income: The company's total earnings, reflecting revenues adjusted for costs of doing business, depreciation, interest, taxes and other expenses. Do not confuse net income with operating income.

off-balance sheet financing: The way a company raises money that does not appear on the balance sheet, unlike loans, debt, or equity that do appear on the balance sheet. Examples are joint ventures, research and development partnerships, and leases (rather than purchases of capital equipment).

operating income: Revenue less the cost of goods sold and normal operating expenses.

operating margin: Calculated by dividing a company's operating profit by net sales.

price-to-book ratio: Used to compare a stock's market value to its book value, calculated by dividing the closing stock price by the latest quarter's book value.

price-to-earnings ratio: A stock analysis statistic in which the current price of a stock is divided by a company's earnings per share.

profit margin: Net earnings after taxes divided by revenues, usually displayed as a percentage.

return on equity: A measure of a company's profitability, calculated as net income divided by shareholder's equity.

return on investment: The profit or loss resulting from an investment transaction, usually expressed as an annual percentage return.

revenue: The money generated by a product or service over a period of time.

shareholders' equity: A firm's total assets minus total liabilities. It is the amount of the company that is financed through common and preferred shares. Also known as capital.

share repurchase plan: A company's plan to buy back its own shares from the marketplace, reducing the number of outstanding shares, and typically an indication that the company's management thinks the shares are undervalued.

REFERENCES

Barnhart, B. (2001, August/September). Financials tell tales, not analysts. *The Business Journalist.* p. 1.

Borden, W. (2002, November 26). UnitedHealth: Profit at high end of view. Reuters.

Clayton, M. (2002, November 19). Home Depot 3rd-qtr earnings rise 21% on cost controls. Bloomberg News.

Coca-Cola Company. Form 10-K. Coca-Cola Company. (2002, March 11). (SEC Publication No. 0000021344-02-000011, pp. 1–30). Washington, DC: Securities and Exchange Commission.

Coca-Cola Company. From 10-Q. Coca-Cola Company. (2002, August 13). (SEC Publication No. 0000021344-02-000027, pp. 26–27). Washington DC: Securities and Exchange Commission.

Commerce Group Incorporated. Form 10-Q. Commerce Group Incorporated. (2001, August 13). (SEC Publication No. 0000811612-01-500048, pp. 14–15). Washington, DC: Securities and Exchange Commission.

Elam, S. (2002, March 1). Publix Super Markets annual profit unchanged at $530.4 million. Bloomberg News.

Erie Indemnity Company. Form 10-Q. Erie Indemnity Company. (2001, July 19). (SEC Publication No. 0000922-621-01-500002, pp. 20–21). Washington, DC: Securities and Exchange Commission.

Gassman, K. (2002, April 7). Investor, trust thyself: Proxies, annual reports (usually) reveal. *Richmond Times-Dispatch.* p. D-1.

Home Depot. Third-quarter 2002 earnings release. November 19, 2002.

Intel Corporation Third-quarter 2002 earnings release. October 15, 2002.

Markel Corporation. Form 10-Q. Markel Corporation. (2001, August 8). (SEC Publication No. 0000916641-01-500824, pp. 13–14). Washington, DC: Securities and Exchange Commission.

MetLife Incorporated. Form 10-Q. MetLife Incorporated. (2001, August 14). (SEC Publication No. 0000950123-01-505612, pp. 20–22). Washington, DC: Securities and Exchange Commission.

PXRE Group Limited. Form 10-Q. PXRE Group Limited. (2001, August 20). (SEC Publication No. 0000950117-01-501018, pp. 15–16). Washington, DC: Securities and Exchange Commission.

St. Paul Companies. Form 10-Q. St. Paul Companies. (2001, August 14). (SEC Publication No. 0000086312-01-50012, pp. 23–25). Washington, DC: Securities and Exchange Commission.

UnitedHealth Group. Corporate news release. November 26, 2002.

Other Books on Understanding Company Finances

Apostolou, N., & Crumbley, D. L. (1994). *Keys to understanding the financial news* (2nd ed.). Hauppauge, NY: Barron's Educational Series.

Bandler, J. (1994). *How to use financial statements: A guide to understanding the numbers.* New York: McGraw-Hill.

Godin, S., & Lim, P. (1998). *If you're clueless about accounting and finance and want to know more.* Chicago: Dearborn Trade Publishing.

Schilit, H. (2002). *Financial shenanigans: How to detect accounting gimmicks & fraud in financial reports* (2nd ed.). New York: McGraw-Hill.

Tracy, P. (1999). *How to read a financial report.* New York: Wiley.

Warfield, G. (1994). *How to read and understand the financial news* (2nd ed.). New York: HarperCollins.

SUGGESTED EXERCISES

1. Find a local public company. If your area doesn't have public companies based in the area, it may have a location of a public company such as McDonald's or Wal-Mart that would suffice. Read the 10-Q filing for the company and write a 400-word analysis of its income statement and balance sheet. Then review this analysis in class together.

2. Review a cash flow statement of the same company. Take turns explaining what a line in the cash flow statement means. Then vote as to whether

the cash flow statement is from a company whose health is improving, or declining.

3. Find the earnings press release and a Form 10-Q for the same company on its Web site. Compare the financial information disclosed in both. If possible, find a press release that does not include a balance sheet or cash flow statement.

4. Compare and contrast a company's analysis of its performance in an earnings news release to its discussion in the Form 10-Q for the same time period. Are there issues discussed in the filing that aren't discussed in the news release?

5. Calculate the profit margin, operating margin, price-to-book ratio and price-to-earnings ratio for a company. Take 10 minutes, and then compare the numbers to a competitor.

6. Read the 10-Q and 10-K filings for a company. List three potential news stories from the narrative information provided in the filing.

5

Writing Company News

SEC FILINGS ARE THE REPORTER'S BEST FRIEND

Before the Internet, it was tough to convince some publicly traded companies to provide copies of their SEC filings to reporters. Many companies knew that if you were not in Washington, DC or New York, it was often hard to get your hands on these documents. Services that would make copies of filings and mail them to newsrooms typically charged $25 a pop. For many penny-pinching newspapers, that was a lot of money for a boring regulatory filing that may—or may not—contain news that would end up in the paper.

Never, however, did a business editor object to spending the money on a Form 8-K filing. That is because Form 8-Ks contain more actual news than any other form companies file with the SEC. In legal lingo, a Form 8-K is a "current event report" for a "materially important" occurrence in the life of a corporation. This means that the 8-K may disclose just about anything. An event that requires disclosure is documented under one of the following categories: change in control, acquisition or disposition of assets, bankruptcy-court filing, change in accounting firm, resignation of directors, financial statements and exhibits, change in fiscal year, waiver of a company's code of ethics for an executive, suspension of trading in its employee benefits plan, operational or financial results, or any other event deemed important to the company. The filing of an 8-K separates the business news wheat from the chaff. There used to be a saying at newspapers: If the event does not merit the filing of an 8-K, regardless of what the company PR person might be pitching as a story, then it probably does not merit being on the front page of our business section.

Quite often, the 8-K filed is simply a copy of the news release issued by a company. However, sometimes the 8-K will contain extra information not provided in the release. And at other times, the 8-K will be filed without a release being issued. Those are, quite often, the best for news. As a general rule of thumb, when a company files an 8-K, but does not issue a release about the news in the filing, it means generally that the information therein is information the company must disclose, but may not want to.

Many 8-Ks are filed on Friday afternoons, particularly if the news is bad. Companies hope that the business reporter forgets to look for the filing and is instead thinking about the weekend. With more and more reporters becoming aware of these filings, however, such moves typically fail. In addition, services that alert reporters whenever a company on their beat files a document with the SEC help prevent news from flying under the radar.

There are dozens of documents that companies and their executives must file with the SEC that disclose vital information to reporters. In chapter 4, the valuable information that a 10-Q and a 10-K can provide is explained. This chapter discusses the important information that gets disclosed in proxy statements, as well as forms filed by executives whenever they purchase or sell company stock.

Simply put, SEC documents can be a reporter's best friend. These pieces of paper—although most of these forms are now filed electronically—disclose news and information that can detail valuable insights into how public companies, and some private companies, operate. Although many of these documents are written in legalese that can be hard to understand, they often disclose the key details of the inner workings and important decisions made in a business, as long as the reporter understands what is being explained.

In stark contrast to 15 and 20 years ago, SEC documents for companies can now be obtained in a variety of ways. Many companies make their most recent SEC filings available on their Web sites. In fact, the SEC is currently considering a rule that would require all public companies to post filings on their corporate Web sites. If this rule is passed, reviewing documents will be much easier for reporters. Not all filings are, or will be, available however, so it is sometimes valuable to check a second source as well. Many companies provide the most common filings, such as the 10-Q, 10-K, and proxy statement, via the Internet. But they will not provide insider trading filings made by executives or filings made by investors.

The easiest place to review all of a company's SEC filings is by going to the agency's Web site at www.sec.gov and clicking on "Search for Company Filings."

From there, reviewing filings is as easy as typing in the name of the company and clicking on the "Find Companies" link. Another site that many reporters use to read SEC filings is www.freeedgar.com, a site run by a Norwalk, Connecticut-based company, EDGAR Online Incorporated. This site requires the user to register. The company also runs pay sites that use information and data from SEC filings. Interestingly, EDGAR Online itself is a public company, and its SEC filings are available on its Web site. A third site that some advanced business reporters use to examine filings is www.10Kwizard.com. Many reporters use this service because it allows a journalist to search a specific company's filings for certain words and phrases. For example, if a reporter wants to review all Coca-Cola filings to see if they mention Pepsi, a search on this Web site could tell you where the competitor is discussed. Like some of EDGAR's services, however, this site charges for detailed searches.

Reading SEC filings can be a valuable resource tool for reporters, particularly those new to their beats because these new journalists need to learn and understand the companies about which they are going to be writing stories. Reading an SEC filing may not result in a story every time. In fact, it is unlikely that reading SEC filings will result in a story for a reporter even half of the time. But it is a good practice for reporters to read the filings of companies on their beats every time. Such diligence pays off when a story does appear buried in the back of a filing. And reading the filings will help paint a picture about the company for the reporter that will give him or her the understanding needed to produce stories that show the writer knows his or her stuff.

CORPORATE EVENTS PUBLIC COMPANIES ARE REQUIRED TO DISCLOSE

In the last few years, public companies have dramatically increased the number of times they file 8-Ks. First, it is important to know the various reasons why a company must file a Form 8-K and when it must be filed. According to current SEC regulations, companies are required to file 8-Ks within 5 business days or 15 calendar days of a "materially important" event, depending on the type of event. Sometimes companies file 8-Ks on the day the event occurs. But many times, companies wait a few days, or even a week. This is important to note, especially if the company issues a news release: A follow-up story may be waiting in the filing.

Certain events in a company's operations trigger the requirement that an 8-K be filed. Many of these events are important changes in a company that regulators have determined investors have a right to know about. Business writers should take their cues from the regulators—these disclosures are often important news that should be reported by media outlets. One of these events is when the company names a new leader. Because a new CEO or president is almost always announced by a news release, the filing of an 8-K with this information rarely becomes a newsworthy event. However, sometimes an 8-K about an executive change discusses important information. For example, note the details filed in this 8-K by Chubb Corporation on January 21, 2003 about the pay package of its new CEO, who had been named to the post months earlier:

- His starting base salary is $1.2 million;
- He may receive bonuses up to 2.5 times his salary;
- His stock options are currently worth $6 million;
- He may use a company car and driver, and a company aircraft for business travel he will be provided with a membership and club dues at one country club, and he will receive free financial counseling.

The new CEO's compensation package is important information for the business reporter to write about because this disclosure can help investors and employees determine whether a company is spending money wisely. In addition, whenever a company acquires or disposes of assets—buys or sells a business—it is required to file an 8-K detailing the transaction. Quite often, the 8-K about a transaction discloses financial details of the deal not included in the release. Other items may include the merger agreement, including the stock option agreement if there is one, any amendments or modifications to the merger, the closing of the deal, financial statements of the company being acquired, and financial statements of the combined operations.

Sometimes an 8-K may even disclose a potential acquisition. For example, note the beginning of this story from the *Denver Post*:

Williams Cos., an energy trader and pipeline operator, may jump into the bidding for Barrett Resources Corp.—a move disclosed Tuesday when "outside individuals" got onto a conference call among Williams directors.

Denver-based Barrett on Monday rejected a sweetened $2.4 billion takeover bid by a unit of Royal Dutch/Shell Group and has put itself up for auction.

Williams, based in Tulsa, Okla., held a board meeting by telephone Tuesday to consider a bid to buy Barrett, the company disclosed in a filing with the Securities and Exchange Commission. Terms weren't specified. Disclosure of a possible Williams bid was made unintentionally when "outside individuals were mistakenly connected by a conference call vendor" to the company's board meeting Tuesday, the filing said.

"Before this error was discovered, officers of Williams stated that the board meeting had been called to consider Williams' potential proposal to acquire Barrett," said the filing, an 8-K report to the SEC.

Barrett has said it will continue to accept bids until today.

The company reported first-quarter profit rose more than sixfold because of higher prices.

Denver-based Barrett posted net income of $57 million, or $1.67 a diluted share, up from $7.8 million, or 24 cents a share, a year ago, the company said in a statement on PR Newswire. Sales more than doubled to $161.4 million.

Barrett shares rose 52 cents to $64.87—an indication investors consider it likely the company will receive a higher offer than Shell Exploration and Production Co.'s bid of $60 per share.

Williams shares rose $1.21 to $43.38.[1]

Without the filing of the 8-K, it is unlikely that this important news of an offer for Williams would have been disclosed in the media until a news release was issued.

When a company files for bankruptcy-court protection or is the recipient of regulatory action, it must file an 8-K. These filings can often contain valuable information for reporters covering companies with operations in other states, or companies incorporated in a state other than the one in which its headquarters is located. For example, thousands of companies are incorporated in Delaware because of its friendly corporation laws, so a large amount of bankruptcies (and lawsuits, for that matter) are filed in that state. Thus, a reporter in Portland, for example, probably will not know what has been filed by companies in Delaware courts, or by regulators across the country.

Writing stories from these types of filings should be basic reporting because the disclosures spell out what is going on at a company. For instance, when CyNet Incorporated, a provider of Internet, voice, and fax messaging software, filed for Chapter 11 bankruptcy protection, the event was detailed in its 8-K filing, which was covered by reporters. Other 8-K filings might include documents such as letters from regulators to companies detailing limits placed on their future operations, or restraining orders preventing companies from continuing to do business. In many of these cases, the companies do not issue news releases, which makes it vitally important for reporters to read 8-K filings.

Another reason a company is required to file an 8-K is when it changes its accounting firm. The accountants may have resigned, or they could have been fired. In either case, this event leads to a filing, even if the parting is amicable. It should be noted that an accounting firm often ends its relationship with a client when there is a disagreement or a discrepancy with the company's financial statements. Given what happened between Enron and Arthur Andersen, its former accountants, reporters should expect more companies to take a closer look at their relationships with their auditors. In addition, look for more accounting firms to reassess relationships with clients with whom there has been friction.

Writing a story about a company changing its auditors may not seem like an exciting day in the newsroom. But a change such as this may hint at further problems within the company, particularly if the business is struggling. Accounting firms used by companies are approved each year at the company's annual meeting. If an accounting firm declines to put itself up for reelection at the annual meeting,

---

[1]From "Liberty takes On Command reins; Hotel room movie firm may be merged with rival," by J. Beauprez, May 2, 2001, *Denver Post*, p. C-1. Copyright 2001 by *Denver Post*. Reprinted with permission.

that decision could be a sign that there has been a disagreement. A small story in the newspaper about a change in auditors could lead to a call from a source—either at the company or at the accounting firm—who wants to tell the reporter more about what happened. Check the company's proxy statement, or DEF 14A, to see if there are new accountants up for election at the annual meeting.

An 8-K must also be filed when a member of the board of directors resigns. This is not typically a front-page story for a business section either, unless the board member was well-known and carried some clout on the board. Typically such resignations are simply a brief, no more than two or three sentences. But again, the sudden resignation of a board member may signal growing discord between the board and the executive team at the company. If several board members resign at the same time, that may also indicate conflict between the board and company management. A brief in the *Rocky Mountain News* from the Associated Press on June 26, 2002 is typical of the coverage of an 8-K disclosure of a board member resignation. It stated that Hewlett-Packard President Michael Capellas was resigning from energy company Dynegy's board as a result of the increased demands on his time and his new responsibilities at the computer company.

A company also files an 8-K for its financial statements and exhibits, and when it changes its fiscal year. Rarely do these disclosures result in a story, but they could. For example, an exhibit could be something such as an employment agreement with a new executive, and if the details have not been disclosed before, a story could be written. The financial statements are typically from the most recent quarter, and if they were not included in the company's earnings release, they should be reviewed.

The SEC also requires that other events material to a company's business be disclosed in an 8-K filing. Whether an event is "material" enough to be disclosed is up for interpretation by company executives. But, as a result of recent events, many companies have been criticized for not disclosing information, which, in turn, caused a number of businesses to file 8-Ks just to be on the safe side of federal regulation. For example, Nathan's Famous Incorporated, a New York-based hot dog restaurant chain, filed an 8-K noting that Home Depot terminated eight restaurant license agreements at some Home Depot stores in which Nathans operated, accounting for about 15% of the company's total sales. This information was valuable enough to be picked up in the *Atlanta Journal-Constitution,* for which a reporter covers Home Depot.

Other times, companies file 8-Ks projecting earnings for the next quarter, or for the next year. Many times, these projections are given to analysts and investors at conferences or presentations. Thus, in these instances, 8-Ks are filed so that the information is given to everyone at the same time.

When MONY Group Incorporated, New York-based life insurer and asset manager, filed an 8-K on January 16, 2003 it provided the SEC with the slides from a presentation that it was giving to investors and analysts later that day. Wire service reporters and others immediately reviewed the filing to determine whether there was news in the slide show.

The following is how Michael Crittenden, who follows MONY for the online news site Insurance Investor Interactive, led his story that day:

> Life insurer MONY Group Inc. suggested in a Jan. 16 regulatory filing that its fourth-quarter operating earnings could easily beat Wall Street expectations.
>
> In the Form 8-K, the New York-based company said that its preliminary fourth-quarter results yielded pretax operating earnings in a range of $8 million to $13 million, or 11 cents to 18 cents per share. That range is well ahead of the Thomson First Call consensus estimate of 3 cents per share, with a high estimate of 11 cents and a low estimate of breakeven. MONY Group said preliminary net income for the fourth quarter should be between $9 million and $14 million, or 12 cents to 19 cents per share.[2]

Interestingly, Dan Lowrey, a reporter for Dow Jones, chose to focus on other disclosures in the filing in his lead the same day. His lead noted the company's earnings estimates for 2003—$.30–.35 per share—compared with the average earnings estimate by Wall Street analysts, which was $.33 per share. Both reporters reviewed the entire filing, which, in this case, was more than 30 pages because of the length of the slide show. And in both cases, the reporters found news that was important to their readers.

Other times, the 8-K may disclose financial results that can be important in assessing how a company is performing. For example, the Associated Press reported that computer networking equipment maker Cisco Systems Incorporated noted in an 8-K filing that 5% of its $275 million quarterly loss provision was related to customer accounts. The company set aside $14 million for losses on doubtful accounts, up from $5 million in the same quarter the previous year. In writing about this disclosure, the reporter nicely compared Cisco's first quarter loss provision with the loss provision for the first quarter of the previous year. That comparison shows the reader that the company is setting aside nearly three times as much money to pay for overdue payments than it had previously, an indication that maybe its customers are having trouble paying their bills.

A brief in the *Pittsburgh Post-Gazette* in 2002 used information from a from 8-K filed by Adelphia Communications Corporation to show that the cable company was losing subscribers and now projecting lower earnings.

The brief story took the earnings projections for Adelphia and shows why the company is lowering its estimates. It is important for any business reporter writing a story based on an 8-K to explain why the news is happening.

Also note that all of the stories used as examples in this chapter cite the documents in which the information was obtained. Doing so lends credence to the report, and to the reporter, by showing readers that he or she is tracking the

---

[2]From "MONY sees fourth-quarter results ahead of estimates, in line 2003," from M. Crittenden, January 16, 2003, Insurance Investor Interactive. Copyright 2003 by SNL Financial. Reprinted with permission.

company closely. Often, a reporter has to read through numerous pages in the filing to find snippets of news here and there, and then combine that information into a compelling story. A reporter has to condense thousands of words and numbers into a story that often is no longer than 300 to 400 words.

The SEC is currently considering adding 11 new events in a company's operations that would require the business to file an 8-K. These events include entering into or terminating a material agreement not made in the normal course of the company's business, defaulting on a loan, terminating a customer resulting in a loss of revenue, a change in a company's debt rating by a rating agency, or if the company's stock no longer meets the requirements for its exchange. In addition, the SEC is proposing changing the time period for when an 8-K is filed to within two days of the event. Both of these changes would give the business reporter more information about a company's operations on a more timely basis.

The following story from the *Chicago Tribune* helps explain why such disclosures would be considered important, and how they may help journalists do their jobs:

> While wary investors watch for the next corporate scandal, federal regulators are quietly moving ahead with controversial plans to significantly broaden the information that companies must disclose to the public.
>
> The Securities and Exchange Commission has proposed tripling the number of "events" that a company must disclose in a prompt regulatory filing, adding 11 new items, including a change in credit rating or when a firm enters into or terminates a material agreement. It also wants the forms filed within two days, instead of the current five to 15.
>
> The proposal has touched off an important debate in the business world. Everyone, it seems, favors improved disclosure. But a split has emerged over how to decide what is sufficiently "material," or important to tell investors.
>
> It's a vague standard at best, defined by court rulings and SEC staff interpretations. In essence, various rulings say something is material if a "reasonable shareholder" would consider it important in forming an opinion about a company, or if it's something about which "an average prudent investor ought reasonably to be informed."
>
> Some companies use a rule of thumb that the item must affect revenue, profits or assets by a certain percentage, sometimes 3 percent or more. But the SEC and some court rulings have stressed that such tests are usually not enough. Now, however, some of the items in the nearly 100-page SEC proposal have specific thresholds.
>
> In issuing the proposal, commissioners, as always, asked for comment. They got an earful.
>
> Some, including several accountants, have criticized the idea of such specific triggers, saying they're too rigid to cover all circumstances. Others, including Financial Executives International, say the proposal's definitions of material aren't nearly specific enough.
>
> "We believe the proposed rule should apply a consistent materiality threshold for required disclosures," James Bell, finance vice president at Chicago-based Boeing Co., wrote to the commission. "The lack of uniformity in materiality guidelines could create inconsistencies in the disclosures provided."
>
> Others said they feared the inconsistency would confuse or overwhelm investors—and, for that matter, companies.

"Without further clarification of what is deemed material, we are concerned that companies may provide disclosure for every exit activity or impairment charge in order to avoid potential liability issues, resulting in 'disclosure overload,'" auditor Deloitte & Touche wrote.

Others, while not making formal comment to the SEC, are watching what happens.

"You look at the specificity of the proposal, and your jaw just drops," said Stephen Presser, a law professor with Northwestern University's Kellogg School of Management.

"All through the years with the SEC disclosure policies, no one has ever been certain that an individual investor is equipped to assess these things," he said.[3]

An individual investor may not be able to assess this kind of information. But a business journalist, with the help of experts and a proper understanding of what he or she is writing about, can properly assess the information and write a story telling the investor why the disclosure is important.

RESIGNATIONS OF BOARD MEMBERS AND EXECUTIVES

The previous section mentions that an 8-K must be filed for numerous reasons, including when a company changes its executives and when a board member resigns. These are, arguably, the most important disclosures under the SEC rule because the executive team and the board are the people in charge of running the company, the people responsible for ensuring that the business is making money and running smoothly. However, if one or more of them leaves, it should not be automatically assumed that something is wrong.

Many times, company executives change for reasons that have nothing to do with how the company is performing. A CEO or board member may reach retirement age. In some cases, a CEO will leave a company for health reasons, or decide that it is simply time to let someone younger have a chance to run the shop. A board member may take on a new commitment with another business opportunity, and feel as if he does not have the proper time to devote to the board, as in the example involving the president of Hewlitt-Packard.

These are all good reasons for a changing of the guard at a company. But in an increasing number of cases, a CEO or a board member moving on may be an indication that there is unrest.

The first time business journalists might have thought there was trouble at Enron was when its CEO, Jeffrey Skilling, abruptly resigned shortly before its accounting problems were disclosed. At the time, Skilling said in a statement that

---

[3]From "SEC proposal becomes a material issue; critics complain rules not uniform," by A. Countryman, Sept. 29, 2002, *Chicago Tribune*, p. C1. Copyright 2002 by *Chicago Tribune*. Reprinted with permission.

he was leaving the company for personal reasons that had nothing to do with the company. Although "personal reasons" may be true in a number of cases, it is also the terminology, unfortunately, that many companies use to mask tense situations that could range from a board becoming dissatisfied with the CEO's performance to an outright coup forcing executives into retirement.

In many cases, writing about boardroom intrigue can be one of the most fascinating stories for a business reporter. Executives and directors are only human, just like journalists, and they have personalities that can often clash. Those personalities often drive a company, which takes on the personal styles and mannerisms of the executives. Writing a story about a resignation from a news release or a filing may just be the beginning of a bigger story that delves into a number of other issues, such as who will replace the deposed executive or why the board member left.

An enterprising reporter reading in an 8-K the explanation for a CEO's departure should become curious enough to want to find out more about the review of the executive's performance. In fact, the following story from the *Tampa Tribune* about the resignation of a CEO implies that more than meets the eye was going on behind the scenes.

The recently announced resignation of Tropical Sportswear International Corp. Chief Executive Officer William Compton raises the question of how much publicly traded companies are required to disclose to regulators and shareholders.

Although they don't have to disclose everything that goes on within the business, companies must notify the Securities and Exchange Commission of "material events," corporate governance experts said.

That means disclosing information "a reasonable investor would deem important in making an investment decision," said Charles Elson, director of the University of Delaware's Center for Corporate Governance and a former professor at Stetson University College of Law in Gulfport. In the case of a material event, the filing, on a document known as Form 8-K, must be made within 10 days after the close of the month in which the event occurred. A similar filing must also be made with the stock exchange on which the company's shares are traded.

In Tropical Sportswear's case, the company filed a Form 8-K on Nov. 19, the day after Compton's resignation.

It disclosed Compton's resignation and included his severance agreement and a company press release announcing that Compton had agreed to resign "following a review by a committee of the board of directors of recent management issues related to Mr. Compton."

The release did not elaborate on the management issues leading to Compton's departure other than to say they were "not systemic to the company and will not result in any adjustments to or restatements of the company's financial statements."

The definition of what is material, and required to be disclosed, has been refined by the courts over the years on a case-by-case basis.

It "leaves a lot of latitude in the judgment of the company" about what it must report, said Willis Riccio, a securities law partner with Adler Pollock & Sheehan in Providence, R.I., and a former New England regional administrator for the SEC.

"They can make a good-faith judgment about whether what has occurred is material, in terms of disclosure," Riccio said.

Reforms in Congress, including the recently enacted Sarbanes-Oxley Act, are likely to shorten the amount of time companies have to make disclosures, Riccio noted.

Companies also have a continuing duty to supplement their filings if they obtain important new information about a material event.

"What is clear, is that when they say something, it has to be correct in all material respects," Elson said.[4]

In addition to explaining what must be disclosed, this story raises the question as to why Compton left Tropical Sportswear. It is a question that many investors in the company would obviously like to have answered, thus, it is probably a good question for reporters to be asking.

Other times, the filing may show the specific reasons why board members want to get rid of executives, as was the case with this Colorado-based company in the following story from the *Denver Post*:

Three directors of an Arapahoe County technology company recommended that the company's top managers resign as a result of long-term accounting problems in the firm, according to the directors' letters of resignation, filed with the Securities and Exchange Commission this week.

Laser Technology Inc.'s chief executive officer, David Williams, who spoke to The Denver Post on Wednesday, said everyone's overreacting to a problem caused when a sale was logged as having occurred in the 1993 fiscal year but possibly should have been recorded in fiscal 1994. He wouldn't give details.

Richard B. Sayford, F. James Lynch and William R. Carr quit the board of Laser Technology after the company's full board of directors rejected the recommendations, the Jan. 11 letters said. The company, which makes laser speed- and distance-measuring devices, filed the letters this week as an amendment to its form 8-K. The three directors' proposals came out of their investigation, begun in October, into the company's accounting practices.

The recommendations, according to the letters, called for the resignations of Williams, Chief Financial Officer Pamela Sevy, Director H. DeWorth Williams and Secretary and Director Dan N. Grothe.

They also stated that David Williams "pay all amounts, if any, that are due from him to the company," that the company hire a new CEO and CFO from outside the company, and that Laser immediately retain a reputable accounting firm that's independent from any of the company's officers and directors.

Asked if he planned eventually to resign, Williams said: "Not today."

It's the latest installment of Laser's turmoil, which began when the company's accounting firm, Chicago-based BDO Seidman, quit Dec. 21 and disclaimed its audits of Laser's financial statements for fiscal years 1993 through 1997. Laser's stock has not traded on the American Stock Exchange since Dec. 22.

At the heart of the dispute, Williams told The Post, is a sale that was logged as having occurred in the 1993 fiscal year but possibly should have been recorded in fiscal 1994. He wouldn't give details.

---

[4]From "Firms base disclosure on relevance to investors," by C. Haber, December 10, 2002, *Tampa Tribune*, p. 4. Copyright 2002 by *Tampa Tribune*. Reprinted with permission.

"It's difficult for me to get into that without going into a lot of explanation, which unfortunately I can't do," Williams said.

When it stopped working for Laser, however, BDO Seidman told the SEC, "Information has come to BDO's attention which indicates that they can no longer rely on management's representations."

While Sayford declined to comment Wednesday on the situation, he said he stands by the statements in his letter of resignation. Carr declined comment and Lynch could not be reached.

Sayford, Lynch and Carr formed a Special Audit Committee in October to begin investigating Laser's accounting practices. The three directors brought in their own legal counsel, accounting firm and interim CFO, all of whom reported directly to the special committee.

BDO Seidman quit in the midst of the investigation.

Trading in the stock halted and the special committee continued its work, recommending to the full board on Jan. 7 that Williams and Sevy be retained only long enough to find a new CEO and CFO, and that Williams pay what—if anything—he owes the company.

"There is an issue as to whether the company owes me some money or whether I would potentially owe the company a small amount of money" stemming from the disputed sale, Williams said.

The matter in question is a bookkeeping misunderstanding, he said, not malfeasance.

"I wouldn't say it's a small issue, but it's an issue that has kind of blown up into a big deal and it's not as big an issue as some people would think that it is," he said.

Neither the accounting dispute nor the nearly month-long trading halt has had a negative impact on the company's business, Williams said. "Business is proceeding well. The company is doing very well," he said.

Though the company's results for 1993 and 1994 may end up being restated, Williams said the aggregate amount of business the company reported for the entire five-year period remains accurate. He also said the company's recent announcement of net income of $738,508, or 15 cents per share, on sales of $8.1 million for the nine months ended June 30, 1998, is accurate, as is its prediction of record sales of $11.7 million for the full year ended Sept. 30.

Laser retained the firm Jones, Jensen & Co. as new auditors last week and hopes to have its books in order in two or three weeks, Williams said, after which trading could resume.[5]

Clashes between board members and executives can occur for several reasons. The company may not be making as much money as the board expects. Or the CEO and president may be running the company with a style that upsets other employees, lowering morale and hurting the company's performance because the workers have no incentive to better the business. Executives may also have reasons to be upset with board members. Coca-Cola CEO Doug Ivester left the top spot at the company in 1999 after only two years on the job because he felt board members interfered with his ability to run the company. Because executives run

---

[5]From "Laser Technology execs' exit urged," by L. Kokmen and E. Hubler, January 21, 1999, *Denver Post*, p. C1. Copyright 1999 by *Denver Post*. Reprinted with permission.

the company on a day-to-day basis, they may have a better feel than the board for what the company needs.

In either case, it is wise to watch for such disagreements between the executive suite and the board room, even if they are not events disclosed in an 8-K. Infighting, no matter what size the company, can turn into a gripping story about the control of a business that often becomes the best-read story in the business section. The clues can be found in 8-K filings as long as the reporter knows what to look for.

Many investors—and therefore readers—want to know the price of getting rid of an executive. In some cases, the 8-K provides the details. If not, the next proxy statement, discussed in more detail in chapter 8, could provide the information.

The following excerpt shows how the beginning of a story in the *Sun-Sentinel* in Fort Lauderdale handled the price of a company getting rid of its chief operating officer:

> Fort Lauderdale-based staffing and recruitment giant Spherion Corp. said Tuesday it will write off an additional $250 million to $300 million for the value of goodwill in acquisitions—on top of the $692 million it wrote off earlier in the fiscal year.
>
> In the same announcement, Spherion said Chief Operating Officer Robert Livonius has left the company, a departure that will cause the company to take an additional $3.5 million charge in the fourth quarter.
>
> Spherion filed an 8-K report with the Securities Exchange Commission disclosing both events before the market's opening. Its stock closed down 42 cents at $6.21.
>
> Company spokeswoman Patricia Johnson said Livonius' position was eliminated in an effort to reduce layers of management and to flatten the organization. Livonius had been with the company since 1991 and was appointed executive vice president and COO in 1997 under former CEO Raymond Marcy.
>
> Livonius, with an annual salary of $495,000 plus options, was the second highest paid executive in the organization, after the chief executive. The company will give him a $3.5 million severance agreement.
>
> CEO and President Cinda A. Hallman said in a statement on Livonius' departure that she will assume direct responsibility for business operations.
>
> "We sincerely appreciate Bob's many contributions to the company and wish him well in the future," she added.[6]

The charge mentioned in the second paragraph of the above example essentially states that the executive received $3.5 million to leave the company. Exorbitant pay to leave a company is often criticized by investors and executive pay experts. Disclosures like this should be reported, because investors and employees of the company want to know if it is spending money wisely. Thus, business reporters covering events such as these should find out whether the company will receive benefits totaling more than the severance package as a result of getting rid of the

---

[6]From "Spherion taking $250 m goodwill charge; COO post eliminated to cut costs," by J. Fleischer Tamen, January 8, 2003, *Sun-Sentinel*, p. 10. Copyright 2003 by *South Florida Sun-Sentinel*. Reprinted with permission.

executive. In October 2003, the SEC proposed rules that would require companies to send out ballots listing shareholder nominees for the board in addition to the company's list. If enacted, these new rules could provide another story regarding company board members.

WHEN COMPANIES AND ACCOUNTANTS COLLIDE

The relationship between a company and its accounting firm has come under increasing scrutiny in recent years. Before the collapses of Enron, WorldCom, and other companies, a company and its auditor were closely tied together. A company would pay its accounting firm millions of dollars to audit its financial records and to provide a statement in its SEC filings giving it a clean bill of health. The accounting industry's role was to provide some sense of comfort to investors and others who did business.

What actually happened, it turns out, is that accounting firms were going along with what company executives wanted to do as far as reporting revenues, sales, and other financial numbers because they feared losing their income if they said no. In other cases, companies hid the actual financial performance of their operations from their auditors, making it nearly impossible for the accountants to properly do their job.

Still, the auditors must take some blame. According to a study by Weiss Ratings, a Florida-based firm, accounting firms gave a clean bill of health to more than 90% of companies that later had accounting irregularities uncovered. The Weiss research also disclosed that few companies that announced accounting problems had a statement from their auditors expressing concern. These companies had a market capitalization of more than $1.9 trillion on Wall Street before their accounting irregularities were uncovered. Afterward, their value on Wall Street fell by more than $1.2 trillion. That is a huge story for business journalists and shows how important it is to understand the relationship between companies and accountants.

Under these circumstances, business reporters are also put in a difficult position. How can a business journalist trust a company's numbers or uncover a wrong doing if the company's own auditors are not being told the truth? There are still a number of documents that a journalist showed examine to determine whether the relationship between a company and its accountants is legitimate.

Most important, the reporter should review the accountant's statement in a company's 10-Q and 10-K filings. Sometimes the auditor's statement discusses concerns about a company's continuing ability to operate, in which case the writer has not only a story for tomorrow's newspaper or evening newscast, but a clear indication that the relationship between the company and accountants is legitimate.

The following excerpt from the *San Jose Mercury News* illustrates how an auditor statement expressing concern about the future of a company is a story.

At Home, the nation's largest provider of high-speed Internet access, is at risk of being buried under its heavy debt and operating losses, the company said in an updated annual report filed Monday with the Securities and Exchange Commission.

The Redwood City company, once a high-flying player in the Internet economy, said auditors Ernst & Young have expressed "substantial doubt" about its ability to continue as a "going concern."

Shares of At Home lost nearly half their value Monday, falling 46 cents to 47 cents a share.

The company, which does business as Excite@Home, faces a possible delisting from the Nasdaq stock market, which would trigger a $100 million payment to its convertible bondholders. With only $183.4 million in cash as of June 30, At Home would soon run out of money and be forced to declare bankruptcy if it had to make the payment, analysts said.

In June, At Home obtained through a convertible bond a crucial $100 million injection from two investment firms that specialize in financing struggling companies. That deal included a requirement that the company stay listed on one of the major stock exchanges.

At Home currently fails to meet Nasdaq's minimum requirements for continued listing. Its stock price has dropped below $3, the lowest bid price allowed under one of Nasdaq's standards. Alison Bowman, an At Home spokeswoman, said the company has not received a delisting notice from Nasdaq.

In July, At Home's board of directors authorized a 1-for-4 reverse stock split. However, at Monday's closing stock price of 47 cents a share, the reverse split would still leave the company short of the $3 threshold.

At Home's financial problems stem, in part, from the collapse of online advertising, which has battered its online media properties. The company has been trying since April to sell its media division, which includes the Excite portal and the Blue-Mountain online card site.

Henry Blodget, a Merrill Lynch analyst, last week wrote in a note to investors that he believes At Home hasn't closed its media operations because of contractual obligations to advertisers; it would cost even more to shut down than to keep running at a loss, he said.

The company lost $346.3 million in the second quarter on revenue of $138.6 million. Its debt was about $1 billion.

Blodget warned that "the company's prospects are even worse than expected," questioning the company's ability to raise additional funding and detailing the bleak outlook for both its media and Internet access businesses.

In the spring, At Home said it would need to raise $75 million to $80 million in funding to stay afloat into 2002. In June, the company raised $85 million from restructuring a lease of fiber-optic lines from AT&T and $100 million more in convertible bonds.

In July, At Home stunned analysts by saying that wasn't enough.

At Home wrote in its latest SEC filing that it may not have sufficient cash to fund operations through the end of the year.

While At Home's future is dark, analysts said the lights won't necessarily go out for its Internet subscribers.

Blake Johnstone of Davenport & Co. said he doesn't think At Home's biggest partners—AT&T Broadband, Comcast and Cox Communications—would stand by while they lose a lucrative revenue stream and their subscribers lose Internet connections.

AT&T owns 23 percent of At Home, but has a 74 percent voting interest.

A source close to AT&T Broadband said, "No matter where this turns out, customers will not be impacted."

One option is for the cable giants to keep At Home operating until subscribers could be switched to another Internet service provider, most likely AOL Time Warner's Road Runner service, Johnstone said. AT&T owns a 25 percent stake in Road Runner, and subscribers to its MediaOne cable network already use the Road Runner service.

Although AT&T has an exclusive contract with At Home, it has been working to open its cable network to other Internet service providers in anticipation of the contract expiring in April. AT&T, the cable operator for most of the Bay Area, has been testing a system in Boulder, Colo., that allows subscribers to smoothly transfer from one ISP to another.

At Home was formed in May 1999 through the merger of Excite, one of the first and most popular Internet search engines and portals, and At Home, which offered high-speed Internet access through cable systems.[7]

It is always important to read the auditor's statement, particularly if the company has been losing money for the last few years. Most companies receive a clean bill of health from their accountants, so it is a major development when the statement raises questions about the company. Other companies receive qualified opinions, which typically means the company's financial books are not up to par.

In addition, if a company's future viability is questioned by its accountants, reporters should check the statements in the 10-K or 10-Q to see if the language in the statement has changed. If it has—for better or worse—then a story updating the company's condition is likely warranted.

When the ongoing concern statement is made, it may be filed in an 8-K, as it was in the case with Boston Chicken, disclosed in the following *Denver Post* story:

Boston Chicken Inc.'s auditor has filed a statement with the federal Securities and Exchange Commission saying there is "substantial doubt" that the restaurant chain can stay in business.

In the SEC document, dated May 19 and filed Wednesday, auditor Arthur Andersen LLP gives a detailed account of Boston Chicken's financial woes.

The auditor describes how Boston Chicken's money problems could trigger default on hundreds of millions of dollars in debt. There can be "no assurance," the document says, that the company will be able to "meet its financial obligations." On the 8-K form, Arthur Andersen says it has included a paragraph in its 1997 audit report that "there is substantial doubt about (Boston Chicken's) ability to continue as a going concern."

The same statement is included in Arthur Andersen's assessment of Boston Chicken's franchisees—called area developers. Andersen, the company that also audited each of the franchisees, questions each franchisee's ability to continue "as a going concern."

---

[7]From "At Home warns it may run out of cash," by J. Kwan, August 21, 2001, *San Jose Mercury News*, p. 1C. Copyright 2001 by *San Jose Mercury News*. All rights reserved. Reprinted with permission.

An 8-K is a form a publicly held company files with the SEC to report on any events that might affect its financial situation or the value of its shares of stock.

An auditor's inclusion of the "going concern" statement in a financial audit is "serious," according to a partner at KPMG Peat Marwick, a national auditing firm.

The statement is meant to alert creditors, vendors, shareholders and anyone else with a stake in the company that the company is in financial trouble, said Rick Connor at KPMG Peat Marwick's Denver office.

"You don't take the 'going concern' opinion lightly," Connor said. "The explanatory paragraph is an extra paragraph in an accountant's report that alerts the reader there is an uncertainty at that point in time whether the company will continue. But it doesn't necessarily mean the company won't survive."[8]

It is also wise for a business reporter to check with the suppliers, competitors, and government agencies, who know a company's operations. Competitors often know if another company is experiencing difficulty or losing market share. In writing about many companies, suppliers are particularly important sources because they can tell you if the company pays its bills on time. If a company pays late that may be an indication that there are financial problems that the accountants have not uncovered or mentioned in the filings. One should also look for lawsuits to see if a company is being sued for nonpayment.

Sometimes the SEC initiates investigations or actions against companies that it believes may have improperly stated financial problems. The results of SEC actions can be disclosed in 8-Ks or filings such as the 10-K or 10-Q.

The following is an example of how Bloomberg News reported the disclosure of a look into a company's books:

Alpharma Inc. said the Securities and Exchange Commission has begun a formal investigation of the company's methods for recognizing revenue.

Alpharma shares declined 13 percent, falling $2.75 to $17.90.

The Fort Lee, New Jersey, manufacturer of generic drugs and animal health products last November restated its earnings. The investigation, reported in a filing with the Securities and Exchange Commission, involves to revenue recognition practices connected with the restatement.

Shareholders had alleged in a class action lawsuit that the company used improper revenue recognition policies in regard to its animal health business in Brazil. The U.S. District Court for the District of New Jersey dismissed the class action suit, the company reported today.

Alpharma in October said it would revise its earnings statements because some sales of animal products were billed when the orders were recognized, not when they were actually shipped. The problem was corrected by the third quarter of last year, the company had said.

Alpharma in November restated earnings to report 59 percent more net income, or $35.7 million, for the first half of 2001, and lower earnings than reported for the previous three years.

---

[8]From "Boston Chicken woes mount," by P. Parker, May 29, 1998, *Denver Post*, p. A1. Copyright 1998 by *Denver Post*. Reprinted with permission.

Net income in 2000 was $55.5 million, Alpharma said, not $61.1 million as it had reported. In 1999, the company earned $29.9 million, $7 million less than reported, and in 1998, it earned $22.8 million. It had reported $24.2 million for that year.

Once the commission approves the opening of a formal examination, staff members have the authority to subpoena information.

Alpharma anticipates cooperating with the SEC investigation, according to the filing.[9]

An investigation like this can lead a company to restate its financial results, lowering its revenue or its earnings. When this happens, a company is essentially admitting that its accountants goofed. However, investors are not humored by the event. They will usually dump the stock, sending its price downward. That is why a business reporter should always be on the lookout for any hint of impropriety in a company's financial statements. The writer who is first to report an investigation or a problem does his or her readers a great service.

Earlier, the "corporate events public companies are required to disclose" section of this chapter mentioned that companies must file an 8-K when they part ways with their auditors. It cannot be emphasized enough that when a company fires an auditor or an auditor declines to work with a company is one of the best indicators that there may be some future problems. (An exception to this is when an accounting firm such as Arthur Andersen goes out of business, forcing all of its former clients to find a new auditor to review its books.) Often, the 8-K discloses that there was a disagreement between the company and its accountants that led to the parting. Other times, a reason is not given. It is still an important event, and one that a reporter should watch closely and perhaps even call sources to determine the real reason for the switch.

Below is a story from *The Tampa Tribune* in which a company in bankruptcy court picked a new auditor. It is implied in the story that the new auditor was selected to provide a fresh look at the company's financial situation:

Anchor Glass Container Corp. has dismissed Andersen as its independent public accountant but said the decision has nothing to do with Andersen's recent troubles.

The loss deprives Andersen of a Tampa Bay client that paid $503,000 in fees in 2001, Securities and Exchange Commission records show.

Anchor retained PricewaterhouseCoopers for 2002, according to an SEC 8-K filing April 15.

"It has nothing to do with Andersen; we would have done this regardless," said Dale Buckwalter, chief financial officer for Anchor Glass. "It reflects we have a new owner and a new law firm," Carlton Fields in Tampa.

The SEC filing states Anchor's board made the decision April 11.

"There were no disagreements with Arthur Andersen on any matter of accounting principle or practice, financial statement disclosure or auditing scope or procedure," the SEC filing states.

---

[9]From "Alpharma says SEC investigating its revenue methods." by M. Weiss, June 3, 2002, Bloomberg News. Copyright 2002 by Bloomberg L. P. All rights reserved. Reprinted with permission.

Anchor was forced to file for protection from bankruptcy April 15 because its parent company, Toronto-based Consumers Packing Inc., filed for bankruptcy protection, company officials said.

Business at the Tampa-based subsidiary is the best it's been in two decades, Anchor Chief Operating Officer Richard M. Deneau said last week.

PricewaterhouseCoopers, which gains Anchor's business, is the largest accounting firm in Tampa Bay.

"Obviously, Anchor Glass is a large and important client for us," said Andrew McAdams, office managing partner for PricewaterhouseCoopers' Central Florida practice.

In an indictment March 14, a federal grand jury accused Andersen of destroying "tons of paper" and deleting computer files in the financial collapse of Enron Corp.[10]

With the increasing scrutiny of the relationships between companies and accountants, many hope that auditors will become more vigilant in reviewing the financial statements of their clients. Such a development could lead to more auditors making disclosures about problems at companies.

The SEC appears to be taking a more aggressive stance in (a) reviewing business dealings between auditors and companies, and (b) fining and censuring accountants whose dealings call into question their independence as auditors. Another important step that could prove valuable for business reporters is a measure designed to increase the clout of the auditing committee on a company's board of directors. The auditing committee reviews the relationship between a company and its outside accountants. Rules proposed by the SEC would require that this committee consist of board members from outside the company, and give the committee the responsibility of hiring and firing auditors. The last measure may not seem important, but many companies hire CFOs from accounting firms with which they do business. That relationship has been criticized by some reviewing corporate governance. (It should be noted that the SEC has also encouraged many large private companies to adopt some of the proposed rules to improve the relationship between public companies and their auditors.)

One more interesting development in the relationship between companies and auditors is that executives at the largest companies are now required to certify that their financial statements are as correct and accurate as possible. Though this certification applies to the 900 largest companies, or those with more than $1.2 billion in assets, other smaller companies have also had executives attest to their results. This means that the onus is now on company executives to provide accurate financial statements that reflect the true picture of the company to auditors and the general public.

Most companies try to give as accurate a picture of their financial results as possible. But there will always be a few businesses that stretch the limits of

---

[10]From "Anchor Glass drops Anderson, retains PricewaterhouseCoopers," by T. Jackovics, April 23, 2002, *Tampa Tribune*, p. 5. Copyright 2002 by *Tampa Tribune*. Reprinted with permission.

accounting rules in a bid to make themselves appear better than they actually are. The relationship between a company and its outside accountants is important to understand, particularly for the business journalist, so one can assess whether the business is being truthful, or if it needs closer examination.

REGULATION FD AND CONFERENCE CALLS

Remember the example earlier in this chapter when MONY Group disclosed in an 8-K filing its projected earnings? Why did the company disclosed such information?

A news release issued two days before the filing provides a clue. It mentioned that the company was going to hold its annual meeting with investors and analysts, and that its management team would provide an "overview and outlook for the company and its business units" (MONY Group, 2003). The release also mentioned that the meeting could be heard via the Internet from its Web site. So, at the same time the 8-K was filed, the company held a meeting to discuss the information in the filing. The meeting, the release, and the 8-K filing by MONY Group were done to comply with a set of SEC rules called Regulation Fair Disclosure (Regulation FD) that went into effect in 2000 and profoundly changed how Wall Street and the business media obtained information from companies.

Amid opposition from companies and Wall Street firms, Regulation FD was enacted to bring a level playing field to the investment community. Regulators saw companies providing information about their financial performance and their business operations to favored analysts and investors, allowing them to trade in the company's stock before the information was shared with others. Regulation FD now prevents companies from providing information to a select few on Wall Street. A company or executive must now provide the information to everyone at the same time.

Companies have chosen to comply with Regulation FD in a number of ways. One of these ways has been through filing information in an 8-K. Another way has been to open conference calls discussing quarterly earnings or other important developments to anybody who wants to listen via the Internet or a toll-free telephone number. This includes the media and small-time investors. In the past, companies limited who could listen to these conference calls to analysts and investors. Although some companies allowed reporters to listen to these calls, others such as Anheuser-Busch did not. If a reporter noticed a company's stock rising or falling while a conference call was ongoing, he or she would have to wait until the call was over to call analysts and investors he knew were listening to find out what had caused the stock to move.

The business journalism community rallied strongly behind Regulation FD. Bloomberg News wrote countless stories about companies that did not allow broad access to their conference calls. The Society of American Business Editors and

Writers wrote letters in support of the legislation. The reasoning was simple: In addition to helping investors, Regulation FD gave reporters more information as well. Reporters can now listen to the calls that were previously just the territory of Wall Street insiders. Though many times they cannot ask questions during the calls, business journalists can use the conversations among executives, analysts, and investors on the calls to improve the content of their stories, explaining why people on Wall Street are angry or happy with a company's performance. The result has been more-detailed stories, making listening to the conference call an important part of the business journalist's daily routine. Some reporters often have several conference calls to listen to in a single day, particularly during earnings season. And most companies provide information about how to access their conference calls directly to journalists in the form of releases.

But the increase in conference calls as a result of Regulation FD, some argue, has not had the intended effect of providing more information. The executives now read from carefully worded scripts and do not provide any out-of-the-ordinary information when discussing their companies. And the major analysts and investors who follow that company still ask the bulk of the questions on the call. Many companies limit the number of questions that a single person can ask during the call, and with prepared remarks sometimes lasting as long as 30 min there is little time to answer all questions on a call that is usually limited to an hour. Conference calls about quarterly earnings results, in particular, can be extremely boring, especially if the company reported earnings in line with Wall Street estimates and is not expected to reveal any surprises on the call. It takes a savvy reporter who has followed a company for years to listen to such a call and determine whether there has been any news disclosed. Many times, the only news on such calls comes during the question-and-answer period. But increasingly, analysts and investors do not want to ask probing questions for their competitors to hear. Then, the news is typically if a company provides any sort of earnings guidance during its call. If that happens, the company has usually provided the news in a release and in an 8-K filing. Often if a company executive, in answering a question on the call, provides information that the company determines is material to its performance, the company will later file an 8-K.

Still, listening to conference calls can be a valuable experience for business reporters, even if the time spent on the call does not result in a story. The journalist can assess how the CEO or CFO interacts with analysts and investors by noting whether the questions are hostile or friendly. The tone of the questions, and the responses, can tell the reporter whether Wall Street is happy or upset with the company. How an executive responds to a question can also be an indicator of how he thinks the business is performing, or what he thinks about the company's future prospects.

Anyone who went back and listened to the first-quarter 2001 earnings conference call for now-bankrupt energy giant Enron would have run across this exchange between Highfields Capital Corporation analyst Richard Grubman and CEO Jeff

Skilling on why the company had not released a balance sheet along with its earnings statement.

> Grubman: Yes, good morning. Can you tell us what the assets and liabilities from price/risk management were at quarter-end, what those balances were?
> Skilling: We don't have the balance sheet completed. We'll have that done shortly.
> Grubman: But you're the only financial institution that can't produce a balance sheet or a cash flow statement with their earnings.
> Skilling: You—thank you very much. We appreciate it.
> Grubman: Appreciate it.[11]

Skilling then muttered an expletive. Less than a six months later, he resigned from the company, which then restated its earnings and filed for bankruptcy-court protection. The tense conversation between Skilling and Grubman could have been an indicator to anyone listening that maybe someone needed to take a closer look at Enron's performance.

Sometimes, the conference call can provide some unintended results. The following Bloomberg News story illustrates a case in which shareholders disclosed information on a conference call about a relationship between the company and its CEO:

> Insignia Financial Group Inc. Chief Executive Andrew Farkas' compensation was criticized by two of the property broker's biggest investors, who said he is profiting from company partnerships at shareholder expense.
> An arrangement giving Farkas a 22 percent share of profits from a company managed investment fund after a certain return is met isn't in the best interests of shareholders, Daniel Loeb of Third Point Partners LP, said on a conference call.
> Insignia also shouldn't have paid Farkas $950,000 for company use of a personal plane and boat he owns, Loeb said. The compensation arrangements put Insignia, whose Insignia/ESG unit is New York's biggest broker, at risk of "a major backlash" from shareholders at a time when the company's shares are down 24 cents for the year, said Loeb, whose firm had a 4.9 percent stake in Insignia at the end of March.
> "Right now you're in a position to make a lot of money while your stock is languishing," Loeb told Farkas on the call.
> Company officials declined immediate comment. On the call, which was held to discuss Insignia's second-quarter results, Farkas said Loeb's analysis wasn't "entirely accurate."
> I "believe that the interests of shareholders and the interests of management, including all those who participate in promote programs, are in fact very much aligned," he said.
> Insignia's counsel and compensation committee, which consist of Related Cos. Chairman Stephen Ross and H. Strauss Zelnick, former head of Bertelsmann AG's BMG Entertainment music unit, reevaluate its "programs on a regular basis," Farkas said.

---

[11]From "Any more questions? Company conference calls still leave investors out," by M. Barbaro, October 6, 2002, *Washington Post*, p. H1. Copyright 2002 *Washington Post*. Reprinted with permission.

Insignia yesterday said it had second-quarter net income of $3.18 million, or 12 cents a share, compared with a loss from continuing operations of $1.75 million, or 9 cents, a year earlier. Losses on Internet-related ventures reduced results for the latest quarter by $2.6 million, Insignia said.

The company's shares fell 30 cents to $8.20 on the New York Stock Exchange. Another shareholder, hedge fund manager David Einhorn of Greenlight Capital LLC, joined Loeb in his criticism on the call. Greenlight owned a 7.4 percent stake in Insignia at the end of March, making it the company's third-largest shareholder.

"We feel similarly to him," Einhorn said. "And we think the company should come back promptly with how to fix its corporate governance issues before this turns into some sort of media circus."

Before taking personal benefits from new ventures, Farkas should first make sure Insignia recoups its losses, Loeb said. Insignia has taken $34.7 million of charges for failed Internet ventures spearheaded by Farkas, including EdificeRex.com, which sought to provide services to apartment renters.

"It seems like you can keep setting up these partnerships one after another and if one doesn't work well, so be it," Loeb said. "You go on to the next one. What I'd rather see is us all sitting at the same table and eating from the same trough, if you will."[12]

A month later, Insignia Financial filed an 8-K disclosing that it would no longer reimburse its CEO for the company's use of his personal boat, and would stop paying for the plane he co-owns. (That resulted in another story for the Bloomberg reporter covering the company.) This is a case in which the investors in a company, not the executives, used the conference call to make news.

For most business reporters, accessing these calls is as simple as finding the company's Web site. Most companies include a link to the conference call via the Internet. Others provide the phone number that can be called at the end of a news release. But there are also Web sites that specialize in providing access to company conference calls. One of the best free sites is www.investorbroadcast.com. Another good site—although it is a pay site—is www.analystcall.com because it also provides transcripts of calls.

It has now been three years since the SEC imposed Regulation FD. It took regulators more than two years to crack down on companies suspected of violating the rules. Even then, the companies received little more than slaps on the wrist, as the following *San Jose Mercury News* story explains:

Siebel Systems agreed to settle a federal charge that it had violated a Securities and Exchange Commission regulation prohibiting companies from selectively disclosing information to favored Wall Street analysts before releasing the news to ordinary investors.

The agreement with the San Mateo software company marked the first litigation brought to enforce Regulation FD (for Fair Disclosure), which was adopted

---

[12]From "Insignia Financial CEO's pay package criticized by shareholders," by D. Levitt, July 25, 2002, Bloomberg News. Copyright 2002 by Bloomberg L. P. All rights reserved. Reprinted with permission.

in August 2000 in order to ensure the public equal access to important investment information.

The SEC also announced Monday the settlement of administrative proceedings against Secure Computing, a San Jose security-software maker, and Raytheon, a Lexington, Mass., defense contractor.

All three companies agreed to cease and desist from any future violations of Regulation FD without admitting or denying any wrongdoing. Siebel Systems also agreed to pay a civil penalty of $250,000.

"They are trying to send a message that SEC is serious about enforcing the Regulation FD," said Gordy Davidson, chairman of Fenwick & West, a Silicon Valley law firm that emphasizes its technology practice.

The three cases illustrate how broadly Regulation FD has affected the way companies communicate with investors. Before it was adopted, analysts generally relied on private conversations with executives to form an opinion about a company's financial prospects. Analysts at larger, more prestigious firms often received special guidance.

"These cases, and Raytheon in particular, describe the kind of conduct that Regulation FD was supposed to prevent," said Mark Schonfeld, associate regional director of the SEC's Northeast Regional Office.

According to SEC documents, Raytheon Chief Financial Officer Franklyn Caine called individual analysts following a February 2001 earnings call to let them know their estimates for first-quarter earnings were "too high" or "very aggressive."

After speaking with Caine, who was named as a party in the SEC action, analysts lowered their estimates, enabling Raytheon to beat the consensus estimate by a penny a share when it announced financial results three months later.

Regulators said Motorola avoided becoming the subject of a similar action because the company's in-house legal counsel told a senior executive it was OK to telephone selected analysts.

In the case involving Secure Computing, Chief Executive John McNulty told selected analysts about a deal the company had made to bundle its software with products made by Cisco Systems before it issued a press release, according to SEC documents which named McNulty as a party.

Though regulators determined the initial disclosure was accidental, McNulty continued to talk about the deal with still more analysts as his employees prepared a press release, said Robert Mitchell, assistant district administrator of the San Francisco District Office. "That was a particular problem for them," Mitchell said.

Tom Siebel, CEO of Siebel Systems, was not named in the action brought against his company, though it concerned statements he made during a Goldman Sachs technology conference in November 2001.

On a public earnings call three weeks before the conference, Siebel had spoken pessimistically about "an exceptionally soft market" and a tough business environment. But a few days before the conference, the company's director of investor relations told a Goldman Sachs analyst that business was looking up. When Siebel struck an optimistic tone during his 10 a.m. presentation, the company's stock took off. It closed more than 16 percent above the previous day's close.

According to SEC documents, attendees at the conference began trading the stock even before Siebel finished speaking, and Goldman Sachs was the most active firm trading Siebel Systems stock that day.

A company press release Monday said Siebel's remarks "were deemed to be in violation of Regulation FD because the presentation was not Webcast or otherwise simultaneously broadcast to the general public." The company said Siebel did not know the conference was not being transmitted on the Internet.

"This is a great reminder to management teams everywhere that they better be careful what they say in question-and-answer sessions and in breakout sessions at conferences," said Patrick Walravens, an analyst at JMP Securities.[13]

It is hoped that this regulatory move will give a company some guidance about the what and how of information it is supposed to provide to the public. As the corporate world moves forward and understands these regulations better, companies are likely to move back to pre-Regulation FD days and become more comfortable and forthcoming in providing information during conference calls.

Understanding the important ways companies make news and disseminate that information to the rest of the world can help business reporters, making it easier for them to cover the news in ways that show they know what they are talking about. Nothing hurts a business journalist more than botching an explanation of what it means for a board member to resign, or for an auditor to express doubt about a company's future.

GLOSSARY

adverse opinion: An opinion made by an auditor indicating that a company's financial statements are misrepresented, misstated and do not accurately reflect its financial performance and health.

auditor: An outside firm that conducts an unbiased examination and opinion of the financial statements of a business or other organization.

auditor's report: Recorded in the annual report, it tests to see that corporation's financial statements comply with generally accepted accounting practices, or GAAP. This is sometimes referred to as a "clean opinion."

bankruptcy: When a person or company is unable to repay debts. In most cases, ownership of the firm's assets are transferred from the stockholders to the bondholders.

conference call: An event in which investors can call into a special phone number and hear the management of their company comment on the financial results of the recently completed quarter, or another important corporate event.

Form 8-K: A report of unscheduled material events or corporate changes that could be of importance to the shareholders or the SEC. Examples include an acquisition, bankruptcy or a change in fiscal year.

---

[13]From "Siebel to pay fine to SEC; $250,000 settles charge of disclosure violation," by E. Ackerman, Nov. 26, 2002, *San Jose Mercury News*, p. 1. Copyright 2002 by *San Jose Mercury News*. All rights reserved. Reprinted with permission.

ongoing concern: A statement made by a company's independent auditors that raises doubts about the company's ability to function in the future.

qualified opinion: Written upon the front page of an audit done by a professional auditor, a qualified opinion suggests that the information provided was limited in scope of the company being audited has not maintained GAAP accounting principles. Contrary to its connotation, a qualified opinion is not a good thing. Auditors that deem audits as qualified opinions are stating that the information within the audit is not complete or that the accounting methods used by the company do not follow GAAP.

Regulation Fair Disclosure: A rule passed by the Securities and Exchange Commission in an effort to prevent selective disclosure by public companies to market professionals and certain shareholders.

REFERENCES

Ackerman, E. (2002, November 26). Siebel to pay fine to SEC; $250,000 settles charge of disclosure violation. *San Jose Mercury News.* p. 1.

Associated Press. (2000, December 5). Cisco prepares for delinquent accounts.

Associated Press (2002, December 27). CyNet files for Chapter 11 bankruptcy protection. *San Jose Mercury News.* p. 2.

Barbaro, M. (2002, October 6). Any more questions? Company conference calls still leave investors out. *Washington Post.* p. H1.

Beauprez, J. (2001, May 2). Liberty takes On Command reins; Hotel-room movie firm may be merged with rival. *Denver Post.* p. C-1.

Countryman, A. (2002, September 29). SEC proposal becomes a material issue; Critics complain rules not uniform. *Chicago Tribune.* p. C1.

Crittenden, M. (2003, January 16). MONY sees fourth-quarter results ahead of estimates, in line 2003. *Insurance Investor Interactive.* Retrieved January 30, 2003 from http://www.snl.com.

Form 8-K. Chubb Corporation (2003, January 21). (SEC Publication No. 0000950123-03-000485, pp. 1–22).

Haber, G. (2002, December 10). Firms base disclosure on relevance to investors. *Tampa Tribune.* Washington, DC: Securities and Exchange Commission. p. 4.

(2002, September 21). Home Depot ends 8 Nathan's licenses. *Atlanta Journal-Constitution.* p. 2F.

(2002, June 26). H-P head resigns from Dynegy board. *Rocky Mountain News.* p. 10B.

Jackovics, T. (2002, April 23). Anchor Glass drops Andersen, retains PriceWaterhouseCoopers. *Tampa Tribune.* p. 5.

Kokmen, L., & Hubler, E. (1999, January 21). Laser Technology execs' exit urged. *Denver Post.* p. C1.

Kwan, J. L. (2001, August 21). At Home warns it may run out of cash. *San Jose Mercury News.* p. 1C.

Levitt, D. M. (2002, July 25). Insignia Financial CEO's pay package criticized by shareholders. Bloomberg News.

Lowrey, D. (2003, January 16). Mony Group 2003 earnings outlook tracks estimates. Dow Jones Newswires.

MONY Group. (2003, January 14). Corporate news release.

Parker, P. (1998, May 29). Boston Chicken woes mount. *Denver Post.* p. A1.

Subscriber loss hurts Adelphia. (2002, November 6). *Pittsburgh Post-Gazette.* p. D-4.

Fleischer Tamen, J. (2003, January 8). Spherion taking $250M goodwill charge; COO post eliminated to cut costs. Fort Lauderdale, FL: *Sun-Sentinel.* p. 1D.

Weiss, M. (2002, June 3). Alpharma says SEC investigating its revenue methods. Bloomberg News.

SUGGESTED EXERCISES

1. Find examples of each of the seven reasons an 8-K is filed, along with stories that were written from those filings. This could be a project that is spread out among an entire semester.

2. Write a 500-word essay explaining the increase in 8-K filings due to Regulation FD. Explain Regulation FD and give examples of the types of 8-Ks being filed as a result and why they're stories.

3. Obtain SEC proposal to add additional reasons requiring a company to file an 8-K and what type of information those filings might contain. Write a fictitious disclosure for a company under one of these new guidelines.

4. Find a company where a top-ranking executive has recently left or been replaced. Compare the information disclosed in the company's news release disclosing the change to the information disclosed in the Form 8-K.

5. Listen to a company's conference call and write a story based on what you thought was the news disclosed during the call. After the story is turned in, compare the prepared remarks at the beginning of the call to the Q&A session at the end of the call.

6

Mergers and Acquisitions

WHY COMPANIES BUY EACH OTHER

At some point in time, virtually every business reporter will write a story about one company buying another. It is like a police reporter writing a story about a murder. Both of these news events happen with regularity. In 2001, there were more than 8,600 mergers or acquisitions valued at more than $640 billion. In 2003, there were more than 7,300 mergers or acquisitions of U.S. companies, worth more than $470 billion, according to www.mergerstat.com, a Web site that tracks merger and acquisition (M&A) activity. Although those numbers seem large, they are actually down from previous years. These figures exclude deals in Europe, where the number of M&A transactions, and their values, were higher in both 2001 and 2002.

Simply put, mergers and acquisitions occur with such regularity that they have become a staple of business reporting. And because of the frequency, it is important for journalists to understand how and why M&A occur, and what information is important for readers and viewers to receive. Virtually every huge company, and plenty of small ones too, were created by a merger or an acquisition, sometimes several. Citigroup is the combination of the former Citibank and Travelers; AOL Time Warner was created by the merger of America Online with Time Warner, itself the creation of a deal between Time and Warner Brothers; and Disney bought television network ABC, which brought ESPN into the new company.

Most companies, whether they are public or private, like to get bigger. Many of them make acquisitions under the belief that a larger company can spread its expenses around more efficiently. For instance, why have two CEOs and two CFOs when two companies can be combined to only have one of each? Why operate two headquarters when one would suffice? That is what most companies hope for. But, in reality, mergers and acquisitions do not always work out that way.

First, the terms should be defined. Although the terms merger and acquisition are sometimes used interchangeably, there is a big difference. Merger refers to when two companies agree to combine their operations into one company. In a true merger, the past owners of the two companies will each own 50% in the new company. However, that is not always the case. In a merger, the combined company's board of directors is also typically split among the board members of the two old businesses. In many cases, the management teams of the old companies also combine to form one new executive team. That is how it is supposed to work. However, despite how hard companies try to make mergers equal, one company typically has the upper hand. For example, its headquarters becomes the new headquarters for the combined operation, its CEO takes over running the new company, or its shareholders may end up owning 55% of the new company.

Acquisition refers to when one company buys a controlling interest in another company. An acquisition does not always mean that one company purchases 100% of another company. Sometimes, one will just purchase 51% of another, but as long as one company becomes the majority owner, it can control how the entire company is operated.

Companies buy other companies for various reasons, one of which may be because the CEO wants to see it grow. Sometimes, the easiest way to grow a company is to acquire another company. But sometimes an acquisition is not a smart move for a company to make. The acquired company may not fit in with the business, either operationally or culturally. In most cases, however, mergers or acquisitions take place for specific reasons. An acquisition may be part of a company's expansion strategy. For example, in the mid-1990s, Coca-Cola wanted to round out its portfolio of beverages. One of the biggest holes in its product line was in root beer. The company sold a brand called Ramblin' Root Beer in a handful of locations, but its competitors all had better-known brands such as Mug, Dad's, and A&W. So Coca-Cola looked around until it found a root beer company it could buy. In 1995, it purchased Barq's, a New Orleans-based company.

Other times, companies like to make acquisitions to expand into new geographic territories. Maybe the company's operations are primarily in the Midwest and the West, but it would like to expand into the Mid-Atlantic. The following is a story from *The Washington Post* written about one company's acquisition of another that helped it move into new markets:

Trigon Healthcare Inc., the largest health insurance company in Virginia, agreed yesterday to be acquired by Anthem Inc., the fifth-largest publicly traded U.S. health insurer, for $3.8 billion in cash and stock.

Both Blue Cross Blue Shield companies formerly operated on a not-for-profit basis but converted to stockholder-owned enterprises. In recent years, many regional Blue Cross plans have announced plans to merge with larger "Blues" to better compete with big insurers such as Aetna Inc. and UnitedHealth Group Inc.

Indianapolis-based Anthem serves 8 million customers in eight states. If approved, the merger would give Anthem 2.2 million members in Virginia and the District and a foothold in the Southeast and Mid-Atlantic, where it does not have a presence. Under terms of the deal, Trigon stockholders would receive $30 in cash and 1.062 Anthem shares for each Trigon share they own. Based on Friday's closing prices, the package is worth $105.08 a share to holders of Trigon.

Trigon stock surged $14.62 a share, or 17.4 percent, to $98.87 yesterday on the New York Stock Exchange. Anthem shares fell $4.05, or 5.7 percent, to $66.65.

Trigon chief executive Thomas G. Snead Jr. said the deal would have no immediate impact on premiums the company's customers pay. He said he expected double-digit premium increases "for at least the next couple of years."

"Premiums are set as a result of the underlying medical costs and administrative costs that are required to service the product," he said.

But over time, he said, the merger would create a stronger health insurer with greater financial resources and technological capabilities.

"This is a strategic alliance," Snead said. "Both parties sat down and figured out what we could look like together versus separate and, I got to tell you . . . this makes an awful lot of sense."

The merger agreement is subject to approval by Virginia insurance regulators.[1]

Note that the lead paragraph of this story begins with the company being acquired, Trigon, not the company making the acquisition, Anthem. That is because the reporter knows what his readers will care about the most. With a large contingent of readers in Virginia, the *Post* focuses its coverage of this acquisition on the Virginia-based company. The lead paragraph also details how much money is being paid for the acquired company. The price is the most important detail in any merger and acquisition story. The money being paid places a value on the transaction. If a company does not disclose how much it is paying for another company, the reporter should ask. For mergers and acquisitions involving public companies, disclosing the price is required by regulators. Only in a transaction involving a private company is the price not required to be disclosed, but sometimes companies will release that information.

The story also explains that the company is being purchased with a combination of cash and stock. This is another important detail that should be disclosed in most merger and acquisition stories. It lets the reader know where the money is coming from to fund the acquisition. Public companies often use their stock to help pay for

---

[1]From "Indiana company to buy Trigon: Insurers agree to $3.8 billion deal," by B. Brubaker, April 30, 2002, *Washington Post*, p. E1. Copyright 2002 by *Washington Post*. Reprinted with permission.

a deal. The exchange ratio is also detailed in this story. For mergers and acquisitions in which stock is being used, this is vital information. It informs the shareholders of the company being acquired how many shares they will receive in the combined company. In the case of the Trigon/Anthem deal, it is slightly more than one share in Anthem for every share of Trigon stock they own, in addition to the cash. With mergers, this exchange ratio is often one share for one share, or a ratio close to 1:1.

This story also informs readers how the deal values the acquired company on a per share basis. For readers of the *Post* who also owned Trigon stock, this is important information. This tells them how much money they will receive for each share of stock they own, and it enables them to assess whether the deal is a good one. In this case, most investors in Trigon likely were happy with the price being paid by Anthem. Trigon stock was trading for about $84 before the deal was announced, yet Anthem paid $105 per share for the company, a 25% gain for investors. This 25% is considered the premium paid by Anthem for Trigon. A premium is how much more the acquirer is willing to pay for a company than the company's current value.

Companies pay premiums to acquire other companies for various reasons, but many of these can be tied into their overall merger and acquisition strategies. Maybe the management of the acquiring company thinks it can do a better job of running the acquired company, increasing its sales and profits. If the acquiring company is right, then the company being acquired is probably worth more than it is currently valued. Or maybe the executives at the purchaser think that they can cut costs out of the bought company by combining the two operations, thus lowering the expenses related to running the company. This is called synergy.

The acquisitions that have been referenced so far are what are typically called friendly takeovers, which means the acquiring company negotiates with the board of the company being sold, and they come to an agreement on the purchase price before the acquisition is announced. But this does not always happen. Sometimes a company will want to acquire another company that does not want to sell. Or sometimes a company will negotiate to acquire another company, but those talks will end without an agreement. When that happens, sometimes the company wanting to make the acquisition launches what is called a hostile takeover.

A hostile takeover attempt can even occur when a company has reached an agreement to acquire another. A third company may enter the fray, offering more money or a different structure than the original merger or acquisition. Such an event occurred in the Southeast in 2000 and 2001, when Wachovia and First Union agreed to merge and create one bank. However, another bank, SunTrust, became upset with the transaction and made a separate offer for First Union. In the end, Wachovia won the battle. Such hostile takeovers are great news stories for business reporters because they typically involve competitors and angry CEOs who want to talk to the media to get their side of the takeover out for discussion. In many cases, CEOs, in the hopes of convincing people their bid is better, use the media to speak directly to the shareholders of the company up for sale. This is just one of the many types of stories that can be written about mergers and acquisitions. Large acquisitions typically are announced on late Sunday or early Monday after negotiations are finalized during the weekend. This often happens because the

---

The following *New York Times* story from 2001 helps explain why companies sometimes use publicity to make their case in a hostile takeover attempt:

The big hostile takeover is coming back, but it is warmer and fuzzier this time. They even call it the bear hug.

So far this year, unsolicited offers account for 19.5 percent of the value of all deals, compared with only 2.9 percent during the corresponding period a year ago, according to Thomson Financial Securities Data. In past years, many of these offers came in the form of tender offers, in which the bidder went straight to the shareholders of a company. But recently, many of the most publicized bids have been made not to shareholders but to the companies' managements, in some cases because they could not go directly to shareholders. But unlike quiet, behind-the-scenes takeover talks, these "bear hugs" are made in a very public way.

EchoStar Communications' unsolicited $30 billion offer this week for Hughes Electronics, is one example. Comcast's takeover bid for AT&T's cable-television business is another. A third is the toolmaker Danaher Corporation's unsolicited $5.5 billion bid for a rival, Cooper Industries, which rejected it yesterday.

In each of these cases, the bidders knew they stood little chance of winning. They also knew that even if they lost, in many ways they would still win.

Take EchoStar's bid. The chairman, Charles Ergen, took his proposal public partly to get the attention of the board of General Motors, parent of Hughes. He had held discussions with executives at Hughes, but said he was worried that G.M.'s board had not reviewed the proposal.

Yesterday, Mr. Ergen said he was "encouraged that G.M. is taking our proposal very seriously," after a decision by G.M.'s board on Tuesday to review the offer.

The publicity of a bear hug is also meant to stir shareholders to apply pressure to the company's board. Since EchoStar made its bear hug, four lawsuits have been filed against G.M. by shareholders effectively pushing the company to consider EchoStar's offer.

Comcast's public offer for AT&T Broadband forced AT&T to postpone spinning off the unit, putting the business in play. And while Cooper Industries may have rejected Danaher's offer, Cooper did say it will consider a variety of alternatives to increase shareholder value, effectively putting the company up for sale. Cooper also postponed a vote to move the company to Bermuda, where a takeover would be much more difficult.

The biggest problem with making such a public offer is that it reduces a suitor's chance of being able to negotiate for the target without competition. Since Comcast made its offer for AT&T Broadband, half a dozen suitors have begun circling the business, some discussing forming consortiums to buy the business simply in an effort to keep it from Comcast.

In another situation, the Shell Oil Company, the United States arm of the Royal Dutch/Shell Group, made an offer for the Barrett Resources Corporation. Barrett rejected Shell's offer, but decided there was enough pressure from shareholders to put itself up for sale. In the end, the Williams Companies, an energy trader and pipeline operator, won control of Barrett.

Companies also like the bear hug because it is easier and cheaper than a tender offer, which can involve a costly, lengthy appeal to thousands of shareholders. All it requires is a press release and a postage stamp to send the proposal to the company's board.

Some companies are also more comfortable about going public with their offers because they aren't worried about losing.

'The old rule of thumb that you don't start something publicly you can't finish doesn't seem to hold anymore,' said Donald Meltzer, global head of mergers and acquisitions at Credit Suisse First Boston. 'More acquirers are prepared to go public with an offer and take the risk of losing, demonstrating they are disciplined about the price they are willing to pay.'

When SunTrust lost its fight against First Union for control of Wachovia, SunTrust's chairman, L. Phillip Humann, said the loss was acceptable.

'Clearly we would have preferred a different outcome to this contest, but not if it meant abandoning our business discipline to pursue an acquisition at a price that did not make sense for our shareholders," he said. "Now we'll do just what we said we would in this situation—close the book.'[2]

companies involved in the deal want as much coverage from the media as possible. Because little business news occurs during a weekend, the companies know that they are likely to get stories written about their deal. They also realize that *The Wall Street Journal* reporters that specifically cover mergers and acquisitions could give the deal good play. The *Journal* does not publish during the weekend, so its editors look for the latest news for its sections.

Like snowflakes, every transaction is different. But stories about mergers and acquisitions should be written so that they should answer these questions:

1. What is the total price and per share price of a deal?
2. Is the acquisition being paid for with cash, stock, debt, or a combination?
3. If it's a stock transaction, what is the exchange ratio?
4. What is the price compared to similar transactions in the industry?
5. When will the deal be completed, and who must approve the transaction?
6. What is the reason for this deal? Does it make the company the largest in its industry, or business line?
7. How did investors react to the acquisition announcement?
8. Will specific competitors be affected by the merger or acquisition?
9. Did the trading activity of the stocks of the companies involved in the transaction increase shortly before the deal was announced?
10. Will the deal be accretive or dilutive to the acquiring company?

---

[2]From "The warm and fuzzy version of the hostile takeover bid," by A. R. Sorkin, August 9, 2001, *New York Times,* p. C1. Copyright 2001 by New York Times. Reprinted with permission.

Anytime a deal is announced, the reporter covering the story should ask him or herself why the transaction makes sense for both the acquiring company and the selling company. Many times, executives at the companies will hold a conference call to explain to Wall Street and others why they think the move is a good one. Always listen to these calls. If the analysts and investors are skeptical about the deal, then there's probably a good reason why you should be also.

HOW DEALS ARE FUNDED: STOCK, CASH, AND DEBT

Companies use various ways to fund the purchase of another business. The three most-common methods of payment a company would use to acquire another company is cash, stock, and debt. A company can also use a combination of two or more of these methods to raise the cash needed to buy another company.

First, cash is the easiest to understand. Basically, if a company has enough cash sitting in its banks to make an acquisition, it has enough money to pay for the acquisition. Business writers can look at the company's cash flow statement filed with its quarterly or annual financial statements to determine whether it has the cash to do a proposed deal. Sometimes companies announce that they will use cash to pay for an acquisition, though they do not actually have that cash in their accounts. The money can come from bonds, debts, or offerings, as discussed in chapter 7. This is similar to borrowing the money from a bank.

At other times, a company will pay for an acquisition by using its stock. This means that the company will give the owners of the company it is acquiring shares of stock. To do so, the acquirer will often have to file documents with the SEC to sell the additional shares. These filings disclose lots of information about the transaction. Companies often like to use stock to pay for acquisitions when their stock price is high compared with its historical valuation. The rationale behind such transactions is this: The higher the stock price, the fewer shares a company has to issue to fund an acquisition. If Company A agrees to buy Company B for $100 million, it would have to issue 10 million shares at $10 each. But if its stock is trading at $20, then it would only have to issue 5 million shares to fund the deal. That is an important consideration for many companies and their existing shareholders who do not like to see their holdings diluted by the company issuing more stock.

Companies can also factor in debt as part of the purchase price. If the company being acquired has money it owes to banks or other lenders on its books, it may want the acquiring company to assume the debt and pay off those loans as part of the acquisition. If the acquirer is not assuming the debt from the seller, and there are debts on the seller's books, it would be important for a reporter covering the story to find out how this debt will be repaid, particularly if the coverage is focused more on the seller than the buyer. Assumed debt is often considered part of the purchase price of a company. If a company buys another company for $150 million in cash plus the assumption of $50 million in debt, the total purchase price is often considered $200 million. That is the total amount of money the acquiring company will eventually have to pay for the deal.

Not all acquisition prices are this cut and dried. As with the Anthem/Trigon acquisition, Anthem agreed to purchase Trigon for a combination of cash and stock. Other times, an acquisition will be for cash and assumed debt, or stock and assumed debt. Other deals could be a mix of all three. Obviously, what the buying company wants to do is structure how it pays for another company in a way that is most advantageous to itself. If its stock price is low, it may want to avoid using stock, particularly if it thinks that the stock price is going to go up soon. Stock may also be used to entice the management of the selling company to remain with the operation. If the management of the selling company are shareholders and they receive stock in the acquired company as part of the deal, then they have an incentive to remain with the company and to try to drive the stock price higher by improving the results. Shareholders of the selling company, in turn, may negotiate to receive more cash from the acquirer if it believes that the stock price of the buyer is not going to get any higher. Or they may ask for more stock if they believe that the stock price could rise soon.

The balance between cash, stock, and debt is part of the negotiating process between the buyer and the seller. In addition, taxes may play a part in whether a transaction uses cash, stock, or debt. Many owners of small companies sell for cash, which is taxed as a capital gain, although higher capital gains rates might deter some deals. Often, however, in smaller transactions, owners of private companies may look for strictly cash deals because they are not looking to remain stockholders in the purchasing company. If they do receive stock, many times the owners will sell their holdings within a year or two of the deal.

Often, a company determines what it is willing to pay to buy another company with the help of an investment banker. An investment banker comes in and reviews the performance of the business being acquired compared with other companies in the same industry. The bankers also review the target's future prospects, other acquisitions in the industry, and give the potential acquirer a range of prices to pay. Typically, the board of the acquiring company, on the basis of the information from its investment banker, makes an offer to the board of the company it wants to buy. This can often be in the form of a letter, often later released in SEC filings if the companies are public. Occasionally, in the letter a buyer will offer what is known as a collar. A collar is often offered to guarantee a minimum payment to the seller and can be used as incentive for management/owners to stay on board rather than to leave to perhaps start a competing business.

The target can choose to accept the offer, or reject it and hold out for a higher price. When the two companies finally agree on a price, a news release is typically issued with glowing praise for how the combined operations will be a success for many years to come. But, as any skeptical business writer knows, the proof is in the results a year or two later.

GOOD DEALS AND BAD DEALS

As mentioned earlier, not every merger or acquisition works for both the acquiring and selling company. And with just a basic knowledge of how mergers and acquisitions work, a business reporter can determine if the deal was good or bad.

The first indicator of whether a transaction is going to be successful for the acquirer is if it is immediately accretive or dilutive to the acquiring company's earnings. An acquisition that is accretive is one that immediately adds to the acquiring company's earnings per share. This happens when the price-to-earnings (P/E) ratio is higher at the acquiring firm than the business being purchased. If the acquiring company has a P/E ratio of 18, but the company being acquired has a P/E ratio of 14, then it is an accretive acquisition. (For a review of P/E ratio, see chap. 4.) A dilutive acquisition is one in which the acquiring company's earnings per share decrease as a result of the deal. This happens when the P/E is lower at the company making the purchase than at the company being sold. Typically, a company will state in the release announcing the acquisition whether the acquisition is accretive or dilutive. If this information is not in the release, the question as to whether the deal will be accretive or dilutive is likely to be asked by an analyst or an investor on the conference call discussing the transaction.

Investors typically want mergers and acquisitions to be accretive, or at least neutral, to earnings. After all, these are the people who buy a company's stock on the basis of the belief that earnings will rise. A dilutive acquisition makes earnings go down. As a way to appease its investors, a company making a dilutive acquisition will often state that the deal will begin to add to earnings in the next year or the year after that. It can turn a dilutive acquisition into an accretive acquisition by improving the results of the acquired company.

After the acquisition is complete, a reporter should follow the company's progress in integrating the purchased business into its own operations. Watch its quarterly earnings for any indication of whether the acquisition actually was accretive to earnings. Often, companies trumpet the success of their deal making in earnings releases. If that information is not in a release, an analyst or investor typically will ask for updates on an acquisition's progress during an earnings conference call. If that does not happen, a reporter can always ask the company the question. If a deal that was supposed to be accretive has not been, that is a potential story and warrants further investigation.

Deals also go bad because they are a bad strategic fit. Companies acquire other companies believing that they need to expand their operations to continue to be successful. But that does not always happen. Just because a company has been successful in one business does not mean it can translate that success into another operation.

Consider what happened to First Union, the Charlotte-based bank, before it ended up merging with Wachovia, as was noted earlier in this chapter. In 1998, First Union decided it wanted to expand its lending operations and become a major player in that business. So it purchased The Money Store. Two years later, however, First Union shuttered its lending business, effectively saying that the acquisition of Money Store was a colossal flop. Heather Timmons (2000) of *BusinessWeek* explained why this deal failed in a story soon after the announcement. She noted in her story that First Union took a $2.6 billion charge to earnings to shut the consumer lender, and her reporting disclosed that First Union's $34-a-share offer for the company was 25% more than what the company would have accepted. In addition, First Union paid about 20 times Money Store's earnings, whereas rival Bank of America paid about 8 times earnings for a similar company. This deal failed because First Union paid much more for Money Store than competitors were paying for similar operations. Timmons uses P/E ratios to compare what First Union paid to what others paid. She also noted that First Union underestimated the business of lending to low-income consumers.

In a story, it is always important to compare what one company is paying in acquisition to what other companies have paid to acquire similar businesses. Such a comparison of P/E multiples, or other barometers, gives the reader an indication whether a company is overpaying. Another example of this is illustrated by the Anthem acquisition of Trigon earlier in the chapter. In the managed care business, companies base their acquisitions on the price per member in the managed care plans. Anthem paid more per member for Trigon's operations than competitors had paid for similar companies. Reporters who knew the importance of such a comparison dutifully reported the high price for their readers.

The *BusinessWeek* story mentions a writedown, or a charge to earnings, which is an important factor for any business writer looking to determine whether a merger or acquisition was successful. A deal that worked for the buyer will not have any writedowns, which is exactly what it sounds like. It is when a company reduces the value of an asset on its financial statement because it is overvalued compared with market values for similar assets. This typically shows up on the income statement as an expense, thereby lowering net income.

In the case of acquisitions, the assets that get written down are often the assets of the business that was purchased. When the assets are written down, what a company is essentially saying is that it paid too much for the business when it was acquired, and is now being forced to lower the value of the assets it purchased. In other words, the deal was a flop. Business reports should look at any company writing down its assets as a sign that an acquisition it made in the recent past has failed. Conversely, if a company is not writing down its assets, that means it probably made an acquisition that fit nicely into its operations and is working. Writing down assets is commonly called goodwill impairment charges because what is being written down is the value of the goodwill purchased. Goodwill arises when more was paid for the business than you would expect from just looking at the value of its assets and liabilities. Goodwill can be considered to be the loyalty of a company's customers or the locations of its stores.

The following 2001 article in the *San Francisco Chronicle* does an excellent job explaining why companies take goodwill charges to earnings, and how it affects a company's performance:

> "Goodwill impairment" sounds like a good topic to bring up if you want to shoo off somebody at a cocktail party.
>
> It's one of those subjects stock investors would rather not think about, right up there with margin calls and capital gains taxes.
>
> But as one company after another writes off billions of dollars worth of impaired goodwill, you have to ask yourself what the heck is going on here, and should I care?
>
> JDS Uniphase last week announced a record-breaking goodwill write-down of $44.8 billion, which is less than a billion shy of the amount California will spend on K-12 education in the next year.
>
> Other companies taking large goodwill charges in the latest quarter include include Nortel Networks ($12.4 billion) Corning ($4.8 billion) and VeriSign ($9.9 billion). But the write-downs we've seen so far might be the tip of the iceberg.
>
> "In the first quarter of next year—wow, you won't believe it. There will be hundreds of billions of dollars" in goodwill write-downs, says Robert Willens, a tax and accounting analyst with Lehman Bros.
>
> Here's why:
>
> Goodwill is created when a company buys another firm for more than the value of its identifiable assets minus its debts. Goodwill supposedly represents a company's unidentified intangible assets, such as its reputation, customer base and workforce.
>
> "It's what makes the whole worth more than the sum of the parts," says Kim Petrone, a project manager with the Financial Accounting Standard Board. The FASB recently changed the way companies must account for goodwill.
>
> Under the old rules, a company has to "amortize" or write off a fixed portion of goodwill over time. This write-down reduces a company's operating earnings. The hope is that the merger will create enough earnings to exceed the added charge.
>
> Companies are supposed to take an additional write-down any time they discover their goodwill has become "impaired," which means the purchased company isn't worth as much as they originally thought.
>
> Because goodwill charges don't represent cash outlays such as salaries or Super Bowl ads, analysts often ignore them when valuing a company's performance and prospects. But that doesn't mean you should.
>
> PURCHASE VS. POOLING: Goodwill is only created when a company treats an acquisition, for accounting purposes, as a "purchase" transaction.
>
> Under accounting rules, acquisitions treated as "pooling of interests" do not generate goodwill. Although pooling deals have drawbacks, many companies have preferred them because they could avoid goodwill charges.
>
> To create a more level playing field, the FASB recently adopted a new rule— Statement 141—that outlaws pooling. All acquisitions announced after June 30 must be accounted for under the purchase method, which means all mergers will potentially create goodwill.

The FASB's other new rule—Statement 142—says companies will no longer have to amortize goodwill on a fixed schedule.

Instead, they will only have to take write-downs when they determine goodwill has become impaired under a new method spelled out in Statement 142. The new method replaces several different methods companies use now.

Companies whose acquisitions haven't gone sour will benefit from the new rule because they won't have to take quarterly goodwill charges. Genentech, Marriott and other companies have already estimated how much the accounting change will add to earnings next year.[3]

There are a couple of other considerations for business reporters to consider in addition to bad strategic fits, accretion/dilution, and writedowns when assessing acquisitions. Sometimes, how the acquisition is structured can be vitally important to its future success.

In the 1980s, many companies were acquired in what is called a leveraged buyout, or LBO. An LBO typically occurs when the company is sold to its management and other investors who put up part of the cost to buy the company but fund the rest of the acquisition price by borrowing money, or issuing debt such as bonds. The management then hopes that it can raise enough cash by managing the company to repay the debt or bonds. Often, the management sells parts of the company to help raise the cash. Some of these LBOs of the 1980s failed when the company was not able to generate the cash to repay the debt. This can happen if a company cuts expenses such as advertising and store employees in a bid to control costs, but the result is lower sales in its stores. If a reporter is writing about an acquisition, particularly one in which the management has been involved in buying the business, he or she should always look at how the transaction is structured. Not all LBOs failed. But many resulted in companies that ended up in bankruptcy court or were forced to sell operations to raise money.

LBOs became popular because management teams could run the companies for several years and then offer stock in the company in an initial public offering— essentially selling the company to the public. In doing so, many executives became rich by selling their stock. Although LBOs do not occur with as much regularity as they used to, some acquisitions are still structured in ways that allow management to gain financially. Some companies add so-called "golden parachute" language into their corporate bylaws that allow management to receive millions of dollars should the business be sold. A golden parachute is often implemented by a company to fend off an unwanted takeover, such as a hostile takeover. But should a company decide to sell itself and its bylaws contain this language, its executives would receive stock options, bonuses or lump-sum payments should they lose their jobs as part of the transaction. In some cases, executives have received tens of millions

---

[3]From "Large goodwill write-downs a sign company made bad buyouts; JDS uniphase leads list of firms posting charges," by K. Pender, November 4, 2001, *San Francisco Chronicle*, p. E1. Copyright 2001 by San Francisco Chronicle. Reprinted with permission.

of dollars. Business reporters should look for golden parachute language in the SEC filings from the companies detailing specifics behind their deals. If reporters find such agreements in the filings, then they have got a story.

Transactions also have what are called break-up fees built into them. A break-up fee is money that a company involved in an acquisition must pay to the other company in the deal should the transaction fall through for some reason. In some cases, the break-up fee is set high to discourage a company from breaking the deal. Like golden parachutes, these break-up fees are often disclosed in the SEC filings for a deal. The existence of a break-up fee, or a golden parachute for that matter, does not mean that a deal is bad or good. But they are important potential payments of large sums of money that could result in stories.

Another important factor to consider is whether a company has adopted a poison pill statement. This allows a company to fend off an acquisition from another company if it does not want to sell. The poison pill allows a company's shareholders, other than the potential acquirer, to purchase additional shares in the company at a lower price. This forces the potential acquirer to have to pay much more than it typically would want.

Sometimes deals do fall apart even before they are completed. Another buyer may step in and offer more money, and the original buyer may bow out of the agreement. Or a company making an acquisition may run into financial difficulty and be forced to back away from a transaction. In other instances, government regulators may scuttle a deal. In some cases, the purchase price may be renegotiated if the performance of the company being sold changes dramatically. These are also details that reporters can find in a company's filings.

FINDING OUT HOW THE DEAL WAS NEGOTIATED

A story in the *San Francisco Chronicle* in late 2001 about the acquisition of Compaq by Hewlett-Packard leads with an anecdote of a financial analyst asking Hewlett-Packard President Michael Capellas if he could dance, a reference to the fancy footwork done by the executive to ensure his company's acquisition of Compaq. "I have been known to do whatever it takes," replied Capellas before breaking into a dance. This anecdote came from a private meeting between company executives, analysts, and investors. These meetings between analysts, shareholders, portfolio managers, and company executives are not typically open to the public or reporters. But there is a way for a savvy business reporter to find out what was said during those meetings, particularly if they involve a merger or acquisition. The *Chronicle* reporter makes a brief mention of where this information can be found at the end of his second paragraph (Pimental, 2001, p. E1).

Many business desks do not pay much attention to S-4s when they are filed with the SEC. But they should. These documents are important because they do the best job of any SEC filing at telling a story. First, an S-4 is filed when a company wants to sell more shares of its stock and needs shareholder approval to do so. The most common reason a company would want to sell more stock is that it wants to make an acquisition. For example, Illinois-based Arthur J. Gallagher & Company filed an S-4 in 2001 to sell an additional 12 million shares of its stock. Gallagher, which operates insurance agencies across the country, has been an active acquirer of smaller agencies in the past couple of years. In 2000, it made or announced 16 deals. The year before, it made or announced 6 deals. Just after this filing, Gallagher completed deals to buy three more agencies.

So it should come as no surprise that Gallagher's S-4 filing contains the following language:

> We expect to offer and sell the shares covered by this prospectus in connection with future acquisitions within the next two years. We anticipate that our future acquisitions will consist principally of additional insurance brokerage and related businesses. The consideration for acquisitions may include cash, including install-ment payments, shares of common stock, other securities including securities which may be converted into common stock, guarantees, assumptions of liabilities or any two or more of the foregoing, as determined from time to time by negotiations be-tween us and the owners or controlling persons of the businesses or properties to be acquired. In addition, we may enter into employment contracts and non-competition agreements with former owners and key executive personnel of acquired businesses. At this time we are engaged in preliminary discussions with a number of candidates for possible future acquisitions.
>
> In general, the terms of a future acquisition will be determined by negotiations between our representatives and the owners or controlling persons of the businesses or properties to be acquired, and the factors taken into account in an acquisition may include the established quality and reputation of the business and its management, gross commission revenues, earning power, cash flow, growth potential, location of the business and properties to be acquired and geographical and service diversification resulting from the acquisition. We anticipate that shares of our common stock issued in any future acquisition will be valued at a price reasonably related to the current market value of the common stock as reported for securities listed on the NYSE, either at the time the terms of the acquisition are tentatively agreed upon or at or about the time or times of delivery of the shares. We do not expect to receive any cash proceeds, other than cash balances of acquired companies, in connection with any such issuances. (Form S-4, Arthur J. Gallagher & Co., p. 5)

True, this is not Hemingway. And it is probably not enough by itself to warrant a story in virtually any publication. But it does give some insight into Gallagher's ac-quisition strategy and how it goes about negotiating deals with potential acquirees. It also tells readers that it is likely to announce more deals in the near future. A business reporter can use that information whenever he or she talks to Gallagher's CEO about its acquisition strategy.

Other S-4 filings can be more juicy. Consider the S-4 filed by Radian Group Incorporated on December 27, 2000 regarding the stock it was issuing as part of its acquisition of Enhance Financial Services Incorporated. It gave the reader a lot of background about the deal that had not been previously disclosed. The result was a nice story written by Dail Willis, a former *Baltimore Sun* reporter who is editor of *Insurance Mergers & Acquisitions.*

Her story told us that Radian and Enhance negotiated back and forth for months, with Enhance lowering its price more than once. The following excerpt from her story reads:

> The SEC filing states that the company engaged investment banker Morgan Stanley & Co. in late February to help it find a buyer for either the whole company or parts of it. . . . Morgan Stanley contacted 45 companies—22 possible buyers of Enhance in its entirety and 23 prospective buyers of one or more Enhance subsidiaries, the filing shows. Eight companies offered written expressions of interest. Among them was Radian, which retained investment banker Goldman Sachs & Co. to help it evaluate a possible acquisition of Enhance.
>
> On May 19, the two companies signed a confidentiality agreement and Radian began its "review of Enhance Financial Services' insurance business and some of its non-insurance subsidiaries," according to the filing.
>
> Negotiations proceeded through the summer, with Enhance also considering three other prospects—not identified in the filing—who had notified Morgan Stanley in June of their interest "regarding possible acquisitions of Enhance Financial Services or its insurance subsidiaries." In addition, Enhance in August signed a letter of intent to sell its interest in Credit-Based Asset Servicing and Securitization LLC ("C-BASS") to Residential Finance Corp., a subsidiary of General Motors Acceptance Corp.[4]

Note that sometimes S-4 filings will include competing bidders for the selling company. In the case of the Radian filing, it did not name names, but it did say there were other interested buyers. There were other juicy parts to the filing, according to the story:

> On Sept. 20, Enhance's board of directors met informally over dinner to hear Morgan Stanley's evaluation of the Radian deal. The next day, the board met again, this time formally, and discussed alternatives to the Radian deal, including merging with someone else and remaining independent.
>
> At the conclusion of the meeting, the board authorized management and Morgan Stanley to pursue a transaction with Radian, according to the filing.
>
> The discussions continued through the end of September, when Radian sent Enhance Financial Services a draft merger agreement, and on through October and into November. So did the due diligence.
>
> The terms of the agreement were revised, and revised again. Radian adjusted its initial offer of 0.2375 share of Radian stock for each Enhance share down to 0.225, with its agent Goldman Sachs citing "consideration of certain due diligence matters," according to the filing.
>
> On Nov. 8, saying "it appeared likely that the costs incurred because of the merger were likely to be greater than had been anticipated," Radian lowered its offer again— to 0.22 share of Radian for each Enhance share, according to the filing.

---

[4]From "SEC filing connects some dots in the Radian-Enhance deal,"by D. Willis, December 28, 2000, *SNL Insurance Daily*, pp. 1–2. Copyright 2000 by SNL Financial. Reprinted with permission.

Four days later, Enhance's board met by telephone to discuss the final offer, and received a fairness opinion from Morgan Stanley. Minor adjustments were made to the deal agreement on Nov. 13 and on Nov. 14 the two companies announced the deal.[5]

Although it could have been obvious to some reporters following Enhance during 2000 that the company was in some financial distress and a willing seller, the S-4 details exactly how distressed the company was, and how badly it wanted to make a deal with Radian. That is a story.

Note that these documents can often be the only source of information detailing the negotiations between acquirer and acquiree. Many times, company executives are not willing to talk about negotiations that occur in acquiring another company or selling their company. Sometimes, they will give the excuse that the transaction has not yet closed.

For the reporter trying to write a story about how an acquisition came about, the S-4 is the best place to look for background information and details about the negotiations. If executives are not willing to talk, they should be politely reminded that the information will come out when the S-4 is filed. It is surprising how many executives suddenly want to talk. Sometimes the level of detail in the negotiations and the background in an S-4 can reveal stories that should have been reported months earlier.

The American International Group Incorporated S-4 filing from September 2000, filed to sell shares as part of its acquisition of HSB Group Incorporated, however, did not warrant a story from many business reporters, and maybe it should have. The filing included previously undisclosed details such as the fact that HSB CEO Richard Booth was basically installed as the company's CEO just to sell the company. However, Booth neglected to expose this to reporters when he was interviewed after being named to the position a year earlier.

The following S-4 goes into detail about when and where Booth and AIG CEO Hank Greenberg met and what they talked about:

As part of the process Mr. Booth undertook, he met with a number of entities with which HSB then currently had or might form strategic relationships, joint ventures or other alliances. One such meeting occurred on April 13, 2000, between Mr. Booth and Mr. Maurice R. Greenberg, Chairman and Chief Executive Officer of AIG, at AIG's headquarters in New York. They discussed industry conditions, strategies being pursued by AIG and HSB and the competencies of each company in their respective marketplace. Both prior and subsequent to this meeting, Mr. Booth met with other industry senior executives to discuss potential relationships which could provide a strategic breakthrough for HSB.

---

[5]From "SEC filing connects some dots in the Radian-Enhance deal," by D. Willis, December 28, 2000, *SNL Insurance Daily*, p. 2. Copyright 2000 by SNL Financial. Reprinted with permission.

    At a June 5, 2000 meeting, Mr. Booth discussed with the HSB Board the results of
his review to date, the various strategic options available to HSB and an evaluation of
the various operating risks facing HSB. Representatives of Goldman Sachs discussed
various shareholder value issues with the HSB Board. After a thorough discussion,
the HSB Board instructed and authorized Mr. Booth to explore all strategic options,
including the possible sale of HSB. On June 14, 2000, HSB engaged Goldman Sachs
as its financial advisor in connection with possible strategic transactions, including
a possible sale of HSB. Goldman Sachs contacted nine entities regarding potential
interest in a strategic transaction with HSB. At a July 24, 2000 meeting, Mr. Booth updated the HSB Board on strategic options and Goldman Sachs reviewed shareholder
valuation issues with the HSB Board. After considerable discussion, an indication
of interest from AIG was judged to be superior, based on price and currency, to
indications of interest from other potential bidders. The HSB Board authorized Mr.
Booth to proceed with discussions with AIG.
    On July 26, 2000, Mr. Booth, Mr. Saul L. Basch, Senior Vice President, Treasurer
and Chief Financial Officer of HSB, and Mr. Normand Mercier, Senior Vice President
and Chief Global Insurance Officer of HSB, met with Mr. Greenberg and other
members of AIG senior management in New York to discuss corporate strategies and
the potential benefits of a business combination. Thereafter, AIG and HSB conducted
due diligence. AIG was provided with a form of proposed merger agreement by HSB.
Following several days of intensive negotiations, commencing early in the week of
August 13, 2000, the principal elements of a transaction and related documentation
were agreed upon.[6]

Nowhere else can a business reporter get a first-hand account about with whom
a CEO the stature of Hank Greenberg is meeting and what they are talking about
unless the CEO lets the reporter sit in on the meetings. Unfortunately, this filing
does not detail the haggling about the purchase price the way the Radian/Enhance
filing did. Maybe that is because Greenberg could have told Booth, "This is how
much I'm willing to pay for your company, and not a penny more." Sometimes
that information is in the filing, and sometimes it is not.

In this case, it was not there. For the reporter writing about a merger or acquisition, it is vitally important that he or she be on the lookout for the filing of
the S-4. Often the filing contains many more details about the transaction than
the companies released in their announcements of the deal. Likely, the filing will
divulge who other bidders were for the company, and whether the purchase price
was negotiated higher or lower during the process. In addition, the reporter can
likely get an important glimpse into the process of how a merger or acquisition
was structured. However, S-4s are often ignored by reporters who do not know to
look for them. Those that do know what they are and the information they contain
will likely make their editors happy.

All filings related to an acquisition should be reviewed, not just the S-4. An
acquisition could upset some shareholders, who could make it known through

---

[6]From Form S-4, by American International Group Incorporated, September 15, 2000,
SEC Publication No. 0000950123-00-008562, pp. 26–30. Washington, DC: Securities and
Exchange Commission.

filings that they intend to fight the deal. Such a case occurred with Hewlett-Packard's acquisition of Compaq, when a relative of one of the company's founders decided the deal was bad for the company. His filings with the SEC led to stories like the following Bloomberg News report:

Hewlett-Packard Co. director Walter Hewlett, the son of company co-founder William Hewlett, will lobby shareholders to fight the planned acquisition of Compaq Computer Corp., according to a regulatory filing.

Edwin van Bronkhorst, a shareholder and Hewlett-Packard's former chief financial officer, two sisters of Hewlett and the William R. Hewlett Revocable Trust also will participate in the proxy fight, the Securities & Exchange Commission filing said.

Hewlett and David Packard, the son of the company's other co-founder, have criticized the $23.3 billion purchase, saying it would make Hewlett-Packard more reliant on personal-computer sales and require too many layoffs. A shareholder vote is expected early next year.

"Hewlett coming out against the deal definitely raised a number of questions," said David Katz, chief investment officer at Matrix Asset Advisors Inc., which owns Hewlett-Packard shares and opposes the purchase. "Clearly, he is going to try to stop the deal."

Last week, Hewlett hired proxy-solicitation firm MacKenzie Partners Inc., which started speculation that Hewlett would go on the offensive to try to lure other shareholders to his side.

Hewlett may decide not to pursue a proxy fight, said Hewlett spokesman Todd Glass. The filing was meant to keep Hewlett's options open, Glass said, adding that "Mr. Hewlett has not decided on a course of action."

Van Bronkhorst is a former trustee of the David and Lucile Packard Foundation, which owns 10.4 percent of Hewlett-Packard's shares and hasn't said how it will vote on the deal. The two Hewlett sisters are Eleanor Hewlett Gimon and Mary Hewlett Jaffe.

Shares of Palo Alto, California-based Hewlett-Packard fell 59 cents to $21.50. Houston-based Compaq fell 40 cents to $10.30, 24 percent less than the per-share value of Hewlett-Packard's acquisition offer.

The acquisition of Compaq is "unattractive" because Hewlett-Packard's business portfolio will become worse, strategic problems won't be solved, integration risks will be "substantial" and the deal will hurt shareholders, a report prepared by Friedman Fleischer & Lowe and The Parthenon Group said. The report, commissioned by Hewlett, was filed with Hewlett's SEC statement today.

Hewlett-Packard Chief Executive Carly Fiorina is pushing investors to accept her plan to acquire Compaq. She has said the combination would broaden Hewlett-Packard's product line and emphasize more-profitable services such as consulting.

"We remain convinced the transaction is the best way to create value for shareholders, employees and customers," said Hewlett-Packard spokeswoman Rebeca Robboy. Compaq spokesman Arch Currid declined to comment on Hewlett's SEC filing.[7]

[7]From "Hewlett-Packard director to wage merger proxy fight," by P. Horvitz, November 16, 2001, Bloomberg News. Copyright 2001 by Bloomberg News. All rights reserved. Reprinted with permission.

When a company is involved in an acquisition, it is extremely important that business writers review anything that might seem remotely involved with the deal. They may be surprised at what they find.

REGULATORY OVERSIGHT OF M&A

Just because an acquisition has been agreed upon by the board of directors of both the buying and selling companies does not mean that the transaction is complete. In virtually every case, other participants in the deal must also approve the transaction. For example, shareholders vote whether to approve or turn down a deal before it goes through. Often, a company's management will line up agreements from large shareholders to get them to vote for a deal. When Hewlett-Packard announced its acquisition of Compaq, its management then spent a lot of time wooing shareholders to vote for the deal.

But there is another important player that typically has the final say on many mergers and acquisitions, particularly those that involve the two biggest companies in a certain industry or business. State and federal regulators review many acquisitions each year to determine whether the deal will hinder competition in a certain field, or whether consumers will be hurt by a transaction through unfair or deceptive acts or practices, such as higher prices by the elimination of a competitor.

All mergers and acquisitions, no matter what industry the companies are involved in, must be reviewed by the Federal Trade Commission (FTC). When a deal is announced, the FTC as well as the Department of Justice have 30 days to review the transaction. They can request an additional 30-day review period if the deal is complicated. That is why it is typical to see the statement in many news releases announcing transactions that says, "The transaction is subject to shareholder and regulatory approvals." A review by the FTC involves the filing of a Hart-Scott-Rodino report, which is confidential and almost always a formality.

Still, the FTC plays an important part in reviewing deals. According to testimony by the FTC's chairman to Congress, the number of merger filings reported to the government agency tripled between 1991 and 2000, from 1,529 transactions to 4,926 transactions. The agency's Bureau of Competition was spending more than two thirds of its resources on merger enforcement, compared with an historical average of closer to 50%, in 2001. That percentage has likely dropped in the last few years as the slowing economy has forced many companies to reconsider an acquisition or merger strategy. Still, the chairman noted that recent mergers and acquisitions are larger and often raise complex competitive issues that take more time to understand.

If the FTC reviews an acquisition and decides to oppose a deal, it can seek a preliminary injunction against the companies in federal court. The court can then grant a temporary restraining order preventing the deal from being completed until the FTC files an administrative complaint or begins an administrative proceeding. Sometimes, the FTC can simply imply to the companies involved in a transaction that the deal is unlikely to be approved. That nudge can scuttle a deal—and create a story for a business writer tracking the progress of a merger or acquisition.

The following shows a case reported in the *Washington Post* in the summer of 2002 in which communication between the federal agency and the companies ended a deal:

Less than a week after the Federal Trade Commission voiced its opposition, Gaithersburg-based Digene Corp. terminated its agreement to be acquired by Cytyc Corp.

The deal would have combined the biggest U.S. maker of Pap tests with the maker of a follow-up test. The FTC last week cited antitrust worries for its decision to block the merger.

"It's not in the best interests of the company to go through a potentially protracted and uncertain dispute in the courts with the FTC," said Charles M. Fleischman, Digene's president, chief financial officer and chief operating officer. "Instead of combining our operations with Cytyc we will continue as an independent company." Cytyc officials did not return calls seeking comment.

The two medical-testing companies reached an agreement in February, but FTC information requests pushed the acquisition deadline back to June 28 before Cytyc extended it again—for the eighth time. Either company had the right to kill the deal after June 28. Digene did so formally on Sunday.

Digene and Cytyc make medical tests for cervical cancer. Cytyc's product has a 93 percent market share for liquid-based Pap tests, according to the FTC. Digene sells a DNA-based test that detects the virus believed to cause cervical cancer. Digene's test is mostly used as a follow-up test to Cytyc's, but in the future the two could compete directly.

The FTC argued that an acquisition of Digene would eliminate Cytyc's only competitor and also hamper future competitors by limiting access to Digene's test. The merger would ultimately lead to reduced competition in the market for cervical cancer tests, the FTC said.

Digene lost $3.3 million in the three months ended March 31, and it had $18.4 million in cash. Although it is not hard pressed to raise additional financing soon, the company eventually will need help through additional funding or partnerships, according to Scott Keller, an analyst at research firm DealAnalytics.com.

"Digene is a tiny company, and they're not exactly printing cash," he said. "They're going to clearly need a partner at some point."

Digene officials, however, are committed to running the company independently now, after the failed acquisition by Cytyc.

"We have a strong company and a strong market position," Fleischman said. Cytyc would have issued 23 million shares of stock and paid $76.9 million for all of Digene's outstanding shares. When announced, the deal was valued at $553.7 million. Since then, however, shares of Boxborough, Mass.-based Cytyc have fallen more than 60 percent, cutting the deal's value to less than $250 million.

Digene stock fell $2.50, or 21.3 percent, to $9.26 a share. Cytyc fell 32 cents, or 4.2 percent, to $7.30.[8]

Digene will hold a conference call for investors and analysts on July 10 to discuss the decision to cancel the merger.

The Department of Justice also reviews large mergers and acquisitions, and may also challenge them by seeking an injunction in federal court. When a deal has been completed, the Department of Justice may require a company to divest, or sell, some of its operations. The Justice Department often works with the FTC in reviewing mergers and acquisitions, and quite often it does require changes in a deal before it can be completed. When Exxon and Mobil combined operations into one company, federal regulators forced them to sell more than 2,400 gas stations in the Northeast, Mid-Atlantic, California, and Texas because it was determined that the resulting company would have too much of the gasoline business in those markets. BP and Amoco were also required to sell some of their gas stations when they merged.

There are other regulatory agencies that look at mergers and acquisitions. The Federal Communications Commission, for example, reviews deals that involve radio and television stations. The Federal Reserve Board has a say in transactions involving banks and thrifts, as does the Office of the Comptroller of the Currency. Regulators in Europe also review transactions that involve a U.S. company buying another company with large operations there. In general, American mergers and acquisitions that would result in a company with more than $225 million in annual revenue from Europe falls under the domain of the European competition commissioner. That is how General Electric's proposed $45 billion acquisition of Honeywell International was scuttled, even though U.S. regulators had approved the deal.

State regulators also often have a say in whether a transaction goes through. The insurance industry is still largely regulated by state insurance commissioners, so any transaction in that field is approved by the regulators in the states where the companies are based. Banks also must receive state regulatory approval for mergers and acquisitions.

Business reporters should know the regulators that must approve any deal and should find out if these regulators plan to hold a public hearing on a merger or acquisition. Such hearings often occur at the state, not federal level. As in the Anthem/Trigon acquisition at the beginning of the chapter, before that deal was completed, the State Corporation Commission—a regulatory agency in Virginia where Trigon was based—held a public hearing in which a number of doctors

---

[8]From "Digene calls off merger with Cytyc, citing FTC opposition," by N. Johnston, July 2, 2002, *Washington Post*, p. E6. Copyright 2002 by *Washington Post*. Reprinted with permission.

spoke out against the deal. A reporter attending the hearing would have ended up with a nice story.

If there are no public hearings, reporters should find out what documents about the transactions are available. The FTC and the Department of Justice often ask for comments from other companies when an acquisition occurs in their industry. When Coca-Cola announced its agreement to purchase Barq's, the head of the company that owns A&W opposed the deal in a statement to the FTC. For the reporter at the *Atlanta Journal-Constitution* covering Coca-Cola, the comments made by John Brock, president of the U.S. soft drinks business of Cadbury Schweppes, turned into a story.

If the public comments for a transaction are unavailable, the reporter can simply call the companies that are the biggest competitors for the businesses involved in the transaction. A company spokesman will likely be able to divulge whether they have opposed the deal with federal regulators, and on what grounds.

As with any other business story, reporters should think about who might be affected by a merger or acquisition. In many cases, it is the other companies in that business. If a reporter can think about the effects of a deal, he or she is one step ahead of competitors at another newspaper.

GLOSSARY

accretive: An acquisition that will increase the acquiring company's EPS. As a general rule, an accretive merger or acquisition occurs when the P/E ratio of the acquiring firm is greater than that of the target firm.

acquisition: When one company purchases a majority interest in another company.

break-up fee: A fee paid by a target company to bidders (during an acquisition) if the pending deal is terminated.

dilutive: An acquisition that will decrease the acquiring company's EPS. As a general rule, a dilutive merger or acquisition occurs when the P/E ratio of the acquiring firm is less than that of the target firm.

exchange ratio: The number of shares of the acquiring company that a shareholder will receive for one share of the acquired company.

fairness opinion: An opinion developed by qualified analysts or advisors with the purpose of providing key details and factual proof to the decision makers of a merger or acquisition.

golden parachute: Lucrative benefits given to top executives in the event a company is taken over by another firm, resulting in the loss of the job. Benefits include items such as stock options, bonuses, severance pay, etc.

leveraged buyout: A strategy involving the acquisition of another company using borrowed money, i.e. bonds or loans. The acquiring company uses its assets as collateral for the loan in hopes that the future cash flows will cover the loan payments.

merger: The combining of two or more companies, generally by offering the stockholders of one company securities in the acquiring company in exchange for the surrender of their stock.

poison pill: A strategy used by corporations to discourage the hostile takeover by another company by making its stock less attractive to the acquirer.

premium: The difference between the actual cost for acquiring a target firm versus the estimate made of its value before the acquisition.

synergy: Used mostly in the context of mergers and acquisitions, synergy is the idea that the value and performance of two companies combined will be greater than the sum of the separate individual parts.

takeover: When an acquiring company makes a bid for an acquiree. If the company is publicly traded then the acquiring company will make an offer for the outstanding shares.

tender offer: An offer to shareholders to purchase some or all of their shares in a corporation. The price offered is usually at a premium to the market price. Tender offers may be friendly or unfriendly.

writedown: Reducing the book value of an asset because it is overvalued compared to market values.

REFERENCES

Brubaker, B. (2002, April 30). Indiana company to buy Trigon; Insurers agree to $3.8 billion deal. *Washington Post.* p. E1.

Form S-4. American International Group Inc. (2000, September 15). (SEC Publication No. 0000950123-00-008562, pp. 26–30). Washington, DC: Securities and Exchange Commission.

Form S-4. Arthur J. Gallagher & Co. (2001, February 9). (SEC Publication No. 0000950131-01-000770, pp. 4–5). Washington, DC: Securities and Exchange Commission.

Form S-4. Radian Group Inc. (2000, December 27). (SEC Publication No. 0000950123-00-011830, pp. 23–29). Washington, DC: Securities and Exchange Commission.

Horvitz, P. (2001, November 16). Hewlett-Packard director to wage merger proxy fight. Bloomberg News.

Johnston, N. (2002, July 2). Digene calls off merger with Cytyc, citing FTC opposition. *Washington Post.* p. E6.

Pender, K. (2001, August 2). Large goodwill write-downs a sign company made bad buyouts; JDS Uniphase leads list of firms posting charges. *San Francisco Chronicle.* p. B1.

Pimental, B. (2001, November 4). Selling the deal; HP-Compaq road show fails to convince many analysts that merger is the solution. *San Francisco Chronicle.* p. E1.

Sorkin, R. A. (2001, August 9). The warm and fuzzy version of the hostile takeover bid. *New York Times.* p. C1.

Timmons, H. (2000, June 10). How the Money Store became a money pit. *BusinessWeek.* p. 62.

Uchitelle, L. (2000, Frbruary 13). As mergers get bigger, so does the danger. *New York Times.* p. C4.

Willis, D. (2000, December 28). SEC filing connects some dots in the Radian–Enhance deal. *SNL Insurance Daily.* pp. 1–2.

Other Books on Mergers and Acquisitions

Foster Reed, S. and Reed Lajoux, A. (1998). *The art of M&A: A merger acquisition buyout guide.* New York: McGraw-Hill.

Gaughan, P. (2001). *Mergers, acquisitions, and corporate restructurings* (3rd ed.). New York: John Wiley & Sons.

Paulson, E. (1999). *The complete idiot's guide to buying and selling a business.* New York: Macmillan.

Rickertson, R., Gunther, R. & Lewis, M. (2001). *Buyout: The insider's guide to buying your own company.* New York: AMACOM.

Sherman, A. (1998). *Mergers and acquisitions from A to Z: Strategic and practical guidance for small- and middle-market buyers and sellers.* New York: AMACOM.

SUGGESTED EXERCISES

1. Find a news release for a recent merger or acquisition in your area. Answer the following questions: What information did the company disclose about the sale price? What information was released about how the acquired company will be integrated into the purchasing company? Why do you think the purchasing company decided to buy the acquiring company?

2. Find a Form S-4 for an acquisition involving stock. Review the section of the S-4 that discusses how the negotiations for the acquisition occurred. Write a 500-word analysis of the negotiations, including whether there were any other potential suitors and whether the acquired company was able to negotiate a higher stock price.

3. Discuss the differences between accretive acquisitions and dilutive acquisitions with another student. List reasons why a company would make an acquisition that was dilutive.

4. Assess the recent rise or decline in the stock price of a company making an acquisition. Do they attribute the rise or fall to the acquisition? What details about the acquisition are making investors nervous or happy?

5. Find an acquisition where the acquiring company used all stock or all cash to pay for the acquired company. If the company used all cash, assess the

company's stock price at the time of the acquisition to historical levels. If the stock is down from its all-time high, discuss whether the stock price played a part in how the acquisition was funded. If the company used stock, do the same assessment and ask why cash was not used. This exercise might require reviewing the acquiring company's cash flow statement.

7

Wall Street and IPOs

DEFINING WALL STREET, STOCKS, AND BONDS

Nothing dominates business coverage in mass communication like Wall Street. During the day, viewers of CNBC or Bloomberg TV are bombarded with live reports from the trading floor of the New York Stock Exchange, along with a rolling tape of stock prices on the bottom of the screen. Yet few beginning business reporters, let alone experienced journalists, understand enough about what is happening to be able to write a cohesive and clear story about how the stock market performed in a single day, and why the stock prices of particular companies might have risen or fallen.

In actuality, the basic principle behind Wall Street is not that complicated. Reporters should think of Wall Street as a huge marketplace, where investors from all over the world gather each day to buy and sell stocks. Although there is an actual Wall Street, a lot of the trading occurs via computer from offices around the globe. And though the U.S. exchanges—New York Stock Exchange, American Stock Exchange, and NASDAQ—are open Monday through Friday from 9:30 a.m.– 4 p.m. for trading, trading in stocks of American companies now occurs virtually 24 hrs a day in overseas exchanges and after-hours markets using computers.

Investors buy and sell stocks on the basis of how well they believe a company might perform in the future. If an investor believes that Vanilla Coke is going to boost Coca-Cola's sales and profits, he or she might be willing to buy the company's stock at $60, even though it began trading in the morning at $58. The higher the earnings in the future, the higher the stock price might rise. If another investor samples Vanilla Coke and does not like the taste, he or she may believe the product could be a failure, and sell some stock. (For a refresher on how a company's performance affects its stock price, see chap. 4.)

The old adage "buy low and sell high" was created on Wall Street because every investor buys and sells stocks, as well as other investments, to make money. The investor who purchased Coca-Cola stock at $40 per share may be willing to sell some of it at $60. In doing so, he or she has realized a 50% return on his investment. But the investor who bought Coca-Cola stock at $58 per share may want to hold onto it a little bit longer, hoping that it will rise above $60. At that price, he or she has only realized a return of 3.4%.

The trick for investors, of course, is that not all stock prices rise. Many investors who entered Wall Street in the late 1980s and rode the spectacular gains throughout the 1990s and into the 2000s came to expect double-digit gains in their stock portfolios every year. But the performance of the stock market for much of 2001 and 2002 shows that Wall Street will not always go up, and only the experienced and smart investor can continue to find and invest in stocks that will rise.

The exchanges where stocks are bought and sold are like huge grocery stores that offer every possible food and drink available. The only difference is that the consumers, or investors, are determining how much they are willing to pay. Each day, hungry investors come to the exchange, wanting to buy and sell stocks. But many of them have a set price for those stocks. If they want to buy Microsoft stock, but think that the company's shares are worth only $50 per share, then they may not be purchasing any stock. There must be a buyer for every seller of stock. Thus, the stock market operates under the economic idea of supply and demand. If there is a demand for stock in a company, then the supply of stock available to purchase at a low price might be minimal. But if the supply of stock in a company is large because many investors want to sell the stock for one reason or another, they may have to sell it at a lower price than they expected.

Stock gives an investor a piece of ownership in the company that is selling the stock. Shares are sold by businesses to raise money so that they can expand by building a new plant or buying another company. The stock is sold to investors under the idea that the money given to the company will be put to good use, resulting in higher profits and more sales that will, in turn, make the stock price go up because other investors will see the company's success and want to buy the stock too.

That is not always the case, however. Some companies fail in their strategies to expand their business. And when that happens, stock prices begin to fall as well.

For example, a widget company sells 1 million shares of stock at a price of $20 per share to a number of investors. At that price, the company has raised $20 million to expand its business. Imagine that one of those investors bought 100,000 shares, spending $2 million. That investor now owns 10% of the company, which would require him to file certain disclosures with the SEC (which are discussed in chap. 8). As the owner of 10% of the stock, the investor would be entitled to 10% of the company's assets should it be liquidated.

The prices of stocks rise and fall on the basis of a number of factors that all boil down to one overriding reason: investor sentiment. If investors believe that a stock is going to go up for whatever reason, then they are willing to pay more for that stock. The opposite also holds true. Investors may believe a stock will fall because the company is unlikely to report higher profits than in the past or because the CEO is leaving to run another company.

Investors look at a number of factors in determining whether a stock is worth buying. Some of these factors are fundamental numbers, such as the price-to-earnings (P/E) ratio and the price-to-book (P/B) value discussed in chap. 4. Others may look at quarterly earnings results, or earnings projections from analysts for future quarters or years. Still others use qualitative reasons for buying and selling stocks, such as whether they like the CEO or how often they purchase the company's products.

A business reporter asked to write a story about the stock market's performance during a day, week, month, quarter, or year will want to look at the factors that caused stocks to rise or fall. Many newspapers ask their markets reporters to focus their stories on how local stocks performed. But even in those cases, stocks could go up or down on the basis of a number of factors, many of which may not be directly related to the company. Maybe investors have become skittish about the economy or fear a war with Iraq may cut off oil supplies from the Middle East, raising the cost of doing business for many companies. Or maybe the government has released a report on spending or consumer confidence that came in below projections. Or maybe the president urged the passage of a tax cut designed to put more money into the pockets of consumers, hoping that they will go out and spend it on products and goods.

Understanding why the broader stock market rises or falls on a given day is not as easy as assessing the performance of a single stock, or the stocks of companies in a specific industry. But often, a single stock or stocks in a sector may cause the overall market to fall. For example, the Dow Jones Industrial Average is perhaps the best-known barometer of stock performance on Wall Street. Every day, hundreds of reporters detail how the Dow moved up or down. But the Dow includes just 30 stocks, albeit 30 stocks of companies that are well-known, such as Coca-Cola and Walt Disney. But if one of the stocks in the Dow happens to fall dramatically one day, it could cause the overall index to drop.

Other indexes may not fluctuate as much on the basis of the performance of a single stock. The Standard & Poor's 500 Index is made up of 500 stocks, while the

Russell 2000 Index includes the stocks of 2,000 small companies. Other indexes exist for certain industries and for specific markets.

The following excerpt is an example of a Bloomberg News story that explains why some of these indexes declined:

> U.S. stocks fell as a drop in orders for durable goods and disappointing retail sales during the holiday season gave investors new reasons to avoid equities. Financial shares including Citigroup Inc. led the decline.
>
> As the Standard & Poor's 500 Index and Dow Jones Industrial Average complete their first three-year losing streak since 1941, mounting tensions in Iraq, North Korea and Venezuela are adding to concern that growth in companies' earnings is slowing.
>
> "It's all going to add up in the negative column for the moment," said Erick Maronak, director of research at NewBridge Partners, which manages $3.5 billion. "Does it mean that we're going to get thrown back in a recessionary environment? That's tough to say."
>
> The S&P 500 fell 4.91, or 0.6 percent, to 892.47. Financial stocks accounted for one-third of the drop. The Dow Average shed 45.18, or 0.5 percent, to 8448.11, its fifth loss in six days. The Nasdaq Composite Index slid 9.22, or 0.7 percent, to 1372.47.
>
> Today was the slowest session since Christmas eve last year as trading on the New York Stock Exchange totaled 461 million shares. U.S. markets shut at 1 p.m. in New York and will remain closed tomorrow for Christmas. About eight shares fell for every seven that rose on the exchange.
>
> All three indexes have declined so far this month after gaining in October and November. For the year, the Dow has lost 16 percent, the S&P 500 22 percent and the Nasdaq 30 percent.
>
> "Everyone wanted to get excited as we finished the third down year of the market," said Crit Thomas, who helps oversee about $26 billion at National City Investment Management Co. "The market really wanted to rally, but it's having a hard time in the face of more negative news."[1]

Later in the story, the writer explains that stocks of retailers such as Best Buy, Lowes, and Target declined on the day as investors became worried about slow sales at their stores during the Christmas shopping season.

Bloomberg's handbook for reporters, called *The Bloomberg Way*, lists four questions that should be answered early in a story about the market. Those questions are the following:

- What happened to my investments today?
- Why did it happen? (theme of the day)
- How does today's move compare with the past?
- Who said what? (key quote) (1995, p. 100)

---

[1]From "U.S. Stocks fall as durable, retail data lag: Citigroup drops," by S. Fu, Dec. 24, 2002, Bloomberg News. Copyright 2002 by Bloomberg L. P. All rights reserved. Reprinted with permission.

Each of these questions are answered early in the story. It is not until the fourth paragraph that the reader is given the specific numbers indicating how the broad indexes fell on the day. *The Bloomberg Way* later advises reporters in answering the third question to consider the following comparisons:

- Biggest advance/decline since when?
- How many days in a row up/down/little changed?
- How much have prices/yields changed in that time?
- Highest/lowest level since when?
- Narrowest/widest range since when? (1995, p. 101)

Bloomberg News does perhaps the best job in writing about the market because its primary audience are the traders and investors buying and selling stocks every day. Its reporters and editors know this is a demanding reader who wants to know what is happening and why in a clear and concise manner. Too many stories about the stock market dance around the "why" without fully explaining why the market rose or fell.

Twenty and 30 years ago, reporting about the stock market was not considered important to many media outlets. But as more people across the country poured their retirement savings into 401K plans and variable annuities that invested in Wall Street, more readers wanted to know how the stock market was performing. Now, it can be argued that writing about Wall Street is one of the most important stories in mass communication today.

Investors do not just buy stocks in companies. They can also purchase another investment called bonds. A bond is considered a loan given to a company by an investor. An investor purchases the bond, and the money goes to the company. In return, the company pays the investor interest on the bond, and at the end of the bond's term, pays the balance of the bond. To illustrate, a company sells $100 million in bonds at an interest rate of 6.75% over a 30-year period. Each year, the company pays the interest to investors, and at the end of 30 years, pays the $100 million back. A company hopes to recoup the $100 million and the interest paid by using the money during that time period to expand its operations into new businesses that will bring in much more than the cost of the interest. The longer the time period for the bond, the higher the interest rate the company will pay. For example, a one-year bond may only give an investor a 3% yield. But the 30-year-bond would pay 6.75% a year. So-called junk bonds are issued by companies that have low credit ratings from companies such as Standard & Poor's or Moody's. Because of their low ratings, these companies must offer higher yields to attract investors. Some bonds issued by these companies may offer returns of more than 10%.

Bonds are traded every day in the market, just like stocks. But what usually trips up business reporters is that when the price of a bond goes up, the yield declines, and vice versa. For example, if one investor buys a $1,000 bond from a company with a 7% return, he would receive $70 a year from the company until the bond matures, when he would receive his $1,000 back. But if the investor sells that bond for $999, the yield goes up slightly, because the new bondholder would get the $1,000 back when the bond expired—more than what he originally paid—in addition to the interest payments.

One important distinction between bonds and stocks occurs when a company files for bankruptcy court protection. When this happens, a bondholder is usually first in line to be repaid what he is owed. But a stockowner rarely, if ever, gets anything in a bankruptcy proceeding. (For more on bankruptcy court, see chap. 11.)

But bonds and stocks are alike in a fundamental manner: They are both sold by large Wall Street firms known as brokerage houses or investment banks. Many of these firms have long-standing relationships with the companies whose stocks and bonds they are selling to investors. And they have offices across the country where their stockbrokers try to get investors to purchase shares in these companies. When investors want to purchase stock, they place orders with their stockbrokers. The orders are typically for a set number of shares (e.g., 1,000) for a specific dollar amount (e.g., $20 per share). The broker then goes out to find a buyer willing to sell those shares at that price. These firms do not buy stocks and bonds, they only sell and receive commission fees on the shares they sell. The more shares they sell, the more money they make. That is why these companies have stockbrokers and people called sell-side analysts who peddle these stocks to investors. Whereas local stockbrokers primarily spend their time selling stocks to local, small-time investors, analysts focus on selling these stocks to large investors known as institutional investors. An institutional investor is someone who buys and sells stocks for a living. He or she may work for an insurance company, or a mutual fund operation. But the job is to find stocks before they go up in price, and sell them before they fall. Sometimes institutional investors are successful in accomplishing that task, but other times they are not.

The analysts at a stock brokerage house will research the companies in which their firm is selling stock and determine which ones are the best investments. Recent investigations into this practice, however, discovered the secret that most professional investors on Wall Street already knew—that analysts were influenced by the firms to push stocks of companies with which their employer did business, such as helping it find potential acquisitions or sell more stock and bonds.

Because of these investigations, the credibility of Wall Street has suffered in the eyes of many consumers, and with business reporters as well. Some media outlets now require their reporters to divulge the potential conflicts of interest between an investment banking firm's analysts and its other businesses when quoting the analyst. Stories now typically read something like the following:

> "Widget Co.'s earnings were much stronger than its competitors because it's built a better widget," said Fred J. Muggs, an analyst at Salomon Smith Barney who owns shares in the company. However, his firm has not done investment banking business for the company.

A business reporter needs to know the relationship between an analyst and the stocks he or she is following to help determine whether the analyst is as objective as possible. See the "sell-side and buy-side analysts" section later in this chapter for a closer look at sell-side analysts and the role they play in business reporting.

WHAT INFLUENCES INVESTOR DEMAND FOR STOCKS

Demand for a stock can rise and fall from one day to the next. But over months and years, there are some stocks that are constantly in demand by investors. All stocks are not created equal, and how the companies that issue these stocks perform typically determines what investors are willing to buy them, and at what price.

Investors come in all shapes and sizes, and with all kinds of preconceived ideas about what stocks perform better than others. It is important for a business reporter to understand the connections among a company's business strategy, its size, its management team, and its past history and whether investors would be willing to purchase its stock. Some investors may want to acquire stocks in companies where there is great potential for future growth.

In the mid-1990s, a grocery store chain in Atlanta called Harry's Farmers Market went public, selling shares to investors with the promise that it was going to revolutionize the grocery industry in much the same way that Home Depot had changed the do-it-yourself business. Early investors in Home Depot, after it went public in 1981, became millionaires many times over as a result of the company's rapid growth, which made it one of the top 10 retailers in the world. But Harry's was not able to follow up on its promise. It never expanded outside of the Atlanta market, and many of its investors lost money.

For every Harry's, however, there is a Home Depot or a Microsoft. Investors who like to buy stocks of companies in which there is a lot of growth potential look for what are called growth stocks. Investors in growth stocks are looking for the price of the stock to rise because of the increase in the company's revenue profits as a result of an expansion plan. Most growth stocks do not pay dividends to their investors. Growth companies are businesses in which revenues or profits are typically increasing at multiples of the rest of the company. Revenues may be rising by 30% every quarter, and profits may be increasing by 25% or more.

The opposite of a growth-oriented investment strategy is one that focuses on buying stocks in companies on the basis of their value. So-called value investing looks at the worth of the stock price compared with quantitative barometers. For example, a value investor may look to purchase stocks that appear cheap on the basis of the P/B value.

If a company's P/B value is below that of its competitors or the overall market, then an investor may consider it to be cheap. A value investor may also look at a stock on the basis of its P/E ratio. If a stock price of a company is trading at around

10 times its earnings, but the rest of the stock market is trading at around 15 times earnings, then that stock may be considered to have value.

The opposite is also true. If the P/B or P/E of a company gets to be higher than the rest of the market or competitors, then an investor may consider selling his holdings. It is wise for reporters to track these values of the companies on their beats to look for potential stories about why the stock price is rising or falling.

Other value investors prefer to purchase stocks in companies that pay dividends to their investors. A dividend is a payout to investors, often done on a quarterly basis, that serves as an incentive to own the stock. For example, Atlanta-based Southern Company, a power company, currently pays the people who own its stock about $ .34 as a quarterly dividend for every share they own. Many investors purchase stocks just to receive the quarterly dividend check from a company. That is why it is always a story when a company decides to cut its dividend and use that money elsewhere. Cutting a dividend will cause investors to sell the stock, leading to a drop in the stock's price.

For the most part, investors who take a growth-oriented strategy to investing are taking a greater risk than value investors. Growth means that a company is expanding, and growing means that there is always the chance of something going wrong. Maybe a retailer is putting its stores in the wrong place. There is less risk with value investing, in general, because these are companies looking to entice investors with their slow, methodical growth. However, a growth-investing strategy may also pay greater rewards for the investor if the company is successful in growing itself at a fast rate.

Another quantitative attraction for investors to a stock is reputation, or reliability. For most of the 1990s, GE and Coca-Cola were attractive stocks to own for many investors because they routinely reported earnings that met or beat Wall Street expectations. Although these companies were criticized for sometimes using accounting changes to control their earnings growth, investors appreciated their ability to match what Wall Street predicted. Investors do not like negative surprises, and if a company can report earnings that are in line with estimates, then the stock price is unlikely to fall.

Investors, and business reporters, can measure this reliability simply by comparing the numbers. If Company X reports second-quarter earnings of $.25 per share, but was expected to report earnings of $.27 per share, investors may be scared off. But if the company was expected to report earnings of $.24 per share, then investors are more likely to be happy. This last point is an important one for business reporters to consider, particularly when they are writing stories about a company's earnings performance. A strong earnings performance could cause its stock price to rise, but weak results could lead to a drop in the stock price. If either one of these is the case, it is good to call an investor and talk to him or her about the stock's movement.

The size of a company can also be a determining factor in whether an investor purchases its stock. Some investors refuse to even look at the stock of any company that has a market capitalization of less than $1 billion. The market capitalization is the value of the company on Wall Street, and is computed by multiplying the current stock price by the number of shares outstanding. Other investors like to purchase stock in companies that have small market capitalizations. Some mutual funds, for example, specialize in investing in companies with market caps, as they are called, of less than $500 million.

Other investors may be looking solely at the company's strategy or how it is structured. There are a number of investors spread across the country whose strategy is simply to purchase stock of thrifts that convert from being owned by the depositors into one that sells its shares on the market and is owned by stockholders. These investors have made money in the past on these conversions, and they are willing to bet that others will also make them money.

Many investors also look at the company's business strategy with regard to how it sells its product or services. Investors are often more willing to purchase a stock in a company if they use that company's product. Many investors look at how a product is sold, or at a company's local store. For example, an investor may go into a Gap store and see many customers, but if he or she notices that a number of those shoppers walk out without buying shirts and jeans, then the investor may think about selling some of his or her stock. Another investor may want to buy stock in Starbucks because he or she has to wait in long lines every day for a cup of coffee.

Another qualitative measure that many investors consider is a company's management. Like business reporters, investors like to meet and talk with a CEO and a CFO of a company. How an investor perceives management's ability to run the company and espouse a coherent strategy can go a long way in determining whether he purchases stock. If an investor comes away from a meeting with a CEO thinking that the company leader does not have a firm grasp on its operations, then he is unlikely to buy the stock. Conversely, if the CEO can explain his vision for the company in a way that makes sense, investors will be more likely to purchase the stock.

There are other investors that simply look for companies that might be acquired by other companies. Because acquiring companies often pay more than the value at which a selling company's stock is currently trading, a savvy investor who can find companies that are for sale or could be bought if the right buyer came along can make a lot of money. After the Gramm-Leach-Blilely Act was passed by Congress in 1999, many investors looked to purchase stock in insurance companies and financial services companies because the new law allowed banks to own these companies for the first time. A reporter who recognizes the significance of such an event can find a nice story that will inform readers through interviewing investors who will make decisions on buying and selling stocks on the basis of new development.

There are still other investors who look for companies of which they believe that the stock price is actually going to fall. These investors are called short-sellers, and are not actually purchasing the stock of the company. Instead, they are borrowing stock from a stockbroker, betting that the price is going to fall. This investment strategy can be extremely risky, because if the stock price rises, the short-seller continues to lose money until he stops borrowing the stock. Many such investors spend intense weeks and months examining a company's financial statements to find a business that may be having problems and could see its stock price drop.

By now, it should be evident that it is important for a business reporter to understand the different reasons for why an investor becomes attracted to buying stock in a company. If a business reporter can develop sources among investors that only buy stocks in companies that might be sold, then he or she is likely to be able to write a story about that company being sold days and even weeks before an official announcement is made.

Or take the case of Bethany McLean, the *Fortune* writer credited with detailing the potential problems at Enron less than nine months before it reported huge losses and filed for bankruptcy court protection. McLean was initially tipped off that Enron may need closer examination by an investor, Jim Chanos of Kynikos Associates, who was shorting the company's stock. Chanos suggested that McLean review the company's Form 10-K.

McLean said she found "strange transactions," "erratic cash flow" and huge debt. "It made you wonder, if their business was so phenomenally profitable, why they had to be adding debt at such a rapid rate," said McLean in a *Washington Post* article about how she wrote her story. (Kurtz, 2002, p. C1)

Now, the motive behind Chanos' discussion with McLean is obvious. He was interested in seeing a story in print which was critical of the company in the hopes that it would cause the stock to fall. As long as a business reporter understands that an investor always has a motive, then these people can be valuable sources of information. For instance, when working on any type of story that involves a public company, a reporter should consider calling investors. They often know more about the company than the business reporter, as they have researched the company's strategy, management, past performance, and operations.

To be sure, all investors have a vested interest in what a reporter is writing. Many of them want to see the stock price of the company go up, whereas others want to see the stock price fall. But an investor may also have more access to company management than a reporter, and thus may be able to provide more insight into what is going on at a business, particularly if the company is not talking. A large investor in a company typically gets his phone calls returned quickly from a CEO or a CFO. In addition, just because an investor has a vested stake in the performance of a company does not mean he is going to gush about its performance. Many investors, particularly those who believe management is not doing enough to increase the stock price, will be honest in talking to reporters assessing a company. Many large investors freely and openly criticize companies in which they are investors. They may be upset that the stock price is falling.

Notice how the following story from the *San Jose Mercury News* uses an investor to explain why other investors should be upset. The story also explains why the investor was interested in buying the stock in the first place:

When Internet software company Unify Corp., of San Jose, admitted Monday that it had overstated its revenue for its last fiscal year and possibly the previous fiscal year as well, it looked like other cases in which ambitious executives at high-tech companies may have engaged in creative accounting.

But over the last few days, upset investors in the company have focused on another unsettling fact: At the same time the company was overstating its revenue—and thus boosting the market's valuation of the company—the company's CEO Reza Mikailli was busy selling, or otherwise disposing of, many of his 1.4 million shares.

In fact, according to his filing with the Securities and Exchange Commission and confirmed by the company, Mikailli had sold all of his shares in the company by June 20—about six weeks before the company announced its revenue problems and Nasdaq halted trading in the company's shares this Monday. All told, since June 1999, he has sold shares valued at $7.34 million. "Can this be normal?" said Mark Gardy, a partner at Abbey, Gardy & Squitieri, a law firm that has also filed a class-action lawsuit on behalf of Unify's investors. "I don't believe in coincidence when you reduce your holdings to zero just before bad news comes out."

On Monday, the company put Mikailli and the company's chief financial officer, Gary Pado, on leave and announced it had engaged in "improper accounting practices." This meant the company had "improperly recognized" revenues during the last fiscal year, and perhaps the one before that.

The company's board said the company's audit committee is investigating the matter, and that it has retained Gray Cary Ware & Freidenrich as counsel. Gray Cary, in turn, has asked PricewaterhouseCoopers to assist with the investigation as independent auditors.

Unify's outside auditors, Deloitte & Touche, are also participating.

The company has provided no other information on why it chose to put the two executives on leave, or why Deloitte & Touche had not discovered the revenue mis-stating problem earlier. Mikailli did not return a phone call to his Saratoga residence, and his lawyer could not be reached for comment.

Eleven law firms representing shareholders have already filed lawsuits against the company, most of them alleging that the executives sought to profit by wrongfully boosted revenue.

"As a result of Unify's alleged misrepresentations and omissions, the price of Unify's stock was artificially inflated," alleges a class-action suit by Kirby McInerney & Squire, in New York, "allowing insiders to receive artificially high prices for selling their stock and forcing investors to pay artificially high prices to buy the stock."

A number of questions are hanging over the stock sales of Mikailli and other company's insiders. Mikailli suffered a heart attack June 5, and the company announced he was taking medical leave June 6, though the company says he is currently at home.

On Friday, company spokeswoman Deb Micciche said many of Mikailli's sales came to light only three weeks ago, when he was apparently "catching up" on some of his filings to the Securities and Exchange Commission of stock sales. Only then, during the week of July 17, did his disposal of between 700,000 and 900,000 shares suddenly show up in public documents, she said.

At least 163,000 shares were categorized by Mikailli in his filings as "disposed via transfer," though Micciche says the company still has no idea to whom or where the shares were transferred. Normally, such a category refers to a transfer to a relative or to a personal trust.

Pado, the CFO, sold 14,595 shares in May, or about a fourth of his total holding of 53,115 shares, according to the Web site insiderwatch.com. Vice President Frank Verardi sold 50,000 shares in May, about two-thirds of his holdings of 77,850 shares.

Investors, meanwhile, were broadsided. David Kupler, a Hayward investor in Unify, said he was tracking insider sales at Unify on insiderwatch.com and saw that Mikailli still appeared to have about half of his position left in May. He went to the company's annual reports, checked its debt and cash levels, and concluded that the company's shares looked like a good buy.

"I bought the stock," said Kupler, "but I based my analysis on public documents. If the company cooks the books, how can I make the right decision?" Kupler spent $12,000 to buy the shares at about $6 each. They slid to $3.94 on Monday when Nasdaq stopped their trading.

"This is extraordinarily suspicious," Kupler says. "Insiders sell their shares in their own company all the time, but they usually hold on to a few."[2]

This story has plenty of skepticism about the stock trading. That's a sign of a good reporter.

SELL-SIDE AND BUY-SIDE ANALYSTS

For decades, sell-side analysts who track stocks and bonds have been the business reporter's best friend. Analysts regularly take phone calls from reporters wanting to talk about everything from a company's CEO to the new potato chip it is rolling out next month. Become friendly with analysts, and quote them fairly, and they will return reporters' phone calls and likely tip them off to potential news at a company. In return, the media made analysts such as Henry Blodgett, Mary Meeker, and Jack Grubman stars, trumpeting their bold prognostications that a stock was going to double in the next year. As the stock market rose higher and higher, so did the public stature of the sell-side analyst.

Analysts, however, have come under increasing scrutiny as to whether they are an objective voice in discussing the companies and stocks they cover. Some of the analysts who made bold predictions about the future of technology or telecommunications companies came under fire when those businesses failed or filed for bankruptcy court protection. Many of them privately thought the companies they covered were feeble, but maintained bullish recommendations of "strong buy" or "buy" because of financial relationships their firms had with the companies.

Any business reporter who covers a public company followed by sell-side analysts should now be well aware of the inherent conflicts of interest. It is the job of the analyst to sell stock of the companies they cover to investors. However, the analyst's firm may have other business relationships with the companies they cover.

_____

[2]From "Stock sale jolts Unify investors," by M. Marshall, August 5, 2000, _San Jose Mercury News_, p. 1C. Copyright 2000 by _San Jose Mercury News_. Reprinted with permission. All rights reserved.

The firm may be the company's investment bankers, which means it receives fees anytime the company decides to sell more stock, issue additional debt, or make an acquisition. As such, many analysts in the past have received pressure to paint a rosy picture about a company's future.

With hundreds of millions of dollars in fines now levied against Wall Street firms for these unethical practices, sell-side analyst research operations are overhauling how they do business. More of them are now grading stocks as "sell" or "neutral," which means that the shares of the company are not worth buying, at least in the mind of the analyst. Other firms have created stricter separations between their research departments and their investment banking outfits.

A business reporter should still value the sell-side analyst as a source of information. In a way, both the reporter and the analyst are in the same job. They both inform people about companies, and they both go about their jobs by asking questions and examining a company's operations. The only difference is that a reporter does his or her job to better inform readers, whereas the analyst does his or her job to better inform investors. Good analysts for the business reporter are those that know inside and out the companies they follow. They are willing to criticize a company when it is warranted, and praise it when laudatory remarks are warranted. Like a business reporter, an analyst should call a spade a spade.

In addition, analysts are like reporters in that they write about the companies they track. The analyst's report can be a revealing insight into what a Wall Street pro thinks about a company's future. Any reporter writing regularly about a public company should be reading research reports about the operation to get a feel for what the investment community thinks. Some reports are short, no more than a page. They sing with their simplicity. Other reports, particularly reports in which an analyst is initiating coverage on a company, can be long documents, often 30 pages or more, and filled with charts and data. Some analysts are excellent writers and do a great job in explaining the rationale behind their feelings about a company. Others have subordinates write the reports. A company often lists the analysts who follow its stock and issue research reports on its Web site under the "Investor" section. The number of analysts following a company can range from one or two to nearly three dozen for a large company such as GE.

Virtually all analysts issue recommendations for the stocks they cover. At most Wall Street firms, the top recommendations are "strong buy" or "buy." This means that the analyst believes that the company's stock will outperform a broader market index, such as the Standard & Poor's 500 or the Dow Jones, during the next 12 months. These are the stocks that the analysts are pushing their clients to acquire. Many times, an analyst will own the stock in his personal investment portfolio, though some Wall Street firms now require analysts to disclose what stocks they own.

Lower ratings from analysts for stocks could be "outperform" or "accumulate." These rankings are not as strong as the "strong buy" or the "buy" ratings, but they still indicate the analyst believes the stock is likely to beat the performance of the overall market. Lower ratings are "neutral" or "hold." In previous years, these ratings often meant that an investor should sell the stock. But as many Wall Street brokerage houses attempt to overhaul their rating system, these ratings may begin to mean what they actually state, that the stock has become fully priced in relation to the rest of the market and is unlikely to rise soon. The lowest rating from an analyst is a "sell" rating. Studies showed that only about 1% to 2% of all analysts' ratings were the equivalent of a "sell" shortly before the market fell in 2000. Although the number of these ratings has increased in recent years, stocks with "sell" ratings only accounted for about 8% of the total 24,000 stock recommendations made by analysts in late 2002, according to a *Los Angeles Times* article on the subject (Peltz, 2002, p. 4). And many of those lower ratings were put on companies only after their stock prices fell by 50% or more.

It is important for a business reporter to know what an analyst's rating is on a company's stock if he or she plans to quote that person in a story. If an analyst is making very positive comments about a company during an interview but has a "hold" rating on its stock, then that should raise questions in the reporter's mind as to whether the analyst is accurately portraying his or her feelings, in either the interview or the report. The same questions should arise if an analyst makes negative statements about a company but gives it a "strong buy" rating. If the reporter does not know what the analyst's rating is on a company, he or she should always ask during the interview. Many analysts provide copies of their research reports to reporters via mail or e-mail. A reporter should ask to get on the analyst's mailing list. Reporters should read analyst reports thoroughly and look for clues about changes in an analyst's thinking about a stock. The most obvious change would be if the analyst downgrades his rating on a company from a "buy" to a "hold," for example. Upgrades from the analyst should also garner some attention. If the change in the rating is based on newsworthy information about the company, then the reporter should write a story like the following one written by this *Baltimore Sun* reporter about a shopping mall developer:

A financial analyst accused Rouse Co. yesterday of improperly accounting for $25 million in expenses, a move that allowed the shopping mall giant to report record quarterly earnings to the public.

David Fick, an analyst at Legg Mason Wood Walker Inc., said investors were being misled by the company and recommended they sell the stock.

Rouse executives said the company did nothing wrong but acknowledged that they did not follow industry guidelines by excluding such expenses as bonuses and retirement costs from funds from operations, a benchmark of performance used by most real estate investment trusts.

"We felt what we were doing was providing the best measure of recurring income," said David Tripp, a Rouse vice president and director of investor relations. "We were upfront in how we were calculating our results. We don't think it would have given you a very good big picture to have added those charges." The sell order did not appear to affect Rouse stock, which closed yesterday at $29.40, down 20 cents.

Fick made his recommendation a day after Rouse released its third-quarter earnings. The company reported Monday that in the quarter that ended Sept. 30, its funds from operations were $96.8 million, or $1.03 a share, compared with $69.9 million, or 92 cents a share, in last year's third quarter.

Fick said the company was able to report record results only because it excluded the $25 million it planned to spend by the end of year on a signing bonus for a new executive and costs related to buyouts, retirements and layoffs.

Rouse took an $8.6 million third-quarter charge and said it would take a $16.4 million charge this quarter. Had Rouse included the expenses in funds from operations, Fick said, the costs would have reduced per-share earnings by 12 cents, or 19 percent, in the third quarter.

"They should not be allowed to get away with this kind of misleading financial report," Fick said. "We ultimately believe that they reported their earnings incorrectly."

Fick's sell rating was also based on other factors, such as the company's handling of its development pipeline, he said, adding, "This is not a crash and burn by Rouse by any means. Our view is that over the next 18 months to two years Rouse will underperform its sector. But it's not a cancerous situation."

Funds from operations are not reported to the federal Securities and Exchange Commission, although they are a key gauge used by analysts and investors. The benchmark was developed by the National Association of Real Estate Investment Trusts to better represent the year to year earnings of companies by excluding such noncore and sometimes fluctuating expenses as depreciation of property.

Others agreed that Rouse did not adhere to industry standards.

"Severance to people who are laid off is probably appropriately a one-time cost, but bonuses to executives and that kind of stuff are not," said Howard Schilit, head of Center for Financial Research & Analysis Inc. "It seems interesting to even have those two things in the same sentence."

Matthew Ostrower, an analyst with Morgan Stanley in New York, said Rouse's expenses should have been included in the earnings. He has a positive rating on the company's stock.

"We do not agree with the way Rouse accounted for" funds from operations, he said. "We believe the $25 million charge should have been included in FFO. However, if we were to downgrade every mall REIT that violated the FFO rules at one time or another, we would likely have a sell recommendation on every mall REIT."

During a conference call to analysts Monday evening, Rouse Chairman and Chief Executive Officer Anthony W. Deering characterized the third- and fourth-quarter charges as one-time restructuring costs. He said it was proper to exclude them from funds from operations. However, he acknowledged to an analyst that challenged the accounting that the calculation violated the industry association guidelines.

Some analysts expressed surprise at the size of the one-time charges. But Rouse said it believes Fick was the only analyst to downgrade the stock yesterday. Some charges stem from a major restructuring uncommon at Rouse, known for its executives' decades-long tenures and promotion from within.

The company, which develops shopping malls and communities such as Columbia and Summerlin, Nev., is facing a depleting pipeline of development because the nation has enough shopping centers. Rouse has hired a new vice chairman and chief financial officer from outside the company, merged two divisions and has promoted a number of high-level staffers. Two senior executives have announced their retirements.

Fick and other analysts have praised the moves, which aim to reduce the company's costs by $5 million a year and infuse new leadership. But Fick noted other challenges facing the company in recommending that investors sell the stock.

He said some Rouse centers, such as Owings Mills Mall, continue to do poorly and that the general retail climate is not improving. Office building vacancies are up, and new malls in Coral Gables, Fla., and Las Vegas will require a few years to lease and start contributing to earnings.

Land sales fueled by a hot residential market will begin to decline if interest rates rise, he said. Rouse credits those sales for the record quarter reported yesterday.

Also, Fick said, Rouse is carrying a lot of debt, partly to pay for the acquisition of all or parts of eight premier shopping centers purchased this year. The debt will hamper further acquisitions, he said.[3]

This story explains why the analyst downgraded the stock, and adds comments from another analyst who did not lower his rating. That is the type of information from an analyst report that leads to a story. In addition, many analyst firms have simplified their rating systems because many technology stocks fell precipitously in the early 2000s. Many stock ratings are not as hard to decipher as they were before.

Another potential story in an analyst report could be written when the analyst changes his earnings estimates for a company. The best reports changing quarterly or annual earnings per share estimates come out before the company issues an earnings advisory stating that it will be unable to meet the consensus analyst estimate—the average earnings estimate for a company on the basis of the predictions of all of the analysts covering the company. Research reports that change estimates after the company issues its guidance are merely following the herd, and are not likely worth a story unless the new estimate from the analyst is dramatically lower than the number given by the company.

Also, a reporter should be wary of an analyst's report that changes a company's earnings estimates downward after a company has issued an earnings warning, but does not downgrade the rating, especially if that rating is a "strong buy" or "buy." An earnings warning is a company's way of telling Wall Street that the fundamentals of its operations are not clicking on all cylinders.

Most analyst reports also have a price target noted on them. This is the price that the analyst thinks the stock will hit sometime in the next 12 months. If a report does not have a price target, it will often be because of an overall "neutral" or "avoid" rating on the stock. Beware of analyst reports that do not have a price target, but also have a "strong buy" or "buy" rating. If it is really such a strong buy, the analyst would tell investors, or business reporters, how strong he or she thinks it will be. Reporters should always look at the company's current stock price in relation to the price target. If the current stock price is near the analyst's price target, then the reporter should expect the analyst to raise the price target if he or she thinks the stock can go even higher. Or the reporter should expect the analyst to downgrade the stock because he or she now believes the stock is fully valued.

---

[3]From "Legg analyst accuses Rouse of a misleading 3Q report," by M. Cohn, October 30, 2002, *Baltimore Sun*, p. 1C. Copyright 2002 by *Baltimore Sun*. Reprinted with permission.

Most analysts estimate revenue, income, earnings per share, and other numbers for a company in their reports for the next year or two years. These numbers are quite often a better barometer of how well the analyst thinks the company is going to perform going forward. If the analyst has a "strong buy" rating on a company, but is only projecting 5% earnings growth, something is wrong.

There are other analysts who follow the stocks of public companies. These analysts are called buy-side analysts and credit analysts. A buy-side analyst is someone who works for an investment firm such as a mutual fund company or even a local university's investment operations. These analysts can also be valuable sources for business reporters, but few of them issue reports on the stocks that they follow for the outside world. Buy-side analysts provide their research on companies to investors within their company.

A credit analyst is someone who tracks the debt offerings for a company. These analysts often work for the same Wall Street firms as the buy-side analysts, but they are analyzing the debt, not the stock, issued by a company. They may also work for a credit rating agency. Analysts for rating agencies did a much better job of raising concerns about Enron and other companies that recently encountered problems.

IPOs AND THE INFORMATION THAT
GETS DISCLOSED

When a private company wants to convert and become a public company, it makes a large filing with the SEC. A Form S-1 filing can be the most important filing for a business reporter because it gives the first glimpse of a company that has previously been private and has not disclosed any financial information or analysis of its performance. The S-1 is the statement filed with the SEC that tells the world: "We want to sell stock in our company to the public, and we think there are enough people out there willing to take a chance on our future." The Wall Street community then reviews the filing and determines whether it wants to invest money in the company. Often, a company will amend these filings, adding more information.

For a business reporter, the S-1 can provide some valuable information. We can find out how much money a private company has made, or lost, in the past. Reviewing the financial performance disclosed in this filing is the first step any business reporter should take. A reporter always wants to read this over very carefully, and compare (a) how the company did in its most recent quarter with how it did the same quarter a year ago, and (b) how it did in its most recent full fiscal year with the previous year's performance. That will give the reporter a good indication as to whether the company's earnings are increasing. For example, the initial S-1 statement for Hartford-based Phoenix Companies, which went public during the summer of 2001, did not disclose its first-quarter 2001 financial performance, but an amended statement filed in May 2001 did disclose those numbers. The company reported loss in the first quarter, compared with a profit in the same quarter during 2000.

How does a business reporter take this information and write a story about it? The *Hartford Courant's* Diane Levick wrote a story on the day the filing occurred, leading with the fact that the company reported a net loss of $157.5 million in the first quarter because of losses in its venture capital investments. (Levick, 2001)

The second paragraph of Levick's story mentions that the company had reported a profit in the same quarter the previous year—another fact disclosed in the filing—and then the story mentions that the company faces two lawsuits challenging its initial public offering (IPO).

Levick read the entire filing and compared what was in the filing with information disclosed in an earlier filing. By taking the time to read and analyze the filing, she wrote a story that was helpful to readers in explaining the company's performance.

It is also good to note dramatic shifts for the positive. London-based Willis Group Holdings' F-1 statement (similar to an S-1, but filed by foreign companies) disclosed that the company reported net income of $9 million, or $.07 per share, in 2000. In 1999, the broker lost $132.0 million, or $1.11 per share. Willis' profits are still below the range of competitors, so it is also good to compare profits and profit margins with comparable companies. The filing often details the company's plans for future growth, as well as potential pitfalls in its strategy.

The initial S-1 statement may not always include the specific amount of money the company wants to raise by going public. And it may not initially include the stock price range at which the company believes it can sell its stock, or the total number of shares it plans to sell. But these are the most important numbers, and the numbers that every investor wants to know because the number of shares that a company hopes to sell in its IPO can give investors an indication of how popular this offering might be. The more shares a company sells, in general, the more interest the underwriters are having in getting their clients to buy the stock.

The stock price range is also important because it can be an indication of the demand for the offering. In Levick's story (2001), she noted that Phoenix initially filed its S-1 and gave a stock price range of $9 to $16 per share. Later, it increased the range of the offering to $14.50 to $17 per share in an amended S-1 filing. That shows people who track these things that the underwriters are getting a lot of interest from investors in the stock. And that is the kind of information that business reporters should be tracking and writing stories about.

But it is not that simplistic. Note that the changes in the stock price range should be looked at in conjunction with the number of shares being offered. At the same time Phoenix increased the stock price range of its offering it also decreased the amount of shares in the IPO, from 73.8 million to 48.8 million. It upped the price but lowered the amount of shares it is going to sell. This is a case of basic supply-and-demand economics. The fewer shares, the greater the demand from investors; thus, in all likelihood, Phoenix will up the price. It is important to always check for amended S-1 filings to see if the stock price range or the number of shares being offered has changed. And the total amount of money that the company hopes to raise in the IPO may also change.

Normally included on the bottom of the first page of the S-1 statement is a list of the underwriters of the stock offering. The underwriters are the Wall Street firms that will sell chunks of the company's stock to investors. This is important information for a business journalist to assess because the listing of the underwriters will indicate how successful the company could be in selling the stock. If big Wall Street firms like Goldman Sachs, Salomon Brothers, JP Morgan, and Morgan Stanley are listed as underwriters, the disclosure should be a sign that these firms will be selling as much of the offering to their institutional clients as possible. That increases the chances of the IPO rising shortly after the stock begins trading. It is important to note, however, relationships between the underwriters and the company going public detailed in the S-1 filing. Sometimes that tells a better story of why a Wall Street firm is an underwriter in the offering.

Consider the following nugget from a recent S-1 filing by Max Re Capital:

> Mr. Mario P. Torsiello, one of our directors, currently serves as a Managing Director of Dresdner Kleinwort Wasserstein, Inc., an affiliate of which, Dresdner Kleinwort Wasserstein Securities LLC, is acting as an underwriter in this offering. Salomon Smith Barney Inc., an affiliate of Citigroup, Inc., acted as placement agent for our second private equity offerings, for which it received $5.8 million in fees, and is also acting as underwriter for this offering. Mr. William H. Heyman, one of our directors, is the Chairman of Citigroup Investments, Inc., an affiliate of Salomon Smith Barney Inc. and one of our principal shareholders.
>
> Bank of America, N.A., an affiliate of Banc of America Securities LLC, one of the underwriters in this offering, and Citibank, N.A., an affiliate of Salomon Smith Barney Inc. and Citigroup, participate in our syndicated U.S. bank $300 million letter of credit facility. Each of Bank of America, N.A. and Citibank, N.A. committed $100 million to the facility.[4]

This is obviously a case of "you scratch my back, and I'll scratch yours." In today's business world, such relationships are coming under increased scrutiny by regulators. And if regulators are interested in such information, then it is obvious that a business reporter should also care about these disclosures, and likely should be writing stories about them.

One of the most important disclosures a company makes in an S-1 is its tangible book value. This is what every investor wants to know, and this information will tell people buying the stock whether the shares are worth more or less than the company's actual value.

An investor would like to buy stock at a price near the tangible book value. But that is not what happened with the Willis Group Holdings' IPO. Its F-1 filing noted

---

[4]From Form S-1, by Max Re Capital, May 31, 2000, SEC Publication No: 0000950130-01-502080, p. 81. Washington, DC: Securities and Exchange Commission.

that it had a negative net tangible book value (note the numbers in parentheses) before it went public. Following is what the filing said:

> After giving effect to 20,000,000 shares of common stock which we are selling under this prospectus at an assumed initial public offering price of $11.00 per share, the midpoint of the range indicated on the cover page of this prospectus, and after deducting an assumed underwriting discount and estimated offering expenses and giving effect to the intended use of proceeds assuming that we used all the net proceeds to purchase preference shares of TA II Limited, our adjusted net tangible book value as of March 31, 2001 would have been approximately $(838) million, or $(5.82) per share. This represents an immediate increase in net tangible book value of $2.55 per share equivalent to existing shareholders. This also represents an immediate dilution of $(16.82) per share to new investors purchasing shares under this prospectus.[5]

In other words, investors who bought the Willis stock during its IPO did so at a price much higher than the value of the company. That is something that a business reporter would want to write a story about.

Reporters also need to let readers know if control of the company will change after the IPO. Shareholders who buy stock in a company going public may not always have any say as to what is going to happen with the operation going forward. In some cases, other companies will maintain majority control. This means that, as in the case of a New York company called Odyssey Re, its former parent Fairfax Financial is still pulling the strings after the IPO. According to Odyssey's S-1 statement, a unit of Fairfax Financial Holdings Limited retained a majority stake in the company after its offering. TIG Insurance Company controls more than 70% of the stock. And investors should not expect Fairfax to cede control of the company any time soon. In Odyssey's filings, Fairfax states that it "cannot foresee any circumstances under which it would sell a sufficient number of shares of our common stock to cause it not to retain such control." (Form S-1, Odyssey Re Holdings, p. 14)

In addition, the filing states the following:

> In order to retain control, Fairfax may decide not to enter into a transaction in which our stockholders would receive consideration for their shares that is much higher than the cost of their investment in our common stock or the then current market price of our common stock.[6]

This is the type of disclosure to which business reporters should pay attention. With this information, they can write stories explaining to their readers

---

[5]From Form F-1, by Willis Group Holdings, May 15, 2001, SEC Publication No: 0000912057-01-516288, p. 25. Washington, DC: Securities and Exchange Commission.

[6]From Form S-1, by Odyssey Re Holdings, March 26, 2001, SEC Publication No. 0000947871-01-000156, p. 16. Washington, DC: Securities and Exchange Commission.

that investors may not be interested in buying stock in this company for these reasons.

Another good section to read in S-1 statements is the "Risk Factors" section, in which every company going public has to list anything and everything that could possibly go wrong that would result in its stock price going down. Some of these risk factors are basic and are included in virtually every S-1. They talk about how a downturn in the overall market would hurt a company's business, how higher rates being charged would increase profits, as well as the company's competition. In addition, a company's proverbial dirty laundry is also aired here. So, what a reporter should look for are risk factors that are unique to the company. Understanding what risk factors are unique is a skill that takes some time to develop, but after reading a few of these filings, the reporter will begin to pick up on what is normal and what is not.

The following excerpt from a recent S-1 statement noted a company's high debt levels, which may limit its ability to finance growth and make acquisitions.

> Our debt level reduces our flexibility in responding to changing business and economic conditions, including increased competition in the insurance brokerage industry. . . . And our debt level limits our ability to pursue other business opportunities, borrow more money for operations or capital in the future and implement our business strategies.[7]

It is also important to find the company's dividend policy, which is another important disclosure in the S-1. This will disclose plans on offering a dividend after it becomes a public company. A dividend is often a quarterly payment to investors to entice them to purchase and hold the stock.

There are plenty of other sections within an S-1 that can also provide valuable information. Most S-1 statements include the first disclosures about executive compensation, stock options, loans to corporate executives, and other juicy tidbits. When reporting on an S-1 statement, it is important to read the entire document because some information that might be included in one section may not be there, but could be included elsewhere. For example, an amended S-1 statement filed by Phoenix included a paragraph in the "Underwriting" section about how the company asked the IPO syndicate to set aside 5 million shares of stock for one buyer—State Farm. That is information that most frequent S-1 readers would have wanted to read in the summary that begins each S-1 because it is significant news that one company, particularly one as large as State Farm, wants to invest in another. That is the type of story the business reporter should be writing.

---

[7]From Form F-1, by Willis Group Holdings, May 15, 2001, SEC Publication No. 0000912057-01-516288, p. 11. Washington, DC: Securities and Exchange Commission.

UNDERSTANDING DEBT OFFERINGS

Most of this chapter evaluates how the stock market works, and how and why investors, analysts, and even company executives pay a lot of attention to stocks. But another important investment vehicle that many companies use to raise money that is often ignored by the business media is debt.

A debt, or bond offering, often comes from a company. But they can also be issued by local or state governments as a way to fund building projects such as new hospitals or new roads. Although writing stories about issuing bonds to finance construction projects may seem like drab reporting, some of the best business journalists learned the craft while working at *The Bond Buyer*, a newspaper dedicated solely to reporting, writing, and editing stories about all kinds of debt issues.

Watching the debt market can be very similar to analyzing the stock market. In both cases, companies—or government entities, in the case of bonds—are reliant on finding enough buyers to purchase shares or bonds to allow them to do what they will with the incoming money. And in both cases, investors expect to receive a return on their investment. That return, however, is where stocks and bonds differ. Historically, stocks have given investors a larger return than bonds. However, bonds are considered the safer investment. Rarely does a government entity, be it city, county, state, or federal, fail and become forced to file for bankruptcy court protection. To be sure, businesses that issue debt do sometimes go into bankruptcy court, but even in such cases bond holders are more likely to be repaid than owners of the company stock.

Understanding how the bond market works is also important for another reason that differs from the stock market: Private companies frequently issue debt to fund projects. And when a private company issues debt, it must often disclose information about its past performance.

A bond is like a mortgage, similar to one people may take out to purchase a home. A bond is also similar to a loan one may use to buy a first car. The company or government body that issues the bond needs money for some reason, so they sell bonds to investors, typically worth $1,000 each. In return, the company or government promises to pay the investor a certain amount of money each year. This payment is known as a coupon. On a $1,000 bond with a 7% annual interest rate, the coupon is $70 each year. At the end of the time period of the bond, known as the maturity date, the company or government repays the bondholder the $1,000, plus the coupon.

Companies and governments issue bonds because it can sometimes be difficult for them to go to a bank and ask the bank to loan them $500 million to build a new bubble gum factory. Most banks are not large enough to loan a single company that much money. Banks do not want to make such a large loan to one company because they fear that if the business is unable to pay the loan back, the bank itself will be stuck. So, instead, companies and governments issue bonds and spread the risk around to hundreds and sometimes even thousands of investors.

The following excerpt from an Associated Press story about the building of the Florida Aquarium in Tampa explains how bonds work, why they were issued in this case, and how the bonds were expected to be repaid:

> Most of the money for the glass-domed structure was raised through the sale of $84 million in revenue bonds that are partly backed by the city, a package that Racanelli said he wouldn't have recommended if he had been on board at the time.
>
> The public financing package means the aquarium essentially borrowed money from the bond-buyers—individuals and corporations—and must pay it back with money it takes in from visitors.
>
> That seemed easy before the aquarium was built. Studies showed that it would draw 1.8 million visitors a year. By charging $13.95 for each adult admission, the aquarium would raise enough money to cover its $7.2 million annual bond payments.
>
> But in hindsight, the figures seem questionable. The attendance figure was dependent on state tourism increasing 4 percent. Also, the admission price at Florida Aquarium is the highest in the country.[8]

This story is an example of a bond issued by a state or local government. But two types of bonds are also widely issued and written about. These two types are bonds issued by corporations and bonds issued by the U.S. government, sometimes known as treasury bills.

Corporate bonds fall into two main categories—investment grade and junk bonds. When a company issues a bond, the bond is given a rating by an agency such as Standard & Poor's or Moody's. The rating determines whether the offering is investment grade or junk. To be considered investment grade, the bonds must be rated BBB or higher. Higher ratings include AAA, AA, and A. Lower ratings are BB, B, C, and D. When bonds are given these lower ratings, they are considered junk.

The higher the rating, the lower the yield. When companies have high ratings, they can offer bonds at a lower interest rate. Companies with junk bond ratings are typically newer companies or companies that have had recent financial trouble. To entice investors into purchasing these higher-risk bonds, the companies offer higher yields.

The ratings that companies receive are often important stories, and should be watched by business reporters. When a rating agency lowers a company's credit rating, that means the company will have to spend more money paying interest the next time it wants to borrow money. If a company's credit rating rises, then its cost of borrowing money will go down. That could be a good story too, particularly if the company can tell you what it plans to do with the extra money.

In addition, the ratings analysts at the agencies that issue the ratings are good sources, because they have looked at the company issuing the bonds and know its performance. These analysts are similar to sell-side analysts in some respects,

---

[8]From "Flagging crowds make aquarium a Florida flop," by Lisa Holewa, March 17, 1996, Associated Press. Copyright 1996 by Associated Press. Reprinted with permission.

but they are not pushing investors to purchase the bonds, so they may be more objective. However, their firms do receive money from the companies issuing the bonds in exchange for the ratings.

Investors in these bonds are good sources as well. Just like investors in stocks, bondholders have typically done extensive research into the companies of which they are purchasing bonds. Sometimes, these investors purchase bonds that can later be converted into company stock, so they are looking for the company to perform well and have its stock price go up. These bonds are called convertible bonds.

The prices of corporate bonds do not fluctuate as much as the price of stocks. A bond that sells above its face value is considered to be selling "at a premium." But there are many instances when the price of corporate bonds rarely moves despite large fluctuations in the company's stock price. And a corporate bond can sell close to its face value even when the stock price of the company falls dramatically.

The municipal bond market is smaller than the corporate bond market, but still provides plenty of good stories. Whereas state and local governments are typically covered by reporters writing for the news section, these reporters too need to know how bond offerings work and how the money is being spent. A municipal bond is often favored by investors over corporate bonds because municipal bonds are tax exempt. This means that the interest paid to investors is exempt from federal taxes. However, municipal bonds typically offer lower rates than corporate bonds. Just like corporate bonds, agencies issuing municipal bonds have to repay their investors. Sometimes state and local governments must find other ways to raise cash to repay their bondholders.

The following is a Bloomberg News story that explains how a state water agency in Massachusetts that issued bonds is looking to raise its rates and cut its expenses to help it repay its bonds:

> The Massachusetts Water Resources Authority, Boston's water and sewer utility, plans to raise rates, fire 50 employees and spend more of a $135 million reserve fund to meet a $48 million budget deficit.
>
> The authority's board voted to fill the deficit with $16 million in spending cuts, including the firings, $16 million by increasing rates 4 percent, and by using $16 million from a reserve fund, according to authority spokesman Jonathan Yeo.
>
> Earlier this year, acting Governor Jane Swift and the state legislature eliminated the authority's $48 million subsidy.
>
> The authority, which supplies sewer and water to 61 municipalities, spends about 60 percent of its operating budget to repay its $5.1 billion of outstanding debt. The authority's senior debt is rated AA by Standard & Poor's, Aa3 by Moody's Investors Service and AA- by Fitch Ratings.
>
> "We're very keen on maintaining our strong bond rating, and I think that was shown in the board's judicious use of reserves," said Yeo, who also noted that the authority has about $350 million in reserves that are required by bond covenants.
>
> U.S. states are cutting subsidies and programs as they deal with budget deficits brought on by a loss of tax revenue from the decline of the economy and stock market. Massachusetts has a budget deficit of at least $300 million this fiscal year, and is projecting a deficit that could exceed $2 billion next year.

Yeo said the board now plans to spend its $135 million reserve fund, which was created for rate relief, over four years rather than five as it had planned.

The rate increase, which could go into effect by February, comes mid-year and will be on top of the 2.9 percent increase passed before the fiscal year began July 1. So rates from February through June will be 6.9 percent higher than the previous year.

The authority's 5.25 percent coupon note maturing in 2012 rose 0.3 cent on the dollar to 111.5, yielding 3.767 percent, according to Bloomberg data.[9]

This story provides the reader with the bond rating, as well as what the yield is on the bond. By detailing the ratings and the price information, the reporter helps the reader understand the soundness of investing in these bonds.

The last type of bond is a U.S. Treasury bond. These come in different denominations with different maturity dates and are issued by the federal government to help fund U.S. government projects. A Treasury bill is issued with a maturity date of a year or less, and has a price of $10,000. A Treasury note is issued with a maturity date ranging from one year to 10 years, and has a value of $1,000. A Treasury bond will have a maturity date ranging from 10 years to 30 years, and can be purchased in $1,000 denominations. The later the maturity date, the bigger the yield. These bonds are considered some of the safest investments in the world, because the U.S. federal government has never defaulted on a payment.

It is important to assess economic factors with all types of bonds. If interest rates are rising, then corporations and governments may pull back from issuing bonds because their cost will increase.

There is also a connection between corporate bonds and Treasuries, as the following story explains:

U.S. Treasuries headed toward their biggest weekly decline in more than two months on increasing signs the economy is gaining strength.

Demand for Treasuries fell today after the Commerce Department said construction spending rose for a third month in November. The benchmark 10-year note had its largest drop in more than a year yesterday, ending a four-week rally, after an industry report showed the biggest increase in a manufacturing index in 11 years and as stocks surged.

"The tone for the first six weeks of this year could be positive for the economy, which is good for corporate bonds and not so positive for Treasuries," said Dan Shackelford, who helps invest $6 billion of bonds at T. Rowe Price Group Inc. in Baltimore. He said the firm has added higher-yielding corporate and asset-backed debt at the expense of Treasuries.

The benchmark 4 percent 2012 note this week lost $1^3/_4$, or $17.50 per $1,000 face amount, to $99^{25}/_{32}$ at 3:15 p.m. in New York, its biggest slump since the week ended Oct. 18. The note's yield rose 22 basis points to 4.03 percent. The $1^3/_4$ percent 2004 note fell about $^3/_8$ to $99^{15}/_{16}$ as its yield grew 18 basis points to 1.77 percent. A basis point is 0.01 percentage point.

On the day, prices were little changed. The 10-year note rose $^1/_{32}$ while the two-year note was unchanged.

The interest-rate differential between the two securities grew 5 basis points this week to 2.26 percentage points, the widest in two weeks. A wider gap suggests traders see the Federal Reserve's target overnight lending rate, at a 41-year low of 1.25 percent, underpinning an economic recovery.

Some investors sold Treasuries this week to make room in their portfolios for an expected increase in the supply of corporate debt, analysts said. Trump Hotels & Casino Resorts Inc. and Kreditanstalt Fuer Wiederaufbau, Europe's fourth-largest seller of debt, are among companies slated to sell about $4 billion of bonds in coming days.

The average investment-grade corporate bond yields 1.81 percentage points more than Treasuries, according to a Merrill Lynch & Co. bond index.[10]

Treasury bonds provide a lower yield than corporate bonds, so when corporate bonds are sold, some investors dump Treasuries to purchase them. This is a trend in the bond market that business reporters should watch, because it might affect the bond issue of companies they cover.

Although the majority of Wall Street coverage focuses on the rise and fall of stocks, it is still vitally important for any business reporter to understand the bond market as well. Bonds can often tell a broader and clearer story about a company or government body. If a company is issuing a large amount of bonds, it may be gearing up for a large expansion. Or it may be getting ready to make an acquisition. For one reason or another, it needs money. It is the business reporter's job to find out why and for what.

WHAT COMPANIES DO WITH THE MONEY THEY RAISE

The bulk of this chapter explains why and how companies raise money through the stock market and the bond market, and how this process is important to the success of the business. Companies that perform well by increasing profits and sales will likely see their stock price rise, allowing them to sell additional stock and use the stock to compensate their employees.

But where does this money that's raised in the stock and bond markets go once it gets into the bank accounts of the companies? And how is it used?

---

[10]From "Treasuries fall in week on expectations economy growing faster," by H. Bandur, January 3, 2003, Bloomberg News. Copyright 2003 by Bloomberg L. P. All rights reserved. Reprinted with permission.

Companies sometimes are not specific in telling their shareholders what they plan to do with the money. Typically, the money goes to one of four uses: to pay off past loans and debt; to acquire another company or business; to build something, such as a new plant or headquarters; or simply to sit in the company bank account and be used to fund expenses when necessary.

As mentioned earlier, by going public, companies sell shares of ownership to investors. Often, the S-1 will explain what the company intends to do with that money. For example, New York-based Cosi Incorporated, a casual restaurant chain, went public in 2002. In the following excerpt from its filings, it explained how it intended to use the money from the sale of its stock in broad terms, explaining that:

> Our management has broad discretion as to the use of the net proceeds that we will receive from this offering. We cannot assure you that our management will apply these funds effectively, nor can we assure you that the net proceeds from this offering will be invested in a manner yielding a favorable return.[11]

This statement is about as nebulous as it can get. But elsewhere in the filing, the company provided more detail that explains how the money was going to be spent, that is, opening new restaurants:

> The addition of new restaurants has been our primary source of growth historically and we anticipate that it will be the primary source of growth in the near term. We believe that we have adopted a manageable growth strategy and intend to develop many of our new restaurants in our existing markets, and selectively enter new markets, to gain operational efficiencies, enhance convenience for our customers and increase brand awareness. We do not utilize a commissary system and thus our expansion is not restricted by geographic proximity to commissary kitchens. Our site selection criteria is flexible and allows us to adapt to a wide variety of real estate paradigms including central business districts, urban and suburban residential locations and suburban shopping centers. We plan to open approximately 25 new restaurants during fiscal 2002, and approximately 53 to 59 new restaurants in fiscal 2003. We expect the majority of our restaurants to be opened in the future will be in the Cosi all-day format.[12]

Another company that sold stock in late 2002, California-based Impac Medical Systems, was also similarly vague about its intended usage of the millions of dollars it received from its offering. It mentioned a number of potential possibilities shown in the following excerpt, but gave no specifics:

---

[11]From Form S-1, by Cosi Incorporated, April 17, 2002, SEC Publication No: 0000950123-02-003869, p. 12. Washington, DC: Securities and Exchange Commission.

[12]From Form S-1, by Cosi Incorporated, April 17, 2002, SEC Publication No: 0000950123-02-003869, p. 3. Washington, DC: Securities and Exchange Commission.

Our management could spend the proceeds from this offering in a manner that our stockholders may not desire or that does not yield a favorable return. You will not have the opportunity, as part of your investment in our common stock, to influence the manner in which the net proceeds of this offering are used. We currently intend to use the net proceeds from this offering for general corporate purposes and working capital. We may also use the net proceeds in future strategic acquisitions or investments, but currently we do not have any specific acquisitions or investments planned. Until we need to use the net proceeds of this offering, we plan to invest the net proceeds in investment grade, interest bearing securities, but these investments may not produce income or may lose value.[13]

The bottom line is that many companies raise money because they can. Often, they do not have a specific usage for the money, but they want to have the money available when they need it.

Anytime a company announces a major initiative that will cost money—everything from a new national advertising campaign to the construction of a new factory to the acquisition of another company—a business reporter should ask where the money is coming from. If the company does not say how much the new initiative is going to cost, the reporters should ask for an estimate. If it does not give you an estimate, find an expert in that business to provide a ballpark figure. Then look at the company's financial statements to see if it has enough money to fund the project. If it does not, then the company could borrow the money from a bank, or sell stock or bonds.

The money for businesses to expand has to come from somewhere. Most often, it comes from investors buying and selling stocks and bonds on Wall Street. A business reporter who can follow the money trail from how the cash was raised to how it will be spent can provide a valuable service to readers and listeners by writing stories that help explain if the money is being spent wisely.

The money trail is the most important aspect of being a business journalist. This chapter explains how money flows from investors into companies, and why companies sometimes need money. Later chapters discuss other ways companies spend their money.

GLOSSARY

American Stock Exchange: The third-largest stock exchange in the United States. The AMEX is located in New York and handles approximately 10% of all securities traded in the States. The exchange is primarily for smaller companies and derivatives.

bond: A bond is considered a debt investment—you are loaning money to an entity (company or government) that needs funds for a defined period of time

---

[13]From Form S-1, by Impac Medical Systems Incorporated, June 4, 2002, SEC Publication No. 0000898430-02-002259, p. 16. Washington, DC: Securities and Exchange Commission.

at a specified interest rate. In exchange for your money, the entity will issue you a certificate, or bond, that states the interest rate you are to be paid and when your loaned funds are to be returned, otherwise known as the maturity date.

buy-side analyst: A term used to describe the analysts at investing institutions like mutual funds, pension funds, and insurance firms, that tend to buy large portions of securities. These analysts provide research for the firm's money managers.

consensus analyst estimate: The average earnings estimate for a company based on the predictions of all of the analysts covering the company. The estimate could be for a quarter or for a year.

coupon: The interest rate stated on a bond when it's issued. The coupon is typically paid semiannually.

dividend: A cash payment using profits that's announced by a company's board of directors to be distributed among stockholders. Dividends may be in the form of cash, stock or property.

Dow Jones Industrial Average: A price-weighted average of 30 significant stocks traded on the New York Stock Exchange and the NASDAQ. The DJIA was invented by Charles Dow back in 1896. It is the oldest and single-most watched index in the world.

exchange: A market where securities, commodities, options and futures are traded.

Form S-1: A document filed with the Securities and Exchange Commission by a company desiring to go public. This is also known as the registration statement.

initial public offering: The first sale of stock by a private company to the public. IPOs are often smaller, younger companies seeking capital to expand their business.

institutional investor: A non-bank person or organization that trades securities in large enough share quantities or dollar amounts that they qualify for preferential treatment and lower commissions. Institutional investors face less protective regulations because it is assumed that they are more knowledgeable and better able to protect themselves.

investment banker: A person representing a financial institution that is in the business of raising capital for corporations and municipalities. Investment bankers do the grunt work behind IPOs and debt offerings.

lead underwriter: The managing underwriter who maintains the books of securities sold for a new issue. Also known as the book runner.

maturity date: The date the borrower has to pay back the money it has borrowed through the issue of a bond

mutual fund: Fund operated by an investment company that raises money from shareholders and invests it in stocks, bonds, options, commodities or money market securities.

NASDAQ: Created in 1971 as the world's first electronic stock market, the NASDAQ is a computerized system that facilitates trading and provides price quotations on some 5,000 of the more actively traded over-the-counter stocks. Its largest stocks include Microsoft, Dell, and Cisco.

New York Stock Exchange: A corporation, operated by a board of directors, responsible for setting policies and supervising the stock exchange and its member activities, and listing securities. The NYSE also oversees the transfer of members' seats on the Exchange and judging whether a potential applicant is qualified to be a specialist.

sell-side analyst: Used to describe the retail brokers and research departments that sell securities and make recommendations for the brokerage firm's customers.

short selling: The selling of a security that the seller does not own, or any sale that is completed by the delivery of a security borrowed by the seller. Short selling is a legitimate trading strategy. Short sellers assume the risk that they will be able to buy the stock at a more favorable price than the price at which they sold short.

stock: Ownership in a corporation that is represented by shares. A holder of stock (a shareholder) has a claim on a part of the corporation's assets and earnings. Also known as equities.

yield: In general, a return on an investor's capital investment. For bonds, the coupon rate of interest divided by the purchase price, called current yield. Also, the rate of return on a bond, taking into account the total of annual interest payments, the purchase price, the redemption value, and the amount of time remaining until maturity.

REFERENCES

Baeb, E. (2002, December 27). Massachusetts water taps reserves, raises rates and fires 50. Bloomberg News.

Bandur, H. (2003, January 3). Treasuries fall in week on expectations economy growing faster. Bloomberg News.

Cohn, M. (2002, October 30). Legg analyst accuses Rouse of a misleading 3Q report. *Baltimore Sun.* p. 1C.

From S-1. Cosi Incorporated. (2002, April 17). (SEC Publication No. 0000950123-02-003869, pp. 1–45). Washington, DC: Securities and Exchange Commission.

Form S-1. Impac Medical Systems Incorporated. (2002, June 4). (SEC Publication No. 0000898430-02-002259, pp. 1–50). Washington, DC: Securities and Exchange Commission.

Form S-1. Max Re Capital. (2001, May 31). (SEC Publication No. 0000950130-01-502080, pp. 1–83). Washington, DC: Securities and Exchange Commission.

Form S-1. Odyssey Re Holdings. (2001, March 26). (SEC Publication No. 0000947871-01-000156, pp. 1–37). Washington, DC: Securities and Exchange Commission.

Form F-1. Willis Group Holdings. (2001, May 15). (SEC Publication No. 0000912057-01-516288, pp. 1–96). Washington, DC: Securities and Exchange Commission.

Fu, S. (2002, December 24). U.S. stocks fall as durable, retail data lag; Citigroup drops. Bloomberg News.

Holewa, L. (1996, March 17). Flagging crowds make aquarium a Florida flop." Associated Press.

Kurtz, H. (2002, January 18). The Enron story that waited to be told." *Washington Post.* p. E1.

Levick, D. (2001, May 12). "Phoenix lists a loss of $157 million for quarter." *Hartford Courant.* p. E1.

Marshall, M. (2000, August 5). "Stock sale jolts Unify investors." *San Jose Mercury News.* p. 1C.

Peltz, J. F. (2002, October 14). Analysts' tougher ratings take toll on Wall Street. *Los Angeles Times.* p. 4.

The Bloomberg Way. (1995). New York: Bloomberg Business News. pp. 100–101.

Other Books on Understanding Wall Street and IPOs

Apostolou, N. G., & Crumbley, D. L. (1994). *Keys to understanding the financial news* (2nd ed.). Hauppauge, NY: Barron's Educational Series.

Warfield, G. (1994). *How to read and understand the financial news* (2nd ed.). New York: Harper Collins.

Wurman, R. S., Siegel, A., & Morris, K. M. (1989). *The Wall Street Journal guide to understanding money & markets.* New York: AccessPress.

SUGGESTED EXERCISES

1. Compile a list of local stocks and how they performed during a day. Write a story based on the gains and losses in the individual stocks and the indexes. Then compare the stories to the stock market story in the local newspaper.
2. Review a research report for a local company issued by a sell-side analyst. Write a 250-word analysis on the analyst's rating for the company, and whether you believe the rating is justified.
3. Discuss the differences between sell-side analysts and buy-side analysts. Compile a list of five ways a sell-side analyst can help a business reporter, and five ways a buy-side analyst can help a business reporter. Think of ways both analysts might use reporters to their advantage.
4. Review the S-1 registration statement for a company that has recently gone public. Assess the size of the offering and the initial stock price. List five items in the filing that are newsworthy and should be included in a story about the stock offering.
5. Pretend you are the editor of a magazine that follows bank stocks. You arrange a Q&A interview with the manager of a mutual fund that invests in

bank stocks. The mutual fund is part of the magazine's 401(k) retirement plan, and the editor is part of the plan. Should you conduct the interview, or should you find a staff member who is not invested in the retirement plan to conduct the interview? If you find a staff member to conduct the interview should you be involved in editing the transcript?

6. Find the chief investment officer of your university. Ask him or her to explain the rationale behind the stocks or bonds currently in the school's portfolio. Then write a story based on the interview, assessing the performance of the stocks or bonds in the university's portfolio during the past 12 months.

8

The Executive Suite

THE CEO AS ROCK STAR

During the 1990s, it became popular to write profiles about the CEOs of major corporations, treating them like movie stars or rock icons. The business media lauded the exploits of GE's Jack Welch and Coca-Cola's Roberto Goizueta, to name two. Many CEOs were given credit for the company's successes, even though they oversaw operations with thousands of employees who contributed to the companies' position as industry leaders. The coverage was perhaps a bit over the top. Certainly, it was not nearly as critical as it should have been. We now see business reporters taking a harder look at the successes and failures of a CEO in running his or her company.

Tyco International's Dennis Kozlowski was considered one of these rock stars in the 1990s. His face adorned the cover of many business publications, and his strategy of building a conglomerate was praised. Now, Kozlowski no longer leads Tyco. The disgraced executive resigned from the company shortly before he was indicted for tax evasion in 2002. In addition, he now stands charged with looting the company of $600 million to sustain an extravagant lifestyle that included a $15,000 umbrella stand and a $6,000 shower curtain. Ozzy Osbourne likely lives with such amenities, but when a corporate executive uses money from a public corporation to buy them, he is playing with fire and should draw the scrutiny of the business media.

Kozlowski's business strategy is also in tatters. Under Kozlowski's direction, to raise cash, Tyco sold operations at less than half of what it paid a few years earlier. Nonetheless, just months before his arrest, Kozlowski was named one of the country's best managers by *BusinessWeek.* He is not alone, unfortunately. Former Enron CEO Kenneth Lay apparently used the corporate jet to transport his daughter's furniture. Ex-Adelphia Communications head John Rigas took $13 million from the cable company to build a golf course.

Even former icons such as Welch and Goizueta are facing a reevaluation of their performances. Welch retired from GE, but the company has since struggled to maintain the growth rate it had under his reign, primarily because it can no longer make acquisitions big enough to fuel higher earnings, and also because it can only squeeze so much excess spending out of its existing businesses. And Welch had his excesses too. After Welch had an affair with an editor of the *Harvard Business Review,* his wife—a former Wall Street lawyer—sued for divorce, seeking half of his holdings. As part of the divorce negotiations, it was disclosed that GE had given him a generous retirement package, including paying for items such as a Manhattan apartment and country club fees.

The performance of Goizueta, who died as Coca-Cola's CEO in 1997, now is also being examined under a new light. A man who once easily obtained meetings with presidents of countries around the world, Goizueta led Coca Cola on an overhaul that was supposed to ensure its future success for decades to come. Just more than two years after taking over for Goizueta, however, Doug Ivester resigned as Coca-Cola's CEO. The job was too much for the Georgia-born accountant, who was Goizueta's hand-picked successor. He was unable to withstand the spotlight brought on by a racial discrimination lawsuit, a tampering scare in Europe, and sluggish sales, as suggested in a December, 1999 story in the *Atlanta Journal-Constitution,* which called Ivester's resignation a "surprise" and noted that his tenure as leader of the company was "tumultuous" (Unger, 1999, p. A1). The story also noted that Ivester resisted pressure from the board of directors to name a No.2 executive.

In many of these cases, business reporters appear to have been all too willing to give the CEO the benefit of the doubt when documenting his company's performances. Powerful CEOs and their public relations staffs often coddle reporters with grand visions of future corporate glory that will ultimately result in shareholders becoming unbelievably rich. Their promises are seldom realized, however. Few companies have been able to sustain repeated growth over a long period of time that makes their shareholders wildly rich. Even Coca-Cola and GE, regular visitors to *Forbes'* list of most admired companies, stumble.

Talkative and quirky CEOs also get a fair amount of attention. But is it warranted? In many cases, it may not be, a senior writer for TheStreet.com, an online business news service, Dagen McDowell, wrote in a column on the site:

A company also will get a lot more attention from the media if it's run by a colorful personality who could serve as an engaging character in an otherwise dry financial story. . . . A corporate executive who is blunt, outspoken, opinionated and maybe even a little nuts will get a lot more media time than someone who is, well, boring. Unfortunately for investors, an outsize personality doesn't always mean a great corporate leader. (McDowell, 2002)

Every rock star has his or her critics. The same should hold true in the corporate world. Business journalists should learn from the recent disclosures of excess and hold executives accountable for their actions. To be sure, some CEOs and other executives act in the best interests of their shareholders and their employees. But there are enough who do not that all merit more scrutiny by reporters.

Reporters can dig into the world of corporations and write stories that expose what is going on inside the executive suite and the boardroom. In the case of public companies, laws require them to disclose salaries and bonuses, as well as stock options and other perks, to their top executives every year. In the case of some private companies, salaries and bonuses and other compensation are disclosed to state regulators, and that information can be obtained if a reporter knows where to look or whom to ask.

The question is: Why have boards allowed their CEOs to get away with spending corporate money on personal items? The answer is that many boards, including members of the Tyco board, have professed ignorance to what their CEOs have done. Many boards are now aggressively looking at such spending, which can be good news for business reporters looking to find such information. A friendly board member might provide the documents for a story.

Another question might be: Why do boards agree to pay executives such large sums of money? In many cases, successful executives receive seven-figure salaries and bonuses to keep them at the company. But executive compensation has become an increasingly controversial topic that business reporters are now covering with more diligence. Later chapters detailing real estate records and court filings can also help to uncover an executive's financial holdings as they relate to his company. But before any reporter begins to interview executives and write stories about what they are doing, it is important to understand how a company is structured.

WHO DOES WHAT?

The CEO is the most important person in any business, no matter the size. This is the executive who sets the strategy for the company, and everyone underneath on the organizational chart eventually must answer to the CEO.

In many companies, the CEO can hold other titles. A lot of times, the CEO is also the chairman of the board of directors. Many companies have boards, which are set up to provide guidance to the executive team. If the CEO is the chairman of the board, he also often wields great influence in setting the company business strategy given other executives.

But not always. Consider the story of Coca-Cola's CEO. The new CEO is Doug Daft. Daft also holds the title of chairman of the board, as did his predecessors. But the Coca-Cola board also includes Warren Buffett, one of the richest men in the world who owns 8% of the company's stock. Many believe that Buffett's stature gives him more power in making important decisions for Coca-Cola than Daft, who owns much less of the company. There were reports that it was Buffett and other board members who turned down Daft's request to buy Quaker Oats in 2001 (Valdmanis and Howard, 2000). Instead, rival Pepsi bought the company, which included Gatorade.

A board of directors is typically made up of other CEOs and executives at other companies, friends of the company CEO, or people who have business relation-ships with the company and executives. Many boards, spurred by regulators and investors seeking more independent boards willing to speak up and hold CEOs accountable for excessive spending and other decisions that may affect the com-pany's future, are adding members from outside the company who have no ties to the CEO. Others are adding minority and female board members to add different perspectives.

If the CEO is not the chairman of the board, it is important for these two people to have a good working relationship. The chairman is essentially the CEO's boss, and if the chairman does not have confidence that the CEO is doing the job, he or she may ask the other board members to help find a new CEO.

Another interesting relationship with CEOs and boards sometimes occurs when a CEO retires from that position but maintains the title of chairman of the board. Many former CEOs turned into chairmen have been unable to let go of the reins and allow their successor a chance to run the company without interference. When reviewing a board's composition, it is important for a journalist to see if there are former company executives lingering.

Board meetings for companies, even public companies, are not open to re-porters. Depending on the company, boards get together on average about once a month or every other month and often meet for an entire day, hearing reports on the performance of the company's operations or discussing managerial changes. Boards vote to approve major company moves, such as building a new plant or hir-ing a new CFO. Boards also vote on matters such as whether to split a company's stock or to raise the dividend paid to investors. Companies will typically disclose newsworthy events decided at board meetings via a news release.

It is smart for business reporters to know the board members of the companies they are writing about. Most companies provide a list of board members on their Web sites and at the back of their annual reports. Board members may often speak to reporters about the CEO's job performance, and they often can give insights into boardroom discussions related to acquisitions. Later this chapter details how to find more information about board members.

Corporate Organizational Chart

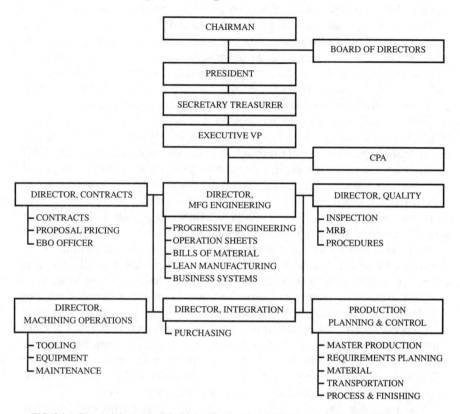

FIG. 8.1. From Air Industries Machining Corporation, 2003. Copyright 2003 by Air Industries Machining Corporation. Reprinted with permission.

The CEO, the top executive of a company, may also hold the title of president. A president of a company typically is the person in charge of the day-to-day operations, overseeing major divisions and manufacturing. If the two jobs are split, the president typically reports to the CEO. The major difference in these two jobs—if held by separate people—is that the CEO is often more focused on a company's plans, whereas a president oversees the current, running businesses.

Figure 8.1 is a typical organizational chart for a manufacturing company. The chairman in this company is also the CEO.

If a company does not have a president, it may have a chief operating officer, or COO. These jobs are similar, and often one person may hold both titles. If a company has a COO, but not a president, that is not significant. However, a company with a COO and a president may be having a power struggle near the top. Or it could be setting up those two executives in a horse race to replace the current CEO. That is something that bears watching and could lead to a story.

The relationship between the president/COO and the CEO is important in a company. A CEO will often pick someone as his or her right-hand for that slot, knowing that he or she needs a No. 2 executive that can execute orders effectively and quickly. A CEO and president often meet regularly to discuss corporate strategy and a company's operations. At Coca-Cola, for example, the CEO and president get together weekly with other executives at lunch to discuss business.

Typically at the same level as the president and COO is the CFO, who is charge of keeping the company's books together. The CFO typically has a better handle on the financial performance of the company than most other executives. The CFO typically is involved in preparing a company's quarterly earnings statement and will quite often discuss those results when the company holds a conference call for analysts and investors.

Below the president and COO can be a number of positions, depending on how a company is structured. A company like Coca-Cola that is heavily focused on marketing and its geographic operations has executives in charge of its North American, European, Middle Eastern, and Asian operations, as well as a chief marketing officer. All of these executives report to the president. Another company may be structured differently and have executives in charge of manufacturing or specific products reporting directly to the president.

A reporter should understand the relationships among these executives. A chief marketing officer and the head of an operating unit at a company may need to spend a lot of time together. When a company unveils a new product, it wants to sell as many of them as it can. So the operating executive will need to discuss the selling points for the new product with the chief marketing officer.

Other important relationships exist in a company. An operating executive may need money to expand a plant or to develop a new product. To get that money, he or she will have to go to the president or the CEO. At a company like Wal-Mart, the head of the Sam's Club division may want to install new computers in the stores to track the sales of various products. To get those new computers, he or she will need to ask the head of information systems, also sometimes called the chief information officer.

Or if Wal-Mart is opening a new location, it will need to hire new employees. A vice president of human resources will need to know from the head of the retail division where the store is located, when it is expected to open, and how many full-time and part-time employees will be needed.

It is important to know the responsibilities of each executive. For a reporter writing a story about Microsoft's business in Brazil, it is probably better to interview the head of the company's South American operations than to talk to Bill Gates. Most companies have other executives who can also be important for a business reporter. A reporter covering a drug company such as GlaxoSmithKline may want to cultivate a relationship with the head of research, a person who might be willing to talk about drugs being developed for future sale. A reporter writing a story about how the automated teller machines failed at a bank may want to interview its chief information officer or vice president of information systems.

Larger companies have corporate communications staffs that handle media requests. The better corporate PR staffs work to put the business reporter and executives together, rather than talking themselves. They realize that it is the executives who know what is going on at the company better than anyone else, and can give better answers. In most cases, these executives are trained to answer questions in a specific manner. Reporters should be diligent in their interviews to ensure that questions are answered satisfactorily. Sometimes executives can be like politicians: They try to answer a question that was not asked, not the one that was. It is important for reporters to listen to the answers during the interview and return to questions that go unanswered. Often, just asking the question again will get an answer; sometimes it takes two or three times.

Executives are busy people. In many cases, they have multibillion dollar corporations to manage. They tend to be focused and quick to be impatient about a reporter's repetition of questions or poorly framed questions. A reporter should prepare for interviews by conducting background research on the executive so that time is not wasted on basic questions. A reporter should ask about the exec's strategy for the company, not how long he or she has been CEO. The reporter who shows that he or she is prepared and knows the business will be more likely to get an interview the next time.

Figure 8.2 is another typical organizational chart for a company. (The CEO in some countries is called the executive director.) Note that the head of communications for this company reports directly to the company leader, but is at a lower level of power than the director of operations or the CFO. Often, a vice president of corporate communications will work directly with a president or CEO in setting the company's strategy with handling media requests.

SALARIES, BONUSES, AND STOCK OPTIONS

Companies are in the business of making money. So are their executives. A company CEO knows that the more successful he makes his company, the more likely he is to get a pay raise or a higher bonus. A CEO will take on projects or business ventures for a company that have the best possibility of succeeding and being profitable, knowing that his wallet stands to benefit as well.

The SEC requires every public company and some private companies to disclose information about their operations to investors. That disclosure of information includes the compensation packages of top executives. Increasingly, the disclosure of this information is becoming a major business story because of some of the examples described at the beginning of this chapter.

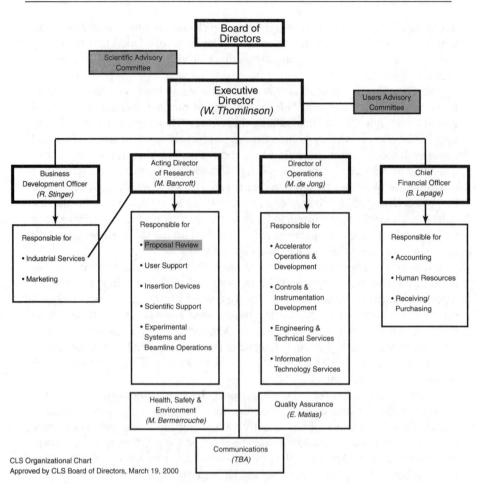

FIG. 8.2. From Canadian Light Source Incorporated, 2002. Copyright 2002 by Canadian Light Source Incorporated. Reprinted with permission.

A business reporter can find this salary information in several places.

Every year, public companies send a filing called a proxy, or a 14A filing, to every registered shareholder of that company about six weeks before the annual meeting. A separate voter card asks shareholders to vote on various items detailed in the proxy. This mailing typically happens in late February and March. A business reporter should check with the companies that they track to see when they expect to release the proxy. Often, the proxy contains news that the reporter's newspaper will want in tomorrow's business section.

Typically, several members of the board of directors are up for election. Board members are often elected in staggered terms, so the majority of a board rarely changes in a year. Often, companies will ask shareholders to approve executive option plans. Typically, companies also ask shareholders to vote against proxy proposals presented by dissident shareholders—such as unions—that they think could limit executive control over the company's affairs. A common dissident shareholder proposal is to ask a company to increase the number of outside directors on the board and decrease the number of company executives on the board. This information can often result in good stories for busines reporters.

The following example shows how Bill Barnhart of the *Chicago Tribune* looked at a variety of dissident shareholders proposals related to corporate auditors and turned them into a broad story about this trend:

> The implosion of energy trader Enron will provide new vigor to this year's round of shareholder meetings.
>
> Proponents of the status quo will finger Enron's current and former senior management as negligent or fraudulent—the so-called bad apple theory. But shareholder activists will use the Enron case to demand systematic reforms in corporate governance procedures.
>
> In doing so, activists preparing for the annual meeting season, which peaks in April and May, will build on gains made last year in educating shareholders and asserting their rights.
>
> A major advance was a new rule by the Securities and Exchange Commission requiring public companies to disclose payments to their independent auditors, broken down into money paid for audit services and money paid for "other" work, such as consulting services, which could pose a conflict of interest with the audit. The requirement, adopted during the past year, represents a compromise between those who wanted no change and those who wanted to ban auditors from engaging in non-audit work for their clients.
>
> "In view of past auditing scandals at Sunbeam, MicroStrategy, Cendant and Waste Management and the ongoing horror of Enron's collapse, shareholders naturally began to question how "independent" their auditors were," Chicago-based Marco Consulting Group, a consultant to union pension plans, said in its annual review of shareholder rights issues.
>
> In what could become a trend, activists are doing more than asking questions at entertainment giant Walt Disney. The proxy statement for the company's Feb. 19 meeting contains a shareholder proposal asking that independent auditors, currently PricewaterhouseCoopers, be barred from performing other work for Disney.
>
> In addition to accounting shenanigans, shareholder activists remain concerned about executive compensation. Many studies have demonstrated that what the chief executive is paid bears no relation to how well the company's stock performs.
>
> At least 13 times last year, shareholders defeated management-proposed stock option plans that threatened to dilute the stakes of shareholders. In some cases, the options proposals allowed options to be exercised at prices below the market value of the stock at the time of the options grant, according to the Marco Group analysis.
>
> Using the Internet, shareholder activists were successful last year in rallying votes for dissident board members at several companies. The Marco report mentions Lone Star Steakhouse & Saloon, Alltrista, Hercules, Willamette Industries and ICN Pharmaceuticals.[1]

---

[1] From "Activist shareholder forcing change," by B. Barnhart, January 8, 2002, *Chicago Tribune*, p. 8. Copyright 2002 by *Chicago Tribune*. Reprinted with permission.

This story takes the trend of increasing shareholder agitation and focuses on why shareholders may be proposing more limits on company control of selecting auditors and determining executive compensation in future years. Barnhart put his knowledge of proxy statements and the shareholder requests in them to good use. Those types of proposals should be written about every time a business reporter finds them in a proxy.

There is plenty of other information in a proxy filing to interest business readers. Most business reporters immediately turn to the compensation chart of a proxy when they receive it. How much a CEO's salary or bonus rose or fell in the past year is obviously news. The hard part is deciphering the numbers and explaining them to readers who also want to know this information, but do not have access to the proxy, or investors who have not yet received their proxy.

Compensation stories are among the most widely read in the business section. Executives at other companies want to know what their counterparts are making down the street. Employees of that company want to know what their boss is pulling in. And shareholders of that company want to know whether the executive is worth his salary. This last one can often be determined by comparing the percentage increase or decrease in the CEO's compensation package in any given year with the percentage increase or decrease in the company's stock price for the same year. What most investors would like to see is an executive's total compensation package—his salary, bonus, stock options, and other pay—rise somewhat in line with how the company performed for the year. For example, if a CEO's pay increased 75% during a year in which the company's stock price fell 40% and profits dropped 50%, then an investor is likely to be upset and could ask questions at the annual meeting.

The proxy is the only place in which public companies annually release executive compensation. It explains who is making the big bucks, how much of a bonus was awarded in the past year, and whether stock options were granted. A category called "All other compensation" is often the most interesting section.

Figure 8.3 is an example of what one of these charts looks like. Figure 8.3 came from Conseco, and during the 1990s it was an aggressive purchaser of other companies in life insurance and consumer lending. Stephen Hilbert, its chairman, CEO, and president, led this aggressive expansion plan, and was paid handsomely as a result. Figure 8.3 is from the company's 2000 proxy filed with the SEC and sent to shareholders.

A number of potential stories should jump out at even the first-time proxy reader when looking at this figure. For one, Hilbert was making a ton of money before he resigned from his job under pressure later in 2000. At more than $835,000, his "all other compensation" is more than three times the salary of his executive vice presidents. The footnotes below the chart, not shown in Fig. 8.3, show why Hilbert is being paid so much money. In this case, the dollar amount includes the premiums for split-dollar life insurance the company paid on behalf of Hilbert. But these footnotes often include

NAME AND PRINCIPAL POSITION	YEAR	ANNUAL COMPENSATION			LONG-TERM COMPENSATION AWARDS NUMBER OF RESTRICTED SECURITIES UNDERLYING		ALL OTHER COMPENSATION
		SALARY	BONUS	OTHER	STOCK AWARDS	OPTIONS/SARS (IN SHARES)	
Stephen C. Hilbert, Chairman of the Board, President and Chief Executive Officer	1999	$1,000,000	$7,895,391	$123,254	$1,192,369	2,047,443	$835,974
	1998	1,000,000	13,500,000	130,714	1,275,891	2,571,897	754,568
	1997	250,000	15,000,000	163,240	4,156,373	2,561,792	4,297
Ngaire E. Cuneo, Executive Vice President, Corporate Development	1999	250,000	4,500,000		390,635	221,814	4,745
	1998	250,000	1,235,000		109,718	422,967	4,991
	1997	250,000	2,612,000		80,035	621,859	4,983
Rollin M. Dick (5), Executive Vice President and Chief Financial Officer	1999	250,000	3,800,000		333,041	609,812	592,360
	1998	250,000	3,816,000		302,094	741,635	554,510
	1997	250,000	3,816,000		1,108,184	853,452	20,669
Thomas J. Kilian (5) (7), Executive Vice President and Chief Operations Officer	1999	250,000	2,000,000		185,023	5,447	3,570
	1998	237,148	1,262,852		56,520	352,576	3,896
Maxwell E. Bublitz(7), Senior Vice President, Investments	1999	250,000	1,800,000		168,576	5,447	3,227
	1998	250,000	1,400,000		28,558	201,785	3,608

FIG. 8.3. Source: Form DEF 14A, Conseco Incorporated, Filed with Securities and Exchange Commission, May 23, 2000

such items as a company buying the home of an executive, paying for cars and airplanes, or relocations.

Hilbert's bonus is very large, but it declined by almost half in 1999. A footnote explains why, stating the following:

> Mr. Hilbert agreed that his bonus, after reduction for cash to pay taxes, relating to the last three quarters of 1999, was to be paid in shares of Common Stock valued at the higher of $50 per share or market. Consequently, his bonus for 1999 consisted of 108,221 shares of Common Stock (which are reflected in the table at the values at the respective dates of issuance) and $5,466,056 in cash. (Form DEF 14A, Conseco Incorporated, 2000, p. 9)

In other words, Hilbert's bonus for 1999 was partly paid in stock and partly in cash. In previous years, it was paid in all cash. Conseco's stock was declining at this time, making his bonus worth less.

After reading enough proxy statements, the reporter will begin to establish some patterns. One is that many companies give stock options to their executives as part of their compensation packages. The stock options are a way to provide an incentive to the CEO and other executives to improve the company's performance, which should lead to a higher stock price—and higher assets for the CEO.

Consider a fictitious company called ACME Inc. ACME's compensation committee decides to give its executives some stock options. The CEO is granted 100,000 stock options, allowing him to purchase the stock at $25 per share. He typically has a certain amount of time, perhaps 10 years, to exercise those options at $25 per share, regardless of how high the stock is valued. What the CEO wants to do is exercise his options and buy the stock when it is at a price much higher than $25 per share because he will only be paying the prearranged $25 price.

He wants to do this because if he can get ACME's stock price up to $50 per share, those 100,000 shares of stock are now worth $5 million. Mr. CEO will spend $2.5 million to buy those shares at $25 per share, on the basis of the agreement struck with the compensation committee. He has just pocketed a profit of $2.5 million, minus taxes, in this transaction. Many times, executives turn around and sell the stock at the higher price immediately after exercising the options. That is a story for a business reporter.

Of course, the opposite often happens. The CEO and other executives are unsuccessful in raising the stock price above the option price, making the options worthless. Who would purchase stock for $25 per share if it were trading at $15 per share? What sometimes happens, though, is companies change the stock option agreement, lowering the price at which executives can purchase shares. That is a move that upsets investors and should be front-page news.

It is also significant when the options expire. If the expiration date is coming up soon, and the company's shares have not yet reached the option price level, the

CEO may seek to find another company willing to purchase the entire company at a price tag above the option price. That way, he or she can exercise the options before they expire.

It is important to know whether executives are exercising options. If they are not exercising options when the exercise price is below the current price, that is a sign that they feel more comfortable putting their money elsewhere. Later, this chapter examines how to find out if an executive is buying or selling stock. These items are of particular interest because options are a way for companies to pay their executives additional "compensation" in addition to salary and bonuses. Shareholder rights activists also criticize large stock option awards to executives as being excessive because company executives are already being paid multimillion dollar compensation packages.

Companies also give executives what is called restricted stock. Restricted stock has more limits than stock options. Most companies that give executives restricted stock set limits that the executive cannot sell the stock prior to retirement. If the executive leaves the company before retirement age, the restricted stock is then forfeited. In most cases, however, the executive receives dividends paid on the stock, despite the fact he or she does not actually control the stock. The granting of restricted stock and stock options to executives often adds millions of dollars to an executive's compensation package. That is news.

A reporter should look elsewhere in the proxy for explanations about compensation and why executives are receiving stock options and restricted stock. A reporter's best bet is what is called the "Compensation Committee Report." The compensation committee is composed of board members. This report on executive compensation is not usually found with the chart on executive compensation. Instead, it will appear elsewhere in the proxy. Some companies place it early on in the proxy with all of the other board-of-director-type information. Others place it way in the back, assuming that many proxy readers will fall asleep before they get to it. But a reporter should look for the report from the members of the board of directors who sit on the compensation committee and who decide how much or how little executives get paid.

For example, the Conseco compensation committee report informs readers of the following:

> In 1998 Conseco and Mr. Hilbert entered into a new employment agreement (the "CEO Contract"). The CEO Contract provided for an annual salary of $1 million. In addition, Mr. Hilbert was entitled to receive an annual bonus equal to the lesser of a non-discretionary amount ($13.5 million for 1999 prior to the revision described below) or 3 percent of Net Profits. Mr. Hilbert was entitled to receive an additional bonus for any year in excess of this amount only if payment of that additional bonus amount would not cause the total bonus to exceed 3 percent of the annual Net Profits and the Company's return on equity ("ROE") for such year after giving effect to such bonus would be at least 15 percent. In addition, the Compensation Committee had the authority under the CEO Contract to reduce any such additional bonus.

The Company's ROE for 1999 was less than 15 percent. Consequently, Mr. Hilbert's bonus for 1999 would have been $13.5 million, but Mr. Hilbert agreed that his bonus, after reduction for cash to pay taxes, relating to the last three quarters of 1999, was to be paid in shares of Common Stock valued at the higher of $50 per share or market. Consequently his bonus for 1999 consisted of 108,221 shares of Common Stock and $5,466,056 in cash. (Form DEF 14A, Conseco, Incorporated, 2000, p. 9)

Although it includes a lot of legal mumbo jumbo, the report does tell why Hilbert's bonus was reduced in 1999 as compared with the year earlier—his bonus for 1999 included stock, which a reporter would have discovered had dropped in value.

A story written about the Conseco proxy might begin the following way:

The chief executive officer of struggling Conseco Inc. received a lower bonus in 1999 than two years ago due to the company's lagging stock price, according to a proxy statement filed by the company with regulators.

However, Stephen Hilbert's $1 million salary and bonus of nearly $7.9 million, down more than 41 percent from his $13.5 million bonus in 1998, still makes him one of the highest-paid executives in the country.

In addition, Hilbert received other compensation of more than $835,000, a figure higher than the salary of any other company executive, and restricted stock awards worth more than $1 million. Hilbert was also granted options to purchase more than 2 million shares of Conseco stock.

SWEETHEART DEALS AND BOARD MEMBERS

Another eyebrow-raising section of the proxy, normally found right after the list of the members of the board of directors, is a section called "Certain Relationships and Related Transactions." It details business relationships between board members and the company. For example, if a board member is an attorney, this section will detail, in dollar amounts, how much the company is paying his or her law firm in annual fees.

Former U.S. Sen. Sam Nunn is an attorney in the Atlanta-based law firm of King & Spalding. Nunn also happens to be a board member at Coca-Cola. King & Spalding, you guessed it, does legal work for the company. So in this section of the 2002 proxy, the company discloses that relationship:

In 2001, we paid King & Spalding fees totaling approximately $7.56 million for legal services which represents less than 5 percent of King & Spalding's gross revenues for 2001. We expect that King & Spalding will provide services to the Company and its subsidiaries in 2002. Mr. Nunn does not personally provide any legal services to the Company. (Form DEF 14A, Coca-Cola Company, 2002, p. 16)

On its own, this is probably not something worth reporting, given that the law firm was doing legal work for Coca-Cola long before Nunn joined the board. (A business reporter can look this up by going back and reading old proxies.) Still, it is worth remembering should the reporter run across a story involving Coca-Cola and its attorneys.

The section in Coca-Cola's proxy detailing its relationships with Warren Buffett's companies is more detailed. Buffett is chairman of Berkshire Hathaway, an Omaha company that owns dozens of companies, from carpet makers to jewelers. This disclosure states the following:

> International Dairy Queen, Inc. ("IDQ") is a wholly owned subsidiary of Berkshire Hathaway. In 2001, IDQ and its subsidiaries made payments totaling approximately $1.12 million to the Company and its subsidiaries directly and through bottlers and 15 other agents in respect of fountain syrup and other products in the ordinary course of business. Also in 2001, IDQ and its subsidiaries received promotional and marketing incentives (such as funding and loans for menu boards bearing the Company's logo) for corporate and franchised stores totaling approximately $1.3 million from the Company and its subsidiaries in the ordinary course of business. This business relationship was in place for many years prior to Berkshire Hathaway's acquisition of IDQ and is on terms substantially similar to the Company's relationships with other customers. FlightSafety International, Inc. ("FlightSafety") is also a wholly owned subsidiary of Berkshire Hathaway. For the years 1998, 1999 and 2000, the Company paid FlightSafety approximately $207,000, $262,000 and $347,000, respectively, for providing pilot training services to the Company in the ordinary course of business. In 2001, the Company paid FlightSafety approximately $269,000 for these services. Berkshire Hathaway holds an equity interest in Moody's Corporation, to which the Company paid fees totaling approximately $242,000 in 2001 for rating our commercial paper programs and other services in the ordinary course of business. Berkshire Hathaway also holds an equity interest in The Dun & Bradstreet Corporation. In 2001, the Company paid approximately $200,000 to The Dun & Bradstreet Corporation for providing credit reporting services and other services in the ordinary course of business. (Form DEF 14A, Coca-Cola Company, 2002, pp. 15–16)

Again, all of these relationships between Coca-Cola and Buffett's companies seem legitimate. But this section of the proxy is required reading for any business reporter because it could detail business dealings that might raise questions.

A reporter will also find interesting transactions such as the one below, which was detailed in Progressive Corporation's 2000 proxy. At the time this document was filed, Peter Lewis was the company's CEO.

> On April 23, 1999, the Company sold its corporate airplane, a Canadair Challenger 601-1A, to a company independently owned by Peter B. Lewis. The airplane was sold to Mr. Lewis for $12.1 million, the fair market value as determined by JetPerspectives, Inc., an independent aircraft appraiser. The net book value of the airplane was $6.9 million at the date of the sale. Operation of the airplane is supported by two pilots and a mechanic, who are employees of a subsidiary of the Company. Mr. Lewis reimburses the Company for the salaries and all other payroll costs of such employees and pays directly or reimburses the Company for all operating and other costs that the Company incurs in connection with the storage, maintenance, use and operation of the airplane. The Company reimburses Mr. Lewis at the rate of $3,567 per hour, the air charter rate for comparable aircraft (based on the quotes obtained from three

air charter companies selected by JetPerspectives, Inc.), for his use of the airplane on Company-related business or as a member of the Board of Directors. (Form DEF 14A, Progressive Corporation, 2000, p. 5)

This seems like a reasonable arrangement, at least at first reading. The statement clarifies the relationship between the company and the CEO, in case questions should arise regarding the airplane sale. But an inquisitive reporter may want to make a few phone calls on the value of this model airplane and the going rate for chartering planes.

Health care provider Aetna Incorporated also disclosed some interesting relationships among board member Leonard Abramson and his relatives in its 2000 proxy statement.

Those disclosures stated the following:

A subsidiary of the Company paid Richard Wolfson, a son-in-law of Mr. Abramson, $150,469 under an independent contractor agreement for services rendered in 1999.

During 1999, the Company and its subsidiaries paid $7,068,958 to Criterion Communications, Inc. pursuant to a service agreement. Marcy Shoemaker (a daughter of Mr. Abramson) owns 100 percent of the outstanding voting securities of Criterion. (Form DEF 14A, Aetna Incorporated, 2000, p. 16)

That may be a story. Such financial arrangements smack of nepotism at its worst. And when Abramson resigned from the board in June of that year, these relationships were reported in an Associated Press story and in a June 8 *Philadelphia Inquirer* story. The fourth paragraph of the *Inquirer* story stated the following:

Abramson's two daughters and son-in-law also were paid more than $18 million by the insurer since 1996, according to the Associated Press, which cited financial statements filed by the company with the U.S. Securities and Exchange Commission. (Stark, 2000)

Later, the story quotes shareholders criticizing the consulting fee arrangements.

Other sections of the proxy can provide clues as to how much power certain board members have. It is important to see what board members belong to what committees. Membership on certain committees such as compensation can result in power.

It is also important for a business writer to review the "Chart of Principal Ownership," which lists the largest shareholders of the company. The list should include the number of shares owned by every board member, every top executive, and the largest institutional investors. The more shares owned by a board member, the more power he or she is likely to wield at meetings.

The company CEO or a former CEO should be, typically, one of the largest individual shareholders. In addition, board members should increase their stock ownership annually. A reporter should check the stock ownership chart for the current year with the one from the previous year to determine if board members are buying more stock. If they are not, then maybe they should be asked why. If a board member's stock holdings are going up, that could indicate a bullish future.

This chart is also valuable for another reason. It lists the largest shareholders who are not company executives or board members. That is whom reporters should call when the company implodes. Sometimes the footnotes of this section contain home addresses for these shareholders, which should help reporters dig up some phone numbers for them.

INSIDER TRADING

Ask the average person on the street about insider trading, and many of them will make the uninformed comment that they believe it is immoral and that the government should step in and be more aggressive in prosecuting cases. Many of them probably know that home maven Martha Stewart was accused of obstruction of justice in an investigation into insider trading of ImClone stock based on a tip she might have gotten from the company's former CEO, Sam Waksal, who stepped down from the company and pleaded guilty to insider trading.

What people do not realize is that more than 99% of all insider trading is perfectly legal. And insider trading records are an excellent way for a business reporter to assess what a company executive, board member, or investor thinks about a company.

According to the rules used by the SEC to govern investing, an insider is defined as an officer or director of a public company or an individual or entity owning 10% or more of any class of a company's shares. In Martha Stewart's case, she would be considered an insider because she allegedly received information from an insider—Waksal—and acted upon that information.

Those executives, board members, and institutional investors are allowed to buy and sell stock in these companies as long as they file a Form 4 with the SEC following the transaction. If an insider buys or sells stock in the open market, he or she must file with the SEC by the 10th day of the month following such a trade. Insider trading becomes illegal when the executive, director, or outside investor buys or sells stock in the company on the basis of nonpublic information that is, or could be, considered material in nature—generally anything that would require the company to file a Form 8-K, covered in chap. 4.

For example, if an executive at HSB Group Incorporated told an investor in the spring of 1999 that the company would be acquired by American International Group Incorporated for $60 a share, and the investor bought the stock with the intention of profiting from this information, he or she would be in serious trouble. The feds would be coming after him or her with handcuffs.

The following is the type of story that most casual business section readers equate with insider trading:

Investor John D. Weil of St. Louis has agreed to pay $93,424 to settle an insider-trading suit brought by the Securities and Exchange Commission.

The SEC alleged that Weil had profited illegally from a tip that Kaye Group Inc., an insurance brokerage based in New York, might be acquired.

Without admitting or denying the allegations, Weil agreed to give up $46,712 in profits and pay a civil fine of an equal amount.

Weil could not be reached for comment.

David Horowitz, assistant district administrator for the SEC in Philadelphia, said the Nasdaq Stock Market became aware of suspicious trading in Kaye's stock as part of its normal surveillance process. The Nasdaq then alerted the SEC, he said.

According to the SEC, Weil learned in late November or early December of 2000 that another company was interested in buying Kaye Group. The information came from Ned L. Sherwood, a director of Kaye Group.

The SEC says that Weil, who owned 10 percent of Kaye Group's stock, talked regularly with Sherwood about the company, and had assured Sherwood that the conversations were confidential.

Using brokerage accounts in his future wife's name, Weil bought 7,400 shares of Kaye Group between Dec. 28, 2000, and Jan. 17, 2001, at prices ranging from $7.44 to $7.94 a share.

Kaye Group announced on Jan. 20, 2001, that it had accepted a $14-a-share buyout offer from Hub International Ltd., another insurance brokerage.

The SEC also accused Rand E. Shapiro of Orlando, Fla., of making $35,804 in illegal profits on Kaye Group's stock. Shapiro's inside information came from another director, Howard A. Kaye, the SEC said. Like Weil, Shapiro agreed to settle the charges, return his profits and pay a fine.

The Kaye Group directors weren't accused of wrongdoing because they thought their conversations were confidential, and they didn't expect anyone to trade on the information, Horowitz said.

The SEC's allegations were included in a civil lawsuit filed Tuesday in federal court in Orlando.[2]

These stories are valuable and important to write when covering business news. But the facts for such stories do not come from SEC filings. Instead, they come from an SEC complaint, which is often available on the agency's Web site at www.sec.gov. (For more information about obtaining information from Web sites, see chap. 15.)

Again, virtually all stock trades done by company executives, board members, or other investors are perfectly legitimate and typically are not worth writing about. But it is a story if a board member or company executive is selling the majority of his or her stock holdings in the company, or buying a large chunk of stock.

There are legitimate reasons for an executive or board member to sell stock. It might be time to pay for junior's college tuition. Or maybe they are buying a vacation home on the water. It might even be time to diversify the investment portfolio and not hold too much of their net worth in one stock. These are all valid reasons for an insider to sell stock. But business reporters should watch for insider

---

[2]From "St. Louis investor John D. Weil settles SEC insider trading suit," by D. Nicklaus, December 14, 2002, *St. Louis Post Dispatch*, p. 2. Copyright 2002 by St. Louis Post Dispatch. Reprinted with permission.

selling. When it happens, a reporter should call the company to find out why. If the executive can give a good reason for selling, then it is not likely a story. But if there is no good reason, it might mean that he or she does not think the price is going to get higher anytime soon. Executives know more about the future prospects of a company than anyone else. Also, reporters should watch for executives buying large amounts of company stock. That could be an indication that these executives think good things about the company's future prospects and believe the stock price is going higher sooner rather than later. The temptation for the business reporter might be to act on this information and buy some of the stock also. This should be avoided, because it will likely result in the reporter being fired from his job. No media outlet allows its reporters to actively buy and sell stocks of companies they are reporting on. Now, where can a reporter find this information? Again, the SEC comes to the rescue. It requires executives, board members, and other investors to disclose their transactions in a variety of forms.

The Form 4 is a two-page document filed by directors, officers, or owners of more than 10% of the stock in a company. The report contains information on planned purchases and sales of certain equity securities. The form also contains information on the reporting person's relationship to the company. In addition, the form will disclose whether shares were bought or sold, how many shares were bought or sold, and the price. The form will also state how many shares the person still owns.

Reading the forms can be valuable because they also typically contain street addresses for the filer. If a reporter is having trouble tracking down a company board member, this form can help find them. Sometimes, however, Form 4s simply use the company's mailing address when they are filed by executives or board members. However, one problem for reporters in tracking these trades is that insiders have until the 10th day of the month following their trades to file their Form 4. By that time, the conditions causing the buying or selling may have changed.

Anytime a reporter is writing a story about a company's strategy or the CEO, it is wise to check the insider trading. If CEOs gush about a new product or a change in a company that is expected to produce better results, they should be willing to put their money where their mouth is. If a CEO is not buying his or her own company's stock on the basis of those prospects, a reporter should ask why.

Watching insider trading is also helpful in a broader sense. Wall Street experts who track insider trading want to know if more buying than selling is occurring. If that is the case, it may be an indication that the broader stock market could be headed higher.

The following is part of a story about another company that documents insider trading by investors during the last six months of 2000:

> A number of institutional investors have been adding to their positions in Trenwick in recent months, according to SEC filings.
> During the third quarter, New York-based Jennison Associates LLC purchased more than 1 million shares. Trainer Wortham & Co., another New York-based money

manager, purchased more than 686,000 shares. Over the same period, Memphis-based New South Capital Management Inc. added to its position as Trenwick's largest institutional investor, purchasing an additional 457,915 shares. New South, a long-term investor in the company, now owns more than 3.5 million shares.

More recently, Lord Abbett & Co. purchased more than 240,000 shares in the fourth quarter, bringing its total holdings in Trenwick to more than 1 million shares. The Teacher Retirement System of Texas bought 97,000, bringing its total position to 240,000 shares. And Palisade Capital added 43,400 shares to its position.

According to the most recent SEC filings for the firms, only two of Trenwick's top 10 institutional shareholders have lowered their holdings in the past six months. In the third quarter, Reich & Tang sold 51,525 shares, less than 4.0% of its total holdings. New York-based Royce & Associates Inc. trimmed 289,600 shares from its Trenwick holdings in the fourth quarter, but the firm still owns more than 905,000 shares.

Yet as Trenwick's market capitalization nears $1.0 billion, the company still attracts little interest from the sell-side analyst community on Wall Street. Three of the five analysts who follow Trenwick currently give it a "hold" rating.[3]

This is the kind of insider trading activity that readers of business stories want to know about, but quite often do not have the time to look up themselves. If reporters can provide more such information in their stories, they will better serve their readerships. In addition, they will show company executives that they know the most meaningful measure of performance—whether investors are willing to buy stock. An increase or decrease in these filings can be an indicator of what Wall Street pros think about a certain stock.

There are several other important filings for stock trades to note, although they do not directly involve company executives or board members. Investors who are not connected to a company are also required to file documents with the SEC when they purchase and sell company stock.

A Schedule 13D is filed when a shareholder or a group of shareholders acquires more than 5% of a company's stock. These filings must be made within the first 10 days of the investment. In addition, someone filing a 13D typically wants to affect a change at the company. These are most often disgruntled shareholders. Because investors have to file a 13D when they acquire 5% of a company's stock, many times they will purchase shares up to 4.9% so that other investors do not know of their interest in the company, which might drive the price up.

There is another form that is also important for business reporters. The SEC notes that institutional investors and professional investors acquire stock in the course of their business and not with the idea of changing the control of the company. When this happens, an institutional investor files a Schedule 13G. A Schedule 13G must also be filed within 10 days of the end of the quarter when the

---

[3]From "Trenwick Group's growth spurt: The reinsurer has added new businesses through acquisition and is seeking more deals. Can CEO Jim Billett keep the stock price rising?" by C. Roush, March 2001, *Insurance Investor*, p. 1, Copyright 2001 by SNL Financial, Reprinted with permission.

transaction occurred. But even though they are not filed as quickly as some other documents, a 13G can still provide good information.

How much of a treasure trove are these files? Schedule 13Gs and Schedule 13Ds typically include the name of the investor's company, how many shares were purchased, purchase dates and prices, and quite often, the name and the phone number of someone at that institutional investor who is in charge of the specific investment.

For example, consider the excerpt from the Schedule 13G below. A reporter found this filing while doing research for an article about American Physicians Capital Incorporated, a Michigan-based company. All the reporter had to do was look up the phone number for Greenlight Capital and had David Einhorn on the other end, more than happy to talk, even though he had never heard of or seen the publication for which the reporter was writing.

Item 1(a) Name of Issuer. American Physicians Capital, Inc.

Item 1(b) Address of Issuer's Principal Executive Offices. 1301 North Hagadorn Road East Lansing, Michigan 48823

Item 2(a) Name of Person Filing. Greenlight Capital, L.L.C. ("Greenlight"), David Einhorn and Jeffrey A. Keswin

Item 2(b) Address of Principal Business Office, or, if none, Residence. 420 Lexington Ave., Suite 1740, New York, New York 10170

Item 2(c) Citizenship or Place of Organization. Greenlight is a limited liability company organized under the laws of the State of Delaware. David Einhorn and Jeffrey A. Keswin are the principals of Greenlight and are United States citizens.

Item 2(d) Title of Class of Securities. Common Stock, no par value per share (the "Common Stock").

Item 2(e) CUSIP Number. _____

Item 3 Reporting Person. Inapplicable.

Item 4 Ownership. (a)Greenlight and Messrs. Einhorn and Keswin are the beneficial owners of 990,000 shares of Common Stock.

(b) Greenlight and Messrs. Einhorn and Keswin are the beneficial owners of 9.9 percent of the outstanding shares of Common Stock. This percentage is based upon the outstanding shares of the Issuer equaling 10,000,000 shares, the amount of shares initially offered in connection with the Issuers initial public offering (the "IPO"). Mr. Keswin has been informed that underwriters of the IPO have elected to subscribe for an additional amount of shares causing the outstanding shares to equal 11,450,254 as of December 14, 2000. Based on this revised number of outstanding shares, Greenlight's and Messrs. Einhorn's and Keswin's percentage ownership would be equal to 8.6 percent.

(c) Greenlight has the sole power to vote and dispose of the 990,000 shares of Common Stock beneficially owned by it. As the principals of Greenlight, Messrs. Einhorn and Keswin may direct the vote and disposition of the 990,000 shares of Common Stock beneficially owned by Greenlight. (Schedule 136, Greenlight Capital L.L.C., 2000)

The story was a look at American Physicians Capital's strategy for improving its performance. And, likely, the only person better to quote assessing that strategy than an investor who has purchased a large amount of stock in the company is the CEO himself. The valuable information in this filing that allowed the reporter to find Einhorn was the name of his company, Greenlight Capital, its mailing address, and Einhorn's name. The firm's phone number was obtained with a quick call to directory assistance.

Writing about company executives, boards, and investors can be detailing one of the most fascinating relationships in business reporting. These people are all human, and they are all driven by certain factors. The CEO may be driven by the need to have power or control. Or he may be driven by the desire to provide a good working environment for his employees and a favorable return for his investors. Board members are often driven by the same factors. Investors are driven by one factor—to make money. How the three interact often results in fascinating stories.

GLOSSARY

board of directors: People selected to sit on an authoritative standing committee, or governing body, taking responsibility for the management of an organization. Board members are chosen by shareholders, but in practice they are usually selected by the current board's recommendations. The board usually includes major shareholders as well as executives of the company.

bonus: A financial incentive given to employees in addition to their base pay in the form of a one-time payment.

chairman of the board: The most senior executive in an organization. The chair of an organization is responsible for running the annual meeting, and meetings of the board of directors. He or she may be a figurehead, appointed for prestige or power, and may have no role in the day-to-day running of the organization. Sometimes the roles of chair and chief executive are combined, and the chair then has more control over daily operations, and sometimes the chair is a retired chief executive.

chief executive officer: The person with overall responsibility for ensuring that the daily operations of an organization run efficiently, and for carrying out strategic plans. The chief executive of an organization normally sits on the board.

chief financial officer: The officer in an organization responsible for handling funds, signing checks, the keeping of financial records, and financial planning for the company.

Form 4: A document required by the SEC and the appropriate stock exchange to announce changes in the holdings of directors, officers, and shareholders owning 10 percent or more of the company's outstanding stock.

insider trading: Trading in securities by executives, board members or large shareholders. When insider trading is based on privileged information, it is illegal.

president or chief operating officer: The officer in a corporation responsible for the day-to-day management of a company and usually reporting to the chief executive officer.

proxy statement, or 14A: A notice that a company sends to stockholders allowing them to vote and giving them all the information they need to vote knowledgeably.

restricted stock: A Restricted Stock Award is a grant of stock by an employer to an employee in which the employee's rights to the shares are limited until the shares "vest" and cease to be subject to the restrictions. Typically, the employee may not sell or transfer the shares of stock until they vest—frequently a defined period of time—and forfeits the stock if the employee's employment terminates before the stock vests.

salary: A form of earnings given to employees at regular intervals in exchange for the work they have done. Traditionally, a salary is a form of remuneration given to professional employees on a monthly basis.

Schedule 13D: A form filed by anyone acquiring a beneficial ownership of 5% or more of any equity security registered with the SEC. If the company is listed on an exchange, the form must be filed with the exchange too.

stock options: A stock option is the opportunity, given by your employer, to purchase a certain number of shares of your company's common stock at a pre-established price, known as the grant price, over a specific period of time, known as the vesting period.

REFERENCES

Barnhart, B. (2002, January 8). Activist shareholders forcing change. *Chicago Tribune.* p. 8.

Form DEF 14A. Aetna Incorporated (2000, March 22). (SEC Publication No. 0000914039-00-000119, pp. 15–16). Washington, DC: Securities and Exchange Commission.

Form DEF 14A. Coca-Cola Company. (2002, March 4). (SEC Publication No. 0000950144-02-1998, pp. 13–16). Washington, DC: Securities and Exchange Commission.

Form DEF 14A. Conseco Incorporated. (2002, May 23). (SEC Publication No. 0000950124-00-003401, pp. 10–19). Washington, DC: Securities and Exchange Commission.

Form DEF 14A. Progressive Corporation. (2000, March 16). (SEC Publication No. 0000950152-00-001752, pp. 4–5). Washington, DC: Securities and Exchange Commission.

McDowell, D. (2002, January 18). Confessions of a securities writer. TheStreet.com. Retrieved Sept. 15, 2002 from http://www.thestreet.com/funds

Nicklaus, D. (2002, December 14). St. Louis investor John D. Weil settles SEC insider trading suit. *St. Louis Post Dispatch.* p. 2.

Roush, C. (2001, March). Trenwick Group's growth spurt: The reinsurer has added new businesses through acquisitions and is seeking more deals. Can CEO Jim Billett keep the stock price rising? *Insurance Investor.* p. 1.

Roush, C. (2001, March). Bill Cheeseman enters the fray: The CEO of American Physicians Capital wants to buy other medical malpractice insurers. The line forms to the left. *Insurance Investor.* pp. 6–8.

Schedule 13G. Greenlight Capital, L.L.C. (SEC Publication No. 0000941302-00-500113, pp. 1–6). Washington, DC: Securities and Exchange Commission.

Stark, K. (2000, June 8). Abramson quits Aetna Inc. board; he sold U.S. Healthcare to the insurer in 1996. *The Philadelphia Inquirer.* p. C1.

Unger, H. (1999, December 7). Coke's shocker: Ivester retiring after 2 years under pressure. *Atlanta Journal-Constitution.* p. 1A.

Valdmanis, T., & Howard, T. (2000, November 22). Coke plan to buy Quaker for $16B stock collapses; Disagreement over price, strategic direction bring startling about-face. *USA Today.* P. 1B.

Other Books on CEOs and Management

Bossidy, L., & Charan, R. (2002). *Execution: The discipline of getting things done.* New York: Crown Publishing.

Charan, R. (1998). *Boards at work: How corporate boards create competitive advantage.* New York: Jossey-Bass.

Charan, R. (2001). *What the CEO wants you to know: How your company really works.* New York: Crown Publishing.

Collins, J. (2001). *Good to great: Why some companies make the leap . . . and others don't.* New York: Harper Collins.

Ellig, B. (2001). *The complete guide to executive compensation.* New York: McGraw-Hill.

Greising, D. (1999). *I'd like the world to buy a Coke: The life and leadership of Roberto Goizueta.* New York: Wiley.

Slater, R. (1998). *Jack Welch & the GE way: Management insights and leadership secrets of the legendary CEO.* New York: McGraw-Hill.

SUGGESTED EXERCISES

1. Review the organizational charts of two different companies. Write a 500-word analysis of why the organizational structures differ, focusing on job titles and who reports to whom, with emphasis on the relationship between the CEO, president and executive vice presidents or division presidents.

2. Review the executive compensation for a public company. Compare the bonus and salary increase for the CEO and president of the company to the increase in net income and stock price for the same fiscal year. Discuss why there may be a discrepancy between the compensation and the company's performance.

3. Examine a company's board of directors. List the directors who may be considered to have financial ties to the company, and those that don't. Discuss whether the financial connections might have a bearing on the decisions made by the board member.
4. Review a list of the top shareholders for a company. Take 30 minutes to determine which shareholders are outside investors, which ones are board members and which ones are current or former executives. Compare the amount of stock held by board members to the amount of stock held by outside shareholders. Discuss whether a large outside shareholder deserves a seat on the board.
5. Examine the insider buying and selling by a single company's executives and board members for the past 12 months. Total the number of shares sold by the entire group to the number of shares purchased. Is the insider trading for the company in the past year a reflection of the company's future performance?

9

Private and Small Companies

A VITAL PART OF LOCAL ECONOMIES

Private and small businesses are the backbone of the nation's economy. Without them, many towns and communities would not exist. They provide stable jobs for millions, and help the economy grow.

Yet read the nation's newspapers, Internet sites, and magazines, listen to its radio news or watch its television news, and the bulk of the business news coverage ignores small and private businesses. Part of the reason is that many reporters believe that there is no news in these companies, they are too small to be making news, or they are not interesting enough.

At first glance, they may be correct. Big companies whose products and services are used by millions around the country—and the world—have more of an impact on more people. Small businesses do not sell products that have a huge impact.

But if a small business develops a product that is going to have an impact on a large part of the population, they will become one of those big companies. Bill Gates started his company in his garage, and now Microsoft is one of the biggest companies in the world, dominating the computer software industry. Wal-Mart started with one store. Coca-Cola started by selling its soft drinks at one drug store. Ford started by selling its first car. These companies were not created as multibillion dollar operations with tens of thousands of workers. They began as tiny operations with dreams of becoming something bigger.

The other argument against covering small and private businesses in the media is that it is tough to find information about them that is objective. Virtually all private and small companies are not required to file financial information with the SEC, for example, so that everyone can see how much revenue and profits they have. When the CEO of a small company says that his or her company's revenues grew by 50% in the past year, it would seem that a reporter has no way of verifying that information unless the executive shows him the books. But, there are plenty of ways to find out financial information about small and private companies across the country. All it takes is some thinking and research, as this chapter shows later on. No company is completely private. And no business, no matter how small, leaves a cold trail without leaving background information somewhere. The reporting can be done. Many just do not know how to do it.

There is another, more important, reason why mass communication outlets should likely pay more attention to small and private businesses and the issues that affect their operations. As mentioned earlier, small and private businesses are vital to the economy.

According to the U.S. Small Business Administration, there were approximately 22.9 million small businesses in this country in 2002. Small businesses provide 75% of the net new jobs added to the economy, and represent 99.7% of all employers. More than half of the private work force is employed by a small business, and small businesses accounted for 52% of the private sector output in 1999.

Some media outlets—particularly those in large metropolitan areas—virtually ignore businesses that collectively employ more than half of the country's work-force and account for more than half of all private sector output. To be sure, a number of newspapers and other media outlets do have a reporter assigned to cover small business issues. And small-town newspapers such as the *Statesville Record & Landmark* in western North Carolina have a reporter assigned to cover business in a community where it is virtually all small business news. But for the most part, business journalism has overlooked many small and private businesses when compared with the coverage of public companies and well-known private corporations.

That is despite the fact that Americans have a higher opinion of small businesses than they do of better-known corporations and labor unions, according to a survey by the American Enterprise Institute in Washington. Ninety percent of Americans have a favorable opinion of small business, according to the survey in a compilation of polls by Gallup, Harris, National Opinion Research Center, and RoperASW. The figure has hovered between 84% and 94% for the last quarter century.

In comparison, the latest Harris poll showed that 66% of people have a great deal or some confidence in labor unions. The confidence level for large companies was 72% in the Harris poll.

Small businesses have been revered—and feared—in this country for more than a century. When Congress first passed antitrust laws in the 19th century, they did so to protect small and private businesses. The U.S. Small Business Administration was created in 1953 to aid and assist small companies.

Because of their collective interests, small business has also grown into a powerful lobbying force in state legislatures and in Congress. The National Federation of Independent Business has more than 600,000 members and offices in all 50 states. Its lobbyists fight for small business rights with state and federal authorities.

The following story from CBSMarketWatch.com shows how regulatory agencies have catered to small business interests in the past—with one notable exception:

Call it the red tape wars. Rules and regulations churned out by the government are the bane of most small businesses. For more than 20 years, they've fought a running battle with federal bureaucrats over the daunting process of complying with the edicts emanating from Washington.

Make no mistake; small businesses have won a significant round or two along the way. Yet the war continues in all its pencil-snapping frustration. The latest skirmish unfolded last week before the House Committee on Small Business. The target: the Internal Revenue Service.

By way of background, an armistice in the red tape wars was supposed to have been reached back in 1980. That's when the White House Conference on Small Business serve as a catalyst for three significant new laws–the Regulatory Flexibility Act, the Equal Access to Justice Act and the Paperwork Reduction Act.

Together they were supposed to insure that government agencies took the concerns into account of anyone afflicted by federal rule making. The Regulatory Flexibility Act, in particular, was key. It exacted a pledge that agencies would study proposed regulations—before they were issued—to assess how they affected small businesses. The goal was to find ways to limit the impact, if regulation hit small firms disproportionately.

As we all know, no federal agency seems to pile on the paperwork quite like the IRS. Yet when it comes to complying with regulations itself, the nation's tax revenuers have proved to be particularly resistant to change. "If avoidance of the RFA has been the Service's implicit goal, they have been unquestionably successful; but for those who care about the efficacy of the RFA, the overall record has been dismal," said Dan Mastromarco, Principal of The Argus Group, a Phoenix, Ariz., company that provides insurance to small businesses.

Congress last tightened the RFA's legal standards in 1996, following a bruising four-year legislative battle. Perhaps not surprisingly, the IRS triggered the reform effort when it issued supposedly innocuous changes to the payroll tax deposit system. "What they put out as a proposed rule can best be described as gibberish," said former Congressman Andy Ireland, who was involved in the fight. "I couldn't understand it. And, when I went to testify at a hearing before the staff of the IRS Commissioner none of his people seemed to understand it," he told the committee. "Yet these same people were confident that the average small businessperson would have no problem complying."

Unfortunately, the IRS's disdain for the RFA is still evident, said Frank Swain, a partner in the law firm of Baker & Daniels in Indianapolis. In fact, of the 286 regulatory projects it's working on right now, the IRS says that only two merit a regulatory flexibility analysis, according to the agency's most recent semi-annual regulatory agenda, which it published in the Federal Register in December. "Whatever the IRS's reading of the law is, in the real world it defies credibility to say that [it] is only working on two of 286 regulatory matters that it believes merit a regulatory flexibility analysis," said Swain, a former Chief Counsel for the Small Business Administration.

To understand how seemingly innocuous IRS proposals often have broad over-reaching consequences, consider an IRS proposal last June to eliminate a regulation exempting certain mobile machinery, such as cranes, from certain fuel and other excise taxes. Although the measure, known as the mobile machinery exemption, had been on the books since 1977, the IRS said it would have an insignificant economic impact on small businesses. It never bothered to conduct an RFA analysis, said Swain. As it turned out, many affected industries, including construction, well digging and services, and mobile-crane operators, include a significant number of small businesses, Swain said.

While the IRS didn't bother with a study, the Federal Highway Administration separately conducted its own review in 1999 and discovered that the change would cost businesses more than $250 million annually. An updated analysis now pegs the cost at $462 million a year.

Starting Jan. 29, Massachusetts businesses will be able to file required reports to the secretary of state's office online and pay related fees by credit card. Secretary of State William F. Galvin said electronic filing was "another way to make government more user-friendly for business." Corporations will be able to go to www.state.ma.us/sec/cor to file.

Starting next month, Uniform Commercial Code filings by creditors to protect their interest in a debtor's property can be done on the Web, too. By summer, the public will be able to research corporate filings online. Galvin said the state would continue to accommodate companies that wish to file "the old-fashioned way."[1]

Writing about small and private businesses can be different than covering large, public companies. For one, many small and private businesses are not seeking publicity to help pump up their stock price. Many of them do not want a reporter poking around, looking for stories. Whereas many public companies have public relations personnel to handle media inquiries, most small and private businesses do not. When a reporter calls, the president or CEO often takes the call.

Business reporters do not necessarily have to write stories about what is going on at small and private businesses to write stories that include them. A retail reporter writing about Christmas sales can call the private storeowner as well as the publicly traded department store chain and Wal-Mart. A banking reporter will want to write about how a private community bank is adding branches to compete against Bank of America and BankOne.

Private business owners and executives can also sometimes be willing to grant interviews to talk about the local and regional economy, or for stories assessing

---

[1] From "The battle rages on: Small business squares off against IRS rulemaking," by K. Girard, May 5, 2003, CBS.MarketWatch.com. Copyright 2003 by CBS.MarketWatch.com. Reprinted with permission.

issues such as a shortage of experienced workers or how they will be affected by new laws. With each story, the reporter is not writing about the business, but is gaining the trust of the small and private business owner or executive. Then, when news specifically about the company merits coverage, they will be more likely to open up.

Like most businesses, the small and private companies need to understand the role of the media. Many of them will expect to receive glowing or positive coverage, and when they do not get it, they will be mad. Some of them may even believe that positive coverage is a quid pro quo in exchange for their advertising.

The reporter should make the ground rules clear. With any business story, the job of the reporter and of the media outlet is to inform the public. Some stories are written about small and private businesses if they are unique to the market. *The Door County Advocate* in Sturgeon Bay, Wisconsin covered the opening of the first car wash in the county north of Sturgeon Bay in its March 29, 2002 issue. But that is because of its uniqueness—it is the only car wash for miles. It should be clear that the media outlet decides what is news.

Writing about small and private businesses can be done to show how they are changing and evolving with the community. The *Southeast Missourian* in Cape Girardeau, Missouri, published a story about the influx of immigrant small business owners and international workers in its area in a front-page story on April 21, 2002 that helped explain to its readers why these businesses were opening around town.

Many small business reporters focus on issues and trends instead of profiling companies. They are looking at how these small companies are struggling to make it in the business world. They are writing about the decision to provide health insurance and other benefits to workers, and how the cost of doing so can cripple a small operation. They are writing about the struggle of a small business owner to hand his operation over to the next generation after 40 years of running the company. They are assessing the impact of the new Home Depot in town on the local hardware stores that have been part of the community for a half century.

Writing about small and private businesses can be fascinating because it forces the reporter to dig deeper into analyzing a company's situation. He or she cannot rely on SEC filings to provide the facts. They have to interview competitors, interview customers and clients, assess the market and look for clues as to why a small business is successful—or struggling to make ends meet.

The reporter should think of him- or herself as a small business. The reporter has revenue—a paycheck—and expenses, such as rent, electricity, and gas, just like a small business. What is left over is the money that can be used to expand operations by buying a new television or some furniture or even a new car. The more money left over from the paycheck, the more the reporter can expand his or her "business." But if there is no money left over, then the "business" is struggling, and may have to go into debt to make ends meet. That may mean making purchases with credit cards, or asking the bank for a loan to buy that car.

Small and private businesses operate much the same way. And when they struggle, they have to borrow money too. If they continue to struggle, they may be forced
to go out of business. If the reporter's financial situation continues to flounder, he
or she too may be forced to go out of "business"—and find a new job that pays
more money.

Small and private businesses have ups and downs, just like any business. Those
ups and downs can be news.

FINDING INFORMATION

Many reporters mistakenly believe that private companies are just that—private.
And while private companies do not often willingly hand out information about
their operations, there are plenty of other places to go to get that information.

Reporters should consider what information would be good to know about a
small or private business, and then ask the company for the information. (The CEO
of watchmaker Timex once told me the private company's revenues and profits just
because I asked.) If the business declines to provide the information, then think
about where that information might be found.

Some private companies are willing to give a range of revenue and profits to
publications such as the local business journal. In other cases, revenue and earnings
may be estimated on the basis of knowledge of the company's operations. When
reporters use numbers like these, they must make sure to attribute them to the
source.

Still, it is not hard to find information about small and private businesses if
the company is not forthcoming with it. Government agencies are the best places
to look for most of this information. Basic information about small and private
companies, such as articles of incorporation, is filed with the Secretary of State's
office. This will get you the names of the executives and owners, as well as phone
numbers and mailing addresses. That is the first place to start when researching
information about a small or private business. Sometimes the incorporation records
may not be up to date, and maybe the state has listed the company as not in good
standing. This could be a sign that the business is having financial trouble.

Another good place to find information is local government records. The local
building department will have building permit and inspection records, for example.
A county clerk or register of deeds will have information about real estate deeds,
mortgage agreements, and fictitious name registrations. The names may be important when a company is operating its business under one name but incorporated at
the state level under another name.

While a reporter is at the courthouse, he or she should not forget to check to see
whether the business has been sued in the past. The reporter should read the lawsuits
and check the names of the lawyers suing the company. They should be called and
asked about their dealings with the business. If there are a lot of lawsuits against

a company in the last few months or year, that could be a sign that the business is having trouble paying its debts. Also check to see if the business is litigious itself and is filing lawsuits against others. Lawsuits can provide information about small and private businesses that may have otherwise gone undisclosed.

Reporters should not forget about the criminal side of the courthouse either. If a CEO or small business owner has been arrested, that is often news. CEOs and company executives also occasionally find themselves in civil suits unrelated to their business in which information about their company is disclosed. Divorce filings are a prime example. A spouse may be seeking half of the worth of the business, and may file detailed information about its financial performance in the filings.

There is much other information also available at the local level. The local health department will have health inspection records and some permits. Health records are important for many industries such as restaurants. The *Loveland Daily Reporter Herald* in Colorado, for example, lists restaurant and food service inspections throughout the county every week, ordering them from those that received "excellent" ratings to those that received "marginal" and "inadequate" ratings.

The planning or zoning department will have information about development permits and bonds posted to guarantee construction. This information can be helpful for reporters writing about a local commercial or residential developer. In addition, the property appraiser or tax assessor's office will be able to provide the assessed value of a property as well as property and building descriptions.

Local real estate transactions can also be telling for a small or private business. Reporters should check to see if the company has been making any purchases recently. If so, where is the land, and what does the company plan to do with the land? If the purchases are near its current location, the company could be planning an expansion. It is also important to check to see if a small or private business is purchasing residential property. If it is, who is living in the houses? If the residents are employees or executives of the company, why are they receiving this special treatment?

Small and private businesses also come into contact with state regulatory agencies that could provide information. In addition to the Secretary of State's office, other state agencies that might have records on a business include the attorney general's office, which might have investigated consumer complaints against the business or prosecuted the company, and an economic development office, which has a goal of keeping businesses happy in the state and attracting new companies to come to a state. If the business has ever received a tax break or other financial enticement, the economic development office would have a record.

The Hartford Courant reported in April 2003 that Connecticut officials assisted a small Pennsylvania company seeking state funding to help it expand. In addition, the company helped close relatives of those officials invest in the private company. The value of their investment skyrocketed shortly thereafter. That story came from looking at the state economic development agency.

State licensing agencies are also an important source of information for small and private businesses. They regulate businesses ranging from barbershops to doctors, and many of their records are public information. Fines and suspensions against the medical profession, for example, can be obtained in some cases.

Reporters should also check the state legislature to see if there have been any hearings related to the company or its industry. The state environmental protection agency may have records of pollution on the business, whereas the department of labor may be able to tell whether the company has been laying off workers. The state purchasing office can tell whether the business has any contracts with the state, and for what goods or services.

Uniform Commercial Code (UCC) filings are also important documents that can help tell a story about a small or private business. The UCC has a body of laws that has been adopted in virtually every state in the country. A UCC filing occurs when one business sells something to another business on credit. The business that sold the tractor to the farmer, for example, filed a UCC form showing that the tractor is collateral for the loan. If the business that purchased the tractor fails to pay the loan, the other business can repossess the tractor. UCC forms can show whether a business is borrowing a lot of money to make purchases. This could be a sign that the company plans to expand its operations.

State regulators who track the banking and insurance industry can also be important sources of information, even for small businesses like insurance agencies. They will also have financial reports for every bank and insurance company operating in the state. If the bank or insurer is private and not willing to disclose its revenue and profits to a reporter, it has given this information to regulators. That information should be readily available—reporters should let the company know they are going to get the information and use it. They might open up more after a few calls to the state. The same goes for utility companies such as electricity and water operations. They are regulated by a state public service commission, which keeps financial records.

State tax records can also be valuable when researching small and private businesses. Jim Hoffer of WABC in New York searched state tax records and discovered that many Manhattan restaurants owed thousands in back taxes. "From fast food to some of the city's finest restaurants, our investigation found nearly 200 establishments that have collected from their customers a combined total of about $10 million," noted Hoffer (2003). "It's money collected through the 8.25% sales tax. But instead of passing it on to the city and state, these restaurants kept it." Armed with this information, Hoffer confronted some of these restaurant owners, all small, private businesses, many who claimed to be working to pay off the debt. One said he used the sales tax as a loan to help make it through the aftermath of the September 11, 2001 terrorist attacks, fully understanding he would be paying a penalty (Hoffer, 2003).

Federal agencies might also have information on small and private businesses, depending on what they do and what they sell. The Environmental Protection

Agency, for example, issues permits to businesses that discharge environmentally sensitive liquids, and they also investigate spills. The Consumer Product Safety Commission will have records on a company if it has ever had a product recalled because of safety concerns. (For more information about regulatory agencies, see chap. 14.)

For employee-related matters, the Equal Employment Opportunity Commission and the Occupational Safety and Health Administration are excellent places to check for information. These agencies investigate complaints of job discrimination and harassment and unsafe working conditions. If the business has ever had a worker injured or hurt on the job, or ever faced a claim from an employee who alleged unfair treatment, then there is a record of an investigation into the matter. Also check the National Labor Relations Board if the business has unionized workers.

If the company is involved in technology or another specialized business, it may have patents on inventions that are being used to help it make money. The Patent and Trademark Office will have a record of every patent issued to the company. If the company does not want to talk about its products, this could be a way of getting information about them. However, it may take an engineer or a scientist to help explain what the patent means.

Federal agencies also regulate specific industries. For example, financial information about a credit union is available from the National Credit Union Administration. Many journalists do not know this, and rightfully think that credit unions are nonprofit organizations owned by their depositors. Yet, many credit unions are very profitable. A reporter should find out how profitable the one in his or her own town is. That may be a story waiting to be written.

The Federal Aviation Administration has information about airports that can be useful in writing a story, particularly for a reporter interested in topics related to transportation or tourism. The agency also has enforcement information against airlines, pilots, mechanics, and others in the industry, as well as a registry of all aircraft owned in this country. The Federal Communications Commission has tons of information about each and every radio and television station in the country, as well as documents on telephone and cable companies.

Reporters looking for information about private mining companies can check with the Mine Safety and Health Administration. And the Nuclear Regulatory Commission has records about operators of nuclear plants. As these two examples show, there is likely a regulatory agency for any type of industry. For the reporter trying to write a story about a gun store in town, the Bureau of Alcohol, Tobacco, and Firearms maintains a database of federally approved gun dealers across the country. If the gun store is not on that list, then the reporter has a better story than he or she may have originally thought.

Or maybe a reporter is writing about a small business that has gotten some help from the Small Business Administration (SBA) in the form of a loan guaranteed by the agency. The SBA has a database that details the size of loans, when the loan was approved, whether the loan has been paid or become delinquent, what bank made the loan, the number of jobs the company promised to add to its employee base because of the loan, and other information. The SBA also administers another program that encourages the federal government to award contracts for work to small and minority businesses. Similar information is available on these contracts. If the business you are writing about mentions that it has done work for the federal government, then a lot of information should be available. That information includes revenue for the company, and where the revenue is coming from—even for private businesses.

Other good information about small and private companies is available from other sources. For example, credit reports from companies such as Dun and Bradstreet can be purchased for a fee. These reports can sometimes tell a journalist if the company has had problems repaying its debt.

A private company may have made a debt issue. If it has, then it may have filed information with the SEC. In addition, bond rating agencies will likely have reviewed the debt issue and issued a rating on the bonds. They may have also written a report about the company and its financial status.

Small companies do not always have to go through the same steps as larger companies when filing documents with the SEC to become public companies. If it had less than $25 million in revenue or its stock is worth no more than $25 million, the company can file a Form SB-1 to raise $10 million or less. This form allows the business to provide information in a question-and-answer format. A Form SB-2 is used by a small business when it wants to raise an unlimited amount of cash in a stock offering, but still requires less disclosure than what the SEC requires for larger companies. For example, the small business will have to provide two years of audited financial statements, whereas large companies must provide three years of audited financial statements.

There are other sources for ferreting information about a small or private business. If the business has issued a news release about anything, the document should be available from PR Newswire or Business Wire. Reporters should check his or her media outlet's library to see if it has done a story on the company in the past, or do a broader search on a database such as Nexis to check for other articles or mentions. If the small or private business is part of a niche industry that has a specialty publication such as a newsletter or monthly magazine, reporters should check it to see if it has ever been mentioned. Every little bit helps when you are gathering string on a company that is not divulging any information.

Again, competitors may be able to provide valuable information. Suppliers such as advertising firms and distributors of the company's products or goods can provide information as to what it is like to do business with the company. Public interest groups may also have information. It is a good idea to check with the local Chamber of Commerce or Better Business Bureau to see if there have been complaints filed against the business.

Another valuable source is employees. They may be disgruntled or unhappy. Although they may not talk on the record about their employer for fear of losing their job, they may seek retribution for bad treatment by providing internal documents or company information that could be damaging. Reporters should tread lightly here. If an employee balks, he or she may go to their superior and tell them that a reporter has been snooping around.

A recent survey of visitors to the *Forbes* magazine Web site resulted in 53% of the respondents replying that private businesses should not be required to disclose revenue, profits, assets, and employees, whereas 29% believed they should. It is unlikely that any laws will be passed requiring private companies to do so. But the notion that small and private businesses are closed doors when it comes to information should be dispelled. Plenty of information can be obtained. It certainly takes some legwork, and most of the legwork may not result in any information that will make it into the story. But the one fact that does makes the story worthwhile.

Public records for private companies: What to look for

1. **Local government**—real estate transaction records; register of deeds, health department records, planning department records, property appraiser or tax assessor; civil and criminal litigation.
2. **State government**—Secretary of State's office for incorporation records; Uniform Commercial Code filings, economic development records; state legislature; professional licensing boards; state regulatory agencies for insurance and banking.
3. **Federal government**—Consumer Product Safety Commission, Environmental Protection Agency, Equal Employment Opportunity Commission and Occupational Safety and Health Administration for worksite-related records, Federal Trade Commission, Patent and Trademark Office, specific federal agencies for certain industries such as energy and aviation.

UCC CODE FILINGS

UCC filings were mentioned as being a source of information for small and private businesses. This cannot be emphasized enough.

UCC filings are some of the best documents available for a reporter, but they are seldom used to tell the story about a business—public or private, big or small—or an individual. That is disappointing because these filings help tell the reporter vital information about a company and a person. A reporter should likely look at UCC filings each time he or she writes a story about a company or a person.

UCC filings are available from the Secretary of State's office in each state. Many of these are available online, and can be searched by lender name as well as by the borrower's identity.

As mentioned earlier, UCC filings are made with the state to show when money has been borrowed to make a purchase or for another reason. UCC filings show what company or business holds a lien on a corporation or a home. Sometimes, the filing will disclose the amount of the loan and what was used as collateral for the loan. No one would want to buy a house that has a lien on it from a creditor of the previous owner. A UCC filing can disclose this information, and it can tell a business owner how many loans, and sometimes for what amounts, a potential business partner has. Many business owners check the UCC filings of other businesses before they sign a contract. They want to know that the company is going to be able to fulfill its end of the deal.

The North Carolina Secretary of State's office explains the usefulness of reviewing UCC filings in the following way:

> Such information may be used to determine whether a lender would be interested in extending credit to the small business owner to, for example, provide capital for purchasing equipment or raw materials. The small business owner may, in turn, access the Section's records to determine whether to extend credit to customers by taking a security interest in the finished product to be sold. Without the services offered by the UCC Section, the lender or small business owner might be required to check county lien records in several counties in order to get a true financial picture of the person or business involved in the potential transaction. (North Carolina Department of the Secretary of State, 2003)

These filings can be helpful in a number of ways. When writing about a business or an individual, reporters can find out how much and to whom the person or company owes money. When *USA Today* researched disgraced former WorldCom leader Bernie Ebbers, they pored through UCC filings around the country to get a detailed list of everything he had invested in or purchased during the last decade. That helped show the reader where the money he had made from WorldCom had gone. Another example of the benefits of looking at UCC filings can be illustrated by the *Pittsburgh Post-Gazette* investigation into a church that wanted to redevelop a shopping center. The reporter looked at the church's UCC filings and discovered that banks and other lenders had given it seven loans despite the fact that it had fallen behind in paying its taxes and other debts.

There are two main types of UCC filings. The first one is called a UCC-1 and is the original finance statement being recorded for the first time. A UCC-3 filing is a statement that continues, terminates, amends, or releases the debt or loan.

UCC filings may seem intimidating, but all they are doing is recording simple business transactions. Reporters should use them to their advantage. When a small or private business owner—or anyone for that matter—discovers that a reporter has taken the time to look at its UCC filings, they suddenly realize that that reporter is serious about finding information. The *St. Petersburg Times* used UCC filings to track down information about a company providing water to the city of Port Richey. The owner of the company was surprised that she had been found.

PRIVATE COMPANY OWNERSHIP AND STRUCTURE

Knowing the structure of small or private company ownership may be almost as important as the facts about the business and its operations. The ownership of a company will tell you who is calling the shots for the business. If a business is owned by one person, it is likely that he or she is also the president or CEO and is making all of the major decisions for the business.

But sole proprietorships often change ownership structure as the business becomes more successful. For instance, if the small business needs money to expand, the sole owner may decide to sell a stake in his or her fledgling company to investors in return for the cash. These investors now may want a say in how the company is operated so as to boost the value of their ownership in the company. Or a business may actually sell itself to its employees. Thus, the employees have a vested interest in how the business performs as well.

A recent study on private businesses by accounting firm PriceWaterhouse-Coopers discovered that the typical private company has about 200 employees and annual revenue of about $47 million. For a reporter in a small town, the average small or private company may not be that big. Private companies in larger cities may be much bigger than that, however.

About half of the private companies in the PriceWaterhouseCoopers survey are what are called close corporations, meaning that the businesses only have a small number of shareholders, usually no more than 50. These businesses also have no ready market for the corporation's stock, and a majority of the shareholders are active in the management of these corporations.

The survey found that about 40% of the private businesses are what are called S corporations, which provide the benefits of incorporation but eliminate double taxation, which can occur when the profits of a company are taxed as a corporation and then as income for the shareholders of the corporation. An S corporation is limited to no more than 75 shareholders.

The survey also found that about 4% of private businesses were partnerships, such as limited liability corporations. This business structure provides limited liability to the members, and also taxes like it is a partnership, eliminating double taxation. These businesses are often law firms or accounting businesses. And about 3% of private businesses are sole proprietors, meaning there is just one owner of the company.

Other small and private businesses take the strategy of offering ownership in the company to employees through a program called employee stock ownership plans, or an ESOP. About 11,000 companies now have ESOPs covering more than 8.5 million employees.

Employees can receive stock in an ESOP a variety of ways. They can purchase the stock directly, or be given the stock as a bonus. They can also obtain stock through a profit sharing plan in which the profits of the company are divided up among shareholders.

ESOPs are commonly used by private companies to allow the owners to sell their stake in the company and motivate their remaining employees at the same time. In almost every ESOP, all full-time workers above the age of 21 participate in the plan. They receive stock in the company on the basis of their payrate or another formula. Employees are then vested—which means they then own the stock—within a 5 to 7 year time frame. If an employee leaves the company, then the business buys back the stock on the basis of an outside valuation of the shares. Sometimes this valuation can be obtained from the company or from employees.

ESOPs are designed to encourage employees to consider the best interests of the business, but that is not always how it works. Some ESOPs have failed to turn around struggling companies. Between 1994 and 2000, workers at United Airlines accumulated 55% of the stock in its parent company in exchange for pay and benefit cuts totaling $4.8 billion. But critics say that the ESOP eventually failed because it excluded the flight attendants and did not allow employees who owned the stock to vote for directors. And employees who joined the company after 2000 were not allowed to join the ESOP at all, which created a rift between employees. But, other ESOPs have been successful. Simmons, the mattress company, was majority owned by an ESOP for a decade before selling to other investors for a profit.

The risk of an ESOP structure to a private business is that the employees are putting all of their retirement eggs in one basket. If the company should struggle and begin to lose money, then the value of the stock in the plan is going to go down, just as the value of stocks traded on Wall Street decline when a public company performs badly.

The following story illustrates how the ownership structure of a private company can change, and the causes behind that change.

> Alion Science and Technology Corp. said yesterday that its employees bought the company from the Illinois Institute of Technology, using $130 million from their retirement funds to create an independent defense contractor.
>
> McLean-based Alion, with 1,650 employees, has been a consultant to the Pentagon on military strategy and has developed modeling software for soldiers training on new weapons.
>
> Company executives said the change in ownership will give Alion an edge in keeping talented employees in an increasingly competitive market where it faces industry giants such as Science Applications International Corp. and Booz Allen Hamilton Inc.
>
> "When IIT professors launched this venture during the Depression, it was a different era in research and development," said Bahman Atefi, president of Alion.
>
> "Nowadays, competition for R&D dollars and people is fierce. Rather than face losing some of our key people to private companies, it's critical that we ourselves become private and for-profit, as a way to retain the best and brightest."
>
> Alion, shedding its nonprofit status, will use stock to lure employees with military experience or a scientific and research background, said Barry Watson, Alion's technology systems sector manager.
>
> The company accelerated hiring last year when work on several projects stepped up because of the Sept. 11, 2001, attacks. Alion recently won a Defense Department

contract to develop technology concerning chemical and biological weapons, arms control, and homeland defense, Watson said.

The company has about 100 job openings, he said.

For most of its history the company was known as IIT Research Institute and did most of its business with the government. With the new ownership, the company changed its name and moved its headquarters to Northern Virginia, where it had offices for several years.

Several other major defense contractors are employee-owned, including Reston's DynCorp and SAIC. Computer Sciences Corp. plans to buy DynCorp for $950 million in cash and stock.

Lawyers working on the deal could not find another instance of a nonprofit entity created by a university becoming a private, employee-owned company, Watson said. Alion reported $201 million in revenue during fiscal 2002 and $4.7 million in profit.

More than 20 percent of its revenue is from a single contract with the Defense Department to run an Annapolis facility that manages wireless service for the agency, including finding available frequencies for communications, an Alion spokesman said.

Fifteen percent of revenue is from a contract to develop modeling and simulation software for the military, according to a Securities and Exchange Commission filing.

For the Illinois Institute of Technology, the sale provides money for its endowment, which stood at $150 million before the deal, said Lew Collens, the Chicago university's president. The deal also includes a warrant, worth $100 million, that the university could exercise in five years if Alion meets certain financial goals, Collens said.

"We talked about whether to sell it outright or to sell it to employees," Collens said "Our trustees thought we should give first crack to the employees," he said.[2]

The value of this acquisition is disclosed, even though neither the seller nor the buyer is a public company. Still, the transaction does not say who among the employees will be the largest shareholder.

Changes in ownership structure such as a shift from a nonprofit company to a for-profit business should merit closer scrutiny. Some businesses have trouble making the change after running themselves a certain way for so long. Many businesses have made the switch in recent years from being owned by their customers to being owned by stockholders. This change has occurred most commonly in the insurance and banking industries, in which savings and loans and insurance companies that were owned by their depositors and their policyholders have converted to a stock ownership structure.

These thrifts and insurers were previously known as mutual companies. A mutual company is one where the customers have an ownership interest and is operated for the benefit of the customers. But their ownership ends if they should terminate their insurance policy or withdraw their money from the bank. Some of the largest companies in the country are mutuals, including State Farm and

---

[2]From "Employees buy tech firm for $130 million; Va.-based Alion was Depression-era creation of Illinois Institute of Technology," by R. Merle, January 8, 2003, *Washington Post,* p. E5. Copyright 2003 by *Washington Post.* Reprinted with permission.

Northwestern Mutual. In the last few years, many thrifts have converted from a mutual company structure to a public company structure. In such a conversion, the depositors are offered stock in the public company.

Many of the largest insurance companies, including MetLife, John Hancock, and Prudential, have also converted from a mutual structure in recent years. As part of the conversion, they distributed millions of shares of the new company to their policyholders. These conversions are approved by state regulators, and the process can be lengthy.

A number of small and private businesses have a unique structure in which their performance is tied to a much larger company. These smaller businesses are called franchisees. A franchisee is formed by entering into a contractual relationship with a franchise business that already has a product or a service to sell. The franchisee then operates under the trade name of the franchise, and often with its guidance, in exchange for a fee.

Franchisees can take all kinds of different shapes and forms. They are predominantly used in industries such as fast-food restaurants for companies such as McDonald's and Burger King, although it should be noted that these companies sometimes also operate locations that they own themselves. Franchisees are predominantly privately held businesses, although there are some franchise operations that are publicly traded. Papa John's pizza chain based in Birmingham, Alabama, is an example of a franchisee that was at one time publicly traded, but it is now a private company.

Running a franchise operation requires an up-front amount of money to be paid by the owner. McDonald's estimates that the cost for a new restaurant ranges between $461,000 and $788,500, and that an initial fee of $45,000 is paid to McDonald's for all new restaurants. The initial cash investment for a McDonald's franchise is a minimum of $175,000. The rest of the expense can be paid with a loan.

McDonald's acquires the property for the location and builds the building. The franchisee is then responsible for equipping the building with the kitchen equipment, the seating, signs, and landscaping.

Why do franchise owners go into such business operations? For one, all of the decisions about products and operation have been made for them. All they have to do is run the business, executing the plan, to make money.

Franchisees can be important sources for reporters covering the larger company. The parent may make decisions that affect the franchisees, upsetting the franchise owners. Sometimes, the franchisees may revolt against the bigger company and force it to make changes.

According to *Bond's Franchise Guide,* there are more than 560,000 franchise locations in the country, and they generate more than $1 trillion in sales. Franchising is regulated by the Federal Trade Commission, and some states have also passed franchising laws. Many of them are designed to protect the franchisee, requiring the franchisor to disclose the costs associated with the business and make fair assessments of the earnings potential of the business.

Once a reporter knows the structure of the small or private business he or she is reporting about, some questions should emerge. For example, if it is a private company that has sold a stake to an investor to help fuel growth, how does it plan to manage that growth without losing money? If the growth is successful, how big does the company plan to get? If the business is a franchisee, does it have plans to add more locations to the business? If the business is a mutual company, is it considering changing its structure? In some of these cases, the structure of the small or private business may be the story.

PROFILING A PRIVATE OR SMALL BUSINESS

Many times a media outlet will profile a small or private business. These stories may seem innocuous, and they are often written as flattering, positive stories that tell the story of how a business is thriving because of its products or its services. Many times, these stories can read like advertorials, copy that the business should have probably paid the newspaper to run.

Profiles of small and private businesses, however, do not always have to be this way. Like the business reporters who fell all over themselves in the 1990s writing about the latest Internet company to go public and make millionaires of its workers, many reporters who write stories about small and private businesses are not being as critical as they can and should be.

Writing about small and private businesses should reflect the local economy. If the economy is going bad in a town because a plant has closed, putting 400 workers out of jobs, then that is going to affect the surrounding small businesses that depended on these workers to spend part of their income buying their goods and services. If things are not going well, the reporter should not sugarcoat it. If a particular industry is suffering, reporters should not buy the story that one small business owner in that industry is telling you when he or she remarks, "We've never had a better season." He or she is probably lying.

The following story from the *Petersburg Pilot* in Alaska, which focused on the struggles of local salmon fisheries in its June 20, 2002 paper, did not mince words:

> Wave after wave of bad forecasts are rocking Alaskan's salmon fishery as fisherman and processors scramble for that miracle seasick curing patch. The amount of fish not returning is not enough to cause this nausea; the price heaved at the independent fisherman, however, leaves them weak-kneed with sea legs.
>
> "Price on all species is down," commented Icicle Seafood's John Baird. "There's oversupplies of canned salmon. Farmed salmon are cutting into our frozen stuff, and recently the European countries have put a ban on Chinese-bought fish into the European market. The Ikura market for chum roe is off and is expected to start at less than last year, there's no reason to think that will change much."

"Prices are the biggest concern I have heard from fishermen," commented State House Representative Peggy Wilson on a recent stop in Petersburg. "Permits were bought at an outlandish price and they are not worth even half that now. Traditionally, all gear groups have had their own problems. Now they are trying to come together and solve one. The salmon task force is probably going to be our best bet, but it's in limbo right now."

Southeast crews could harvest 25 to 36 million pink salmon this summer. The statewide harvest is believed to be 87 million, down from a five-year average of 104 million.

Said NorQuest plant manager Dave Ohmer, "The parent year for the run coming in this year is not very large. Last year was a huge year, that may not present itself this season. The price is reflective of the huge supply left from last year and the results of the market place from last year."

The sockeye harvest might be the smallest in 24 years. Chum projection catches are down 15 percent from 2001 and coho catch predictions are consistent with last year. The King salmon quota has actually been revised upward.[3]

Stories about small and private businesses are reported for a number of reasons. Maybe the business is new to the town or city and is unique. Maybe the company is in conflict with another company. Maybe the business is fast growing and adding many local employees. Or maybe the business is struggling and may not be around in six months.

Whatever the reason, reporters should think about small and private businesses the same way they think about larger and public businesses. They are just as important to the reader and viewer, and because the stories are being written about a business that probably has not had much exposure, the piece will probably have more readers wanting to learn about a company they have not heard about before. In addition, reporters should not forget about these businesses after the story has been written. They could just be headed for bigger fame or notoriety, and journalists will want to be there to report it. Imagine a reporter in a small town of about 15,000 people. A few years ago, a chocolate shop opened downtown making truffles and other exotic desserts. The reporter wrote a short story about the shop, and afterward forgot about it. Then, one morning, that same reporter walks into the newsroom to discover that the chocolate shop is on the front page of *The Wall Street Journal*. It is now famous around the world because of its delicious sweets and cannot keep up with its orders for Valentine's Day because of the demand. The owner would like to expand, but he cannot because there are not enough hours in the day to make as many truffles as he needs.

Perhaps the local newspaper did not have that story before the large, national media because the local reporter did not keep in touch with the storeowner or check in regularly just by walking into the store and chatting with the employees. As a result, a great story was missed.

---

[3]From "Storm on the horizon for salmon fisheries," by K. Stolpe, June 20, 2002, *Petersburg Pilot*, p.1. Copyright 2002 by Pilot Publishing. Reprinted with permission.

The following story is from *The Herald-Sun* in Durham, North Carolina, which won first place in a Society of American Business Editors and Writers contest. It is about a private company, but the detail in this story makes it read as if the business was publicly traded. The reporter followed up on the disclosure that the company was delinquent in paying its loans from a bond-rating agency to discover there were even more troubles than had been disclosed. Armed with the bond-rating agency information, he was able to garner interviews that showed just how serious the problems were.

After rapidly growing into the nation's second-largest privately owned convenience store chain, Durham-based Swifty Serve Corp. is fighting for its life.

The chain, which at one time had more than 600 stores throughout the Southeast, has closed between 70 and 100 locations and cut about 1,000 jobs as it fights the red ink flowing from money-losing stores.

Swifty Serve, like the rest of the convenience store industry, has been hit hard by a shrinking profit margin on gas sales and dropping cigarette sales—two of the core businesses of convenience stores.

The 5-year-old company is talking with lenders to help finance a plan for remaking Swifty Serve, but something has to be resolved "in weeks, not months," said Jeff Hamill, a former 7-Eleven executive who became the company's president and CEO in April.

If something can't be worked out, "I don't know if it's bankruptcy or additional changes we'll have to make," Hamill said from the company's headquarters on Hillandale Road.

Durham developer W. Clay Hamner started building the Swifty Serve chain in 1997 with his longtime business partner, Wayne Rogers. Hamner is best known for playing a lead role in the Treyburn residential development and the retail center Brightleaf Square while Rogers is the actor who played Trapper John in the television series M*A*S*H.

From their initial purchase of the 62-store Swannee Swifty chain for $5 million in 1997, Hamner and Rogers grew the Swifty Serve chain into a company with more than 600 stores, 4,500 employees and $850 million in annual revenues.

Hamner, who initially served as Swifty Serve's chief executive, and Rogers are not involved in the day-to-day operations of the company but both serve on the company's board. The two business partners also head up a group of investors that owns 29 percent of the company. Three other investment firms own the rest of the company.

Hamner said Swifty Serve, which has only four Triangle locations, is facing the same challenge as other convenience store owners—the business model for the industry has been turned on its head.

"It's just like in the grocery store business and movie house business—you'll see larger, fewer convenience stores," Hamner said. Small stores won't survive, he said.

The Durham businessman said the number of convenience stores nationally has dropped from about 234,000 in 1994 to about 200,000 currently. He estimated there will be fewer than 100,000 within five years.

The industry's business model has been changed by retailers like Wal-Mart, Costco and some grocers that have started selling gas at low prices, Hamner and Hamill said. "The issue is what I call cents per gallon—what [we] make off selling gas," Hamill said. "[They've] gotten into the gas business and started undercutting it and that puts a lot of pressure on us."

Over the past several years wholesale gas costs have risen while the price at pumps has remained fairly constant because of aggressive pricing by competitors like Costco, he said. That's cut into the company's profit margins on gasoline sales.

Many of the company's underperforming stores are located in small towns, where the problem is particularly acute when big retailers begin selling gas. It's those stores that have been closed as Swifty Serve tries to adjust its organization.

The losses—which Hamill said rose following the terrorist attacks last September—have hit the company's balance sheet hard. As of Sept. 5, Swifty Serve was delinquent on $125 million in long-term loans, according to Fitch Ratings, a bond rating service.

But Hamill stressed that over the past four months he's hammered out a plan for reviving the company by keeping profitable stores, focusing on core "categories" like cigarettes, beer and gas and developing proprietary products.

"I was brought in to help turn this around. In four months all I've been working on is a plan that has tremendous opportunity," Hamill said. "That's why to use words like bankruptcy doesn't fly with me."

Hamner said he's optimistic the company will rebound. "For us it's one of our portfolio companies," he said. "I'm confident the management team can change the business model to meet the current convenience store model."

Swifty Serve is headquartered on Hillandale Road, across from Loehmann's Plaza—the shopping center Hamner bought, renovated and resold. The office at one point had some 160 workers but that work force is down to about 120, Hamill said.

There's only one Swifty Serve in Durham, located near Streets at Southpoint on Renaissance Parkway near its intersection with N.C. 751.

The Swifty Serve chain operates in about seven states under the names E-Z Serve, Swifty Serve, Swifty Mart, Country Cupboard and Majik Mart.[4]

Despite the fact that the CEO calls the company a "tremendous opportunity" and the owner of the business is "confident" of the management team, the reader of this story gets a vivid picture that this convenience store chain is in trouble because of changes in the industry that have affected its performance. This story does not use any specific figures for revenues and profits (or losses) to detail the trouble, but cogently explains how competitors are undercutting it in pricing and building bigger stores. Even without the numbers, the writer is able to make a case that the business is in trouble on the basis of the quotes he uses—and the one single number he does have about the delinquent loans from the bond-rating agency.

Other media are able to effectively report about small and private businesses the same way. The *Loveland Daily Reporter-Herald* in Colorado focused on the problems its local travel agencies were having after airlines announced they were eliminating commissions. The *Antelope Valley Press* in California focused

---

[4]From "Swifty Serve Corp. is in fight for its life; Durham-based convenience store chain has closed stores, cut jobs," by J. Zimmer, Sept. 27, 2002, *Durham Herald-Sun,* p. A1. Copyright 2002 by Durham Herald Company Inc. Reprinted with permission.

on the local minor league baseball team not as a sport, but as a business, and wrote about how the Lancaster JetHawks were trying to boost attendance. Although the team did not cite any numbers, the reporter was able to quote a source within the organization saying that the team had lost money the previous year.

When writing profiles of small and private businesses, reporters should think of them as being companies that might be sold, go out of business, or go public in the future, which would put them in the public eye. Because stories have already been written about the company, the reporter's media outlet will have the background to cover future stories more thoroughly about the company.

Small and private businesses like the media to write stories about them when they are new and trying to attract customers. But rarely do they want the attention when they are going out of business. Still, these stories can also be important because they might reflect on the broader town or county economy. If a store could not make it in the town, what does that say about the future of similar stores in the area?

Reporting about small and private businesses often requires the journalist to focus on the founder or owner of the business. They are often the ones that control the company. Without that interview, though, where would a reporter turn? If possible, he or she should find out where the founder used to work. Maybe someone there can tell you about his or her work habits or business ideas. Maybe he or she was fired or dismissed from the previous job, or left the previous employer to start a competing business.

Small and private business owners are often proud of what they have accomplished in building a company from a simple idea. Many of them are very protective of their business, and want a reporter to recognize the long hours and the tough times that were put in to make the business successful, or at least survive. If a business owner is reluctant to give an interview, the reporter must understand why they are leery. One way for reporters to get past the hesitation is to let the business owner see that they recognize the pain that went into building the operation. That does not mean the story has to be positive. But a good point to make in most profiles of small and private businesses is how they were started and lasted as long as they have.

Reporters should not hesitate to ask for information. All the owner or president can say is "yes" or "no." Reporters must ask for letters or other documents from companies that do business with the company they are reporting about. Maybe a competitor has a letter or document that would make a good story about the business.

Consider the lead of the following story from the *Rochester Business Journal:*

Excellus Inc. deliberately has sabotaged important Strong Health initiatives and continues trying to subvert the University of Rochester's health system, a top Strong Health executive claims.

In a Jan. 4 letter to Excellus CEO Howard Berman, obtained by the Rochester Business Journal, and Berman's reply three weeks later, reflect a massive rift between Strong and Excellus, the parent of Blue Cross Blue Shield of the Rochester area. They are the area's two most powerful health care organizations.

Berman's response letter contains a point-by-point refutation of the charges in the earlier missive from Steven Goldstein, Strong Memorial and Highland hospitals CEO. Berman also offered to meet with Strong officials to further discuss the issues.[5]

The story is about two private companies. But because the reporter was able to obtain the first letter, the CEO supplied the response letter after being questioned about it. That is how obtaining one document can lead to another.

Writing a story about a small or private business should not just consist of interviewing the owner or the president of the company. That is not going to give

---

The Dirty Dozen: 12 questions for the small or private business owner.

Many small business owners are wary of questions from reporters, particularly when they've never been interviewed before. These questions will show the owner that you're genuinely interested in telling readers about his company.

1. Where did you get the idea to start your business? How does your background fit into the company idea?
2. How did you fund the business? Did the money come from savings or relatives?
3. How soon after you first opened your doors did your business first make a profit? How did you celebrate?
4. What was the hardest obstacle to overcome in getting the business off the ground?
5. Who do you consider to be your biggest competitor and why?
6. How have you grown the business? Has it been through advertising or customer recommendations?
7. Who is your biggest customer? What would you do if you lost that customer?
8. What is your best-selling item?
9. How would you react if a similar business opened nearby? How could you handle the increased competition?
10. How big do you foresee your company becoming in the next five years? In the next 10 years?
11. What would make you sell your business to another company?
12. How are your employees involved in the day-to-day decision making for the business?

---

[5]From "Letter underscores UR-Excellus feud," by W. Astor, March 15, 2002, *Rochester Business Journal*, p.1. Copyright 2002 by *Rochester Business Journal*. Reprinted with permission.

the reader or the viewer the balance and objectivity that the story demands. Think of other people to interview that know the business and where other information about the company can be obtained. Putting all of the pieces together will make for a story that tells the complete picture.

GLOSSARY

conversion – The process where a company changes its ownership structure, typically from one where the business is owned by customers to one where the business is owned by stockholders.

corporation – The most common form of business organization. The organization is ongoing, and the owners face limited liability.

employee stock ownership plan – A plan where the company allows its employees to buy shares of the business. These plans are increasing in popularity with small and private businesses.

franchisee – A businessman who pays a larger company, known as the franchisor, to run one of its locations in exchange for a fee.

limited liability corporation – A business structure with corporation and partnership qualities. Often a business will become a limited liability corporation to receive the tax advantages of a partnership and the liability advantages of a corporation.

mutual ownership – An ownership structure commonly found in the insurance and thrift industries where the company is owned by the policyholders and depositors.

partnership – A business organization in which two or more people manage and operate the business. All of the owners are equally liable for the debts of the business.

profit sharing plan – A plan where the employees of a company share in its profits. The business typically decides what profits will be shared.

S corporation – A company that has met the requirements under subchapter S of the Internal Revenue Service code. This allows the company to be taxed as if it were a partnership. These businesses must be domestic, have 75 or fewer shareholders, and only one class of stock.

Uniform Commercial Code – A set of laws regulating commercial transactions, especially those involving the sale of goods where money is borrowed.

REFERENCES

Astor, W. (2002, March 15). Letter underscores UR-Excellus feud. *Rochester Business Journal.* pp. 1, 17.

Fitzpatrick, D. (1999, July 21). Petra Ministries battles financial woes; back taxes, lack of experience as a developer raises concerns about the independent church's ability to revitalize the former East Hills Shopping Center. *Pittsburgh Post-Gazette.* p. B-1.

Girard, K. (2003, May 3). The battle rages on: Small business squares off against IRS rulemaking. CBS.MarketWatch.com. Retrieved May 27, 2003 from http//cbs.MarketWatch.com/news

Hoffer, J. (2003, April 27). Too common restaurant practice is costing New York City. WABC-TV. Retrieved May 28, 2003 from http://abclocal.go.com/wabc/news/investigators/wabc_investigators_042803restaurants.html

Kleinbaum, J. (2002, July 7). A minor struggle . . . JetHawks deal with smaller crowds. *Antelope Valley Press.* p. A1.

McIntire, M., & Lender, J. (2003, April 13). Family ties and hefty profits; as a food company seeks state aid, investments in its stock benefit some close to the circle of power. *Hartford Courant.* p. A1.

Merle, R. (2003, January 8). Employees buy tech firm for $130 million; Va.-based Alion was Depression-era creation of Illinois Institute of Technology. *Washington Post.* p. E 5.

Mickelson, C. (2002, April 21). Taking a shine to it. *The Door County Advocate.* p. 6.

Moyers, S. (2002, April 21). Cape's global economy: Business owners from afar take a chance on Missouri. *Southeast Missourian.* pp. 1A, 6A.

North Carolina Department of the Secretary of State (2003, January 1). Important notice to UCC record filers. Raleigh, NC: Author.

O'Donnell, J., & Backover, A. (2002, December 12). Ebbers' high-risk act came crashing down on him. *USA Today.* pp. 1B, 2B.

Stolpe, K. (2002, June 20). Storm on the horizon for salmon fisheries. *Petersburg Pilot.* pp. 1–2.

Waite M., & Glenn, B. (2000, April 2). Well deal unearths murky ties. *St. Petersburg Times.* p. 1.

Zimmer, J. (2002, September 27). Swifty Serve Corp. is in fight for its life; Durham-based convenience store chain has closed stores, cut jobs. *Durham* (N.C.) *Herald-Sun.* p. A1.

Other Books About Private and Small Businesses

Gerber, M. (1995). *The E-Myth revisited: Why most small businesses don't work and what to do about it.* New York: Harper Business.

Hartley Smith, P. (2003). *Board betrayal: The Weirton Steel story: Failed governance and management hand in hand with Arthur Andersen: An ESOP fable.* Belgrade, MT: Wilderness Adventure Books.

Sutton, G. (2001). *How to use limited liability companies & limited partnerships.* Reno, NV: SuccessDNA Inc.

SUGGESTED EXERCISES

1. Find a small business owner in your city and conduct an interview. Ask them how they started their business and why. See how much financial information the owner is willing to disclose about the business. If he's not willing to

disclose revenues and profits, then ask if there's any financial information that will be disclosed, such as an increase in sales or profits.

2. Take the name of the small business that you interviewed the owner and search for information about the business in public records with the Secretary of State's office and at the county courthouse. Don't forget to check lawsuits, UCC filings and federal records as well. After you've collected the information, go back to talk to the business owner and show them the information. Is the owner now more forthcoming about providing additional information on the company?

3. Many small companies rely on college students. Find a handful of these businesses–restaurants, bookstores, bars, copy centers–near your campus and ask them what percentage of their business comes from college-age students. What does this tell you about the economy of the town or city in which you're living?

4. Ask other students in the class if they have part-time jobs at small businesses. If they do, ask them if they know the owner of the company, and how often he or she works at the business. If they don't know the owner, how many hours does the manager or supervisor spend at the business?

10

Nonprofit Organizations

OPERATING LIKE A FOR-PROFIT BUSINESS

So far this book has ignored one important segment of the business world, and one that is often underreported because of its unique structure. But there are thousands of businesses and other organizations operating like businesses, offering goods or services to the public, that do not fit into the structure of being a public company or a for-profit private enterprise.

There are more than 1.3 million entities in this country that are classified as non-profit organizations by the Internal Revenue Service (IRS). Collectively, nearly a half million of them file financial disclosures with the IRS that show they have more than $2.7 trillion in assets, according to the National Center for Charitable Statistics. California has the most nonprofit organizations, whereas New York's nonprofit organizations have the most reported assets.

These nonprofit organizations include everything from the National Council of YMCAs and the American Red Cross and Goodwill Industries International to local child care centers, homeless shelters, health insurance plans, community health care clinics, museums, hospitals, churches, schools, performing arts centers, and conversation groups. They are some of the largest organizations in a town or a community, and often they can be some of the most powerful as well. In many cases, these are organizations that are competing against public and private companies. The local YMCA, for example, competes with for-profit workout centers to attract fitness nuts. The nonprofit managed care plan such as Kaiser competes with for-profit companies such as CIGNA and Aetna. Hospitals run by Catholic groups compete against hospitals managed by multibillion dollar hospital corporations. Many times, the for-profit companies will complain that their nonprofit competitors are taking advantage of their status to undercut them and steal business.

A nonprofit organization is a corporation formed to carry out a specific purpose, whether it is educational, religious, scientific, or community related. The corporation does not pay any taxes to the state or federal government because of its status. The IRS and state regulatory agencies have determined that the public's benefit from these organizations entitles them special tax status.

However, forming a nonprofit organization does not guarantee tax-exempt status. The corporation must make a request with the IRS, which will then determine whether the organization merits tax-exempt status. If the IRS agrees, then the organization receives the designation of filing financial documents under section 501c3 of the tax code. That is why these companies are often referred to as 501c3 businesses.

Just like public and private for-profit corporations, nonprofit businesses must incorporate with their state's secretary of state's office. And every state has laws and administrative rules governing nonprofit organizations that they must follow. Typically, a state department of justice regulates charitable activities as well. Most nonprofit organizations also have a president or CEO who oversees the day-to-day operations, and they hire and fire staffs that sometimes can total in the thousands. They recruit executives from the for-profit world, and often look at the for-profit sector for strategies and tactics that they can adapt to their organizations.

But they are different as well. Nonprofits are allowed to raise funds from the public and from private business and government agencies. In addition, nonprofits are required to conduct themselves in the same manner as many for-profit businesses. They must hold board meetings and keep records of those meetings for their corporate records. However, they are not allowed to make political lobbying a significant part of their operations, and they cannot conduct their business in a way that would benefit its directors or officers. And nonprofits are not allowed to distribute their profits to members.

Nonprofits are not actually owned by anyone, and cannot be sold. If the directors decide to dissolve the organization, it must pay off all of its debts and distribute the remaining assets to another nonprofit organization. The focus is on the nonprofit aspect of the business. Many people donate their time and money to nonprofits under the idea that these organizations are performing functions for the benefit of the community and are not in existence to make as much money as possible. The money that is made by a nonprofit organization must be used to further develop its programs and services.

Having explained the function and structure of a nonprofit organization, understand that many of them are very profitable ventures. Some of them are more profitable than their public and private competitors. The YMCAs around the country reported more than $4.1 billion in revenue in 2001, with nearly 70% of that money, or $2.8 billion, coming from payments by its members around the country to work out and for its kids to attend camps and sports programs. However, YMCA's expenses for the year totaled $3.8 billion, meaning that there was nearly $350 million left over as "profits."

They are not the only ones. The Boys and Girls Club of America had nearly $1 billion in revenue in 2001 and nearly $926 million in expenses, leaving them with $70 million in profits for the year. Indeed, most of the large nonprofit organizations reported more in revenue than they did in profits in 2001. A notable exception is the Public Broadcasting Service, which reported $536 million in revenue and $565 million in expenses for the year. Nearly half of its revenue came from memberships, although its programs cost more than $543 million.

Where do these profits go? The same place they go to for most for-profit companies, that is, into making the organization stronger by adding additional services or building new facilities, or rewarding excellent employees with higher pay. The point to take away from these examples is that nonprofit organizations can often be as huge—and as profitable—as many for-profit enterprises. Yet the media often looks at these ventures as different entities that are not always covered by business reporters.

That is a mistake. These organizations are major players in specific industries such as health care and insurance. In many towns and cities, they may have the dominant market share for their business. And sometimes, a nonprofit organization can violate its agreement with the public by misusing its money, or by not adhering to regulatory standards.

The Seattle Times reported that local public television station KCTS was suffering from financial woes. Shortly before their report ran, the station's president resigned. The story noted, "Employees, former executives and the station's own paid consultants say [the president] runs the public entity like a private fiefdom." (Phillips and McFadden, 2003, p. A1). Their reporting noted that the station's losses totaled $3.4 million in 2001 even though the president was receiving a $268,000 salary and that the Corporation for Public Broadcasting was withholding funding because it had not turned in financial statements. And the *Journal Star* in Peoria, Ill., documented how the local CrimeStoppers organization was spending 55% of its expenses on fundraising, which is a high percentage compared with other nonprofit organizations. In 1998, executives at Minnesota Public Radio were widely criticized when it was disclosed that they had personally earned more than $7 million when they sold a for-profit mail-order subsidiary. And in April 2003, the U.S. Food and Drug Administration issued a consent decree against the American Red Cross requiring the organization to improve its method of reporting information about the handling of blood or face severe fines. The decree, in which the American

Red Cross neither admitted nor denied any wrongdoing, followed a lengthy battle between regulators and the group.

From those examples, we see that nonprofit corporations are not exempt from some of the same problems and issues that plague the for-profit world. There are still allegations of misuse of money and disobeyance of rules governing the business. Such events are newsworthy, no matter where they happen.

To be sure, nonprofit organizations are performing great deeds and services to the communities in which they exist. They are helping millions of people live better lives, and they are doing so under the concept that their organization should not be making a profit from others. But they are also newsworthy organizations, and they should be covered aggressively by media outlets. However, most do not have a full-time nonprofits reporter, and many mass communication organizations do not even cover this sector of the economy by a business reporter.

But the reporting and writing tactics in covering the nonprofit world should be the same as it is for writing about for-profit businesses. In many cases, it is the financial performance that tells the clearest picture of how well—or how poorly— the organization is performing. And the competition between the two business structures is increasing, as the following *Dallas Morning News* story suggests, leading to the argument that nonprofits should be covered by the business staff:

> The slogan might not have saved the Oldsmobile, but a new upscale concept among Goodwill Industries has left the venerable charity boasting that "this is not your grandmother's Goodwill store."
>
> Indeed, a new superstore approved by the Hurst City Council on Tuesday night will feature 22,000 square feet of retail space, a coffee shop, a high-end used bookstore and a fashion boutique.
>
> "We envision people shopping at Neiman Marcus in the morning and at Goodwill in the afternoon," said David Cox, director of community relations and marketing for Goodwill Industries of Fort Worth Inc. "You will find Mercedes, Lexus and Beamers in our parking lot any day."
>
> The council action cleared the way for a new so-called superstore at 825 W. Pipeline Road. The new store, part of a growing national trend for Goodwill, will be nearly three times as big as traditional Goodwill retail centers and should open in the 33,000-square-foot former Food Lion by July.
>
> The charity isn't forsaking its century-old tradition of selling second-hand clothes and used furniture and appliances to raise money to put the disabled to work. It's just adding a little twist picked up by watching the agency's upscale thrift stores in Portland, Ore., thrive, Mr. Cox said.
>
> "Our mission is still the same," he said. "We're a hand-up rather than a hand-out organization. We take the money [the stores' profits from the sales] and train handicapped people to work. We give them a job rather than a new shirt."
>
> Indeed, the Fort Worth agency took in $10 million last year, with $6 million coming from its retail sales and salvage operation, said Erin Quillian, director of retail sales.
>
> Dave Barringer, a spokesman for Goodwill Industries International, said the northeast Tarrant County superstore is a first for Texas, but it is following in footsteps of a growing number of the charity's approximately 1,800 stores across the nation.

"The better we compete with the other discounters–from Wal-Mart to Kmart–and add all the bells and whistles the better we will be able to serve our people," he said. "The stores have two main purposes: They are usually funding mechanisms for our other programs, and they often provide work opportunities for our clients as well."

Rod Ginther, president of the Dallas Goodwill, said such superstores were the newest stage of an evolution that has been changing Goodwill's retail operations. Dallas stores have been on a larger scale, with bookstores and other amenities, for 10 years, he said.

Mr. Ginther said Dallas Goodwill stores have moved into middle- and upper-income neighborhoods over the years because research showed shoppers spent more in those stores than in similar ones in lower-income neighborhoods.

He disputed a popular notion that Goodwill stores provide low-cost used items to low-income people.

"We are about selling the goods to make money so we can put people to work," Mr. Ginther said. "The more money we make on retail sales the more we can pay our people and the more jobs we can create."

Still, he said the new Hurst store will be larger than Dallas' stores and will be unique in offering a coffee shop.

Fueling all of this goodwill is a remarkable amount of unwanted clothes. Last year donors nationwide provided Goodwill Industries more than 1 billion pounds of clothes.

"That 1 billion pounds equaled $800 million in sales," he said. The government contracts, fees from employers who place their employees and various smaller amounts equaled another $800 million in revenue, he said.

The significant capital required for expanding into an upscale thrift market—and in a growing number of locations, including Fort Worth, buying discounted new merchandise—is an investment needed to help those retail-sales figures grow, he said.

"It's always a balance between trying to build the nicest store we can and trying to conserve money on construction costs," he said. "But the better store we have the better we can compete with the other retailers."

Of the $10 million the Fort Worth agency brought in last year, Mr. Cox said, a full 80 percent was spent on services for its clients. He also said 80 percent of the local organization's workforce could be classified as disabled according to the Americans with Disabilities Act.

Mr. Cox said his agency operates seven stores—the new superstore will be its eighth—and 23 trailers where donors can drop off goods to be sold. (Dallas stores took in about $8 million in retail sales, Mr. Ginther said.)

He said as part of the agency's efforts to change its image, those trailers will be phased out, and replaced by air-conditioned buildings. He and Ms. Quillian also said the superstores likely would become the model for growth in the area.

One Hurst council member, Richard Ward, voted against the minor zoning change required for the store, and said he did so because he did not receive answers to how much the Fort Worth agency's CEO made, and how many of its executives were disabled themselves.

Bernard Kern, who was the agency's president at the time, earned $130,752 in 1999, according to the agency's most recent IRS Form 990. Figures for the number of disabled executives were not immediately available.

Mr. Ward said he was somewhat troubled by the fact that Goodwill, a tax-exempt charity, would compete with tax-paying for-profit retailers in the city.

But Mr. Barringer said such criticism is rare.

The Goodwill stores "are not that close" to the Wal-Mart and Kmart models they are compared to, he said. "People have been supporting us for 99 years—we are going to celebrate our centennial this year—and they see that any way we can grow our retail sales will help us serve the disabled."

The store also will sell new computers and computers built by handicapped employees of Goodwill Industries. The superstore is expected to generate about $1.2 million annually in sales and have about 30 employees.

Mr. Cox said the Hurst location stood out because of high-end demographics in northeast Tarrant County.

"We have a big map in our office and this area, northeast Tarrant County, was our first choice," he said.[1]

After reading this story, can anybody question that non-profit organizations are an important business story waiting to be told? They are expanding, and they're competing more directly with public and private companies. Look at the names of the other retailers mentioned in this story—Neiman Marcus, Wal-Mart, Kmart. These are some of the biggest companies operating today. Yet Goodwill Industries sees itself as fitting in a retailing niche that these others aren't fulfilling.

FOUNDATIONS

Foundations are similar to nonprofit organizations in that they are entities that are not interested in making a profit. Foundations, in fact, simply exist to give money away, not make it. But that does not mean they fall outside of the business world.

Many foundations are the result of the profits made by for-profit corporations and the executives that previously ran them or made their fortunes from the company's stock. The largest foundation in the country is the Bill and Melinda Gates Foundation, named after the founder of Microsoft and his wife. The foundation had more than $32 billion in assets at the end of 2001, the latest statistics available at this time. Other large foundations read like a Who's Who of the business world, with names such as Lilly, Ford, Johnson & Johnson, Kellogg, Packard, Hewlett, Duke, Getty, and Mellon attached to them.

According to The Foundation Center, there are more than 56,000 foundations in this country with more than $486 billion in assets. In 2000, they handed out more than $27 billion in gifts to nonprofit organizations and other individuals and groups. A foundation is established as a nonprofit organization or a charitable trust, but its primary obligation is different than the nonprofit organizations such as hospitals and Goodwill Industries discussed earlier. A foundation's primary purpose is to give away money and sometimes equipment such as computers by way of grants to organizations or individuals who request help. By law, a foundation must give

---

[1]From "Goodwill to open megastore: Retail supercenter will be area's largest," by M. Lindenberger, February 15, 2001, *Dallas Morning News*, p. 1N. Copyright 2001 by *Dallas Morning News*. Reprinted with permission.

away 5% of its assets every year to maintain its tax-free status. (Foundations also apply for 501c3 status with the IRS.) The higher the level of assets, the more money in total dollars is given away.

There are different types of foundations. An independent foundation is the most common. These types of foundations are not associated with a company or a family. Corporate foundations are those connected with a business, quite often a for-profit company that makes grants to the communities in which it operates. Family foundations receive their money from an individual family and its members, and its grants may be tied to family interests. Famous athletes and celebrities also create foundations, and sometimes these organizations can result in stories for the business writer as well, depending on what the foundation is doing with its money. When football star Marshall Faulk was voted the NFL Player of the Year, his foundation received $30,000 to give to organizations.

Foundations could be considered huge investment businesses. Although they give away billions of dollars each year to worthy causes, they are designed to exist forever. Foundations, particularly those funded by private investments, most likely will never give away all of the money and assets that they have. Foundations invest their assets in stocks, bonds, real estate, or other investments designed to build the assets. The money that is given away in the form of grants typically comes from the income and gains on these investments. Therefore, the stock market and the economy are closely watched by foundation managers, particularly investment officers. Their jobs can be similar to mutual fund managers or Wall Street investment pros.

Ups and downs in the stock market and other investments can affect the worth of a foundation's assets. The Robert W. Woodruff Foundation in Georgia sees its asset value fluctuate with the value of Coca-Cola stock. Woodruff once ran the soft drink company and funded the foundation with stock. The J.A. & Kathryn Albertson Foundation was funded partly by stock in the Albertson's grocery store chain.

Foundations have limits on how much ownership they can have in for-profit businesses. The Tax Reform Act states that a foundation can not own more than 20% of the voting shares in a public or private corporation. Some foundations have gotten around this limitation and received a 5-year extension to divest by showing regulators that they have made a good-faith effort to sell the stake.

Understanding how foundations work and where their money comes from can be important. Foundations can have a major impact on a local economy and business community, particularly if small businesses are receiving grants or funding from foundations to survive. Many times, foundations will give grants to needy business groups that will help minority-owned ventures. Foundations also give money to scientific and research organizations that may be seeking to develop drugs to treat major diseases or illnesses. Their success could spur the drug industry.

The following excerpt how a local from the *Kansas City Star* shows how a local foundation might be affecting the Kansas City economy:

After deciding last year to phase out small grants for local social service needs, the Ewing Marion Kauffman Foundation has decided this year to boost such small grants.

The foundation, the region's largest philanthropy, has announced a $2.5 million annual commitment in coming years to a special fund dedicated to non-profit agencies. This money could end up extending Kauffman's traditional support for urban youth, in activities ranging from leadership camps to art classes.

In 2001, Kauffman dedicated about $1.8 million a year in small grants to local non-profits, according to a Kansas City Star analysis of Kauffman's grant-making. So the foundation's new commitment represents at least a 36 percent increase in the total amount dedicated to small grants, those of $25,000 or less.

Kauffman's turnaround on such grants evolved because the foundation figured out how to dispense them while still downsizing, and because the foundation wanted to respond to the worsening economy. Carl Schramm, Kauffman's new chief executive, said foundations have a traditional obligation toward the less-fortunate, and that duty is heightened in bad economic times.

"We see the recession as an opportunity to expand social welfare," Schramm said.

In the non-profit community, Kauffman's announcement comes at a time when social service leaders are collectively holding their breath. They are waiting to see how Kansas City's philanthropic behemoth will change under Schramm, who took over from longtime civic leader Louis Smith last spring.

Schramm has indicated he wants the foundation to get more bang for its bucks, to basically put more money into fewer programs.

He also has promised that when the foundation's new "business plans" get approved later this year, more money will end up going into Kansas City, not less. Kauffman's new commitment to small grants is the first tangible follow-through of that promise.

So while some non-profit leaders hailed Kauffman's action, they wondered what will happen with larger grants.

"It's a good move to make a gift to the (small-grant) fund so that pool grows," said Mary Lou Jaramillo, executive director of the Mattie Rhodes Art Center, which gets Kauffman funding. "We're all waiting in the non-profit community for the direction Kauffman is going."

For years now, Kauffman has fulfilled a role as sort of a societal caretaker. The foundation assumed responsibilities that used to be primarily the province of local governments. These duties ranged from training public school principals to helping to subsidize social service agencies.

In doing this, Kauffman handed out small grants for smaller community needs in two ways. One way was through its Kauffman Fund, held at the Greater Kansas City Community Foundation and administered by a community advisory board. The other way was through the foundation's own entrepreneurship and youth development operating divisions.

The foundation has bankrolled the Kauffman Fund with $1 million a year. As for small grants funneled through foundation operations, a total of $838,000 was disbursed to local causes and local non-profits in the 2001 fiscal year, according to the Form 990 that Kauffman filed with the Internal Revenue Service. That amount does not include small grants to public schools as part of a larger Kauffman program.

Kauffman officials said they could not comment on the $838,000 amount, because the foundation did not keep its own tally of small grants for local causes.

Now Schramm is revamping Kauffman's entire organization while cutting the staff nearly in half. In doing so, he previously announced a desire to phase out the small grants administered at the foundation. He still intends to do this even with the new $2.5 million annual commitment, by channeling that money through the Kauffman Fund at the community foundation.

So Kauffman will be increasing its monetary commitment—for at least the next three years—while also increasing its efficiency.

"That may be a happy outcome of this. This is a very efficient way to get these grants into the community," Schramm said.

What remains uncertain is what will happen to some of the Kauffman operating programs that gave out small grants. One program, for instance, is a youth advisory board. It is made up of high school students who discuss and select grant applications for many youth volunteer activities. Most grants are less than $1,000.

If the youth board or other small-grant programs continue under Schramm, then Kauffman's small-grant commitment would end up exceeding $2.5 million.[2]

This story explains how the shift in grant giving by the Kauffman Foundation, which received its funding from its founder's pharmaceutical company stock, is affecting local organizations.

Foundations are also major donors to universities and schools. Colleges and universities often undergo major fundraising initiatives and target foundations to make donations. These donations could spur major growth at a local university, leading to the construction of new buildings and the hiring of new employees. When writing about major grants or gifts given by foundations, reporters should assess the local economic impact.

Foundations and their money can also be important to current business executives looking to leave their mark long after they are gone. CEOs and others will create foundations and donate their stock holdings in their companies to these foundations. The ownership transfer of the stock can be traced by checking SEC filings. In addition, a company executive may continue to lease office space for his or her foundation in the company's headquarters even after they have left the business. These agreements are also often disclosed in SEC filings.

Foundations, however, are also prone to some of the same issues that nonprofit organizations encounter. They can be mismanaged or misuse their money.

The *San Jose Mercury News* noted in April 2003 that the head of a local foundation lost 25% of its assets and laid off staff members while its president received a compensation package that could have faced sanctions if it had been audited by the federal authorities.

And *The Baltimore Sun* reported in May 2003 that the tax records of local foundations showed that many paid their trustees to do work that many other foundations consider volunteer work. The move attracted IRS attention.

Foundations are run like businesses, with an eye toward expenses and a focus on where the money goes. They're not actually selling a product or a service, but they are important operations that control billions of dollars in some cases.

---

[2]From "Kauffman Foundation will increase small grants to non-profits," by J. Spivak, January 24, 2003, *Kansas City Star*, p. A1. Copyright 2003 by *Kansas City Star*. Reprinted with permission.

The media, with a few notable exceptions, ignores foundations, or downplays their coverage to focus on large grants or gifts handed out. While those stories are news, there's more going on within these organizations that merit coverage.

In the next section, we'll see how to find specific financial information for foundations and non-profit organizations.

FINDING INFORMATION: THE FORM 990

The perception among many journalists is that foundations and nonprofit organizations are secretive entities just like private businesses, with no real way to assess their financial performance.

That belief, however, is wrong, just as it is regarding small and private companies. There is plenty of information available for a reporter to gather about foundations and nonprofits. Just like businesses, these groups are required to file documents with the Secretary of State's office in the state in which they are located. They may also have to file information with the state office that tracks charities. These documents will help a reporter learn a nonprofit organization's board members and attorney, but may not provide much else.

Many nonprofit organizations also receive funding or have contracts with state, city, or federal governments. The documents related to these arrangements are public record. Sometimes, the government agency that has the contract or provided funding to the nonprofit organization will also perform an audit on the group to make sure that the money is being spent in accordance with the agreement.

Other groups also keep track of specific nonprofit information. The Better Business Bureau, for example, has a philanthropic advisory service that evaluates the performance of nonprofit organizations. It measures groups on the basis of their management, their fundraising practices, how money is spent, and other items. It stipulated that 60% of donations must be used in providing services, and no more than 35% of a group's budget should be spent on fundraising. Many of its reports on nonprofits can be obtained by going to http://www.give.org.

However, any reporter truly interested in finding detailed financial information about a foundation or a nonprofit organization must examine one document that will provide most of what they need. The IRS has required a Form 990 be filed by foundations and nonprofit organizations since 1942, and is a public record.

A Form 990 shows how much money the nonprofit organization collected within the last year and from what sources, and where it spent its money. These expenses are divided among program expenses, management expenses, and fundraising expenses. The Form 990 also details what kind of programs the organization is running, and how much it spends on them. In addition, this document details information such as the group's board members and how much its management is paid. There are also disclosures that show if the organization had any transactions in the last year and whether it lobbies.

The Form 990 should be thought of as the equivalent of a Form 10-Q or 10-K for a public company, with some of the functions of other SEC filings—such as proxy statements—rolled in for good measure. The Form 990 is one of the most all-encompassing financial documents available for a reporter.

Regulations in 2000 greatly expanded access to Form 990 documents. Nonprofit organizations are required to provide their three most recent Form 990 filings as well as their original filing for tax-exempt status to anyone who requests them. They must be made available the same day of the request from the foundation's office, and within 30 days by mail. The documents can also be obtained directly from the IRS by using Form 4506A or by writing a letter. The IRS may take up to six weeks to reply, however. Many states are also keeping Form 990s on file for foundations in their state. Many foundations are also now posting their Form 990 each year on the Internet, making them accessible to anyone. However, organizations can be fined for not making their Form 990 filings available to the public.

Most nonprofit organizations must file their Form 990 with the IRS within six months after the end of their fiscal year. However, the document may not be immediately available, as it can take the federal government agency several months to scan the document. Nonprofit organizations can also file for extensions, which may delay when the document is filed.

Most religious organizations are not required to file Form 990 documents. And organizations with less than $25,000 in receipts in a year are also exempt. But nonprofit organizations with more than $100,000 in receipts or more than $250,000 in total assets must file a Form 990, whereas nonprofit organizations with receipts less than $100,000 but at least $25,000 and assets of less than $250,000 must file a Form 990-EZ.

Unlike financial statements from companies, Form 990 filings for nonprofit organizations do not offer a comparison with financial figures from the previous year. To make a valid comparison about a nonprofit group's finances, a reporter needs to look at the financial information for several years to analyze the changes through time. A single Form 990 only provides a snapshot of an organization's finances at the end of the year, much like a balance sheet or cash flow statement for a public company. The Form 990 for the Chapel Hill-Carrboro YMCA near the University of North Carolina shows that the facility had more than $1.9 million in revenue in the fiscal year ended 2001, more than $1.6 million in expenses, liabilities of $831,000 and assets of more than $3.5 million.

The top of a Form 990 looks just like the tax return you file each year. The nonprofit lists its name, address and phone number, as well as its Web address. The first part of the document shows the group's revenue and expenses, as well as changes in its net assets. For example, the Form 990 from 2001 for the Better Business Bureau Wise Giving Alliance, the nonprofit group that tracks other non-profit organizations, listed total revenue of $1.27 million (see Fig. 10.1). But its expenses for the year totaled $1.64 million, meaning that it spent $371,000 more

Form 990 — Return of Organization Exempt From Income Tax

Form 990

Department of the Treasury
Internal Revenue Service

Return of Organization Exempt From Income Tax
Under section 501(c), 527, or 4947(a)(1) of the Internal Revenue Code (except black lung benefit trust or private foundation)

▶ The organization may have to use a copy of this return to satisfy state reporting requirements.

OMB No. 1545-0047

2001

Open to Public Inspection

A For the 2001 calendar year, or tax year period beginning ___ and ending ___

B Check if applicable:	Please use IRS label or print or type. See Specific Instructions.	C Name of organization		D Employer identification number
☐ Address change		BBB WISE GIVING ALLIANCE		52-1070270
☒ Name change		Number and street (or P.O. box if mail is not delivered to street address)	Room/suite	E Telephone number
☐ Initial return		4200 WILSON BOULEVARD	800	(703) 276-0100
☐ Final return		City or town, state or country, and ZIP + 4		F Accounting method: ☐ Cash ☒ Accrual
☐ Amended return		ARLINGTON, VA 22203-1804		☐ Other (specify) ▶
☐ Application pending				

● Section 501(c)(3) organizations and 4947(a)(1) nonexempt charitable trusts must attach a completed Schedule A (Form 990 or 990-EZ).

G Web site: ▶ WWW.GIVE.ORG

J Organization type (check only one) ▶ ☒ 501(c) (3) ◀ (insert no.) ☐ 4947(a)(1) or ☐ 527

K Check here ▶ ☐ if the organization's gross receipts are normally not more than $25,000. The organization need not file a return with the IRS; but if the organization received a Form 990 Package in the mail, it should file a return without financial data. Some states require a complete return.

H and I are not applicable to section 527 organizations.

H(a) Is this a group return for affiliates? ☐ Yes ☒ No

H(b) If "Yes," enter number of affiliates ▶ ___

H(c) Are all affiliates included? N/A ☐ Yes ☐ No
(If "No," attach a list.)

H(d) Is this a separate return filed by an organization covered by a group ruling? ☐ Yes ☒ No

I Enter 4-digit GEN ▶

M Check ▶ ☐ if the organization is **not** required to attach Sch. B (Form 990, 990-EZ, or 990-PF).

L Gross receipts: Add lines 6b, 8b, 9b, and 10b to line 12 ▶ 1,270,313.

Part I Revenue, Expenses, and Changes in Net Assets or Fund Balances

1	Contributions, gifts, grants, and similar amounts received:			
a	Direct public support	1a	814,725.	
b	Indirect public support	1b	452,088.	
c	Government contributions (grants)	1c		
d	Total (add lines 1a through 1c) (cash $ 1,266,813. noncash $ ___)			1d	1,266,813.
2	Program service revenue including government fees and contracts (from Part VII, line 93)			2	2,207.
3	Membership dues and assessments			3	
4	Interest on savings and temporary cash investments			4	1,293.
5	Dividends and interest from securities			5	
6 a	Gross rents	6a			
b	Less: rental expenses	6b			
c	Net rental income or (loss) (subtract line 6b from line 6a)			6c	
7	Other investment income (describe ▶ ___)			7	
8 a	Gross amount from sale of assets other than inventory	(A) Securities 8a	(B) Other		
b	Less: cost or other basis and sales expenses	8b			
c	Gain or (loss) (attach schedule)	8c			
d	Net gain or (loss) (combine line 8c, columns (A) and (B))			8d	
9	Special events and activities (attach schedule)				
a	Gross revenue (not including $ ___ of contributions reported on line 1a)	9a			
b	Less: direct expenses other than fundraising expenses	9b			
c	Net income or (loss) from special events (subtract line 9b from line 9a)			9c	
10 a	Gross sales of inventory, less returns and allowances	10a			
b	Less: cost of goods sold	10b			
c	Gross profit or (loss) from sales of inventory (attach schedule) (subtract line 10b from line 10a)			10c	
11	Other revenue (from Part VII, line 103)			11	
12	Total revenue (add lines 1d, 2, 3, 4, 5, 6c, 7, 8d, 9c, 10c, and 11)			12	1,270,313.
13	Program services (from line 44, column (B))			13	1,175,478.
14	Management and general (from line 44, column (C))			14	259,560.
15	Fundraising (from line 44, column (D))			15	206,520.
16	Payments to affiliates (attach schedule)			16	
17	Total expenses (add lines 16 and 44, column (A))			17	1,641,558.
18	Excess or (deficit) for the year (subtract line 17 from line 12)			18	-371,245.
19	Net assets or fund balances at beginning of year (from line 73, column (A))			19	82,274.
20	Other changes in net assets or fund balances (attach explanation) SEE STATEMENT 1			20	114,446.
21	Net assets or fund balances at end of year (combine lines 18, 19, and 20)			21	-174,525.

(Revenue — lines 1–12; Expenses — lines 13–17; Net Assets — lines 18–21)

123001 01-04-02 LHA For Paperwork Reduction Act Notice, see the separate instructions.

Form **990** (2001)

FIG. 10.1 From Better Business Bureau Wise Giving Alliance, 2001, filed with Internal Revenue Service.

254

BBB WISE GIVING ALLIANCE   52-1070270   Page 2

Part II Statement of Functional Expenses

All organizations must complete column (A). Columns (B), (C), and (D) are required for section 501(c)(3) and (4) organizations and section 4947(a)(1) nonexempt charitable trusts but optional for others.

Do not include amounts reported on line 6b, 8b, 9b, 10b, or 16 of Part I.		(A) Total	(B) Program services	(C) Management and general	(D) Fundraising
22 Grants and allocations (attach schedule)	22				
cash $ noncash $					
23 Specific assistance to individuals (attach schedule)	23				
24 Benefits paid to or for members (attach schedule)	24				
25 Compensation of officers, directors, etc.	25	0.	0.	0.	0.
26 Other salaries and wages	26				
27 Pension plan contributions	27				
28 Other employee benefits	28				
29 Payroll taxes	29				
30 Professional fundraising fees	30				
31 Accounting fees	31	11,375.		11,375.	
32 Legal fees	32	11,797.		11,797.	
33 Supplies	33	55,286.	51,893.	1,714.	1,679.
34 Telephone	34	10,735.	9,254.	333.	1,148.
35 Postage and shipping	35	77,009.	21,684.	3,269.	52,056.
36 Occupancy	36	95,130.	80,861.	2,949.	11,320.
37 Equipment rental and maintenance	37	20,912.	17,775.	648.	2,489.
38 Printing and publications	38	139,286.	103,971.		35,315.
39 Travel	39	19,038.	13,695.	4,369.	974.
40 Conferences, conventions, and meetings	40	1,050.	1,050.		
41 Interest	41				
42 Depreciation, depletion, etc. (attach schedule)	42	2,988.	2,539.	93.	356.
43 Other expenses not covered above (itemize):					
a PERSONNEL SERVICES	43a	851,028.	723,656.	26,189.	101,183.
b OTHER SUPPORT SERVICES	43b	189,354.		189,354.	
c SURVEY RESEARCH	43c	149,100.	149,100.		
d STATE REGISTRATION	43d	7,470.		7,470.	
e	43e				
44 Total functional expenses (add lines 22 through 43) Organizations completing columns (B)-(D), carry these totals to lines 13-15	44	1,641,558.	1,175,478.	259,560.	206,520.

Joint Costs. Check ▶ ☐ if you are following SOP 98-2.

Are any joint costs from a combined educational campaign and fundraising solicitation reported in (B) Program services? .... ▶ ☐ Yes ☒ No

If "Yes," enter (i) the aggregate amount of these joint costs $ _____ ; (ii) the amount allocated to Program services $ _____ ;
(iii) the amount allocated to Management and general $ _____ ; and (iv) the amount allocated to Fundraising $ _____ .

Part III Statement of Program Service Accomplishments

What is the organization's primary exempt purpose? ▶ SEE STATEMENT 2

	Program Service Expenses (Required for 501(c)(3) and (4) orgs., and 4947(a)(1) trusts; but optional for others.)
All organizations must describe their exempt purpose achievements in a clear and concise manner. State the number of clients served, publications issued, etc. Discuss achievements that are not measurable. (Section 501(c)(3) and (4) organizations and 4947(a)(1) nonexempt charitable trusts must also enter the amount of grants and allocations to others.)	
a SEE STATEMENT 3 (Grants and allocations $)	1,175,478.
b (Grants and allocations $)	
c (Grants and allocations $)	
d (Grants and allocations $)	
e Other program services (attach schedule) (Grants and allocations $)	
f Total of Program Service Expenses (should equal line 44, column (B), Program services) .... ▶	1,175,478.

123011 01-02-02   Form 990 (2001)

FIG. 10.1   (Continued)

than it took in. Its expenses included $1.18 million for its programs, $259,000 for management salaries and general expenses, and $206,000 on fundraising.

Again, look at these numbers in comparison with the previous year's filings. If expenses rose dramatically and the money being brought into the organization did not, the reporter should examine where the expenses rose and ask someone at the nonprofit why this happened. Or if the amount of money that the group took in during the year increased dramatically from the previous year, the reporter should find out why. Was there an increase in government funding? Or did the nonprofit receive more in private donations? These large increases or fluctuations can often be a story.

The bottom of the first page of the Form 990 lists the organizations net assets at the beginning of the year and the net assets at the end of the year. These can be important numbers to assess the future viability of the group. If its net assets are rising, then it is a strong organization. But if the assets are falling, or have become a negative number, this may be an indication of future financial problems. The Better Business Bureau Wise Giving Alliance reported a net assets of $-\$174, 525$ at the end of 2001, compared to net assets of $82,274 at the beginning of the year, according to its Form 990 (see Fig. 10.1).

The second page of the document breaks the expenses for the organization down into further categories, including legal expenses, supplies, postage and telephone, rent, printing and publications, and travel. These expenses are broken down for programs, management, and fundraising. According to Web site http://www.guidestar.org, many organizations will lump most of their expenses into the "Other Expenses" category and detail those expenses in an attachment, even though most of the expenses could be included in a category. That suggests it would be wise to look at the attachment. Indeed, the largest expense for the Better Business Bureau Wise Giving Alliance—more than $851,000—is something called "personnel services" that is listed under "Other Expenses" (see Fig. 10.1).

Also pay attention to the amount of money spent on fundraising in relation to the total expenses for the year. Some believe that fundraising expenses should be a small percentage of the total expenses of a nonprofit group. However, fundraising may represent a majority of the expenses for some organizations, particularly new groups or those that are promoting an unpopular cause. If a nonprofit is spending a lot of money on fundraising but its revenue is not increasing, that could be a sign that the fundraising has not been effective.

The next section of the Form 990 is where many nonprofit organizations can list their accomplishments for the previous year, but it is only about a third of a page and does not provide enough room for many groups to detail what they have done. Part IV of the form is a balance sheet, showing the nonprofit groups assets and liabilities. This can be basic information that may not lend itself to a story. But Part V is a section of the Form 990 that does draw attention. Part V is where officers, directors, and key employees and their compensation and expense account allowances are listed in the filing. In past years, nonprofit organizations have been offering larger compensation packages to attract managers from the for-profit world. These can provide stories for many media outlets. The Form 990 for the Better Business Bureau Wise Giving Alliance showed that the group paid CEO Herman Taylor a salary of $86,923 for seven months of the year as well as a $2,000 expense account, and paid COO Bennett Weiner a salary of $90,448 for the entire year. Executive Director Candace McIlhenny received a salary of $59,796. None of the board members were paid a salary. The filing also notes that the salaries came from the Council of Better Business Bureaus Incorporated.

Reporters should compare the salaries for any nonprofit organization with those from previous year. If the salaries have not increased or have gone up only slightly, then there is likely nothing to write about. But if the salaries have increased dramatically, or a new CEO is making much more than the previous CEO, there may be a story.

Reporters should also watch for discrepancies between what is in the documents and what the organization is saying. The beginning of the following *Washington Post* story notes how the Form 990 filings of Jesse Jackson's nonprofit organizations omitted the salary of one of its top executives:

> More than 100 pages of tax records and auditors' reports have been released by Jesse L. Jackson as questions mount about the finances of his organizations. But they make no mention of the woman with whom he fathered a child during an extramarital affair even though federal tax law required that she be listed on one form because of the amount of money she earned.
>
> Jackson's tax-exempt Citizenship Education Fund (CEF), which received more than $10 million of the $17 million collected last year by his four charitable groups, failed to list its former executive director, Karin Stanford, on a 1999 Internal Revenue Service form that required the names of all staff members who earned more than $50,000.
>
> Stanford, according to a spokesman for Jackson's Rainbow/PUSH Coalition, earned $120,000 when she resigned in 1999, the year she had Jackson's baby. The controversy surrounding Stanford intensified after it was disclosed that CEF gave her a "draw" of $40,000 against future consulting fees to help her buy a house in California, according to a Sept. 10, 1999, letter to Stanford from a top Jackson aide. Jackson said he gives Stanford $3,000 monthly from his personal funds.
>
> Billy R. Owens, vice president and chief financial officer of Jackson's four interlocking organizations—Rainbow/PUSH Coalition Inc., the CEF, People United to Serve Humanity and Push for Excellence—said today that tax accountants are trying to determine whether they need to amend the IRS Form 990 on which Jackson aides declared "NONE" when asked to list the top five staff members who were paid more than $50,000 by CEF.
>
> "The guys who prepared it are looking at everything to see if there are issues that need amending," Owens said.
>
> The 1999 tax return also did not list the names of any firms or individuals with outside consulting contracts even though Rainbow/PUSH and related groups reported

paying nearly $1 million in consulting fees. Owens's "Financial Report to Donors" said the Jackson groups paid $1.3 million in consulting fees last year.[3]

If a reporter finds a Form 990 that does not have all of the information that is required by the IRS, there might be a story. All the reporters in this case had to do was compare public statements with what was reported in the document.

Part VI of the Form 990 shows how much money the nonprofit organization spent on lobbying. Many groups spend little or no money on lobbying public officials. However, if there is a filing in which a large amount of money has been spent on lobbying compared with other expenses, a reporter should check into it. If nonprofit organizations lobby too much, they may put their tax-exempt status in jeopardy.

Part IX of the form is also of potential interest to reporters. This is where nonprofit organizations disclose information about for-profit subsidiaries. Some groups operate for-profit businesses on the side to help them raise money for their programs and services. Check this section to see if the nonprofit you are investigating has one of these companies, and how much money it made.

Each year, thousands of Form 990 documents are filed with the IRS. A recent report by the General Accounting Office, however, suggested that the regulatory agency may not be reviewing all of them to find wayward nonprofit organizations, according to the following *USA Today* story:

Don't count on Uncle Sam to spot potential scams involving charities.

Internal Revenue Service oversight of charities is lagging, even as the number of non-profits is rising, a federal study shows. Conducted by the General Accounting Office, the investigative arm of Congress, the study found the IRS lacks data to determine the type and extent of possible tax reporting violations by non-profits. Other findings:

- IRS staffing for oversight of non-profits fell roughly 15 percent in federal fiscal years 1996–2001, even as the number of new charities seeking tax-exempt status grew 9 percent.
- The rate at which the IRS examined charities dropped to less than 0.5 percent during the past two years and stands at a six-year low.
- The IRS does not routinely alert state-level monitors about denials and revocations of charities' tax-exempt status—information the state officials said could be used to help protect contributors.

"The bad apples get headlines after they've cheated people. Clearly, we need to reverse that order," said Sen. Charles Grassley, R-Iowa, ranking minority member of the Senate Finance Committee. "More oversight from the IRS is critical."

---

[3]From "Missing information noted in Jackson's tax records," by W. Claiborne, March 7, 2001, *Washington Post*, p. A 3. Copyright 2001 by *Washington Post*. Reprinted with permission.

Grassley and the Senate panel requested the study after a USA TODAY investigation last year showed some wish-granting charities spend far more on fundraising, salaries and other costs than on their professed mission—fulfilling dreams for seriously ill children. The paper also found that the IRS audits only a fraction of the annual tax returns filed by charities.

The GAO study said the tax agency's examinations have found repeated examples of charities that improperly under-report fundraising expenses or misrepresent spending on fundraising and other costs as part of their philanthropic mission. But the IRS does not know "the extent of misreporting" and "generally has not established results-oriented goals for its oversight," the analysis found.

However, the IRS, coping with multiple oversight and collection missions, plans to study 35 segments of the charity industry to address tax misreporting by non-profits. The report concluded the IRS should also get reliable data on tax law compliance by charities, expand oversight staffing and improve information-sharing with state charity monitors.

In a written response, IRS Commissioner Charles Rossotti agreed with the general findings and recommendations. But he cautioned that the agency must cope with "considerable resource constraints" and "competing priorities" as it tries to improve oversight.[4]

Business reporters are increasingly reviewing SEC documents for public companies in the wake of scandals at Enron, WorldCom, Adelphia, and others. Yet few stories have been written analyzing a nonprofit organization's Form 990 filing in any depth. This area of financial reporting is ripe for aggressive reporters. Their story research does not have to find major misdeeds; the media could simply do a better, more thorough job of writing about nonprofit organizations and foundations.

In addition to Form 990 and the other suggestions on finding information about nonprofits, a number of Web sites are also available to help a reporter analyze IRS documents. The Guidestar web site, mentioned earlier, is by far and away the most comprehensive. It helps reporters understand what the numbers mean. A similar site can be accessed at http://www.grantsmart.org. A third, http://www.charitynavigator.org, has evaluated more than 1,000 organizations and provides tips and resources.

Acquiring the Form 990 filings of a nonprofit organization shows its management team that a reporter is serious about writing a story that is fair and balanced but also uses the best information available to provide the most complete picture of its performance (see Fig. 10.1).

BLUE PLANS AND HEALTH CARE PROVIDERS

One industry above all others has seen a number of major players that are nonprofit organizations. Within the health care industry, major hospital systems, health

---

[4]From "IRS oversight of charities falls behind," by K. McCoy, May 28, 2002, *USA Today*, p. 1B. Copyright 2002 by *USA Today*. Reprinted with permission.

maintenance organizations, nursing homes, and other groups are nonprofit businesses.

Kaiser Permanente is a large managed care operation that has more than 90,000 employees and covers more than 8 million consumers. The Catholic Health Association of the United States has more than 2,000 facilities in the country, ranging from nursing homes to hospitals. The Veteran's Health Administration (VHA) system contains some of the nation's best known hospitals, including the Mayo Clinic and Cedars-Sinai Health. Many Blue Cross–Blue Shield plans across the country are also not-for-profit operations.

Nonprofit health companies are in every state of the country and nearly every market. In many cases, they are competing directly with for-profit businesses for patients and members. And in many cases, they are holding a dominant market share. In Alabama, for example, the Blue Cross–Blue Shield plan has an 80% market share in the state. Nonprofit health organizations do not worry about making a profit or satisfying shareholders. Their mission is to provide quality health care at the lowest cost available. This is a laudable concept, but in reality these are often huge businesses with billions in revenue and millions in profits. And during the last decade, many not-for-profit hospitals and health insurance companies have converted their ownership structure into a for-profit company. Some have even sold themselves to for-profit corporations.

Nonprofit health businesses are run just like other not-for-profit organizations. In many cases, they have tax-exempt status from the federal government, although Blue Cross–Blue Shield plans lost their full exemption from federal income taxes in 1986. They file documents with the IRS reporting their financial performance and executive compensation. St. Joseph's Hospital in Tampa, for example, reported revenue of $388 million in 2001 and expenses of $356 million in the same year, according to its Form 990. Martha Jefferson Hospital in Charlottesville, Virginia reported revenues of $109 million and expenses of $104.6 million for the same year. In many cases, these not-for-profit health businesses are also reporting financial information to state regulators who oversee insurance and health care.

Nonprofit hospitals and other health care businesses have many of the same issues as their for-profit competitors. They must keep costs down to survive. Strong management can make the overall company better. Acquisitions or expansions help these organizations grow into new businesses and new markets. They also have advantages. Whereas for-profit hospitals and insurance companies can tap the equities market and raise money by selling stock, nonprofit organizations can sell tax-exempt bonds. And studies have shown that for-profit health companies have higher costs. But non-profits also face problems just like any other business venture. An expansion did not work out like it was planned, or an executive brought in to turn the business around failed and is asked to leave, as the following *Boston Herald* story shows:

Staff at the UMass Memorial Health Care Inc. report a sense of relief that Dr. Arthur R. Russo is leaving the beleaguered hospital.

Hospital directors pushed Russo to resign late Wednesday after his 14-month tenure.

He was criticized for his attempts to reorganize the hospital, including cutting a popular liver transplant program at the institution. He also oversaw more than 200 job cuts and backed an executive who lied on his resume.

"The mood is much lighter today than it was yesterday," said Dr. Eliezer Katz, head of the liver transplant program, which was ultimately saved. "There is cautious optimism that we will see a change for the better."

The staff has confidence in Dr. Marianne E. Felice, who has taken over as interim chief executive, Katz said. "She has a lot of respect and trust," he said.

A search is planned for a permanent replacement for Russo.

The 761-bed, eight-hospital group lost an estimated $24 million on operations for the just-ended fiscal year, on revenue of $1.07 billion, spokesman Mark Shelton said. The loss would top last year's $9.4 million deficit on revenue of $1.06 billion, he said.

In an attempt to stop the bleeding, officials of the 10,000-employee non-profit hospital network brought in the Hunter Group, a Florida health care consulting firm. Hunter made a number of controversial recommendations including 500 job cuts and eliminating liver transplants.

The decision to cut the liver transplant program drew criticism from doctors and former patients, who picketed the hospital. Eventually, hospital executives conceded and kept the program.

Russo also backed Michael Greene and kept him on staff after it was revealed that he fabricated his education credentials on his resume. It's not certain whether Greene will remain on staff, a spokesman said.

A severance package for Russo, who made $680,000, is still being negotiated, a spokesman said. He is expected to stay on and advise Felice through the transition.

Felice is chief of pediatrics at the medical center and a professor at the affiliated University of Massachusetts Medical School. She has been with the center for three years.[5]

In addition to this story, *The Star Tribune* in Minneapolis noted in November 2001 that a number of top executives at nonprofit health care companies in the state were receiving larger compensation packages than disclosed in their operations' Form 990s.

The number of not-for-profit health operations, however, is declining. A General Accounting Office report in December 1997 found that 192 of the more than 5,000 not-for-profit hospitals in the country converted to for-profit status between 1990 and 1996. In 1996, more than 60 converted. Today, the number of nonprofit hospitals is less than 3,000 of the 5,800 hospitals in the country, according to the American Hospital Association.

The same move is occurring in the health insurance industry, in which non-profit plans are converting to for-profit status, particularly among Blue Cross–Blue Shield operations. The Blue plans in North Carolina filed plans to convert to for-profit status but then withdrew its plans, whereas similar operations in New York,

---

[5]From "UMass hospital ousts embattled Russo as CEO," by J. Heldt Powell, Nov. 2, 2001, *Boston Herald*, p. 38. Copyright 2001 by *Boston Herald*. Reprinted with permission.

Georgia, Missouri, and other states have converted. Some Blue plans, it should be noted, have stated that they will not convert to a for-profit company.

As nonprofit organizations, these businesses belong to the community and their customers. There are no shareholders. But by converting, they are taking that community "ownership" and giving it to stockholders. Many states passed legislation in the 1990s requiring these nonprofit health groups to give some back to the people in exchange for this conversion.

Now, plans by a not-for-profit health care company to convert to for-profit status must be approved by state and federal regulators. In many cases, public hearings must also be held. The process of the conversion can result in good stories, from the initial filing of the conversion plan to the public hearings, at which consumers are likely to speak about the rising cost of health care and how turning the company to a for-profit venture will increase their medical costs.

Regulators throughout the years have required the not-for-profit health company to set up a foundation with the value of the organization that has been built during its time as a benefit to the community. The valuation of the company—and therefore the amount of money that the foundation receives—can be a sticking point in the conversion plan. In some states, the foundation received a small amount of money only to see the for-profit health care business sold for much more several years later.

In other cases, nonprofit organizations have been criticized for selling themselves for much lower than what many believe they are worth. One of the issues is that executives of not-for-profit ventures do not have an ownership stake in the entity. CEOs of public companies often own stock and want to sell their companies for the highest price so that they receive as much as possible for their stock. But executives at nonprofits do not have such an incentive.

In some cases, regulators have stepped in and prevented acquisitions of nonprofit health care operations because they felt the price was too low. The California attorney general stopped the sale of a hospital to Columbia/HCA because its offer was $200 million less than competing bids. And the Maryland insurance commissioner turned down a 2002 request to sell the not-for-profit Blue Cross–Blue Shield plan in the state to for-profit WellPoint. When this happens, it is obviously a story, particularly the facts surrounding the scuttling of the deal. The companies are also likely to seek another deal, which may result in another story.

Although these nonprofit organizations looking to convert are required to file their financial performance with the IRS, many of them also issue releases showing their performance just like for-profit companies. They are gearing up for the switch, and begin performing some of the functions used by a public company.

The following excerpt shows how a reporter analyzed the earnings release from a Blue Cross–Blue Shield company in the midst of a conversion process, providing the context through statements from benefits consultants and historical comparisons to show the reader the impact the large profit might have on regulators and other interested parties:

With its for-profit conversion serving as a backdrop, Blue Cross reported an $85.6 million profit for 2001—the biggest bottom line in the 69-year-old insurer's history.

While company officials described the historic high in terms such as 'a continuation of the company's improving operating performance,' a health care advocate was more succinct: "Holy moley."

However you describe it, the number indicates more than a good year for the state's largest insurer at 2.5 million members.

"They are simply not acting like a non-profit company, they are focused on bringing in profits and building the business," said the health care advocate, Adam Searing, who is project director of The N.C. Health Access Coalition in Raleigh. "It makes me think even more they should be allowed to convert."

The large profit—the closest rival was a $75.6 million profit in 1993—also raises the question of why Blue Cross and Blue Shield of North Carolina needed the double-digit premium increases it sought and recently won from state insurance officials, a health benefits consultant in Charlotte said.

"I think that will bring the question from the public—what's really the story?" said Steve Graybill, a senior benefits consultant with William M. Mercer.

Dan Glaser, the chief financial officer at Blue Cross, said premiums are based on medical costs, which have been trending up in recent years. Medical cost trends rose 13.9 percent in 2001 and 8.8 percent the previous year, he noted Tuesday.

Graybill agreed that medical costs are increasing between 12 percent and 16 percent.

"But how do you get to a 33 percent increase on a given product—are they losing their rears?" Graybill asked.

Blue Cross has an array of health plans it sells to employers and other groups, as well as to individuals. A majority of those plans got premium increases that range from 27 percent to 47 percent on average, according to N.C. Department of Insurance information.

The Chapel Hill insurer's 78,000-member HMO, Blue Care, won an average premium increase of 47 percent that goes into effect in July and its 105,000-member Blue Choice plan premium will go up an average of 37 percent in July, according to insurance department information. Other Blue Cross plans that represent about a quarter of the insurer's business aren't going up as much this year, with rate increases varying between 5 percent and 8 percent.

While the insurance department has approved the rate increases, it is keeping an eye on the issue as Blue Cross works through the process of converting to a for-profit company.

"We're looking at is there a comprehensive plan here to raise rates, preconversion," said Mollie Doll, a spokeswoman for the department.

One of the issues that has slowed down the negotiations between the department and company is Blue Cross has yet to provide a premium rate analysis that looks three years prior and post conversion, she said. The company has said it is compiling the information.

In January, Blue Cross filed a plan to convert to a for-profit company. It hopes to complete the conversion by late spring or summer.

The conversion will follow the plan laid out in a 1998 state law that calls for the creation of one of the largest health care foundations in the state using proceeds from the sale of Blue Cross stock. The plan calls for the foundation to receive all of the initial company stock issued—which could mean more than $1 billion as most of the stock is sold off over five years.

Blue Cross would retain its reserves, now valued at $715 million and could raise capital through secondary offerings.

While investors warm up to stock issued by companies with a proven track record of financial success, a spokesman for Blue Cross said it did not plan to make $85.6 million to ensure a successful public launch of the company.

"The conversion to for-profit had no bearing on how we performed in 2001 or how we determined premiums for this year," said spokesman Kyle Marshall.

Graybill, the benefits consultant, said the fact is Blue Cross has been acting like a for-profit company for years, although a big profit wouldn't hurt its efforts to sell stock. "That might have been one motivating factor, but I think they'd be doing it even if they weren't going for-profit," he said in an interview last week.

A leading force in the for-profit makeover of Blue Cross is Robert Greczyn Jr., who became chief executive in 2000, Graybill said. "The whole culture Greczyn has been trying to establish there is a more for-profit culture, even though they haven't reached that status," he said.

One of the more obvious ways Blue Cross has embraced the practices of its for-profit competitors is its performance-based incentive system, which rewards employees for a strong financial performance by the company.

Some $14 million in bonuses went to Blue Cross employees, including $2 million for nine of the top executives. Greczyn received the largest bonus—$571,500—which boosted his total pay to $1.1 million for 2001.

Glaser, the non-profit insurer's chief financial officer, noted that it was Blue Cross' massive $700 million investment portfolio that pushed profits so high, with dividends, interest and gains from a large stock sell-off alone generating $85.9 million. And Blue Cross operating income—the barometer of the company's principal business of providing health insurance—remained in the black for the second year in a row, producing $48.6 million.

Factor in $46.2 million in income taxes and $2.8 million in interest expense and out comes an $85 million profit.

That profit even takes into account last year's acquisition of Partners National Health plans of North Carolina, a $202 million deal that had Blue Cross buying the state's largest for-profit HMO. Blue Cross paid $102 million in cash raised from its investment portfolio and will pay the balance over 10 years.[6]

This story ends with the mention that a not-for-profit business bought a for-profit operation. In many states, as noted earlier in the chapter, a nonprofit organization can own a for-profit subsidiary.

If a not-for-profit health care company in a community plans to convert, one of the first steps it will take as part of the process will be to hire a new leader with for-profit experience. That CEO will come into the nonprofit and make changes. The next step will be to file their intent with regulators.

Reporters should be on the lookout for any indication that their local not-for-profit health care company may be thinking about a change. The decision

---

[6]From "Blue Cross racks up record $85.6M profit; as non-profit eyes for-profit status, question arises about a need for large rate increases," by J. Zimmer, March 20, 2002, *Durham Herald-Sun*, p. C1. Copyright 2002 by Durham Herald Company Inc. Reprinted with permission.

could have broad implications for the community. As a for-profit venture, the hospital or health insurer may raise rates. Also, it now has the ability to raise cash through the stock market and use that money to make acquisitions or to expand its existing operations. And as a for-profit, it could also provide stock options and other incentives to its executives. These moves bear watching.

Attorneys general and labor unions have also begun to criticize the nonprofit status of many health care businesses, according to the Coalition for Nonprofit Health Care. In some cases, they have forced the breakup of a nonprofit, whereas in other cases a divestiture has been forced. Regulators have also threatened to remove the board of a not-for-profit health business.

YMCAs AND OTHER NONPROFITS

Many other nonprofit businesses also fall under the radar of most media outlets. Yet they can be a surprising source for news.

Nonprofit organizations and foundations can often make great profiles for the work that they do. They are almost always trying to better the community that they are in, or help someone else. Find the work that they do and the people that they have helped. A *USA Today* profile in January 2002 of a former Cisco Systems executive who started her own foundation to help technology start ups by women is a perfect example. ABC News profiled how other high-tech executives in the Seattle area have started foundations to help others with the millions they made.

The relationship between nonprofits and for-profits can also yield interesting stories. *The Wall Street Journal* reported how some entrepreneurial scientists were receiving government grants through nonprofit organizations and then using the money to fund for-profit biotechnology companies. In some cases, the nonprofit and the for-profit shared office space and were run by the same person. These types of connections should raise eyebrows with anyone.

And like with for-profit businesses, stories can come from executive salaries, illegal activities, major campaigns to raise money, and changes in leadership. A *San Jose Mercury News* story focused on the salary of a swim coach at a nonprofit organization. The following is the beginning of that story:

> In the world of swimming, Pete Raykovich gets much credit for building the once-tiny De Anza Cupertino Aquatics program into the sixth-largest club program in the United States. But head coach Raykovich is enjoying more than just praise: Last year he was paid $353,518.
>
> That's far more than the CEOs of many larger and better-known non-profit organizations. It's twice the salary made last year by Gov. Gray Davis.
>
> DACA's board of directors says Raykovich is well worth the money he gets, under a contract that gives him a percentage of the swim club's net revenues. But his pay raises eyebrows in non-profit circles, where talented executives have typically

accepted lower salaries than they could make elsewhere in order to plow money back into their programs.

Experts say it is nearly unheard of for a non-profit group to tie an executive's salary to his organization's revenues.

"I'm not saying he's not doing good work and shouldn't be adequately compensated," said Pablo Eisenberg, a regular columnist for the Chronicle of Philanthropy and a senior fellow at the Georgetown University Public Policy Institute. "But, if he wants to make money, let him go work for a for profit organization. . . . In my view, it's excessive."

DACA's gross income was $2.7 million last year. According to the 2002 Wage & Benefit Survey of Northern California Non-profit Organizations, executive director salaries for non-profit organizations with budgets between $2.5 million and $4 million range from a low of $49,920 to a high of $127,050, with the median at $93,964. The range for youth and recreation-type non-profit executives was $38,500 to $128,102, with a median of $64,700.

But if Raykovich's compensation is large, so—say supporters—is his contribution to the program.

"It's almost like an entrepreneur story,' said board member Matt Sanders. 'Pete built the business, and his compensation has grown along with its success."[7]

The story then goes on to compare the swim coach's salary with the salary of the heads of other nonprofit organizations in the area. And it quotes parents who have sent their kids to the club for swim lessons and who believe that the coach is worth his salary.

Reporters should check for stories about nonprofit organizations in unusual places. The YMCA in Chapel Hill decided to build a child-care center in a retirement home center recently. The uniqueness of putting young kids with old adults made for an interesting story. Or reporters can check to see if a nonprofit organization is buying land by reviewing local real estate records. If there is a recent transaction, the reporter should ask what they plan to do with the land.

Covering nonprofit businesses and foundations should be just like writing stories about for-profit companies. In many cases, you are looking in the same places for information—courthouse records, federal filings, lawsuits, etc. Reporters need to look for trends. If all of the nonprofit organizations in the area are seeing their assets decline, reporters should ask why that is happening. Is it because they all heavily invested their assets in the stock market? Or has gift giving slowed? How do they plan to correct the slowdown? Does the decline in assets mean that they will be giving out fewer grants this year? Or is there a foundation or nonprofit group bucking the trend, showing strong growth in its total assets and the amount of its giving while others in the same field or region have seen drops? What is this organization doing that others are not?

---

[7]From "Is swim coach worth $353,318?; Board says yes, but some experts question salary," by M. Cronk, April 14, 2003, *San Jose Mercury News*, p. A1. Copyright 2003 by *San Jose Mercury News*. All rights reserved. Reprinted with permission.

Many nonprofit groups also have Web sites with information about their programs and services. If there is a new program being added, a reporter should interview someone at the organization to find out what the potential is to bring in additional revenue. An executive director or program director might be the first place to start.

Covering nonprofits can be just like any other beat. The reporter has just got to know what to look for and what questions to ask.

GLOSSARY

conversion – The process by which a not-for-profit company switches to a for-profit structure where it has stockholders.

Form 990 – A document filed with the Internal Revenue Service by virtually every nonprofit organization and foundation. The filing discloses revenue, expenditures and salaries for management.

foundation – A nonprofit organization created to give money away. Foundations are required to grant 5% of their assets annually.

Internal Revenue Service – A federal regulatory agency that collects taxes from businesses and individuals. The IRS also determines the tax status of a business, and reviews documents to determine if a company is in compliance with federal laws.

nonprofit organization – A business created to provide a good or service to the community without making money. Many nonprofit organizations, however, do have more revenue than expenses.

REFERENCES

Adams, C. (2001, January 30). Laboratory hybrids: How adroit scientists aid biotech companies with taxpayer money. *Wall Street Journal.* p. 1A.

Claiborne, W. (2001, March 7). Missing information noted in Jackson's tax records. *Washington Post.* p. A3.

Cronk, M. (2003, April 14). Is swim coach worth $353,518?; Board says yes, but some experts question salary. *San Jose Mercury News.* p. A1.

Howatt, G. (2001, November 30). Health-care executives were paid more than reported; The non-profit companies vary in their interpretation of an IRS rule on disclosing deferred compensation. *The Star Tribune.* p. 1A.

Lindenberger, M. A. (2001, February 15). Goodwill to open megastore; Retail supercenter will be area's largest. *The Dallas Morning News.* p. 1N.

McCoy, K. (2002, May 28). IRS oversight of charities falls behind. *USA Today.* p. 1B.

Nalder, E. (2003, April 27). CEO's rewards at non-profit. *San Jose Mercury News.* p. 1A.

Okeson, S. (2002, August 4). Stopping crime has "shocking" price tag—CrimeStoppers defends spending 55 percent of expenses on fund-raising. *Peoria Journal Star.* p. 1A.

Heldt Powell, J. (2001, November 2). UMass hospital ousts embattled Russo as CEO. *Boston Herald.* p. 38.

Phillips, C., & McFadden, K. (2003, April 18). Head of Seattle's public-TV station to step down amid devastating debt. *The Seattle Times.* p. A1.

Shatzkin, K. (2003, May 11). Some foundations spend lavishly on own board members; Most in U.S. pay nothing, but in some cases, fees exceed amount of gifts. *The Baltimore Sun.* p. 1A.

Spivak, J. (2003, January 24). Kauffman Foundation will increase small grants to non-profits. *Kansas City Star.* p. A1.

Wang, D. (1999, August 4). A boom in giving. ABCNews.com. Retrieved Nov. 29, 2002 from http://abcnews.go.com/sections/tech/DailyNews/hitech_philanthropy990804.html.

Zimmer, J. (2002, March 20). Blue Cross racks up record $85.6M profit; as non-profit eyes for-profit status, question arises about a need for large rate increases. *Durham Herald-Sun.* p. C1.

Other Books About Nonprofits

Carver, J. (1997). *Boards that make a difference : A new design for leadership in nonprofit and public organizations.* Hoboken, NJ: Jossey-Bass.

Dowie, M. (2001). *American foundations: An investigative history.* Cambridge, MA: MIT Press.

Drucker, P. (1992). *Managing the non-profit organization: Principles and practices.* New York: Harper Business.

Weinstein, S. (2002). *The complete guide to fund-raising management.* (2nd ed.). New York: Wiley.

Wolf, T. (1999). *Managing a non-profit organization in the twenty-first century.* New York: Fireside Books.

SUGGESTED EXERCISES

1. Go around the class and ask if anyone has ever donated money to a non-profit organization. If they did, what made them decide to donate money to that particular entity? Did they think about what their money would be used for? Did anyone consider looking at the financial statements of the organization to see if it was using money properly?

2. Find a Form 990 of a non-profit organization or a foundation on the Internet. Many groups now post these documents online. Read the filing and if possible compare the numbers to the Form 990 for the previous year. Write a 500-word essay analyzing what the document tells you about the revenue for the organization and how the expenses were divided among programs, management and fundraising. Conclude with a statement on the organization's financial condition at the end of the year.

3. Go to a local non-profit organization and ask for a copy of their Form 990. The next day, report to the class whether you received the form, and how easy

it was to obtain. Did the organization have the document readily available, or did it take some time for them to find it? Did the organization deny you access to the filing? If so, what reasons did they give? Some suggestions would be the local YMCA, a public television or radio station, the local Salvation Army or Goodwill organization or the local American Red Cross.

4. Find a non-profit organization that has spent a large amount of money recently on fundraising and compare that increase to its revenues for the last three years. Did the fundraising have any impact on revenue? Do you think that the fundraising used by the organization was effective? Why or why not? What else could the organization have done to raise money?

5. Look for a local hospital or health insurance plan that is not-for-profit. If you can find one, ask yourself whether it competes with another hospital or insurance plan that is a for-profit company. Can you tell if they're operated any differently? What is the perception among local residents about the differences between the not-for-profit business and the for-profit entity?

11

Business in the Courthouse

WHY COMPANIES SUE EACH OTHER

The courthouse can be one of the best places for information about how businesses operate. In addition to all of the filings regarding business licenses and deeds for property purchased in the course of business, companies often head to the courthouse to file a lawsuit when they have a dispute with a customer, a supplier, a competitor, or an employee. In addition, people who come in contact with a business may also find the need to file a lawsuit against a company.

Litigation as a business tactic and as a way to redress a wrong committed by a company is on the increase, making an understanding of how the court system is used in the business world vital to any reporter.

In the federal court system, there were more than 274,000 civil case filings in 2002, a 9.5% increase from the previous year. Although there is no breakdown in what percentage of those cases involved businesses, it is fair to say that the increase in business-related litigation has contributed to the rise. In addition, there were 1.5 million bankruptcy cases filed in 2002, a 7.7% increase from the previous year. (For more on bankruptcy cases, see chap. 12.)

Hundreds of thousands of business-related lawsuits are also filed in state and local courts each year as well, although there are no recent statistics. The 1992 Civil Justice Survey of State Courts discovered that there were 762,000 tort, contract, and real property cases around the country. Of those, only 2% went to a jury. In 1996, there were an estimated 15,636 tort, contract, and real property trial cases in the 75 largest counties in the country. In some states such as New York, there are special courts set up to specifically handle business-related lawsuits that may be too complex for other courts to handle in an effective manner.

Out of all of those cases filed every year, there has got to be a great business story or two—or a thousand—waiting to be written. Business lawsuits may disclose to the world the first glimpse into a major business conflict or disagreement, or a company's struggles.

The difference between business-related lawsuits filed in federal court and cases filed in state court is simple. Cases are filed in federal court when the company or person suing the business is based in another state. Cases are filed in state court when both the plaintiff and the defendant are based in the same state.

Some businesses spend a large amount of time in the courtroom. In 2000, retailer Wal-Mart Stores Incorporated was sued 4,851 times, or once nearly every two hours, according to a *USA Today* account of its legal tactics. Legal analysts believe that Wal-Mart is sued more often than any other entity in the country except the U.S. government. The Arkansas-based company has recently taken the strategy of fighting most of the lawsuits against it instead of settling. These lawsuits run the gamut from shoppers injured while inside one of Wal-Mart's stores to a husband whose wife was abducted in a Wal-Mart parking lot and later killed.

Business executives make decisions every day that can end up in a lawsuit. In fact, some businesses today are facing lawsuits for decisions made by company executives that have been dead for more than 100 years. In 2002, insurer Aetna Incorporated, railroad operator CSX Corporation, and bank FleetBoston Financial Corporation were sued by descendants of slaves seeking compensation from these businesses for profiting from slavery. Manufacturers are now facing multi-million dollar lawsuits for decisions made more than a half century ago to construct buildings with asbestos, later discovered to cause serious illness and death after inhalation.

Other lawsuits may result from what may seem like innocuous, but illegal, decisions. A manager for a company may decide to build a new product using technology patented or owned by another company but has not sought its approval. Another manager may share information from a former worker's personnel file with a potential new employer. Or a manager may ask a female potential job candidate her age and whether she plans to have a baby in the next 12 months. All of these incidents may lead to a lawsuit filed against a company.

Businesses also sue other businesses. One business may enter into a contract with another business to supply it widgets for a set price. But if the price to produce widgets goes up, the other company may seek to break the contract because it is losing money under the old arrangement. The business receiving the widgets may file a lawsuit seeking to force the company that signed the contract to honor the obligation.

A business may also sue another business if it is owed money and the other company refuses to pay. Maybe the company built decks on the backs of houses for a homebuilder in a new subdivision. But the homebuilder believes the decks were built sloppily and may collapse, so they refuse to pay. The deck builder may sue the homebuilder in court to attempt to collect the money.

Or a business may sue another business if it believes that its proprietary product information is being violated. Companies own patents on inventions and trademarks on brand names so that other businesses cannot use them for their gain. When a company believes another company has infringed on its products, it will file a lawsuit, as happened between two software companies, according to the following Bloomberg News report:

> Novell Inc., whose software is used to manage computer networks, challenged claims made by SCO Group Inc. that the Linux computer operating system violates SCO's intellectual-property rights.
>
> Novell retains patents and copyrights to the Unix operating system, Provo, Utah-based Novell said in a statement. SCO has said the Linux system contains some Unix code and companies that use or promote Linux may owe SCO Unix royalties. Unix was created by AT&T Corp. in the late 1960s. Novell bought Unix patents in 1992, and in 1995 sold some Unix-licensing rights to SCO.
>
> "The 1995 agreement governing SCO's purchase of Unix from Novell does not convey to SCO the associated copyrights," Novell Chief Executive Jack Messman said in a letter to SCO Chief Executive Darl McBride.
>
> SCO, which last week changed its name from Caldera International Inc., is suing International Business Machines Corp., charging that the Linux software sold and promoted by IBM contains some of the Unix code and that IBM owes SCO royalties. SCO has warned 1,500 other companies that they may face lawsuits. IBM and Oracle Corp.'s campaigns to get companies to embrace Linux may be crimped by SCO's legal threats, analyst have said.
>
> "SCO's lawsuit against IBM does not involve patents or copyrights," SCO said in a statement, adding that the IBM complaint "specifically alleges breach of contract."
>
> SCO said it "has the contractual right to prevent improper donations of Unix code, methods or concepts into Linux by any Unix vendor."
>
> Novell shares rose 11 cents to $3.11 at 10:33 a.m. New York time on the Nasdaq Stock Market. Shares of Lindon, Utah-based SCO dropped 21 cents to $8.50 and had more than doubled this month.
>
> SCO today said it had a second-quarter profit as sales rose 38 percent. Net income was $4.5 million, or 33 cents a share, in the period ended April 30, compared with a net loss of $6.63 million, or 47 cents, a year earlier. Sales increased to $21.4 million from $15.5 million.[1]

---

[1]From "Novell says it owns unix rights, challenges SCO claim," from J. Kelly, May 28, 2003, Bloomberg News. Copyright 2003 by Bloomberg L. P. All rights reserved. Reprinted with permission.

Businesses will also file lawsuits against another business if it believes that the business is interfering with its ability to operate as a business. A business may be stealing its customers, another company may believe. Or a business may have entered into an arrangement that prevents it from doing business. Such a lawsuit was filed in the San Francisco area about the rights of tour companies to access Alcatraz Island, a popular tourist attraction and home of a former federal prison. A June 2000 article in the *San Francisco Chronicle* noted that Jeffrey Sears' A American Tours and Elric Leano's San Francisco Magical Mystery Tours filed suit in San Francisco Superior Court against Blue & Gold Fleet, which has an exclusive contract with the National Park Service to ferry visitors to the island. The other tour companies also want a piece of the rock.

A business such as a bank or another lender may file a lawsuit against another business if that company is not repaying its loan. The January 24, 2002 front page of *News-Register* in McMinnville, Oregon, carried the news that Bank One filed a lawsuit against Hillside Communities, a not-for-profit retirement center in the town, after it missed loan payments for the previous three months. According to the lawsuit, the center put its land, buildings, and retirement business up as collateral against the loan.

Or a business may sue another business in which it is an investor. The July 12–18, 2002 issue of the *Boston Business Journal* contained a front-page story about a private equity company suing a company it helped grow by investing in it, claiming that the business falsely lowered its earnings report to avoid paying millions of dollars to the investor when it sold its stake in the company. The worth of the investor's ownership position was based on a formula that included the company's earnings.

Other business lawsuits may be related to pending mergers and acquisitions. In June, 2003 after software maker PeopleSoft agreed to acquire rival J.D. Edwards for $1.7 billion, another computer company, Oracle, then made an offer to purchase PeopleSoft. Oracle said if its acquisition were successful, it would attempt to switch PeopleSoft customers to its software. PeopleSoft and J.D. Edwards then sued Oracle, accusing it with interfering with its business and tampering with its customers.

Many business-related lawsuits may not merit a story at all, or even a one-paragraph brief. It is up to the reporter and the editor to decide if the allegations in the lawsuit warrant coverage. *The Washington Post* is not likely to write a story about a small convenience store in Bethesda, Maryland, filing a lawsuit against its potato chip supplier for failing to provide a shipment one month, causing it to lose sales. But that lawsuit may be news in a small town where the store could be one of the few places to buy potato chips.

With any litigation involving a business, a reporter should read the entire filing, assessing the seriousness of the allegations and what damages are being sought. Multiple allegations may be mentioned in the original filing. The plaintiffs and the defendants—there can be more than one on both sides—are also specifically identified. In many business lawsuits, their headquarters location is named, and an address is also given. This can help a reporter find someone to talk to at the company to get a response.

In some corporate lawsuits, a business may ask in its initial complaint of a lawsuit for a judge to issue a temporary restraining order preventing another company from taking some action that may hurt the business. In March, 2003 a Missouri circuit court issued a temporary restraining order against Med 4 Home Pharmacy, its owner and its head pharmacist for failing to comply with a state Board of Pharmacy request to recall contaminated drugs. The order was covered by the *Kansas City Business Journal*.

Many lawsuits simply ask for damages. In some filings, a monetary amount may be mentioned as what the business is seeking to correct how it has been damaged. This amount should be included in any story about a business-related case.

Important information to be included in any story about business litigation includes:

- The name of the plaintiffs and the defendants, and their business relationship;
- Background on these businesses, which is often contained in the lawsuit;
- The type of damage alleged in the case. For example, when Liggett Group and Brooke Group, two cigarette makers, sued two-dozen insurance companies, they alleged the insurers were refusing to pay claims to smokers that should have been covered under their policies.
- When the lawsuit was filed and in what court;
- History between the two parties of the lawsuit, again sometimes detailed in the initial complaint;
- Any special considerations, such as permanent or temporary injunctions or restraining orders, sought in the filing.

Writing stories about business-related lawsuits also requires the reporter to call both the plaintiff and the defendant to obtain a reaction. Company executives often will not comment. It is best to go to the public relations staff or the lawyers representing the company. The reporter should try hard to get a comment from both sides to make the story fair. After the original complaint has been filed, the defendant will have a chance to respond to the charges with their own filing. Most of the time, they will deny any wrongdoing. If the case is large enough, their response should also be reported.

Many times, the case will be settled before it goes to court. In December, 2002 the *Miami Herald* and other media reported that insurance company CIGNA Corporation had reached a settlement with doctors in Illinois to settle a lawsuit. But a judge in Miami issued a ruling ordering the company to halt the settlement talks and accused the company of trying to go around the jurisdiction of the Florida court. The report took advantage of a judge's ruling in the case as the major basis for the latest story tracking the case. Judges will often be asked to issue rulings in business-related cases that can be newsworthy, and often will be asked to approve settlements.

Settlements and rulings usually come after hearings related to the case in which both sides of the lawsuit argue their point of view. The hearing, as well as the ruling, might be newsworthy, and the reporter should keep up to date on such developments.

There are many hearings involved in court cases that might be newsworthy. Journalist should not just report on the initial filing of the lawsuit and then wait until the trial begins. There is plenty of news occurring between the two.

The rest of this chapter contains tips and advice on covering specific types of litigation involving companies.

Different Court Systems

1. County and state courts: Will often handle complaints between businesses that are both from the same jurisdiction, or complaints by consumers who live in the same county as the business.
2. Federal courts: Often handles class action lawsuits filed by employees and consumers against businesses, as well as business litigation against another business when the plaintiff is located in another state from the defendant.
3. Bankruptcy court: Part of the federal court system, bankruptcy court handles cases when a business or individual can not repay its debts to lenders and suppliers. For more information, see Chapter 12.
4. Small claims court: Typically covers disputes under $5,000. Any individual or business may use small claims court, sometimes conducted in the evening for the convenience of the public. Most litigants appear without an attorney.

SHAREHOLDER, REGULATORY, AND CONSUMER LAWSUITS

Businesses and companies are not always sued by other businesses. They face lawsuits every day from a variety of other constituents. Most prominently, businesses and companies are sued by shareholders who own their stock, regulators for allegations of violating some law, and consumers who have used one of their products.

Shareholder lawsuits are often cases seeking class-action status in which a handful of shareholders sue the company representing all shareholders. Such suits are often filed against a public company after its stock has fallen dramatically following the release of bad news.

Federal securities class-action litigation suits increased by 31% in 2002 to 224 filings, according to the Stanford Law School Securities Class Action

Clearinghouse. (The number of lawsuits excludes those filed against analysts and Wall Street investment houses.) Suits filed in 2002 were against companies in a variety of industries, but were prominent against communications, consumer products, and financial services companies. More than 80% of the cases filed accuse the companies of fraud or failure to disclose material information, and more than 80% cited misrepresentations in financial documents. Illegal insider trading was alleged in a quarter of the cases.

The increase in shareholder litigation in recent years is despite the efforts of lawmakers, who passed the Private Securities Litigation Reform Act of 1995, which sought to make it harder for shareholders to bring securities fraud cases by requiring stronger evidence that companies acted with knowledge that they were violating the law.

Companies who face lawsuits from shareholders often settle these cases before they reach trial. More than a dozen class-action shareholder lawsuits have been settled for more than $100 million, according to the clearinghouse. In a survey of board members by *Corporate Board Magazine*, 40% of the board members who responded saying their company had been sued by shareholders said the case was settled, whereas another 23% noted the case had been dismissed.

The basic shareholder lawsuit occurs when a company's stock drops precipitously after it discloses negative news. Shareholders become upset with the company because the worth of their stock has dropped. Many of them sue under the belief that company management knew the negative information but failed to disclose it to investors. They file a lawsuit to recoup some or all of their losses from their investment.

To the businesses, filing such a lawsuit violates the concept of taking risk when an investor purchases stock. By filing a lawsuit, the shareholder is eliminating the risk. From the stockowner's perspective, they feel the lawsuit has merit because they have not been allowed to properly measure the risks of the company because of the withheld information.

These lawsuits are often newsworthy, particularly if they occur against a major company or allege serious wrongdoing. The following is a typical story written about these lawsuits:

> Bank One is being bombarded with class-action lawsuits stemming from the bank's mishandling of First USA, its credit-card company.
>
> Former Chief Executive John B. McCoy is named as a defendant in 17 suits filed in the U.S. District Court of Northern Illinois from Dec. 14 to Jan. 19. The complaints allege that McCoy and other officers of the bank inflated Bank One's financial results by improperly recording revenues at First USA.
>
> The suits cover shareholders who purchased stock in Bank One between Oct. 10, 1998, and Nov. 10, 1999. The suits seek hundreds of millions of dollars in compensatory damages.
>
> McCoy, who resigned in December, is one of several Bank One executives to be named as defendants in the lawsuits.
>
> Bank One spokesman Tom Kelly said the bank has nothing to say about the cases.

"We don't comment on pending litigation," Kelly said.

Bank One's stock price has fallen nearly 50 percent since Aug. 24, when the bank said 1999 earnings would be hurt by poor performance at First USA. The class-action suit cutoff date of Nov. 10 is the day after Bank One lowered its earnings estimates a second time. Share prices fell 11 percent that day.

The crux of the class-action cases—and the reason First USA's performance has suffered—is that the credit-card company eliminated a grace period for monthly payments. That forced many customers to incur late fees and higher interest rates. They left in droves, driving down First USA's revenues.

One of the lawsuits alleges that Bank One improperly recorded revenues from late fees, penalties and interest.[2]

Shareholder lawsuits such as these often divert management from the task of running a company, but are often also the result of management making statements to analysts or at investor conferences that the company cannot back up later with its performance. In addition, these lawsuits can be costly to defend, leading some companies to settle before the case goes to trial.

Some consider shareholder litigation to be a nuisance. But they are important news to other shareholders of a company who may not be aware of the allegations. And they are important news to potential investors in a company. Some investors may avoid buying stock in the company, whereas others may see the decline in the company's stock price as a result of the lawsuit or the negative announcement that triggered the lawsuit as a buying opportunity to purchase shares cheaply.

Companies can also be sued by regulatory agencies for alleged violation of a multiple number of laws. The agencies can be either state regulators or federal regulators, and the allegations can be either civil or criminal.

Federal regulators can sue a company to prevent it from misleading consumers, or from selling an unauthorized product. They can also sue a company or its executives and allege illegal insider trading or that the company's financial statements have inflated earnings or revenue. They can sue a company that they believe has engaged in discriminatory or harassing employment practices. They can sue a company or its executives if they believe they have made false statements to the government during an investigation.

A story based on such a lawsuit typically begins with the allegations from the government, and also tries to get a response from the company. The following Bloomberg News story succeeded on both counts:

The U.S. Federal Trade Commission has accused a Canadian company of falsely claiming that its Quick Slim product helps people lose weight without diet or exercise.

The FTC claims in a lawsuit that Quebec Inc., conducting business as Bio Lab, advertised in the U.S. a product that doesn't work, selling it for $70 for a bottle of

---

[2]From "Shareholders' lawsuits piling up at Bank One," by M. Pramik, February 5, 2000, *Columbus Dispatch*, p. 1H. Copyright 2000 by *Columbus Dispatch*. Reprinted with permission.

180 caplets. The U.S. agency sued Sept. 3 in federal court in Albany, New York, and has received a restraining order barring the company from disseminating misleading information, the FTC said.

"Quick Slim does not cause rapid or significant weight loss without the need for diet and exercise, and does not cause permanent weight loss," the FTC said.

The company also marketed its Cellu-Fight, which it claims eliminated cellulite without any effort, the FTC said. That sold for $40 for 60 tablets. The product was also sold on the Internet and by direct mail.

"The ads falsely claim that the product is clinically proven to eliminate cellulite from the stomach, backside, hips, and thighs," the FTC said in a statement.

There was no Bio Lab or Quebec Inc. listed by directory assistance in Quebec.

The company's ads, in publications such as Glamour, TV Guide, the Los Angeles Times, and Washington Post, claimed to "Lose Up to 2 Pounds Daily" without exercise and that the weight loss would be permanent, FTC officials said. The company's president, Jean-Francois Brochu, is also listed as a defendant.

Quick Slim is a dietary supplement advertised as a "fat blocker" that uses apple pectin to control weight.

On Sept. 6, U.S. District Judge David Hurd in Albany froze the company's assets, the FTC said.[3]

State regulators can also file lawsuits. They can allege violations of state laws by a company, or even by a firm hired to do work for a company. For example, state and regulatory agencies have been increasingly targeting accounting firms and other consultants who did work for businesses that later collapsed. Regulators are attempting to hold these firms accountable.

The beginning of the following *Kansas City Star* story explains how one accounting firm is being charged with failing to prevent the collapse of an insurance company:

Accountants in the local office of KPMG Peat Marwick contributed to the collapse of one of the largest life insurers in the United States, a lawsuit filed last week alleges.

The lawsuit, brought by the Missouri Department of Insurance, contends that KPMG failed to disclose the risks associated with an investment product issued by General American Life Insurance Co.

The Missouri-based insurer, which at one time ranked among the biggest life insurers in the country, collapsed after a credit-rating downgrade led to a run on the product in August 1999 as investors tried to get their money back.

The run prompted General American's parent, General American Mutual Holding Co. of St. Louis, to file for receivership. The life insurance company was later purchased by Metropolitan Life Insurance Co. for $1.2 billion. General American Mutual was liquidated.

The insurance department's 68-page lawsuit accuses KPMG Peat Marwick, which did auditing and consulting work for General American, of conflicts of interest,

---

breaches of ethical standards "and other gross departures from the most basic of auditing and professional obligations."

"KPMG's desire to make money was so insidious," the lawsuit states in its introduction, "that it believed that a conflict could never exist for the situation where KPMG provided business consulting or financial advisory services to a company at the same time it was auditing the company."

The six-count action seeks unspecified actual and punitive damages "in an amount sufficient to punish defendants and to deter others from like conduct," as well as interest and costs.

A spokesman for KPMG, Alec Houston, said the firm stood behind its work and would defend itself "vigorously."

"We deny the allegations that KPMG contributed in any way to the liquidity issues faced by General American in 1999," Houston said.

The insurance department's lawsuit comes amid heightened scrutiny of the dual auditing and consulting roles played by many accounting firms and as accounting scandals continue to unfold at WorldCom Inc., Enron Corp. and other large public companies.

The Securities and Exchange Commission has filed several cases in the last year against accounting firms, including KPMG, for maintaining business ties with the companies they audited.

The insurance department's lawsuit against KPMG was filed in Jackson County, which the department said was where portions of KPMG's audit and other work for General American took place. The lawsuit also names six individual KPMG accountants, some of whom worked in the firm's Kansas City office.

One of them, Thomas R. Kochis, was the engagement partner for General American in the late 1990s. Kochis, who is now retired and lives in the Minneapolis area, could not be reached for comment.

Among other allegations, the insurance department says that KPMG concealed material financial information, failed to disclose the risky nature of General American's Stable Value product and failed to exercise due care in performing audits.

The Stable Value product offered relatively high interest rates and was redeemable on only seven days' notice. It was popular among institutional investors, eight of whom owned $3.5 billion worth—or about half of General American's Stable Value portfolio in 1999, according to the lawsuit.

In August 1999, Moody's lowered General American's credit rating. More than three dozen institutional investors, most of them money market funds, sought to redeem the Stable Value investments, but General American was unable to raise funds quickly enough to cash them out.

The company went into receivership on Sept. 15, 1999. Ten weeks later, former Jackson County Prosecuting Attorney and Missouri Court of Appeals Judge Albert Riederer was named special deputy liquidator to oversee the receivership.

Riederer, from his office in downtown Kansas City, said Wednesday that the lawsuit was filed only after the receivership had conducted 'a very thorough investigation to make some kind of determination why and how this company got into financial distress.'

"And on that basis," he said, "we concluded that KPMG had some liability. And obviously, we think we can prove that."[4]

---

[4]From "KPMG accused of conflicts; Missouri alleges liability in collapse of life insurer," by D. Margolies, Dec. 19, 2002, *Kansas City Star*, p. C1. Copyright 2002 by *Kansas City Star*. Reprinted with permission.

More information about how and why regulators sue companies is available later in this chapter under the 'Business and criminal charges' section. Regulators suing companies is occurring with increasing regularity. In general, when regulators file a lawsuit against a company, it should be a serious sign that something could be amiss with the business.

Consumer protection laws exist in all 50 states and have also been passed by the federal government. And though regulators often file claims against companies for consumer protection reasons, many times consumers take matters into their own hands and file lawsuits themselves.

Consumers sue businesses for a variety of reasons. The consumer most likely has been a customer of the business. Maybe the consumer has discovered that the business has taken advantage of them by using deceptive marketing to get them to purchase the product. Or maybe a consumer has purchased a product from a company and then found that it does not work. The consumer could have also purchased a product that has made them sick or given them an illness. The product could have caused serious physical or mental maladies that are irreversible. Other consumer lawsuits can allege wrongdoing for something a business has not done. The business may be a bank that declines to loan money to a consumer with an excellent credit rating simply because of where they live. Or the business may be an insurance company that has declined to pay a claim to cover medical care. Consumers have also successfully sued insurers for using imitation parts to repair their vehicles.

Some consumer lawsuits may seem frivolous when first announced, such as the consumer who filed a case against McDonald's alleging that the food they served made her obese. (Another consumer had previously sued McDonald's for serving hot coffee that burned her skin. She won.) And to be sure, some of them may be stretching the interpretations and limits of the law.

But it is not up to the reporter to decide if the lawsuit has any merit. Consider the facts in the following case:

> Loews Cineplex Entertainment Corp., the No. 3 U.S. movie theater chain, was sued in Illinois state court by a moviegoer angry at having to sit through four minutes of advertisements before the scheduled feature began.
>
> The lawsuit, which seeks to represent all affected Loews patrons across the country, said the chain deceives moviegoers as to the actual starting times for films, to generate a captive audience for ads.
>
> Though it may irritate some moviegoers, the practice of showing advertisements before movies is a trend that's taking hold, as movie chains search for new sources of revenue beyond ticket sales and popcorn, industry analysts say.
>
> "It's a way of maximizing the real estate," said Kavir Dhar, a media analyst for Jeffries & Co. "You can go to an advertiser and say, 'Look, we have a captive audience here.'"
>
> Loews emerged from bankruptcy in 2002, along with rival movie chains Regal Cinemas Corp. (now Regal Entertainment Group) and Carmike Cinemas Inc. Dhar noted that movies are one of the brighter spots in the U.S. economy, as people look for a way to escape.

Loews spokesman John McCauley said he was not familiar with the lawsuit and declined to comment.

Plaintiff's attorney Douglas Litowitz, a visiting professor at Lewis & Clark Law School in Portland, Oregon, said showing ads at the time the movie is supposed to start is a breach of contract and a deceptive consumer practice.

"It is completely ludicrous to have moviegoers pay good money to watch commercials—they can do that at home for free," said Litowitz, who filed the suit on behalf of Miriam Fisch, a Chicago-area high school English teacher.

Fisch complained that she went to a scheduled 4:45 p.m. showing of "The Quiet American" on Feb. 8, at a Chicago theater, and had to sit through ads for such products as Coca-Cola for four minutes, until 4:49 p.m. The suit does not complain about coming attractions.

Litowitz said he would likely target other movie chains in the future. He said that some chains are "a little more fastidious" about showing the ads before the scheduled start- times of the movies, which would put them outside the scope of the lawsuit.

Regal, the world's largest movie chain, has stated that it shows its ads before the posted movie start-times—during the period theaters use to project slides of trivia games or ads for the local dentist, Dhar said.

Pre-movie ads are viewed as a "pretty decent growth opportunity" by theater chains, said Glen Reid, a media analyst with Bear Stearns & Co. "It's still a small part of the business."

Loews, based in New York, has backed away from last year's plan for a $300 million initial public stock offering.[5]

Whether the reporter agrees that movie theaters should not be wasting a consumer's time by showing these ads before the feature presentation is irrelevant. The reporter presents the facts, and then gets comments about the case to let the reader decide.

One area of consumer litigation that is having a major impact on an industry is the field of medical malpractice litigation. The issue is not that more consumers are suing medical doctors and hospitals because of poor treatment. In many states, the issue has become that juries in medical malpractice cases have returned large verdicts, which have raised the insurance premiums paid by physicians and medical facilities. In some states, insurance companies have raised their rates exponentially or left the state altogether.

The issue, which landed on the front page of *Time* magazine in spring 2003, has caused many doctors to lobby state legislatures in a bid to cap jury awards or to limit the amount that a lawsuit can seek. Although there is no doubt that many patients have sued to redress valid injuries and suffering, doctors in many states have threatened to stop practicing medicine or to limit their procedures until new laws are passed.

Reporters covering the health care industry should look at these cases in their area to see if there is a growing concern about medical malpractice litigation. Reporters should talk to doctors and lawyers representing patients as well.

There is also a growing chorus among the business community for tort reform at the federal level that would limit litigation against companies. Many chief executives and business leaders have advocated limits on business litigation in the past. These efforts have not had any effect, but if passed could have a chilling effect on business-related litigation.

THE MOST FRIVOLOUS LAWSUIT AWARD
GOES TO ...

The Olympics are over. But there's one more medal to hand out in the nation's stiffest competition of all.

The most frivolous lawsuit.

As it did in the Olympics, Florida once again proves it is home to gold.

So many lawsuits fought for the honor of most frivolous.

But first, the runners-up from other states.

The silver medal goes to a man who sued McDonald's because it failed to warn customers about the dangers of eating and driving. According to the man's complaint, a customer who had purchased a milkshake at the restaurant's drive-up window spilled the cold drink in his lap, then collided with the plaintiff's car.

The bronze medal goes to an Idaho college student who fell out of his third-floor window while "mooning" his friends, then sued the college for not providing warnings about the perils of upper-story windows.

These are the easy lawsuits to lampoon. They remind us this is not the legal community's finest (pick one: hour, year, decade).

Before unveiling the gold, a little perspective. In the business world, new litigation that often should be considered frivolous—or sheer overkill, at the least—crops up almost daily. Many of these suits seek class-action status and are brought on behalf of investors against companies whose stock prices have not lived up to expectations.

Tampa Bay area companies are awash in such lawsuits. Just look at the past few weeks.

Three law firms in New York and Philadelphia ganged up to sue Tampa's Sykes Enterprises for misguiding investors. Sykes already is buried under class-action suits from earlier accounting missteps.

Milberg Weiss Bershad Hynes & Lerach, America's class-action king, and Baltimore law firm Charles J. Piven are suing St. Petersburg's Insurance Management Solutions Group for misleading investors about its securities.

These cases do not include the multitude of past class-action lawsuits filed against St. Petersburg's Danka Business Systems, Clearwater's Digital Lightwave Inc. and Tampa's PowerCerv Corp., among others.

No question, some business-related lawsuits truly try to right a wrong.

But more and more suits are just copycats going along for a piece of the settlement pie.

The bay area has its own historic collection of frivolous litigation.

- In 1994, Joe Hindman admitted he stole from parked cars on his way to work, lifted thousands of dollars from the purses of fellow workers in the office and kept a handgun hidden in his briefcase. But when GTE Data Services fired Hindman from his computer programming job two years ago, he sued.

  Hindman claimed the firing was illegal discrimination against the disabled, since he argued his behavior was due to a chemical imbalance caused by the anti-depressant Prozac. The case was dismissed in 1995.

- Earlier this year, a Florida jury awarded $5.2-million to the family of a slain Dutch tourist after finding that Alamo Rent-A-Car failed to warn the victim and her husband about a high-crime area near Miami. The death was a tragedy, but the tourists had rented the car across the state in Tampa.

  (Notes litigation expert Walter Olson: What kind of legal trouble would Alamo have gotten into if it had warned its customers to stay out of certain neighborhoods?) Alamo has appealed.

- Ed O'Rourke sued Tampa Electric, along with six bars and stores that sold him alcoholic beverages, over a 1996 incident. He allegedly was hit by 13,000 volts of electricity after breaking into a fenced, gated and locked utility substation and climbing up a transformer in a "drunken stupor." The suit further alleged that local bars and stores negligently served O'Rourke liquor even though he was "unable to control his urge to drink alcoholic beverages."

So many suits. So many frivolous contenders.

That brings us to the gold medal winner. Right here in Manatee County.

The lawsuit was chosen by an Internet poll of several thousand voters among five cases picked from James Percelay's book, Whiplash! America's Most Frivolous Lawsuits. The poll was conducted by M-Law, Michigan Lawsuit Abuse Watch.

In the mid-1990s, a blind man was given the gift of a Seeing Eye Dog. But on a maiden voyage to DeSoto Square Mall in Bradenton, the dog allegedly stepped on the foot of a woman.

After learning that the blind man had no money, the woman sued the dog's owner, Palmetto-based Southeastern Guide Dogs, for "loss of earning capacity . . . and mental pain and suffering." The case: Susan Faith and Reverend Ian Faith, plaintiffs, v. Southeastern Guide Dogs, Inc., defendant.

Kimberly Marlow, Southeastern Guide Dogs' development director, recalls the suit well. The non-profit group had to gather extensive documents in anticipation of a trial.

But the suit never made it to court. After being ridiculed in newspapers and on CNN, the plaintiff dropped the lawsuit. And the plaintiff's law firm donated $1,000 to Southeastern Guide Dogs.

If only more frivolous suits went away this easily.[6]

---

[6]From "The most frivolous lawsuit award goes to," by R. Trigaux, October 4, 2000, St. Petersburg Times, p. 1E. Copyright 2000 by St. Petersburg Times. Reprinted with permission.

EMPLOYEE-RELATED LITIGATION

A female worker walks into a break room and finds male workers reviewing nude pictures of other women in a magazine. A male worker wants a job at a restaurant, but the restaurant declines to hire him, saying that they only hire females for the job that he wants. A male supervisor makes suggestive comments to a female subordinate who is married and asks her out for a drink after work. Another worker asks for training so that she can be considered for future promotions, but is denied the opportunity. A factory worker spends 60 hours on the job one week, but is only paid for 40 of those hours. Another worker becomes seriously ill because of the dust inhaled while on the job and has to spend three weeks in the hospital recuperating.

All of the above are examples of incidents that may lead an employee to sue their employer to recoup damages suffered while on the job. The number of employee lawsuits filed in federal courts tripled between 1990 and 1998, according to a U.S. Department of Justice study. They likely increased in state courts around the country as well.

Employee lawsuits against businesses make for good stories. They are David versus Goliath all over again. For example, an average employee sues a multibillion dollar corporation that views him as an ant to be used to increase its profits and improve its productivity. If only employee lawsuits were that black and white. Too often, there are many shades of gray when it comes to employee litigation. Yes, an employee might have been mistreated. But is the company responsible?

To be sure, in thousands of cases workers have defeated their current or former employer and won damages. They sue and win for not receiving overtime pay, such as what happened to Wal-Mart as described in the following excerpt:

Wal-Mart, the world's largest retailer, forced employees in Oregon to work unpaid overtime between 1994 and 1999, a federal jury found Thursday in the first of dozens of such lawsuits across the country to come to trial.

A separate trial will be held to decide how much Wal-Mart Stores should pay in damages. More than 400 employees from 24 of Wal-Mart's 27 Oregon stores sued the retailer.

"I guess, basically, we are disappointed with the verdict. Wal-Mart has a strong policy of paying its associates for all the time they work," said spokesman Bill Wertz. "We would emphasize that this ruling affects only approximately 350 workers out of 15,000 in Oregon."

The lawsuit was filed by Carolyn Thiebes and Betty Alderson, who worked in managerial positions at Wal-Mart stores in the Salem area.

The lawsuit alleged that managers got employees to work off the clock by asking them to clean up the store after they had clocked out and by deleting hours from time records.

It also said Wal-Mart reprimanded employees who claimed overtime. Workers felt forced to work after clocking out because managers assigned them more work than they could complete in a regular shift, the plaintiffs said.

Wal-Mart conceded during opening arguments Tuesday that some off-the-clock work occurred but said company policy expressly prohibited it.

Wal-Mart, a $218 billion company, employs 1 million workers in 3,250 stores in the United States.

Rudy Englund, Wal-Mart's attorney, had no comment after the verdict was read, but referred questions to Wal-Mart headquarters.

Wertz said the company is considering whether to appeal.

The verdict came after the close of the stock market. Wal-Mart finished the day down 22 cents at $50.16 on the New York Stock Exchange.

Thirty-nine other class-action lawsuits are pending against the company in 30 states. Those suits, from California to New York, involve hundreds of thousands of workers seeking tens of millions in back pay.

Previously, Wal-Mart settled two similar overtime cases in Colorado and New Mexico.

The company reportedly paid $50 million two years ago to settle an off-the-clock lawsuit covering 69,000 workers in Colorado, and it recently settled for $500,000 a case involving 120 workers in Gallup, N.M., said one of the plaintiffs' attorneys.

The trial lasted about four weeks, and jurors took four days to arrive at their decision.

"About once every one or two years, Wal-Mart suffers a minor black eye about something relating to labor relations," said Philip Romero, dean of the Lundquist College of Business at the University of Oregon. "Yet they keep growing and growing. So I don't believe this will materially affect their image and their sales."[7]

Note the details in this story, such as how long the case took to hear, and how long the jury deliberating. Also note the comment from the business school dean. Getting analysis from a law expert or a business expert always lends credence to the writing and helps explain the bigger picture.

The story also provides the perspective of what is happening to Wal-Mart in similar cases in other parts of the country. If a reporter is tracking a case of a large company that operates throughout the country, it might be smart to see how the business has fared in similar cases in other states. A story about those lawsuits might give readers a fresh viewpoint on the case.

Sometimes suits filed by employees against companies begin as one lawsuit by one employee, and then other employees who believe they have been treated in a similar manner join as plaintiffs. Sometimes these suits are classified as class-action lawsuits to represent a body of former workers. Cases like this can involve discrimination, harassment, or other hiring practices.

Employee-related cases often require the reporter to dig deeper into the workplace environment. If a reporter is interested in giving readers or viewers a broader picture of what it is like to work at a company, they can review other documents such as Equal Employment Opportunity Commission filings, other lawsuits filed against the company, and Occupational Safety and Health Administration records.

---

[7]From "Wal-Mart guilty in overtime case," by W. McCall, Dec. 20, 2002, Associated Press. Copyright 2002 by Associated Press. Reprinted with permission.

Employee-related lawsuits may not always be decided by a trial jury. In December, 2002 an arbitration panel ordered stockbroker Salomon Smith Barney to pay $3.2 million to a female stockbroker as part of a settlement of a sex discrimination class-action lawsuit against the firm. The three-member panel's decision was the first to come out of a dispute resolution process for plaintiffs who could not come to terms with the company.

Cases sometimes will be referred to a mediator or an arbitrator to resolve the dispute. Mediation and arbitration are also often used in international business litigation. Many times, one side or the other will suggest this procedure to settle a case as a way of lowering the costs.

In addition, employee-related lawsuits often include other documents related to a company, such as employee contracts, and internal memos that may give a better indication of working conditions. These contracts and documents should be read carefully. They might add good color and anecdotes to a story.

Those employee contracts can also lead to a business suing current and former workers. Businesses will sue a former employee if they believe that the ex-worker has stolen information or documents and taken it to a new job, particularly a job where the person is working for a competitor. Many companies use noncompete agreements or clauses in contracts requiring their workers to abstain from working for a direct competitor for a certain amount of time.

Noncompete agreements protect trade secrets. A trade secret can be information that gives a company a competitive advantage because it is not generally known and cannot be readily learned by other businesses that could benefit from it. It can be a formula, pattern, compilation, program, device, method, technique, or process that a company has made reasonable efforts to keep secret.

For example, Coca-Cola limits who at the company knows the secret formula to make its famous soft drink. If one of those employees were to leave the company, they would likely have a noncompete agreement preventing them from using the formula. (California law excludes noncompete agreements except in narrow instances.)

The following excerpt details a case in which a noncompete agreement became a major story regarding the hiring of an executive by one telecommunications company away from another:

Sprint Corp. on Sunday said William T. Esrey plans to step down as chief executive and the company has offered the job to Gary Forsee, vice chairman of BellSouth Corp.

BellSouth, however, is trying to block Forsee's move in court.

In a brief statement released Sunday evening, Sprint effectively confirmed days of speculation.

The statement said its "independent directors have been evaluating management succession alternatives." It did not say whether the board asked Esrey to leave, or if the chief executive is resigning for other reasons.

The statement said Esrey will be chairman of Sprint "for a transition period." For now, Esrey and president and chief operating officer Ronald T. LeMay will "remain in their current positions with Sprint," the statement said.

LeMay, long considered Esrey's successor, also is expected to leave the company.

Sprint officials declined Sunday to shed further light on an increasingly murky management situation.

"I'm just going to tell you the statement speaks for itself," said board member Irvine O. Hockaday Jr. "As events progress and it becomes either required or appropriate, even if not required, to offer additional information, that will be done."

Sprint's hands apparently are tied for the moment by legal issues.

Atlanta-based BellSouth over the weekend sought and got a temporary restraining order from a Georgia superior court judge that prevents Forsee, 52, from accepting Sprint's job offer.

BellSouth spokesman Jeff Battcher said the temporary order was signed late Friday after the regional Bell company filed suit "in the interest of our shareholders." The lawsuit was based on a clause in Forsee's employment agreement that prevents him from joining a competing company for 18 months after leaving BellSouth. Forsee's employment agreement is detailed in documents filed with the Securities and Exchange Commission. A hearing on the matter is expected in the next several days.

The court fight leaves Sprint's leadership in a quagmire. Esrey and LeMay still are piloting the company, but the actions of the independent directors on the board have placed them in lame-duck status.

The independent board members appear to have lost control of the management succession situation because of news leaks and litigation.

The board has eight members—four from the Kansas City area, three from Florida and one from Connecticut. Esrey and LeMay sit on the board.

In the meantime, insiders are worried that the leadership issue could overshadow positive news as the company reports its fourth-quarter financial numbers on Wednesday. Those numbers are expected to be generally positive.

Reports that Esrey and LeMay are stepping down surfaced last week. Sprint's statement, however, is the first public confirmation that Esrey will no longer be the company's top executive. The company acknowledged last year that Esrey had been diagnosed with lymphoma, which has been seen as a possible reason why he would be replaced as chief executive. But Sprint's statement did not cite health as a factor.

LeMay had been expected to replace Esrey as chief executive. A clause in his employment contract gives him the right to leave with a year's pay and the ability to exercise his stock options if he is not named CEO upon Esrey's departure.

The board's decision to look outside the company for the top post could reflect frustration with Sprint's dropping stock price and uncertainty about how the company will fare in a rapidly changing industry.

Sprint's FON tracking stock, which was trading at more than $74 a share in November 1999, closed Friday at $12.14. Sprint's PCS tracking stock, which was over $64 in March 2000, closed Friday at $3.76.

Forsee, who worked at Sprint before joining BellSouth, would bring a fresh perspective to the company, some shareholders said.

Jack Markham, who worked for United Telecom, Sprint's predecessor, for 21 years, said the company needs new leadership. The board, he said, waited too long. "It's about time they got starch enough to do something and bring someone in who could do something with the company," said Markham, now retired and living in Arizona.

But Forsee's prospective move back to Sprint is being aggravated by court proceedings in Atlanta.

The restraining order BellSouth won this weekend bars Forsee "from accepting employment with Sprint or any other BellSouth competitor." The lawsuit was filed in Fulton County Superior Court in Atlanta.

Such legal maneuvers are fairly routine in cases where a top executive leaves one company to work for another. Forsee and BellSouth Chairman and Chief Executive Duane Ackerman are said, however, to have a good relationship, and Sprint and BellSouth are trying to resolve the situation amicably.

The lawsuit was filed to protect the intellectual property and knowledge that Forsee has developed as a BellSouth executive. Forsee joined BellSouth in 1999 as executive vice president before rising quickly to vice chairman in charge of the company's domestic operations.

Noncompete clauses are common in employment contracts.

Forsee had a similar court fight when he moved to Sprint from AT&T, where he worked in the 1970s and 1980s. AT&T threatened to sue Forsee for breaching a confidentiality agreement. Forsee went to court first, and a judge refused to stop Forsee from taking the job.

And in 2000, when Martin J. Kaplan, Sprint's chief technology officer, resigned and accepted a top job at WorldCom, Sprint went to court to have a noncompete clause enforced. Sprint won a temporary injunction, which barred Kaplan from his new duties. Kaplan eventually backed away from the WorldCom job.[8]

Other companies require employees, particularly executives, to sign agreements when they leave the company that set out postemployment guidelines. These agreements may provide the executives a monetary settlement in return for certain conditions, such as not publicly talking to the media about their tenure while at the company. Some companies have sued former employees who have broken these severance package deals.

On the other side, executives can also sue businesses after they have left the job if the company has not lived up to its side of the agreement. A business can be sued if its executives talk disparagingly about the former coworker, hurting his or her ability to get another job. Or a former executive can sue a company if the business does not uphold the terms of the severance agreement by providing payments or other terms agreed upon in the contract.

Allen Questrom, the former CEO of Federated Department Stores, was widely celebrated for saving the operator of Macy's and Rich's department stores from bankruptcy. But he sued the company after retiring in May, 1997 saying the company owed him more than $45 million in back pay. A judge ruled against his case, and Questrom later became the CEO of rival J.C. Penney.

A former Sears executive sued that retailer over comments made by another executive. The story was covered the following way:

> Sears, Roebuck & Co., the largest U.S. department store chain, was sued by the former president of the retailer's credit division for breach of contract and defamation after being fired in October.
>
> Kevin Keleghan, who had worked at Sears since 1996, is also suing to receive severance pay he says is due under an agreement signed in September, according to

---

[8]From "CEO change near, Sprint says: Esrey stepping down; Forsee offered job, but BellSouth gets court order to keep him," by D. Hayes and S. King, February 3, 2003, *Kansas City Star*, p. A1. Copyright 2003 by *Kansas City Star*. Reprinted with permission.

documents filed with the Circuit Court of Lake County, Illinois. The retailer asked the court to throw out the suit.

Sears Chief Executive Alan Lacy said after the firing that Keleghan "wasn't forthcoming" and was a "barrier" to getting accurate information about the credit-card business, which accounts for about two-thirds of overall profit. Sears has been relying on income from its expanding Gold MasterCard program whiles working to revive flagging apparel and appliance sales.

"I can't see how a lawsuit against the CEO or corporation isn't going to distract you," said analyst Steve Barker at the Public Employees Retirement System of Ohio, which has about $45 billion assets under management. The system has sold some of the 759,600 shares it held in December. "It's taking up time you could be using to focus on aspects of the business that need to be worked on."

Sears, based in Hoffman Estates, Illinois, asked the court to dismiss the defamation counts on the grounds that Lacy's comments were "protected expressions of opinion," according to a court filing. Keleghan "fraudulently induced" the company to sign the severance agreement without disclosing facts he "feared would lead to his termination," the filing said.[9]

This Bloomberg story succinctly covers the issues surrounding the case, and provides the company's response to the allegations.

Defamation lawsuits such as the Sears' case often seek damages of lost earnings, mental anguish, and sometimes punitive damages.

Employers can also get themselves into trouble by disclosing information about a worker's personal life. In many cases, businesses are not allowed to discuss a former worker's financial status, marital status, or other personal issues unless there is a legitimate business reason for disclosing them. And in some states, an exworker can sue his or her former place of employment if they give false information to a potential new employer in a bid to interfere with his or her job prospects.

And in a majority of states, it is illegal for an employer to "blacklist" a former worker if they participate in union activities. This law can apply to letters of recommendation, requiring them to be written without false and defamatory statements.

BUSINESSES AND CRIMINAL CHARGES

Andrew Fastow, the former CFO of Houston-based Enron Corporation pleaded not guilty to fraud charges. Former Tyco International CEO Dennis Kozlowski and the company's CFO were charged with stealing $600 million from the conglomerate. Scott Sullivan, the former CFO of telephone company WorldCom, and another company executive have been charged with fraud.

---

[9]From "Sears sued by fired credit president for defamation," by R. Katz, January 29, 2003, Bloomberg News. Copyright 2003 by Bloomberg L. P. All rights reserved. Reprinted with permission.

Former Imclone Systems CEO Sam Waksal was sentenced to seven years in prison after pleading guilty to insider trading charges. Nearly a dozen former executives at rehabilitation hospital chain HealthSouth have pleaded guilty to criminal fraud and conspiracy charges. And five former executives of cable company Adelphia Communications have been indicted for fraud.

All of these cases involve major companies and their executives. And all of these cases involve criminal charges of wrongdoing. Increasingly, state and federal government agencies are bringing criminal charges against company executives for defrauding investors, accountants, business partners, and others. And some of these executives are going to prison as a result.

Crime reporting has never been common in the business world, but sometimes it becomes a major part of the story. Criminal behavior in business in this country is more than a century old, and has been part of business reporting for nearly as long, from the Ponzi schemes of the early 20th century that stole money from investors to the latest accounting shenanigans that have brought down huge corporations and forced accounting firms out of business.

These stories often become front-page news at newspapers and the top stories for television and radio news broadcasts. They are often a major development for a company, and signal that the business may be in financial trouble.

The SEC and the Justice Department can launch criminal investigations into public companies suspected of wrongdoing, as they did in June, 2003 with Freddie Mac, the mortgage company that ousted three top executives as a result. The Criminal Division of the Justice Department investigates business crimes such as corporate fraud schemes, financial institution fraud, securities fraud, insurance fraud, fraud involving government programs such as Medicare and international criminal activities, including bribery of foreign government officials in violation of the Foreign Corrupt Practices Act.

Increasingly, businesses are actually facing charges in addition to executives. In January, 2003 Deputy Attorney General Larry Thompson distributed an 11-page memo to U.S. attorneys across the county that detailed a revised set of principles for filing charges against a business organization. Among the guidelines were that corporations should not be treated leniently—or be subject to harsh treatment. In addition, prosecutors were asked to apply the same factors in determining whether to charge a corporation as they do in charging an individual. Prosecutors can also review a corporation's history of past criminal, civil and regulatory actions against it in determining whether to bring charges.

In addition, the SEC's Division of Enforcement investigates violations of the federal securities laws, and prosecutes cases using civil lawsuits in federal courts. It often seeks injunctions, and a person who violates an injunction can be subject to fines or a prison term. Many of its cases involve fraud such as fraudulent stock offerings, manipulations, illegal insider trading, or conduct by brokers in violation of securities laws.

The SEC filed securities fraud charges against three former employees of energy company Dynegy Incorporated in June, 2003 accusing them of disregarding advice from the company's outside auditors, establishing secret side agreements to conceal their improper conduct, authorizing the elimination or risk in a special-purpose entity and concealing the transaction from the company, its auditors, and investors. The regulators are seeking fines and the repayment of the defendants' gains, including bonuses and trading profits. At the same time, the Justice Department also unsealed an indictment against the three former employees.

In recent years, the Justice Department has also developed cases directed at schemes such as telemarketing fraud, identity theft, and Internet fraud. Justice Department attorneys may also work with other federal agencies to prosecute companies. In June, 2003 a manufacturer of heart surgery devices pleaded guilty to hiding malfunctions in its products that may have caused a dozen deaths. Endovascular Technologies, a subsidiary of Guidant Corporation, agreed to pay more than $92 million for civil and criminal penalties. The investigation of the case was handled by the Food and Drug Administration and the Justice Department.

In addition, the IRS can investigate and prosecute companies for attempting to evade taxes, willfully failing to file returns, submitting false tax forms, and otherwise attempting to defraud taxpayers.

So-called white-collar crime cases can result from a number of different areas—and do not always have to involve a business executive. Criminal business cases can also involve consumers defrauding companies.

Check fraud can result from forging, altering, or counterfeiting a check on an account that has been closed or has insufficient funds. Credit card fraud occurs when someone uses a credit card that has been stolen, cancelled, or reported lost. Disaster fraud occurs when someone attempts to defraud businesses or the government after a natural disaster such as Hurricane Andrew, which struck south Florida in August, 1992 and caused more than $15 billion in damages. Although thousands of businesses and homeowners reported credible losses, others reported damage and losses for property they did not own.

Fraud occurs in many other areas, such as health care and insurance. Health care fraud can result when someone misrepresents an injury or treatment to receive payment. Insurance fraud can result when a consumer or business files a claim for a loss that did not actually occur.

Even small-town newspapers and radio stations can produce compelling stories about business crime, as the following story from the *Lexington News-Gazette* in rural western Virginia illustrates:

> White-collar crime can be as annoying as a bounced check, or as dangerous as a person posing as a paramedic.
>
> In September, Carolyn Kate Smedley was sentenced in Rockbridge County to eight years in prison on 32 counts of forging checks, with five years and four months of that sentence suspended. She was also ordered to make restitution of $4,148.64.

Forged documents allowed a North Carolina man to join not only the Lexington Lifesaving and First Aid Crew, but the staff of Stonewall Jackson Hospital. David Harold Sult, 34, answered about 60 calls between May and July 2001 on the bogus documents. One of those calls was to Interstate 81 when VDOT worker Denny Kegley was struck by a truck. Because Sult said he was certified as a paramedic, he was in charge of rescue squad members on the call. Kegley died at Carlton Roanoke Memorial Hospital a few days later.

Sult received a five-year prison sentence for forging public documents and 12 months for a misdemeanor charge of obtaining property by false pretenses.

Earlier this month the Southwest Regional Crime Prevention Association presented ways local merchants may reduce the risks of these crimes at a day-long seminar at the Virginia Horse Center. More than 60 law enforcement and retail representatives from across the region attended.

Speakers with the association examined policies for checks and credit cards, reduced computer sabotage and embezzlement and security against counterfeit credit cards and currency.

Speakers were Investigator Steve Funkhouser, Rockbridge County Sheriff's Office; Sgt. Marcus Vaught, Vinton Police Department; Spencer Wilcox, Lynchburg Police Department; Clinton Rogers, Roanoke City Police Department; and Gerald W. Orndorff, CPA, M.Ed, forensic accountant and private investigator.

Reported incidents of white-collar crimes are on the increase across Virginia and the nation. Cases of embezzlement more than doubled between 1999 and 2000, according to the Virginia State Police Web site. Incidents of fraud rose from 4,397 in 1999 to 8,193 in 2000. In that same time period, forgery and counterfeiting incidents increase from 4,903 to 6,954. In Rockbridge County about 45 cases of white-collar crime passes through the circuit court since the beginning of the year.

Losses from employee embezzlement may be as high as $20 to $40 billion annual in the United States, according to statistics provided by Orndorff.

In Rockbridge County, convictions were handed down in two high profile cases of embezzlement this year.

Patricia Truslow was convicted in February of 28 counts of embezzlement. In her capacity as bookkeeper of North Fork Lumber, she stole more than $365,000 from her employer between January 1999 and April 2001. She wrote checks to herself and third parties which she cases. She is serving 14 years in a state penitentiary.

A month later, Gregory Pearce was found guilty of embezzling nearly $70,000 from Washington and Lee University. He used his position as executive chef to sidetrack case reimbursements from vendors to W&L for his personal use between August 1996 and 2001. Pearce received a 20-year suspended sentence and must pay $68,419.90 in restitution.

In the most recent case in Rockbridge County Circuit Court Monday, Mary Francis Teaford pleaded guilty to two counts each of embezzlement and prescription fraud. In a plea agreement, she was sentenced to a four-year suspended sentence and ordered to repay $12,652.12 to the Carilion Obstetrics and Gynecology office in Lexington.[10]

As this story notes with excellent examples, white-collar crime does not always happen by business executives. In many cases, it can be perpetrated by a

---

[10]From "Regional seminar here focused on ways of reducing the risk," by M. L. DiBiase, October 31, 2002, *Lexington News Gazette*, pp. D1–D2. Copyright 2002 by The News-Gazette Corporation. Reprinted with permission.

lower-ranking employee. The examples for this story came easily obtainable from court and police records.

There are many other types of criminal cases that involve business. Money laundering, as defined by the U.S. Criminal Code, involves the concealment of the source of money or its destination, or money gained through illegal activities. In the early 1990s, some banks were accused of helping drug dealers launder money received from selling drugs.

The term white-collar crime can be used to identify counterfeiting, particularly if one business has been hit hard with the passing of fake bills.

Organized crime cases can also involve businesses. Organized crime is defined as when a business is maintained through the use of force, threats, monopolistic control, or the corruption of public officials.

Reporters should also check the criminal records of many of their sources, particularly if a criminal background might add to the story or shed light on a person's character. For example, say a reporter is covering the election of the new president for the union that represents the workers at Tropicana, the orange juice manufacturer. The reporter checks the criminal records of the two candidates at the courthouse and discovers that one of them was once arrested and convicted of cocaine possession. That should likely be in the story, as well as a response from the candidate.

It sometimes even pays to check the criminal records of executives, including CEOs. If a reporter is writing a story about how a CEO is mismanaging a company, one of the ways in which he can help describe the CEO's personality in the story is by including his arrest for speeding 110 miles per hr in a 35 mile per hr zone. That police report helps give readers an understanding of the CEO. A CEO of a New Jersey-based company was charged in November, 1999 with growing marijuana in the attic of his house. The company placed the executive on a leave of absence after his arrest, and he did not return to his position.

Reporters should not forget about the criminal side of the state and federal courthouses. They are often where the most interesting business stories are found. A criminal case against an insurance agent accused of selling fictitious insurance policies to businesses throughout Tampa caused local businesses to check their coverage more carefully.

DEPOSITIONS AND EXHIBITS

After the lawsuit is filed and the defendant has issued a reply to the charges, both sides may begin to prepare their cases. Although many business-related lawsuits do not go to trail, the parties and their attorneys must prepare for that likelihood. There will be motions for information or to suppress information from the case. In addition, lawyers will begin taking depositions of key people involved in the case, and also ask for documents from the defendant. The plaintiffs side will also file documents in the case.

These depositions, which can be lengthy interviews of potential witnesses in a case, can yield valuable information and provide the public a glimpse of what might happen once the case goes to trial. The documents, known often as exhibits, can also help or hurt a case, depending on what they contain.

A reporter should take the time to read through these depositions and exhibits, particularly if they are interviews with corporate executives or documents such as memos written by management. Taken separately, they may not say anything. But put together, they could connect a story that paints a picture of a company or business previously unrevealed to the rest of the world.

Depositions can often last several days in complicated business cases, and attorneys for both sides ask questions. A deposition is a pretrial proceeding in which one person is questioned under oath. A stenographer is present to record the statements. Depositions are used to collect information and facts about the case. Sometimes they are taken to discredit the testimony of the witness if the case goes to trial.

Lawyers often prepare a business executive or another person on how to answer questions before a deposition. For many companies, the depositions taken by their executives can help frame the case in their favor, or against them if the answers hurt their case. Lawyers will look for different answers at a trial than what was stated during a deposition. If they can find such an incident, a case against a business may be strengthened or hurt, depending on whether the deposition was given by an executive for the plaintiff or defendant.

Reporters may not always be allowed to sit in on the depositions while they are occurring. But often transcripts of the depositions are filed as part of the public record in a case. They can be lengthy documents, and often may not contain much valuable information. But sometimes there are statements that warrant news coverage.

The PBS show "Frontline" went through the depositions taken by cigarette company executives in lawsuits filed by state attorneys general in the late 1990s to recoup expenses for Medicaid costs paid by the states for sick smokers. Among the statements the show found in the depositions was that Geoffrey Bible, the CEO of Philip Morris, the largest cigarette company in the world, (a) denied ever hearing of the committee of counsel, a lawyers group that met for more than 30 years to discuss tobacco industry strategy; (b) claimed not to have any knowledge of how many teens smoke Philip Morris cigarettes; and (c) claimed not to have ever asked his employees about it. Alexander Spears III, the chairman of Lorillard Tobacco Company, said in his deposition that he did not believe that smoking caused emphysema or lung cancer, that smoking was not addictive, and that his company had never done a study to determine if teens smoked its brands.

Sometimes businesses will try to limit access to depositions. Microsoft moved in 2002 to have its depositions barred from public access in an antitrust case brought by states around the country. Microsoft did this because depositions often tell the inside story of what went on inside a company that the business may not want disclosed. For reporters, depositions can be a great way to obtain quotes from company executives or other employees who are not willing to talk to a journalist. By using a deposition, a reporter can use quotes and statements made without any doubt as to what was said or who said it.

The *Memphis Business Journal* covered the case of some employees who left one local investment bank to go work for another, and allegedly took documents with them that would help obtain business for their new employer. The documents included contact lists to details of bond underwriting transactions not yet completed. According to the deposition of the administrative assistant of one of the employees, her boss ordered her to destroy copied documents.

"Mac was running around like a chicken with his head cut off, going, 'Get everything off the computer,' " said Kelli Feathers in a deposition that the Memphis publication reported about in its September. 20–26, 2002 issue (Perkins, 2002, p.14). " 'I don't care what it is. I don't care if it's labels, but get it off because I don't want to give anybody any reason to think that we stole anything, because they can take something and turn it into something else, and I don't want any manipulation going on.' "

Depositions taken in a lawsuit against grocery store chain Supervalu alleging age discrimination show that company executives had discussed making employee information sheets that include birthdates available to supervisors. Leland Dake, a Supervalu senior vice president, told another vice president, Randy Wiegand, "Let's do it right so we can get rid of the garbage and save some money," according to Wiegand's deposition, which was reported in the *Minneapolis Star Tribune* (Forster, 2003, p. 1D).

Wiegand said later in his deposition that he had another meeting where he questioned the process. "I told him about my dissatisfaction, dislike, concern for the process that was taking place," said Wiegand in his deposition. "He quickly got off that subject, obviously, and the meeting wound up very shortly thereafter" (Forster, 2003, p. 1D).

Other documents filed in support of allegations made in business lawsuits can also be helpful to a reporter looking to better understand an issue and disclose to readers an inside look at Corporate America. Many business stories have been reported and written solely on the basis of these documents, commonly known as exhibits.

When Tyco sued its former CEO Dennis Kozlowski, it added more than 100 pages of exhibits to its allegations. Those documents showed that the former executive had approved a number of perks for himself and other executives paid for by the company, from a $2.5 million Trump Tower apartment in Manhattan to spending nearly $14 million to buy homes for a dozen employees.

These documents can also include items such as contracts or other agreements. When a Miami music industry executive sued his former business partners in 2001, he included copies of contracts and loan agreements in which he was never paid the money agreed upon in the deals.

And when Northwest Airlines sued its flight attendants' union regarding a "sickout" staged during a New Year's holiday, it used postings on Internet message bulletin boards and forums as exhibits to support its case.

The *St. Paul Pioneer Press* reported in its writing of the case about Kevin Griffin, a 19-year Northwest flight attendant who started the Rank and File site to give Northwest flight attendants a forum. Griffin's site, not affiliated with the union, featured lengthy anonymous memos to flight attendants describing how to call in sick and avoid being called for duty. One memo on the site details the "Rank and File call in sick program." Another link on the site urges flight attendants to "Join the HAVOC Team" (Torbenson, 2000, p. 1C).

Depositions and exhibits may not always be newsworthy. And some of them may be hard to understand out of context. But they can also provide an inside look at developments leading up to a lawsuit, and they can give readers and viewers an idea of what may be said if a case goes to trial.

The entire court system can be viewed as another layer of business regulation. Lawsuits and their related documents are filed as public records to help a company prove itself or defend itself against allegations that may hurt its operations.

GLOSSARY

arbitration: A smaller version of a trial held in an attempt to avoid a court trial. In some contract cases, arbitration may be binding for both parties.

breach of contract: Failing to live up to the stipulations set forth in a written or verbal contract, such as not completing a job by a deadline or failing to pay for services rendered.

civil litigation: Laws that encompass business, contracts, estates, accidents and negligence that is not criminal law. In a few areas civil and criminal law may overlap or coincide.

class action: A lawsuit filed by one or more people on behalf of other people who may be in a similar situation. Class action lawsuits may be difficult and are expensive, but allow people who may not have been able to file a lawsuit individually to band together.

criminal litigation: Charges dealing with crimes against the public or members of the public, filed by government authorities.

damages: The amount of money a plaintiff may be seeking or awarded in a lawsuit. Punitive damages may be awarded in some cases to set an example against the defendant.

defamation: Making untrue statements about a person that damages that person's reputation. If printed, the statements can be considered libel.

defendant: The individual or business sued in a civil lawsuit, or charged with a crime in a criminal case.

deposition: Taking or recording of testimony by a witness away from the courtroom before a trial. Deposition statements may be used by the plaintiff or defendant to prepare their case. Depositions can be made available in the public court file.

exhibit: A document or object introduced as evidence. In civil lawsuits, a plaintiff's case may be supported by exhibits filed along with the allegations.

mediation: An attempt to settle a lawsuit by an independent third party who attempts to find common points of agreement in order to reach a fair result for both sides.

medical malpractice: Allegations against a physician or medical provider that the care provider did not meet the standards of professional conduct or caused damage.

noncompete agreement: A contract signed by an employee that prohibits them from working for a competitor or using the knowledge gained with one employer to go work for a competitor for a certain time period.

out-of-court settlement: An agreement reached between the plaintiff and the defendant outside the realm of the court system. Such settlements often require a judge's approval, but the terms can also be confidential.

plaintiff: The individual or business who files the charges in a lawsuit against another party asking for damages or a court ruling.

REFERENCES

(2003, March 11). Court issues restraining order against KC pharmacy. *Kansas City Business Journal.*

DiBiase, M. L. (2002, October 30). Regional seminar here focused on ways of reducing the risk. *Lexington News-Gazette.* pp. 01–02.

Docherty, N. Inside the tobacco deal. (1998, May 12). Retrieved May 25, 2003, from http://www.pbs.org/wgbh/pages/frontline/shows/settlement/

Forster, J. (2003, April 28). Written off: A lawsuit filed by seven former employees of Supervalu Inc. that accused the company of age discrimination has been cleared for trial in August. *Minneapolis Star Tribune.* p. 1D.

Hayes, D., & King, S. (2003, February 3). CEO change near, Sprint says; Esrey stepping down; Forsee offered job, but BellSouth gets court order to keep him. *Kansas City Star.* p. A1.

Katz, R. (2003, January 29). Sears sued by fired credit president for defamation. Bloomberg News.

Kelly, J. (2003, May 28). Novell says it owns unix rights, challenges SCO claim. Bloomberg News.

Margolies, D. (2002, December 19). KPMG accused of conflicts; Missouri alleges liability in collapse of life insurer. *Kansas City Star.* p. C1.

Martinez, B. (2002, December 13). Cigna hits snag in effort to settle billing lawsuit. *The Wall Street Journal.* p. B6.

Mason, E. (2002, July 12). Charlesbank sues portfolio firm over accounting issues. *Boston Business Journal.* pp.1, 53.

McCall, W. (2002, December 20). Wal-Mart guilty in overtime case. Associated Press.

McQuillen, B. (2002, September 17). FTC sues Canadian company over weight loss claims. Bloomberg News.

Montesano, N. (2002, January 24). Bank seeks Hillside foreclosure: Retirement community residents assured of seamless transition. *McMinnville News-Register.* pp. A1–A8.

Perkins, T. (2002, September 20). Report: Duncan Williams staff stole, copied and deleted files. *Memphis Business Journal.* p. 14.

Pramik, M. (2000, February 5). Shareholders' lawsuits piling up at Bank One. *Columbus Dispatch.* p. 1H.

Sinton, P. (2000, June 21). Rivals challenge Blue & Gold Fleet over access to Alcatraz. *The San Francisco Chronicle.* p. C1.

Torbenson, E. (2000, January 7). Did the Northwest Airlines flight attendants union indicate that its members should stake a sickout? The union says it did not. The airline, in a lawsuit, disagrees. *Saint Paul Pioneer Press.* p. 1C.

Trigaux, R. (2000, October 4). The most frivolous lawsuit award goes to . . . *St. Petersburg Times.* p. 1E.

Wisniewski, M. (2003, February 19). Loews Cineplex sued by Illinois moviegoer over pre-feature ads. Bloomberg News.

Other Books on Business-Related Litigation

Bogus, C.T. (2001). *Why lawsuits are good for America: Disciplined democracy, Big Business, and the common law.* New York: New York University Press.

Howard, P. K. (2001). *The lost art of drawing the line: How fairness went too far.* New York: Random House.

Olson, W. (2003). *The rule of lawyers: How the new litigation elite threatens America's rule of law.* New York: Truman Talley Books.

Schweich, T. A. (2000). *Protect yourself from business lawsuits: An employee's guide to avoiding workplace liability.* New York: Fireside Books.

SUGGESTED EXERCISES

1. Pretend that you're shopping in the local Wal-Mart one weekend when you slip on a toy left in an aisle and break your leg. Do you sue the retailer for the pain and suffering caused by your injury, and for the lost wages for being unable to work in a restaurant on nights and weekends? Why or why not?

2. Imagine you're working in a store, and an irate customer walks in on your shift and demands $500 because the lawn mower they purchased last month no longer works. The customer says that if they don't get the money now, they'll sue the store. The only person authorized to make such decisions is

the store manager, and he's out to lunch for the next two hours. What do you do?

3. You're a reporter for a local newspaper, and you're checking the courthouse one day for lawsuits that may be potential stories. You find that a convenience store chain is suing a local doughnut manufacturer to terminate a contract requiring that only its doughnuts be sold at the store's locations because sales have dropped. The convenience store chain wants to start selling Krispy Kreme doughnuts as well. The file includes documents from the doughnut manufacturer that are marked "confidential" and "private" submitted as evidence by the convenience store chain. Do you use them as part of your story?

4. The state insurance department has filed charges against a local insurance company alleging that it doesn't have enough assets to cover its policies and needs to be placed into regulatory supervision. You call the insurance company and talk to the CEO, who tells you that if you write a story about the allegations, the insurer will likely go under because policyholders will get scared and take their money out of the company. He even gets the company's attorney on the phone via conference call, and the attorney makes similar claims. Do you write the story and run it in tomorrow's newspaper?

5. Criminal charges have been filed against the CEO of a company that you cover. The charges have nothing to do with the CEO's management of the business. However, the company has announced that the CEO is taking a leave of absence to take care of some personal issues. Do you write a story that includes details of the criminal charges?

12

Bankruptcy Court

BUSINESS GONE BAD

Not all companies and corporations are successful. Many of them, including those with the smartest business plans and the best managers, struggle to make money, and some of them actually lose money. This happens to public and private companies.

What causes the problems leading to a company losing money can be wide and varied. A company could have missed a paradigm shift in its industry that caused competitors to take business away from it. A corporation could have decided to enter a new line of business that resulted in disaster, leading to huge losses. Or a business could have acquired another company, taking on debt and other financial obligations that it is no longer able to meet.

These are just a few examples of why a business goes bad. When a company in dire financial straits gets into a position where it is no longer able to pay its bills and loans in a timely manner, it often files papers with the court allowing it to continue operations but reorganize the money it owes, making those payments more manageable. This is called entering bankruptcy court.

Bankruptcy court is a federal court system, and it is not just for businesses. Individual people can also file with the bankruptcy court. But what a bankruptcy court filing allows a company to do is to allow it to have some or all of its debts eliminated or reduced dramatically.

At first glance, such a proposition does not seem fair to the people or other businesses that are owed money. And many of them complain bitterly that they will not be repaid what they should receive. But from the perspective of the business in bankruptcy court, going into the court process to eliminate some of its debt allows it to repay some of the money it is owed. Without such a process, the people and companies owed money may not have received anything if the company simply went out of business. In addition, the bankruptcy court process attempts to find a fair method for compensating creditors. Some people and businesses owed money by a company in bankruptcy court receive compensation before others.

Increasingly, bankruptcy filings have become a major story for business reporters. Six of the 13 largest bankruptcies in terms of company assets were filed in 2002 (Fig. 12.1). Those major companies included WorldCom, Enron, Global Crossing, Conseco, and Kmart.

And even for smaller companies seeking bankruptcy court protection, the story can be important to a local town or city. When companies go into bankruptcy court, they typically try to cut expenses by closing locations and firing workers. That can have an affect on any economy.

Understanding how bankruptcy court works and why businesses file for bankruptcy court protection is important for any reporter, not just those working on the business desk. When businesses file for protection from their creditors, those that are owed money could range from government entities, such as the local school board, to a federal agency that contracted with the business to perform services or provide goods. Or it could be a business that was planning to revitalize a depressed part of downtown.

Bankruptcy courts are located in most major cities in every state. Typically, companies and individuals file for bankruptcy-court protection at the bankruptcy courthouse located closest to its headquarters. But that does not always happen. Sometimes, companies file for bankruptcy-court protection in the state where they are incorporated. That may not always be the state where their headquarters is located.

Bankruptcy courts operate similarly to other federal courts and to state courts. There is a clerk who handles all of the incoming filings as well as the documents filed in existing cases. It is important for a business reporter to know that these bankruptcy court filings are considered public record and should be accessible. The U.S. Bankruptcy Code allows a court to prevent public access to filings if they include trade secrets or confidential information about a company's operations, or if scandalous or defamatory information about a person is filed.

Company	Bankruptcy Date	Total Assets Pre-Bankruptcy	Filing Court District
Worldcom, Inc.	07/21/02	$103,914,000,000	NY-S
Enron Corp.*	12/2/01	$63,392,000,000	NY-S
Conseco, Inc.	12/18/02	$61,392,000,000	IL-N
Texaco, Inc.	4/12/1987	$35,892,000,000	NY-S
Financial Corp. of America	9/9/1988	$33,864,000,000	CA-C
Global Crossing Ltd.	1/28/2002	$30,185,000,000	NY-S
UAL Corp.	12/9/2002	$25,197,000,000	IL-N
Adelphia Communications	6/25/2002	$21,499,000,000	NY-S
Pacific Gas and Electric Co.	4/6/2001	$21,470,000,000	CA-N
MCorp	3/31/1989	$20,228,000,000	TX-S
Mirant Corporation	7/14/2003	$19,415,000,000	TX-N
First Executive Corp.	5/13/1991	$15,193,000,000	CA-C
Gibraltar Financial Corp.	2/8/1990	$15,011,000,000	CA-C
Kmart Corp.	1/22/2002	$14,600,000,000	IL-N
FINOVA Group, Inc., (The)	3/7/2001	$14,050,000,000	DE
HomeFed Corp.	10/22/1992	$13,885,000,000	CA-S
Southeast Banking Corporation	9/20/1991	$13,390,000,000	FL-S
NTL, Inc.	5/8/2002	$13,003,000,000	NY-S
Reliance Group Holdings, Inc.	6/12/2001	$12,598,000,000	NY-S
Imperial Corp. of America	2/28/1990	$12,263,000,000	CA-S
Federal-Mogul Corp.	10/1/2001	$10,150,000,000	DE
First City Bancorp.of Texas	10/31/1992	$9,943,000,000	TX-N
First Capital Holdings	5/30/1991	$9,675,000,000	CA-C
Baldwin-United	9/26/1983	$9,383,000,000	OH-S

*The Enron assets were taken from the 10-Q filed on 11/19/2001. The company has announced that the financials were under review at the time of filing for Chapter 11.

FIG. 12.1. The largest bankruptcies 1980–present. From BankruptcyData.Com. 2003. Copyright by New Generation Research Inc. Adapted with permission.

This initial filing is an important document for any reporter writing about a bankruptcy because it will list the company's total assets and debts, and later every single person or company that the company owes money. This list of creditors can be valuable because it often leads to sources willing to talk about how the company in bankruptcy court has not been paying its bills or is reneging on some sort of business arrangement.

All bankruptcy cases are overseen by a judge. A U.S. bankruptcy judge is a judicial officer of the U.S. district court who is appointed by the majority of judges of the U.S. court of appeals to exercise jurisdiction over bankruptcy matters. The number of bankruptcy judges is determined by Congress. The Judicial Conference of the United States is required to submit recommendations from time to time regarding the number of bankruptcy judges needed. Bankruptcy judges are appointed to 14-year terms.

Some critics complain that the number of judges has not kept pace with the increase in bankruptcy cases. This could lead to backlogs of cases in some jurisdictions, which could also be a story for a reporter to follow.

When a company files for bankruptcy-court protection, its assets are frozen. After the filing, there are hearings to decide whether a company can spend large amounts of money.

The beginning of a *Pittsburgh Business Times* story illustrates the typical first-day bankruptcy-court structure that details the company that has filed for protection from its creditors and totals its debts and assets for the world to see.

The lead notes that RedZone Robotics Incorporated, a company that designs and manufactures robots to clean hazardous environments such as nuclear plants, filed for Chapter 11, and then the second paragraph states in what bankruptcy court the case was filed. The fourth paragraph lists the company's assets and debts. The rest of the story quotes the company's president and mentions that its employment is down.

The reporter actually looked at the court filing to give the reader a sense of the value of the company's assets and the worth of its debt. The reporter also contacted the company to get a comment on the cause of the filing, although the president was not forthcoming. The story, however, does not explain what caused this robotics company to need to go into bankruptcy court.

The following excerpt is the beginning of a story from the *Boston Herald* does a good job explaining what led to a company's downfall. In any story reporting the bankruptcy court filing of a company, the reasons for the problems should be explained prominently.

Kmart Corp. yesterday became the largest U.S. retailer to seek Chapter 11 bankruptcy protection, a move sources say could trigger the closing of up to 600 stores.

The Troy, Mich., retailer, the second-largest U.S. discount chain, with $37 billion in revenue last year, was battered by weak sales, mounting losses, a disastrous holiday shopping season and the erosion of supplier confidence. It has also suffered at the hand of giant rival Wal-Mart Stores Inc.

Kmart yesterday said all 2,114 Kmart stores will remain open until further notice as it seeks to reorganize under court protection. But it will close a number of unprofitable and underperforming stores this year. Kmart operates 29 stores in Massachusetts, with an estimated 3,000 local employees.

Retail sources said they expect Kmart will close several hundred stores—perhaps as many as 600.

Yesterday, Kmart said it will terminate 350 leases for already-closed stores or for locations that are leased to other tenants, resulting in an immediate savings of $250 million.

The company has 69 stores in New England, with an average of 100 employees each.

Some observers have criticized the chain lately for carrying unpopular merchandise in cluttered aisles, for having outdated inventory technology and not keeping pace with today's consumer demands.[1]

The Boston newspaper reporter wrote the Kmart story to reflect how the region would be affected. With any bankruptcy-court filing, it is smart for the writer to note for the reader what the company's local operations are, and how many workers it employs.

The initial filing helps businesses in an important way. A company's supplier must continue to provide products or other materials to the business in bankruptcy court. Companies in bankruptcy court go through a lot of court hearings as part of the process. There are hearings to determine whether a company should be closing locations or factories. There are hearings to decide how much compensation should be paid to executives, and how much in fees should be paid to the bankruptcy lawyers representing the company.

In addition, it is important for a reporter covering a business bankruptcy case to know some other vital parts of what can appear to be a complicated court system.

For example, there is the decision to file for bankruptcy-court protection. Sometimes, that decision is not made by the company but by some of its creditors. This is called an involuntary bankruptcy. At least three creditors owed money by a company can join together and force a company into bankruptcy court. The company can contest the involuntary filing.

And it is vital that a reporter understands who is running the company after it has filed for bankruptcy-court protection. In some cases, the court will appoint a trustee to oversee a company's operations.

Assets, which can be defined as a resource or item owned by a business that can be expected to benefit its operations, are important to assess for a company. Many times a company in bankruptcy court will look to sell some of its assets to help raise cash and turn its operations around.

When Conseco Incorporated decided to sell part of its operations, reporters from Bloomberg, Dow Jones, Reuters, and the Associated Press reported its deal to sell its Conseco Finance unit for more then $700 million to CFN Investment Holdings LLC and its Mill Creek Bank assets to GE Consumer Finance for $310 million. The agreements were reached as part of its bankruptcy-court proceedings in an auction process. They still had to be approved by the bankruptcy-court judge overseeing the case.

A company filing for bankruptcy-court protection should be considered major news, particularly for a large company, and should be displayed prominently in a business section or Web site. However, a company filing for bankruptcy-court protection often does not mean that the company is going out of business—a common

---

[1]From "Kmart enters bankruptcy; Retail giant Kmart is bankrupt; No immediate loss seen of any of its 29 Mass. stores," by G. Gatlin, January 23, 2002, *Boston Herald*, p. 27. Copyright 2002 By *Boston Herald*. Reprinted with permission.

misperception made by many readers and even some journalists. Reporters should make sure that their copy clearly states that the company remains in business, if that is in fact the case.

CHAPTER 11 VERSUS CHAPTER 7

Indeed, the U.S. bankruptcy code has many different parts. One section allows companies seeking to reorganize its debt and emerge from court supervision with less debt to file under one part of the law. Another allows companies to simply pay off as much as its debt as it can and close shop under another part of the law.

Chapter 11 court filings are of the former category. This bankruptcy filing allows a corporation, or an individual, to reorganize without have to liquidate all of its assets. The debtor maintains control of the business—unless the court appoints a trustee. The company typically goes into bankruptcy court to come up with a debt payment plan to submit to its creditors. If the creditors approve the plan, and if the court agrees that the plan is fair, then the company is allowed to reorganize its debts and emerge from bankruptcy court.

Chapter 7 court filings, however, are more drastic. When a company has filed under this part of the bankruptcy laws, it means that all of the company's assets will be sold to pay its debts and that the company is going out of business. This part of the law can also be used by individuals who want to eliminate debt.

A third type of bankruptcy filing that occurs that can be relevant to business reporters is a Chapter 13, where the person filing repays their debts during a three- to five-year time period.

When a reporter is examining the initial filing of a company at bankruptcy court, one of the first facts he or she should determine is whether the business is filing under Chapter 11 or Chapter 7. The differences between the two are important, and getting this vital piece of information wrong could hurt a company, not to mention severely hamper a reporter's relationship with the sources that will help him or her understand the filing and hearings in the future.

Chapter 11 is the most common filing for many medium- and large-sized businesses, although it is not the most common filing for all businesses. In the fourth quarter of 2002, there were 9,500 filings of bankruptcy protection by businesses, and more than 385,000 filings by individuals. More than 70% of the filings, or nearly 276,000, were Chapter 7 filings.

Less than 1% of all bankruptcy-court filings, or 2,772, in the fourth quarter of 2002 were for Chapter 11 protection. That seems like a small amount, but upon examination of the recent cases under Chapter 11, a reporter will discover that there are billions of dollars in assets owned by companies in the process of seeking to reorganize debt and continue to exist as viable companies. For example, at the time of its filing, WorldCom had $103.9 billion in assets, whereas Enron had $63.4

billion in assets. It would take many small companies filing for bankruptcy-court protection to equal those amounts.

Finding out that a company has filed for bankruptcy-court protection may not seem as easy as just going to the courthouse and looking through the filings each day, though that is a good place to start. If a reporter is hearing rumors that a company may be seeking bankruptcy-court protection, he or she should do some background work.

First, the journalist should find out the name of the company as it is incorporated with the state. Sometimes the company's incorporated name may not be the same name under which it is doing business. This is typical for businesses such as restaurants.

Second, the reporter needs to know where the company is incorporated. That will help determine what bankruptcy court the filing can be found. It is frustrating for a reporter to go looking for an initial filing at one court and not find the document, only to be scooped by another reporter who fount the filing at another court. Clerks at the court can often be helpful in cases like this and provide the location at which a company has filed.

And last, businesses—particularly those prominent in a local community—will file for bankruptcy-court protection at the end of the day or on a late Friday, hoping that the filing will escape notice. Reporters should ask for all of a previous day's filings if they cannot wait around the clerk's office every day until closing time.

Other times, however, a company will simply issue a news release announcing that it has filed for bankruptcy-court protection. The following excerpt is an example of how one of these releases reads:

[Company X] announced today that it has reached an agreement in principle with representatives of its banks and bondholders on a financial restructuring of the Company's capital that would substantially reduce the Company's debt. To facilitate the restructuring, the Company and certain of its subsidiaries filed voluntary petitions for reorganization under Chapter 11 of the U.S. Bankruptcy Code.

The Company emphasized that the filing includes only certain holding companies, certain non-operating subsidiaries and certain entities related to [Company X] Finance Corp., the Company's finance subsidiary. [Company X]'s insurance companies, [Company X] Services, LLC and [Company X] Capital Management are separate legal entities and are not included in the filing.

President and Chief Executive Officer [name deleted] stated, "We believe we have achieved a major step toward what we set out to do in August. We have reached an agreement in principle with the bank and bondholder representatives to reduce the company's leverage to a level that, together with our targeted operating performance, will support the efforts by the Company's insurance subsidiaries to reclaim an 'excellent' financial strength rating from A.M. Best following the restructuring." Shea further emphasized that the agreement in principle with the bank and bondholder representatives should significantly expedite the restructuring process.

While negotiating with its major creditor constituents, the Company has worked closely with state insurance regulators. The Company believes the insurance subsidiaries are adequately capitalized, and that policyholders will not be affected by the parent company restructuring.

[Name deleted] further stated, 'Our business leaders have done an outstanding job during this difficult period. We continue to drive our businesses for improved results, both at the top and bottom line. We have terrific franchises with outstanding people. We intend to do everything we can to maximize their potential.'

'While we recognize the hardship that has been placed on our employees and many of our constituencies during this period, we believe we have made the hard decisions necessary to position [Company X] for future success.'

The petitions were filed in the U.S. Bankruptcy Court for the Northern District of Illinois.[2]

This bankruptcy-court protection filing was not considered a surprise by many who followed the company. Some Wall Street analysts, in written research reports, even predicted the company would take such action, and the company also hinted in its SEC filings that it was considering bankruptcy-court protection. Still, the company chose to issue this release at 3 a.m, eastern time. Because the company's stock was publicly traded, it also filed a form 8-K disclosing the filing.

The following excerpt shows how the Associated Press covered the filing, and subsequent hearing later that day:

Conseco said Wednesday it plans to make a quick exit from bankruptcy court protection, even though a group of creditors who were late to the table threaten to delay and potentially tangle the insurance and finance company's reorganization.

Conseco, mired in debt from 1990s acquisitions that backfired, late Tuesday because the third-largest U.S. company to file for bankruptcy protection.

The Carmel, Ind.-based company, which employs about 14,000 people and had $8.1 billion in revenues last year, expects to emerge from Chapter 11 protection during the second quarter of next year, if not earlier, the company's lead attorney told a bankruptcy court in Chicago.

Banks and bondholders reached a tentative agreement on bankruptcy terms with Conseco over the $4 billion those groups are owed.

But a group of preferred shareholders—who initially were left out of talks begun in August to restructure Conseco's debt, but eventually won a seat under protest–have held out. They continue negotiations with Conseco.

Preferred securities holders carry privileges over owners of common stock in recovering their investments from failed companies, but rank below banks and bondholders. Common stockholders are expected to recover little if any of their investments in Conseco.

Details of Conseco's Chapter 11 plan, which have yet to be filed, must be approved by members of investor groups before a reorganization plan can be submitted for the court's approval. A filing outlining specifics could be submitted within four to six weeks, Conseco spokesman Mark Lubbers said.[3]

---

[2]From Conseco Incorporated news release, Dec. 18, 2002. Reprinted with permission.

[3]From "Conseco promises swift bankruptcy," Dec. 18, 2002, Associated Press. Copyright 2002 by Associated Press. Reprinted with permission.

Conseco's bankruptcy-court filing, as the above story points out, is unusual for Chapter 11 cases in that the company negotiated with its largest lenders before it actually sought court protection from its debtors. In some cases, a company will take such a strategy. This is commonly called a prepackaged bankruptcy filing, which means that much of the negotiation that takes place during bankruptcy court supervision has already occurred. In many of these cases, the time a company spends in bankruptcy court is shorter. To do such a plan, the company must get the approval of a majority of credits representing two thirds of its total debt to agree to the plan.

Often, however, a company does not negotiate with its creditors before entering bankruptcy court. The negotiations typically occur in the court, often through hearings. Committees of creditors are appointed, and they often meet. These committees are represented by attorneys, who often can be valuable sources, letting a reporter know if the creditors like or disapprove of a reorganization plan floated by the company.

The following excerpt details a case of a not-for-profit company filing for bankruptcy-court protection. The reporter for the *Louisville Courier-Journal* wrote the story like it would be written for a private or public company. The assets and debts were listed, and the cause of the problems leading to the filing is toward the beginning of the story:

> When it opened in 1990, the Oxmoor golf and steeplechase development in eastern Jefferson County was another success among the vast holdings of HFH Inc., the Louisville real-estate developer that soared during the golf course and residential building boom in the late 1980s and early 1990s.
>
> Today Oxmoor Golf & Steeplechase Inc., which operates Oxmoor Country Club at 9000 Limehouse Lane, is proceeding through bankruptcy after running up debts to nearly 200 creditors and facing four lawsuits by suppliers seeking to recoup their money.
>
> The not-for-profit corporation filed for protection from its creditors in U.S. Bankruptcy Court for the Western District of Kentucky on July 5, a move that shields its assets while it attempts to reorganize. In a petition entered with the court, Oxmoor Golf & Steeplechase claimed debts of $5 million and assets of $1 million. The debts are the result of escalating rent payments on the land Oxmoor Golf & Steeplechase leases from trusts established by the Bullitt family, said attorney David Cantor, who is representing the club. When HFH experienced financial problems in the mid-1990s, Oxmoor members took over the club's operations.
>
> They inherited a modern clubhouse and a challenging 18-hole golf course—and a 37-year lease with ballooning payments of about $30,000 a month, coupled with $17,500 in monthly mortgage payments.
>
> "You're looking at close to $50,000 in debt service alone before you . . . pay the greenskeeper," Cantor said.
>
> "What we're going to try and accomplish in the Chapter 11 (bankruptcy) is obviously not only to keep the club open and running," he said, "but to see if there's some room to negotiate with the two major creditors and to try to get these payments reduced to a more realistic figure."

Cantor said the bankruptcy filing is expected to be completed this week. The first meeting of Oxmoor Golf & Steeplechase creditors is scheduled for Aug. 8.

Among the major unsecured creditors listed in the filing are the Kentucky Revenue Cabinet, owed $132,333; the estate of Harry S. Frazier, owed $87,500; and PNC Bank, owed $61,717.

John Osborn, a Louisville attorney who represents Stock Yards Bank, trustee of the Thomas W. Bullitt trust, and PNC Bank, trustee of the William Marshall Bullitt trust, said the lease stipulates that the land must be used for a golf course.

"We hope and expect that the club and its reorganization will continue to make the ground lease payments," he said.[4]

The story lists some of the largest creditors for Oxmoor. There are two different types of creditors in bankruptcy-court cases. The secured creditors have claims against the company backed by collateral. This is similar to a car loan or a home loan, that is, if one does not make the payments on his or her car or home loan, the loan is backed by the car or home.

The other types of creditors are unsecured creditors. These are creditors with no collateral against their claim. Investors who purchased stock in a public company via a stockbroker fall into this category. Secured creditors are paid before unsecured creditors in bankruptcy cases.

The length of a company's stay in bankruptcy court can vary depending on the negotiations with its creditors. Some bankruptcy-court proceedings have lasted for years, whereas others have taken months. As a reporter, it is important to stay on top of a company's case and its progress, or lack of progress. Some bankruptcy-courts now post court hearing times and filings on the Internet. For others, however, reporters need to go to the courthouse to check the docket.

It is also vitally important to know the players, particularly the attorneys. The company will be represented by attorneys during hearings, as will creditors and others. Company executives will not always show up for hearings, particularly for cases involving large businesses.

Reporters should know the judges as well. Remember the warning about companies filing for bankruptcy-court protection at the end of the day to avoid publicity? Some judges have even allowed filings to be sent to their homes late at night, long after the court has been locked and the lights turned off. Although judges will rarely talk on the record, they and their clerks will often let a reporter know what is happening with a case.

Companies often file for Chapter 11 bankruptcy protection hoping to emerge from the proceedings as a better company that has learned from its mistakes. A number of companies such as Kmart seek to become successful after bankruptcy court.

---

[4]From "Oxmoor club hopes to survive bankruptcy," by M. Green, July 30, 2002, *The Courier-Journal*, p. 1D. Copyright 2002 by *The Courier-Journal*. Reprinted with permission.

But that is not always the case. A number of companies that look for Chapter 11 to reorganize their debt end up converting their case to Chapter 7 when it becomes apparent that they cannot reach an agreement with creditors, or their business deteriorates so much that it becomes obvious that the best course of action for the creditors is to go out of business.

The decision to liquidate is often forced upon the company and its management by creditors, or by the court. The following excerpt details case in which creditors pushed for a Chapter 7 liquidation:

> Wade Cook Financial Corp. was ordered liquidated by U.S. Bankruptcy Judge Thomas Glover after the money-losing stock-market seminar company's chief executive failed to provide testimony requested by creditors.
>
> The creditors of Seattle-based Wade Cook Financial asked the court Dec. 19 to force the company and its subsidiary, Stock Market Institute of Learning Inc., into bankruptcy, alleging employees hadn't been paid back wages and that their health insurance was canceled after the company collected and pocketed premiums.
>
> Wade Cook Financial's "failure to respond to the discovery requests have prejudiced and irreparably harmed" the creditors "by denying them the ability to adequately prepare for trial," wrote Glover in ordering the Chapter 7 bankruptcy.
>
> In Chapter 7, the bankrupt company is liquidated by a trustee. The trustee supplants the existing management and is legally obligated to serve the best interests of creditors.
>
> Chief Executive and founder Wade Cook said he will ask the judge to convert the case to a Chapter 11 reorganization in which the company can continue to operate. He said he would consent to the appointment of a trustee to oversee operations.
>
> "Nobody is saying we haven't been struggling financially," Cook said in a brief telephone interview. "We've got plenty of assets."
>
> Cook predicted a year ago that the company would earn $6 million in 2002. The company lost $6.2 million in the first nine months of the year, according to a filing with the U.S. Securities and Exchange Commission.
>
> The company had $16,000 in the bank on Sept. 30, according to an SEC filing. The filing showed liabilities of $11.5 million and assets of $5.7 million, leaving a working capital deficit of $5.8 million.
>
> Michelle Carmody, an attorney for the creditors, said the company failed to provide any financial records requested under bankruptcy law.[5]

As with all bankruptcy-court stories, it is critical that the reporter get in touch with the company to get their response to the court proceedings. The Bloomberg News reporter called the CEO directly.

In other cases, however, a company will file for Chapter 11 protection and warn creditors that it could convert its case to Chapter 7 liquidation. In a December, 2002 interview with the *New York Times*, the CEO of United Airlines warned that the company might switch its Chapter 11 bankruptcy-court case to a Chapter 7.

---

[5]From "Wade Cook Financial ordered liquidated by judge." by David Evans, Jan. 17, 2003, Bloomberg News. Copyright 2003 by Bloomberg L.P. All rights reserved. Reprinted with permission.

Many bankruptcy court experts believe that a company often mentions the possibility of a liquidation in an attempt to win concessions from creditors or from employees to lower its costs. In the case of United Airlines, the CEO could have been making the assertion to get labor unions to agree to lower wages. Wire reports in March, 2003 noted that the company filed in court records that "liquidation is a distinct possibility if United does not achieve its proposed labor cost reductions" (Associated Press, 2003).

When a company begins talking about Chapter 7, even though it has filed a Chapter 11 case, a reporter needs to look at the motives and reasons. Often, there is one that should be covered in the story. Chapter 7 cases mean the end of the line for a company. By reviewing the court documents and talking to sources, a reporter can write a compelling story about the rise and fall of a company, large or small.

THE REORGANIZATION PLAN

Companies that do enter bankruptcy court with the idea that they will reorganize their debt and leave court protection rely on building a relationship with their creditors to work toward a common goal—coming up with a reorganization plan that allows the business to lower its debt while repaying some of the money owed.

The reorganization plan is vital to the future success of a company. A reorganization plan that weakens a company can lead to the business falling back into the habits that caused its initial problems and leading to yet another bankruptcy-court filing. A reorganization plan that gives little or nothing back to creditors often results in investors not wanting to be involved in the new company.

One of the important initial steps taken by a company after it enters bankruptcy court is to find financing that will allow the business to continue operating while it reorganizes its debt. This decision to provide financing to a company is approved by the court, and is often discussed at a hearing.

The financing is just one of the first steps along a path toward the reorganization plan. The plan is developed with a committee of creditors. Some of the creditors may want to be repaid as much money as possible, and may try to force the company to sell some assets to use the money to pay debt. Other creditors may look to exchange the money they are owed for an ownership stake in the company once it exits bankruptcy court.

A company will file a reorganization plan with the court. It is important for a reporter to determine the deadline for the plan, and to make sure he or she gets a copy of the plan as soon as it is filed. The plan is likely a story because it discloses for the first time how much money the company is proposing to repay its creditors. A reorganization plan often also discloses whether a company will close locations, fire workers, cut salaries for executives, and other steps to reduce expenses.

The plan is then reviewed by the creditors, and some of them may balk at the terms and ask the company to present a different plan. Reporters should find out the creditor's objectives and analyze whether they have any basis.

A reporter should try to maintain contacts with creditors. If creditors are balking at a reorganization plan proposed by the company, their hesitation could mean that they do not trust the executives and believe they are being taken. If creditors are receptive to a reorganization plan, a reporter should ask what they are getting in return for forgiving some of the money that they are owed.

The reorganization plan must be accepted by creditors, bondholders, and stock-holders. Understand that in most bankruptcy cases, the stockholders typically get nothing as part of a reorganization plan. After a plan has been approved by these groups, it must then be approved by the judge.

Bondholders may have the biggest incentive to get a company in and out of bankruptcy court as fast as possible. When a bankruptcy case is filed, bondholders stop receiving interest and principal payments. (Shareholders stop receiving dividends as well, though most companies about to file for bankruptcy-court protection have already halted dividend payments.) In some cases, bondholders will receive stock in the reorganized company when it emerges from the court.

The following details the case of a North Carolina company in which a reorganization plan gave bondholders stock:

> SpectraSite Holdings won court permission Tuesday to eliminate $1.8 billion of its debt, setting the cell-phone tower operator on a course to emerge from bankruptcy court next month.
> The U.S. Bankruptcy Court for the Eastern District of North Carolina approved the Cary company's plan to give bondholders all new stock in the business in exchange for relinquishing their rights to get repaid.
> The decision by Judge A. Thomas Small clears one of the final, and biggest, hurdles for SpectraSite, which sought Chapter 11 bankruptcy protection two months after a failed struggle with its finances.
> "While it's been a tough road, we've come through it," Chief Financial Officer David P. Tomick said after the hearing. "I think we, today, will be one of the success stories that comes our of the other side of the telecom bubble."
> Although company executives are optimistic, SpectraSite will face some of the same challenges that led to its financial troubles in the first place.
> The mobile-phone industry is adding customers at the slowest pace ever, and some carries, such as Cingular Wireless, are evening losing subscribers. They're trying to combat waning demand by paring expansion and spending.[6]

Note that the reorganization plan is approved in a court hearing that should be attended by the reporter. Such hearings often result in nice quotes from creditors and company executives and could also give the reporter an idea of some of the

---

[6]From "Judge OKs stock plan; spectrasite free to move forward," by J. Cox, January 29, 2003, *The News & Observer*, p. D1. Copyright 2003 by *The News & Observer.* Reprinted with permission.

sticking points in the negotiations among the creditors, the company, and the judge. For example, the story above, from the *News & Observer* in Raleigh, notes that the reorganization plan would pay the CFO and the CEO bonuses totaling more than $2 million to pay off debts they incurred to buy company shares once the company exited bankruptcy court. The story noted that the bonuses drew the ire of the judge, but approved it after attorneys for the company explained that the executives would repay the money. However, the repayment is based on stock options, and the reporter accurately pointed out that the options may never be worth enough to repay the bonuses.

For private companies in bankruptcy court, ownership of stock is not as big an issue. But it is still important for a reporter covering such a case to determine who will be the owners of the business once it leaves court protection.

Stories are also written when a company leaves bankruptcy court, which typically happens within a month after the reorganization plan is approved.

The following shows how the same *News & Observer* reporter covered the same case when the company emerged from bankruptcy court:

SpectraSite Holdings completed its reorganization Monday, emerging from bankruptcy protection with less debt, a new stock and a modified name. The operator of cell-phone towers shed about $1.8 billion in liabilities during the three-month process, and it now shows just more than $700 million in debt on its balance sheet, said David P. Tomick, the chief financial officer.

The Cary company will issue 23.75 million new shares, which could begin trading today under the ticker symbol SPCSV, and changed its legal name to SpectraSite Inc.

The moves reflect a new beginning for the beleaguered company, which fell upon hard times when growth slumped in the mobile-phone industry. As carriers such as Cingular Wireless won fewer customers, they cut spending, leaving SpectraSite with a $2.6 billion debt it couldn't manage.

"We now have a balance sheet that can handle what the level of business is today," Tomick said. "Even if didn't get better, or worsened, you can hang in there a long time."

SpectraSite was able to complete bankruptcy—the largest Chapter 11 case ever by a publicly held company based in the state—quickly because it reached a deal with bondholders before filing for protection.

In exchange for relinquishing their claims for repayment, bondholders were promised all the stock in the company.

Old shareholders effectively lost their investments. They get to buy one share for every 133 they owned, provided the price reaches $32 before Feb. 10, 2010. There's no guarantee that will happen.

Shares won't immediately trade on a major exchange because SpectraSite hasn't met all conditions. For example, about 150 people own the stock, too few for it to be posted on the Nasdaq. It must wait for a market to develop in less formal bulletin-board trading before it can be listed there.[7]

---

[7]From "Chapter 11 done for tower operator; SpectraSite out of bankruptcy" by J. Cox, February 11, 2003, *The News & Observer*, p. D1. Copyright 2003 by *The News & Observer*. Reprinted with permission.

In many bankruptcy cases for public and private companies, creditors or bond-holders became the majority owners of the new company. This is a major point in any reorganization plan that should be reported. It should also be reported whether the old shareholders receive anything.

It is also important for reorganization stories to point out how much the company's debt was reduced as part of the plan. An inability to pay the money it owes is the primary reason why a company enters bankruptcy court. If the debt has not been reduced enough, the company could face trouble down the road.

A Reuters story explained all of these points in describing the reorganization plan for map maker Rand McNally. Its report noted that the company would convert $350 million of its debt into equity ownership in the company and exit bankruptcy court with $100 million remaining in debt. The story noted that the company would also have a $10 million credit facility to allow it to operate.

The end of the Reuters report stated, 'The company had invited prospective acquirers to submit bids for the company by September 12, 2001. A planned auction was scrapped after the September 11 terrorist attacks" (Reuters, 2003). Sometimes, a reorganization plan will result in a company being sold, either piecemeal or as a whole operation. A story in the October 18, 2002 *Triangle Business Journal* points out that ArgoMed Incorporated, a medical device company, was sold for $3.15 million in a bankruptcy-court auction. And bankruptcy-court documents revealed that Swifty Serve, the nation's second-largest privately owned convenience store chain, was being sold off to hundreds of buyers, as reported in the *News & Observer* on December 27, 2002.

INTERESTED PARTIES

When a public company files for bankruptcy-court protection, its stockholders usually get nothing in return. Bondholders often get paid, but typically receive less than 100% of what they invested.

There are other groups involved with the bankruptcy filing of a company that also have a vested interest in the proceedings. Lawyers, accountants, investment bankers, turnaround consultants, and even company executives often receive millions of dollars in return for their services in helping steer the company through the legal maze. These groups of interested parties often clash with each other and the company during bankruptcy-court proceedings. Therefore, it is important to understand what role they play in the process.

The stories that result from understanding these relationships and roles can often bring out the reporting that best explains some of the problems with bankruptcy court. A company often lands in bankruptcy court because it is unable to pay its expenses. But bankruptcy court itself can result in some large expenses. Critics would argue that the bankruptcy-court system is flawed, and some of these flaws become apparent during the numerous hearings and motions filed in cases involving companies.

For example, attorneys, consultants, and others performing work for companies in bankruptcy court are required to have their fees approved by the judge presiding over the case. These fees can sometimes raise the ire of judges—and readers.

The *Denver Business Journal* noted how much in fees and expenses were being paid to local attorneys, property valuation experts, and other consultants in a story in its November 15, 2002 issue about the bankruptcy case of Colorado's Ocean Journey, an aquarium. The fees and expenses totaled more than $241,000 for late October and September, including $135,581 paid to its bankruptcy attorney for four months' work.

International wire service Bloomberg News went a step further in discussing fees for attorneys. In its exhaustive research published February 26, 2003 Bloomberg disclosed that the 25 largest bankruptcies in 2001 and 2002 had resulted in a total of $235 million in legal fees as of January 31, 2003 for the lead law firms for the companies.

Some of the fees charged by its lead law firm, Weil, Gothsal & Manges LLP in the Global Crossing bankruptcy case included $21,694 for meals, $73,182 for computerized research, and more than $24,000 for activities that included composing its fee applications for the bankruptcy-court judge to approve.

The Bloomberg report of the large fees drew criticism from the Texas attorney general, who said he saw "little accomplished" for the fees and that the "creditors and other people who deserve this money are seeing it depleted" (St. Onge, 2003).

Reporters following a bankruptcy case should always look for the filings and motions by attorneys and others working for the company to examine how much they are being paid and whether the services they are providing are needed. Often, these filings and motions can make interesting stories similar to the ones mentioned.

But it is not just paying attorneys and others with money from companies in bankruptcy court that draw the ire of those involved. Sometimes, the court-appointed overseers of bankruptcy cases can object as well to money being spent, particularly if they believe that the money could be spent more efficiently elsewhere.

The following *News & Observer* story portrays one such case, and how a disagreement about a company spending money can come up during a court hearing:

> The administrator for Midway Airlines' bankruptcy is worried that the carrier may be piling up too much debt too fast as it gears for its new life as a US Airways commuter.
>
> On Wednesday when Midway proposed buying two expensive airplanes, she opposed the purchase until the airline could show how its existing creditors will be repaid.
>
> "We've got a situation where the debtor is in a hole with regard to expenses," Marjorie Lynch, the administrator for the Eastern District Bankruptcy Court, told the judge. "The debtor's ability to pay is doubtful."

Judge A. Thomas Small ruled Midway could buy the aircraft after the carrier's attorney said they were needed for current operations and that they could eventually be sold to pay creditors if needed.

"This seems in agreement with the overall plan with US Airways, whish is the backbone of Midway's reorganization," Small said.

Morrisville-based Midway faces a Feb. 21 court deadline for filing a reorganization plan, and bankruptcy code guidelines require that administrative expenses be paid when the plan is filed. Administrative expenses range from attorney fees to leases for jetliners that Midway operated before it grounded itself in July.

The amount won't be known until the plan is filed, but the carrier's December expense report listed $10.2 million in past-due administrative expenses.

How much more the two jets will add to Midway's debt is unclear. New regional jets sell for about $20 million apiece but the sales price of the two planes, to be paid in monthly payments over 10 years, have been blacked out in court documents.[8]

This story was the result of a reporter sitting in on the hearing and then looking at the filings in the case to determine the company's expenses and when the reorganization plan was going to be filed. A judge ruling for or against allowing a company to pay for an expense should be noted high up in such stories.

In other bankruptcy cases, investors and creditors may clash. Because creditors are often secured creditors and thus first in line ahead of investors to be repaid, their interests are often catered to by the company more so than the interests of investors. Investors may object to plans to repay creditors if they feel they are getting the short end of the stick.

This happened in the Conseco bankruptcy and lead to stories by reporters who were vigilant in obtaining the court documents outlining those concerns. The following excerpt is one example from the *St. Paul Pioneer Press:*

Berkadia Equity Holdings, a group controlled by investor Warren Buffett's Berkshire Hathaway, led the bidding late Tuesday in a spirited auction to buy Conseco Finance Corp. out of bankruptcy.

Berkadia presented the highest bid of $1.2 billion as of 7 p.m. The bid is equal to the book value—or the value of the assets—of St. Paul-based Conseco Finance as of Sept. 30, according to court documents.

However, Berkadia could yet be topped by a higher bid. Bidding by parties interested in buying Conseco Finance's mobile home, credit card, home equity and home improvement lending businesses continued well into Tuesday night.

The sale is part of bankruptcy proceedings for Conseco Finance, the nation's largest mobile-home lender, and its Indiana-based parent, Conseco Inc., which both filed for Chapter 11 protection on Dec. 17 in Chicago. The companies and subsidiaries listed $51.1 billion in debts in the filing, making it the nation's third-largest bankruptcy. The sale will raise cash to help pay creditors.

Once a winning bid is reached, there's still a major hurdle: The bid or an alternative must be approved by the U.S. Bankruptcy Court in Chicago. A hearing is scheduled for today.

---

[8]From "Midway to get 2 new airplanes, after opposition." by D. Price, February 6, 2003, *The News & Observer*, p. D1. Copyright 2003 by *The News & Observer.* Reprinted with permission.

Four parties bid for all of Conseco Finance: Berkadia, which includes New York financial services firm Leucadia National Corp. as a partner; CFN Investors Holding, a New York-based joint venture; a consortium of Bear Stearns in New York, Charlesbank of Boston, and General Electric Capital Corp.; and Residential Funding Corp. In addition, Fannie Mae, the government-sponsored mortgage purchaser, bid $70 million for just one part of Conseco Finance's business.

CFN, which consists of Fortress Investment Group, J.C. Flowers & Co. and Cerberus Capital Management, has had a pending purchase agreement for Conseco Finance since December. It was revealed during the auction that CFN's first purchase offer made for Conseco Finance in December was $750 million plus assumed debt. The auction was held at the request of some creditors groups to try to raise a higher price for the company.

As of 7 p.m. Tuesday, CFN's last bid was $933 million plus assumed debt of about $200 million. The last bid made by the consortium of Bear Stearns, Charlesbank and General Electric Capital—three firms that initially bid separately on pieces of Conseco Finance—was $932.5 million.

Of that consortium, it's likely that General Electric's unit is bidding on Conseco Finance's bank unit, which also controls the private-label credit card business; Bear Stearns is interested in Conseco Finance's home equity and home improvement loan business; and Charlesbank, a boutique private investment firm, is bidding on the company's $23 billion mobile-home loan portfolio, said Anup Sathy, a partner at Kirkland & Ellis, the Chicago law firm representing Conseco Finance and hosting the auction.

It's not unusual for an auction of this size and complexity to be so lengthy, said Sathy. More than 200 people—from Conseco Finance officials to creditors to lawyers—attended the auction held at the law firm's Chicago office.[9]

Earlier, it had been creditors who were upset with a move by Conseco to sell part of the company. In each of these cases, money is the cause for the disagreement. Reporters should always follow the money, looking for who is getting more than they should, or not getting the money that they think is rightfully theirs. The following is an example, also from the Conseco case:

Going once. Going twice ... Hold.

Objections to the $1 billion-plus sale of Minnesota-based Conseco Finance by one of the losing bidders Friday delayed a potential approval of the deal in U.S. Bankruptcy Court.

Attorneys for billionaire investor Warren Buffett's Berkadia LLC—whose $1.2 billion bid for Carmel-based Conseco's consumer finance unit was tossed out of Wednesday's auction—lost their argument before Judge Carol A. Doyle that the bidding had not legally ended.

But the fact that the winners, CFN Investments LLC and GE Consumer Finance, still wrestled with contractual details well into Friday cast a shadow over the whole deal—one that Berkadia predicts that Doyle ultimately will revisit next week.

"The contract (Conseco's attorneys) wish to present is not sufficient to meet the conditions of creditors—nor is it capable of being considered," said David N. Missner

---

[9]From "Conseco bidding fierce," by S. Jean, March 5, 2003, *St. Paul Pioneer Press*, p. 1C. Copyright 2003 by *St. Paul Pioneer Press*. Reprinted with permission.

of Chicago-based Piper Rudnick, which represents Berkadia. "To consider it further is simply a waste of time."

Berkadia said a post-auction deal it reached with Fannie Mae for nearly $1.15 billion should be considered since CFN boosted its $1.01 billion proposal by $30 million after the auction's conclusion, in turn raising the question of when bidding legally ends.

But Doyle stuck fast to "very high standards" that must be met to overrule an auction—demonstrated harm to a company or its protected assets or fraud.

"I don't remember you saying anything about the bid process being violated. I remember you saying, 'Don't pay attention to it,'" Doyle told Missner.

Doyle also admonished Berkadia for its last-minute purchases of distressed claims against Conseco two days after the auction to win standing as a legal creditor.[10]

The executives of a company in bankruptcy court also come under scrutiny. As in the SpectraSite example earlier in the chapter, their compensation must be approved by the judge handling their case. Sometimes, a judge will decide that the salary and benefits paid to executives is too much. Other times, the company may go to the court and seek money from its executives. In January, 2003 then bankrupt retailer Kmart demanded that five executives repay loans not approved by the board, and fired some of the executives who had received the loans. The story, which came from bankruptcy-court documents, was major news for the mass communication outlets covering the case.

It has been argued by some bankruptcy-court experts that the real winners in any filing are the people hired by the company to turn around its performance, and because the money paid these experts can often run into the millions, creditors are hurt. Others argue that without these experts working long hours to salvage what they can from a company in bankruptcy-court protection, creditors, bondholders, and shareholders might not receive anything in return. Carefully toeing the line between these two viewpoints is the job of the journalist. Reporters who can carefully watch a bankruptcy case unfold and document how money is spent go a long way in explaining to their readers this complicated process of reorganization. It is not an easy job, but with some basic understanding of relationships and how the court works, it can be explained in stories that help readers understand how they might be affected.

PERSONAL BANKRUPTCIES

As noted earlier in this chapter, not all bankruptcy-court filings are made by public and private companies. In fact, more than 95% of all proceedings in bankruptcy court involve individuals.

---

[10]From "Detail delay Conseco Finance sale's OK; Judge rejects Berkadia's objection to auction deal; winning bidders stall working out terms," by B. Hornaday, March 8, 2003, *Indianapolis Star,* p. 1C. Copyright 2003 by *Indianapolis Star.* Reprinted with permission.

These are cases that can also be valuable for a business reporter, especially one who is interested in putting a human face on economic conditions in their region. In addition, checking the details of individual bankruptcy-court cases can lead to important facts for stories about businesses.

Tracking the ups and downs of personal bankruptcy filings in a region can help a newspaper document its local economy. If more people are seeking bankruptcy-court protection in a three-month time period than they were the same time a year ago, that is a good indication that people are struggling with their finances. They may have been laid off from jobs and are now unable to pay their credit card bills. Or they may have found a job, but one that pays much less than their previous job.

Most bankruptcy courts keep tallies of how many cases have been filed during quarterly and annual time periods (Fig. 12.2). By asking the clerk for these numbers, a reporter has a good start on a story. The reporter could then look through a few filings and write down names of people who have recently filed for protection. After talking to a few of these debtors or their attorneys, the reporter could likely write a story similar to the following one in the *Indianapolis Star* in January 2003:

Layoffs, overspending and mortgage debt helped drive a 13 percent increase in personal bankruptcy filings in the southern two-thirds of Indiana in 2002, although the size of the jump was less than half of the 28 percent rise in 2001.

The 32,158 filings in the year ending Dec. 31, up from 28,551 in 2001, "is still a huge increase," said Kevin P. Dempsey, U.S. bankruptcy trustee for Indiana and part of Illinois.

"We're at record levels. It is, by far and away, a record level."

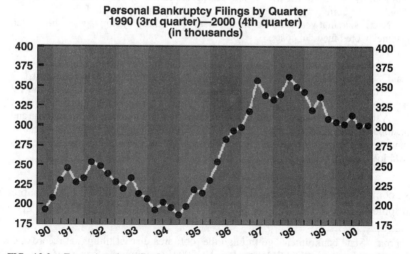

FIG. 12.2. From American Bankruptcy Institute, 2003. Copyright 2003 by American Bankruptcy Institute. Reprinted with permission.

Personal bankruptcy filings in the southern district of Indiana were at twice the national rate during the federal fiscal year that ended Sept. 30: up 15.9 percent versus the U.S. rate of 7.8 percent, according to the Administrative Office of the U.S. Courts.

The southern district, which includes Indianapolis, ranked eighth highest in bankruptcy filings during the fiscal year among 75 federal bankruptcy districts. Northern Indiana filings rose 17.5 percent in the fiscal year, or fourth highest.

"Indiana was at or near the top in percentage increases in 2002," Dempsey said. Bankruptcy experts said last year's increase was fueled by the same problems they saw in 2001, including a rise in layoffs during the sluggish economy.

"Indiana has always been a major manufacturing state, and we have lost so many jobs in the past few years," said Indianapolis bankruptcy attorney Mark Zuckerberg. "I think people have held on as long as they can."

"Usually they have used all the resources they have because nobody wants to file for bankruptcy. By the time I see clients, they have no more money to pay their bills," he said.

Many took advantage of low interest rates to tap an equity line of credit on homes to pay credit-card and other debt. Indiana led the nation last year as the state with the highest home foreclosure rate.

"You can see the (home-equity loan) billboard on the highway right now. No, it's not eliminating your debt. It's just putting your house in jeopardy," said Indianapolis bankruptcy attorney Mike Norris.

Some who rolled credit-card debt into home equity loans lacked discipline and again ran up balances on charge cards.

"Now their credit-card balances are back to what they were, and now they've dug a hole deeper than before," said Paul Ramnarain, vice president of Credit Counselors Corp. in Indianapolis.

"Once the cards are paid off, you better not use them again. That's a trap."

It's not just credit cards that ensnare. Ramnarain sees a proliferation of same-as-cash offers by retailers that delay payments by 90 days or more as another debt bomb. Some of these deals charge interest rates of 20-plus percent if the balance is not paid by the end of the free period. That could turn a $2,000 balance into $2,480, "and you're going to get charged 24 percent on that" going forward.

Norris said that years ago a common theme to bankruptcy filings was a blow such as unexpected medical costs.

Today, the "vast majority" of bankruptcy cases involve credit cards.

"People are making conscious, voluntary choices that really hurt them," Norris said. "It's not a disease that hit them one day. . . . It's greed, lust. Consumer lust."

"The problem our consumers have is they run out and buy a ($10,000) plasma TV and then, a month later, they're short on money and don't make a connection" to why.

A strong economy in the late 1990s followed by a downturn that hurt overtime and crimped budgets in recent years has revealed shortfalls in personal finance education and preparedness, said Rebecca Haynes Bordas, an educator at Purdue University's Marion County extension service.[11]

Like company bankruptcies, consumers file either under Chapter 11 or Chapter 7, and sometimes personal Chapter 11 cases will convert to Chapter 7 cases. Personal

---

[11]From "State bankruptcies go through the roof; area district filings set record and are twice national rate," by C. O'Malley, Jan. 10, 2003, *Indianapolis Star*, p. 1C. Copyright 2003 by *Indianapolis Star*. Reprinted with permission.

cases go through many of the same steps that business filings encounter, including negotiations with creditors. And personal cases are filed at the same place as company filings. Some states have more filings, however (Fig. 12.3).

One major difference is that unlike corporate cases, there are few lenders willing to give consumers financing to help them make it through bankruptcy-court. Bankruptcies can stay on an individual's credit report for up to 10 years.

Personal bankruptcies can also be important sources of information for other stories, particularly stories about companies. Investors who own stock in a company run by an executive who filed for personal bankruptcy in the past would want to know that information.

Households per filing, Rank
During the 12-Month Period Ending June 30, 2002

Region	Households Per Filing	Rank	Region	Households Per Filing	Rank
Nationally	68.9		Missouri	67.3	20
Alabama	42.4	5	Montana	88.4	34
Alaska	165.3	51	Nebraska	88.9	35
Arizona	66.3	19	Nevada	37.1	3
Arkansas	45.1	7	New Hampshire	128.9	48
California	80	27	New Jersey	74.3	23
Colorado	83.5	29	New Mexico	78.8	26
Connecticut	112.3	45	New York	103.4	42
Dist. of Columbia	94.1	37	North Carolina	84.1	31
Delaware	98.4	40	North Dakota	128	47
Florida	68.3	21	Ohio	59.9	15
Georgia	39.8	4	Oklahoma	56.9	11
Hawaii	85.7	32	Oregon	58.5	14
Idaho	54.7	9	Pennsylvania	90.9	36
Illinois	58.5	13	Rhode Island	80.7	28
Indiana	44.7	6	South Carolina	96.3	39
Iowa	101.5	41	South Dakota	109.1	44
Kansas	72.4	22	Tennessee	34.6	2
Kentucky	57.9	12	Texas	96.2	38
Louisiana	62	17	Utah	33.6	1
Maine	115.6	46	Vermont	143.7	50
Maryland	56.3	10	Virginia	63	18
Massachusetts	142.8	49	Washington	60.3	16
Michigan	74.7	24	West Virginia	75.9	25
Minnesota	103.7	43	Wisconsin	88.3	33
Mississippi	46	8	Wyoming	83.7	30

American Bankruptcy Institute
Statistics based on data from the Administrative Office of
The U. S. Courts (2002 bankruptcies) and the U. S. Bureau of
The Census (most recent household figures from 1998)

FIG. 12.3. From American Bankruptcy Institute, 2003. Copyright 2003 by American Bankruptcy Institute. Adapted with permission.

When the *Atlanta Journal-Constitution* asked its retail reporter to investigate the problems at local grocery store chain Harry's Farmers Market Incorporated, one of the steps the reporter took was to run the names of its top executives through the computers at the local bankruptcy court. What the reporter found was that the acting CFO and a vice president of merchandising had been involved in personal bankruptcies.

By reporting these facts, the story used the bankruptcy-court cases to call into question the ability of these executives to run a multimillion dollar public company. If they could not manage their personal finances well enough to avoid bankruptcy court, how would they be able to oversee the spending of millions of dollars on goods and services each week for Harry's?

In some cases, the filing of a personal bankruptcy is the precursor to problems at an executive's company, particularly if it is a private company. Many owners of small and private businesses intermingle their personal finances with their corporate operations. When one or the other—or even both in some cases—start to falter, a bankruptcy-court filing could be looming.

A reporter in rural Hernando County, Florida, discovered just this when a large construction company in the area filed for Chapter 11 protection. The owner of the business had earlier filed a personal bankruptcy case:

> The future of one of Hernando County's most prominent businesses was thrown into doubt Monday when Grubbs Construction Co. filed for Chapter 11 bankruptcy protection.
>
> The company hopes the action will give it enough relief to restore its productivity and pay its creditors. Owner John G. "Gary" Grubbs and his company have accumulated more than $10-million in debts to banks, equipment suppliers, and state and county taxing authorities, according to documents Grubbs has filed in federal bankruptcy court in Tampa.
>
> The debts include a $3-million bank loan secured with his children's trust fund, the court records show.
>
> The documents do not include the names of numerous smaller creditors that will be among the hardest hit if the company fails, said Mike Ebert, owner of Plug Masters sodding company in Spring Hill. Grubbs owes the company about $40,000 for work it did on the Hernando Oaks development, Ebert said.
>
> "I'm not going to see any of it," Ebert said of the debt. "It has put myself, my family and my employees in jeopardy."
>
> Tom Hogan, Grubbs Construction's general counsel, could only assure creditors that Gary Grubbs will try his best to pay them back.
>
> Grubbs "is a very proud person, and he's devastated by the fact that he's hit this obstacle," Hogan said. "But he's going to keep working to try to get past it."
>
> The company's filing on Monday was the most recent in a string of troubles for Grubbs and his company.
>
> • On April 15, the state filed a sales tax lien against Grubbs Construction for $300,000; Grubbs and his company also owe the county about $337,000 in property and intangible taxes, said Hernando County Tax Collector Juanita Sikes.

- On April 23, Grubbs filed for personal bankruptcy protection.
- On Friday, the company closed its asphalt plant north of Brooksville, its largest remaining holding in Hernando County; the company moved last year from its main office in Brooksville to the Sunwest Mine property in Hudson, which the company also owns.

The closing of the asphalt plant is intended to be temporary, Hogan said, and is partly due to a lack of availability of hard rock needed to make asphalt.

But he also said the company's remaining 50 to 60 workers may all be in jeopardy of losing their jobs.

When the company was at its busiest about three years ago, it employed about 300 people, Hogan said. About the same time, its annual revenues peaked at about $60-million, former office manager Kendra Sittig said in an interview late last year.

The company's decline from that crest has been due to both a slowing economy and outstanding debts, Hogan said.

Smith & Company Inc. of Stuart hired Grubbs as the paving contractor for two large jobs in Hernando County.

Smith delayed payment for more than a year on $700,000 it owed Grubbs for paving one stretch of the Suncoast Parkway. Smith still owes Grubbs about $1.2-million for work on the U.S. 41/State Road 50 truck bypass widening project in Brooksville.

In addition, Grubbs has been unable to collect $1.7-million for cleanup work performed in Arkansas after an ice storm in 2001, Hogan said, and has several other smaller outstanding bills that bring its total uncollected assets to about $5-million.

Grubbs recently completed a $2-million project to build the bike path next to the Suncoast Parkway in northern Hernando County and continues to serve as the secondary paving contractor for Hernando County government; it has received $2.3-million for work connected with the county's residential road repaving program so far this fiscal year.[12]

Personal bankruptcy hearings often take up the bulk of a judge's time in court. And although many personal bankruptcy cases are not newsworthy, they do often show the dire financial straits that many people encounter. Sitting in a bankruptcy courtroom for a day will show reporters a side of life they may not have experienced, giving them a broader understanding of how credit cards, loans, and other financial instruments can wreak havoc if not used properly.

GLOSSARY

assets: Generally anything of value, such as property, real estate, cash, notes, stocks, bonds, accounts receivables, securities and any other item of value that could be used to pay off debt.

---

[12]From "Grubbs files for bankruptcy court protection." by D. DeWitt, April 30, 2003, *St. Petersburg Times*, p. 1. Copyright 2003 by *St. Petersburg Times*. Reprinted with permission.

bankruptcy: When a person or firm is unable to repay debts. As a result, the ownership of the firm's assets are transferred from the stockholders to the bondholders.

Chapter 7: A bankruptcy court filing done by businesses and individuals where the assets are liquidated.

Chapter 11: A bankruptcy court filing available to businesses and individuals where the debt is reorganized and some debt is forgiven as part of a plan to rehabilitate the company or person.

Chapter 13: A bankruptcy court filing where a person agrees to repay their debts.

creditor: A person or company owed money from a debtor. The debt occurred before the filing of bankruptcy court protection.

debt: An amount of money owed by a person or a company to another person or company.

debtor: A person or company seeking protection in bankruptcy court from loans and other debts owed.

involuntary bankruptcy: When creditors file a plan to force a debtor into bankruptcy court protection. The debtor can protest and argue before the court.

reorganization: A process designed to revive a financially troubled or bankrupt firm. A reorganization involves the restatement of assets and liabilities, and communication with creditors in order to make arrangements for maintaining repayment.

secured creditor: People or companies owed debt that is backed by collateral, such as a car loan or a home mortgage.

trustee: A court-appointed representative who administers the business or estate. Can be assigned if creditors or others argue that the company is unfit to manage its operations.

unsecured creditor: People or companies owed debt that is not backed by collateral, such as credit cards, medical bills and utility bills.

REFERENCES

(2003, March 5). Conseco in $1 Billion Deal to Sell Unit. Reuters.

(2002, December 18). Conseco promises a swift bankruptcy. Associated Press.

Conseco Incorporated (2002, December 18). Corporate news release.

Cox, J. B. (2003, January 29). Judge OKs stock plan; SpectraSite free to move forward. *The News & Observer.* p. D1.

Cox, J. B. (2003, February11). Chapter 11 done for tower operator: SpectraSite out of bankruptcy. *The News & Observer.* p. D1.

DeWitt, D. (2003, April 30). Grubbs files for bankruptcy protection. *St. Petersburg Times.* p. 1.

Evans, D. (2003, January 17). Wade Cook financial ordered liquidated by judge. Bloomberg News.

Gatlin, G. (2002, January 23). Kmart enters bankruptcy; Retail giant Kmart is bankrupt; No immediate loss seen of any of its 29 Mass. stores. *Boston Herald.* p. 27.

Green, M. (2002, July 30). Oxmoor club hopes to survive bankruptcy. *The Courier-Journal.* p. 1D.

Guzzo, M. Davis, C., & Tascarella, P. (2002, July 12). RedZone files for Chapter 11 reorganization. *Pittsburgh Business Times.* p. 3.

Hornaday, B. (2003, March 8). Details delay Conseco Finance sale's OK; Judge rejects Berkadia's objection to auction deal; winning bidders still working out terms. *Indianapolis Star.* p. 1C.

Jean, S. (2003, March 5). Conseco bidding fierce. *St. Paul Pioneer Press.* p. 1C.

Moore, P. (2002, November 18). Ocean Journey dollars flow to handle bankruptcy fees. *Denver Business Journal.* p. A4.

Nilsen, K. (2003, October 18). ArgoMed garners $3.15M in court. *Triangle Business Journal.* p. 13.

O'Malley, C. (2003, January 10). State bankruptcies go through the roof; area district filings set record and are twice national rate. *The Indianapolis Star.* p. 1C.

Parker, V. L. (2002, December 27). Swifty Serve swiftly split up. *The News & Observer.* p. D2.

Price, D. (2003, Ferbury 6). Midway to get 2 new airplanes, after opposition. *The News & Observer.* p. D1.

(2003, March 20). Rand McNally reorganization approved: Quick exit seen from Chapter 11. Reuters.

St. Onge. J. (2003, February 26). Weil Gotshal Reaps Most Fees on Biggest Corporate Bankruptcies. Bloomberg News.

United Airlines says liquidation possible without labor cuts. (2003, March 18). Associated Press.

Wong, E. (2003, December 10). Airline shock waves: the overview; bankruptcy case is filed by United. *New York Times.* p. A1.

Other Books on Bankruptcy

Baird, D. G. (2002). *Elements of bankruptcy.* (3rd ed.). New York: Foundation Press.

Fusaro, P. C., & Miller, R. (2002). *What went wrong at Enron: Everyone's guide to the largest bankruptcy in U.S. history.* New York: Wiley.

Gilson, S. C. (2001). *Creating value through corporate restructuring: Case studies in bankruptcies, buyouts, and breakups.* Ney York: Wiley.

Roe, M. J. (2000). *Corporate reorganization and bankruptcy: Legal and financial materials.* New York: Foundation Press.

Swartz, M., & Watkins, S. (2003). *Power failure: The inside story of the collapse of Enron.* New York: Doubleday.

SUGGESTED EXERCISES

1. Discuss spending habits as a class discussion. Do your fellow students believe their spending might cause them problems paying debt in the future.

How many credit cards do most students have? Do any of them have car loans?

2. Review an initial bankruptcy petition and write a short story based on the filing, emphasizing the need to list the debtor's assets and debts high up in the story.

3. If a bankruptcy court district is located near your school, attend a hearing one day. During the next class session, discuss what you saw and comment on the relationship between judges, creditors and attorneys.

13

Writing About Real Estate

WHY LAND IS BOUGHT AND SOLD

Every business in this country, and in the world, operates from a central location, often called a headquarters. They have either purchased that land and constructed a building on the property, or leased the property from a real estate company. If their operations become too big, they purchase or lease a building that gives them more space.

Every individual or family is in the same situation. They live somewhere, either in an apartment or a house, either renting or buying. If one thinks about real estate this way—that it is the one necessity for every business and every consumer across the country—then writing about the topic does not seem as boring as it might at first glance. Writing about real estate does not involve just buying and selling homes, or the construction of a new industrial park to attract manufacturers and other businesses to an area. Real estate plays a vitally important role in the business world and in the country's economy.

Real estate transactions can be small deals for less than an acre of land, particularly for residential construction of a new home. Other real estate deals can be extremely large, with the ownership of hundreds of acres being transferred to

327

a developer who plans to turn the land into a giant mall or subdivision. Simply put, real estate is a broad reaching story in business journalism and throughout all reporting.

Retailers need real estate to build their stores. Manufacturers need real estate to build their plants. Farms need real estate to plant their crops and allow their cattle to graze. Trash collectors need real estate to park their trucks and to dump the garbage they collect. Even Internet companies need office space to run their businesses.

Others need real estate as well. Towns and cities need real estate to build parks and schools. State government needs real estate to house its thousands of employees and offices, and to expand public universities and colleges when they outgrow their campuses. Federal government needs real estate for armed forces bases and hundreds of other reasons.

Businesses may also invest in real estate even though real estate is not their primary operation. For example, banks and insurance companies see real estate as an investment that may boost their earnings. Some banks and insurers invested too much in real estate in the late 1980s and early 1990s and suffered when real estate values, particularly the price for office buildings, plummeted.

There are even companies—public and private—the sole business of which is to buy and sell real estate. Their profits come from the rent they collect from apartment complexes and office buildings. The public companies see their stock pricees rise when real estate is in demand and occupancy rates are high and fall when there is a glut of real estate available.

A real estate investment trust, commonly known as a REIT, is a company that owns and operates real estate properties such as office complexes, malls, shopping centers, and apartments. These companies must provide 90% of their taxable income to their shareholders in the form of dividends. There are more than 170 publicly traded REITs with a market capitalization totaling more than $160 billion. There are also private REITs. These companies operate real estate properties in every major metropolitan market.

In addition, there are thousands of other real estate companies that buy and sell commercial real estate. They may only own one piece of real estate. Or they may own hundreds. They may be part of another company.

A commercial real estate transaction is typically reported by disclosing the building being purchased, its significance, the new owner and the seller. A *Chicago Tribune* article on the sale of Aon Center, a so-called "trophy tower" in downtown Chicago, noted that the deal was one of the largest transactions in the city's history. The second paragraph names the buyer and seller and noted that the building had 80 stories. And the third paragraph mentions the price and compares that figure with the original asking price from the seller.

Later, the reporter did some math and told readers the price per square foot of the building. The reporter also tried hard to pinpoint the actual purchase price for the property. In many cases, that price is available in public records that are discussed later in this chapter. But in this instance, the reporter had to rely on industry sources to disclose the price. The price of a real estate transaction is probably the most important fact for any major acquisition, and should be aggressively pursued by the reporter.

Commercial real estate can be divided into several categories. There is the office market, which primarily includes office buildings in which businesses operate. Leasing activity grew in 45 of the 54 metro markets tracked by the National Association of Realtors in the fourth quarter of 2002, the latest statistics available at this time. But the vacancy rate in office buildings rose to 16.7% from 14.5% in the fourth quarter of 2001, and office rents declined by 7.3%. Why did this happen? One answer might be the addition of 25.1 million square ft. in new office space during the quarter. Vacancy rates and average rents can be important barometers for a local commercial real estate economy. Many large brokers have this information.

The warehouse market is another important part of the commercial real estate business. This is where businesses store their finished goods or even unfinished materials, waiting to sell them or ship them to their stores to be sold. The vacancy rate among warehouses grew to 10.4% in the fourth quarter of 2002, up slightly from 10.3% in the last three months of 2001. And warehouse rents declined by an average of 4.3%, according to the National Association of Realtors.

The retail market is also part of commercial real estate. Its vacancy rate was unchanged in the fourth quarter of 2002, standing firm at 12.8%, whereas rental rates increased a half a percentage point. Retail real estate is expected to add 72.6 million square ft. in 2003.

In the residential real estate market, home sales have set records in recent years. There were more than 5.6 million existing homes sold in 2002, up from the previous record of 5.3 million homes sold in 2001, according to the National Association of Realtors. The organization also noted that 2003 was another record-setting year for existing home sales as a result of the drop in mortgage rates. The national median price for an existing home was $158,300 in 2002, up 7.1% from the media of $147,800 in 2001. The increase is the largest since 1980.

Indeed, real estate transactions can be viewed as a key barometer of the economy. If total real estate acquisitions increase, growth in an economy of a region or the country is also likely strong. But if real estate sales slow, then the economy is likely slowing as well. (For more on real estate, particularly new home sales and existing sales, and the economy, see chap. 3.) However, note that residential real estate activity rises and falls with interest rates, which are tied to the Federal Open Market Committee's decisions on where the economy is headed. Reporters should check with a local mortgage lender to find out how rates are moving in their area.

Also understand that residential real estate transactions involve different types of loans. A fixed-rate mortgage is one in which the interest rate remains the same throughout the term of the loan, usually 15 or 30 years. An adjustable-rate mortgage is one in which the interest rate fluctuates on the basis of the Fed's moves, and sometimes other factors. With interest rates near all-time lows in 2001 and 2002, many homeowners refinanced their mortgages to receive better interest rates, thereby paying less interest on their mortgages.

Reporters who follow and report about the activity of real estate in their town, city, county, state, or region of the country can help tell readers and viewers how the economy is performing. If there are large commercial real estate transactions occurring in a specific market, that means business executives believe the market can grow. But if there are large commercial real estate properties for sale for an extended period of time, that could mean buyers of large real estate are betting that the prices will come down and that economic growth could be slowing.

The type of commercial real estate being built or added to a community is also important. Is the new commercial buildings office space for corporate headquarters, or is it for industrial parks where warehouses and manufacturing plants will likely be constructed? The rent paid for office spaces is quite often more than warehouse buildings.

Reporters should also watch for any incentives that a local or state government might be providing for new commercial real estate construction. Often, a government entity will offer tax breaks to entice a business to move to its area and build. This is because the new business means more jobs, which will provide an overall boost to the local economy.

These tax breaks must often be approved by a local government body, such as a city council or county commission. A government reporter may not fully understand the ramifications of the tax break, and may need help from a business reporter who understands real estate.

The following story shows how one of these tax breaks for a new real estate development and its tenant was covered by the *Kansas City Star*:

> A plan to bring HOK Sport Venue Event to the River Market advanced Friday when a city agency approved a trailblazing tax break for the development.
>
> Opus Northwest, the developer of the proposed $40 million mixed-use project, got the full 25-year property tax abatement it wanted from the Planned Industrial Expansion Authority.
>
> "It's a unique project and a great tenant we're working with," said Dave Harrison, Opus' director of real estate development. "We're hopeful this time next year there will be a lot of activity on the site."
>
> It was the first time the expansion authority had approved a 100 percent tax break for a project. It followed the authority's adoption of a policy to cover what it called extraordinary tax abatements.
>
> Opus wants to erect a six-story building at Fourth and Wyandotte streets that would house the 250 employees of HOK and two dozen condominiums on the upper two floors. A public 300-space garage would occupy the lower levels.
>
> Though a final deal has not been reached with HOK, which currently is at 323 W. Eighth St., the architectural firm has signed a letter of intent to occupy 80,000 square feet.
>
> "All is continuing to move forward well," Harrison said, adding that construction could begin late this year or early in 2004.

HOK officials said they hoped to sign a lease soon with Opus.

"We're happy because it means progress," said Richard A. Martin, senior principal and chief administrative officer. "We want to get this resolved and get moving."

Consideration of the proposal had been delayed at the last meeting of the expansion authority because of the unprecedented tax abatement request. The authority previously has limited abatements to 100 percent for 10 years and 50 percent for 15 years.

Board members decided they wanted to adopt policy guidelines to review the Opus request, as well as future requests for full tax abatements. That policy was approved unanimously before the vote on the Opus development.

The new policy is based on a draft economic development policy proposed last winter by the City Planning and Development Department.

The Kansas City Council has delayed consideration of the policy.

Vicki Noteis, city director of planning and development, was on hand for the discussion of the new policy and generally praised it.

"This is a step in the right direction," she said. "It's not perfect, but neither was our draft."

One difference between the authority's new policy and the one advocated by city planners is that the new policy doesn't call for limiting 100 percent tax abatements to projects within the downtown freeway loop.

Noteis said her department continues to believe the downtown loop deserves help beyond that given other areas of the city.

"We feel the need to reserve one or two tools in our arsenal for them," she said.

Noteis said it would dilute the effectiveness of full tax abatements and so-called Super TIF city incentives if they were to be available to nonloop areas, including the River Market, Crossroads and West Bottoms.

In a related matter, board members urged Opus Northwest to cooperate with the developer of another nearby River Market project, River View Central, to help each other meet their parking needs.

The River View proposal calls for the old Adams Transfer Co. building at 228 W. Fourth St. to be converted into office and retail space. The project, however, needs substantial publicly financed parking to proceed.

Ed Drake, the expansion authority chairman, said his agency wants both projects to work together to provide adequate parking.

Jim DeTar, development coordinator for River View, said his firm was working well with Opus. The River View project would need a simpler, less expensive garage if more cars could be accommodated in the Opus development, he said.[1]

This story shows the precedent for the approved tax break. Anytime one of these tax breaks has been approved, reporters should see if other developments have received similar deals. If they have not, then other real estate developers and their tenants might go asking for a similar break.

Residential real estate can also be important for business, particularly developers such as D.R. Horton who build subdivisions. But other businesses are interested in the residential real estate market as well. Some technology companies in the

---

Silicon Valley of California had trouble attracting employees during the 1990s because of the high cost of homes in the area. Businesses want their employees to be able to move into a neighborhood or region with which they are comfortable. They also want housing that fits the price range of workers they are hiring.

Residential real estate can also be important to business in other ways. Downtown retailers like to see apartments, townhouses, condos, and other residential housing built near downtown so that their shops will be visited. Without residents living near their locations, retailers would close.

But real estate is much more than just the buying and selling of property. As rest of this chapter details, the actual transaction is just the end of a long process that started months earlier. Negotiations likely occurred, particularly for commercial space. The buyer or the renter likely reviewed multiple sites. And, along the way, public records were there to record much of the process of a real estate transaction.

REAL ESTATE TRANSACTIONS

The bread and butter of the real estate beat are the multiple transactions that occur each day. If a reporter finds the transactions that will make a difference in his or her community, or that have impact on other pieces of property, and writes stories about them, he or she will provide a service to readers.

Imagine that a developer has been quietly purchasing property in a specific area of town with plans to revitalize the area. He has purchased all of the land for several blocks, except for one property owner who does not want to sell. By following the previous transactions, a reporter knows that this is the one plot of land that the developer does not have. A visit to that property owner could yield an interesting story.

A developer could be purchasing property for other reasons. The *Triangle Business Journal*, researched property records in Raleigh, North Carolina, and discovered that one company owned within blocks of the Exploris museum complex 33 pieces of property valued at about $6.9 million. The owner of that development company was Gordon Smith III, the chairman of Exploris. Smith told the paper that he was hoping that plans to revitalize the area would make the property valuable. He suggested erecting sculptures, housing, and offices in the area.

Big real estate deals can be considered huge scoops for mass communication outlets. Find out about a deal that a competing media outlet has not reported about yet, and they will likely scramble to follow the story the next day.

Steve Cannon, the real estate reporter for *The News & Observer* in Raleigh, competes with the *Triangle Business Journal*, also located in Raleigh, for real estate news. He said that the best sources for him are commercial real estate brokers who know what properties are for sale, what real estate is about to be sold or leased, and who is looking for additional real estate for their operations.

"The brokers are more in contact with news than the developers are," said Cannon (personal communication, May 15, 2003). "The developers have their projects, but that pretty much takes most of their time. The broker is always having people knock on the door asking for space. And then the broker knocks on doors looking for space, but those people may say they do not now have any space because they just gave it to another company. The most important sources are the ones who see that big picture, have the historical context, and can see that every deal is part of a larger pattern, that there were things that came before it and things that it would lead too."

"It's a long process of building up that source list for a little bit more than a year," added Cannon (personal communication, May 15, 2003). "I made a point every week, I would try to meet two new people. I would try to have breakfast or lunch with two new people, whether it was a developer, someone in the banking community, or a broker. And from that, you just work the source list over and over again. You call 25 people a week, which covers things pretty well."

In addition to relying on sources, all real estate transactions are recorded at the county courthouse, typically with the clerk's office. They may not be filed for several days after the transaction, however. But for reporters looking for who bought a piece of property and who sold it, and for how much, there is no better place. Increasingly, some counties have begun putting this information on the Internet.

Unfortunately, real estate transactions are not so simple. Sometimes, a company will purchase a piece of property using another name it has incorporated with the state so that no one will know who is buying the property. It can be hard to track who these buyers actually are. Reporters often need to go to the Secretary of State's office to look at the incorporation filing for the company and review the names of its executives and its mailing address. The mailing address may be the same as a well-known business in the community, and the executives may be the same executives of a better-known company. That is one way a reporter can discover the actual buyer, or at least get a good hint.

The seller of the property may also be an unknown. Sometimes, the name listed as the seller could be an attorney, or another name that is not well known. Again, corporation records can help. Calling the attorney does not hurt either. The reporter should ask him or her whom they represent.

Going to the real estate records may not always be necessary. If the land or building transferring ownership is a major deal, then the buyer or the seller may announce it with a release. Again, the dollar amount changing hands may not always be disclosed. If it is not, get a real estate expert in the community to estimate the price. This can easily be done if the expert knows the square footage of the building or the number of acres and the location of the property. Often, someone from either the buyer or the seller will disclose the amount off the record.

In addition to the selling price, the acreage and the square footage of the building, or the planned building, there are also other important facts that should be in any real estate transaction story. Compare the price per square ft. or per acre of the transaction with other similar transactions in the market. If the buyer is paying more—or less—than recent deals, that could be an indication of where the local real estate market is headed. It could also be a significant sign of how much the purchaser covets the property.

Where the property is located and what its current zoned usage allows are also vital facts for an acquisition. If the buyer is not willing to disclose what they intend to do with the property, then the reporter should keep calling them after the deal closes until they are willing to talk, or regularly check the local zoning commission or planning commission records to see if any proposals for the property have been submitted.

If the buyer is willing to talk about what they are planning to build on the property, they might already have architectural drawings and other specifications for the building such as when construction might begin and be completed. As always, reporters should ask for as much information as they can get.

The beginning of the following story from the *Northglenn-Thornton Sentinel* in Colorado emphasizes what the property being acquired will be used for, how much acreage is being purchased, and how many square ft. of commercial building space will occupy the land:

> The developer of Northglenn's highly successful Marketplace of Northglenn has inked a deal with Thornton to create a regional retail center at Highway 7 and Interstate 25.
>
> Jordon Perlmutter and Co. is acquiring four parcels of land to meld into a 120-acre retail center with an expected 500,000 square feet of commercial space.
>
> Perlmutter's son and business partner, Jay Perlmutter, said the area will be like Park Meadows Mall, with a Highlands-Ranch-size residential area surrounding it.
>
> "This will spawn a whole new economy out there," Perlmutter said.
>
> He pointed out that most of the land surrounding the proposed retail center is owned by major residential developers, and thousands of homes are planned for the area.[2]

Note that the lead of this story also tells readers where the property is located. Also, the story explains what the surrounding property might be used for—to build homes.

If an acquirer is making a lot of acquisitions, then that should be reflected in the story as well. It does not matter if all of the acquisitions are small, they could reflect a trend by the buyer to purchase specific types of property, or to purchase property in a specific area. Reporters should look at the big picture. If the purchaser is making his or her first real estate deal in a market after making lots of deals in other markets, then that should also be a signal that the transaction is part of a strategy.

The following is the beginning of a story that reflects the importance of the acquisition:

> The speed at which Madison County snatched up the Florists' Mutual Insurance Co. building shows how great the need is for office space in downtown Edwardsville, real estate experts said.

---

[2]From "Thornton lands Perlmutter mall," by N. Bachlet Snyder, Dec. 12, 2002, *Northglenn-Thornton Sentinel*, p. 1. Copyright 2002 by *Northglenn-Thornton Sentinel*. Reprinted with permission.

County Board members approved a plan Wednesday to purchase the 32,000-square-foot building at 500 St. Louis Street.

The county will pay $2.23 million and collect rent from the insurance company for about 18 months.

County Administrator Jim Monday said the county made an offer May 17, and the two parties agreed on a purchase price within a week.

The county plans to renovate the building into a criminal courthouse.

Commercial developers said the county got a good deal on the property considering that the market for office space in downtown Edwardsville is hot these days.

There is a lot of demand for space near the public administration buildings, and there is not a lot of new space available," said Phil Polite, president of Amerivest Reality Inc.—a commercial property developer and broker in Edwardsville.

His company is developing the second-story office space in the Manhattan's Restaurant building.

He said the owners just completed their renovations, and they have already leased about 65 percent of the space with other deals in the works.

"Our plan from the beginning was to build space, then advertise for tenants," he said.

"But before we had even hired a contractor, we had two leases in the works."

Polite said he contacted Florists' Mutual two years ago representing a St. Louis firm interested in purchasing a building that size.

But the insurance company was not ready to move.

But Florists' Mutual, led by President and Chief Executive Robert McClellan Jr., signed a deal last year to build a $25 million office park and new headquarters at Illinois Route 143 and Interstate 55.

Before the company put its 30-year-old building on the market, it came knocking at the county's door.

Representatives for the company spoke to County Board members at a buildings committee meeting last fall, Monday said.

County officials looked at purchasing St. John's United Methodist Church on Second Street for a court building but the cost was too high, Monday said.

"It was pretty much public knowledge that we had been talking to people at the church across the street for about five years," Monday said.

Architects who briefly surveyed the Florists' Mutual building said the county could feasibly renovate the structure for courtrooms for about $3 million.

Florists' Mutual said it wanted $2.6 million for the building and the county offered $2 million.

The purchase includes 170 parking spaces, a small house for storage and a fiber-optic cable.

Officials will close the deal by July 15.[3]

This story does an excellent job of explaining the real estate market in this town, the reasons why the purchaser wanted the building, and why the seller was ready to get rid of the property. In addition, note that the last paragraph states when the deal will close, and an earlier paragraph includes the owner's asking price

[3]From "Madison County agrees to purchase Florists' Mutual Insurance building," by H. Ratcliffe, May 22, 2000, *St. Louis Post-Dispath*, p. 1. Copyright 2000 by *St. Louis Post-Dispatch*. Reprinted with permission.

and the purchaser's offer. These are details that add to a story if they can be obtained.

Be on the lookout as well for real estate companies that have been selling property in the past, but are now interested in buying buildings and other real estate. The *Dallas Business Journal* notes such a shift by Crescent Real Estate Equities Company in its February 1, 2002 issue. The company decided to sell properties in Omaha and New Orleans to focus on other markets.

There are other real estate records that might help a reporter follow the industry and its players. Realtors and real estate brokers are licensed and regulated by state laws. In some cases, complaints filed against them may be public record. For reporters who believe that a Realtor or broker may be in trouble, they should check these records. Sometimes the story may not be what the brokers are telling a reporter, but the broker himself.

Other real estate transaction stories may not necessarily involve a purchase or the sale of a property. Many real estate stories are written about new developments. When a new office complex is approved for construction can also be an important development for a local real estate market.

Real estate transactions and developments can seem to be difficult to write about. They are often complex deals. The trick is to write the story in a way that the reader will understand.

"The work that you do to find information can be fairly specialized," said Cannon (personal communication, May 15, 2003). "But the actual writing of the story should not be specialized. It should be important to almost everyone. If it's hard to explain, then maybe I shouldn't be writing it.... sometimes I have guys that tell me stuff about how a lease is put together, and it's important to understand that, but I would never write about it."

ZONING AND PLANNING DEPARTMENTS

Before a building can be sold or leased, and before a home can be bought and sold, local governments typically must first approve the construction plans before dirt is broken and concrete is poured. These government agencies can be a zoning commission or a planning commission. In some areas, they may take on different names as well. Zoning and planning departments at town and city governments can be great places for a real estate reporter to find news. Often, the submission of plans for a new office building or a new subdivision is the first public disclosure by a developer of its intentions for a piece of property. These plans can be interesting stories. They will often disclose how big the building will be in terms of square footage and when the construction might begin.

Zoning commission and planning commission functions differ in many localities. The zoning commission decides on approved uses for land. An owner of a piece of property on a major street that is currently zoned for residential housing may request by application that the zoning be changed to commercial so that he can sell the property to someone interested in building a gas station or convenience store on the property.

Zoning commission meetings are public, and they typically review dozens of zoning applications at each meeting. The applicant often makes a presentation before the zoning board and then the body opens the discussion to allow residents or others to speak. Sometimes, neighbors of the property being rezoned will appear and speak against the proposed rezoning. The zoning commission then votes on the proposal. In many communities, the proposed rezoning then goes before a city council or county commission for final approval.

Planning commissions operate in much the same way. An owner of a piece of property may decide that he or she wants to construct a building on the land. Before he or she can begin construction, an application must be filed with the local planning commission detailing the type of building and how it will be built. If the landowner wants to build a car repair center on a piece of property surrounded by homes, the proposal may meet some resistance. Planning commission meetings are also public hearings where residents and others often attend to speak against proposed developments.

Coverage of zoning and planning authorities is often done by the city desk or government reporters at many media outlets. But these agencies should also be covered by business-related reporters as well because of the development and commercial aspects of most construction.

The zoning application process and the planning application process should be followed from the beginning to end, particularly for large commercial developments that may mean hundreds of new jobs for an area, and new subdivisions that will add hundreds of homes to a community. In some cases, these new developments will be bitterly opposed by homeowners worried about increased traffic congestion, pollution problems to local creeks and rivers, and overcrowded schools. Millions of dollars are often at stake, however. The developer has likely purchased the land with the specific intent of building a development. If the plans are turned down by a local agency, the developer is left owning vacant property that cannot be used for the intended purpose.

The following is the beginning of a front-page story about a major development announced in Louisville, Kentucky, before it was filed with the zoning commission and the planning department. Perhaps the developers were promoting their plans before filing them with the local authorities to let them know they were coming.

The largest piece of privately owned undeveloped property in Louisville, the Oxmoor Farm, would be developed over the next 25 years under a plan unveiled yesterday.

The 450-acre project would contain estate homes, upscale apartments, stores, offices and hotels, attorneys for the farm's heirs said.

The plan would be tied to new roads Mayor Dave Armstrong said he has been working on developing across Oxmoor since he was Jefferson County judge-executive in 1994.

Armstrong called the plan "about the best compromise possible. . . . It will be a wonderful and spectacular campus that will blend green space with progress."

About one-third of the land would be protected from development, including the old Bullitt estate and land along two forks of Beargrass Creek and around a small cemetery.

The preliminary plan for 450 acres of the farm includes:

- A string of about 10 office buildings, most four to six stories, along both sides of Interstate 64.
- A retail area with at least four buildings, each housing several stores, behind Oxmoor Center and serving as an expansion of the mall.
- A string of expensive homes on large lots and a retirement center on the east side of the farm, serving as a buffer for estate homes in nearby Hurstbourne and Oxmoor Woods.
- A large 'commons' in the center of the development, with hundreds of apartments, dozens of small retailers, walking paths, an athletic club and potentially a hotel and conference center.

Officials with the William Marshall Bullitt and Thomas Bullitt trusts, which own the farm, plan to begin discussing the farm's development next week with the Louisville-Jefferson County Planning Commission and to file a rezoning application in about a month.

Because of the project's scope, the commission might need several months to sort out the regulatory issues, said Rick Northern, an attorney for the farm's heirs. The full commission might hear the rezoning case next spring, the trusts' attorneys said.

The board of Aldermen will decide on the rezoning of 405 acres on the farm. Jefferson Fiscal Court would have final say on the rezoning of 45 acres of unincorporated county land.

For now, the entire development plan is conceptual, Northern said. The Planning Commission will be asked to approve a general district development plan. Specific development will proceed as the roads are built and the market demands, Northern said.[4]

Approval of this project is months away. And yet the developer has the local mayor on board. In many cases, zoning and planning requests can be political. Sometimes, politicians want to be known as the ones who approved a great development for the community. They can also use the zoning and planning approval process to force a developer to make other changes, such as improving paved roads in the area or adding sidewalks from a development to another area.

Some communities may have additional review boards for construction projects. There may be design review boards that ensure that the new construction is built with a façade that blends in with the rest of the buildings in the area.

The zoning and planning approval process sometimes can hit snags. The body may ask for more information from the developer on the project. Or it may ask

---

[4]From "Development of Oxmoor Farm proposed; plan calls for stores," by S. Shafer and B. Pike, Oct. 13, 2001, *Louisville Courier-Journal*, p. 1A. Copyright 2001 by *Louisville Courier-Journal*. Reprinted with permission.

for a delay in the hearing to give the developer time to make changes in their proposal to satisfy concerns. If the zoning commission or planning authority delays a vote on a major project, there is usually a reason why. Reporters can find out by talking to the commission members, the developer, and opponents of the project.

Crain's Detroit Business reported in its November 4, 2002 edition that the Ann Arbor Planning Commission tabled two residential developments because of concerns about providing affordable housing. The story was based on information from the city planner, the director of the planning department, and an independent real estate broker.

Some local media outlets report all zoning and planning commission decisions, much the same way that they report all real estate transactions and all building permits. The final approval of a development could also be news because it signals government approval. The stories are also important to readers because they may foretell that jobs are coming to the local economy, or that a major construction project is about to begin on a road they use for travel that they now may want to avoid.

The following is a story about a residential development that was approved that includes the significance for residents in the area—a connector road:

Preliminary plans for the Smokey Row Estates subdivision have been approved, along with a controversial road that would connect Smokey Row with the Water's Edge development.

The Johnson County Department of Planning and Zoning gave the go-ahead for the 76-lot, 38-acre subdivision to be located 2,000 feet east of Morgantown Road along Smokey Row Road.

The location is adjacent to the south side of Water's Edge in White River Township.

Next up for the subdivision—being developed by the Nichols Group LLC, of Scottsdale, Ariz.—is a review by the County Commissioners.

Water's Edge residents have spoken against the connecting street, fearing it would become a shortcut for rush-hour motorists who want to avoid a four-way stop at Morgantown and Smokey Row roads.

Part of the planning department's approval requires a stop sign to be added along the street, which will be called Streamside Drive. The stop sign would be placed one lot south of Water's Edge, according to county planner Joanna Myers.

Water's Edge abuts the northern boundary of Smokey Row Estates. The main entrance to Water's Edge is off of Morgantown Road.

Water's Edge residents had been successful on another front. On June 3, County Commissioners rejected a request by the Nichols Group to rezone 38 acres for Smokey Row Estates from R-1 to R-2.

If that request had been granted, 83 homes could have been built on the 38 acres. Plans call for two units per acre, or 76 lots on 38 acres.[5]

---

[5]From "Planners give approval for Smokey Row Estates," by J. Thomas, June 26, 2002, *The Indianapolis Star*, p. 15. Copyright 2002 by *The Indianapolis Star*. Reprinted with permission.

Residents of neighborhoods next to proposed developments will virtually always come to a zoning or planning commission meeting and voice their opposition to a construction project. Many times they have valid complaints, such as increased traffic and overcrowded schools, but other times they just do not want more homes built around their area. Other groups such as environmental organizations may also attend these meetings and voice opposition.

Zoning and planning departments can also be good sources of information for the building permits they issue. A building permit is required for any new construction, demolition, remodeling, expansion, or repair to a building. Most city and county governments require that a permit be obtained before the work begins. Without the permit, the contractor and the building owner could face fines.

Building permits ensure that the construction will be done in a safe manner and that the structure will not collapse the next time a strong wind comes through town.

Watching building permit activity can show a reporter the activity of the local real estate industry. If the number of building permits is increasing in a specific area, then that is an indication that the local economy is growing. If the number of building permits is declining, then maybe the economy is slowing.

Often, a local zoning or planning department will have statistics on building permits for an area. Reporters should check these numbers regularly to see if they are showing any trends in construction that may be newsworthy. The following shows how one newspaper noted the fluctuation in permits:

Contractors slammed the brakes on commercial construction last year amid a slow-down that has office, warehouse and apartment vacancies at record levels.

In Wake County, where the Triangle's commercial construction is concentrated, the value of commercial building permits dropped to $210.6 million in 2002, down 61 percent compared with 2001. The decline was even more dramatic in Raleigh, where building permits for new commercial construction declined 74 percent to $102.8 million, according to the Wake County tax assessor.

"Except for college and institutional work...we've seen a slowdown in every sector of the market," said Scott Cutler, vice president of marketing for Clancy & Theys Construction Co. in Raleigh, the Triangle's biggest construction company.

"With the broader economy [slowdown] and the tech meltdown, the office market has evaporated, and every other segment has been hit," Cutler said. "Travel and tourism and hotels aren't booming."

Municipalities and the counties don't break down types of commercial projects on the permits. But office and retail construction sectors have been hit particularly hard by the economic slump and a shaky recovery in which businesses are reluctant to add jobs and merchants slow to open new stores. Warehouse construction has ground to a halt.

Commercial construction hasn't fallen as sharply in Durham County, but building permit totals still declined 14 percent to $141.1 million last year, compared with 2001. Together, commercial construction for Wake and Durham counties in 2002 was down 70 percent from the $1.2 billion total value of permits recorded in 2000.

New home construction, which has been bolstered by some of the lowest mortgage rates in decades, also declined in the two counties.

The total value of building permits for new homes in Wake was down 1.3 percent to $1.29 billion last year, compared with permits in 2001. Permits were issued for 9,214 homes last year, compared with 9,467 the year before.

The value of new home permits in Durham County declined 8.5 percent from 2001 to $317 million in 2002. Permits were issued for 2,762 new homes in 2002 compared with 3,643 homes a year earlier.[6]

Although most real estate reporters focus on the commercial side of the business because deals there are often huge, trends in residential construction can be just as important to a local community.

PROPERTY DEEDS

Property deeds can be helpful to reporters working on a variety of stories. They show who actually owns a piece of property.

A deed is a legal document conveying the title, or ownership, of a piece of property. It contains a legal description of the property being acquired. If there is an error in the legal description, the purchaser may have trouble selling the property later. The deed should also spell the name of the buyer and the seller correctly. If a name is misspelled, this could also cause problems when the property is later sold.

Deeds, like most real estate documents, are public records typically filed with the county recorder. In addition, other documents recorded include mortgages and liens against a piece of property. Each time a property owner refinances a mortgage, a new public record is created.

The availability of property deeds and other real estate records allows reporters to trace the history of a piece of real estate, tracking previous owners and how much a piece of property is worth. Reporters have used deeds to find out other information as well, noted the *News & Observer's* Cannon.

"There was a property right in downtown on Fayetteville Street mall," said Cannon (personal communication, May 15, 2003). "The people who had the building didn't own the land, they were leasing the land, and wouldn't tell me anything about it. But the land lease was filed with the county, and I was able to see how much they were paying for it and how much longer the lease was going to last."

Deeds can be important documents, especially for the lender of the money that allowed that the purchaser to acquire the piece of real estate, whether it was a huge office complex of a single-story ranch home. If the owner falls behind in making

---

[6]From "Drop in building permits tells story of decline," by D. Price, February 5,2 2003, *The News & Observer*, p. D1. Copyright 2003 by *The News & Observer*. Reprinted with permission.

loan payments or stops making these payments, then the lender may foreclose on the property. To do that, the lender may foreclose on the property, taking ownership—and receiving the deed to the property—and reselling the property to help pay the loan.

When a property owner stops making payments on its loan, or falls behind in those payments, they are considered in default of the loan. Although many real estate loans that go into default do not lead to foreclosures, a default is usually the first step in the process. Real estate lenders such as banks and commercial finance companies will often disclose the default rate for their loan portfolio. If the defaults are increasing, then the lender may have made a number of bad real estate loans.

A deed can be transferred from the real estate developer to the lender without a foreclosure as well. The developer may run into financial difficulties and simply transfer the ownership to the lender as a way of satisfying the loans. Many lenders are not in the business of managing real estate properties, so when a deed is transferred to a lender, it is often a major development.

Sallye Salter, a former real estate reporter for the *Atlanta Journal-Constitution*, uncovered such a case by reading the deed documents related to Peachtree Center, a downtown complex created by developer John C. Portman Jr. She discovered that the ownership of much of the development had been turned over to two insurance companies who were Portman's lenders. The transfer was recorded in deed documents.

In addition, the deed documents can be valuable tools for other reasons; a *Tampa Tribune* reporter used them to determine who actually owned the home of a former corporate executive:

Corporate raider Paul Bilzerian's trophy mansion in north Hillsborough County is for sale, but he may never see the money.

A federal judge ordered Tuesday that the proceeds of any sale should be frozen until he rules on a contempt hearing against the convicted former chairman of Singer Co. in March.

U.S. District Court Judge Stanley Harris cited Bilzerian's "initial lack of candor" regarding sale of the home as one of the reasons for his order. Bilzerian couldn't be reached Thursday.

No one has made an offer on the 36,000-square-foot home yet, said Bob Glaser, president of Smith & Associates Investment Co. Realtors in Tampa.

"We're still marketing the property," Glaser said.

The 11-bedroom home, considered the largest in the Bay area, is appraised at $3.4 million by the Hillsborough County Property Appraiser.

Bilzerian, in bankruptcy since 1991, was convicted of securities fraud in 1989 for failing to properly report stock transactions. The Securities and Exchange Commission fined Bilzerian and now claims $33 million in fines, plus $29 million in interest.

The SEC asked the judge to hold Bilzerian in contempt for failing to pay the fine and report assets like the Tampa home that could be sold to pay it.

SEC officials discovered Bilzerian's Avila home was for sale when they saw it advertised without a price in January's edition of Unique Homes, an upscale home magazine distributed to wealthy prospective home buyers.

"We want him to give a full accounting," said Judith Starr, SEC assistant chief litigation counsel in Washington.

In court filings, Bilzerian has denied he owns the home.

He transferred ownership to a limited partnership in March 1997, but Starr said there is evidence Bilzerian controls the partnership. The partnership's business address is the same as Bilzerian's home, the deed shows.[7]

The *Fulton County Daily Report*, a daily newspaper in Atlanta that tracks the legal and real estate community, was able to search deed records to show that 8% of foreclosures in the area were connected to one developer. Their research and understanding of deeds showed that the developer acquired real estate by assuming the mortgages of the developers who owned them or by purchasing blocks of condos in the same development. Their survey of deed records suggested that the developer secured the funding to pay for the properties by first selling them. But the sales were a sham, according to lawsuits. Deed records show that the mortgages were for higher interest rates than the going market, and that the developer arranged to have the mortgages refinanced at lower rates even before the transactions closed, and pocketed the proceeds from the transactions.

All of the details of these transactions were laid out for the reporters to uncover through the deed records and other public real estate records. It took them some digging, but resulted in a story that shook the local real estate community. (The story also noted that the developer's $5.1 million home was being foreclosed.)

Properties can also be foreclosed by the government if the owner has not paid taxes on the real estate. This can result in a new owner. Public foreclosures such as this are commonly advertised in advance to drum up interest from potential buyers in acquiring the property.

Checking deeds should be the backbone of the work done by any real estate reporter. Quite often, the trip to the local courthouse will not yield a story. But regularly reviewing deeds for commercial and residential real estate transactions will keep the reporter in touch with the market. By tracking the deed activity and looking for trends, the reporter will be able to give his readers insight into a real estate market that another reporter ignoring the deeds might not be able to offer.

Tracking deeds also gives the reporter plenty of examples to pick from to use as anecdotes for stories about residential and commercial real estate. By looking at the deeds on a regular basis, the reporter is able to use these transactions to illustrate broader trends. To be sure, reading real estate deeds is boring work. But it is also the best way to learn about real estate transactions. And reporters will show sources that they are serious about the industry when they call brokers or developers and mention their latest deed filing.

---

[7]From "Court sews up mansion proceeds," by J. Gruss, February 18, 1999, *The Tampa Tribune*, p. 1. Copyright 1999 by *The Tampa Tribune*. Reprinted with permission.

TAX ASSESSMENTS

Another important place to find real estate information is with the local tax assessor's office. The tax assessor is charged with assessing the value of property throughout their jurisdiction for tax purposes. Those taxes are then collected from the property owners, and the money is used to pay for government services to the community such as schools, law enforcement, hospitals, road building and maintenance, and parks. The assessed value of a property is a public record available from the tax assessor's office. Increasingly, property values are made available online through searchable databases.

Some property may be exempt from paying taxes. If that is the case, a reporter should find out why, particularly if the property is being used for a commercial purpose.

The tax assessor's office does not set the tax rate. That is typically done by a county commission or city council. What the tax assessor does is visit the property and estimate the amount for which the property might be sold in a transaction. Owners can contest the assessed value of their property if they believe it is too high.

Typically business and industrial property is assessed at a higher rate than residential real estate. Often, the property is being used for business reasons that make it more valuable than a home. A $150,000 home may be assessed at 8%, meaning the tax bill would be $12,000. But a business building appraised at the same value may be assessed at 15%, making its tax bill $22,500.

The assessed value of a piece of property can become an important fact in a real estate story, and it should be looked up for virtually every major transaction. If a purchaser is acquiring a piece of property for $2 million, but the local tax assessor's office only values the property at $1.5 million, then what made the acquirer pay 33% more than the appraised value? The same question can be asked of the seller if they are unloading a piece of property for less than its appraised value. Why are they selling it for the lowball price? Of course, not every property will sell for the assessed value, and a sale price slightly above or below the tax assessor's valuation is not likely to warrant a mention. But how much people pay for property is important because that tells how they value it.

In addition, whether the taxes on a piece of property are being paid can often become an interesting development, as the following story reported:

> The West Allegheny School District and Allegheny County are embroiled in a dispute over the taxes owed on the Hyatt Regency Hotel property at Pittsburgh International Airport.
>
> The school district has filed a lawsuit against the county in Common Pleas Court seeking to collect $791,777 in real estate taxes it says are owed on the property for 2000 and 2001.
>
> But the county, which owns the land on which the hotel sits, says it doesn't owe the district anything.

The Dauphin County Municipal Authority built the hotel and leases the land from Allegheny County. In 1998, the authority, Allegheny County, Findlay Township and the school district all agreed that the land would not be subject to property taxation. Instead, the parties agreed that the municipal authority would make annual payments of $460,000 to be divided between the county, the township and the district.

But the next step of making such a deal legal never took place, according to West Allegheny Solicitor Ira Weiss. He said the parties would have had to declare the property tax exempt in order for that to work.

Besides that, the $460,000 payments that were supposed to be made instead of taxes weren't made anyway.

In a letter sent to the county last spring, Thomas Smida, solicitor for the Dauphin County General Authority, said there were "insufficient funds" available to make the payment. He said the authority lost an estimated $1.4 million to $3.1 million in income operating the hotel last year.

But that doesn't matter to Weiss.

An agreement for payments in lieu of taxes "without the exempt status is a nullity," he said. "The county never took the step it needed to take to get the property declared exempt. The school district believes it is owed this money."

On the county's real estate Web site, the hotel is listed as taxable with an assessed value of $23.8 million.

Weiss said the school district is obligated under law to collect taxes on properties listed as taxable, regardless of the agreement for payments in lieu of taxes.

Assistant County Solicitor Craig Stephens said he does not know why an application never was filed with the Office of Property Assessment to get the exemption. Weiss was not impressed by the county's claim that the district should be going after the Dauphin County authority. He said county assessment records list the county as the legal owner of the property.

Stephens said, however, that under the county's lease agreement with the Dauphin County authority, the authority is obligated to pay any real estate taxes owed on the property. He said the county intends to bring in the authority as a defendant in the lawsuit.

"The county's not on the hook for these taxes," he said.

The various claims will have to be sorted out by a judge. A hearing is scheduled for Dec. 11.

Weiss said the district is willing to honor the agreement for payments in lieu of taxes once the property is declared exempt. But that doesn't mean the county or the Dauphin County authority will be forgiven for the taxes currently owed. Weiss said any exemption cannot be made retroactive under law.[8]

As this story and others in this chapter illustrate, writing about real estate requires becoming familiar with government records and how local regulatory authorities oversee real estate developments and transactions. It can be argued that nowhere else in business journalism does a reporter have to become as knowledgeable about the inner workings of local government than in real estate. Some real

---

[8]From "Dispute arises over taxes on airport hotel," by M. Belko, Oct. 18, 2002, *Pittsburgh Post-Gazette*, p. C-14. Copyright 2002 by *Pittsburgh Post-Gazette*. Reprinted with permission.

estate reporters might gain more expertise in this area than the reporter covering city hall or the county commission.

GLOSSARY

assessed value: The value of the property as determined by the county tax assessor for tax purposes.

broker: A Realtor who puts together a buyer and a seller for a real estate transaction. Brokers often specialize in commercial real estate transactions.

building permit: An approval by a local government allowing a contractor to construct, expand or demolish an existing structure.

deed: A legal document conveying title to a piece of property. It transfers ownership from one owner to another.

default: When the owner of a piece of property falls behind in making payments on the loan used to acquire the property, or stops making payments altogether.

foreclosure: A court proceeding where the property owner's rights are terminated in order to sell the property to satisfy lenders.

lease: An agreement where the owner of a piece of property agrees to allow another party to inhabit the property for a specified period of time.

lender: A financial institution that has financed the loan allowing a buyer to purchase a piece of property.

real estate broker: An agent who buys and sells real estate on a commission basis. The broker does not have title to the property, but generally represents the owner or the buyer.

zoning: A legal mechanism to regulate the use of real estate. All privately owned land within a jurisdiction is placed within designated zones that limit the type and intensity of development permitted.

REFERENCES

Bailey, L. (2002, November 4). Affordable-housing request delays 2 Ann Arbor projects. *Crain's Detroit Business.* p.17.

Belko, M. (2002, October 18). Dispute arises over taxes on airport hotel. *Pittsburgh Post-Gazette.* p. C-14.

Collison, K. (2003, June 21). Tax break passed for HOK relocation; Architecture firm would move to site in River Market. *Kansas City Star.* p. C1.

Corfman, T. (2003, May10). Aon Center brings $465 million price; Atlanta firm pays less than expected. *Chicago Tribune.* p. C 2.

Gruss, J. (1999, February 19). Court sews up mansion proceeds. *Tampa Tribune.* p. 1.

Nilsen, K. (2003, June 30). Firm called Wood Pile owns 33 properties near museum. *Triangle Business Journal.* p. 1.

Perez, C. (2002, February 1). Crescent is "done selling," ready to spend. *Dallas Business Journal.* p. 10.

Price, D. (2003, February 5). Drop in building permits tells story of decline. *The News & Observer.* p. D1.

Ratcliffe, H. (2000, May 22). Madison County agrees to purchase Florists' Mutual insurance building; Site in downtown Edwardsville will serve as courthouse; price tag is $2.33 million. *St. Louis Post-Dispatch.* p. 1.

Renaud, T., McDonald, R. R., & Ramos, R. (2002, May 16). Deals send $75 million in properties to foreclosure. *Fulton County Daily Report.* pp. 1,3,4,7.

Salter, S. (1995, April 14). Two lenders get more Portman holdings; Downtown complex: Much of Peachtree Center has been transferred to new owners to meet debt agreements. *Atlanta Journal-Constitution.* p. 1E.

Shafer, S. S., & Pike, B. (2001, October 13). Development of Oxmoor Farm proposed; plan calls for stores. *The Louisville Courier-Journal.* p. 1A.

Bachlet Snyder, N. (2002, December 12). Thornton lands Perlmutter mall. *Northglenn-Thornton Sentinel.* p. 1.

Thomas, J. (2002, June 26). Planners give approval for Smokey Row Estates. *The Indianapolis Star.* p. 15.

Other Books About Real Estate

O'Donnell, J. R., Rutherford, J., & Towle, P. (1991). *Trumped!: The inside story of the real Donald Trump—His cunning rise and spectacular fall.* New York: Simon & Schuster.

Pacelle, M. (2002). *Empire: A tale of obsession, betrayal, and the battle for an American icon.* New York: Wiley.

Schachtman, T. (1991). *Skyscraper dreams: The great real estate dynasties of New York.* New York: Little Brown & Co.

Sobel, R. (1990). *Trammell Crow, master builder: The story of Americas largest real estate empire.* New York: Wiley.

Tauranac, J. (1995). *The Empire State Building: The making of a landmark.* New York: Scribner.

SUGGESTED EXERCISES

1. Find the real estate records of the home of one of your professors or the dean of your school. In some counties, these records may be available on the Internet, so look there first. Write down how much the home was purchased for and what year. Also look for the appraised value of the home. What is the difference between the appraised value of the home and the purchase price?

2. Check local real estate records to see if your university has made any acquisitions recently. If you find some, has the university disclosed what it plans to do with the property? Who sold the property to the university? Did this person have any prior connection to the university?

3. Find out when the local city or county government will hold its next fore-closure auction for properties where taxes have not been paid. Attend the auction. What types of property was sold? Was it primarily commercial property or residential property? See if you can talk to some of the buyers. Who are they, and what was their interest in the property?

4. Attend a meeting of the local zoning commission or planning board, and write a 500-word report on the types of properties that went before the council that evening, noting whether there was any opposition to the developments and whether they were approved or not. If some requests were voted down, what were the reasons against the project?

14

State and Federal
Regulatory Agencies

AGENCIES THAT REGULATE AND WHERE THEIR POWERS ARE DERIVED

Throughout many of the earlier chapters, the SEC and its powers in regulating businesses and stocks are discussed, particularly how those regulations can help business journalists do their job in informing the public.

But there are plenty of other federal regulatory agencies that also have a hand in overseeing businesses and corporations. And state and local government bodies are also involved in ensuring that Corporate America does not run afoul.

Business regulation is the passing of rules, procedures and laws to govern business and industry. Although many business executives might argue that regulation limits their ability to produce a profit, the laws and rules do serve a purpose. Most laws and regulations governing businesses are enacted to protect other businesses, consumers, employees, and competitors.

Business regulation has not been around that long in the United States. Most laws governing the business world were not enacted until the 19th century, long after proprietors set up shop and began selling their goods and services to consumers. In fact, it took the misdeeds of some major businesses to lead lawmakers into creating rules and restrictions on companies. Even world-wide government organizations now play a part in overseeing how businesses operate.

U.S. government regulation of business developed with the Industrial Revolution in the late 19th century. As some businesses became bigger and bigger, other businesses wanted protection so that their rights would be covered. In addition, regulation also came about because some companies misused their power. They neglected the working conditions of their employees and attempted to break unions. Some businesses physically harmed and killed their workers.

State politicians tried to regulate businesses, but they were limited in what could be done. States could only pass laws regulating businesses that operated within their borders.

Before the 1880s, the federal government played a minor role in American business. The first major legislation regulating business was the creation of the Interstate Commerce Commission in 1877. The commission regulated the railroad industry, then the major transportation mode for goods across the country.

With the passage of the Sherman Antitrust Act in 1890, federal authorities took a major step in regulating business. The law prohibited large trusts of businesses. The law initially had little effect, as the Supreme Court prevented its usage by regulators. But by the turn of the century, the government won out. In 1904, it was allowed to break up Northern Securities Company, and in 1911 the Supreme Court sided with the federal government in its breakup of Standard Oil Company and American Tobacco Company.

Small businesses wanted protections against larger competitors who were squeezing them out by underpricing them. And consumers wanted protection from monopolistic operations raising prices. Not surprisingly, large business opposed this legislation.

Since then, more legislation has been passed at the federal level giving the government more powers. In 1914, Congress created the Federal Trade Commission when it passed the Clayton Antitrust Act, which amended the Sherman legislation by outlawing predatory pricing and making illegal other business tactics.

Other regulators also sprung up. Although the Food and Drug Administration traces its roots back to a single chemist in the Department of Agriculture in 1862, the Federal Foods and Drug Act in 1906 gave it regulatory authority. This act was spurred by Upton Sinclair's *The Jungle*, an account of workers in an unsanitary meat packing plant.

Franklin D. Roosevelt's presidency saw another flurry of legislation creating laws governing business. Sparked by the October 1929 crash that led to the Great Depression, Congress created the SEC to oversee the stock markets and public companies. The Communications Act of 1934 established the Federal Communications Commission to regulate radio and television industries. And Congress created the Federal Deposit Insurance Corporation around the same time to stabilize the country's banking industry.

The Wagner Act of 1935 created the National Labor Relations Board, which prevented companies from interfering with the rights of workers to organize into unions and to investigate complaints of unfair labor practices. The law also allowed the board to issue cease and desist orders against companies.

Other regulatory bodies have been added throughout the decades. The Department of Transportation was not created until the 1960s, although some of its units have longer histories. The Occupational Safety and Health Act passed in 1970, giving the federal government the authority to set and enforce workplace safety and health standards.

The 1970s, however, saw the beginning of a period of deregulation by the federal government. In 1978, Congress passed the Airline Deregulation Act, which meant that the market would set prices for airline tickets, not the government. Opposed by the industry, the legislation led to a number of new airlines, and a number of airline company failures.

Federal regulation, however, is still alive and well. In 1984, the antitrust laws were successfully used to force the breakup of AT&T just as they had been used 70 years earlier in Standard Oil and American Tobacco. And the Federal Trade Commission took on reviewing all mergers and acquisitions in the late 1970s.

State and local government agencies have also had a hand in regulating business for more than a century. States, for example, began regulating utilities near the beginning of the 20th century. The Oregon Public Utility Commission, for example, began as the State Board of Railroad Commissioners in 1887, but was abolished and then recreated as the Railroad Commission of Oregon in 1907. Four years later, its jurisdiction was expanded to include utilities.

Across the country, public service commissions and public utility commissions oversee how much electrical companies, water companies, and other utilities charge their customers. They also often set limits on how much of a profit these companies can make. Sometimes, these companies can get in trouble with the regulatory agencies that oversee their business. A utility in North Carolina was found to have made too much money recently, causing the *Charlotte Observer* to write one front-page story that began the following way:

Federal investigators will review thousands of additional documents in a deeper probe of Duke Power's accounting than the one Carolinas regulators conducted last year, sources close to the investigation say.

Federal prosecutors and FBI agents will scour more than 40,000 documents, including a controversial spreadsheet unearthed during the states' investigation, as they evaluate whether Duke intentionally and inappropriately altered its accounting and committed any crimes, according to sources.

After a 10-month investigation last year, independent auditing firm Grant Thornton LLP said Duke underreported $124 million in regulated profits over three years. Duke changed its accounting methods to fall under the profit margin mandated by regulators, the firm said.

When Duke goes over its allowed limit, utility commissioners can lower the power bills for Duke's 2.1 million Carolinas customers.

Duke says it made unintentional, one-time errors but committed no crime. Duke Power, the Carolinas' largest utility, is a subsidiary of Charlotte-based Duke Energy Corp., which is No. 118 on the Fortune 500 with $15.2 billion in revenue last year.

Federal investigators began their probe after The Observer published stories in October about Grant Thornton's allegations of Duke wrongdoing. In February, Duke announced it had received a grand jury subpoena requesting documents related to the Grant Thornton audit.

Days before receiving the subpoena, Duke hired former U.S. Attorney Mark Calloway to represent the corporation. The company also helped assemble A-list criminal defense lawyers for more than a dozen employees. Companies and their employees typically hire lawyers when they learn they're under investigation.[1]

The story later quotes the executive director of the South Carolina Public Service Commission saying that documents he reviewed convinced him there was an obvious effort to underreport profits.

States also play a major role in regulating other industries, such as banking and insurance. Unlike most industries that are regulated by the federal government, regulation of the insurance industry is done on a state-by-state basis. Each state has its own insurance commissioner who regulates the companies doing business in that state. Some states, such as New York, have laws governing insurance companies that are more strict than other states, forcing some insurers to create separate subsidiaries to do business there or to eschew the state altogether. States also require each and every business that operates in its territory to register with the state. This information can be valuable, and is discussed later in this chapter.

Last, some counties, cities, and towns also have laws and rules that businesses must follow. Developers, for example, must get plans to build a new subdivision approved by a town council or a city commission before they can start bulldozing. Expanding a building to handle the growth of a business also takes a permit.

All of the rules, laws, regulations, and other requirements that government agencies require of businesses attempt to balance the interest of the public with the need of a business to grow, expand, and continue to be a thriving part of the community. Sometimes, a government entity will even try to get legislation passed that will bring new business into the area, or improve the quality of existing businesses.

The following excerpt is an example of the beginning of a business story that comes from following bills introduced in a state Legislature to change how businesses would operate:

North Carolina businesses that improve workplace safety could be rewarded with a tax break if Labor Commissioner Cherie Berry has her way.

---

[1]From "Fed deepens Duke probe" by S. Choe and G. L. Wright, May 11, 2003, *The Charlotte Observer*, p. 1A. Copyright 2003 by *The Charlotte Observer*. Reprinted with permission.

Berry is pushing for bills that have been introduced in the House and Senate that would give tax credits to companies that voluntarily improve safety in factories, offices, stores and construction sites where several million North Carolinians spend their working hours.

The idea, Berry said Tuesday, is to reach smaller employers that don't have a safety director on board or fear that by asking the labor department for help they might be forced to make improvements they can't afford.

"We're trying in this business climate to do as much as we can to promote safety and health and reward businesses that take that step," she said. "It shows that we're trying to reach out, rather than, as in the past, just go out and enforce with that big hammer and club."

Voluntary compliance has been a mission of Berry's since she took office two years ago. One of her first moves was to roll back ergonomics rules that her predecessor, Harry Payne, had sought to make businesses pay closer attention to repetitive stress injuries. Her agency has worked with employers to help them reduce such injuries, reporting strong results in certain cases.

But some question the fairness of the tax credit bills, as well as the timing of such legislation during a budget crisis.

"You don't want to create a system where companies that have already invested in safety get nothing," said John Hood, president of the John Locke Foundation, a conservative think tank in Raleigh. "And now that they're coming in after the law is passed, they get money. The impulse here is commendable, but I would be hesitant to go into the tax code to find a tool to pursue policies other than raising revenue."

The bills, HB 919 and SB 680, are before the House and Senate finance committees. They have not been placed on the calendar for consideration by state lawmakers.

Sen. David Hoyle, a Gastonia Democrat who sponsored the Senate version and leads the Senate Finance Committee, said the proposal has a "great chance" of becoming law this session, though it would deprive the state of revenue.

"We're $400 million in the hole, so what's a couple of hundred thousand?" he said. "We're not talking about a lot of money."

But it's unclear what the cost of the program would be, labor department officials acknowledge. That would depend on how many businesses ask for the agency's assistance in identifying safety problems and what it would cost to get such employers up to code.

North Carolina is believed to be the first state to consider a safety tax credit. But the idea has sparked interest at the U.S. Department of Labor, which is contemplating a national version of the program, said John Johnson, state deputy commissioner for occupational safety and health.[2]

In addition, many states have recently become aggressive in prosecuting companies for wrongdoing, with New York Attorney General Eliot Spitzer being a prime example of a regulator filing charges for alleged crimes by business.

Following how government regulates business can turn into exciting business stories. Government and business often clash, and that conflict results in good

---

[2]From "Labor Department tries carrot: It recommends tax breaks for companies that willingly improve safety," by K. Rives, May 7, 2003, *The News & Observer*, p. D1. Copyright 2003 by *The News & Observer*. Reprinted with permission.

copy. The rest of this chapter explores how government regulation is an important part of writing stories that explain the ins and outs of covering business and the economy.

REGULATORY INFORMATION ABOUT PRIVATE COMPANIES

Following the government trail of regulation is important to a reporter who writes stories for the business section, particularly for a writer who spends most of his or her time covering private companies.

Most private companies do not have to report on their financial performance and other major moves like public companies do to the SEC. But knowing and understanding what private companies do have to disclose to government regulators can help a reporter uncover the news at private businesses.

Even though it may seem that private companies are not all that forthcoming in providing information, the truth is that there is plenty of information available if you know where to look.

All companies, public and private, are required to register certain information with their Secretary of State's office, for example. Reporters researching any company for an article should look up the company's incorporation records with the state, which will provide the mailing address, phone number, and officers. This can be important information, for example, if a reporter is writing about a company that has been sued but has been unable to contact anyone at the business for comment. Incorporation records are also required of nonprofit organizations and limited liability corporations such as law firms.

There are plenty of other public records available on private companies at the state level. In every state there are occupational licensing boards that require many businesses, from barbershops to hearing aid providers, to obtain a license before opening shop. These boards may have additional records on the company a reporter may be writing about.

Private companies must also register their business name if that name is not the same name as the corporation. In many places, this is done with the Register of Deeds office, or a similar courthouse office, at the county level. This is a good place to find out who is the actual owner of a company.

Real estate records are another good place to look for information about private companies. Reporters should check these transactions to see if a company owns any land or buildings. It is also good to check these records under the name of the company president or CEO. This can be done at the county courthouse, or the county, in which the business is buying or selling property.

Private companies are also required to disclose information about layoffs and working conditions. These records can be obtained through your local Department of Labor or Occupational Safety and Health Administration (OSHA) office.

For example, mass layoffs and firings of workers are typically disclosed to labor regulators, and OSHA conducts inspections on factories and plants, particularly after an accident or death. Obtaining those records can be as easy as one phone call.

State regulators of specific industries also require many companies to file information about their financial performance. Some of these regulatory agencies include those that oversee banks and insurance companies, as well as water and electrical utilities. Private companies document their profits and revenues to these regulatory agencies. Reporters who find out where these records are kept will likely get information that the company otherwise would not be willing to disclose.

Private companies come under the jurisdiction of federal regulators at numerous levels. Even the smallest companies, such as nonprofit institutions and credit unions, are required to file financial information about their operations. For more information about nonprofits, see chap. 10.

All credit unions across the country are governed by the National Credit Union Administration. Credit unions are required to file information to this federal agency on a quarterly basis. The information includes total assets, total loans, total equity, and a breakdown of the loan income.

The business reporter for the *Goldsboro News-Argus* in eastern North Carolina regularly reviews this information for the credit union in his town, North Carolina Community Credit Union. By receiving this information, he discovered that the credit union had reported net income of $124,586 in the third quarter of 2002, but lost $242,469 in the last three months of that year, a dramatic drop.

Privately owned banks and thrifts are also required to provide financial information to federal regulators such as the Federal Deposit Insurance Corporation (FDIC), the Office of Thrift Supervision, and the Office of the Comptroller of the Currency.

The federal government also has other agencies that come in contact regularly with businesses across the country. The Environmental Protection Agency, for example, has information on companies that handle environmentally sensitive chemicals and products. The Food and Drug Administration has information on food products and drugs sold by thousands of companies. The U.S. Patent and Trademark Office maintains filings of patents and trademarks that a company uses to make its products. Reporters should check these filings regularly to see if businesses they write about have received new patents or trademarks that may help their operations.

Sometimes, private companies run into trouble with these government agencies. In addition to checking for simple financial information and background information about private businesses, a reporter should also look for fines and regulatory actions. Unlike public companies regulated by the SEC, private companies do not have to disclose to the government if they want to branch into different business lines—unless, of course, the new business line requires approval of a new product, such as a drug. But "private" companies are not as private as they may seem. With the right research, a reporter can make the operations of a private company as transparent as that of a public business simply by looking at the government agencies that oversee it and following a paper trail. (For more information about private companies, see chap. 9.)

INSURANCE AND BANKING REGULATORS

Sectors of the financial services industry can be daunting beats for any reporter. Banks and insurance companies touch the lives of virtually every user of mass communication. Most people have checking and savings accounts, and automated teller machine cards, everyone has auto insurance, and many people have life insurance policies. Yet banks and insurance companies can be some of the hardest to understand. How do they make money? What do they do with the money that consumers pay them?

Unlike most industries, the insurance business is regulated by state insurance commissioners who often, but not always, agree on regulation. In addition, each state has passed laws to govern insurance companies, and these laws are not the same across the country. So the laws that a national insurance company must adhere to in California might not be the same as the laws in Florida.

Insurance commissioners are politicians. Many of them are elected officials who must win a majority of the votes in their state to hold the position. As such, the people holding these positions may not have had much background in the insurance industry. Some of them may view the office as a stepping stone to something greater, such as governor or senator.

Still, insurance commissioners oversee a multibillion dollar industry in many states. Insurance companies sell coverage for everything from cars and homes to variable annuities used to invest in the stock market. When an insurance company wants to raise the rate it is charging for coverage in a state, it has to file a request with the insurance commissioner's office.

These rate requests are public records, and could be major stories, particularly if the company holds a large market share in the state. If State Farm or Allstate, the two largest auto and home insurers in the country, want to raise rates in a state, that is likely to affect tens of thousands of readers or viewers.

The following story illustrates how one of those rate requests was written up in Florida, one of the country's largest insurance markets:

> Many of the state's Allstate policyholders will see their insurance premiums soar this year.
> Florida's second-largest insurer has two statewide rate requests pending with the Office of Insurance Regulation–an average hike of 44.2 percent for individual condo policies and an average increase of 10.3 percent for nonstandard auto insurance policies.
> While rates usually tend to be higher in South Florida, Allstate declined to say what the average increases would be in Broward, Miami-Dade, and Palm Beach counties.

The company cited rising claims costs as the reason for the requests and expects a decision from the state Office of Insurance Regulation any day now. The company paid out about $1.10 for every $1 it collected in premiums last year, said Kathy Thomas, Allstate spokeswoman.

"Our claims frequency and severity is outpacing the premiums we collected," she said, adding that the insurer has suffered from a rise in water claims, medical costs, repair expenses and auto insurance fraud.

Allstate Floridian Insurance Co., which raised rates 15.7 percent for condos last year, requested another increase earlier this month. The insurer has 203,866 individual condo policies in Florida–60 percent are in Broward, Miami-Dade and Palm Beach counties. An approved hike would go into effect July 30 for new policies and August 24 for renewals, according to documents filed with state regulators.

Allstate Indemnity Co. requested new auto rates in March and hopes to implement approved auto rates May 19 for new policies and June 23 for renewals.

The insurer has 285,523 nonstandard policyholders in Florida, 36 percent of whom are in South Florida. Nonstandard insurance policies have higher rates and are issued to those who don't qualify for standard policies because of poor driving histories, credit problems and high-valued cars, among other risk factors. Allstate's nonstandard auto policyholders saw their rates jump an average 16.5 percent when policies came up for renewal last November.

Consumer advocates said the increase was likely meant to cover investment losses. They said Allstate lost about $23 million in the first half of 2002 invested in Tyco stock that plummeted after news of accounting mismanagement.

"They're going to pass those losses on to consumers," said Bill Newton, executive director of the Florida Consumer Action Network.

While Allstate has experienced investment losses like many others in the sluggish market, the company says its Florida companies are trying to keep up with mounting costs and fraud in the state.

Insurers have been jacking up insurance rates to compensate for the insurance industry's poor 2001.

Allstate Corp. Chairman and Chief Executive Edward Liddy told investors last week that insurance premium hikes last year helped the parent company turn a profit this year. He said the company would likely boost rates more to bolster profits.

The insurer posted a profit for the quarter ended March 31 of $665 million, or 94 cents per diluted share. That's seven times what the company earned during the same quarter a year earlier.

The insurance office is still reviewing the insurer's rate requests and no deadline has been set, said spokesman Bob Lotane. Regulators can grant the requests, approve partial rate increases or reject them. If regulators grant all or part of the rate changes, Allstate will have about 45 days to notify policyholders in writing.[3]

This story does an excellent job of explaining to readers of the *Sun-Sentinel* why Allstate feels the need to raise rates—it is paying $1.10 in claims for every $1 it has collected in premiums. The story also lets readers know that more than 200,000 south Florida residents could be impacted by the request.

---

[3]From "Allstate seeks premium hikes; condo, auto rates targeted," by P. Patel, April 24, 2003, *The Sun-Sentinel*, p. 1D. Copyright 2003, by *The South Florida Sun-Sentinel*. Reprinted with permission.

These rate requests can be checked regularly with any state insurance department. With hundreds of insurance companies operating in most states, it is likely that one of them is filing for a rate hike in one of its insurance lines on almost a weekly basis. In some cases, the entire industry files a rate request. This can happen for workers' compensation coverage or auto insurance policies, for example. The industry has a lobbying group that files requests with the commissioner's office, which then typically gets reviewed by actuaries and other experts. Sometimes, there are public hearings at which company executives and the general public are invited to speak for and against the proposal. The commissioner typically presides over such cases and issues a ruling on the rate request days or weeks after the hearing occurred.

Insurance commissioners are also charged with ensuring that companies in the industry have enough money set aside to pay for claims. This money is often called surplus, and regulators have laws requiring a certain level of surplus to be in an insurance company's bank account. If a company falls below that level, then the insurance commissioner may go to court and ask a judge to allow regulators to take over that company to improve its financial position. This can be called regulatory oversight, or regulatory control.

Insurance companies take the premiums paid to them by consumers and businesses and invest that money. Many of them do not charge enough in premiums to cover their expenses, so they are hoping that their investment income will allow them to report a profit. But if a major storm or natural disaster hits, they could be hit with more claims than they anticipated. Insurers of autos, homes, and businesses paid billions in claims after the Northridge earthquake hit California in 1994, and life insurers did the same after the September 11, 2001 terrorist attacks killed nearly 3,000 at the World Trade Center and the Pentagon.

Insurance commissioners also work with the industry. Insurance commissioners want companies to offer coverage to as many consumers and businesses as possible. If companies begin to drop policies or decide to withdraw from a state because an insurance commissioner will not allow them to raise rates, then the commissioner may have a problem during the next election. Consumers and businesses want a variety of choices and competition in the insurance market.

The banking industry is regulated in a similar fashion. In fact, in some states such as Florida, banks and insurers can be regulated by the same elected official. Although banks are not filing requests to raise or lower the rates they charge consumers, they do file information with state and federal regulators that can give an insight into their performance.

Some of the most valuable information available about banks is market share and branch data. A reporter can determine how much money is held in each branch of a bank with thousands of locations, such as Bank of America, from FDIC records. For a reporter in a small or medium-sized town, following this branch data can show who is winning the banking war in the community. If one branch is gaining market share in the town, while a branch of another bank is losing market share, then there is a story behind those numbers. A reporter should call the banks to find out what strategy the winning bank has been employing, and what new tactics the losing bank is planning to regain deposits.

Surprisingly, few mass communication outlets track bank branch data, although this information helps localize the success or failure of major interstate banks in hundreds of communities across the country. The following excerpt shows how an online Web site that follows the banking industry assessed recent market share changes and branch data in California and New York:

> The United States is more than just New York and California, as most folks who live outside of those areas will be quick to point out. So please forgive us for being a bit exclusionary in choosing those markets for a quick look at deposit market share trends revealed in the latest available deposit data.
>
> The largest banks and thrifts operating in California had little trouble growing deposits between mid-2000 and mid-2001, based on SNL Securities' analysis of the latest branch deposit data from the Federal Deposit Insurance Corp.
>
> According to the newly updated SNL Branch Marketshare DataSource, each of the eight banks and thrifts with the largest deposit market share in California saw their deposits in the state increase in the 12 months preceding June 30, 2001.
>
> By far the largest increase among this elite eight—which held an aggregate of $324.5 billion in deposits at June 30, or roughly two-thirds of all California deposits—came at Comerica Inc. The Detroit-based bank completed its acquisition of Los Angeles-based Imperial Bancorp on Jan. 30, 2001, and now ranks No. 7 statewide in deposits held. The pick-up of Imperial didn't account for the entire boost, however; the company reported an additional $2 billion in deposits above what it and Imperial reported at June 30, 2000. That represents a 19.6 percent year-over-year increase.
>
> Across Comerica's entire franchise, which stretches from Los Angeles to the Midwest, total deposits increased to $37 billion from $32 billion, the bank said in its second-quarter earnings release issued on July 17. Much of that gain was the Imperial acquisition.
>
> Wells Fargo & Co. added $10.6 billion in deposits, pushing its California market share to 13.9 percent from 12.8 percent a year earlier. The increase widened Wells Fargo's statewide position at No. 2, ahead of No. 3 Washington Mutual Inc. WaMu lost deposits in California a year ago, but it posted a 6.61 percent gain this year to register a 12.2 percent share of deposits.
>
> Adjustable-rate-mortgage lender Downey Financial Corp. raked in new deposits during the last two years, posting a 23.0 percent gain at June 30 to follow the 33.2 percent gain seen in the FDIC's prior update. Downey's California deposits increased from $5.5 billion in mid-1999 to $8.9 billion at mid-2001.
>
> "It largely reflects the fact that we've been opening up a lot of new branches," Downey CFO Tom Prince said. "In the year 2001, we opened 23 branches, which put us at 137 total. If you went back to the beginning of 1996, we only had 52 branches."
>
> Most of the new branches have been in-store locations. Prince pointed to Downey's customer-service approach as an advantage in the effort to build deposits, but he singled out no specific competitors from which the thrift has been cherry-picking deposits. New deposits have been of both the core and CD variety, although upwards of 80 percent of the thrift's deposits fall in the latter category.
>
> There remains plenty of room for growth. No. 8 Downey now holds a mere 1.8 percent of California deposits.

"We anticipate this year that we will open an additional 20 branches," he said.

Metropolitan New York is the biggest banking market in the United States, and some would say it is the most competitive. That's certainly the case for several large thrifts—including a handful of the nation's largest mutual thrifts—that operate in the New York Metropolitan Statistical Area.

Washington Mutual now has the largest deposit position in metro New York, thanks to its acquisition of Dime Bancorp Inc., which it completed on Jan. 4. The thrift has been rumored to be an eventual acquirer of GreenPoint Financial Corp., which holds the second-largest deposit franchise among thrifts in the metro New York market.

However, the two largest thrift operations have had trouble holding on to deposits in that market in recent years. Picking away at the top have been a host of somewhat smaller thrifts like Astoria Financial Corp., New York Community Bancorp and Staten Island Bancorp Inc. The latter grew deposits in the market by 7.9 percent year-over-year through June 30; Astoria and New York Community saw gains of 4.9 percent and 3.4 percent, respectively (the latter figure being adjusted for acquisitions).

Dime Community Bancshares Inc. grew its deposits in the market by 16.0 percent to $1.1 billion at June 30 from $947.1 million at the same time a year earlier. Dime Community CFO Ken Mahon attributed the growth to a fundamental change in the thrift's strategy in 1999.

"About two years ago, we embarked on a new strategy here as far as raising deposits," Mahon said. "Our company's a multifamily lender, and that was really our major line of business. For a few years after we went public in 1996, our focus was on originating loans, originating loans, originating loans. And what we were doing was funding with wholesale borrowings."

That strategy came with a price, however, as the thrift's balance sheet began to become unbalanced. So Dime Community decided to become more aggressive on the deposit-taking end as well.[4]

Although this story was written about state market share and how that has changed among the top banks in California and New York, a similar story can easily be written for any town or city in the country with competing banks just by reviewing the same data. It may take some addition and subtraction, and following the numbers for a while, but the story will likely be well read and show readers or viewers what is happening in an important industry used by all consumers.

Bank and thrift regulators, like their insurance brethren, are also charged with making sure that banks have enough money set aside to pay off loans and their depositors. Regulators set certain requirements on capital adequacy levels. If a bank falls below these levels, it could be taken over.

Two barometers a reporter should follow in a bank's filings with regulators are its loan losses and loan loss reserves. When a bank starts setting aside large amounts of money to cover loans that have become past due, that could be an indication that the bank's past lending practices were not sound.

Like insurance companies, banks also invest deposits and other money paid to them by consumers. The investment portfolio can be an indication that a bank is

---

[4]From "Research & Analysis: Latest branch data revealed," by M. Saunders, Jan. 28, 2002, SNL Interactive. Copyright 2002 by SNL Financial. Reprinted with permission.

engaging in risky business practices. If it is investing in high-risk investments such as real estate ventures in shaky foreign economies or volatile currencies, that can be a sign that the bank is trying to make up for other bad investments. A reporter should always review an investment portfolio to see where a bank—or an insurance company—is putting its money.

State regulators of insurance and banking companies are also involved in approving mergers and acquisitions between businesses. If a merger or acquisition is announced, there might be a hearing by the state regulatory agency that should be attended, or the regulators might ask for public comment.

With a little digging some knowledge of the documents that must be filed with regulators, a reporter can piece together enough information about a private bank or insurance company that might otherwise go uncovered. These stories can often tell more about a local economy than anything else.

HEALTH CARE REGULATION

Another industry that is primarily regulated by state agencies is the health care business. Hospitals, doctors, and managed care companies are part of a fast-growing industry that is a vital part of many economies. In many towns and cities, the local hospital is the largest employer. That should be a good reason as to why stories should be written about them.

Hospitals, doctors, and managed care companies have a symbiotic relationship. Doctors and hospitals rely on managed care companies to bring them large amounts of patients. Conversely, managed care companies rely on doctors and hospitals to treat patients as cost efficiently as possible. Sometimes, these relationships can become strained, as each is out to maintain a level of profitability that is dependent on others.

One of the ways to find stories about hospitals, particularly private or non-profit hospitals, is through state regulatory filings. Many hospitals are required to file financial information with state regulations, and the rates that some hospitals charge for operations and other services must be approved by a state agency. (In Massachusetts, the state hospital industry was deregulated in the 1980s. The result caused a number of hospitals to close.)

Reporters should check to see which agency oversees hospitals in their state, then call or visit that agency to find out what information is available about local hospitals. A reporter may find out that the local hospital is losing money and needs to raise its rates to survive, or that the so-called nonprofit hospital has had profits of millions of dollars in recent years.

In many states, hospitals must also receive permission from state regulators before they are allowed to expand and offer new services. In Michigan, for example, a government body called the Certificate of Need Commission approves filings by hospitals across the state asking to build new additions that add beds or services such as cardiac units. The idea behind such regulations is to prevent a glut of hospital services in a certain community. In Florida, the certificate of need process covers new hospital beds as well as the beginning of open heart surgery, organ transplantation, neonatal intensive care, burn services, inpatient psychiatric or substance abuse services, inpatient comprehensive medical rehabilitation, hospice freestanding inpatient beds, and skilled nursing.

The certificate of need process in many states also allows others such as consumers and competitors to argue against an expansion plan by a competitor, as the following story from *Cleveland Plain Dealer* shows:

Without taking a vote, the Parma Planning Commission bounced a controversial proposed 260-bed senior citizen complex back to City Council last night.

After a nearly three-hour hearing attended by 70 persons, the commission said it stands behind its March 9 endorsement of the project proposed by Parma Community General Hospital and Generations Health care, a company formed by members of the Coury family, longtime nursing home operators.

On July 10, residents won at least a temporary victory as council sent the thrice-revised project back to the Planning Commission.

Council did so under the threat of an injunction made by the residents' lawyer, Rodger Pelagalli, who had argued that city laws required any project that has been radically changed since its adoption by the Planning Commission be reviewed again by the panel.

"Residents feel the Planning Commission was just washing its hands of the deal," said Councilman John Stover who said he and others felt the panel should have voted on an array of plan changes since March.

The complex, proposed for vacant land ringing the old Fay Junior High School, would offer a wide range of care, including an Alzheimer's unit.

The old building has been converted to a health education center that would give the proposed senior complex an added dimension, developers have argued. They said they have reviewed alternate sites but ruled them out because of cost.

That drew fire from Ward 5 Councilwoman Michelle Stys, who said: "I'm not concerned about their purse strings. I am concerned about the existing neighbors."

Residents have vowed to continue the fight next month by asking the Ohio Department of Health to not award a certificate of need for the project.

Other opponents, composed mainly of abutting property owners, said the proposal lacks access for emergency vehicles, threatens to overload storm and sanitary sewers, and could erode property values.

Mary Ann Nice, of Sassafras Dr., said Parma Hospital has allowed the Fay property to deteriorate. It is marked with graffiti, smells of raw sewage, is covered in places by broken glass and high grass, Nice said.

The residents picked up support from the city's Engineering Department, which criticized the plan as incomplete. The department reported the plan lacks details on parking, landscaping buffers, erosion and utilities.

Liz Varga, of Brook Park, testified that another Coury-operated nursing home, the EastPark Care Center in her city, has been less than an ideal neighbor.

"I invite the people of Parma to come and take videos of all the trucks going in and out all day," said Varga.

Parma Heights Mayor Paul Cassidy, the hospital's legal counsel, insisted that the Parma Hospital-Generations Health Care design has been changed in recent months to reflect city and resident concerns. He said there are now four buildings instead of five, they have two floors instead of one, and the buffer between senior complex and homes has been widened.[5]

Conflict occurs often in the business world, and the conflict a reporter finds in state documents may not always be between business and regulators. Often, another business is also involved, as the preceding story illustrates.

As in the case with insurance company rate requests and bank branch data, few media outlets actively watch certificate of need filings. But in many cases, these documents can be major news, indicating that a health care facility plans to spend millions of dollars. Where is that money coming from? And is that money being spent wisely? Too often, those questions are not answered.

State medical boards can also be a source of business stories. These organizations regulate doctors and surgeons in an area. They can revoke or suspend the license of a doctor if he or she performed an unnecessary surgery or prescribed the wrong medication for an illness. These are public records, and can be important information about a business in a town. These boards can also oversee other medical workers, such as nurses and nursing home administrators.

One of the biggest players in the health care business can be the managed care operators. In many instances, these are businesses operated by insurance companies, and often they also come under the regulation of the state insurance department.

Managed care companies generally offer two types of plans to consumers, a health maintenance organization (HMO) and a preferred provider organization (PPO). An HMO provides and arranges for coverage with doctors and hospitals for its plan members for a set rate. The HMO must agree on a set of basic and supplemental health maintenance and treatment services. A PPO establishes contracts with doctors and hospitals, and under those contracts the managed care company provides lower co-payments if its subscribers use one of those preferred providers. Managed care companies charge premiums, just like insurance companies. And the for-profit managed care companies expect to make a profit on the basis of the premiums they have collected. Nonprofit managed care companies often also make a profit on their operations. The financial results of managed care companies can usually be found by asking state regulators, probably with the insurance department.

The following is a story that assessed the financial performance of managed care companies operating in Kansas City:

Amid rising premiums, the principal managed care companies doing business in Kansas City on the whole enjoyed a spectacular financial turnaround last year.

---

[5]From "Planners bounce nursing home plans to council; Parma residents vow to continue fighting proposal," by J. Wagner, July 21, 2000, *Cleveland Plain Dealer*, p. 3B. Copyright 2000 by *Cleveland Plain Dealer*. Reprinted with permission.

Eight managed care companies that operate here earned an aggregate net income of $71.9 million last year, compared with an aggregate net loss of $12.7 million in 2001.

The good fortune was not shared by all. Four of the eight big companies were profitable, but the four others reported losses for 2002.

The numbers include results outside the Kansas City area for national managed care companies operating here.

"The HMO industry since 1998 has been focusing on profitability," said Randy McConnell, a spokesman for the Missouri Department of Insurance. "2002 turned out to be a breakthrough year for them on that score."

McConnell said the financial turnaround was largely brought about by HMOs being more selective in choosing the groups they cover, along with "substantial premium increases."

Other numbers pointed to a similar trend. HMOs operating in Missouri earned a record consolidated net income of $167.7 million last year, compared with a $598,287 consolidated net loss in 2001, according to the Missouri Department of Insurance. The numbers include national operating results of some managed care companies.

HMOs operating in Kansas earned a consolidated net income of $93.8 million last year, compared with a $25.9 million consolidated net loss in 2001, based on numbers reported by the Kansas Insurance Department. Those numbers also include the national operating results of some companies.

Beneficiaries of the turnaround included Blue Cross and Blue Shield of Kansas City. Blue Cross earned $31.1 million in net income last year, compared with a 2001 net loss of $6.3 million. The numbers include results from Blue Cross HMOs and PPO networks.

John W. Kennedy, Blue Cross's executive vice president, said the company had benefited from higher premiums and overall growth.

"We sold a lot of business," Kennedy said.

Kennedy said Blue Cross also benefited from dropping its money-losing Medicare HMOs and from lower administrative costs. In addition, he said the 2001 bottom line had suffered a $14 million hit as a result of Blue Cross buying out its partners in the TriSource managed care group.

Other managed care companies did not fare so well. Coventry Health Care of Kansas suffered an $8.6 million net loss last year, compared with a $3 million net loss the previous year.

Coventry's 2002 financial results include those of Mid America Health Partners Inc., which Coventry bought for $38 million last year.

Janet M. Stallmeyer, president and chief executive officer of Coventry Health Care of Kansas, declined to comment on the company's latest figures, except to acknowledge that they represent the consolidated results of Coventry and Mid America Health.

"I'm not in a position to discuss the details behind those filings," Stallmeyer said.

She added: "I believe that we've built a strong platform for moving forward, and our statutory filings will reflect that in 2003."

Coventry Health Care of Kansas is part of Bethesda, Maryland-based Coventry Health Care Inc.

Among the others, Aetna Health Inc., FirstGuard Health Plan Inc. and United Healthcare of the Midwest Inc. reported positive earnings. Cigna Healthcare of Ohio Inc., which does business in Kansas and Missouri, Family Health Partners and Humana Health Plan Inc. reported losses.[6]

---

[6]From "Operating profits" by J. Karash, April 11, 2003, *Kansas City Star,* p. C1. Copyright 2003 by *Kansas City Star.* Reprinted with permission.

Many of the companies mentioned in this story are private companies, or sub-sidiaries of public companies that do not break out the financial performance of subsidiaries in their SEC filings. That shows why getting these records from state regulators can provide a better indication of how a local operation is performing in many instances.

The Blue Cross–Blue Shield system across the country is one of the dominant managed care players, as are national operators such as CIGNA and Aetna. With Blue Cross–Blue Shield plans, each company operates separately, although the plans have been undergoing a consolidation move. When such deals are announced, regulators are typically involved, especially if a for-profit Blue operator wants to acquire a not-for-profit Blue plan. In 2003, Maryland regulators turned down the request by WellPoint, the for-profit Blue company operating in California, Missouri, and Georgia, to acquire the nonprofit Blue operator in that state.

Managed care companies watch medical inflation carefully. If the cost of med-ical goods and services rises too fast, they are unable to keep pace by raising premiums. Many may ask for rate increases from regulators if medical costs start rising.

WATER AND POWER UTILITIES

Every business and homeowner pays electricity, water, and a telephone bills. Some of them also pay a gas bill. What is surprising to many of them is that the rates are regulated by state utility commissions. These regulatory agencies are charged with protecting the consumer by making sure these companies are charging fair rates for their services. In addition, public service commissions also work with the companies to try to make utilities more efficient, thereby lowering the potential for rate increases in the future.

In addition, there is a federal agency that also regulates some utilities. The Federal Energy Regulatory Commission (FERC) regulates the price, terms, and conditions of power sold across state lines and is the federal counterpart to state utility regulatory commissions.

Like their insurance brethren, state public service commissioners must approve any request to raise rates. These rate requests are sometimes accompanied by documents justifying why the electrical company, for example, needs to raise rates. And there is often a hearing to take testimony from the company and consumers before the commission makes its decision.

The filing of these requests, as well as their approval, should be stories, par-ticularly those about rate hikes that affect a large number of consumers. One of these rate requests was covered by a brief item in the *Milwaukee Business Journal*, which notes that Wisconsin Power & Light filed a rate increase with the Public Service Commission of Wisconsin totaling $113.1 million. If the rate increase was passed, the average customer would see a $7.58 increase in their electric bill and a $10.91 hike in their gas bill. Note how this story told the reader how much their average monthly bill would increase if the rate request passed. This is information that is vital to any story about a rate request because it tells the consumer how much they will be affected.

At many rate hearings, the people are represented by a consumer advocate. Often, the consumer advocate is in a government position with the sole job of protecting the interest of citizens. These consumer advocate offices may often conduct their own studies on why a utility needs a rate hike. These studies can be important to read and even write stories about. They are public documents that often paint a different picture than the company's rate filing.

Public utility commissions also hold hearings on other matters. They may feel as if the utility has not treated its customers fairly or acted in the public's best interests. When an ice storm hit North Carolina in December 2002, thousands of residents went without power for as long as a week. Many of them complained that the power companies in the state should have been better prepared to handle the damages and repairs needed to get power restored. Besieged with complaints, the state utilities commission conducted a hearing into the matter while many residents still had branches and trees throughout their lawn.

The following shows how one newspaper covered the proceeding:

Duke Power customers, given the opportunity to confront the utility giant at a state Utilities Commission hearing Thursday, lashed out at the company for poor planning, material shortages and unreliable communications after the Dec. 4 ice storm.

Among the 33 people who signed up to speak before the six-member panel was Joe Capowski, a former Chapel Hill Town Council member and an electrical engineer who criticized Duke Power for not doing more to rebuild Chapel Hill's power distribution system after Hurricane Fran in September 1996.

"Duke Power was not born on Dec. 4, 2002," he said before an audience of more than 150 people in Durham's City Hall. "Their efforts, while indeed heroic, were made so by their own management's lack of foresight and learning."

The ice storm brought the state's fourth largest city to "an abrupt and frigid halt," recalled Durham Mayor Bill Bell, who suggested that the commission analyze work reports of Duke Power personnel to see where they were assigned immediately after the storm. Bell has accused the company of not concentrating enough resources in Durham—where 93 percent, or 107,000 of the company's customers, were without power at the peak.

In the storm's aftermath, the information Duke Power supplied "was often too general to give any value to emergency management operations," Bell said.

E.O. Ferrell, a Duke Power senior vice president, said that although the company's "communication with the elected officials and with the emergency centers did not function the way we would have liked," the utility's efforts were hampered by the magnitude of the damage in the western Triangle.

The hearing, requested by Durham officials, was the first in a series of public meetings the commission has scheduled around the state to evaluate Duke Power's and Progress Energy's emergency preparedness in response to hundreds of complaints about utilities' performance after the ice storm. Earlier this week, Duke Power joined CP&L officials at a hearing before state regulators in Raleigh where both companies defended their emergency protocol.

Complaints have poured in from the western Triangle, where 147,000 customers were affected and power-restoration efforts were the slowest in the Carolinas.

One week after the storm, 20,000 remained without power in Durham and 8,100 in Chapel Hill.[7]

No company likes to be in the public spotlight. They dread it when they are dragged before a state regulatory board and asked to answer consumer complaints. A reporter should be there to document it all.

Although most of the reporting on utility commissions focuses on electrical companies, the commissions also regulate water utilities and phone companies in most states, making decisions on rate requests and disputes in those industries. Like other state regulatory filings, utility commission documents are often a goldmine for stories and are frequently unreported because journalists think they contain boring information.

But tracking the dealings of utilities that affect thousands of consumers can be one of the best services a mass communication outlet can provide to its readers or viewers. It can be argued that no other business beat affects as many consumers as the public utilities beat.

Reporters should not forget that many utilities such as energy and electrical companies are also public companies with shareholders. Information from their SEC filings should be used to supplement information contained in state regulatory filings. Also, reporters should be sure to check with the federal agency as well, particularly for energy companies. The recent rise and fall of many energy companies, led by the collapse of Enron, caused the FERC to become involved in many energy company dealings.

Many of these companies also sign long-term contracts to provide power with states and other major customers. If the cost to power should rise or fall, these companies could reap a financial windfall, or face difficulty.

CONSUMER PRODUCT SAFETY

One of the functions of the government in business is to protect the consumer. And one of the ways regulators go about this job is to make sure that businesses are producing goods, products and services that are safe for consumers to use. When regulators find out that some product or good could harm a consumer, they may ask the business to change the way it is made. If the product or good is causing people to die or become seriously injured, they may even ask that it be withdrawn for sale in the market.

[7]From "Duke Power assailed at hearing: Customers complain about the utility's planning and actions after recent ice storm," by M. Fishman, Dec. 20, 2000, *The News & Observer*, p. B1. Copyright 2003 by *The News & Observer*. Reprinted with permission.

Some of the biggest business stories in the last few decades have involved such stories. The question of whether Firestone tires were causing people to crash and die in their Ford Explorers was first reported by KHOU-TV in Houston before it became a national story. Millions of tires ended up being recalled, Ford posted its largest loss ever and ended its relationship with its longtime tire supplier. The story made drivers of sports utility vehicles across the country check their tires and question whether they were driving a safe vehicle.

One of the biggest business stories of the 1980s occurred after drug maker Johnson & Johnson was forced to recall millions of Tylenol containers after seven people in the Chicago area died as a result of ingesting cyanide-laced pills. The ensuing scare caused drug makers around the world to install tamper-proof seals to their packages.

Concerns about the safety of products occur on a regular basis around the world. In this country, a number of regulatory agencies are charged with making sure the products and goods sold to consumers are safe. The concerns can range from the healthiness of the hamburger at a fast-food restaurant to whether a child can choke on a toy part.

The Consumer Product Safety Commission (CPSC) was created in the 1970s and is the government agency that oversees most products. The products it covers range from adhesives to wood-burning stoves. It does not regulate products such as ammunition, automobiles, cosmetics, drugs, foods, tires, and tobacco, which are under the realm of other regulatory agencies.

The CPSC works with companies and industries to set guidelines as to how products should be manufactured so that they are safe for consumers. It enforces those standards and can ban products if those standards are not met. The agency also conducts research on potential product hazards, and can issue a recall or repairs on a defective product. The agency is run by three commissioners appointed by the president and confirmed by the Senate. One of the commissioners is a chairman, and the agency's nearly 500 employees oversee the safety of more than 15,000 products.

Naturally, some products and the companies that manufacture them fail to meet the CPSC standards. And when that happens, the agency will use its power to protect the consumer. That is when a business reporter is likely to find a story at this agency, particularly if the product is manufactured at a local plant or sold by a company with headquarters located in his or her media outlet's area.

The CPSC remains busy. In May 2003, for example, the commission worked with businesses to announce the recall of 13,000 Stihl chain saws; 38,000 plastic cups for kids at Starbucks; more than 2,000 Catlike Kompact bike helmets; 620,000 Lane Furniture high-leg recliner chairs; 7,100 Sea Gull Lighting ceiling lights; 8,200 United General Supply extension cords; 800 toy drumsticks from the Step2 Company; 126,000 toy vehicles from International Playthings; 25,000 packages of diving sticks from Swimways Corporation; 1,700 gas boilers; 64,000 fabric lanterns sold at Wal-Mart, 4,600 wooden convertible cribs; and 9,500 Ab Swing exercise units. And these were not even all of the product recalls for the month!

The CPSC's Office of the General Counsel also issues advisory opinions about products that may not need a recall to correct a defect.

Product recalls can be stories for almost any newspaper, Internet site, TV station, or radio station because the products are often distributed throughout the country. It is very likely that someone in the outlet's audience has a product that has been recalled.

Product recall stories can also be developed by watching trends to see what type of goods or products have been recalled. A reporter from the *Los Angeles Times* spotted such a trend—the toys that fast-food restaurant chains were giving away with kids meals were being recalled by the millions because of safety concerns. Fast food toys accounted for 77% of all of the toys recalled.

The CPSC is not the only agency that is trying to protect consumers from unsafe products. Cosmetics, drugs, foods, and medical devices come under the watch of the Food and Drug Administration, whereas car seats, tires, and vehicles are reviewed by the National Highway Traffic Safety Administration (NHTSA).

The NHTSA is as busy as the CPSC in announcing recalls. In April 2003, it recalled thousands of cars ranging from BMW and Ferrari to Ford and General Motors, as well as motorcycles made by Indian Motorcycle Company and Kawasaki, to be checked for potential defects and needed repairs.

Major recalls involving thousands of cars or trucks across the country are likely to affect consumers in every state. Although such news may not need to be covered as full stories in many mass communication outlets, they should merit at least a brief mention.

States are also involved in protecting consumers. For example, every state has passed what is known as a lemon law, which allows consumers to return cars and other vehicles that have broken down repeatedly after purchase. Most states have a period where the breakdowns must occur within the first 12 to 24 months of purchase, or within 12,000 to 24,000 miles. If the defect is related to something serious such as brakes or steering, the manufacturer is given one chance at repairing it. If it is another safety-related defect, the manufacturer has two chances to repair the vehicle. The manufacturer is allowed as many as four chances for repair on other defects.

Many other federal and state regulators also act to protect consumers. The Federal Trade Commission (FTC), for example, is active in pursuing Internet fraud. State insurance commissioners prosecute insurance agents who sell fake policies. The Federal Communications Commission (FCC) addresses consumer complaints about telephone companies cutting service without reason and radio stations broadcasting vulgar words. There are even private organizations within the business community that also are involved with consumer protection. The Better Business Bureau also handles complaints against businesses, and tracks the number of complaints that a business receives.

Anytime a reporter is writing about a company, particularly a business which sells products to consumers, it is wise to check to see if there are complaints.

Not every consumer is going to be happy all of the time. If there are a handful of complaints about the products being sold by a huge company, such as Wal-Mart or Microsoft, then there may not be a story. But if there are a number of complaints against any company that are all about the same product or the same defect, then there may be a story.

THE EPA AND FDA

Two other federal agencies that play a vital business regulation role–the Environmental Protection Agency (EPA) and the Food and Drug Administration (FDA)— are often thought of as focusing on nonbusiness topics. But selling foods and drugs are multibillion dollar businesses in this country. And increasingly, business practices that affect the environment are coming under closer scrutiny.

The FDA was formally created about a century ago, while the EPA was not formed until the 1970s. Both of them have thousands of staff members charged with regulating numerous companies—many companies that also fall under regulations from other state and federal agencies.

Rachel Carson's *Silent Spring*, published first in the *New Yorker* in 1962 and later as a book, led to an outcry about the use of pesticides and their effects on the environment. This exhaustively researched reporting can be considered to be what led the federal government to create an agency to protect the environment.

The EPA's job is to protect human health and to safeguard the environment. It carries out its job by enforcing existing environmental laws and setting standards. The agency also sanctions companies that do not meet its requirements and pollute. The EPA is divided into 10 regional divisions across the country, and each region is charged with enforcing the laws.

The EPA has taken measures to ban products sold by companies. In 1972, it banned the use of the pesticide DDT, and two years later it began enforcing the Safe Drinking Water Act. In 1975, the agency banned the use of pesticides heptachlor and chlordane for most household and agricultural uses, calling them a cancer threat to humans. Three years later, the EPA banned ozone-destroying fluorocarbon gases in most aerosol products—such as hair spray and deodorant— produced by large companies such as Allied Chemical, DuPont, Kaiser Aluminum and Chemical, Pennwalt, and Racon.

The EPA has also played a major role in the Superfund program and in the cleanup and removal of asbestos from older buildings. The Superfund program has identified sites across the country in which chemicals and other products are polluting the area and has ordered their cleanup, which can cost millions of dollars. Superfund cleanups have caused controversy in industries such as insurance companies, who have foot the bill to clean up on the basis of old policies. The EPA maintains a list of Superfund sites across the country. If one of them is in a reporter's area, it might be a story.

The biggest environmental issue since the EPA's creation was the spill of 11 million gallons of oil off the coast of Alaska in March 1989 by the Exxon *Valdez*. Two years later, Exxon paid a record $1 billion in fines and damages as a result of the spill for violating numerous EPA regulations and laws.

In 1996, the EPA led the phasing out of leaded gasoline, which had been causing illnesses in children. And in 2000, it eliminated virtually all home and garden uses of Dursban—the most widely used household pesticide in the country and a product of Dow Chemical.

Although most of these stories are national issues, the EPA also regulates many businesses in every town and city in the country. The agency conducts thousands of air, water, and hazardous waste compliance inspections every year, and can fine a business if it is found to be violating the laws. The EPA also grants permits to facilities that are allowed to use certain products and get rid of them in approved methods.

If there is an environmental spill in a town or a city, a reporter covering the story should check these records to see if the business had the proper permits and to see if the business had been fined in the past for violating EPA rules. Sometimes, the bigger story can be found in what happened, or did not happen, in the past.

Virtually every company or business dealing with chemicals, liquids, or other products that can pollute the environment comes into contact with the EPA. If a reporter suspects a company may be polluting, he or she should check with regulators first to see what those agencies have uncovered.

The FDA plays a similar role with companies that manufacture and produce cosmetics, foods, drugs, and medical devices. Its job is also to protect the consumer in many ways. With food products that each of us buy in the grocery store on a daily basis, the FDA ensures that these frozen dinners and packaged meat trays, among other things, are safe, sanitary, wholesome, and properly labeled. With drugs, the FDA reviews medical research on the effectiveness of the drugs and approves them for sale to the general public.

The FDA's oversight also includes the safety and labeling of cosmetics, the manufacturing and performance of medical devices; the safety of radiation-emitting products such as microwaves, x-ray machines, and sun lamps; and the safety of pet foods, veterinary drugs, and devices. All of these products and goods are manufactured by for-profit companies, which means these companies have to receive FDA approval for their products and goods before they can be sold to the public. The labeling must be truthful and not misleading.

The FDA has garnered media coverage in recent years for its role in approving new drugs for pharmaceutical companies, particularly with the increase in the number of AIDS patients in the country wanting medications that can help them combat the illness. Its drug approval process has also garnered attention in other ways, such as when it failed to review ImClone's cancer drug Erbitux in 2001, leading CEO Sam Waksal to sell shares in the company before the information was publicly disclosed, resulting in his eventual arrest and prison term.

The FDA's review process can make or break a drug. A pharmaceutical company submits an application to the regulators with research and background on the drug's effectiveness. The agency can review the filing and ask for more information from the drug company, or it can accept the filing, which then places the drug into its review pipeline.

Approval of a drug for public consumption can make or break a small pharmaceutical company. Many start-up drug companies sell stock to investors on the promise that their drugs will be approved by the FDA before their money runs out. Therefore, drug approval for a small company, or drug approval for a major illness can be an important business story, as the following *San Jose Mercury News* story illustrates:

Gilead Sciences won Food and Drug Administration approval Friday for Hepsera, its new pill for treating chronic hepatitis B, a devastating illness that can lead to liver cancer, liver failure and death.

The agency action is the Foster City biotechnology company's second drug approval in less than a year and is expected to boost Gilead's newfound profitability. The first shipments of Hepsera should reach wholesalers by Tuesday. The annual cost of the once-a-day pill will be $5,353 per patient.

Only about 50,000 of the estimated 1.25 million Americans infected with hepatitis B are currently being treated, so Gilead is planning an extensive campaign to convince physicians of Hepsera's benefits.

"Wall Street is estimating $30 million in sales the first year," said Gilead Chief Financial Officer John F. Milligan. "We will have to grow the market over time working with physicians, getting doctors used to the treatment."

An FDA briefing paper points out that Hepsera slows the progress of the disease by interfering with the duplication of the hepatitis B virus and that it is effective against viruses that have grown resistant to another anti-viral drug, lamivudine or Epivir.

"Today's FDA approval of Hepsera gives physicians and their patients a new weapon in the fight against chronic hepatitis B," said Dr. Eugene Schiff, a liver specialist at the University of Miami and one of the investigators who tested the drug in patients.

Hepatitis B is one of several forms of viral hepatitis. Like AIDS, it is spread through bodily fluids—primarily through unprotected sex and dirty needles.

Gilead will market the drug in the United States and Europe, where the incidence of hepatitis B is more than twice what it is here. Its partner, GlaxoSmithKline, will sell it elsewhere, including Asia, where there are more than 300 million patients.

Hepsera—the brand name for adefovir dipivoxil—was first developed for treating AIDS. But in the doses required to kill the AIDS virus, it proved too toxic.

Researchers showed that in much lower doses, the drug can reverse liver damage in patients with chronic hepatitis B.

Last year, Gilead won approval for Viread, an anti-HIV drug that rapidly became one of the bestselling AIDS treatments and is the cornerstone of the company's profitability.[8]

---

[8]From "Gilead pill wins approval to treat hepatitis B; FDA says Hepsera slows disease's progress," by P. Jacobs, Sept. 21, 2002, *San Jose Mercury News*, p. 1. Copyright 2002 by *San Jose Mercury News*. All rights reserved. Reprinted with permission.

As any story about a pharmaceutical drug should, this report assesses how much in revenue the new drug will add to the company's financial picture, and also evaluates what it will mean to its profits.

The FDA can also file litigation against companies involved in the businesses it regulates, asking them to halt production or dispensing of a product. And it often joins with other regulatory agencies, such as the FTC, to halt misleading advertising of food, drug, or beauty products.

An action would be announced in a news release similar to the following one from June 2003:

> The Federal Trade Commission has charged the marketers of a dietary supplement called Coral Calcium Supreme with making false and unsubstantiated claims about the product's health benefits. This action is part of a series of initiatives the FTC and the Food and Drug Administration (FDA) are taking against the purveyors of products with unsubstantiated health and medical claims. In a complaint filed in federal district court, the FTC alleges that Kevin Trudeau; Robert Barefoot; Shop America (USA), LLC; and Deonna Enterprises, Inc., violated the FTC Act by claiming, falsely and without substantiation, that Coral Calcium Supreme can treat or cure cancer and other diseases, such as multiple sclerosis and heart disease. The FTC charges that these and other claims go far beyond existing scientific evidence regarding the recognized health benefits of calcium.
>
> The defendants promote the product primarily through a nationally televised 30-minute infomercial featuring Trudeau and Barefoot, and through statements made in brochures accompanying the product. The informercial has aired on cable channels such as Women's Entertainment, Comedy Central, the Discovery Channel, and Bravo.[9]

Just like the CPSC and the NHTSA, the FDA will also issue product recalls and safety alerts for products it regulates. These can be food products contaminated with bacteria or other illness-causing organisms such as salmonella, or they may be products with improperly marked packaging that contain ingredients that can cause serious illness or death as a result of allergies.

In each case, reporters should check to see if there is a story for their readership. This is often the case if the product or good has been distributed or manufactured locally, or the company that made the product is located in the area. If local people have become sick or died as a result of the product, it is likely front-page news. *The Detroit Free-Press* ran a series of stories in 2001 about how a Sara Lee meat plant shipped tainted meat, killing 15 and making more than 100 sick.

The recall or banning of a food or drug product can be damaging to the manufacturing company. Many fail to handle the situation properly and blame others for their problem. If this is the case with a business on a reporter's beat, he or she should interview industry experts and scientists to find out what

---

[9]Federal Trade Commission news release, June 10, 2003.

went wrong. The regulators will also talk, as likely will the company. But each side will probably have an agenda, and the independent parties may be more objective.

FCC AND THE FTC

The FCC and the FTC also play important roles in regulating businesses. And both of them have taken high-profile positions in recent years in enforcing and interpreting their laws and regulations.

The FCC's role is to regulate interstate communication by radio, wire, satellite, television, and cable. In other words, in a town with a radio station, television station, or a cable company, the FCC is involved in overseeing those businesses. The commission is run by five commissioners appointed by the president and approved by the Senate to 5-year terms.

Each business that the FCC oversees must have a license from the agency. In addition, the agency handles complaints from consumers and investigates potential wrongdoing. It holds hearings about new regulations for these companies, and can fine companies that violate the laws it oversees. The FCC holds auctions, and the winners of these auctions receive the right to broadcast over the bandwidths on which they bid. Winning these auctions can be an important step for a business. A radio station can not operate unless it has received approval from the FCC to operate on a certain bandwidth.

In mid-2003, the FCC took the step of loosening its rules on ownership of media properties. Previously, ownership of television stations, newspapers, and radio stations had been limited. But the new rules allow for more cross ownership. Many argued against the proposal, and some lawmakers in Congress vowed to repeal it with legislation. Some believe the new regulations will not stand.

The *San Antonio Express-News* published stories about these controversial changes, noting that some newspaper chains, including the company that owns the local paper, might be interested in acquiring television stations in the same markets to allow them to increase their advertising and save on costs by combining the management of various media. The story also quotes a journalism professor who predicted that smaller media companies will have trouble entering markets, and minorities may have a hard time acquiring media operations as a result of the ruling.

To be sure, the FCC wants to maintain competition among the industries that it regulates. Without competition, companies might raise rates. If the FCC is changing the rules for one of the industries it regulates, reporters should check with their local companies to see if it is going to affect them. If the new rules will cause local companies to make changes, then that could be a story.

The FCC can also be a good resource for reporters writing consumer-related stories about phone bills or wireless phone bills, explaining the different charges.

The FCC also is involved in other issues, such as pushing for more rural telecommunication service and promoting rural health-care providers to receive the same rates as those paid to health care providers in urban areas. These are important trends in communities across the country that should be covered as major events for the local business community.

The FCC also regulates telemarketers who make those pesky phone calls trying to get people to accept a new credit card or donate to the local police league. According to the FCC, these calls cannot be made before 8 a.m. or after 9 p.m., and the callers must identify themselves and what organization they are calling for.

In chap. 6 on mergers and acquisitions, the FTC's role in reviewing deals between companies was discussed. But there are plenty more ways that the FTC becomes involved with regulating business. For example, the care labels on the backs of clothing are the result of FTC regulations, as are the stickers on home appliances showing their energy efficiency. The FTC oversees a wide variety of rules and regulations for businesses that are designed to protect the consumer from unfair and deceptive practices. The agency reviews everything from weight loss advertising to the protection of children online. If an online retailer promises to ship a gift before a holiday but doesn't deliver, the FTC steps in and investigates. If a small business is billed for unordered toner or printer cartridges, the agency will review the claim.

The agency also regulates credit laws, such as the Truth in Lending Act, which requires creditors to disclose in writing certain cost information, such as the annual percentage rate (APR), before consumers enter into credit transactions, and the Consumer Leasing Act, which requires lessors to give consumers information on lease costs and terms. Another credit law that the FTC enforces is the Fair Debt Collection Practices Act, which prohibits debt collectors from using unfair, deceptive, or abusive practices, including overcharging, harassing, and disclosing consumers' debt to third parties.

Competition and boycotts are also big issues with the FTC. The agency has challenged boycotts by physicians seeking to prevent the establishment of a competing health care facility. And it frowns upon agreements between cable TV companies not to enter a competitor's territory. Price fixing is also banned by the FTC. It encourages competitors to set rates and terms independently. The FTC has the power to charge businesses with lawsuits to prevent them from using what has been interpreted to be unfair or illegal business practices. Or it may seek to introduce new rules to outlaw a business tactic that it believes is hurting competition or deceiving consumers.

The following recent story shows how the FTC was going after illegal fundraisers trying to get money from unsuspecting consumers by telling them they were donating to needy causes:

> Federal regulators are going to court—and launching a public education campaign— against fraudulent fundraisers charged with bilking millions of dollars out of donors

who thought they were giving to needy veterans, disabled children, police officers and firefighters.

The Federal Trade Commission on Tuesday announced it had charged five operations with fraud. One Florida telemarketer is accused of donors by having its solicitors claim to be firefighters or police officers. One in San Diego falsely said that money raised would benefit veterans, the FTC contends. Another telephone solicitor in Anaheim is accused of raising money for sham non-profits.

In addition to the FTC enforcement actions, law-enforcement officials in 16 states also announced fraud charges Tuesday against what they called sham charities.

"By diverting charitable dollars, these scam artists undermine the public's confidence in legitimate charitable fundraising and injure legitimate non-profit organizations," said Howard Beales, director of the FTC's Bureau of Consumer Protection.

Earlier this month, the U.S. Supreme Court ruled that telemarketers who misrepresent the percentage of a donation that actually goes to charity can be prosecuted for consumer fraud.

In the Anaheim case, the FTC says Tamara Bell created brochures, telephone scripts and Web sites to raise millions of dollars for six non-existent charities: American Veterans Council, Children's AIDS Council, Children's Relief Services, Disabled Children's Charity, Firefighters' Assistance Foundation and Police and Sheriff's Support Fund.

In a civil settlement reached Monday, Bell's organization was banned from telemarketing.

In another case, the FTC charges a San Diego company claimed to raise money for the Junior Police Academy, which would send police officers to schools in the donor's area to give talks on alternatives to drugs and gangs. In fact, the FTC says, no police officers ever visited schools. The company, West Coast Advertising & Marketing, pulled in more than $4 million in contributions from 1998 to 2001, with fundraisers pocketing 85 percent of the amount, the FTC says. The charity, Junior Police Academy, received the remaining 15 percent.

"These are particularly heartless scams," Beales said.

Thirty-four states, including California, joined the education campaign, dubbed, "Operation Phony Philanthropy."

With just a little bit of investigation, donors can quickly sniff out problems, said Dan Moore, vice president of Guidestar (www.guidestar.org), which provides an online listing of tax statements of non-profits.

No more than 33 percent of funds raised in a year should be spent on fundraising, according to standards set by the BBB Wise Giving Alliance (www.give.org)

"The most important thing," he added, "is to ask questions."[10]

The FTC and other regulations went after small companies in this story, not the huge corporations that dominate most business coverage. Many reporters mistakenly think that huge federal regulatory agencies concern themselves only with the biggest businesses. But a large portion of their work is in enforcing the rules against small companies that may have never been covered by the media in the past.

---

[10]From "Charity fraud alleged by FTC; Agency: firm scammed donors," by J. Boudreau, May 21, 2003, *San Jose Mercury News*, p. 1. Copyright 2003 by *San Jose Mercury News*. All rights reserved. Reprinted with permission.

WORKPLACE REGULATIONS

In addition to regulating how companies sell products to consumers and how they manufacture these products, government agencies also ensure that the workplace is safe for workers and that employees will not be harassed by employers.

The government agencies that oversee workplace-related issues include OSHA, the Equal Employment Opportunity Commission (EEOC), and the National Labor Relations Board (NLRB). Although they are federal agencies, they are active in virtually every town and city across the country.

OSHA investigates businesses in which there have been accidents or injuries on the job. It also investigates job-related deaths. If the business has violated OSHA regulations that led to the injury or death, then the company can be fined. Since its creation in 1971, the number of workplace deaths has declined by 50% and work-related injuries and illnesses have declined by 40%.

In 2001, the latest statistics available, the rate of workplace injuries and illnesses was 5.7 per 100 workers, the lowest level ever. And there were 5,900 worker deaths that year, not including the deaths from the September 11 terrorist attacks.

In 2002, OSHA conducted more than 37,000 workplace investigations, with the bulk of those occurring in high-hazard worksites such as construction. The agency found more than 78,000 violations and levied nearly $73 million in fines. State job safety and health plans found another 144,000 violations and handed out almost $76 million in fines.

These workplace investigations and fines are public record, and can be obtained by asking for them. They are important documents, particularly for journalists reporting about workers who were injured or killed on the job. The following excerpt shows how reviewing OSHA records about a workplace can help tell a better story:

> An Italian man working on equipment at the Case New Holland plant remained in a Lincoln hospital Tuesday, two days after he fell into a tank of poisonous potassium hydroxide and suffered severe burns.
>
> Federal officials said the Sunday accident was the third they were aware of in five months at the Grand Island farm-machinery plant, where a subcontracted worker from Mexico fell to his death Oct. 25.
>
> Gerardo Piazza, 38, was in critical condition at St. Elizabeth Regional Medical Center. He suffered second- and third-degree burns over 80 percent of his body, said Jo Miller, a spokeswoman with the Lincoln hospital.
>
> Piazza, whose family lives in Milan, Italy, was flown to Lincoln Sunday by medical helicopter from Grand Island's St. Francis Medical Center.
>
> He apparently fell into the potassium hydroxide tank about 2:30 p.m. that day but managed to get out and yell for help, Grand Island Police Capt. William Holloway said Tuesday.
>
> He said other workers rushed to Piazza, removed his clothing and rinsed him off with water before Grand Island paramedics arrived to treat him. Only Piazza's head and buttocks were not burned, Holloway said.

Potassium hydroxide, sometimes called lye or caustic potash, is a corrosive acid sometimes used for cleaning. It can be fatal if swallowed and can cause severe burns if it comes into contact with living tissue.

Steve Lee, manager of the Case New Holland plant, did not return telephone messages Tuesday.

He said Monday that Piazza's family had been notified and planned to travel to Lincoln.

Lee said Piazza was alone when he fell into the tank, which is behind a safety barrier that requires authorization to cross.

Plant officials didn't know why Piazza was near the tank, in which parts of combines are dipped before painting.

Lee identified Piazza as a project engineer with Comau Geico, a paint-supply firm based in Milan.

That firm and Case New Holland, which employs 700 people in Grand Island, are part of the Italy-based Fiat Group.

New Holland NV belonged to that group before merging with Case Corp. in 1999, according to material on Fiat's Internet site. Both firms had deep roots in U.S. farm-machinery production.

The merger formed CNH Global, which announced in July 2000 that it would consolidate its Case IH and New Holland combine production at the Grand Island plant.

Another Fiat company, Comau Pico, and a subcontractor have been fined for safety problems at the plant related to or predating the Oct. 25 fatality, said Bonita Winingham, assistant Omaha-area director for the U.S. Occupational Safety and Health Administration.

Holloway said Juan Jimenez Lemus, 36, died of head injuries after he fell 12 feet from a scaffolding onto a concrete floor.

He had been working with a piece of sheathed insulation and wore a safety harness, but the harness was unattached, police said.

Lemus, who came from Celaya in the Mexican state of Guanajuato, was employed by a firm called One de Mexico.

Winingham said that firm, which lists a Grand Island address, has agreed to pay fines totaling $24,479 for four OSHA violations found after Lemus' death and six found in inspections between Aug. 7 and Sept. 11.

The earlier inspections were triggered by a July 31 allegation that a worker was hurt during construction of a conveyor system at the plant, she said.

Comau Pico has agreed to pay $7,425 in fines for four violations found in inspections from Aug. 7 to Sept. 17, she said.

The firm has until Jan. 13 to contest $70,000 in fines that OSHA assessed Dec. 16 for eight violations found from Oct. 23 to Dec. 16, she said.

The Case New Holland plant itself has been admitted to OSHA's Voluntary Protection Program, Winingham said. The program, limited to employers with a strong health and safety record, exempts a worksite from programmed inspections by OSHA.[11]

Without the background information about the numerous fines and violations, a reader might believe that the most recent accident was an isolated incident.

---

[11]From " Worker falls into tank of poison; An Italian engineer sustained severe burns in an accident at Grand Island's Case New Holland plant," by T. Van Kampen, Jan. 1, 2003, *Omaha World Herald*, p. 1B. Copyright 2003 by *Omaha World Herald*. Reprinted with permission.

But the story indicates, by using OSHA information, that this workplace may be unsafe for workers and that the company has not done a good job in improving conditions.

OSHA can levy fines on the basis of the seriousness of the violation and whether it is a repeat offense. A violation that the employer willingly or knowingly commits carries a fine between $5,000 and $70,000. A violation in which there is a probability that death or serious physical harm could occur and the employer knows, or should know, of the hazard, can result in a penalty of up to $7,000 per violation.

If a company was found in violation of a regulation on one inspection and then found in violation of a similar rule on a reinspection, it can be fined up to $70,000. Failure to correct a violation can result in a fine of up to $7,000 per day until it is corrected. And violations that have an affect on safety and health, but probably would not cause death or serious injury, can result in a fine of up to $7,000.

A reporter may not get an indication that there is a workplace safety problem at a local company until tipped off by a lawsuit filed against the company by an injured worker or by a union complaint. It is helpful for any reporter covering a large employer to develop relationships with employees to learn about OSHA complaints. In addition, the OSHA Web site can also be searched for complaints by company name.

The EEOC was created in 1964 and prevents businesses from employment discrimination on the basis of race, color, sex, age, religion, or national origin. In 1990, the Americans with Disabilities Act extended the EEOC's regulations to include workers with disabilities. The commission has five commissioners, all appointed by the U.S. president, who serve 5-year terms, as well as a general counsel who serves a 4-year term.

The EEOC receives approximately 80,000 charges of discrimination annually from employees of private businesses. The agency will then investigate, and if it discovers that there is reasonable cause that discrimination has occurred, the EEOC may attempt to reach a settlement with the company. If a settlement cannot be reached, the EEOC may file charges against the business in federal court.

In 2001, the EEOC filed 431 lawsuits against businesses and settled 354 lawsuits, obtaining more than $50 million in damages for workers. These settlements are often newsworthy, and should be reported, as were the following cases in South Florida:

A store manager who alleged she was fired after complaining about sexual harassment that female employees endured from a male manager was awarded $250,000 in back pay and monetary relief after regulators sued her employer.

It was one of three retaliation lawsuits against Florida employers recently settled by the Miami office of the U.S. Equal Employment Opportunity Commission.

"Retaliating against employees for complaining about what they reasonably believed to be employment discrimination is contrary to federal law," said Delner Franklin-Thomas, EEOC regional attorney in Miami.

In Florida, there were 1,725 retaliation filings in 2002, accounting for 29 percent of all discrimination charge filings in the state. Retaliation charge filings with the EEOC nationwide have increased by 33 percent from 17,070 filings in 1995 to 22,768 filings in 2002.

The settlements announced Tuesday were with:

Norstan Apparel Shops Inc., a New York-based chain of women's clothing stores called Fashion Cents. The agency won $250,000 in monetary relief, including back pay and compensatory damages, for a store manager in Tampa. She alleged that she was fired for complaining to district managers about a manager who harassed female workers.

Attempts to reach the company president for comment were unsuccessful.

Marine Bank of the Florida Keys. The EEOC charged the bank with allowing a vice president's sexually offensive conduct to go unchecked and with firing a female employee for complaining about the conduct.

The suit was resolved with the bank agreeing to pay two employees $220,000 as well as do annual training at all facilities and comply with EEOC monitoring.

"We take this very seriously," said the bank's president, Hunter Padgett. "We're glad to have the lawsuit behind us. On April 4, we begin the training, and we've made it clear that we will not tolerate those behaviors."

GeoLogistics Americas, a Santa Ana, Calif.-based logistics and freight forwarder, was ordered by a federal judge to pay $100,000 to an employee who alleged that a branch manager in Jacksonville fired her after she complained of discrimination.

She complained that GeoLogistics provided forklift training and certification to male workers, but consistently denied her requests for the training because she is a woman. The court also required GeoLogistics to do annual training for managers and complete reports to the EEOC.

Attempts to reach the company's director of human resources were unsuccessful.[12]

Again, these cases were against small companies, not the big businesses that dominate coverage. To be sure, the EEOC has filed charges against high-profile employers such as Home Depot and Hooter's. But again, a large amount of its regulatory work is with small businesses that make up the bulk of the economy.

Reporters should find out where the local EEOC office is in their state. That is where complaints are filed by local workers, and where the investigations begin. If the EEOC is going to take action against a business, it will file its lawsuit in federal court. If a reporter suspects a case is about to happen, he or she should check the clerk's office regularly.

The NLRB also protects workers on the job. It oversees the laws governing relationships between labor unions representing workers and corporations. The NLRB has two basic functions: One is to conduct secret-ballot elections to determine whether the workers at a specific employer want to be represented by a union and which one, the other is to investigate unfair labor practices by employers or unions.

---

[12]From "3 employer lawsuits settled; regulators take aim at retaliation," by J. Fleischer Tamen, March 19, 2003, *The Sun-Sentinel*, p. 3D. Copyright 2003 by *The South Florida Sun-Sentinel*. Reprinted with permission.

An NLRB official oversees an election. Sometimes the story with one of these elections is actually the events that caused the workers to consider union representation. It might be beneficial to interview some of these workers to ask them about their working conditions and what they believe they will get out of joining a union. There may be pro-union and anti-union workers at the employer. And the employer may also be campaigning actively to defeat the union. Most businesses do not want their workers represented by a union. They believe it adds additional costs to running their operations.

An unfair labor practice can mean a number of different things. It could be a supervisor threatening workers with the loss of their jobs if they join a union, or threatening to close the plant or warehouse if the workers vote to join the union. Promising benefits to workers if they vote against the union can also be a violation.

Unions can also engage in unfair labor practices that could lead to an investigation. They may threaten workers with the loss of their job if they do not support the union, or they could refuse to file a grievance against a supervisor if the worker has criticized union officials in the past.

After a charge is filed, an investigation is conducted. If a regional director believes a violation has occurred, it will attempt to mediate a settlement. If no settlement can be reached, then the case will go to an NLRB administrative law judge who will issue a written decision. Those decisions can be appealed to the five-member board that oversees the NLRB. About 30,000 unfair labor practice charges are filed each year. And of those, about one-third are found to have merit. More than 90% of those cases are settled.

The relationship between businesses and regulatory agencies can often be adversarial, which makes for stories by reporters who know how to obtain the details leading to the confrontation. Although regulatory agencies may seem boring at first glance, they play an important role in the business world, setting rules and regulations for how Corporate America should operate. Because of that role, they are vital sources of information that should be regularly checked.

GLOSSARY

articles of incorporation: A set of documents filed with state authorities for the purpose of documenting the creation of a corporation.

Consumer Product Safety Commission: The federal agency that protects consumers against faulty products. Its jurisdiction covers product safety for more than 15,000 products, and it can force a recall of a product.

Environmental Protection Agency: The federal agency whose job is to protect the environment and human health by preventing the release of harmful items into the environment. The EPA can ban the use of certain products, and can fine companies for violating environmental laws.

Equal Employment Opportunity Commission: The federal agency created in 1964 to investigate claims of employment discrimination on the basis of race, color, sex, age, natural origin and religion. Its jurisdiction has since been expanded to include discrimination based on age and disability.

Federal Communications Commission: The federal regulatory agency charged with overseeing interstate and international communications by radio, television, wire, satellite and cable.

Federal Trade Commission: The federal agency that works to ensure that the nation's markets are vigorous, efficient and free of restrictions that harm consumers. The FTC enforces federal consumer protection laws that prevent fraud, deception and unfair business practices. The commission also enforces federal antitrust laws that prohibit anticompetitive mergers and other business practices that restrict competition and harm consumers.

National Labor Relations Board: The federal agency created in 1935 to enforce the National Labor Relations Act. It conducts secret-ballot elections to determine whether employees want union representation and investigates unfair labor practices by employers and unions.

Occupational Safety and Health Administration: The federal agency whose job it is to enforce laws to ensure a safe and healthy workplace.

public utilities commission: State agencies that regulate water, electrical and telephone companies. In some states, the agency may be called the public service commission.

Secretary of State's office: The state agency that registers a variety of business organizations including corporations, assumed business names, banks, insurance companies, limited liability companies, limited liability partnerships and limited partnerships. Other business-related filings include trade and service marks, auctioneer's licenses, legal newspaper registrations, among others.

Securities and Exchange Commission: The federal agency whose job it is to protect investors and ensure the integrity of the stock markets. The SEC regulates publicly traded companies, companies who trade stocks and investors.

Superfund: The federal government's program to clean up the nation's uncontrolled hazardous waste sites.

Uniform Commercial Code: A set of laws regulating commercial transactions, especially ones involving the sale of goods and secured transactions.

REFERENCES

Boudreau, J. (2003, May 21). Charity fraud alleged by FTC; Agency: firms scammed donors. *San Jose Mercury News.* p. 1.

Choe, S., & Wright, G. L. (2003, May 11). Feds deepen Duke probe. *Charlotte Observer.* p. 1A.

Federal Trade Commission (2003, June 10). News release. Washington, DC: Author.

Fishman, M. (2002, December 20). Duke Power assailed at hearing: Customers complain about the utility's planning and actions after recent ice storm. *The News & Observer.* p. B1.

Fleischer Tamen, J. (2003, March 19). 3 employer lawsuits settled; regulators take aim at retaliation. *Sun-Sentinel.* p. 3D.

Jacobs, P. (2002, September 21). Gilead pill wins approval to treat hepatitis B; FDA report says Hepsera slows disease's progress. *San Jose Mercury News.* p. 1.

Karash, J. A. (2003, April 11). Operating profits. *Kansas City Star.* p. C1.

Kennedy, S. (2001, August 11). Fast-food toys lead in recalls; Kiddie-meal freebies made up 77 percent of hazardous toys recalled last year. *Los Angeles Times.* p. 1.

Patel, P. (2003, April 24). Allstate seeks premium hikes; condo, auto rates targeted. *The Sun-Sentinel.* p. 1D.

(2001, August 1). Madison utility requests $113.1 million in rate hikes. *Milwaukee Business Journal.* Retrieved Nov. 25, 2003 from http://www.bizjournals.com/milwaukee/stories.

Poling, T. E. (2003, June 4). Big media firms like new FCC rules; Looser regulations have companies discussing mergers, acquisitions, swaps. *San Antonio Express-News.* p. 1E.

Rives, K. (2003, May 7). Labor Department tries carrot: It recommends tax breaks for companies that willingly improve safety. *The News & Observer.* p. D1.

Saunders, M. (2002, January 28). Research & analysis: Latest branch data revealed. SNL Interactive. Retrieved Dec. 23, 2002 from http://www.snl.com

von Kampen, T. (2003, January 1). Worker falls into tank of poison: An Italian engineer sustained severe burns in an accident at Grand Island's Case New Holland plant. *Omaha World Herald.* p. 1B.

Wagner, J. (2000, July 21). Planners bounce nursing home plans to council; Parma residents vow to continue fighting proposal. *Cleveland Plain Dealer.* p. 3B.

Other Books on Business Regulation

Bradsher, K. (2002). *High and mighty: SUVs—The world's most dangerous vehicles and how they got that way.* New York: Public Affairs.

Hilts, P. J. (2003). *Protecting America's health: The FDA, business, and one hundred years of regulation.* New York: Knopf.

Shapiro, S. (1987). *Wayward capitalists: Targets of the Securities and Exchange Commission.* New Haven, CT: Yale University Press.

Yager, D. V. (1996). *NLRB: Agency in crisis.* Washington, DC: LPA.

SUGGESTED EXERCISES

1. Ask five people you know if they would file a complaint with the EEOC if they felt they were being harassed or discriminated against on the job. What circumstances would force them to file a complaint? If some answered that they wouldn't file a complaint, why wouldn't they?

2. What type of bad service would it take from your phone company or cable company to lead you to file a complaint with regulators?

3. How would you know if your electrical company or water company was overcharging you? Where could you go to have your bill checked?

4. If you purchased a product that didn't work, what three steps could you take to try to get your money back from the retailer or the manufacturer?

5. Why does the government play such a large role in regulating business? What would happen if the government didn't regulate how companies sold their products or manufactured them?

15

Finding Information on the Internet

ANALYZING AND DETERMINING RELIABILITY OF SITES

Nowadays, reporters are getting more and more of their information and facts used in stories from the Internet. But is everything on the World Wide Web credible? No, and that is why business journalists conducting research online should be wary of what they are finding.

The Internet has drastically changed how reporters and editors do their jobs in every area of journalism. It used to be that reporters or editors would have to go to the courthouse to find a lawsuit or criminal record, or they would have to send a check to some out-of-town federal agency and wait two weeks for a document to show up in the mail.

The Internet has made it possible for journalists to get much of the information they need to report a story just by clicking on a few favorites on their desktop—without leaving their desk in the newsroom. But, according to the Public Record Research System, only about 20% of public records are available on the Internet. The others are still maintained on paper stored in millions of file cabinets and drawers, unable to be perused with some keyboard clicks.

And even the public records available on the Internet can be hard to find. Many reporters do not know where to begin. Ginger Livingston, a reporter for the *Greenville Daily Reflector* in eastern North Carolina, did not know where to turn when she needed to find out information about the Dutch parent company of a large employer in her town, and the public relations people were not much help. As it turns out, the information Livingston needed was available at several Web sites.

Another problem with researching topics online is that the information may come from a site where it is not clear who is operating the URL. Many young reporters find information on the Internet and believe it must be true if it is available online. That is simply not the case. Information on the World Wide Web may reflect the opinion or biases of whoever is operating the site. And there is plenty of information online that has not been updated in years.

Though it can be reasonably assumed that Web sites operated by state and federal government agencies and Internet domains run by public and private companies for the purpose of disseminating information about their operations, are reliable places to obtain information for a story, millions of other sites are not as trustworthy.

However, there are actually a handful of Web sites that allow a person to check the ownership of other Web sites. This handy tool can go a long way in determining whether the Web site is reliable. One of these sites is located at http://www. whois.net/ which allows people to look at the ownership of a current domain names as well as who owned an Internet site that is now defunct. Other similar sites are located at http://www.allwhois.com and http://www.networksolutions. com/en_US/whois/index.jhtml. Insert a company's Web address into one of these and see what you find.

Most of the time, the administrative contact person will be an attorney for the company, but often they will also include a technical contact. This is the person who probably actually runs the Web site, updating it with information as needed. And the information that comes back from one of these searches could also tell you when was the last time the site was updated.

For a reporter searching the ownership of a Web site of which he or she is unsure of the information and how recent it is, or if he or she is unsure of the Web site's agenda, it can make or break a story, particularly if the reporter plans to use the information in his or her report. Failing to do so could cause the reporter to lose credibility if the information is false.

One last word about searching for information online: Beware of doing basic searches using a common search engine such as Google or Lycos. Although these are great services, they will also give an abundance of information about people or topics that may not be germane to the search.

The following list of Web sites for business journalists is by no means comprehensive. But it does attempt to offer some of the most widely known and used sites by reporters in gathering information about business and economics topics and issues. All of these sites have been reviewed and are credible sources of information. When in doubt, check the site with one of the resources above.

General Business News Sites

http://www.ap.org: The home site of the Associated Press, the international wire service.

http://www.barrons.com/: The weekly business newspaper published by Dow Jones. *Barron's* focuses on the stock market and public companies.

http://www.bizjournals.com: The home site for the American City Business journals chain, publisher of 41 weekly business newspapers across the country. From this site, you can access any of their business publications.

http://www.bloomberg.net: Home page of Bloomberg News, the international business wire service. This site charges to look up old articles, but can be a valuable and quick way to look up a public company's current stock price or to see how the overall market is doing.

http://www.businessweek.com: Home of the weekly business magazine published by McGraw-Hill. Many stories on *BusinessWeek's* site are items that aren't published in the magazine.

http://cbs.marketwatch.com/news/default.asp?siteid=&avatar=seen&dist=ctmw: Founded in 1997, this Web site publishes more than 800 stories, briefs and headlines each day by 70 journalists in nine bureaus. Headquarters is in San Francisco.

http://www.economist.com/: Online source for world business and current affairs with a definite British viewpoint. The site has an archive for old articles, and backgrounders of current events that can be helpful.

http://money.cnn.com/: Web site put together by the editors of *Money* magazine and CNN, both subsidiaries of TimeWarner. This site has nice charts, such as the top 25 deals year-to-date, that can be quick references.

http://news.ft.com/home/us: The online site for *The Financial Times*, the British-based newspaper. Under the business menu, the site has a list of public companies where you can read the latest stories for a particular business.

http://www.forbes.com/: Home page for the New York-based magazine, which has links to the magazine's lists of the richest people and largest public and private companies, as well as access to Reuters business news.

http://www.fortune.com/fortune/: Home page for the business magazine owned by TimeWarner. Site has access to its rankings of the best companies to work for and the most-admired companies.

http://www.investors.com/: *Investor's Business Daily*. The stock chart on the home page shows stocks with abnormally high trading volume, an indication of where investors are putting their money.

http://online.wsj.com/public/us: *The Wall Street Journal's* Web site allows readers to look at stories from that day's issue. The menu on the left-hand side allows you to pick business stories by geography.

http://moneycentral.msn.com/cnbc/tv/default.asp: The Internet location for television station CNBC, which chronicles business news for viewers. The site can tell you what company executives and analysts are slated to appear on CNBC and at what time.

http://www.reuters.com/: Home page for the international wire service. Click on "Finance" near the top left corner of the page to see the latest business stories.

http://www.thestreet.com/: Home page for the online business news service that is primarily subscription based. One of the best free features on the site is a list of Wall Street analyst upgrades, downgrades and initiations.

Basic Journalism Web Site

http://www.businesswire.com/expertsource/: BusinessWire provides a list of expert sources for important topics in the news. This can be helpful when you're writing about a topic and are searching for experts to interview.

http://www.gehrung.com/biznet/biznet.html: This Web site also puts reporters in touch with experts. The sources at this site are from business schools across the country.

http://www.brbpub.com/pubrecsites.asp: One of the best Web sites out there for accessing public records. This site has nearly 1,700 county, state and federal court URLs where you can access public record information for free.

http://www.virtualgumshoe.com: Another excellent Web site for public records and online resources. Virtual Gumshoe has everything from adoption records to where to search for prison inmates by state.

http://www.powerreporting.com: A site managed by Pulitzer Prize winning journalist Bill Dedman. Power Reporting has links on how to find people, government sources and resources divided by individual newsroom beats.

http://journalism.berkeley.edu/resources/car/: Site maintained by the journalism school at the University of California at Berkeley. It has good tutorials and advice on researching information online and how to use the right search engine to find the most information.

http://www.facsnet.org/tools/biz_econ/biz_econ.php3: Site full of business reporting resources maintained by FACS, an independent, non-profit organization that does journalism training. Good articles on reading financial reports and understanding deregulation.

http://www.nfoic.org/: National Freedom of Information Coalition Web site. The Resources page has links to every state in the country. These links provide a handy resource for public records and public meetings, as well as links to state agency. Also included are links on how to write FOI letters.

http://www.sabew.org/: Home page for the Society of American Business Editors and Writers. If you're a member, log in and check out the links and resources for business journalists under the "Members Only" section. There's also a section here to post resumes and to search for jobs.

http://www.ire.org: Investigative Reporters and Editors Web site. This location has copies of thousands of stories, as well as tip sheets and guides to writing stories about any topic, available for free if you're a member.

http://www.journalismnet.com/: Run by a full-time journalist, this site has 300 different Web pages with more than 6,000 links designed to help journalists (and anyone else) find useful information fast.

http://www.mediaresource.org/: Sources for science and technology-related stories are available here for free. Run by Sigma Xi, the Scientific Research Society.

http://www.newstream.com/splash.html: Resource for daily news compiled by online journalists for online journalists. You must register to access this site, which is operated by BusinessWire and MediaLink.

http://www2.profnet.com/: Another good sources for finding experts to interview for stories. This site is operated by PRNewswire, but you may send a query to thousands of information officers without registering in ProfNet.

http://www.journaliststoolbox.com/newswriting/business.html: This site is run by the American Press Institute and includes handy links to business reporting topics such as Enron, small business and backgrounding companies.

http://www.score.org/: Site run by a nonprofit organization of retired executives and small business owners who act as mentors and trainers for other business executives. Can be valuable for experts and for background information on the business world.

http://www.washingtonpost.com/wp-dyn/business/specials/glossary/index.html: The glossary contains more than 1,250 business terms, organized and cross-referenced for your convenience.

http://www.nytimes.com/library/cyber/reference/busconn.html: A selective guide to Internet business, financial and investing resources, compiled by Rich Meislin, editor in chief of the New York Times Electronic Media Co.

http://www.investopedia.com: Good site for tutorials and a business term dictionary. Insert virtually any word, and Investopedia will define it and use it in a business reference.

http://www.investorwords.com/: The biggest, best site for investing terms on the Web. Also very good for looking up any business term you don't understand.

http://www.economist.com/encyclopedia/Dictionary.cfm: Breaks business terms into categories such as accounting, banking, E-commerce, economics, HR, and personnel.

http://www.militarysearch.org: Find out whether a person actually served in the military with a report direct from the Department of Defense. There is a fee to get this information.

Economic Data and Resources

http://minneapolisfed.org/bb/: Archive maintained by the Minneapolis Federal
   Reserve on the Beige Book. The Beige Book is released two weeks prior to
   each FOMC meeting eight times per year. Each Federal Reserve bank gathers
   anecdotal information on current economic conditions in its district through
   reports from bank and branch directors and interviews with key businessmen,
   economists, market experts, and other sources. The Beige Book summarizes
   this information by district and sector. It is not a commentary on the views
   of Federal Reserve officials.

http://www.bls.gov: Tons of information is available at the Bureau of Labor
   Statistics, run by the Department of Commerce. Everything is here, from the
   Consumer Price Index to import/export data to industry information. This is
   one of the most comprehensive sites for government information.

http://www.census.gov/: Home page for the U.S. Census Bureau, part of the Department of Commerce. This is where to begin if you're looking for general
   data or information on the 1992 or 1997 Economic Census, which breaks
   down the country's economy by industry, state, county and metropolitan
   statistical area.

http://www.census.gov/cgi-bin/briefroom/BriefRm: The Economic Briefing
   Room for the Census Bureau. This is where to go to get the latest reports
   from the Census Bureau, such as construction spending, new home sales,
   housing starts and inventories.

http://www.census.gov/epcd/cbp/view/cbpview.html: County Business Patterns is an annual series that provides county and state economic data by
   industry. The series is useful for studying the economic activity of small
   areas; analyzing economic changes over time; and as a benchmark for statistical series, surveys and databases between economic censuses. Businesses
   use the data for analyzing market potential, measuring the effectiveness of
   sales and advertising programs, setting sales quotas, and developing budgets.

http://www.conference-board.org/: Home site of the Conference Board, where
   you go to look at the latest Consumer Confidence Index survey results. It
   also compiles a survey on leading economic indicators.

http://www.econdata.net: Sponsored by the Economic Development Association, EconData.net has 1,000 links to socioeconomic data sources, arranged
   by subject and provider and its own list of the ten best sites for finding
   regional economic data.

http://www.federalreserve.gov: Home page for the central bank of the United
   States. Check out "Economic Research and Data" from the menu on the left,
   as well as the "News and Events" section, which is where you can access
   speeches and testimony by Fed members.

http://federalreserve.gov/otherfrb.htm: Links to the 12 Federal Reserve districts,
   where there is also economic research and data available for that specific

geographic region. Working papers are available on many of these Web sites. They can give you a clue as to what the regional feds are thinking about.

http://www.phil.frb.org: Home page of the Philadelphia Reserve. Singled out here because of its surveys on economic activity indexes and leading indexes for Pennsylvania, New Jersey and Delaware, which sometimes can be a barometer for the rest of the country.

http://www.ny.frb.org: Home page for the New York Reserve. Has a nice section on the banking industry, including memos sent to banks, and a consumer section. Home page has a quick update on foreign currency exchanges and certificate of deposit rates.

http://www.dismal.com: Site run by Economy.com, a Pennsylvania-based company, to provide news and information about economic trends and research for professional investors, government agencies and others.

http://www.imf.org: The International Monetary Fund. A good place to go to if you're writing about a company or business with operations in an international company. This site can give you an indication of that country's economic shape.

http://www.bea.doc.gov: The Bureau of Economic Analysis at the Commerce Department. Go here to get data on the Gross Domestic Product by industry and by state. Also has information on personal income by state.

http://research.stlouisfed.org/system_change_notice.html: Go here to subscribe to an e-mail system that allows you to receive economic data and research publications from the Federal Reserve in St. Louis. (Note: Many of the other Federal Reserve sites also have an e-mail notification system whenever something has been added.)

http://www.stat-usa.gov/: A service of the U.S. Commerce Department, this is a site for the U.S. business, economic and trade community, providing authoritative information from the Federal government. The State of the Nation section has virtually all of the major economic reports from the federal government.

http://www.nber.org: The National Bureau of Economic Research Web site, this is run by a private, non-profit organization dedicated to promoting a better understanding of how the economy works. Two of its best features include a calendar of business cycles for the past two centuries and another calendar showing when key economic data will be released.

http://www.cjr.org/tools/inflation/: From the *Columbia Journalism Review*, this allows anyone to calculate the value of a dollar into present-day values, adjusted for inflation.

http://www.publicdebt.treas.gov/sav/savcalc.htm: The Bureau of Public Debt's savings bond calculator. Helps find what the worth of a bond is today.

http://www.x-rates.com/: Site that tracks the value of the U.S. dollar to currencies from other countries. This site also has a currency calculator and a way to look up the historic value of the dollar.

http://www.newsengin.com/neFreeTools.nsf: A cost of living calculator. Uses the Consumer Price Index to compare the real buying power in historical dollar amounts.

http://www.ficalc.com/: A calculator for the value of bonds, everything from treasuries to municipal and government bonds. Also some European bonds are here.

http://www.smartmoney.com/onebond/index.cfm?story=bondcalculator: A bond calculator offered by *Smart Money* magazine. Begin by entering the bond's coupon rate and maturity. If you then enter a price, the calculator will display the bond's yield to maturity; if you enter a yield, the calculator will show you the corresponding price.

http://www.whitehouse.gov/fsbr/esbr.html: Easy access to current Federal economic indicators. It provides links to information produced by a number of Federal agencies. All of the information included in the Economic Statistics Briefing Room is maintained and updated by the statistical units of those agencies. All the estimates for the indicators presented in the Federal Statistics Briefing Rooms are the most currently available values. The indicators include employment, productivity, transportation, income, international, money, output, and prices.

Business-Related Sites

http://www.analystcall.com: Same-day transcripts of earnings conference calls for most public companies. Username and password required. The transcripts can be invaluable if you're covering several earnings in one day.

http://www.annualreportservice.com/: A free site that provides annual reports for public companies. You need to register to access this site, but it does have access to thousands of annual reports.

http://www.assetalt.com/products/dir/index.htm: Provides information about alternative asset and private equity investments. If you're writing about private companies with venture capital investments, you may want to look at this site.

http://www.bigbook.com: Online directory that lets you look up the mailing address and phone number of any business in the country. Can also search to find what's near an address.

http://www.bizweb.com: Breaks down companies by industries, from antiques to the Web. This site has listings for more than 46,000 companies in more than 200 categories.

http://www.bbb.org: The Better Business Bureau. Check out any business in the nation at this site by clicking on the "Check out a Company" icon near the top left of the home page.

http://www.businesswire.com: Provides news releases from companies and other sources by industry, geography and subject. Also has an events calendar for major industry conferences.

http://www.ceres.org/:The Coalition for Environmentally Responsible Economies, which tries to encourage companies to adhere to an environmental code when conducting business. Also encourages investors and money managers to invest in such companies.

http://www.corptech.com: Has profiles of more than 50,000 U.S. technology companies, their products and the executives who run them. It contains detailed profiles on public and private manufacturers and developers of technology products including smaller, privately held companies. Seventeen high-tech industries are covered from factory automation to biotech, computers to pharmaceuticals and defense to environmental.

http://www.edgar-online.com/people/: Searches SEC filings by a person's name or displays all people associated with a specific company name.

http://www.freeedgar.com: Access to all public company filings. However, you must register and the site has become more pay in recent years. If you need SEC filings for a company and can't pay for them, might need to go to www.sec.gov.

http://www.hoovers.com: Nice background information on all public and many private companies. Includes competitors.

http://www.internalmemos.com/memos/: Bills itself as the Internet's largest collection of corporate memos and internal communication. Recent company memos range from IBM to Western Union.

http://www.mergerstat.com: Web site that tracks mergers and acquisitions activity around the globe. The home page tracks deal flow for the current year to the previous year on a year-to-date basis.

http://www.prnewswire.com: Exactly what it sounds like—press releases on the Internet. As a reporter, you can sign up to receive releases from only the industries and companies you want.

http://www.researchmag.com/: Corporate profiles and fact sheets are available at this site, as well as reports on analysts and industry studies.

http://www.searchsystems.net/: Provides more than 10,000 links to public record databases around the world to help you locate businesses, people and information. There is no cost to use this Web site, but some of the public records databases do charge a fee to access.

http://www.switchboard.com: Find home addresses and phone numbers for company executives and other sources. There are other search engines like this available on the Web, but Switchboard.com is perhaps the most comprehensive.

http://www.tollfree.att.net/index.html: Another online phone book that allows you to search for companies by name or by category, such as all florists or restaurants in a city.

http://www.thomasregister.com: Easy to use searchable database of thousands of companies and the products they manufacture. If you know a product, but don't know who makes it, this is the place to go.

http://www.netronline.com/public_records.htm: Public records online. The best site to use when trying to find someone's house. Has databases for every state. In some states, the search will also give you photos of the house.

http://biz.yahoo.com/i/: Yahoo! company and fund index. Quick and easy reference tool that can take you to information about public companies.

http://finance.yahoo.com/: Home page for finance news on Yahoo! One of its best features is the symbol lookup option, which allows you to find the stock ticker of a public company. (A similar feature is also on the Bloomberg site.)

http://dir.yahoo.com/Business_and_Economy/: Another good Web site that breaks down searching for business information by categories, from ethics and responsibility to transportation to business schools.

http://www.inta.org/tmcklst1.htm: The International Trademark Association's checklist site. Everything from A1 steak sauce to Zippo cigarette lighters.

Industry and Sector Information

http://www.agribiz.com/: News and information about the agriculture industry. Has links to specific agriculture news sources.

http://www.aha.org: Home site of the American Hospital Association. Also has links to state, regional and metropolitan hospital organizations. Also lots of good background statistics and information on the hospital industry, as well as a hospital locator function.

http://www.ama-assn.org/aps/amahg.htm: American Medical Association's web page. Click on "patients" near the top of the home page, and there's a search engine to find doctors throughout the country by name and specialty.

http://info.asaenet.org/gateway/OnlineAssocSlist.html: American Society of Association Executives. Search through more than 6,500 different industry associations and organizations here.

http://www.aba.com/default.htm: The home page of the American Bankers Association. The main site is divided nicely into a number of different industry-related issues ranging from agriculture credit to trust departments.

http://www.opensecrets.org/lobbyists/index.asp: Use this search engine to find out how much a company has been paying lobbyists to take state and federal lawmakers out to dinner to schmooze them.

http://www.mbda.gov/: The Minority Business Development Agency, which helps minority business owners. The MBDA has regional directors located in major cities throughout the country that could be useful sources.

http://www.nfib.com/: The National Federation of Independent Business lobbies for small businesses around the country. Its Web site has a link to find out what it's working on in every state in the country.

http://www.nrf.com: The National Retail Federation looks after the interests of the country's retailers. It also does surveys on consumer spending habits for certain events such as Father's Day that are posted here.

http://www.bankrate.com/brm/default.asp: Good place to go to compare interest rates in your state to the rest of the country. At the top of the page there's a way to select a state. After you've done that, select the product, such as an auto loan or a mortgage loan.

http://www.docboard.org/docfinder.html: Links to state associations of medical board examiners. Many of these state boards have online directors that will allow you to see if a doctor's license is up to date or has expired.

http://www.freep.com/index/autos.htm: Site run by the *Detroit Free Press* that covers the auto industry. If you are not in Detroit and need a quick run-down on the auto business, this is the place to go.

http://www.landings.com/:Database for airplane ownership. Click on "Databases" at the top of the page. Then find out if a company you cover owns a fleet of jets to transport its executives across the country.

http://api-ec.api.org/newsplashpage/index.cfm: Home page for the American Petroleum Institute. The "Testimony/Comments" section has Congressional testimony.

http://acnielsen.com/: ACNielsen provides market research, information, analysis and insights to the consumer products and service industries. The reports are not free, and can be quite expensive. Sometimes a company will provide the market share data for its industry.

http://www.restaurant.org/: The National Restaurant Association has some nice free industry reports under its "Industry Research" header near the top left of the home page. There are also state statistics on number of locations, employees, sales and sales growth available in the same location.

http://www.snl.com: Private company that tracks the real estate investment trust business, banking, financial services, insurance and energy. Its publications aren't free, but it has analysts who aren't tied to companies through investment banking fees willing to talk.

http://www.women-21.gov/index2.asp: Web site operated by the Small Business Administration for women business owners. Good information if you're writing about a business owned by a woman.

http://d2.dir.scd.yahoo.com/business_and_economy/organizations/professional/: Yahoo!'s directory of professional organizations, ranging from accountants to unions. This is a comprehensive guide to industry organizations.

Wall Street

http://www.aimr.org: The Association for Investment Management and Research is an international, nonprofit organization of more than 50,000 investment practitioners and educators in more than 100 countries. Good information on investment professionals, such as pay.

http://www.amex.com: Home page of the American Stock Exchange. Provides access to market and historical data, charts and tools.

http://bigcharts.marketwatch.com/: Great site that can give viewers a quick glimpse of how the NASDAQ and Dow Jones Industrial Average are performing during the day.

http://www.bondsonline.com/: The source for tracking bond prices and bond market news, searching for preferred stocks and convertible preferred stocks, Bondsonline.com has real-time pricing for more than 15,000 bond offerings.

http://www.cbot.com/: The Chicago Board of Trade location. The CBOT is the home to trading for the U.S. Treasury bond futures contract and other U.S. Treasury instruments spanning the yield curve.

http://www.cboe.com/Home/Default.asp: Chicago Board Options Exchange, another futures exchange. The CBOE lists options on more than 1,200 widely held stocks. In addition to stock options, the CBOE lists stock index options (e.g., the S&P 100 Index Option, abbreviated OEX), interest rate options, long-term options called LEAPS, and sector index options.

http://www.cme.com/: The Chicago Mercantile Exchange, which offers futures and options on futures in four basic product areas: interest rates, stock indexes, foreign exchange and commodities. The commodities include beef, dairy, forest and hog.

http://www.dailystocks.com/: DailyStocks.com bills itself as the biggest Web site for stock research. The site does have some research reports available for public companies.

http://www.earningsbase.com/research/index.jsp: Nice news site for Wall Street and economic information. Also provides insight on "Whisper numbers," what analysts and economic experts predict will actually happen as far as corporate earnings and economic indicators.

http://finance.lycos.com/: Home page for Quote.com now. This site allows you to create a portfolio of up to 10 stocks and track them for free. Can also review stock upgrades and downgrades and most-active stocks trading on the day.

http://www1.firstcall.com/index.shtml: First Call compiles analysts' estimates and ratings and provides these numbers. Good to check them when you're writing about a company's earnings estimates or whether the analyst community has actually changed how it rates stocks.

http://www.adviserinfo.sec.gov/IAPD/Content/IapdMain/iapd_SiteMap.asp: The Investment Advisor Public Disclosure web site run by the Securities and Exchange Commission. You can search for an investment adviser firm on this website and view that firm's Form ADV. Investment advisers file Form ADV to register with the SEC and/or the states. Form ADV contains information about an investment adviser and its business operations. Form

ADV also contains disclosure about certain disciplinary events involving
the adviser and its key personnel.

http://averages.dowjones.com/jsp/index.jsp: If you need to find out how one of
the Dow Jones stock indexes is moving, this is the place to go. Tracks the
industry indexes as well as the broader market indexes.

http://moneycentral.msn.com/investor/calendar/insider/top10insider.asp: Nice
site for tracking insider buying and selling. This site lists the top 10
companies for insider buying and insider selling. Click on the stock ticker
for the company to see the actual transactions.

http://www.ipofinancial.com: Good information about private companies
wanting to convert to public status, including a calendar of when they plan
to sell stock to the public.

http://www.kcbt.com/: The Kansas City Board of Trade is used by grain
elevators, exporters, millers and producers to protect their cash positions
by buying or selling futures and options. Stock market investors also utilize
KCBT products. Nonetheless, cash grain trading is still the core business
of many of KCBT's members.

http://www.moneypage.com/: Nice site with basic background on investing as
well as other topics. There is a guide to getting started to investing that is
a primer for everyone new to the stock market.

http://www.moodys.com: Web site for Moody's Investors Service, which
provides ratings and research on bond issues. The Web site allows you to
look for an issue by corporate name.

http://www.morningstar.com: Information about mutual funds and what stocks
they hold. Good way to find investors for companies you are writing about.
Lists the top stock holdings for all mutual funds.

http://www.multexnet.com: Real-time access to sell-side analyst reports from
the big Wall Street firms. Username and password required. Accessing the
analyst reports can cost money, but this service is worth the hassle.

http://www.nasdaq.com: Another good way to find investors of public companies you are writing about and to track their buying and selling of those
stocks.

http://www.nasdr.com/2700.asp: The National Association of Securities Dealers takes disciplinary actions against firms and individuals for violations of
NASD rules; federal securities laws, rules, and regulations; and the rules
of the Municipal Securities Rulemaking Board. Look up any disciplinary
action on this site.

http://www.nyce.com/: The New York Board of Trade is the parent company
of the Coffee, Sugar and Cocoa Exchange Inc. and the New York Cotton
Exchange. Can also be accessed at *http://www.nybot.com*. Has current
market and historical data available.

http://www.nymex.com/jsp/index.jsp: The New York Mercantile Exchange is
the largest physical commodity exchange in the world. It is the preeminent

energy and precious metals market. Agriculture products no longer trade here. Under "Resources," the site has a listing of industry conferences and conventions.

http://www.nyse.com: The New York Stock Exchange has more than 2,800 companies whose stocks trade on a daily basis. The fact book under "Overview" has nice historical data on stock trading. Check out "Daily Statistics" in the pressroom as well.

http://www2.standardandpoors.com/NASApp/cs/ContentServer?pagename= sp/Page/HomePg: Home site for Standard & Poors, which provides credit ratings and research on bonds, as well as equity research. S&P is billing itself as an independent analyzer of the stock market because it doesn't do investment banking for the companies it covers. Search function on this site is particularly useful. Also has access to S&P stock indexes.

http://www.stockpatrol.com/: One of the more skeptical Web sites for investors and those who follow the stock market. StockPatrol.com investigates, researches, and reports on interesting, odd and unusual developments in the securities markets. It believes that such information will enable our readers to thoughtfully assess and address the existence of scams, schemes and scandals in the investment community. Look here to see if a company you're writing about has been the subject of one of its scathing exposes.

http://www.valueline.com: A well-known name in the investment community that publishes research on publicly traded stocks. Accessing these reports requires a subscriber username and password.

http://www.wallstreetcity.com/: A nice site for tracking the news about particular companies. Click on the "News" function and then enter a company's stock ticker to find every story that mentions the business.

http://www.wsrn.com: Wall Street Research Net. Type in a company's stock ticker near the top of the Web site, and this site provides tons of information, including analyst estimates and whether a company is meeting estimates. Also has recent press releases for companies.

http://chart.yahoo.com/d?s: Yahoo! site that allows you to get historical stock prices on any company. The historical stock prices go back to at least 1970.

Regulatory Information

http://www.publicrecordsources.com: Does not provide the public record itself, but it does point you to the agency that houses the record you need (it's got more than 650 listings by state and county). Public Records Sources also informs you of access procedures and restrictions, search fees and more. However, if the agency offers free online access you can link to that site.

http://www.autoexchange.net/dmv/: Links to all state Department of Motor Vehicle departments throughout the country. Some of them have access to vehicle registration information online.

http://www.bls.gov: Bureau of Labor Statistics. Go here to check on information about the unemployment rate, payroll employment, the average hourly rate.

http://www.business.gov/: Created by the Small Business Administration and an interagency task force to help businesses interact better with the federal government. It is also a helpful site for journalists looking for business-related information, particularly the Business Resource Library on the right-hand side of the home page.

http://www.sec.gov: Not just for the filings by public companies. The "Litigation" and "Regulatory actions" sections can also hold great information. The site also contains a daily news digest of information on recent commission actions, including enforcement proceedings, rule filings, policy statements, and upcoming commission meetings.

http://www.10kwizard.com/main.php?g: Subscriber-based site that allows you to access SEC filings. One of the best features on this page is a search that allows you to look for particular words in all SEC filings. Great way to find information about people, or references to towns and cities.

http://www.statelocalgov.net/index.cfm: Access to more than 8,000 state and local government Web sites. This site is useful because it's one of the few places that has links to multi-state government entities and national organizations such as the National Governors Association.

http://www.commerce.gov/: Home page for the U.S. Department of Commerce. The country map on the right of the page has links to local Commerce Department offices that can be helpful. Also go here for economic information on trade.

http://www.csbs.org/links/state_links.asp: Links to state banking regulators provided by the Conference of State Bank Supervisors.

http://www.epa.gov: The U.S. Environmental Protection Agency. Click on the docket to the left on the home page to see Federal Register notices, support documents and public comments for regulations the agency publishes and various non-regulatory activities. Also a nice search engine of environmental information available by ZIP Code, which lists EPA regulated businesses.

http://www.epa.gov/epapages/statelocal/envrolst.htm: Links to regional EPA offices and state environmental regulatory agencies.

http://www.fedstats.gov: The gateway to information from more than 100 U.S. agencies. Allows you to search by topic, state, by region and by agency name.

http://www.fdic.gov: The Federal Deposit Insurance Corp. is a federal agency that oversees bank deposits. One of the best pieces of information here is a monthly list of banks being reviewed for compliance for the Community Reinvestment Act. Go here to find out if a bank in your area is being looked at. There's also market share data on individual banks available under "Bank Data."

http://www3.fdic.gov/idasp//: Financial institutions directory operated by the Federal Deposit Insurance Corp. Can find any bank holding company or location insured by the FDIC. Search results will tell you the bank's total deposits and total assets.

http://www.fdic.gov/bank/analytical/stateprofile/index.html: Another Federal Deposit Insurance Corp. site, this one has banking and economic conditions for each state, updated quarterly. Good, useful information for any banking and finance reporter.

http://www.ffiec.gov/: The Federal Financial Institutions Examination Council is empowered to prescribe uniform principles, standards and report forms for the federal examination of financial institutions by the Federal Reserve System, the Federal Deposit Insurance Corporation, the National Credit Union Administration, the Office of the Comptroller of the Currency, and the Office of Thrift Supervision. Click on "Enforcement Actions and Orders."

http://www.ftc.gov/: The Federal Trade Commission has links to its formal actions, as well as a place to make Freedom of Information requests online for documents.

http://www.govexec.com/top200/2000top/index.htm: Want to know if a company you're writing about does business with the federal government? This Web site lists the largest government contractors by agency.

http://secst.com/StatesMap.htm: This Web site contains links to all Secretary of State Internet Web sites with links to Internet addresses for online access to public records and information on corporations, partnerships, businesses and other entities, plus Uniform Commercial Code (UCC) filings.

http://www.nass.org/busreg/corpreg.html: Another Web site that offers access to Secretary of State records. This one is run by the National Association of Secretaries of State. UCC filings are also available on the left-hand side of the page.

http://www.ncua.gov/: The National Credit Union Administration, governed by a three-member board appointed by the President and confirmed by the U.S. Senate, is the independent federal agency that charters and supervises federal credit unions. Click on "Credit Union Data" on the left-hand side menu to find specific information about any credit union in the country.

http://vocserve.berkeley.edu/CenterFocus/CF8guide.html: A child labor resource guide. This site lists contacts at your state Department of Labor for information concerning your state child labor law.

http://www.bls.gov/iif/oshstate.htm: Bureau of Labor Statistics Web site that tracks occupational illnesses, injuries and fatalities. Click on the state for the information you want.

http://www.labor.gov/: The home page for the U.S. Department of Labor contains information about wages, health plans and benefits, unemployment. Also has a directory of Department of Labor offices around the country. The statistical summary at the bottom of the home page is a nice overview.

http://www.fecinfo.com/: Nice lobbyist directory, as well as information on how much money has been contributed to specific campaigns. See "reporter tips" near the bottom of the page.

http://www.census.gov/econ/www/index.html: An index of U.S. Census Bureau information, from minority and women-owned businesses to building permits and manufacturer survey. Much of this data is broken down by state and county, making it vital information for virtually any reporter.

http://www.irs.gov/taxstats/index.html: Internal Revenue Service tax statistics are available here. Statistics are arranged by the number of returns filed, as well as returns filed by individuals, businesses and tax-exempt organizations.

http://www.uspto.gov/patft/: U.S. Patent and Trademark Office. You can search for issued patents as well as patent applications.

http://www.naic.org/state_contacts/sid_websites.htm: Links to all state Insurance Departments, provided by the National Association of Insurance Commissioners. The information on the individual sites varies, with some having information about individual company rate hikes and others having no information at all about the industry.

http://www.treas.gov/: The U.S. Department of Treasury. Click on "Key Topics" near the upper left side of the page to get discussions on everything from currency and coins to the Treasury Department's Most Wanted List. The Office of the Comptroller of the Currency and the Office of Thrift Supervision, which regulate banks and thrifts, respectively, can be found under "Bureaus."

http://www.fedworld.gov: A site maintained by the Department of Commerce, this has links to thousands of federal government Web locations. Go here if you're stuck and don't know where to find information, or are looking for a government employee.

http://www.usda.gov: Department of Agriculture home page. If you cover the agriculture, food or forest industries, this has plenty of information on recent issues affecting all of them.

http://www.utilityconnection.com/page5.asp#StateRegulation: Links to state utility regulatory agencies across the country. Many of these are public service commissions that have access to dockets and lists of companies they regulate.

http://www.law.cornell.edu/topics/agencies_by_state.htm: The Legal Information Institute maintains this Web site with links to white collar crime enforcement agencies by state. Includes state attorney general offices, securities regulators and others.

Consumer and Labor-Related Sites

http://activistcash.com/: Profiles anti-consumer activist groups, along with information about the sources of their exorbitant funding. Breaks them up among activist groups, foundations, celebrities and major individual players in the activist community.

http://www.aflcio.org: The nation's largest labor union. Nice information on workers' rights, as well as a state-by-state economic snapshot that reviews issues such as poverty, health care coverage and state budget issues.

https://www.alpa.org/alpa/DesktopDefault.aspx: The Air Line Pilots Association has good updates on negotiations between pilots and airlines when they're negotiating new contracts. Speeches and testimony are also available.

http://www.cch.com: The Commerce Clearing House site, which is excellent for summaries on tax rules.

http://www.consumerfed.org/: Consumer Federation of America, which lobbies Congress and other government agencies on behalf of the consumer. Its major concerns are food, finance, health care, privacy, safety and environmental health and utilities, so if you're interested in one of these topics, go there.

http://www.cpsc.gov: Home page of the U.S. Consumer Product Safety Commission, where you can find out information about product recalls. There's also a way to sign up to be notified whenever the CPSC announces a major recall. That is at *http://www.cpsc.gov/cpsclist.asp.*

http://www.cpsc.gov/cpscpub/pubs/amuse.pdf: This file lists who regulates amusement park rides on a state-by-state basis.

http://www.clearhq.org: Council on Licensure, Enforcement and Regulation. The discussion board has interesting submissions from state regulators across the country on how to better serve consumers. You might find a story idea there. Also, click on "Resources" to find regulatory boards of professions.

http://www.ebri.org/publicpr/index.htm: The Employee Benefit Research Institute is the only nonprofit, nonpartisan organization committed exclusively to data dissemination, policy research and education on economic security and employee benefits. Research is available here on employee benefits.

http://www.dot.gov: Looking for information about auto recalls? Go to the Department of Transportation and the National Highway Traffic Safety Administration. This site also has a handy Freedom of Information link that explains how to access information for each of its departments, including the Federal Aviation Administration and the Federal Highway Administration. If you cover the auto industry, or if trucking is a major part of your local economy, look here for information.

http://www.eeoc.gov: The Equal Employment Opportunity Commission investigates charges against businesses for unfair employment practices or discrimination. The "Litigation" section on the left side of the page has a link to a monthly report on all of the actions taken by the agency. There's also an area for statistics on various types of discrimination, ranging from race and pregnancy to age and religious beliefs.

http://www.fda.gov/oc/buyonline/enforce.html: Nice Web site from the Food and Drug Administration about the action taken by the agency against the selling of medicine and medical products online. The FDA's home page, located at *www.fda.gov,* also lists drug recalls.

http://www.fda.gov/default.htm: FDA site that provides access to various issues about its regulation of food, drugs, medical devices, animal food, cosmetics and radiation-emitting products such as cell phones. You can also subscribe to its e-mail newsletters here.

http://www.fda.gov/opacom/campaigns/tobacco/compliancechecker.html: The Compliance Checker database contains the results of FDA's investigations of tobacco retailers for compliance with FDA's age and I.D. tobacco regulations that went into effect on Feb. 28, 1997. On March 21, 2000, the U.S. Supreme Court held that FDA lacked the authority to issue and enforce those regulations, and FDA terminated its investigations at that time. The Compliance Checker database therefore contains historical data that have remained static since March 21, 2000 and will not be updated.

http://www.fraud.org/: The National Fraud Information Center was established by the National Consumers League to combat telemarketing and Internet fraud. Statistics are available on the site.

http://www.ftc.gov/ftc/consumer.htm: The Federal Trade Commission's consumer protection home page has links for topics ranging from identity theft to investments that can be useful for reporters writing about these topics.

http://www1.ifccfbi.gov/index.asp: The Internet Fraud Complaint Center is a partnership between the Federal Bureau of Investigation and the National White Collar Crime Center. Statistics and warning notices are available here.

http://www.ibew.org/: The International Brotherhood of Electrical Workers Web site has information on union membership and negotiations with some larger employers.

http://www.jdpower.com/: Consumer-based ratings on various products, such as cars, boats, homebuilders, financial service providers and travel. The ratings can be viewed for certain markets as well.

http://www.lemonlawamerica.com/state_laws/index.htm: An index of state lemon laws that allow consumers to fight back if they believe they've purchased a defective car, truck, SUV, boat, motorcycle or other consumer product.

http://www.nacaanet.org/: The National Association of Consumer Agency Administrators is a Washington, DC-based non-profit association for government consumer protection agency administrators. This site is best for its "Member" list, which provides links to federal, state and local consumer protection agencies across the country.

http://www.nasuca.org: National Association of State Utility Consumer Advocates, which represents the interest of consumers before state and federal agencies in 40 states and the District of Columbia. Nice list of its testimony and filings.

http://nice.emich.edu/: The National Institute for Consumer Education at Eastern Michigan University has a nice list of links to consumer protection groups and government agencies.

http://www.notice.com/: Two nice search engines here, one for product recalls from the Consumer Product Safety Commission and the Food and Drug

Administration, and another for class action lawsuits. Both can be searched by product or company name.

http://www.osha.gov/oshstats/: The Occupational Safety and Health Administration statistics and data page allows you to look at accident investigation reports and inspection reports for companies by industry.

http://www.osha.gov/cgi-bin/est/est1: This page enables the user to search for OSHA enforcement inspections by the name of the establishment.

http://pueblo.gsa.gov/: The Federal Citizen Information Center has plenty of publications that can be ordered online about a variety of topics, from cars to small business. The site is operated by the General Services Administration.

http://d1.rtknet.org/tri/: The Toxic Release Inventory is a database of information about releases and transfers of toxic chemicals from manufacturing facilities. Facilities must report their releases of a toxic chemical if they fulfill four criteria. This can be searched by geographic regions as well as by facility, parent company and industry.

http://nhtsa.gov: Home site of the National Highway Traffic Safety Administration. Safety problems with specific vehicles and equipment can be found here, as well as regional recalls, which are available here: *http://nhtsa. gov/cars/problems/regional/regional.html*

http://www.nlrb.gov/: The National Labor Relations Board investigates disputes between companies and workers. Its site has a nice weekly summary of cases it's handled, as well as a Freedom of Information link that shows you how to request documents.

http://www.planetfeedback.com/: Search for complaints or compliments about any product and any company at this site. If you're writing about consumer products companies, the postings here might provide some story ideas.

http://www.safetyalerts.com/: Another good Web site that tracks all kinds of product recalls, from automobiles to electric heaters and children's toys.

http://www.uaw.org/: The United Auto Workers home page has information on recent news affecting its members and links to government-related issues it thinks is important.

Legal Information

http://www.abanet.org/home.html: The American Bar Association home page has a lawyer locater service, as well as links to specialty organizations such as minority lawyer and female lawyer groups.

http://www.bigclassaction.com/: Information about class action lawsuits filed against dozens of industries can be found here. Also has a pending list of litigation that can be helpful for industry reporters.

http://www.bmccorp.net/: This site tracks the court filings of some of the country's largest bankruptcy cases, including past cases such as Conseco, TWA and W.R. Grace.

http://www.courtexpress.com: Registration site that allows you to track court cases across the country to see what's been put on the docket. Also provides a document service, which can be pricey.

http://www.courtlink.com: Site run by Lexis Nexis that provides online access to current cases, federal and state court records, E-mail alerts about new case filings and automatic case tracking.

http://www.martindale.com: Find a lawyer anywhere in the country. Can also search by firm or area of practice.

http://www.uscourts.gov/allinks.html: Links to all federal courts, from bankruptcy courts to court of appeals to district courts. Also other helpful links for other federal courts such as the Tax Court and the Federal Claims Court.

http://pacer.psc.uscourts.gov/: The PACER Service Center is the Federal Judiciary's centralized registration, billing and technical support center for electronic access to U.S. District, Bankruptcy and Appellate court records. The service will allow you to search nationwide by name or social security number in the bankruptcy index, name or nature of suit in the civil index, defendant name in the criminal index, and party name in the appellate index. There is a fee for this service, but it is worth it if you're doing serious searches for lawsuit information.

http://pacer.psc.uscourts.gov/lookup.html: Web site that allows you to search for all counties in a U.S. Court district, or to search for a district by county.

http://vls.law.vill.edu/Locator/fedcourt.html: Provided by Villanova University, this is another list of links to federal courts across the country.

http://www.internetlawyer.com: Information about the growing field of Internet law is available here. If you're a technology reporter, this has important trends and issues on the legal aspects of the industry.

http://securities.stanford.edu/index.html: The Securities Class Action Clearinghouse provides detailed information relating to the prosecution, defense and settlement of federal class action securities fraud litigation. The clearinghouse maintains an index of 1,797 issuers that have been named in federal class action securities fraud lawsuits since passage of the Private Securities Litigation Reform Act of 1995. The clearinghouse also contains copies of more than 2,000 complaints, briefs, filings and other litigation-related materials filed in these cases. If you're writing about companies being sued for inflating their stock price, this is the place to go.

http://www.uscourts.gov/Press_Releases/: News releases from the administrative offices of the U.S. Court System. While this is the federal court system, there is plenty of information here that can be localized about the need for more judges across the country.

http://www.westlaw.com: West's online legal research service. It provides fast and easy access to an extensive collection of legal resources, news, business and public records information. However, there is a fee for this service.

Real Estate Information

http://indorgs.virginia.edu/portico/personalproperty.html: State-by-state index
of real estate records. After you click on the state you want, the site takes
you to a county listing, which then takes you to the local property ownership
database. Invaluable for finding the appraised tax value of a home.

http://www.real-estate-public-records.com/RE_free_public_records.htm: This
site has access to free property transactions across the country as well as
plenty of other public records.

http://www.realtor.com: Site of the National Association of Realtors. Helps
locate homes for sale across the country based on price and other factors,
and offers a mortgage lending comparison tool.

http://www.nahb.org: The National Association of Home Builders has some
interesting statistics on the industry in its "Newsroom" under economics
and housing data.

http://www.hud.gov/: U.S. Department of Housing and Urban Development
home page that has reports on topics such as minority homeownership.

http://www.huduser.org/datasets/pdrdatas.html: Provides data from a variety
of surveys, including the American Housing Survey, HUD median family
income limits, as well as data from research initiatives on topics such as
housing discrimination, the HUD-insured multifamily housing stock and the
public housing population. It has great information for low-income housing
stories.

http://dowjones.homepricecheck.com/: Maintained by the *Wall Street Journal*,
this site offers searches to look at the sale of homes on a particular street
or range of addresses, previous sale prices of specific houses and a way to
compare all homes sold in a certain area for a specific price range. Not all
U.S. counties are included in this free service.

http://policy.rutgers.edu/cupr/index1.htm: The Center for Urban Public Research is recognized for its research on affordable housing, land use policy,
the arts and cultural policy, development impact analysis, the costs of sprawl,
transportation information systems, environmental impacts and community
economic development. Go here to see their research on these topics.

http://www.zanatec.com/multiwin.html: Listing of county recorders across the
country maintained by Peelle Management Corp. There are nearly 4,000
recorders to keep track of, so some of the information here will not be
current.

Nonprofit Organizations

http://www.aafrc.org/: The American Association of Fundraising Council has
charts and statistics showing giving by source of contributions and by recipient organizations.

http://www.charitynavigator.org: This Web site has independent evaluations of more than 2,500 charities. Database can be searched by category, region or keyword.

http://www.give.org: The Better Business Bureau Wise Giving Alliance maintains reports on nationally soliciting charitable organizations that are the subject of donor inquiries. These reports include an evaluation of the subject charity in relation to the voluntary BBB charity standards.

http://www.grantsmart.org: Has a searchable database for Form 990 filings with the Internal Revenue Service for more than 60,000 foundations. Can search by name, location or assets. More than one year may be available.

http://www.guidestar.com: The National Database of Non-Profit Organizations compiles information based on Internal Revenue Service documents filed by more than 850,000 organizations. Guidestar is the place to go to look up non-profit information.

http://www.fdncenter.org: The Foundation Directory has a list of foundations throughout the country. However, there is a fee to search its directory database. A free foundation finder service is also available here, as well as lists of Web sites for private, corporate and community foundations.

http://www.philanthropy.iupui.edu/: The Center on Philanthropy at Indiana University has major research projects available online on giving and charitable organizations.

http://www.irs.ustreas.gov/charities/index.html: The Internal Revenue Service home page for information about charities and non-profit organizations. This helps someone understand reports and filing requirements for these companies.

http://nccs.urban.org/: The National Center for Charitable Statistics is the national repository of data on the nonprofit sector in the United States. Its mission is to develop and disseminate high quality data on non-profit organizations and their activities for use in research on the relationships between the nonprofit sector, government, the commercial sector and the broader civil society.

http://www.internet-prospector.org/charities.htm: State charities databases on the Web. Some states do not have an online search for charity information, while others allow you to search by name or word.

Glossary

accretive: An acquisition that will increase the acquiring company's EPS. As a general rule, an accretive merger or acquisition occurs when the P/E ratio of the acquiring firm is greater than that of the target firm.

acquisition: When one company purchases a majority interest in another company.

adverse opinion: An opinion made by an auditor indicating that a company's financial statements are misrepresented, misstated and do not accurately reflect its financial performance and health.

American Stock Exchange: The third-largest stock exchange in the United States. The AMEX is located in New York and handles approximately 10 percent of all securities traded in the States. The exchange is primarily for smaller companies and derivatives.

annual meeting: A meeting held once a year by public companies where shareholders are invited to attend and vote on matters. Company executives typically give presentations about the performance of the company at the meeting and answer questions from shareholders in the audience.

arbitration: A smaller version of a trial held in an attempt to avoid a court trial. In some contract cases, arbitration may be binding for both parties.

articles of incorporation: A set of documents filed with state authorities for the purpose of documenting the creation of a corporation.

assessed value: The property value as determined by the county tax assessor for tax purposes.

assets: Anything owned that has economic value. Asset is also a balance sheet item showing what a company owns. Assets are bought to increase the value of a firm or benefit the firm's operations. They can be anything from real estate to products.

auditor: An outside firm that conducts an examination and opinion of the financial statements of a business.

auditor's report: Recorded in the annual report, it tests to see that corporation's financial statements comply with generally accepted accounting practices, or GAAP. This is sometimes referred to as the "clean opinion."

B

balance sheet: A company's financial statement. It reports assets, liabilities and net worth at a specific time, typically the end of a quarter.

bankruptcy: When a person or company is unable to repay debts. In corporate cases, ownership of the firm's assets are often transferred from stockholders to the bondholders.

board of directors: People selected to sit on an authoritative standing committee, or governing body, taking responsibility for the management of an organization. Board members are chosen by shareholders, but in practice they are usually selected by the current board's recommendations. The board usually includes major shareholders as well as executives of the company.

bond: A bond is considered a debt investment—you are loaning money to an entity (company or government) that needs funds for a defined period of time at a specified interest rate. In exchange for your money, the entity will issue you a certificate, or bond, that states the interest rate you are to be paid and when your loaned funds are to be returned, otherwise known as the maturity date.

bonus: A financial incentive given to employees in addition to their base pay in the form of a one-time payment.

breach of contract: Failing to live up to the stipulations set forth in a written or verbal contract, such as not completing a job by a deadline or failing to pay for services rendered.

break-up fee: A fee paid by a target company to bidders during an acquisition if the pending deal is terminated for any reason. Some companies being acquired may also require a break-up fee clause from the company acquiring it as part of the deal.

broker: A Realtor who puts together a buyer and a seller for a real estate transaction. Brokers often specialize in commercial real estate transactions.

building permit: An approval by a local government allowing a contractor to construct, expand or demolish an existing structure.

buy-side analyst: A term used to describe the analysts at investing institutions like mutual funds, pension funds and insurance firms, who tend to buy large portions of securities. These analysts provide research for the firm's money managers.

C

cash flow: The amount of cash a company generates and uses during a period, calculated by adding non-cash charges (such as depreciation) to the net income after taxes. Cash flow can be used as an indication of a company's financial strength.

chairman of the board: The most senior executive in an organization. The chair is responsible for running the annual meeting and meetings of the board of directors. He or she may be a figurehead, appointed for prestige or power, and may have no role in the day-to-day running of the organization. Sometimes the roles of chair and chief executive are combined, and the chair then has more control over daily operations. Sometimes the chair is a retired chief executive.

Chapter 7: A bankruptcy court filing done by businesses and individuals where the assets are liquidated.

Chapter 11: A bankruptcy court filing for businesses and individuals where the debt is reorganized and some debt is forgiven as part of a plan to rehabilitate the company or person.

Chapter 13: A bankruptcy court filing where a person agrees to repay their debts.

charge: A one-time expense by a company that negatively affects earnings.

chief executive officer: The person with overall responsibility for ensuring that the daily operations of a company run efficiently, and for carrying out strategic plans. The chief executive normally sits on the board.

chief financial officer: The officer responsible for handling funds, signing checks, the keeping of financial records and financial planning for the company.

civil litigation: Laws that encompass business, contracts, estates, accidents and negligence that is not criminal law. In a few areas, civil and criminal law may overlap or coincide.

class action: A lawsuit filed by one or more people on behalf of other people who may be in a similar situation. Class action lawsuits may be difficult and are expensive, but allow people who may not have been able to file a lawsuit individually to band together.

conference call: An event in which investors can call into a special phone number and hear the management of their company comment on the financial results of the recently completed quarter, or another important corporate event.

consensus analyst estimate: The average earnings estimate for a company based on the predictions of all of the analysts covering the business. The estimate could be for a quarter or for a year.

Consumer Confidence Index: A measurement by the Conference Board on whether consumers are feeling optimistic or pessimistic about the economy.

Consumer Price Index: A measure of the price change of consumer goods such as gasoline, food and automobiles.

Consumer Product Safety Commission: The federal agency that protects consumers against faulty products. Its jurisdiction covers product safety for more than 15,000 products, and it can force a recall of a product.

conversion: The process where a company changes its ownership structure, typically from one where the business is owned by customers to one where the business is owned by stockholders.

corporation: The most common form of business organization. The organization is ongoing, and the owners face limited liability.

coupon: The interest rate stated on a bond when it's issued. The coupon is typically paid semiannually.

creditor: A person or company owed money from a debtor. The debt occurred before the filing of bankruptcy court protection.

criminal litigation: Charges dealing with crimes against the public or members of the public, filed by government authorities.

D

damages: The amount of money a plaintiff may be seeking or awarded in a lawsuit. Punitive damages may be awarded in some cases to set an example against the defendant.

debt: An amount of money owed by a person or a company to another person or company.

debt-to-equity ratio: A company's total long-term debt expressed as a percentage of shareholders' equity.

debtor: A person or company seeking protection in bankruptcy court from loans and other debts owed.

deed: A legal document conveying title to a piece of property. It transfers ownership from one owner to another.

defamation: Making untrue statements about a person that damages that person's reputation. If printed, the statements can be considered libel.

default: When the owner of a piece of property falls behind in making payments on the loan used to acquire the property, or stops making payments altogether.

defendant: The individual or business sued in a civil lawsuit, or charged with a crime in a criminal case.

deflation: The opposite of inflation. This is the rate at which the price of goods and services in the economy is falling.

deposition: Taking or recording of testimony by a witness away from the courtroom before a trial. Deposition statements may be used by the plaintiff or defendant to prepare their case. Depositions can be made available in the public court file.

depression: A severe and prolonged recession in the economy marked by lower productivity, higher unemployment and falling prices.

dilutive: An acquisition that will decrease the acquiring company's EPS. As a general rule, a dilutive merger or acquisition occurs when the P/E ratio of the acquiring firm is less than that of the target firm.

dividend: A cash payment using profits that's announced by a company's board of directors to be distributed among stockholders. Dividends may be in the form of cash, stock or property. All dividends are declared by the board of directors.

Dow Jones Industrial Average: A price-weighted average of 30 significant stocks traded on the New York Stock Exchange and the NASDAQ. The DJIA was invented by Charles Dow back in 1896. It is the oldest and single-most watched index in the world.

durable good orders: Measures spending on products consumers purchase that they don't necessarily need, such as dishwashers, sports equipment, jewelry and lawn and garden equipment.

E

earnings guidance: A report by a company that its earnings may vary considerably, either positively or negatively, from expectations, or that earnings will still be in line with expectations.

earnings per share: The portion of a company's profit allocated to each outstanding share of common stock.

economics: The science dealing with the production, distribution and consumption of goods and services and with the issues of labor, finance and taxation.

employee stock ownership plan: A plan where the company allows its employees to buy shares of the business. These plans are increasing in popularity with small and private businesses.

Environmental Protection Agency: The federal agency whose job is to protect the environment and human health by preventing the release of harmful items into the environment. The EPA can ban the use of certain products, and can fine companies for violating environmental laws.

Equal Employment Opportunity Commission: The federal agency created in 1964 to investigate claims of employment discrimination on the basis of race, color, sex, age, natural origin and religion. Its jurisdiction has since been expanded to include discrimination based on age and disability.

exchange: A market where securities, commodities, options and futures are traded.

exchange ratio: The number of shares of the acquiring company that a shareholder will receive for one share of the acquired company.

exhibit: A document or object introduced as evidence. In civil lawsuits, a plaintiff's case may be supported by exhibits filed along with the allegations.

existing home sales: The resale of an existing home by the current owner to a new owner. Not to be confused with new home sales.

F

fairness opinion: An opinion developed by qualified analysts or advisors with the purpose of providing key details and factual proof to the decision makers of a merger or acquisition.

Federal Communications Commission: The federal regulatory agency charged with overseeing interstate and international communications by radio, television, wire, satellite and cable.

Federal Reserve Board: The governing body of the federal reserve system. They are appointed to the Board of Governors by the president, but must be approved by the Senate.

Federal Trade Commission: The federal agency that works to ensure that the nation's markets are vigorous, efficient and free of restrictions that harm consumers. The FTC enforces federal consumer protection laws that prevent fraud, deception and unfair business practices. The commission also enforces federal antitrust laws that prohibit anticompetitive mergers and other business practices that restrict competition and harm consumers.

forecast: A company or analyst's estimate of the company's future earnings.

foreclosure: A court proceeding where the property owner's rights are terminated in order to sell the property to satisfy lenders.

Form 4: A document required by the SEC to announce changes in the holdings of directors, officers and shareholders owning 10 percent or more of the company's outstanding stock.

Form 8-K: A report of unscheduled material events or corporate changes that could be of importance to the shareholders or the SEC. Examples include an acquisition, bankruptcy or a change in fiscal year.

Form 10-K: The annual report that public companies file with the SEC. It provides a comprehensive overview of the company's business. The report must be filed within 90 days after the end of the company's fiscal year.

Form 10-Q: A report filed quarterly by public companies. It includes unaudited financial statements and provides a continuing view of the company's financial position during the year. The report must be filed for each of the first three fiscal quarters of the company's fiscal year and is due within 45 days of the close of the quarter.

Form 990: A document filed with the Internal Revenue Service by virtually every non-profit organization and foundation. The filing discloses revenue, expenditures and salaries for management.

Form S-1: A document filed with the Securities and Exchange Commission by a company desiring to go public. This is also known as the registration statement, and is often amended frequently.

foundation: A non-profit organization created to give money away. Foundations are required to grant 5 percent of their assets annually.

franchisee: A businessman who pays a larger company, known as the franchisor, to run one of its locations in exchange for a fee.

G

golden parachute: Lucrative benefits given to top executives in the event a company is taken over by another firm, resulting in the loss of the job. Benefits include items such as stock options, bonuses, severance pay, etc.

Gross Domestic Product: The monetary value of all goods, services and products made by an economy during a certain time period. It includes purchases, investments and exports minus imports.

H

housing starts: The number of residential buildings that have begun construction in any month.

I

income statement: An accounting of sales, expenses and net profit for a given period.

inflation: The rate at which the average price of all goods and services in the economy from one year to the next is rising, and therefore, purchasing power is falling.

initial public offering: The first sale of stock by a private company to the public. IPOs are often smaller, younger companies seeking capital to expand their business.

insider trading: Trading in securities by executives, board members or large shareholders. When insider trading is based on privileged information, it is illegal.

institutional investor: A non-bank person or organization that trades securities in large enough share quantities or dollar amounts that they qualify for preferential treatment and lower commissions. Institutional investors face less protective regulations because it is assumed that they are more knowledgeable and better able to protect themselves.

interest rate: The rate paid on money borrowed, or received on money lent if you are the lender. It is typically expressed as a percent. $1,000 borrowed at a 6 percent interest rate means the person pays $60 a year in interest.

Internal Revenue Service: The federal regulatory agency that collects taxes from businesses and individuals. The IRS also determines the tax status of a business, and reviews documents to determine if a company is in compliance with federal laws.

investment banker: A person representing a financial institution that is in the business of raising capital for corporations and municipalities. Investment bankers do the grunt work behind IPOs and debt offerings.

involuntary bankruptcy: When creditors file a plan to force a debtor into bankruptcy court protection. The debtor can protest and argue before the court.

J

joint venture: Agreement by two or more parties to work on a project together.

L

lagging indicators: An economic measurement that begins to change after the economy has already moved in that direction.

lead underwriter: The managing underwriter who maintains the books of securities sold for a new issue. Also commonly known as the book runner.

leading indicators: An economic measurement that begins to change before the economy moves in that direction.

lease: An agreement where the owner of a piece of property agrees to allow another party to inhabit the property for a specified period of time.

lender: A financial institution that has financed the loan allowing a buyer to purchase a piece of property.

leveraged buyout: A strategy involving the acquisition of another company using borrowed money, i.e. bonds or loans. The acquiring company uses its assets as collateral for the loan in hopes that the future cash flows will cover the loan payments.

liability: A legal debt or obligation estimated by accrual accounting. Recorded on the balance sheet, current liabilities are debts payable within one year, while long-term liabilities are debts payable over a longer period.

limited liability corporation: A business structure with corporation and partnership qualities. Often a business will become a limited liability corporation to receive the tax advantages of a partnership and the liability advantages of a corporation.

M

market capitalization: Value of a company as determined by the market price of its issued and outstanding common stock. It is calculated by multiplying the number of outstanding shares buy the current market price of a share.

maturity date: The date the borrower has to pay back the money it has borrowed through a bond issue.

medical malpractice: Allegations by a patient against a physician or medical provider that the provider did not meet the standards of professional conduct or caused damage.

mediation: An attempt to settle a lawsuit by an independent third party who attempts to find common points of agreement in order to reach a fair result for both sides.

merger: The combining of two or more companies, generally by offering the stockholders of one company securities in the acquiring company in exchange for the surrender of their stock. Rarely are mergers equal for both companies.

mutual fund: Fund operated by an investment company that raises money from shareholders and invests it in stocks, bonds, options, commodities or money market securities.

mutual ownership: An ownership structure commonly found in the insurance and thrift industries where the company is owned by the policyholders and depositors.

N

NASDAQ: Created in 1971 as the world's first electronic stock market, the NASDAQ is a computerized system that facilitates trading and provides price quotations on some 5,000 of the more actively traded over-the-counter stocks. Its largest stocks include Microsoft, Dell and Cisco.

National Labor Relations Board: The federal agency created in 1935 to enforce the National Labor Relations Act. It conducts secret-ballot elections to determine whether employees want union representation and investigates unfair labor practices by employers and unions.

net income: A company's total earnings, reflecting revenues adjusted for costs of doing business, depreciation, interest, taxes and other expenses. Do not confuse net income with operating income.

new car sales: Reported by the major automobile dealers, typically five days after the end of the month. The sales can give an indication about the economy because they reflect consumer demand.

new home sales: The sale of a newly built home to a buyer from the builder. An increase in new home sales can be a sign of a growing economy.

New York Stock Exchange: The largest stock exchange in the country, which is responsible for setting policies and supervising the stock exchange and its member activities. The NYSE also oversees the transfer of members' seats on the Exchange and judging whether a potential applicant is qualified to be a specialist.

noncompete agreement: A contract signed by an employee that prohibits them from working for a competitor or using the knowledge gained with one employer to go work for a competitor for a certain time period.

nonprofit organization: A business created to provide a good or service to the community without making money. Many nonprofit organizations, however, do have more revenue than expenses.

O

Occupational Safety and Health Administration: The federal agency whose job it is to enforce laws to ensure a safe and healthy workplace.

off balance sheet financing: The way a company raises money that does not appear on the balance sheet, unlike loans, debt, or equity that do appear on the balance sheet. Examples are joint ventures, research and development partnerships, and leases (rather than purchases of capital equipment).

ongoing concern: A statement made by independent auditors that raises doubts about the company's ability to function in the future.

operating income: Revenue less the cost of goods sold and normal operating expenses.

operating margin: Calculated by dividing a company's operating profit by net sales.

out-of-court settlement: An agreement reached between the plaintiff and the defendant outside the realm of the court system. Such settlements often require a judge's approval, but the terms can also be confidential.

P

partnership: A business organization in which two or more people manage and operate the business. All of the owners are equally liable for the debts of the business.

plaintiff: The individual or business who files the charges in a lawsuit against another party asking for damages or a court ruling.

poison pill: A strategy used by many corporations to discourage its hostile takeover by another company by making its stock less attractive. Sometimes, a poison pill will allow existing shareholders to purchase more shares of company stock if an offer is made for the company.

premium: The difference between the actual cost for acquiring a target firm versus its value before the acquisition.

president or chief operating officer: The officer responsible for the day-to-day management of a company who usually reports to the chief executive officer.

price-to-book ratio: Used to compare a stock's market value to its book value, calculated by dividing the current closing price of the stock by the latest quarter's book value.

price-to-earnings ratio: A stock analysis statistic in which the current price of a stock is divided by the company's earnings per share.

private company: A business whose ownership is confined to a handful of people, or whose ownership cannot be traded on a stock exchange.

Producer Price Index: A measure of price change from the perspective of the seller, it measures selling prices for goods and services.

productivity: Output divided by input, with output being the goods and services produced and input being the number of worker hours.

profit margin: Net earnings after taxes divided by revenues. This is a number that is usually displayed as a percentage.

profit sharing plan: A plan where the employees of a company share in its profits. The business typically decides what profits will be shared.

proxy statement: A document sent to shareholders of public companies to invite owners of the company's stock to its annual meeting. The proxy statement will include information about proposals to be voted on at the annual meeting and executive salaries.

public company: A business whose ownership includes stockholders that have purchased shares on Wall Street.

public utilities commission: State agencies that regulate water, electrical and telephone companies. In some states, the agency may be called the public service commission.

Q

qualified opinion: Written upon the front page of an audit done by a professional auditor, it suggests that the information provided was limited in scope or the company being audited did not maintain GAAP accounting principles. Contrary to its connotation, a qualified opinion is not a good thing. Auditors that deem audits as qualified opinions are advising that the audit is not complete or that the accounting methods used by the company do not follow GAAP.

R

real estate broker: An agent who buys and sells real estate on a commission basis. The broker does not have title to the property, but generally represents the owner or the buyer.

recession: A decline in the Gross Domestic Product for at least two consecutive quarters.

Regulation Fair Disclosure: A rule passed by the Securities and Exchange Commission in an effort to prevent selective disclosure by public companies to market professionals and certain shareholders.

reorganization: A process designed to revive a financially troubled or bankrupt firm. It typically involves the restatement of assets and liabilities and communication with creditors in order to make arrangements for maintaining repayment.

reserve: Money set aside by a company from earnings to pay for other expenses, such as a pending lawsuit or other contingencies.

restricted stock: A restricted stock award is a grant of stock by an employer to an employee in which the employee's rights to the shares are limited until the shares "vest" and cease to be subject to the restrictions. Typically, the employee may not sell or transfer the shares of stock until they vest—frequently a defined period of time—and forfeits the stock if the employee's employment terminates before the stock vests.

restructuring: General term for major corporate changes aimed at greater efficiency and adaptation to changing markets. This can also be called a downsizing, a recapitalization and a major management realignment.

return on equity: A measure of a company's profitability, calculated as net income divided by shareholder's equity.

return on investment: The profit or loss resulting from an investment, usually expressed as an annual percentage return.

revenue: The money generated by a product or service.

S

S corporation: A company that has met the requirements under subchapter S of the Internal Revenue Service code. This allows the company to be taxed as if it were a partnership. These businesses must be domestic, have 75 or fewer shareholders, and only one class of stock.

salary: A form of earnings given to employees at regular intervals in exchange for the work they have done. Traditionally, a salary is a form of remuneration given to professional employees on a monthly basis.

Schedule 13D: A form filed by anyone acquiring a beneficial ownership of 5 percent or more of any equity security registered with the SEC. The form must also be filed with the exchange on which the stock is traded.

secured creditor: People or companies owed debt that is backed by collateral, such as a car loan or a home mortgage.

Secretary of State's Office: The state agency that registers a variety of business organizations including corporations, assumed business names, banks, insurance companies, limited liability companies, limited liability partnerships and limited partnerships. Other business-related filings include trade and service marks, auctioneer's licenses and legal newspaper registrations, among others.

Securities and Exchange Commission: The federal agency that protects investors and ensures the integrity of the stock markets. The SEC regulates publicly traded companies, companies who trade stocks and investors. As part of its mission to protect investors and the investment community, the SEC required public companies to file documents disclosing financial information and other material so that it can be read by anyone.

sell-side analyst: Used to describe the retail brokers and research departments that sell securities and make recommendations for the brokerage firm's customers.

shareholders' equity: A firm's total assets minus total liabilities. It is the amount of the company that is financed through common and preferred shares. Also known as capital.

share repurchase plan: A company's plan to buy back its own shares, reducing the number of outstanding shares, and typically an indication that the company's management thinks the shares are undervalued. Also referred to as a buyback plan.

short selling: The selling of a security that the seller does not own, or any sale that is completed by the delivery of a security borrowed by the seller. Short selling is a legitimate trading strategy. Short sellers assume the risk that they will be able to buy the stock at a more favorable price than the price at which they sold short.

shortfall: Amount by which a financial objective has not been met.

stock: Ownership in a company that is represented by shares. A holder of stock (a shareholder) has a claim on a part of its assets and earnings. Also known as equities.

stock options: A stock option is the opportunity, given by your employer, to purchase a certain number of shares of your company's common stock at a pre-established price, known as the grant price, during a specific period of time, known as the vesting period.

stock split: Increase in a corporation's number of outstanding shares of stock without any change in the shareholders' equity or the aggregate market value at the time of the split. In a split, the share price declines. In a reverse split, the stock price rises.

strategic alternatives: Anything up to and including the sale of a company.

Superfund: The federal government's program to clean up the nation's hazardous waste sites.

synergy: Used mostly in the context of mergers and acquisitions, synergy is the idea that the value and performance of two companies combined will be greater than the sum of the separate individual parts.

T

takeover: Change in controlling interest of a corporation. A takeover may be a friendly acquisition or an unfriendly bid that the target company may fight. If the company is publicly traded then the acquiring company will make an offer for the outstanding shares.

tender offer: An offer to shareholders to purchase some or all of their shares in a corporation. The price offered is usually at a premium to the market price. Tender offers may be friendly or unfriendly.

trade deficit: When the buying and selling of goods and services between two economies results in fewer exports than imports.

trustee: A court-appointed representative who administers the business or estate. Can be assigned if creditors or others argue that the company is unfit to manage its operations.

U

unemployment rate: A measure of how many people are out of the labor force but are looking for work.

Uniform Commercial Code: A set of laws regulating commercial transactions, especially those involving the sale of goods where money is borrowed.

unsecured creditor: People or companies owed debt that is not backed by collateral, such as credit cards, medical bills and utility bills.

V

venture capital: Funds made available to start-up companies and small businesses, typically in return for an ownership stake and a say in how the operation is managed. A venture capital firm invests money in such companies, expecting that the company receiving the funds will grow and become successful.

W

writedown: Reducing the book value of an asset because it is overvalued compared to market values.

Y

yield: In general, a return on an investor's capital investment. For bonds, the coupon rate of interest divided by the purchase price, called current yield.

Also, the rate of return on a bond, taking into account the total of annual interest payments, the purchase price, the redemption value, and the amount of time remaining until maturity.

Z

zoning: A legal mechanism to regulate the use of real estate. All privately owned land within a jurisdiction is placed within designated zones that limit the type and intensity of development permitted.

Index